Productivity & Quality Management Frontiers - IV

Productivity & Quality Management Frontiers - IV

Volume 2

Refereed papers presented at the Fourth International Conference on Productivity and Quality Research, Febuary 9-12, 1993, Miami, Florida USA

Edited by

David J. Sumanth, Ph.D., Conference Chairman
Professor and Director, Productivity Research Group (UMPRG)
Department of Industrial Engineering, University of Miami, Florida USA

Johnson A. Edosomwan, D.Sc., Conference Vice-Chairman
President, Johnson & Johnson Associates, California USA

Robert Poupart, Ph.D., Program Chairman
Professor, Montreal Polytechnical School, Quebec CANADA

D. Scott Sink, Ph.D., Conference Vice-Chairman
Associate Professor, Industrial Engineering and Operations Research, and Director, Virginia Productivity Center, Virginia Polytechnic Institute & State University, Virginia USA

Industrial Engineering and Management Press
Institute of Industrial Engineers
Norcross, Georgia USA

Productivity & Quality Management Frontiers - IV, Volume 2
©1993 Industrial Engineering and Management Press. All Rights Reserved.
Printed in the United States of America.

ISBN 0-89806-125-3

The papers in this book comprise the proceedings of the meeting mentioned on the cover and title page. They reflect the authors' opinions and are published as presented and without change, in the interest of timely dissemination. Publication by the Institute of Industrial Engineers does not in any way constitute endorsement or approval of the book's contents.

Additional copies may be obtained by contacting:
IIE, Customer Service Center, 25 Technology Park, Norcross, GA 30092, USA. 1-404-449-0460 (phone) or 1-404-263-8532 (FAX).

TABLE OF CONTENTS

━━━━━━━━━━━━━━━━━━━━ **Volume 1** ━━━━━━━━━━━━━━━━━━━━

x

xi

━━━━━━━━━━━━━━━━━━━━━━ **Volume 2** ━━━━━━━━━━━━━━━━━━━━━━

xvi

Productivity & Quality Management Frontiers-IV, edited by Sumanth, Edosomwan, Poupart, and Sink. ©1993
Institute of Industrial Engineers.

How Are Agencies to Respond to Increasing Demands for Services and Decreasing Resources?

W.H. Flickinger
U.S. Army Construction Eng. Research Lab
Champaign, Illinois USA

K. Fitzpatrick and S.L. Welch
Police Department
Urbana, Illinois USA

ABSTRACT

The current U.S. economic situation requires many public organizations to make tough decisions. Resources are constantly decreasing while the demand for public services grows. It is reasonable to ask whether public service agencies can maintain realistic productivity levels as budgets continue to shrink. Any useful measure of productivity must distinguish between the *quality* and the *quantity* of services. To narrow the broad spectrum of productivity measures that can influence the effectiveness, this paper addresses personnel, facilities, and programs.

Personnel issues are highly visible when funding declines. Another concern is the impact that facilities have on productivity. Discussion includes an analysis of the incentives for implementing any additional programs, and consideration of funding sources. Finally, the authors examine the impact of new programs, or changes in existing ones, on an agency's productivity. Incentives for implementing new programs or altering existing ones are discussed, as are possible sources for funding.

The authors conclude that meeting the demand for more services using fewer resources will require creativity. Additionally, public sector agencies must be willing to learn from the private sector--both it's successes and it's mistakes. In all cases, reevaluation of the agency's mission will be essential.

KEYWORDS: decreasing resources; facilities; personnel issues; productivity; programs; public agencies; resources; services

INTRODUCTION

Government agencies are now facing massive funding cuts while their constituencies demand maintaining, or even increasing, the level of services provided. Managers of public agencies are being forced to reexamine their priorities and develop innovative approaches to providing services. Decreases in funding traditionally result in personnel cuts and poorer quality of service. Creative managers are looking for ways both to maintain a high quality of service and satisfy the public's demand to cut costs.

To accomplish these apparently contradictory goals, effective new measures of productivity must be developed and applied. These measures must differentiate between *quality* and *quantity* of service, but must also recognize both aspects as integral to any true measure of productivity. The results of productivity measurements must be reviewed continually in order to fully understand all factors that affect productivity levels. After an agency learns to effectively evaluate its own productivity, it can then attempt to improve it. The authors identified three different aspects of an agency that may impact productivity: personnel issues, facility quality, and programming. Each topic area was examined in terms of whether it can or cannot affect productivity, how changes in that area would be funded, the incentives for doing so, and whether an agency must modify its current mission in order to make the changes.

PERSONNEL ISSUES

Personnel issues are highly visible during times of reduced funding. Areas of concern to public agencies are quality management, recruitment, training, and retention of qualified employees. Traditional approaches to personnel issues have often not been cost effective. A quality management approach can help improve production, increase job satisfaction, and reduce costs.

Quality leadership addresses the improvement of products and services by improving *how* the work gets done rather than *what* gets done. Quality is defined by the customer's expectations. Improvements are made on the basis of measurable data. Those who conceive and implement the improvements -- the employees -- work together as a team. Traditional "management by results" has consisted of little more than numerical goals, with little attention paid to processes and systems. Problems arising with this management style include short-term thinking, misguided focus, internal conflict, and blindness to customer expectations.

Quality leadership emphasizes results by working on methods. The principles of quality leadership emphasize customer focus, quality, unification of the work force, identifying faults in the system, teamwork, and continuing education and training. By adopting a quality management approach, an organization focuses on making a better product at a lower cost by fully using the skills and resources of all the employees in the organization. Better use of employees already on staff decreases the need to hire more for higher production.

A variety of personnel issues can be addressed in a cost-savings approach. Areas such as recruitment, hiring, training, and retention of public service employees, and use of auxiliary personnel, temporaries, and volunteers must be part of the strategy in cost containment. The challenge to attract qualified individuals into public service and retain them has never been greater. For one thing, the pool of talent continues to shrink: demographic studies show that the number of people who reach age 18 in a given year has declined from about 3 million in the late 1970s to 1.3 million today. Hyams (1991)

If public agencies are to attract talented, dedicated people, the agencies must begin cultivating and developing their own pool of human resources. Training programs can identify interns or cadets who have genuine interest in a particular profession, and can help determine how well the individual may fit into the profession. Applicant profiles must become a part of the employee selection process. Aggressive recruitment campaigns need to be developed. Campaigns must identify public service positions as professional jobs. These campaigns may require higher educational qualifications. Immediate implementation of such qualification requirements could drastically reduce the applicant pool.

The use of contractual agreements with public service employees may offer a way to save money. The average cost for basic academy training for a new police recruit in Illinois is $2,800.[1] When salary is added, the total cost increases to $7,200. Communities employing these recruits do not see a full return on their investment dollars for a number of years, if ever. By entering into a contract with the new officer, the community could ensure a return on the training dollars it invested and prevent depletion of its scarce resources when employees leave to take a higher paying job elsewhere. Another alternative to the expensive entry-level training budget would be to require applicants to obtain training on their own. This requirement would not only lower the cost of new employees, but would also identify people who truly have an interest in the career field.

To continue with the example of police departments, volunteers and auxiliary police officers are increasingly used to perform public service duties in an effort to reduce expenses. Senior citizen volunteer groups are being used by some agencies to assist with recordkeeping functions and various nonsworn activities. Departments are diverting service functions to nonsworn volunteers, which frees the fulltime officer or officers to perform the actual police duties. Reserve and auxiliary police officers can provide additional manpower at reduced costs. Volunteers provide assistance to an agency free of cost.

Reserves enable the agency to handle the sporadic demands for extra manpower at a reduced cost per hour. *Reserve* police officers take the same amount of training as fulltime personnel and have the same law enforcement authority, but they are scheduled to work only as needed such as during major events, disasters, or emergencies. Auxiliary officers can be used to provide technical (but nonsworn) assistance. *Auxiliary* officers are nonsworn employees who work directly under the supervision of a fulltime officer.

---

[1] Police Training Institute, University of Illinois.

699

This concept can also be applied to other positions in a community. The reduction of the greatest cost to any employer -- salaries -- can be achieved.

Another way to reduce personnel costs during the application process is to establish a registry of candidates shared by a number of agencies. In Fairfield County, Connecticut, 10 agencies implemented preapplication testing and screening of police candidates. Rotunda (1990) A standardized certification procedure was used, and the candidate was required to pay for this process. Using a third-party screening organization, candidates were screened using standardized assessment procedures designed to objectively measure the abilities and personal criteria considered necessary for success in law enforcement occupations. The resulting list of candidates was then provided to the hiring agencies, freeing their budget and personnel from the costly and time-consuming tasks of testing and screening. The applicant benefits from the registry because a single application process results in distribution of his or her name to all participating agencies. Agencies would no longer waste dollars on testing unqualified candidates. The registry concept would easily work together with the idea of preservice certification in required training. The registry process could be integrated into the required training process. The end result would be elimination of the cost of applicant testing and entry-level training.

Management changes, recruitment campaigns, and training programs all require funding. Reallocation of existing funds to make them work more efficiently is perhaps the least costly way to pay for these changes. Shared applicant registries coupled with requirements for preservice training eliminate significant costs to the employer. These savings, can be transferred to other critical areas, such as health care, promotion, and training in effective management techniques.

FACILITY QUALITY

Facilities play an important role in the public sector. The work environment can make the difference between a successful organization and one that struggles. As funding decreases and the demands for services remains constant (or increases), it is important to invest money where it will produce the greatest return. Facilities are a good candidate for such an investment. A minor cost when compared to personnel expenses, properly selected facility investments can significantly improve productivity of the workforce. Brill (1986)

Businesses understand the impact of their facilities on their operations. Any spending on facilities must be justifiable. This pertains to the public sector as well as the private sector. Costs must be traced to something that helps the organization fulfill its mission. When funds are invested in equipment, systems, personnel, training, and other "concrete" items whose effects can be measured, there is an audit trail that can justify that expense. The "bottom line" mentality demands a well defined, clearly understood accounting of costs, and how those costs contribute to fulfilling the mission of the organization.

The impact of facilities in the area of public service must be evaluated if agencies are to effectively respond to decreasing resources and increasing demands for services. Investing in facilities to support the public workforce may or may not provide a measurable return on investment. However, facilities *do* play an important role in how employees of public agencies perform their functions. This concept is strongly supported within the nation's military services:

> Military installations are vital to the nation's security, and quality facilities greatly enhance the working and living conditions of our military people and their families....The investment that this country makes in its defense facilities is an investment in its military people--an investment that is repaid in the form of improved pride, greater performance, and better combat readiness. Department of Defense (1988)

The Department of Defense report from which the quote was extracted goes further to state that "All base operating support, either directly or indirectly, contributes to the performance of the military mission." Department of Defense (1988) It is necessary for the Army to support this mission from a fixed base structure. Due to the aging base structure and limited land assets, the Army has defined a policy of maintaining the current facilities, correcting deficiencies, and replacing or renovating deteriorated facilities to provide the best mix of maintenance, construction, and renewal. Department of Defense (1988) Given the relationships between facilities and mission, and the importance of maintaining, renovating, repairing, or replacing the facilities to support the mission, it is obvious that military facilities have a direct link with fulfillment of the military mission. The same holds true for the facilities used by governments at every level around the nation.

Certain facilities must be available to support vehicles and other equipment used in the public sector. Mission essential equipment such as highway maintenance vehicles, police vehicles, and fire equipment require facilities. This illustrates the necessary link between the facility and the mission. What is usually not as obvious is the effect of facility degradation on an organization's mission readiness.

Facility and equipment quality are important to whatever extent they affect employee performance. Facilities that are inadequate or of inferior condition hurt employee morale, thus interfering with productivity. There have been numerous studies involving military installations and the requirements for maintaining a standing Army. The supposition here is that, since so much emphasis has been placed on quality of life and concern for the appearance of military communities, there is indeed a basis for linking a government agency's mission with its facilities. Assistant Secretary of Defense (Force Management and Personnel) Chapman B. Cox stated that attention to the employees' quality of life pays off in retention, increased morale, and productivity. Kline (1988) Mr. Robert P. Stone, as Deputy Assistant to the Secretary of Defense (Installations), also has emphasized that quality of life is impacted by the facilities in which personnel live and work:

> Facility investment is critical, we can't afford not to invest more. Obsolete facilities are expensive because they cost us productivity, quality, and pride-- which means reduced mission capability. Industry invests about three times

as much, proportionally, as DOD. Major companies...invest in quality facilities to get and keep the best people, to get the best from their people, and to accomplish their mission better...These companies know that quality facilities repay their cost in the quality of work done by people who use them. Stone (1989)

As mentioned in the section on personnel issues, retaining a quality workforce in the public sector is critical if the organizations expect to provide the full spectrum of services demanded of them when funding is becoming more and more critical.

PROGRAMS

The third driver of productivity considered here is whether alterations in existing programs or the addition of new programs may enhance productivity levels. Often program changes are the first alternative considered when improvements in productivity are sought. While this discussion has emphasized productivity-related aspects of personnel policy and facility quality not widely discussed, several programming issues are also relevant to examine here. These areas of programming warrant attention: (1) manpower and scheduling, (2) time and money saving, (3) and equipment improvement programs.

Programs that affect manpower levels are the most common productivity improvement methods utilized. Frequently, this amounts to agency heads asking their governing bodies for more personnel. O'Boyle (1991) But, as previously indicated, the current environment requires public agencies to maintain services as funding levels decline. In law enforcement, for example, "Municipal boards and state legislatures are no longer buying into the idea that simply hiring more police officers will improve the level of policing." Rose (1991) Therefore, agencies must try new methods of addressing the need for greater productivity.

Alternative scheduling is one such method. One thing many public service agencies have in common is their need to operate 24 hours a day rather than a standard 8 or 12 hour business day. The public expects this fulltime service from a number of agencies. Traditionally this kind of coverage has been accomplished by working in three 8 hour shifts, for example, 7:00 AM to 3:00 PM, 3:00 PM to 11:00 PM, and 11:00 PM to 7:00 AM.

The rationale for alternative scheduling is based on two premises. First, it recognizes workload differences between shifts; second, it considers the effects of scheduling on individual employees. Clearly, in many public service agencies, workload is different at 3:00 PM than at 3:00 AM. Furthermore, researchers have documented many "negative effects on the human body that ultimately affect the employee's productivity, attitudes, and health." Rose (1991) Taken together, these two points make it clear that productivity may be affected either positively or negatively by scheduling decisions. A complete evaluation of both aspects may lead to more productive scheduling decisions.

Numerous time, and money, saving programs have also been cited as having the ability to improve productivity. Most such programs are successful because they do not require a new funding source. In other words, one thing that successful programs under this heading have in common is that they fund themselves. Productivity levels are improved without incurring the usual cost associated with the addition of a new program. Many public service agencies are constantly looking for new sources of funding, but all too often they fail to look "in their own backyard." Perhaps a public service agency can fund it's own programs while, at the same time, improving the productivity of it's employees.

Law enforcement provides some good examples of self-sufficient productivity improvement programs. Many agencies have instituted Selective Traffic Enforcement Programs (STEP programs), which are self-funding. In order to implement a successful STEP program, a police department must first evaluate it's traffic enforcement productivity in terms of the impact that any current traffic enforcement has on high-accident or high-violation locations within its jurisdiction. Those areas would be targeted for a STEP program. Officers would be assigned to a STEP unit on an overtime basis and would not be required to handle any activity other than traffic enforcement at a targeted location. The revenue generated by the traffic citations written at that location is earmarked to fund the STEP overtime budget. In this way the program is self-sufficient while improving the productivity of the agency as well.

Another example of a self-sufficient program from the law enforcement field involves forfeiture laws that are currently being enacted in many states. Although the laws vary in detail, they are generally similar. In effect, state forfeiture laws and actions filed under federal laws governing racketeering and corrupt organizations (RICO) allow police departments to seize any property used in the commission of a felony and sell it or use it in the conduct of police business. RICO even allows police departments to seize all of the proceeds of a continuing criminal enterprise. For police agencies, self-funding programs such as the forfeiture laws and RICO "have power and potential because they can bring substantial financial penalties against criminals, which in turn can result in substantial financial gains to police departments." Snow (1990) The productivity level of the police agency improves because the consequences of arrest and convictions are more detrimental than they would be otherwise, and often put the offender out of business permanently.

A third area that is being carefully considered by law enforcement agencies is the idea of charging citizens or private businesses to reimburse the police for the cost of certain services. For example, when police respond to a false alarm by a residential security system, the owner of the property may be charged a standard fee for the response. Where this policy is in effect, there are fewer false alarms at the same address because the home owner tends to be more careful with the alarm system. In this manner, police productivity may improve because officers have more time available to handle other calls for service. Also, the additional revenue generated can help fund other crime prevention programs, such as a Neighborhood Watch program. There is great potential for adapting this approach to many other services, both by police departments and public service agencies in general.

As in the programming areas discussed above, equipment improvement programs also have the ability to improve agency productivity. The costs of improvements can easily be offset by the amount of time saved due to the improvements. Hand held police computers that issue parking citations are one such example. Similar devices have been used for several years in both the private and public sectors for tasks such as inventory control and utility billing. Parks (1990) Traditionally, parking citations were handwritten in an inefficient and often illegible manner. The hand held ticket computer eliminates these problems, and its data can be transferred electronically to a desktop computer instead of being transcribed manually.

Another equipment improvement program frequently tried by law enforcement agencies is the audio recording of police reports. This strategy, like those discussed above, "focuses on keeping the patrol units in productive service." Kelly (1990) A great deal of a patrol officer's time is spent writing reports, often by hand. While reports are a necessity, writing them ties up much valuable time. Many departments now encourage officers to record their reports, after which the recordings are transcribed by clerical staff. The pay rate for clerical staff is generally much lower than for patrol officers, and the trained clerical personnel can transcribe a voice recording much faster than an officer can handwrite it. The police department in Fort Collins, Colorado, estimates that the audio taping of police reports has saved the department over $1 million. Kelly (1990)

PRODUCTIVITY AND MISSION

It is readily apparent that there are many productivity incentives for implementing the types of changes discussed throughout this paper, as well as alternative funding methods that place no new burdens on revenue sources that are already overwhelmed. When studying changes such as those discussed, an agency may also need to consider whether its mission must be redefined. In some cases the mission may need to be changed, while in others, it may not. But when funding becomes scarcer as constituents simultaneously demand steady or increasing levels of service, it seems advisable for a public agency to reevaluate its mission. As one police official has noted, "The rapid growth of communities, a constantly changing environment, the challenges of a generation of youth at risk and the increasing evidence that traditional incident-driven policing has failed - all are compelling reasons for police executives to carefully define their agency's mission." Nila (1990) Because the changing environment has impact far beyond the law enforcement profession, this statement contains prudent advice for public service agencies in general.

CONCLUSION

Public service agencies can respond to increasing demands for services with decreasing resources through creativity. Part of this creativity involves looking to the private sector for appropriate solutions. The public sector should willingly learn from both the successes and failures by private sector in its efforts to improve productivity. Implementing the changes discussed in this paper would require an agency to modify its management philosophy and redirect existing funds to support new productivity initiatives. The public agency's mission would not necessarily change, but the methods by which this service is provided would be made more efficient. Nevertheless, reevaluation of missions is essential in all cases wherever the environment is rapidly changing. Ultimately, redefining the mission may be a proper response where the demand for services cannot be met with the resources available.

The 1990s may well be the decade known throughout history as the one that determined the fate of public service. It is clear that most state and federal agencies do not have the resources that were available in previous decades. It is equally clear that the demand for services has not declined: the burden on the public sector is greater than ever. In order to survive the contradictory forces buffeting the public sector, agencies must effectively learn how to maintain and improve productivity.

REFERENCES

Brill, Michael (1986) Designing High-Performance Workspaces for Pacific Bell, Buffalo, BOSTI.

Department of Defense (1988) Department of Defense Base Structure Report for Fiscal Year 1989, Washington, D.C., Department of Defense.

Hyams, M. (1991) "Recruitment, Selection, and Retention: A Matter of Commitment", The Police Chief, p. 24.

Kelly, Patrick T. (1990) "Report Preparation: Easing the Burden - Increasing Productivity by Taping Reports", The Police Chief, pp. 49-50.

Kline, Terry D. (1988) "An investigation into the Predictors of Employment Intentions for Department of Defense Employees", MS thesis, Air Force Institute of Technology.

Nila, Captain Michael J. (1990) "Community Policing- Defining the Police Mission: A Community/Police Perspective", The Police Chief, pp. 43-45.

O'Boyle, Ernest H. (1991) "Manpower", Law and Order, pp. 88-93.

Parks, Commander Charles H. (1990) "On the Cutting Edge- Handheld Police Computers: The Ticket to the Future", The Police Chief, pp. 36-44.

Rose, Deputy Chief Raymond J. (1991) "Enhancing Organizational Efficiency Through Alternative Scheduling", The Police Chief, pp. 60-63.

Rotunda, T. (1990) "The New Tool for More Cost Effective Hiring: The Municipal Registry", The Police Chief, pp. 19-20.

Snow, Robert L. (1990) "Funding by Offenders", Law and Order, pp. 67-70.

Stone, Robert P. (1989) "Excellent Installations", Defense Housing, vol III, no. 6, pp. 18-20.

Productivity & Quality Management Frontiers-IV, edited by Sumanth, Edosomwan, Poupart, and Sink. ©1993 Institute of Industrial Engineers.

Productivity Improvement through Training in the Changing Technologies in Indian Cement Industry

M.B. Patel
Shantilal Shah Engineering College
Bhavnagar, Gujrat State INDIA

J.M. Mahajan and U.R.K. Rao
Indian Institute of Technology
Hauz-Khas, New Delhi INDIA

ABSTRACT

Over the last ten years or so, there has been a significant advance in the development of modern technologies in Indian Cement Industry. This has resulted in the achievement of order, efficiency and control ensuring productivity improvement. However, there exists a need for training the personnel in the industry to cope with these technological developments. For this purpose a Training Master Plan (TMP) has been developed in this paper. Based on this, a Linear Programming Training Model (LPTM) has been developed to decide the number of persons to be trained. The application of the model has been demonstrated through a case study in one cement plant.

INTRODUCTION

In India, the cement industry started in 1904 and grew to a modest capacity of about 75,000 tonnes per year in 1913. The installed capacity of this industry grew up to 29.3 million tonnes by 1981-82[2]. The growth in the capacity was unprecedented after February 1982. The installed capacity thereafter went up further from 29.3 million tonnes in 1981-82 to 61.34 million tonnes by the end of March 1992[1]. This capacity is attributed to the 97 large cement plants in India, excluding the capacity of white and mini cement plants. Out of the 61.34 million tonnes capacity, the share of private sector plants is 51.76 million tonnes and the rest of 9.58 million tonnes share is of public sector plants. The production which was 21.00 million tonnes in 1981-82 went up to 50.61 million tonnes by the end of March 1992[1]. With this, India has emerged self-sufficient in cement production and has attained the fourth position among cement producing nations in the world [1]. The long term strategy of Indian cement industry is to increase the capacity and the production upto 100 million tonnes and 87 million tonnes respectively by 2000 A.D.[2].

TECHNOLOGICAL DEVELOPMENTS AND HUMAN FACTORS IN THE INDUSTRY

Since Indian cement industry has undergone technological improvements from time to time, there are at present all types of cement plants in India based on old wet process technology to most modern dry process technology. In the wake of partial decontrol policy started in 1982 and total decontrol policy in 1989, ambitious and comprehensive modernisation programs have been undertaken by this industry. Thus, over the last ten years there has been a significant advance in the development of modern technologies. A number of new units has come into existance during this time. They are large in size and are based on modern technologies incorporating sophisticated systems and equipments. This has resulted in the achievement of order, efficiency and control ensuring quality and productivity improvements. However, the capabilities of human resource are not at par with technological developments in the industry. Inability to reach expected operating, maintaining and controlling functions in the plants is most often due to the lack of total systems perspectives in which human elements are planned and developed to match the technical elements[5]. The full potential of modern technologies can best be achieved only when the technical and human components are balanced. In this context, there exists a need for higher level of skills and knowledge to balance the technological developments. This can be obtained through a systematic approach to training the total work force at all levels in the industry.

DEVELOPING THE TRAINING MASTER PLAN (TMP)

There is a need for knowledge-intensive skills of a higher
order in the changing scenario of Indian cement industry,
which demands continuous improvements in skills and work
practices with the upgradation of technology [4]. This need
for knowledge-intensive skills is not only limited to
technical personnel at lower levels but is essential for
other personnel including those in management. They also
need to update their knowledge and skills required to
operate and maintain the plant. In other words, training is
necessary for all levels of personnel in the plant. The
authors had the opportunity to visit some of the cement
plants based on traditional as well modern technologies.
The interviews held with many personnel working in these
plants confirmed the impression about the shortfall in
qualified personnel needed to cope with the rapid
technological developments in the industry.

Keeping this in view, it is suggested that a Training Master
Plan (TMP) be prepared for a given cement plant. This can
be looked upon as the human resource inventory for the
entire plant and can provide the targets for training of
workers at all levels. This way of looking at the training
needs may permit the application of the principles of
inventory control to be employed for designing and
regulating the training programmes.

The personnel working in the industry are grouped under the
various categories. The number of training programs and the
number of training categories are finalised in consultation
with the people involved in training in the industry. This
plan has been given in Table-1, which is proposed as the
Training Master Plan (TMP) for the cement industry in
general. The individual cement plant can modify this
training master plan (TMP) as per its own requirements.
The details regarding training programs and training
categories are included in the TMP.

A LINEAR PROGRAMMING TRAINING MODEL (LPTM)

After developing the training master plan (TMP) the
management has to decide the number of persons from various
categories to be trained within the organisational
constraints. Depending upon the commitment to production
targets of individual cement plant, a lot of human as well
as physical resources are needed for training. So before a
commitment is made for training the management has to think
over about the budget. Investment in training is one of the
constraints and hence the decision maker has to allocate his
permissible resources among the various training programs in

Table-1

Training Master Plan

Training Programs in		Training Programs For						
		(X_1)	(X_2)	(X_3)	(X_4)	(X_5)	(X_6)	(X_7)
Management Systems	Y_1	x	x	x				
Maintenance & Spares	Y_2			x		x	x	
Operations Improvements	Y_3		x		x		x	
Management Techniques	Y_4	x	x	x				
Operations & Technology in Cement Plant	Y_5		x		x		x	
Energy Conservation	Y_6	x	x	x	x			
Optimization in Plant	Y_7	x	x	x				
Problem Solving Techniques	Y_8	x	x	x	x			
Communication and Coordination Techniques	Y_9	x	x	x	x			
Cement Technology and Maintenance	Y_{10}		x		x	x		
Safety in Cement Plants	Y_{11}				x	x	x	x
Schedule Maintenance	Y_{12}			x		x	x	
Methods & Instruments	Y_{13}		x	x	x	x		
Quality Assurance	Y_{14}		x		x		x	
Overseas Visits and Training	Y_{15}	x	x	x				
Coaching & Orientattion Programs	Y_{16}				x	x	x	x
Job Rotation	Y_{17}		x	x	x	x	x	
Apprenticeship	Y_{18}							x

X_1 = Persons in Middle Management & above that category
X_2 = Operational Engineers
X_3 = Maintenance Engineers
X_4 = Operational Supervisors and Foreman
X_5 = Maintenance Supervisors and Foreman
X_6 = Skilled Workers
X_7 = Unskilled Workers

a judicious way. A linear programming based training model (LPTM) has been developed for this purpose.

The mathematical statement of the model in linear programming will be -

Find X_1, X_2, X_3, ... X_n which optimise the linear function

$$Z = C_1X_1 + C_2X_2 + C_3X_3 + ... C_nX_n$$

Subject to :

$$a_{11}X_1 + a_{12}X_2 + a_{13}X_3 + ... a_{1n}X_n \leq b_1$$
$$a_{21}X_1 + a_{22}X_2 + a_{23}X_3 + ... a_{1n}X_n \leq b_2$$
$$..$$
$$..$$

$$a_{m1}X_1 + a_{m2}X_2 + a_{m3}X_3 + ... a_{mn}X_n \leq b_m$$
and $X_1 \geq 0$, $X_2 \geq 0$, ... $X_n \geq 0$

where,

Z is the measure of effectiveness of systems performance in achieving the training objectives.

C_j is the relative contribution towards the effectiveness in training the persons in different categories.

X_j is the number of persons being trained in the j_{th} category.

a_{ij} is the amount of resource i consumed by each number of person of the competing category j.

b_j is the amount of resource i available for j_{th} category.
    for   i = 1, 2, 3 .... m and
           j = 1, 2, 3 .... n

The variables X_1, X_2, X_3, ... X_n being solved are called decision variables. They are the number of persons of the j_{th} category to be trained. With the help of Training Master Plan (TMP), a linear programming based training model (LPTM) has been developed which is shown in Table-2.

Any cement industry can use this model to maximize the number of persons in various categories to be trained within the organisational constraints. This model will provide feasible solutions. An optimal solution will indicate the number of persons to be trained from various categories.

Table - 2
A Linear Programming Training Model (LPTM)

Find $X_1, X_2, X_3 \ldots\ldots\ldots X_n$ which optimise the linear function $Z = C_1X_1+C_2X_2+C_3X_3+C_4X_4+C_5X_5+C_6X_6+C_7X_7$

		Middle Management & above category (X_1)	Operational Engineers (X_2)	Maintenance nance (X_3)	Operational Supervisors (X_4)	Maintenance Supervisor (X_5)	Skilled Workers (X_6)	Unskilled Workers (X_7)	Available Resources
Management Systems	Y_1	$a_{11}x_1$	$+a_{12}x_2$	$+a_{13}x_3$	+ - - -	+ - - -	+ - - -	+ - - -	$< b_1$
Maintenance & Spares	Y_2	- - -	+ - - -	$+a_{23}x_3$	+ - - -	$+a_{25}x_5$	$+a_{26}x_6$	+ - - -	$< b_2$
Operations Improvements	Y_3	- - -	$+a_{32}x_2$	+ - - -	$+a_{34}x_4$	+ - - -	$+a_{36}x_6$	+ - - -	$< b_3$
Management Techniques	Y_4	$a_{41}x_1$	$+a_{42}x_2$	$+a_{43}x_3$	+ - - -	+ - - -	+ - - -	+ - - -	$< b_4$
Operations & Technology in Cement Plant	Y_5	- - -	$+a_{32}x_2$	+ - - -	$+a_{54}x_4$	+ - - -	$+a_{56}x_6$	+ - - -	$< b_5$
Energy Conservation	Y_6	$+a_{61}x_1$	$+a_{62}x_2$	$+a_{63}x_3$	$+a_{64}x_4$	+ - - -	+ - - -	+ - - -	$< b_6$
Optimization in Plant	Y_7	$+a_{71}x_1$	$+a_{72}x_2$	$+a_{73}x_3$	+ - - -	+ - - -	+ - - -	+ - - -	$< b_7$
Problem Solving Techniques	Y_8	$+a_{81}x_1$	$+a_{82}x_2$	$+a_{83}x_3$	$+a_{84}x_4$	+ - - -	+ - - -	+ - - -	$< b_8$
Communication and Coordination Techniques	Y_9	$+a_{91}x_1$	$+a_{92}x_2$	$+a_{93}x_3$	$+a_{94}x_4$	+ - - -	+ - - -	+ - - -	$< b_9$
Cement Technology and Maintenance	Y_{10}	- - -	+ - - -	$+a_{103}x_3$	+ - - -	$+a_{105}x_5$	$a_{106}x_6$	+ - - -	$< b_{10}$
Safety in Cement Plants	Y_{11}	- - -	+ - - -	+ - - -	$+a_{114}x_4$	$+a_{115}x_5$	$a_{116}x_6$	$+a_{117}x_7$	$< b_{11}$
Schedule Maintenance	Y_{12}	- - -	+ - - -	$+a_{123}x_3$	+ - - -	$+a_{125}x_5$	$a_{126}x_6$	+ - - -	$< b_{12}$
Methods & Instruments	Y_{13}	- - -	$+a_{132}x_2$	$+a_{133}x_3$	$+a_{134}x_4$	$+a_{135}x_5$	- - -	+ - - -	$< b_{13}$
Quality Assurance	Y_{14}	- - -	$+a_{142}x_2$	+ - - -	$+a_{144}x_4$	+ - - -	$a_{146}x_6$	+ - - -	$< b_{14}$
Overseas Visits and Training	Y_{15}	$a_{151}x_1$	$+a_{152}x_2$	$+a_{153}x_3$	+ - - -	+ - - -	- - -	+ - - -	$< b_{15}$
Coaching & Orientation Programs	Y_{16}	- - -	+ - - -	+ - - -	$+a_{164}x_4$	$+a_{165}x_5$	$a_{166}x_6$	$+a_{167}x_7$	$< b_{16}$
Job Rotation	Y_{17}	- - -	$+a_{172}x_2$	$+a_{173}x_3$	$+a_{174}x_4$	$+a_{175}x_5$	$a_{176}x_6$	$+a_{177}x_7$	$< b_{17}$
Apprenticeship	Y_{18}	- - -	+ - - -	+ - - -	+ - - -	+ - - -	+ - - -	$+a_{187}x_7$	$< b_{18}$

A CASE STUDY

A case study in a cement plant was carried out to show as to how this model can be worked out. A Master Training Plan (MTP) and linear programming based training model (LPTM), were developed for the given cement plant, and the following policy norms were drawn up :

(1) The number of training programs suggested were modified according to the needs as perceived by the management. Table-3 gives the information about the training programs under various categories in the company.

(2) Management did not agree to develop inhouse training programs in company itself. However, they agreed to purchase training modules from experts in the field.

(3) Management did not give any specific time span during which training programs could be conducted and budget allocated. However, they decided to allocate an adhoc amount, which excluded the purchasing cost of training modules, as under :

a)	For training programs	Y_1	–	Rs.20,000.00
b)	For training programs	Y_3	–	Rs.20,000.00
c)	For training programs	Y_4	–	Rs.12,500.00
d)	For training programs	Y_8	–	Rs.12,500.00
e)	For training programs	Y_9	–	Rs.30,000.00
f)	For training programs	Y_{16}	–	Rs.18,000.00
g)	For training programs	Y_{18}	–	Rs.10,000.00

(4) It was impossible for management to spare at a time more than 150 persons from operational categories as well as from maintenance categories (including skilled workers). Total number of persons that management can spare for training were 300, approximately one-fourth of company's strength.

(5) Management expressed it's views about spending money per person on a category basis to meet the personal needs like refreshments etc. It was decided by them to spare money per person as under :

a)	For Category No.1	–	Rs. 150.00 each
b)	For Categories No.2, 3	–	Rs. 200.00 each
c)	For Categories No.4,5,6	–	Rs. 100.00 each
d)	For Category No.7	–	Rs. 40.00 each

The other constraints regarding the number of persons to be trained in each category were incorporated in the upper bound and lower bound constraints respectively. The values

Table-3

Training Model

Training Programs in	Training Programs For						
	X_1	X_2	X_3	X_4	X_5	X_6	X_7
Maintenance and Spares for Maint. Personnel - Y_2			x		x	x	
Operations Improvements for Operational Personnel - Y_3		x		x		x	
Management Technique - Y_4	x	x	x				
Problems Solving Techniques - Y_8	x			x	x		
Communication and Coordination Techniques - Y_9	x	x	x	x	x	x	
Coaching and Orientation Programs - Y_{16}	x	x				x	x
Apprenticeship - Y_{18}						x	x

X_1 = Persons in Middle Management & above that category
X_2 = Operational Engineers
X_3 = Maintenance Engineers
X_4 = Operational Supervisors and Foreman
X_5 = Maintenance Supervisors and Foreman
X_6 = Skilled Workers
X_7 = Unskilled Workers

of C_1, C_2, C_3, ... C_7 which indicate the relative contribution towards the effectiveness of systems performance in training the persons from various categories were determined using a procedure based on Delphi study. The study was conducted in three rounds. The consolidated statistical summary of experts' responses was prepared and the final values of C_1, C_2, C_3, ... C_7 with rounding them off to the nearest multiple of 5 were obtained as 20, 15, 15, 15, 15, 15 and 05 respectively.

Objective Function

The objective function for this case study is to maximize the number of persons in jth category that optimize the linear function :

$$Z = 20x_1 + 15x_2 + 15x_3 + 15x_4 + 15x_5 + 15x_6 + 5x_7$$

Subject to :

(A) Resource constraints :

    1)   For training program in maintenance and spares
$$200x_3 + 100x_5 + 100x_6 \leq 20,000$$

    2)   For training program in operations improvements
$$200x_2 + 100x_4 + 100x_6 \leq 20,000$$

    3)   For training program in management technique
$$500x_1 + 200x_2 + 200x_3 \leq 12,500$$

    4)   For training program in problem solving technique
$$500x_1 + 100x_4 + 100x_5 \leq 12,500$$

    5)   For training program in communication and co-ordination technique
$$500x_1+200x_2+200x_3+100x_4+100x_5+100x_6 \leq 30,000$$

    6)   For training program in coaching and orientation
$$200x_2 + 200x_3 + 100x_6 + 40x_7 \leq 18,000$$

    7)   For training program in Apprenticeship
$$100x_6 + 40x_7 \leq 10,000$$

(B) Capacity constraints :

$$x_2 + x_4 + x_6 \leq 150$$
$$x_3 + x_5 + x_6 \leq 150$$
$$x_1 + x_2 + x_3 + x_4 + x_5 + x_6 + x_7 \leq 300$$

(C) Lower bound constraints :

$$x_1 \geq 5, \quad x_2 \geq 10, \quad x_3 \geq 10, \quad x_4 \geq 20, \quad x_5 \geq 20$$
$$x_6 \geq 35, \quad x_7 \geq 35$$

(D) Upper bound constraints :

$$x_1 \leq 15, \quad x_2 \leq 25, \quad x_3 \leq 25, \quad x_4 \leq 50,$$
$$x_5 \leq 50, \quad x_6 \leq 150, \quad x_7 \leq 100$$
$$\text{and} \quad x_1, \quad x_2, \quad x_3 \ldots\ldots\ldots \geq 0$$

Solution Procedure and Analysis of Results

The problem has been solved with the generalised linear
programming package on the computer using the revised
simplex method for solution. This employs the bounded
variables algorithm for the solution of the problem and
offers the use of upper bounded and equal to number of
variables. The minimum number of persons to be trained or
the maximum number of persons to be trained and constraints
can be taken care with the help of this particular feature,
without adding to the size of the matrix [3]. Changes in
the data matrix, i.e. changing the co-efficient, changing
the R.H.S, addition or deletion of constraints etc. can be
made with ease and speed.

For the case under study the computer tried 18 basic
solutions and the last solution was found to be the optimal
solution to the problem. Accordingly to this solution
management could give training to 275 persons. The detailed
break-up of the persons to be trained from each category is
given in Table-4. This solution utilises 92 per cent of the
total number of persons that could be spared for training.
The value, in terms of index number, of the objective
function is 3650 and there is a surplus budget of
Rs.7600.00. It is up to the management as to how and where
to use this surplus budget. However, in case management
decides to use this surplus budget amount for training, then
it is necessary to carry out the sensitivity analysis.

Sensitivity Analysis

Although optimum solution states what to do, given the
objective function and the constraints, the sensitivity
analysis raises questions about the opportunities and
perhaps about what could or should be done to improve the
solution to the managerial problem. If the management makes
the changes in the cost function of a_{ij} per participant for
training program for the respective category, then it will
be interesting to know the results of these changes through
the model. Hence, two changes were made in the original
model for further investigations about the dynamic
characteristics of the model. The cost per participant
which was Rs.500/- for category X_1 is refixed at Rs.250/-
and the cost which was Rs.100/- for category X_6 is refixed
at Rs.60/-. The program was rerun on the computer. Again
18 basic solutions were obtained. Likewise, changes were
made in other parameters of the model and subsequent results
were obtained. these results are shown in Table-5. The
information in this table gives the insight for deciding the
combination of persons to be spared for training. The
important point is to make the compromise within the
constraints. If management is ready to make the compromise

with it's constraints, sensitivity analysis helps the
management to improve the solution to the managerial
problem. Thus, this model can be used as a managerial tool
in solving such problems.

Table-4

Solution of the Problem using L.P. Based Training Model

Value of the Objective Function	Surplus Budget	Persons to be trained in the respective category							Total
		X_1	X_2	X_3	X_4	X_5	X_6	X_7	
3650	Rs.7600	5	20	20	50	50	80	50	275

Table-5

Sensitivity Analysis

Changes in the model	Value of the Objective Function	Surplus budget	Persons to be trained in the respective category							Total
			X_1	X_2	X_3	X_4	X_5	X_6	X_7	
1. Changes in aij value Rs.250 for category-X_1 Rs.60 for category-X_6	3900	Rs.17,845	10	25	25	50	50	75	65	300
2. Change in total budget Rs. -23,000	2312	Rs.43,000	5	10	10	20	20	54	100	219
3. Change in sponsoring capacity										
a) 175 for Operational Personnel 175 for Maintenance Personnel	4150	Rs.12,345	10	25	25	50	50	100	40	300
b) 125 for Operational Personnel 125 for Maintenance Personnel	3650	Rs.23,345	10	25	25	50	50	50	90	300

REFERENCES

1. Cement Manufactuters' Association (May 1992), "Basic Data - Cement Industry", Vol.1, N. Delhi, CMA Publication. pp.1-2.

2. Chakravarty, S.M. (1989), "Cement Industry - the emerging surplus scenario, Indian Cement Review - Annual 1988", Wadhera Roshan (ED), Wadhera Publication, Bombay.

3. Gillett, B.E. (1986), "Introduction to Operations Research - A computer oriented Algorithmic Approach", Tata McGraw-Hill Publication, New Delhi.

4. Patel, M.B.; Mahajan, J.M.; and Rao, U.R.K. (1988), "Productivity Improvement Through HRD in Indian Cement Industry", XXX, National Convention, Indian Institution of Industrial Engineering.

5. Patel, M.B. (1989), "Human Resource Development in the midst of Changing Technologies in Indian Cement Industry", Ph.D. Thesis, IIT, New Delhi.

DR. M. B. PATEL

Graduated in Mechanical Engineering in 1972. He took his M.Tech. and Ph.D. in Industrial Engineering in 1985 and 1989 respectively from Indian Institute of Technology, New Delhi. He has carried out teaching at various engineering colleges owned by Government of Gujarat. At present he is a faculty member at Shantilal Shah Engineering College, Bhavnagar, a Government of Gujarat Institution. His current interest is in industrial engineering and management.

PROF. J. M. MAHAJAN

B.E. (Mech.), M.E. (Ind. & Prod.) from Rourkee University in 1961 and 1965 respectively and Ph.D. in Engonomics & Work Dsign from Indian Institute of Technology, New Delhi in 1982. He has been carrying out teaching and research at Indian Institute of Technology, New Delhi since 1966. He is consultant to many industries. Currently Vice Chairman of National Council of Indian Institution of Industrial Engineering. His current interests are T.Q.M., Engonomics and Human Factors Engg, Industrial Safety.

PROF. U.R.K. RAO

Took his B.Tech. in Mechanical Engineering and M.Tech. in Production Engineering in 1961 and 1963 respectively from Indian Institute of Technology, Kharagpur. His Ph.D. is from Imperial College, London (1971). He has been carrying out teaching and research at Indian Institute of Technology, New Delhi since 1964. His current interests are in OAD/CAM, CIM and Optimization of Production Systems.

Productivity & Quality Management Frontiers-IV, edited by Sumanth, Edosomwan, Poupart, and Sink. ©1993 Institute of Industrial Engineers.

Quality Engineering, Off-Line Quality Control and the Taguchi Methods

E. Iakovou
University of Miami
Coral Gables, Florida USA

ABSTRACT

The challenge to improve quality during the last few decades has resulted in several exciting and useful developments. The introduction of the Taguchi approaches to "off-line" quality control in the western world is one of the major developments that has been surrounded with controversy.

A process or product design has to provide functional products under normal manufacturing conditions as well as all working conditions throughout the product's specified life. At the same time the development and manufacturing costs related to the product must be low, and the development time must be short so that market changes can be met. Genichi Taguchi of Japan, developed a systematic way to address these issues through optimization of the design process.

Off-line quality control methods and robust design are quality and cost control activities conducted at the product and process design stages to reduce product development and lifetime costs, and to improve product manufacturability and reliability. These methods have been found effective in many areas of engineering design in AT&T, Ford, ITT, Xerox and other major U.S. companies.

In this paper, we first introduce the concepts of off-line quality control and robust parameter design. We distinguish between the Taguchi strategy (the conceptual framework for planning a product or process design experiment) and the specific Taguchi methods. The Taguchi strategy attempts to find product and process designs that are robust over uncontrollable variability in the manufacturing environment and in the product's use environment. The Taguchi methods are the specific techniques proposed by Taguchi to implement this strategy. Such techniques as the signal-to-noise ratios and the orthogonal arrays have drawn lot of criticism for their effectiveness. We present an overview of the limitation of Taguchi's tactics along with alternative statistical techniques (such as exploratory data analysis, computer graphics, data transformation) that could be of great assistance to industrial management.

Keywords : robust design, off-line quality control, parameter design, quality engineering.

1 Introduction :

Fifteen years ago Dr. Genichi Taguchi was virtually unknown in the United states. Nowadays though he is frequently mentioned with such quality experts as W.E. Deming, J.M. Juran and K. Ishikawa. This change is an indication of the success of his quality engineering techniques. Dr. Taguchi created an extremely effective scheme for quality improvement by combining statistical methods with a solid understanding of engineering problems.

It is the purpose of this paper to describe concisely the Taguchi approach to quality engineering. For this we will address the issues involved in the philosophy the conceptual framework, alongwith the specific methods and techniques that Taguchi uses. Although some of these techniques have flaws and could be improved furthermore the basic approach to the "quality" problem is correct.

2 Taguchi's philosophy :

There is still certain mystique and controversy surrounding the Taguchi's quality philosophy. Some of its basic elements are the following :

- There is a societal loss generated by the fabrication of any manufactured product. This loss relates to the quality of that product.

- In a competitive market, where a plethora of new products are introduced rapidly, continuous quality improvement and cost reduction are necessary steps for the survival of any company.

- Variation in a product's performance during the product's life span is of paramount importance to the quality of the product. Furthermore, there is a customer's loss associated with this performance variation.

- The engineering designs of the product and its manufacturing process have a major effect on the quality and the cost of the manufactured product.

- Statistically planned experiments can be used to identify settings of product design characteristics that minimize performance variation.

2.1 Societal dimension of quality :

Quality is a complex concept that has many aspects : performance, durability, serviceability, reliability etc. The weight of its aspect on quality depends on the specific nature of the product and its potential use by the customer. Quality experts find it difficult to encompass all these aspects into a single definition of quality.

Taguchi on the other side, points out an important dimension of quality: the loss that is caused to the society by this product. Taguchi states that "Quality is the loss imparted to the society from the time a product is shipped". The smaller the loss the better is the quality of the product. Some potential components of the societal loss could be of failure to meet the customer's requirements for use or harmful side effects caused by a malfunctioning product.

The concept of societal loss provides us with a new way of tackling quality improvement projects. Let us consider the following case :
A manufacturer ships a product that imparts a loss of $ 1,000 to the customer while the cost to the manufacturer of adapting the manufacturing process and therefore preventing the customer's loss is $ 300. In this case the loss to the society is $ 1,000 - $ 300 = $ 700. The adaptive cost of $ 300 could eventually cost the manufacturer loss of goodwill along with a significant portion of the market share. This way of thinking dictates the use of a long term view when one considers investments in quality improvement.

2.2   Continuous Quality Improvement :

Continuous quality improvement and cost reduction are necessary steps for staying in business. This principle is quite popular today, even among western manufacturers. The only way that a business can ultimately survive is by gaining enough profit. This profit is a function of the market share and the manufacturing and marketing cost. In today's global economy customers are usually well informed and the selling price of a product is determined mainly by the selling price of comparable products that the competitors offer.

Companies that want to be successful have to realize that quality is never good enough and the manufacturing cost is never low enough. Quality improvement and cost reduction should be pursued on a continuous basis.

2.3   Performance Variation :

As it is mentioned above, Taguchi quantifies the quality of a product in terms of the total loss to the society from the time the product is shipped to the customer. This loss could be due to undesirable side effects or functional variation from the target performance. *Performance characteristics* are the characteristics of the final product that determine the product's performance by the customer's viewpoint. If the manufactured product is a TV set then a major performance characteristic will be the sharpness of the TV. If the product is a door of an automobile then the performance characteristics should include the length, the width, the quality of the surface of the door etc. Most products have more than one performance characteristics that are important to the customer. The ideal state of a performance characteristic from the user's point of view is called a *target value*.

It has been a widespread practice in industry to use interval specifications to define target values of performance characteristics. This approach implies that a customer is equally satisfied with the product as long as the values of the performance characteristic fall into the specified interval and becomes immediately dissatisfied when some values fall out of the interval. Rather than doing this Taguchi dictates the use of nominal levels and tolerances around them to define specifications of performance characteristics.

The variation of a performance characteristics from its target value is defined as performance variation. The smaller the variation the better is the quality of the product. This variation should be over the whole span of the product's life and under different operating conditions. For example, the amplification level of a public telephone set may differ from winter to summer, may deteriorate over a period of time and may also differ from one set to the other. In general a product's performance is influenced by factors which are called *noise factors*. There are three types of noise factors :
1. External : These are noise factors external to the product such as humidity, temperature, dust and human errors in operating the product.
2. Manufacturing Imperfections: These include the variation in the performance characteristics from unit to unit. As all manufacturing engineers know this is inevitable in a manufacturing process.
3. Deterioration : As time goes by the values of the characteristics of the different components that comprise the product might change. These changes lead to deterioration of the product's performance.

2.4   Expected loss due to performance variation :

Any variation of a product's performance characteristic from its target value causes a loss to the customer. This loss can be quantified as the *expected loss*, that is the expected value of monetary losses that a user is likely to suffer at any random point during the product's life time due to performance variation. By introducing the concept of expected loss the problem of reducing performance variation becomes more easy to tackle.

Let Y be the value of a performance characteristic and τ its target value. Y

is obviously a random variable that follows a certain probability distribution and its different realization would deviate from τ. This variation cause losses to the product's user. Let $l(Y)$ to represent the loss in dollars by a user at a random point during the product's life due to deviation of Y from τ. The actual form of $l(Y)$ is generally difficult to be estimated. For this, an approximation used widely in statistics is proposed, namely a quadratic approximation to $l(Y)$. That is,

$$l(Y) = K(Y - \tau)^2 \qquad (1)$$

where K is a constant (figure 1). K can be calculated in a simple way as long as $l(Y)$ is known for some value of Y. Suppose that the confidence interval that defines which products will be acceptable by the customer is $(\tau - \epsilon, \tau + \epsilon)$ and that the cost of repairing or discarding the product if Y falls out of this interval is C \$. Then from $C = K\epsilon^2 \Rightarrow K = C/\epsilon^2$.

This form of the loss function is appropriate when a specific target value is desirable and the loss increases symmetrically as the performance characteristic deviates from the target value. We will discuss other scenarios in subsequent sections.

The expected or average loss to customers due to performance variation is obtained by statistically averaging the quadratic loss associated with possible values of Y.

One should note that in this case the measure of variability is the mean squared error (MSE) of Y about the target value τ rather than its variance, since $l(Y)$ is proportional to MSE (Figure 1).

3   Quality Engineering :

One approach to reduce a product's performance variation would be to limit or even more eliminate the noise factors. For the example of the public phone set that would imply to demand tighter manufacturing tolerances or reduce the temperature range over which the device is supposed to be used. With no doubt these are expensive means to reduce functional variation. Taguchi on the other side points out that the final quality and cost of a manufactured product are determined very significantly by the engineering designs of the product and its manufacturing process. He then proposes to find the combination of design parameters that makes the process less sensitive (more robust) to all noise factors.

Taguchi considers three stages in a product's development : *system design, parameter design*, and *tolerance design.*

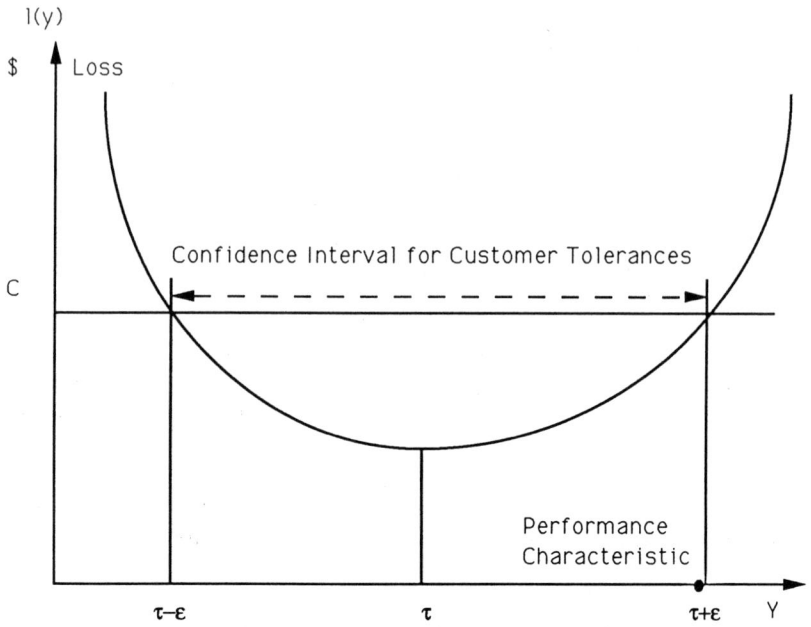

Figure 1.   Customer's Loss due to performance variation.

- *In the system design stage*, engineering and scientific knowledge is used to configure the basic product or process design. For example, in the design of a machining center, at the system design stage, the design engineers could decide about the necessity of a flexible machining cell consisting of lathes, a cell of drilling machines and a cell of presses.
System design requires an understanding of both the manufacturing environment and the customer's needs.

- *Parameter design* is the stage in which the parameters of the system design (values for the design variables) are determined.

- The settings that are chosen are the ones that reduce the sensitivity of the engineering design to sources of variation. In the design of the machining center, the objective of the parameter design stage would be to determine the number of lathes for the lathe flexible cell, the number of drilling machines for the milling cell and the number of presses for the press cell. So the system design stage represents the higher level in the hierarchy of decision during which a more general solution is proposed. At the lower level that represents the parameter design stage the system is optimized with respect to its controllable variables or parameters.

- *Tolerance design* is the process that determines tolerances around the nominal settings identified by parameter design. At this stage there is a tradeoff between narrow and wide tolerances. Too narrow tolerances increase significantly the manufacturing cost and on the other side wide tolerances increase performance variation and therefore the corresponding customer's loss.

We will explore parameter design furthermore since it is the most important and complex of the three stages.

4   Role of Parameter Design for improving Product Designs

4.1   Objective :

Let us recall what we would like to achieve at this stage. At every fixed combination of the design variables there is a distribution of the loss and a distribution of the quality due to manufacturing variations, uncontrollable internal and external variability. The Taguchi approach (strategy) attempts to find the combination of the values of the controllable design variables that minimizes the expected loss over the uncontrollable noise space.

4.2   Problem Structure :

Let τ denote the target value for the quality characteristic. Y is always the value of the quality characteristic. For product design let us assume that we identified the controllable variables $X = [X_1, X_2, ..., X_m]$ that are sufficient for specifying the product design. For each given vector X, there is a distribution of Y. We will use the following notation for the expected value and variance of Y at X :

$$E_\Omega(Y/X) = \eta(X) \tag{2}$$

$$Var_\Omega(Y/X) = E_\Omega[(Y/X) - \eta(X)]^2 \tag{3}$$

where $\Omega = [\Omega_1 \times \Omega_2 \times ... \times \Omega_L]$ stands for the noise parameter space, that is all possible combinations of environmental factors internal deterioration conditions etc.

As we explained before for a particular X there is a distribution of Y given X. To show the dependence on X we will denote the loss function as $l(Y/X)$ and then the expected loss function as

$$R(X) = E_\Omega l(Y/X) \tag{4}$$

Then the objective is to find a product design X that minimizes $R(X)$.

To minimize the expected loss $R(X)$ Taguchi proposes a two stage approach. He first introduces the use of performance statistics which he calls *signal-to-noise ratios*. In the first stage one tries to identify the combination of the controllable variables X_c which optimize a specific performance measure, π. In the second stage the controllable variables that have no impact on π, are used to adjust the expected value of Y close to the target value, that is $\eta(X) = \tau$. Leon, Shoemaker and Kackar(1987) in their paper follow that approach.

4.3   Parameter Design Experiments :

Parameter design is the process that aims to identify settings of product design characteristics that reduce performance variation. For this purpose statistically planned experiments can prove very useful. Parameter design is based on the classification of the variables that affect a product's performance into two categories : *design parameters* and *sources of noise*. Design parameters are those product parameters whose settings can be chosen by the product engineer. A vector of settings of all the design parameters define uniquely (there is one to one correspondence) a product design. The sources of noise are all the variables that cause the performance characteristics to deviate from their target values. They can be divided into *external sources of noise* (temperature, humidity, dust, human variations in operating the product) and *internal sources of noise* (manufacturing imperfections and product deterioration).

Note that in most cases we do not know all of the sources of noise, or in other cases we cannot in an experimental design because of actual physical constraints.

Noise factors are those sources of noise that can be included in an experiment; they should represent the major sources of noise affecting a product's performance in the field.

Taguchi proposes the use of two matrices for the conduct of an experiment : a *design parameter matrix* and a *noise factor matrix*. The first specifies the test settings of design parameters. Its column correspond to design parameters and its rows to different combinations of test settings and therefore to different product designs. Similarly the noise factor specifies the test settings of the noise factors. Its rows correspond to noise factors and its columns to different combinations of noise settings.

The experiment is run by
(1) varying systematically the settings of design parameters and
(2) by exploring the effect of the noise factors on each test run.

Therefore the experiment cannot be modelled as the product of the design parameter and the noise factor matrix (Table 1). Each test run of the design parameter matrix (each row) is tested or evaluated over each of the noise conditions in the noise conditions in the noise factor matrix.

Each $W_i = [W_{i1}, W_{i2}, ..., W_{il}]$, i=1,2,...,$n_w$ represents a possible environmental use condition or noise state. The noise factor matrix in Figure 2 represents n_w distinct conditions that the product might encounter in actual use.

The quality characteristic for each product design in the design matrix is observed n_w times and a performance statistic based on these observations is calculated for each product design (each row of the design matrix). Taguchi recommends the use of criteria he calls signal-to-noise ratios as performance statistics. These performance statistics should be estimators of the expected loss function $R(X)$. Let $Z(X)$ denote the value of the performance statistic calculated over the noise space for a specific product design X. At the completion of the experiment and once the data has been collected and the performance statistics calculated, an analysis of variance (ANOVA) is performed using $Z(X)$ as the dependent variable and the settings X_j of the different design parameters as controllable variables. From this model an "optimal" product design X can be obtained. Taguchi advo-

727

					ω_{11}	...	ω_{i1}	...	$\omega_{n_w 1}$	
					·		·		·	
					·		·		·	
					·		·		·	
					ω_{1s}	...	ω_{is}	...	$\omega_{n_w s}$	
					·		·		·	
					·		·		·	
					·		·		·	
					ω_{1l}	...	ω_{il}	...	$\omega_{n_w l}$	
x_{11}	...	x_{1t}	...	x_{1k}	y_{11}	...	y_{1i}	...	y_{1n_w}	$Z(x_1)$
·		·	·	·	·		·		·	·
·		·	·	·	·		·		·	·
·		·	·	·	·		·		·	·
x_{j1}	...	x_{jt}	...	x_{jk}	y_{j1}	...	y_{ji}	...	y_{jn_w}	$Z(x_j)$
·		·	·	·	·		·		·	·
·		·	·	·	·		·		·	·
·		·	·	·	·		·		·	·
x_{d1}	...	x_{dt}	...	x_{dk}	y_{d1}	...	y_{di}	...	y_{dn_w}	$Z(x_d)$

Table 1:

vocates a confirmation experiment to verify that a better design has indeed been obtained.

The role of the signal-to-noise (s/n) ratios is an important component of Taguchi's approach, since the best design will be the one that maximizes the s/n ratios. For non-negative continuous performance characteristics with fixed target he has defined three s/n ratios, depending on the form of the loss function : the smaller the better, the larger the better, and being closer to a finite target value the better.
For the case that smaller values of Y_{ji} are better, the recommended form of s/n ratio is

$$Z_s(X_j) = -10\log_{10}\frac{1}{n_w}\sum_{i=1}^{n_w}Y_{ji}^2 \tag{5}$$

When the larger Y_{ji} is to be better, then the s/n should be :

$$Z_L(X_i) = -10\log_{10}\frac{1}{n_w}\sum_{i=1}^{n_w}(\frac{1}{Y_{ji}})^2 \tag{6}$$

Finally when being closer to a target value is considered better, then the s/n ratio

$$Z_T = 10\log_{10}[\overline{Y}(X)/S^2(X)] \tag{7}$$

$$\overline{Y}(X_j) = \frac{1}{n_w}\sum_{i=1}^{n_w}Y_{ji} \tag{8}$$

$$S^2(X_j) = \frac{1}{n_w - 1} \sum_{i=1}^{n_w} [Y_{ji} - \overline{Y}(X_j)]^2 \tag{9}$$

4.4   Critique :

4.4.1   Taguchi Design

Taguchi recommends the use of "orthogonal arrays" (OA) for constructing the design parameter and the noise factor matrices. These are standard designs that have been discussed in the literature since the 1940's. All fractional factorials and factorial experimental designs are orthogonal arrays (but not all OAs are fractional factorial designs).

As Pignatiello[1988] points out one of the Taguchi tactics that cause lot of controversy in the suggested universal application of these orthogonal arrays. But these arrays are not a "must" for the implementation of the Taguchi strategy. Other designs can also be used.

Box[1985] and Hunter[1985] point out that Taguchi's designs do not exploit the sequential nature of the experimental investigation. Instead of using first order screening designs followed by designs of higher resolution and composite designs, Taguchi finds the "optimal" settings of the designs variables with a single experiment followed by some confirmation test runs. But again this tactic is not necessary for the implementation of the overall strategy.

Hunter[1985] shows that for certain type of designs, the presence of interactions can seriously bias the estimates of the linear and quadratic coefficients of a model. He then recommends the use of the Box-Behuken and similar designs. Box, Hunter and Hunter(1978) in their classic Experimental Design book discuss extensively the sequential iterative approach in Design of Experiments.

Taguchi also recommends the use of accumulation analysis for the data analysis of ordered categorical measurements. Nair[1986] criticized the technique as inadequate and proposed alternative ones.

Summarizing some of the criticism of the Taguchi techniques :
(1)The sequential nature of experimentation is not used.
(2)A limited choice of design is recommended. Their use does not deal satisfactorily with the presence of interaction.
(3)Complicated Orthogonal array methods for computer optimization are recommended while they exist simpler and more effective constrained optimization packages.
(4)The portmanteau use of signal-to-noise ratios has many flaws.
(5)The use of data transformation for a more efficient analysis is not exploited at

all.

4.4.2 Signal-to-Noise Ratios :

Another issue of much controversy related to the Taguchi tactics is the use of signal-to-noise ratios as performance measures. Box[1988] concludes that it is better to study the sample mean $\overline{Y}$ and the sample variance S^2 separately rather than combine them into a single s/n ratio. Pignatiello and Ramberg[1985] have reached the same conclusion after completing a case study. We fully agree with Box[1985] that "the information in experimental data, both expected and unexpected, is best revealed by data analytic methods rather than in terms of portmanteau criteria decided in advance such as SN_s,SN_L, SN_T." Box also points the importance of data transformation along with the need of using elementary data analysis with computer graphics to obtain an adequate summary of data.

5   Summary :

It is known that one of the key elements in Japanese success is their use of statistical methods to design quality into the product and the manufacturing process placing less emphasis on traditional on line quality control that employs sampling inspection. In this, Taguchi had a lot to contribute. He emphasized : (1) the need to achieve minimum variance at the desired quality level and (2) the need to find product and process designs that are robust over uncontrollable variability in the manufacturing environment and in the product's use environment. His strategy is an empirical application of decision making under uncertainty. And this is clearly his most important contribution. He provides us with a conceptual framework that can be used to design and manufacture a high quality process or product.

The actual tactics that Taguchi uses to implement his strategy have drawn lot of criticism, especially the use of signal-to-noise ratios and the orthogonal arrays designs.

Despite its quite empirical tactics the Taguchi method has been quite successful in the U.S. since Dr.Taguchi was invited by the Quality Assurance Venter of AT&T in the summer of 1980. By combining engineering quality ideas with experimental design techniques Dr.Taguchi showed us that a systematic experimentation (even one that is not very sophisticated) can provide us with valuable information on how to design and build new product or process or how to improve existing products or processes. On the other side it is believed that we can gain much more by adopting more advanced and rigorous statistical techniques in our product or process design experimentation. Management could greatly benefit from the use of computer graphics, exploratory data analysis and statistical computing techniques.

REFERENCES

Box, G.E.P.(1985) "Off-line Quality Control, Parameter Design, and the Taguchi Method, A Discussion ", Journal of Quality Technology, vol. 17, no.4, pp.189-190.

Box, G.E.P.(1988) "Signal-to-Noise Ratios, Performance Criteria and Transformations", Technometrics, vol. 30, no. 1, pp. 247-254.

Hunter, J.S.(1985) "Statistical Design Applied to Product Design", Journal of Quality Technology.

Kackar, R.N.(1985) "Off-line Quality Control, Parameter Design, and the Taguchi Method" Journal of Quality Technology, vol. 17, no. 4, pp. 176-209.

Leon, R.V., Shoemaker, A.C. and Kackar, R.N.(1987) "Performance Measures Independent of Adjustment : An Explanation and Extension of Taguchi's Signal-to-Noise Ratios", Technometrics, vol. 29, no. 3, pp. 253-285.

Nair, V.N.(1986) "Testing in Industrial Experiments with Ordered Categorical Data" Technometrics, vol. 28, no. 4, pp. 283-291.

Pignatiello, J., and John S. Ramberg(1985) "Discussion of Off-line Quality Control, Parameter Design and the Taguchi Method", Journal of Quality Technology (Oct.), pp. 198-206.

Pignatiello, Joseph J.,(1988) "An Overview of the Strategy and Tactics of Taguchi", IIE Transactions, vol. 20, no. 3, pp. 247-254.

Productivity & Quality Management Frontiers-IV, edited by Sumanth, Edosomwan, Poupart, and Sink. ©1993 Institute of Industrial Engineers.

Effective Use of Market Quality Information for Product Planning

M. Iijima
Yokkaichi University
Yokkaichi, Mie JAPAN

M. Inamura
Daihatsu Motor Co., Ltd.
Ikedashi, Osaka JAPAN

ABSTRACT

Making customer oriented high quality products is important. In the past, technical needs and customer wants were not closely integrated in product planning. But now, in Japan, it is becoming normal to make products according to a Customers' Satisfaction Index, especially electronics and automobile companies. This paper discusses market quality information and its effective use for planning and designing Japanese mini-cars. Planning information is usually in the form of statistical data, but planners sometimes misjudge customers' real wants from products. Planning managers must ensure whether future products will satisfy customers or not. Satisfaction is the key to success in sales.

KEY WORDS

market, quality information, customer satisfaction, mini-cars, major-minor feeling, real wants, product planning, Japan

1. Purpose of Study

This paper proposes to clarify methods of obtaining effective market information in order to reflect user needs in product planning, concentrating particularly on how the information is to be gathered, analyzed and utilized in the case of the mini-car.

In the recently deteriorating Japanese business market, it is reported that the commodities based on customer satisfaction are selling well. Not every commodity fits this trend; luxury goods have been affected by the bad business conditions, but the necessities of life have been maintaining constant-level gross sales. In general, Japanese products have hitherto been market needs oriented. Now commodities with a high Customer Satisfaction level are showing a trend towards higher quality and larger size, diversification, and superior quality service. While these products are high in price, their contribution to gross sales is increasing in many cases. Recently automobiles and electronics have been representative of products that strive to meet users' needs. In a former study, Iijima and Hasegawa (1992) treated information networks in the case of electronics products involving the active use of management techniques such as design review.

2. Development of Marketing Research

Marketing research is now considered to be in its third stage of development by Niki and Asano (1991). The first stage was mainly sampling research and statistical estimates which were useful for actual-case studies or so called fact-finding in the 1950's. The second stage was multi-variate analysis approaches such as quantification that were mainly used for motivation research into consumer behavior in the 1970's. In the third stage, since the 1980's, a conjoint analysis has been employed for investigating strategic information, and it has become a key to successful sales strategies.

3. Information Relating to Product Planning

Fig.1 shows the information flow that applies for product planning, especially quality information in the case of automobiles. Hitherto quality information concerning user complaints and that concerning market demand were discussed separately from each other. However, it is now becoming regarded as natural for several departments to work together on customer satisfaction (CS) projects, and discuss them within a project team. Today, there are many company CS systems used in drawing up development plans, such as MTM (Matsushita Market Oriented Total Management System) in Matsushita Electric Industrial Co. in Kojo-kanri journal (1991), QMEDI (Quality Management Determination Education Implementation) in Sony Corp. by JMA management center (1992), CS committees in Toyota Motor Corp. and Nissan Motor Co., Ltd. and CCS (Customer & Communication Satisfaction) in Yamaha Motor Co., Ltd..

4. Customer Satisfaction Index and Product Planning

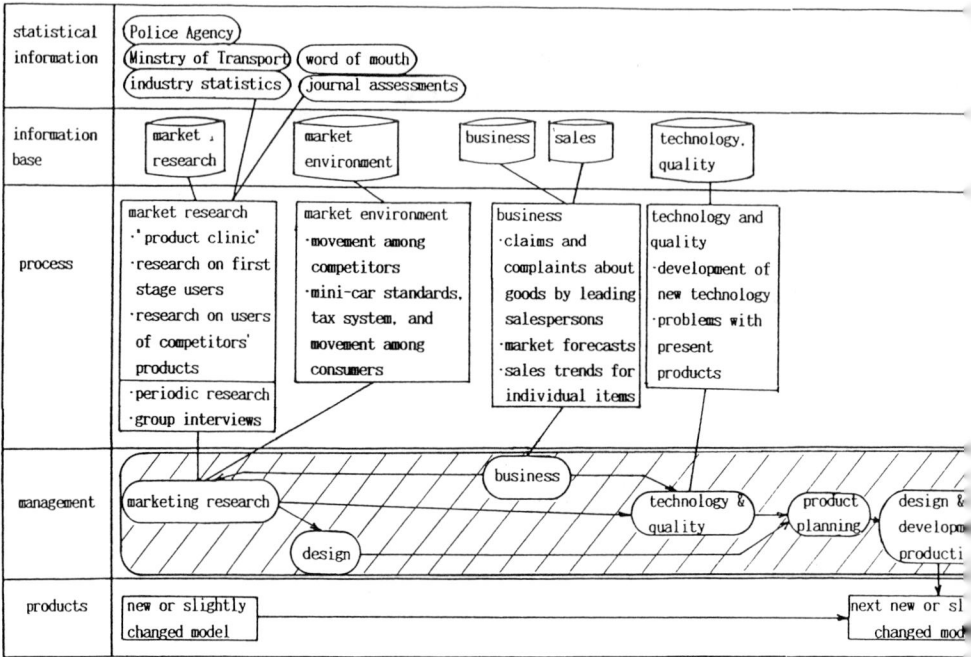

Fig.1 Flow of Information for Product Planning
(hatched area shows the CS project system)

4.1 Two Concepts of Customer Satisfaction

The idea of a customer satisfaction index (CSI) has become familiar since US-Honda's "Acura" was awarded first prize for fou years, from 1987 to 1990, in the CS survey carried out by J.D. Power Co.. This coincided with a large increase in sales of Honda cars. In 1991 the Toyota "Lexus" and Nissan "Infiniti" won the first prize jointly. The method of assessment used by J.D. Power is to "add the demerit points" concerning quality and service in order to compare the average score for a company's products or individual models. This method encourages each company to take remedial action about the items earning the most dissatisfaction points. In other words, it attaches importance to customers' complaints. Sometimes the strategy fails because the improved standard product becomes too expensive.

The alternative method is to "add the merit points" as is done by Matsushita. Up until now, in Japanese companies, technical engineers have been solely responsible for deciding additional values or functions, without systematic reference to customer response. In the Matsushita method, by checking which product achieves an actual high sales score, the company can ensure that customer wishes are reflected in products.

In the past, if sales of a product were bad, the leader of the product development project was considered responsible. But with the new product development system used by both Toyota and Matsushita, project leaders do not need to bear this kind of responsibility for the sales failure.

In the past, meeting customers' wishes, or needs, meant attaching great importance to high quality and high added value. But more recently more than this is involved, as can be seen from Fig.2. Here, "service" includes such items as "attitude towards customer", "after-sale service" and so on, and these items are considered as having equal weight.

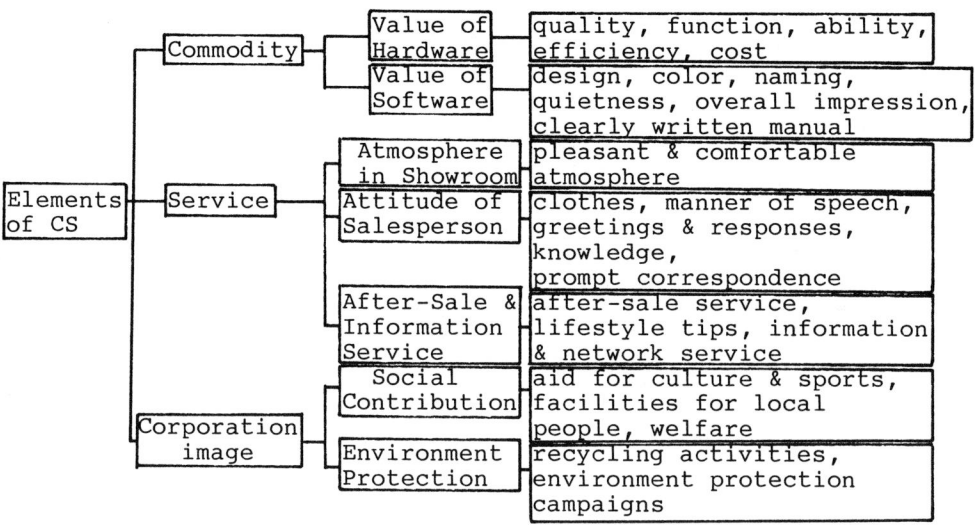

Fig.2 Elements of Customers' Satisfaction
(cited in Hirashima (1992), p.54)

4.2 CS Research for Women College Students Wishing to Own a Car

In Japan, women students usually get their driver's license after graduation from senior high school. Many women students want to buy mini-cars, because of limited parking space and in order to save on maintenance costs. Table 1 shows the ranking of car satisfaction items in the consciousness of such students. The priority items are in the order "style","cost" and "efficiency". The largest deviation is for "make".

Table 2 shows "the students' interest in cars". They want to purchase a second family car for their personal use. Much of the cost is paid by their parents, after direct viewing in showrooms or after seeing TV commercials. But fewer than 1% rely on newspaper information.

5. Product Design in the Case of Mini-Cars

5.1 Generational Changes in Mini-Cars

In this section we shall be considering the product design of Japanese mini-cars as a case example of the gathering and integrating of quality information from market research by a

Table 1 Ranking of Car Satisfaction Items for Women Students

rank	item	mean rank	std. dev.
1	style & design	2.77	2.61
2	cost	4.34	2.98
3	performance	4.94	2.70
4	color	5.98	3.12
5	handling	6.41	2.98
6	size	6.51	3.23
7	safety	6.55	2.98
8	fuel economy	6.67	3.38
9	interior design	7.15	3.20
10	make	8.73	3.93
11	few breakdowns	9.93	3.13
12	utilization purpose	12.02	2.54
13	low pollution	12.20	3.18
14	service	12.60	2.33
15	dealer's manner	14.33	1.89
16	showroom atmosphere	14.76	1.58

Table 2 The Students' Interest in Cars

item	percentage
1 belongs to a car owing family	63 %
2 license holder	67
3 own personal car	16
4 interest in cars	
1) none at all	11
2) some interest	83
3) will purchase	6
5 wish to purchase prompted by	
1) TV commercials	29
2) newspaper	0.5
3) friends	13
4) direct viewing	52
6 approaches the dealer	
1) with parents	82
2) with friends/boyfriend	6
3) by herself	0.5
4) by telephoning	0.5
5) others	2

booklet of Daihatsu (1990). The first mini-car standards in Japan were established in 1951. They fixed the car's length at under 3 meters, and fuel displacement at a maximum of 360 c.c.. Several types of mini-car came on the market, including the Daihatsu "Midget" in 1957, and the Fujijuko "Subaru 360" in 1958. The high economic growth period of the 1960's saw continual appearances of new mini-cars such as the Daihatsu "Fellow" in 1966, the Honda "N-360" and the Suzuki "Fronte", both in 1967. The number of new mini-cars registered came to 1,260,000 in 1970 if both passenger and goods vehicles are included. Fig.3 shows the number of so-called "bonnet-type" vehicles (ie. regular passenger cars and

wagon-style passenger cars) only, which stood at 868,000 in 1970.
But subsequent changes in social circumstances and then the oil
shock adversely influenced sales of mini-cars, which in 1975 fell
to 590,000. The special driver's license category for mini-cars
only was abolished in 1968, and the periodical vehicle inspection
system was extended to this class of car in 1973. Exhaust gas
regulations were enforced in 1978. Honda stopped all production
of mini-cars in 1974, and Mazda followed in 1977. Meanwhile, in
1975, mini-car standards had been revised, and the maximum
dimensions were now 3.2 meters for length and 550 c.c. for fuel
displacement.
   After the second oil shock in 1979, mini-cars enjoyed a revival.
New cars were brought out: the Suzuki "Alto" in 1979, the Daihatsu
"Mira Cuore" in 1980, the Mitsubishi "Minica" in 1981, the Honda
"Today" and the Daihatsu "Mira XX" in 1985 and the Mazda "Carol"
in 1989. In 1989 the special commodity tax on cars was also
abolished.
   Factors that contribute to second big rise in sales of personalized mini-cars include the appearance of less expensive cars and
the advancement of women's position in society. Women have come
to need cars of their own, generally bought as second family cars.
More and more women have obtained drivers' licenses as indicated
in Fig.4.
   In 1990, mini-car regulation standards changed again. Maximum
car length was increased to 3.3 meters and maximum fuel displacement to 660 c.c.. This revision was aimed to allow for greater
engine power to match the increase in weight resulting from the
inclusion of additional safety functions and anti-pollution
devices. With the relaxation of size standards, new standard
mini-cars now offered high performance functions, higher quality,
more interior comfort and more safety.
   In the immediate future, new mini-cars will be developed to

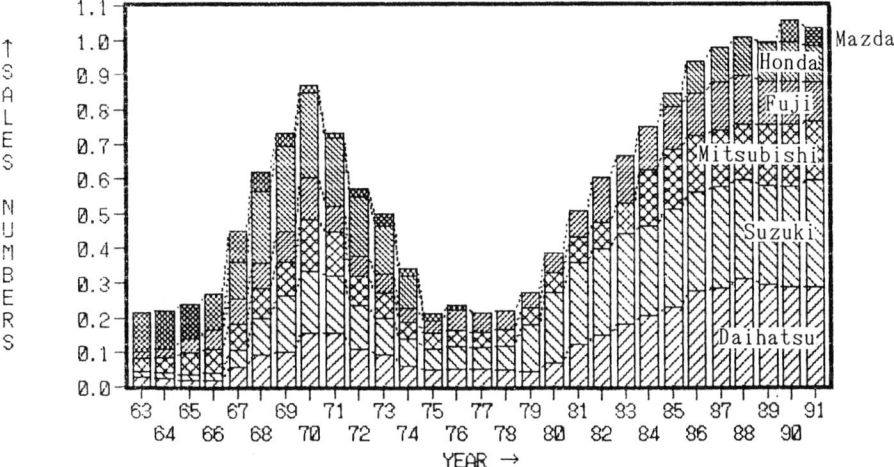

Fig.3 Sales of Registered Mini-Cars

737

Unit;Millions of persons

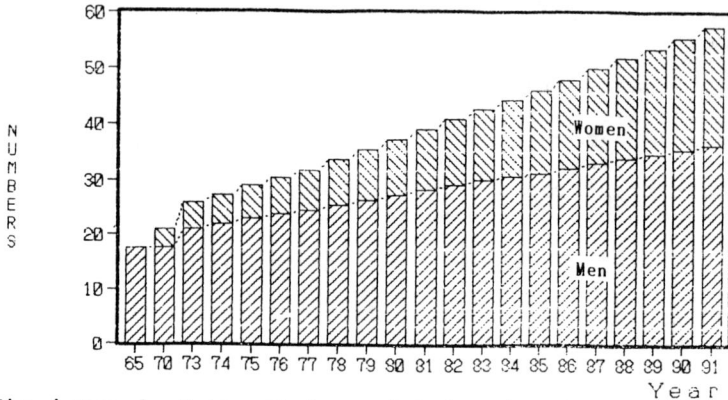

Fig.4 Trend of the Number of Driver's License Holders

use less energy and occupy smaller spaces.
    Daihatsu, with its skillful mini-car sales strategies, has
steadily increased its sales figures for its main product, the
"Mira", and at present, in 1992, the company offers three
personalized types of mini-car, the "Mira", the "Leeza" (brought
out in 1986) and the "Opti" (1992).

5.2 Effective Quality Information for Planning and Developing the "Mira XX"

    The Daihatsu "Mira" has maintained a top share ranking in the
"bonnet type" passenger mini-car class since 1988. Model changes
in the "Mira" and new types of Daihatsu mini-car are shown in
Fig.5.
    The "Mira" has been through several development cycles, and
today's "Mira" represents the third stage. In this section, we
focus on the "Mira XX" which was brought onto the market in 1985.

year	'80	82	83	85	86	87	88	90	91	chracteristics
first stage	①—②—③—○—									①original "1.5 box" design (31HP)
				"Parco"						②automatic transmission
				series						③more spacious version with turbo / 4WD
second stage				④—⑤———○———						④fashionable & high-power (52HP)
				"TR-XX"						·"1.3 box" design, 3 cylinders
										⑤sporty car with personality
third stage							⑥——⑦—			·aero-turbo system
								"Parco"		⑥high total balance
								series		·new standards (64HP)
other K-cars				"Leeza" ○——————————						⑦more spacious version
								"Opti"○		·4 speed / 4WD automatic

Fig.5 Model and Design Changes in the Daihatsu "Mira" and Other Mini-Cars

We shall consider the collection and active use of effective quality related information in the making of the car. The second stage "Mira" had already appeared in 1985, as the result of a full model change, but this included a change from "1.5 box" to "1.3 box" design (i.e. the ratio of the passenger compartment to the engine compartment is 1.0:0.3). As a result, the car shape became unfamiliar to customers, and this led to a decrease in sales. The "Mira XX" was accordingly put onto the market as a more spacious version of the same car.

The model change cycle in Japan is generally 4 - 5 years for passenger cars and 5 - 6 years for commercial vehicles. The model change is intended to coincide with the customer's purchase of of a new car. The important thing from a design point of view is to introduce the latest elements of fashion into the basic concept that forms the product's image.

(1)Market Movements
About 70% of mini-car users are women and in the years around 1985 the relevant background situation was as follows:
1. Women's position in society was rising.
2. The proportion of families owning two or more cars was increasing.

In order to form a profile of these women users, we show the results of CS surveys on the first stage "Mira". Market movements can be read from the time series graph plotted from the scores of the factors, as in Fig.6.

The factors have to do with the "image of the mini-car" in 12 items, "purchase motivation" in 12 items, "utilization purpose" in 12 items, and "user's character" in 4 items. The individual items in each section are:

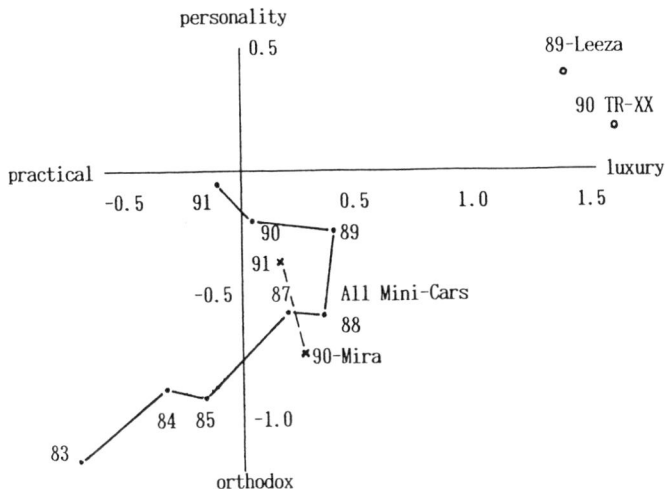

Fig.6 Market Movements in the Image of Mini-Cars

739

(i)"image of mini-car": youthful, cheerful, cute, sporty,
practical, friendly, town car, individual, up-to-date, fashionable, suited for family use, suited for women.
(ii)"purchase motivation": new image, style, interior, fuel
displacement, capabilities, mechanical quality, quietness, front
seats, rear seats, baggage space, color, personal preference.
(iii)"utilization purpose": to work, to school, dropping off and
and collecting, outdoor activities, long drives, short drives,
shopping with family, shopping alone, leisure, drives alone,
work or business, to avoid walking.
(iv)"user's character": length of trips, for own use, for children, for family.
(2)Effective Customers' Information
     The "Mira XX" series was not expected to achieve big sales by
top management, and it was designed by young staff with an eye
on fashion. In the 1980's, the car market was moving into higher
areas of performance and quality, with individualization, remodel-
ing and equipping with aero-parts, so that the "Mira XX", despite
its high price of 850,000 yen ($ 6,500) with aero-parts, was
accepted by young people without reserve. The market research
reported by Umeda (1989) on first stage users revealed an average
age of under 24 years, an average annual income of under 3 million
yen ($ 23,000) and a job not involving intellectual skills. The
development planner in charge of the "Mira" had heard an opinion
from other marketers in the industry that "young people prefer
the 'major-minor feeling'". He pursued this hint and in 1982
developed the "Mira TR-XX". It won great popularity.
     Further research was then carried out to establish the differ-
ence in the users' profile between the "Mira XX" and "Leeza",
which came on sale in 1981. Group interviews were conducted in
the Kobe, Osaka and Nara areas with 40 young women. The results
are set out in Table 3. The "Leeza", which was highly ranked by
critics and prominently advertized on T.V. in commercials featuring the famous actress You Hayami, did not have a strong appeal
to the "quiet young women" users, so that high sales could hardly

Table 3 Classification of the Type of Users
(modified from Umeda (1989))

"Mira XX"	"Leeza"
Conspicuous & extrovert women.	Pretty & aspiring young women.
- Active, assertive personal ity.	- Quiet and feminine character.
- Many friends.	- Small group of friends.
- Greatly valuing judgment of peers.	- Personal and attractive-looking car is a necessary condition.
- No ornaments except dark film window. Clean interior, good for driving with shoes off.	- Space for ornaments and dolls.
- Part-time jobs in conveni- ence stores, coffee shops, and other non-intellectual work.	- Piano teaching, tutoring in private schools, and other intellectual work.

be expected. It was found in the research that the main difference between the users of the two kinds of car was that the "Mira"
users had strong networks of friends in which information
circulated by word of mouth.

The users for the types of car were found to form almost
completely separate groups. This shows that market users may have
quite different view-points covering product information, while
management sometimes misjudges and aims for the wrong group when
developing new products. Market movements for mini-cars show a
trend toward new styles and images, more comfort, higher quality
and easy handling. So mini-cars are also rising in price. But
mini-car developers must always seek the kinds of additional
items that are really wanted by customers.

6. Conclusion

In this paper we have discussed the effective use of market
quality information for product planning in the case of Daihatsu
mini-cars. Marketing research offers several kinds of significant
information, but the interpretation of it is not always correct.
We conclude that much has to be done to keep in touch with changing public needs. For example, senior management sometimes needs
to provide an opportunity for younger generation staff to plan
and design a new car, and, more generally, a key product planning
manager must always seek out the customers' real needs by meeting
and listening to their opinions both before and after making
definitive decisions.

We thank David Dykes of Yokkaichi University for his useful
comments and suggestions on English style, and many staff of
Daihatsu Motor Co., Ltd. for useful information and assistance.

REFERENCES
Hirashima,Y. (1992) "How to Proceed in Customer Satisfaction
Management" (in Japanese), Nihon-jitsugyo-shuppan, pp.58-60.
Iijima,M and Hasegawa,K. (1992) "Quality Information Management
for Improving Productivity in Japan", International Journal of
Technology Management, Vol.7, No.4.
"Japan's Mini" (in Japanese) (1990), a booklet of Daihatsu
Industry.
"MTM Revolution in Matsushita Electrics" (in Japanese) (1991)
special issue of Kojo-kanri, Vol.37, No.17, pp.21-71.
Niki,K. and Asano,H. (1991) "Planning and Practice of Marketing
Research" (in Japanese), Nikkankogyo-shinbun.
Sony Quality Reliability Dept. (1992) "QC Renaissance in Sony"
(in Japanese)", JMA Management Center.
Umeda,T (1989) "The 'Mira' Story" (in Japanese), Daihatsu
Monthly Report NEO, pp.3-9, No.4.

Bibliographic Sketches of Authors
    M. Iijima is an Associate Professor of Management & Information
Engineering at Yokkaichi University. His current research is in
Quality and Maintenance Information Management. He is a senior
member of IIE.
    M. Inamura is a General Manager of Marketing at the Head Office
of Daihatsu Motor Co., Ltd.

Productivity & Quality Management Frontiers-IV, edited by Sumanth, Edosomwan, Poupart, and Sink. ©1993 Institute of Industrial Engineers.

Productivity and Quality Enhancement in Requests for Proposals: Using TQM in Air Force Major Weapon System Procurement

T.S. Graham, C.R. Templin, and M.E. Heberling
Air Force Institute of Technology
Wright-Patterson AFB, Ohio USA

This paper describes recent changes to the Request For Proposal (RFP) process used to acquire Air Force weapon systems. The purpose of this description is to provide an understanding of how TQM and the improved RFP process have enhanced the quality of the products (RFPs, contractor proposals, and military contracts) and the productivity of the customers (the government and the defense industries). Air Force Systems Command has applied the Total Quality Management (TQM) philosophy to define and improve this process.

Just as many U.S. companies have turned to TQM principles in their struggle to regain their competitive positions in the market, the Air Force has aggressively moved to apply TQM principles to restructure its acquisition organizations and processes. It is merging its two main acquisition organizations, Air Force Logistics Command and Air Force Systems Command, into the Air Force Materiel Command to better integrate weapon system acquisition and management as well as to increase efficiency by avoiding duplication of effort. Each of these commands has also been aggressive in the use of TQM to improve its own organization and processes. A critical process team (CPT) was formed consisting of highly experienced, senior civilian and military government leaders as well as their counterparts from the defense industry sector.

This paper focuses on the five management objectives of the CPT to intensify RFP quality improvement and associated productivity of government and defense industry workers. The five objectives were to: 1) to foster awareness and commitment, 2) to work with industry to remove barriers and develop improvement objectives, 3) to develop tools and techniques, 4) to apply the tools and techniques to acquisition programs, and 5) to be able to assess the effectiveness of any recommended changes. In order to accomplish these objectives, the CPT set out to define and map out the process, identify deficiencies or problems with the process, and develop and implement solutions.

Lastly, this paper will describe the background that served as the starting point for the process improvement initiative and the TQM methodology used to analyze the process. It will then focus on the initial findings and conclusions of the study and report the changes that have been made to date to improve the RFP process for acquiring major weapon systems.

PRODUCTIVITY AND QUALITY ENHANCEMENT IN REQUESTS FOR PROPOSALS: USING TQM IN AIR FORCE MAJOR WEAPON SYSTEM PROCUREMENT

This paper describes recent changes to the Request For Proposal (RFP) process used to acquire Air Force weapon systems. Air Force Systems Command has applied the Total Quality Management (TQM) philosophy to define and improve this process. Prior to describing this effort and its initial results, it is important to understand the overall setting in which the initiative was conceived and carried out.

Over the last two decades there has been mounting pressure for reform of the weapons acquisition process in the Department of Defense (DoD). Cost overruns, scandals, overpriced spare parts, and quality problems have created overwhelming pressure from the public and from Congress for major institutional and procedural change. Presidential commissions such as the Fitzhugh Commission (1970), the Grace Commission (1983), and the Packard Commission (1986) have made specific, and in many cases highly consistent, recommendations for organizational and process reform. Academic studies such as Fox (1974, 1988) and Gansler (1980, 1989) and Congressional (1988) studies have concluded that DoD has been unable to fully implement the suggested improvements, in spite of repeated attempts to do so. Fox observed that the repeated failures to solve acquisition problems were undermined due to lack of continuity and the tendency to apply quick fixes or easy solutions, which often attack symptoms rather than solutions (Fox, 1988, pp. 49-51). However, events over the last few years have come to a head so as to create unparalleled pressure for change.

Changing global threats, declining budgets, and downsizing of the force structure have forced major institutional change on both operational and acquisition organizations. While the Persian Gulf War demonstrated the value of technically superior weapons and the ability of the acquisition process to acquire such superior weapons, issues of affordability and extremely tight defense budgets have mandated a more efficient, and affordable way of acquiring and supporting weapon systems. Consider that in 1955 $2 billion (1983 constant dollars) bought this country 7000 tanks. Today, that same dollar amount would purchase only 700 tanks, or 10% of the purchasing power of 1955. In 1951, this country purchased 6300 fighter aircraft for $7 billion (in 1983 dollars), whereas in 1984 it cost $11 billion to procure only 322 fighter aircraft. Part of the reason for this is the growing complexity of our weapon systems. For instance, the F-15 Eagle fighter aircraft has 585,000 different parts and is put together by 22,000 people. The fuel control system alone is comprised of over 5,000 parts. Such complexity and sophistication requires extensive logistical support. The F-15 spends 53 hours undergoing maintenance for every single hour in the air. With weapon system complexity and sophistication and associated acquisition and support costs rising at an exponential rate while defense budgets grow tighter and tighter, acquisition reform has become a matter of survival.

Just as many U.S. companies have turned to TQM principles in their struggle to regain their competitive positions in the market, the Air Force has aggressively moved to apply TQM principles to restructure its acquisition organizations and processes. It is merging its two main acquisition organizations, Air Force Logistics Command and Air Force Systems Command, into the Air Force Materiel Command to better integrate weapon system acquisition and management as well as to increase efficiency by avoiding duplication of effort. Each of these commands has also been aggressive in the use of TQM to improve its own organization and processes. This paper focuses on the efforts of Air Force Systems Command to define and improve the RFP process. It will describe the background that served as the starting point for the process improvement initiative and the TQM methodology used to analyze the process. It will then focus on the initial findings and conclusions of the study and report the changes that have been made to date to improve the RFP process for acquiring major weapon systems.

THE REQUEST FOR PROPOSAL

DoD has two methods of contracting, the solicitation of sealed bids through the sealed bidding process and the solicitation of competitive or noncompetitive proposals using Requests for Proposals. Sealed bidding is a highly structured process where bids are publicly opened and the award goes to the lowest priced offeror who is responsive to the government's requirements and is a responsible (or capable) performer. It is used when the supply or service to be purchased can be well defined and competition exists. In fact, DoD must use sealed bidding if time permits, there is reasonable expectation of competition, it is not necessary to negotiate or conduct discussions with offerors, and the award is to be based upon price and other price related factors (Federal Acquisition Regulation[FAR] 6.401(a)). When one or more of these requirements cannot be met, the RFP process is used. This process provides the freedom to award the contract based upon price and other factors (such as technical approach, quality, past performance, etc.). It also permits the buyer to award with or without negotiation with offerors and permits the government to use the full range of contract types.

The vast majority of defense contract dollars are spent using RFPs (see Table I). In fact, roughly ten times as many procurement dollars are awarded using RFPs versus sealed bids. Thus, just in terms of the magnitude of the dollars involved, the RFP process must be considered a crucial element in the acquisition process. In addition, the complexity, uncertainty, and risk associated with developing and producing today's sophisticated weaponry mandate the use of the RFP in the acquisition and support of major weapon systems.

According to the FAR, an RFP is used in negotiated acquisitions "to communicate Government requirements to prospective contractors and to solicit proposals or quotations from them" (FAR 15.302.a). Communication is the key word. The RFP must communicate the government's requirement so the contracting process will produce the product or service required to satisfy user's needs. It must also obtain all the required information necessary to assess the offeror's capability to deliver the required product or service. To a large extent, the RFP process defines the roles and relationship of the government and the defense industry for the specific acquisition in question. This relationship has not always been as good as it should be. Fox (1973), in his book Arming America, concluded the relationships between the Defense Department and the defense industry effectively prevent the acquisition system from functioning to its best advantage. In 1988, Fox emphatically stated in his book The Defense Management Challenge that this relationship has worsened in the 15-year

Table I
Military Prime Contract Awards

FUNCTION	1986	1987	1988
	($ billions)		
Small Dollar (< $25,000)	13.0	13.9	14.2
Sealed Bidding	5.5	6.0	5.9
Competitive RFP	20.2	29.4	33.5
Noncompetitive RFP	16.9	34.5	37.0

Source: U.S. Bureau of the Census, 1990 Statistical Abstract of the United States (Wash. D.C.: Government Printing Office, 1990) p. 330, Table 534.

interim. Because of this worsening situation, the RFP process has undergone intense scrutiny and substantial transformation over the last two years with the objective of improving the process itself and the relationship between the government and industry.

THE MANDATE FOR RFP IMPROVEMENT

In November 1988, General Bernard P. Randolph, then Commander of Air Force Systems Command (AFSC), had a meeting with Chief Executive Officers of various defense contractors. The purpose of this meeting was to examine the RFP process and decide how to make it better. A critical process team (CPT) was formed in January of 1989, consisting of highly experienced, senior civilian and military government leaders as well as their counterparts from the defense industry sector. The overriding goal of the team was to suggest ways to improve the procedures used to buy major weapons systems so as to benefit both the government and industry. It was termed a critical process because the RFP/Proposal process consumes excessive resources or causes significant "pain" to one or both parties and has a major impact on the delivery of products or services to meet organization objectives.

General Randolph, then Commander of Air Force Systems Command, in association with other senior Air Force and industry leaders, equipped the CPT with the following charter:

> Improve the quality of our RFPs and establish a framework for all of us within Air Force Systems Command to continuously improve our RFP documents and their preparation process. This framework should be capable of promptly adapting to changes in law and policy.

The CPT had five management objectives: 1) to foster awareness and commitment, 2) to work with industry to remove barriers and develop improvement objectives, 3) to develop tools and techniques, 4) to apply the tools and techniques to acquisition programs, and 5) to be able to assess the effectiveness of any recommended changes. In order to accomplish these objectives, the CPT set out to define and map out the process, identify deficiencies or problems with the process, and develop and implement solutions.

DEFINING THE PROCESS

One of the basic tenets of TQM is to satisfy the needs of the customer. One of the first tasks of the CPT was to determine exactly who is the customer of the RFP. Traditional thinking viewed the government, the customer of the goods/services, as the customer of the RFP process as well. The CPT, composed of military and defense industry team members, developed a new paradigm which placed the defense contractor in the role of customer. The government provides a product (an RFP) to the contractor, whereby the defense industry's response is a proposal based on that RFP. If the government delivers an inferior product to the contractor, the proposal submitted to the government will be inferior. This practice has the unwanted effect of increasing the lead time to field a desired weapon system (due to changes, further proposals, etc.), increasing costs associated with the system, and nonresponsiveness to the using units (i.e., those units waiting for the system). Under this shift in philosophy, the government must provide a quality RFP that meets the needs of the contractor and which will enable the contractor to provide better proposals to the government. A critical underlying belief must be that a little more time spent on the front end of a weapon system acquisition will save a lot more time (and money) later.

The CPT faced an arduous task of laying out the myriad of tasks and interfaces which take place from weapon system concept to proposal. There were numerous perspectives to reconcile, each with their own definition and understanding of the process. Eventually, a generic RFP preparation process was developed which recognized inputs and actions by various key team players, such as the using/supporting commands, the Secretary of the Air Force, Air Force Systems Command Headquarters, the Product Division Staff, the System Program Office, and the Contractor. During the CPT's review of the RFP process, problem areas were identified and recorded. These were termed "pains" by the process team members because they caused the government and/or the contractor community some hardships which could possibly be avoided with a better approach to RFP preparation. At every juncture in the RFP process (flow charted for all users for ease of comprehension) where a "pain" occurred, the location of the pain was annotated. Upon completion of the finalized and current RFP process, 115 pains had been annotated. Each pain was examined in detail and addressed in order to make the process better.

IDENTIFICATION AND LOCATION OF "PAINS"

Due to the massive amount of "pains" identified, this paper cannot detail them all. However, a few examples are provided to illustrate the types of problems recognized by the CPT. One pain was the lack of training in RFP preparation. This often results in "cutting and pasting" an old RFP to make the new RFP. This contributes to discrepancies and inadequacies which serve to confuse the contractors. They have to spend precious time deciphering the government's needs and correcting the RFP. One extreme example of the problems with cutting and pasting concerned an RFP for the construction of a new building. Part of this RFP required the contractor to provide a **flight test** plan. The RFP had been "tailored" from an existing RFP for an aircraft.

Another pain was unrealistic schedules. This hurts the government and the contractor. The government rushes RFP preparation to save time, shifting the onus on the contractor to "fix" it; however, what little time is saved with an RFP "rush job" is often more than lost after a vague and lengthy proposal has to be reworked. The contractor loses valuable time and money proposing to a shoddy RFP. Again, this harkens back to the new customer paradigm and TQM concepts whereby the contractor should be the customer of the product (the RFP) and the RFP should be a quality product.

Adding to the contractor frustration is the lack of a standardized RFP format. While FAR Part 15 provides a Uniform Contract Format that is used in RFPs, there is little consistency in they way different buying organizations used each section. As a result, contractors must search through the whole RFP to piece together the information it needs. Most defense contractors want to provide a realistic and quality proposal to the government; however, they are constrained by their inability to find the applicable sections in the government RFPs. If there were a standardized format in which all sections of an RFP contained the same type of information, contractors could evaluate the RFP more efficiently and save much time and effort.

Akin to this is the pain of non-integrated, conflicting sections of the RFP. This results partly from rush jobs and cut and paste operations. It also results from a lack of communication with, and feedback from, contractors during the RFP preparation process. Because of procurement integrity concerns, communication with contractors has traditionally been tightly limited and controlled. The result is that contractors get little or no information prior to release of the RFP. The government constructs the RFP in a vacuum and the contractor proposes with little or no interface during the proposal process. Further, the government usually provides extremely short lead times from RFP release to the required proposal submission date (typically 45 to 60 days later). Since contractors usually need much more time than that to develop a good proposal, they are forced to anticipate the government's requirements for the RFP and start constructing their proposal long before the RFP release date. If contractors had better information up front, they could use their resources more effectively and produce better proposals for the government. The government also misses out on the valuable input contractors could provide in helping the government to better define requirements, eliminate inconsistencies, and clarify ambiguities. The draft RFP is designed to provide contractors the opportunity to comment on proposals. However, the government spends a great deal of time and effort to develop a draft RFP and, in many instances, is reluctant to make significant changes because the draft RFP is sent to the contractor so late in the RFP process. Thus, the draft RFP itself becomes a pain instead of a solution.

After identifying more than 100 pains, the CPT located them as to their occurrence and impact on the RFP preparation process flow chart. They then focused on areas where large numbers of pains were concentrated. In the initial stages of an RFP formation, the contractor community should be providing input into the concept of a new system. Perhaps the contractors' ideas, incorporated early, would shed valuable insight on a particular issue. However, there is no place in the current, established process to institute a teaming arrangement between the government and the defense contractors. Another significant area of impact was the assembling of the government team and associated team building efforts needed to ensure a cohesive and responsive group. This is needed to develop better acquisition strategies and draft RFPs. Other general problem areas included communication with offerors and getting reviews and approvals from higher headquarters. Once the pains were identified and organized, the CPT set out to resolve the pains and improve the process. They vigorously avoided quick fixes which the CPT coined falling prey to the "disease of immediacy". From the team sessions emerged some innovative and insightful recommendations as to how to make the RFP process better. Table II emphasizes the major RFP CPT initiatives. To date, only the first seven items have been completely determined and coordinated by all the players. The remaining six issues are being feverishly, thoroughly, and concurrently worked. As they are concluded, they too will be incorporated into the process of the new RFP process.

LESSONS LEARNED

As of the summer of 1991, the CPT has identified various lessons learned regarding the RFP process. They include the following:

- The new Procurement Integrity Law complicates the improvement process
- Personnel at all levels must be educated before real cultural change can occur
- Industry viewed with suspicion; attitude must be changed by both parties
- The disease of immediacy is counterproductive
- Industry must be involved in a CPT where industry is the customer
- Joint Air Force-Industry teams work well
- Commitment from the commanders and chief executive officers is essential
- The opportunities never end

The RFP is critical to the communication of the government's requirements and the defense industry's capability of meeting the government's needs. It must also provide the offerors ample opportunity to employ the best business and technical approaches. As General Randolph stated in a 1989 letter to all members of Air Force Systems Command:

The focus of this entire improvement project rests on industry-government team-building. Our goal is positive not adversarial business relationships. In the early stages of acquisition planning, we must communicate openly and effectively, and carry that teamwork through the RFP process and into the ensuing program.

For this to fully happen, the precepts of Total Quality Management must continue to be applied to the RFP Process. It provides the framework for the common-sense management and the evolution of an attitude that thrives on continuous improvement. The precepts maintain the adoption of a customer-oriented operations

Table II
RFP Initiatives

1. RFP Process Guide
2. Improved Communications
3. RFP Team Training Process
4. Improved Team Formation Process
5. Dedicated RFP Support Organization and Facility
6. Standardized RFP Format and Instructions
7. RFP Process Measurement
8. Standardized RFP Document Processes and Products
9. Streamlined Document Review, Coordination, and Approval Process
10. Improved RFP Scheduling Process
11. Improved Tailoring, Data, and Data Determination Process
12. Digital Delivery of Data
13. Expanded Use of Electronic Bulletin Boards

philosophy and a commitment to excellence for all products and services. It also demands participation, trust, and teamwork. The RFP improvement initiatives carried out so far, as well as those currently in process, have gone a long way toward moving away from the traditional adversarial, non-participative RFP process toward one that fosters the type of government/industry teamwork and communication that will be required if we are going to field technologically superior but also affordable weapon systems.

ONE YEAR LATER

A longitudinal follow-up study occurred in June of 1992, one year after RFP CPT guidance. Interviews with Air Force users of the progress toward RFP process improvement efforts, such as RFP Process Guide implementation, revealed insightful and applicable information.

Because the initial RFP CPT effort was a joint industry/government team endeavor, the customers of the productivity and quality improvement efforts were identified as industry teams proposing to the government and government program management teams deliverance of RFPs to industry. Overall, the interim year has been extremely fruitful and value has indeed been added to the RFP process. The remainder of this paper will briefly highlight the positive changes which are a direct result of the RFP CPT efforts from last year, and those areas needing further development and attention.

Probably the greatest impact of this government/industry effort emerged in the development and implementation of RFP Support Organizations (SOs) at each major buying center in the USAF. These SOs are in place as advisers to the customers outlined earlier in this section. The SOs assist in the construction of the RFPs and in the RFP implementation process.

On a quarterly basis, there is a meeting of the SOs' "grey beards", a term proudly worn by the support office personnel to connote senior leadership, wisdom, and experience in the preparation and use of RFPs. At that meeting, potential conflicts, changes, and improvements to the entire RFP process are discussed and acted upon. Additionally, the graybeards talk on an almost daily basis to share knowledge gained through the growth and improvement of the RFP process. The RFP SOs offer their customers assistance in RFP team building, construction, process metrics, tailoring and a host of other applicable areas outlined in the process guide. The guide is widely used by all customers!

The RFP SOs, in an ever-present desire to continuously improve the process, are within months of completion of a computerized, on-line, RFP-tailoring data base. The program management teams, as a group, meet in a specially equipped room at the RFP SO to plan and construct the RFP. These will be two-to three-day upfront, RFP team effort, planning periods which will likely yield tremendous benefits downstream - clearer RFPs, better proposals from the contractors, contracts for what the user really wants and needs, and, in turn, a better and smarter buy for the government and the taxpayer.

Aside from the continued movement toward RFP automation, a couple of areas need further development. More use of the developed training modules on team formation should be employed by the program management teams. This may help ensure a cohesive team that knows their strengths and weaknesses from the outset so the teams are better able to plan accordingly. In addition to this improvement, faster turnaround time on the implementation of changes to the RFP Process Guide will ensure the latest information is available to the users of the guide.

These two areas for improvement are far overshadowed by the overwhelming success of the RFP process improvements to date. The TQM philosophy is being fully implemented through continuous improvements at all levels of work, constant self-inspection by the SO personnel and by the customers, and a government/industry team effort to see that RFP horrors of the past stay in the past. The efforts of the RFP CPT in 1991 are extremely helpful and have improved this critical process immeasurably.

The quality and productivity of the RFP process is vastly improved and continues to improve on a daily basis. This success story should be extremely comforting to the general public, especially the skeptics of the professionalism, competence, and dedication of the military acquisition personnel and their desire to do what is best for the country.

REFERENCES

Blue Ribbon Defense Panel (Fitzhugh Commission). Report to the President and the Secretary of Defense on the Department of Defense. Washington D.C.: Government Printing Office, July 1970.

Commission on Government Procurement. Report of the Commission on Government Procurement. Washington D.C.: Government Printing Office, December 1972.

Fox, Ronald. Arming America: How the U.S. Buys Weapons. Boston: Harvard Business School Press, 1974.

------. The Defense Management Challenge: Weapons Acquisition. Boston: Harvard Business School Press, 1988.

Gansler, Jacques S. The Defense Industry. Cambridge: The MIT Press, 1980.

------. Affording Defense. Cambridge: The MIT Press, 1989.

President's Private Sector Survey on Cost Control (Grace Commission). Task Force Report on the Office of the Secretary of Defense. Washington, D.C.: Government Printing Office, July 1983.

President's Blue Ribbon Commission on Defense Management (Packard Commission). A Quest for Excellence: Final Report to the President. Washington, D.C.: Government Printing Office, June 1986.

U.S. Congress. House. Committee on Armed Services. Defense Acquisition: Major U.S. Commission Reports (1949-1988). Washington, D.C.: Government Printing Office, November 1988.

About the Authors

Major T. Scott Graham
Assistant Professor of Contracting Management
Ph.D. in Management from The University of Georgia
Air Force Institute of Technology

Lt. Col. Carl R. Templin
Assistant Professor of Contracting Management
Ph.D. in Purchasing from Arizona State University
Air Force Institute of Technology

Lt. Col. Michael E. Heberling
Head, Department of Systems Management
Ph.D. in Purchasing from Michigan State University
Air Force Institute of Technology

Productivity & Quality Management Frontiers-IV, edited by Sumanth, Edosomwan, Poupart, and Sink. ©1993 Institute of Industrial Engineers.

A Study of Successful Total Quality Management Implementation

V.S. Polivka
PRC Inc.
Arlington, Virginia USA

R. Khorramshahgol
The American University
Washington, D.C. USA

ABSTRACT

The 90s will probably be remembered as the era of Total Quality Management (TQM). Nowadays, TQM is perhaps the most talked about issue in industry, government, and education. Meanwhile, numerous success stories from leading companies and some government agencies demonstrate that Quality process and product is indeed achievable and it has high payback. However, TQM holds promises only for those organizations that implement it properly, otherwise, improperly implemented, TQM can create such a chaos that the business organization cannot possibly survive. To enable proper implementation of TQM, this paper, on the one hand identifies key factors that contribute to its successful implementation, and on the other hand focuses on reasons for its failure. The results reported in this research are based on personal interviews with TQM officials in those U.S. firms which have attained maturity in TQM practices and have a well established implementation record.

Key Words: TQM implementation; Success Factors; Failure Reasons; Proactive vs. Reactive

Productivity & Quality Management Frontiers-IV, edited by Sumanth, Edosomwan, Poupart, and Sink. ©1993 Institute of Industrial Engineers.

Total Quality Management in the Information Systems Function: A Case Study

J.M. Dudziak

Brush Wellman

Cleveland, Ohio USA

For over two years Brush Wellman's Information Services Department has been implementing a new culture and infrastructure based on Total Quality Management (TQM) principles. The goal is to dramatically increase development and maintenance productivity and customer satisfaction (waste elimination, responsiveness, cycle time reduction) by concentrating on Quality.

APPROACH AND DEPLOYMENT - Our approach has focused on a few key strategies continuously fine-tuned. The best way to manage change is from the security of knowing our culture. Culture and strategy must be compatible. We focus constantly on the process and do not rush to CASE (automated) tools. We maintain a customer (internal) focus at all times, and always recognize the difficulty of change! Education and training on quality set the stage for self-assessment. We focused on the cost of quality, involving everyone in regular work sampling to identify rework and value-added work. I.S. process improvement was accomplished through Continuous Improvement Teams. Flowcharting processes, brainstorming, fishbone diagrams and Pareto analysis activities became and are the way we work, think and talk. Trust was built through a series of team recommendations that were accepted by management; one was to purchase and install a new formal System Development Methodology.

A Quality Assurance Committee has worked to "Reward the behavior you want," and establish measurements and metrics which we call "Dashboards". "You get what you measure." Vision and Mission Statements, Quality Policy, and various key indices are posted throughout. A key new culture dimension was a reorganization to semi-autonomous teams from a classic functional structure.

RESULTS - Trouble Reports showed an 18-month decline, "rework" was reduced, customer satisfaction ratings have a positive trend, and national recognition was received.

Over the past three years the I.S. Department of Brush Wellman, a primary metals manufacturing company, has been implementing a new culture and infrastructure based on TQM principles. The goal is to dramatically increase development and maintenance productivity and customer satisfaction (waste elimination, responsiveness, cycle time reduction) by concentrating on Quality.

This paper is an actual case history of our implementation of TQM in the I.S. Department with emphasis on leadership and culture change. Described are the basic approaches and strategies, some specific implementation activities, problems incurred and lessons learned, and tangible results of our efforts to date.

BACKGROUND

American businesses today understand that unless they are getting better, they are not even going to be in the game in the highly competitive '90's and beyond. Brush Wellman is no exception. Recognizing the need for a fundamental strategic change back in 1988, our now retired C.E.O. assigned to me the task of defining and establishing what this fundamental strategy change should be. At that time, it was suggested that it be Computer Integrated Manufacturing (C.I.M.). With a manufacturing background and being responsible for Information Services, the assignment was a natural. But, perhaps in heresy to the I.S. world, it was not an appropriate approach for our company. We evolved during 1988 from discussions of a new strategy called C.I.M. to a strategy called C.I.M./J.I.T. (Just-In-Time), and finally embarked on a "back to basics" company-wide total quality initiative that came to be known as our Continuous Improvement Process, or C.I.P.

Our C.I.P. philosophy statements survived the editing of Senior Vice Presidents, the C.E.O. and the Board of Directors, and the test of time so the statements are a good and fair representation of the depth and breath of our C.I.P.:

Continuous Improvement Process Philosophy Summary
...Creative Involvement of Employees in **Continuous Improvement** in **All Operations** through the **Elimination of Waste** that negatively affects quality, price and service to the **Customer.**
...Requires a new mind set, a **Culture Change** within the Company.
...Focusing the creative energies of **All Employees** requires investments in training, time and resources to institutionalize a culture that emphasizes increasing quality and decreasing costs.

> ...Our approach to all endeavors will be **Simplify,**
> **Automate** and **Integrate**. In that order.

To comment on the highlighted items, it is important to
recognize that C.I.P. is not just another program, it is a
business way of life. It involves the gradual and consistent
mending of problems to achieve higher goals. Unlike "Don't
rock the boat" philosophies of the past, which said, "If it
ain't broke, don't fix it," the new Brush Wellman philosophy
is stated, "If it ain't broke, at least make it better." Or
to paraphrase Tom Peters..."If it ain't broke, you ain't
looked hard enough."

"All Operations" means that everyone in the company is
involved, not just the factory floor or Manufacturing. Cycle
time reduction in paper processing in our order entry system,
for example, is as important as similar efforts on the
factory floor.

How do we continue to improve? Simply stated, we need to
find waste, get rid of it, and keep it gone. Easy to say,
but hard to do. What is waste? One way to look at it is how
things are now versus how we would like them to be, or how
things should be. Waste of all kinds needs to be eliminated.
Wasted material in the broadest meaning, wasted money, wasted
time, waste from lost sales opportunities. It is up to
everyone to find the waste, get rid of it, and keep it gone -
- and forever!

Of course, eliminating defects is not enough to capture
markets. Success depends on how well a company evaluates the
processes, products, and markets of today to determine what
the customer will want tomorrow. It requires a commitment to
long-term strategies and to know where organizational changes
are needed. The C.I.P. hinges on the constant cooperation
of all departments, including research, production, and
sales, so that the corporate focus stays on the customer or
any part of the process that might affect the product being
built.

Our C.I.P. is a "Cultural Change," which means it affects all
functions. It affect the way we think, work, talk and act.
It means doing the right things right the first time.
Continuous Improvement involves "Everyone." It begins with
people. It requires treating people with respect. It
requires a commitment from all the people at all levels, all
functions, all the time. Not just the factory; everyone!
People are not hired "hands"; they are hired "brains"!

Simplify, automate, integrate (in that order). We are trying
to go about using the quality process to simplify things

before we do any automation and that applies to office work especially.

All these efforts come down to two words: "Customer Satisfaction." C.I.P. is fundamentally a customer driven process. Because increasingly in the '90's, we recognize that the Customer is King. Indeed, it has often been said, "no customers, no orders, no jobs."

We selected the internationally recognized quality expert Bill Conway, Conway Quality Inc., to lead us into this new "management system". Bill had the credibility since, as a former C.E.O. of a Fortune 250 firm (who was the first to actually work with Dr. Deming in the U.S.), he had actually done it. Through seminars and videos, Conway Quality helped educate and train our entire work force starting with the C.E.O. and his staff and cascading this education level by level through the entire organization. For us, this was a massive undertaking, unprecedented, and took two years. How to work in teams, group dynamics, how to be a team leader, how to be a team facilitator, etc. is Phase Two of our education, which we are in the midst of now.

Conway's education process broadly covered the what, why, who, how, when, and where. More specifically ,the employees now <u>want</u> to make fundamental changes which is the underlying principle of C.I.P. This fundamental change in attitude is not being satisfied with the status quo, anxious to participate, be part of a team, challenge our thinking to find ways to improve, asking ourselves "How can we do this better?" or "This thing just does not look right; there's got to be a better way;" and, being willing to express those points of view, share these ideas, and to accept change that comes perhaps as a result of the changing of the process.

APPROACH - STRATEGIES

The approach we used in the I.S. Department focused on key strategies which were drafted at the beginning of our initiative and fine-tuned as we proceeded.

o   The best way to manage change is from the security of knowing your culture - who you are and what you value. Thoughtful introspection is crucial.

o   Focus on establishing the culture first, then build an infrastructure (methods, tools, management programs and organization) to support the new culture. Institutionalize the culture. Make it permanent, but self-correcting. Culture and strategy must be compatible; this is critical to successful change!

o   Take a top-down perspective. Create a Vision for the culture and associated infrastructure. A strong, top management concern for the health of the culture is fundamental for enhancing or reinforcing strategy.

o   Make the initiative a process, not a program. Implement in a phased, iterative manner. Make sure each component is/was right before moving on.

o   Obtain creative and continuous involvement from I.S. staff, the user community and outside sources. Build partnerships for continuous improvement.

o   Focus constantly on the process. "Blame" the process, not the people. We want to improve the process, not punish people.

o   Simplify before we automate. Do not rush to C.A.S.E. tools and other technologies to reach our goals.

o   Maintain a customer focus at all times. It is our internal users or clients who are ultimately "paying" us. Treat them as we would treat an external bill paying customer.

o   Recognize the difficulty of change. Expect a three to five-year investment "horizon". Before three years, we should be seeing real, tangible benefits; within five years, results should be pouring in, and quality the only acceptable way to work, forever.

We generally use the term Total Quality Management. Total means everyone in the organization is involved and actively working on improving processes. This includes all employees. Quality means that every process is being continuously improved in order to meet internal (and external) customer expectations. Management is leadership at every level of the organization committed to improvement and creating a positive environment. In our process, leadership is constantly contrasted to the old management way.

DEPLOYMENT - IMPLEMENTATION PROCESS

The process used to implement TQM in I.S. was:

1. Educate and train the staff in TQM principles.
2. Assess where we were.
3. Determine where we wanted to be in 3-5 years.
4. Plan and take measured steps to get to the goals.
5. Assess incremental progress to the goals.

Education and training brought an awareness to the staff of the importance of quality in the work they did and provided them with the belief and wherewithal to improve their environment. This initial step set the stage for a meaningful and objective self-assessment of the I.S. function. The self-assessment was conducted through surveys administered to the I.S. staff and the user community and through an independent review by an outside consultant. These assessments provided us with an understanding of our department's strengths, weaknesses, opportunities and threats and were among the first viable signs from management in proving that people would not be punished for negative input.

Determining where we want to go was perhaps the most important as well as most intriguing step in our process. Within this step, we revised our Mission Statement and, keeping to our strategy of building the infrastructure around the culture, we planned our implementation using the first ever IS Vision Statement as a cultural guideline.

We started our implementation process by developing and focusing on the leadership within the I.S. department. This was accomplished through training courses and I.S. planning sessions. We essentially had the I.S. management team step up to bat and provided the tools to make the right things happen.

Once the Mission Statement was re-developed to reflect TQM, the objectives solidified, we focused on building upon the quality awareness which was introduced in the earlier education and training step. This was accomplished by calculating and advertising the cost of imperfect quality, involving everyone in work sampling to identify value-added work as well as personal rework, and providing TQM training videos to be studied in teams. All of these activities raised the level of staff awareness concerning quality, but it also raised their level of anxiety over the "lack" of quality within the department. We had opened their eyes and now they agreed that something had to be done to improve quality.

We immediately followed up by officially empowering the staff to work on key quality issues. This was met with skepticism by some of the staff initially; they did not trust management's sincerity and intent. How could management simply "give up" power so easily and quickly? Everyone was waiting for the day when the old authoritative style would return. Trust was built through a series of staff decisions that were accepted by management. One was to purchase a project management tool. Another was to select and purchase a System Development Methodology (SDM). Management questioned/challenged the research, analysis and justifications, but did not try to re-assess and re-analyze decisions, and relatively quickly approved the recommendations. Also concerning trust, early on we published an Amnesty Statement which absolved all from blame for any waste - who cares how it got there, just get rid of it, forever! This was a powerful concept we learned from Bill Conway.

Process improvement of various I.S. functions was introduced to the staff through C.I.P. Teams responsible for detailed analysis, simplification, and automation if appropriate. Flowcharting processes, brainstorming, fishbone diagrams and Pareto analysis activities became and are the way we work, think, talk, and act ... i.e., continuous improvement. We created Teams to analyze and recommend changes to our project management, systems development, estimating, quality assurance and maintenance functions. The leadership developed and expressed in the early stages of this initiative allowed these Teams the time and support they needed to reach decisions. Without this leadership, the Teams would have languished indefinitely, postponing the decision until the "right time".

To support process improvement and improve quality awareness, the informal, nonmonetary rewards mechanism was adjusted to recognize quality work. As a result, a monthly quality award was instituted and quality issues became the first agenda item at each meeting. The old adage, "Reward the behavior you want," was never more true. This focus provided the motivation and drive for each employee to strive toward self-improvement with a quality goal. Self-improvement was also supported by the empowerment aspect. A Quality Assurance Committee worked with the entire department as we establish measurements and metrics, which we call "Dashboards". "You get what you measure" is, of course, another very true old adage. Our Q.A. function is managed by committee.

As we empowered the staff to get the job done, we also legitimized personal responsibilities for each staff member. We built this culture dimension through "gripe sessions" and pointed to the need for everyone to pull their own weight. We made it very clear the role that each individual was to play in the new organization, but we encouraged constructive criticism.

To reinforce trust and ensure quality, one milestone event was that a SDM was selected, approved and implemented. This SDM incorporates an engineering mentality which provides the substance to a disciplined, rigorous approach to development and maintenance. Some of the IS staff members initially felt that the new SDM would diminish creativity and innovativeness, thereby reducing our ability to freely improve the process. This resistance was met with the implementation of "practical rigor". Under this principle, the staff was to use the standardization aspects of the SDM, but free to make project tradeoffs if they understood the implications and "managed by fact."

A key cultural dimension which we implemented was a reorganization to self-managing teams, actually we call them semi-autonomous teams. Each of four new teams are now empowered to get the job done in the best way possible. In the past, staff members were accustomed to a hierarchial structure where every decision was scrutinized by a management team often removed from the detail. Now the focus was on the team entity, not the manager. This was and still is not an easy aspect to implement. We focused on improving internal communications within and between the teams to replace the old management flow of control and information.

With the team structure in place today, we are continuing to provide and enable the staff with tools, training and coaching in order to acquire the skills and self-confidence that the individuals need in order to effectively work as a team(s).

Positive reinforcement of behavior is a key tool in improving the environment. This goes from "at-a-boys" all the way up to formal recognition and rewards. Positive reinforcement gets people to repeat desired behavior and, unlike negative reinforcements or punishments, gets people to want to contribute. We found that asking someone to be part of a C.I.P. Team was a positive reinforcement; taking an interest in the team and what they are doing, praising their efforts and especially implementing their ideas are powerful positive reinforcements.

Communications is always a fundamental, critical item. It takes on several levels and begins with the development of good listening skills. We work hard at continuing to seek out employees, ask them about their work, their difficulties, and their ideas and anything we can do to help. The person actually performing the work, as TQM teaches us, (such as the programmer) is closest to it and knows it best. We continually practice that the person closest to the work can provide valuable inside information and it is our responsibility to remove barriers. We also need to let the employee know how he or she is performing. It is a psychological fact that the best way to influence behavior is to impact it at the time it occurs, not six or twelve months later. So, we strive very much to practice "one minute manager type" Performance Management, if you will. In this way, positive behavior is reinforced and negative behavior can be extinguished.

Another communications level is information about the company, its policies, goals and objectives. These must be conveyed to employees on a regular basis so they know the company direction and they know how they can contribute.

Much of what has been said actually involves empowerment, which is built on the existence of good communications and positive reinforcement. Asking for ideas, giving people authority to improve processes and implement ideas all are examples of empowerment and imply a level of trust between management and employees; we have certainly learned by experience that empowerment is a strong motivator in that the person often wants to contribute even more.

This positive environment created through pro-active approaches becomes the driving force for continuous improvement as described by Dr. Deming in the well known plan-do-check-act cycle.

Finally, we are using the Malcom Baldrige National Quality Award (MBNQA) as a guide to the establishment of TQM in I.S., as a guide to the establishment of a Quality Management System within the I.S. function. Having the honor of being on the '92 MBNQA Board of Examiners has convinced us that the Baldrige can help us greatly in further assessing where we are and where we need to direct our efforts to become a world class I.S. function. The Core Values of the MBNQA fit well with our past and planned initiatives.

RESULTS

The success to date of our initiative is shown in the following, and everyone believes that bigger and better results are forthcoming.

O   Incident Reports (emergencies and major problems in production) have shown an 18-month steady decline.

O   Our detailed personal work samples show a definite, overall downward trend in rework and an upward trend in value added work.

O   We had the opportunity over this time period to meticulously document the activities involved in the rewriting and installation of a new system. Phase One of the system showed rework of 32% using all of our old processes. Phase Two used many of our new approaches and attitudes (even though some were in their pilot stage) and resulted in a significant drop in rework from 32% to 18%! This is especially impressive when it is realized that the work in Phase Two was actually twice the scope of that of Phase One. The staff remained the same for both Phases.

o   Our maintenance activity has shown a continuous,
    positive trend in customer satisfaction ratings.

o   A C.I.P. team specifically addressing data center
    operations has shown impressive results, including the
    elimination of almost five hours a night of third shift
    work, considered unnecessary or rework. Those resources
    were channeled into value-added work, again to improve
    our overall quality and productivity. Overtime has
    correspondingly decreased.

o   The I.S. Department received "VP-Bravo Awards", Brush
    Wellman's second highest Quality Recognition, for our
    C.I.P. Teams.

o   We received national recognition with the 1991 Best of
    the Best Award from the 1,000-member Quality Assurance
    Institute for quality initiatives in the I.S. function.

o   Our initiatives have been featured by CIO Magazine,
    Software Magazine, Computerworld and the Quality
    Assurance Institute Journal.

LESSONS LEARNED

For us, an inside/outside combination worked very well in
that a consultant was a good conduit between management and
the organization in the initial stages. It was a safe way to
relay information until we established a better working
relationship, getting rid of the old way and working the new
way. Using an organizational psychologist to assist and
monitor our early team development activities gave us
invaluable insights. The daily work still had to get done;
that is always a problem and we really are not satisfied with
the progress we made. People put a lot of their own overtime
and their own weekends into working on these projects while
the daily work still had to be done. As to momentum, Tom
Peters talks about problems with old "Mo" even at Toyota. No
matter how successful your effort is, you go through peaks
and valleys. Our culture has clearly changed in the
department overall, although not everyone is 100% with the
new. We have what is called in psychology some "unloving"
critics but most of our staff are "loving" critics who really
want to succeed and want everyone to do well in the new way!

Before we started C.I.P., our people may have said
"OPPORTUNITY IS NO WHERE". Now, most in the department would
change the phrase to "OPPORTUNITY IS NOW HERE", which
symbolizes a shift in how we look at things. We continue on
our unending journey in establishing a quality way (not
program) of life!

ACKNOWLEDGEMENTS

William E. Conway - Conway Quality, Inc.   Nashua, NH

Thomas Flecher - CAP Gemini America   Cleveland, OH

Andrew Passan - O'Brien, Passan & Associates   Cleveland, OH

Rebecca Staton-Reinstein - The Paul Hertz Group   Miami, FL

BIBLIOGRAPHY

Burrill, C.W. and Ellsworth, L.W., (1980)
Modern Product Management
Tenafly, Burrill-Ellsworth Associates, Inc.

Conway, W.E. (1992) The Quality Secret
Nashua, Conway Quality Inc.

Davis, S.M. (1984) Managing Corporate Culture
New York, Harper & Row

Kouzes, J.M. and Posner, B.Z. (1987)
The Leadership Challenge
San Francisco, Jossey-Bass, Inc.

James M. Dudziak has been a Corporate Vice President and Officer for ten years. He is on the 1992 Malcolm Baldrige Board of Examiners, teaches part-time at Kent State University and has contributed numerous speeches and articles on TQM. He has an MBA from the University of Florida.

Productivity & Quality Management Frontiers-IV, edited by Sumanth, Edosomwan, Poupart, and Sink. ©1993 Institute of Industrial Engineers.

Optimizing Employee Involvement

M.R. Kelly
Total Quality Management Services, Inc.
Palm Beach Gardens, Florida USA

ABSTRACT

Most organizations, that either have or are considering an Employee Involvement Program, view employee involvement from a traditional management perspective - it will be good for the bottom line. Some organizations go further, envisioning such programs as a means of improving employee morale, or developing employee capabilities. Notice that these are all outcomes that management desires. Objectives like these fail to adequately consider the <u>customers</u> of this management practice - a consideration that is essential if employee involvement is to be optimized.

When management determines to implement an Employee Involvement Program, the customers of the program are the employees whose efforts it is intended to enlist. The program is a management output; a component of the management system; a part of the overall structure management has put in place to operate the business. Therefore, the program must be regarded like any other product or service that has been produced to meet a need. It must adhere to basic quality principles that lead to customer satisfaction. Without satisfied customers, who are the employees in this case, there is no need for the program, and the program will not succeed. This paper identifies four guidelines, that when adhered to, will address the needs of the employees and sustain an effective Employee Involvement Program.

Guidelines for Optimizing Employee Involvement

1. Identify the needs of your employees. Find out what will motivate them to participate, then, envolve them in directing the program to satisfy these needs.

2. Establish indicators and targets to measure performance, analyze results, and take appropriate action to correct deficiencies.

3. Treat people as you would like to be treated. Be honest about your intentions. Reinforce performance that is directed at the achievement of your stated goals.

4. Never be satisfied that your Employee Involvement Program is as good as it can be. Constantly seek to make it better.

Employee Involvement Programs have over the past two decades become an integral part of the way we do business.[1] Whether called Quality Circles, Quality Improvement Teams, participative management, productivity teams, or Employee Involvement, it is an approach that attempts to capture the creative and innovative power of the work force. A magnificent idea, but with over two hundred thousand employee involvement groups in the United States, and several million operating worldwide[2], the question is often asked, "Is our Employee Involvement Program as effective as it can be?" And further, "How can we make our program more effective?"

As with many practices that become popular in business, Employee Involvement Programs are largely models of what other companies have done. The process involves finding companies that are doing employee involvement well, and taking from them ideas to implement in another organization. What evolves are Employee Involvement Programs that represent a collection of several successful programs, or an exact copy of one that worked somewhere else. Will these Employee Involvement Programs work as well in the new organization? What we know about resistance to change[3] tells us that a copied program, placed in a new organization without involving the employees, will not quickly reach its potential.

What then, can be done to improve an existing, or assist with the implementation of a new Employee Involvement Program? The four guidelines outlined in this paper provide practical direction that will lead to an optimized Employee Involvement Program.

BEGIN WITH THE CUSTOMER

Whether you have, or are considering implementing an Employee Involvement Program, start by analyzing the program you now have, or investigating other successful programs. Include in your research the important element of talking with your customer (the employees). Most organizations view employee involvement as a benefit to the employee, something each worker has been longing for, and now, through management's goodwill, a new program is being given to them. The employees, however, may not view the program in the same light. They need to be involved in the development, or refinement of the program in order to have ownership of the concept; to truly see it as a benefit. This is why it is critical to involve a

---

[1] Dewar, D.L. (1980) The Quality Circle Guide to Participation Management, New Jersey, Prentice-Hall.

[2] Aubrey, C.A. II (1988) Teamwork: Involving People in Quality and Productivity Improvement, New York, Quality Resources.

[3] Lawrence, P.R. (1968) "How to Deal with Resistance to Change," The Harvard Business Review, January-February.

representative body of your employees in planning implementation strategies, and developing corrective actions.

Consider this story from a company whose management was attempting to help their field employees. To improve productivity in field operations, management determined that a new vehicle design was necessary. There was adequate justification for this decision, but the employees were never involved in determining what features should be included in the new vehicle. When the new vehicles arrived, management was beaming, anxious to hear how thrilled the employees were about what had been done for them. The employees, however, were only interested in testing the vehicle's capabilities. The first test was to see if the vehicle could reach locations that had previously been inaccessible (a problem that had long hampered field operations). The workers engaged the four-wheel drive mechanism, and proceeded toward their objective. The test vehicle promptly sank so deeply into the bog that even four-wheel drive was ineffective without the help of a large winch truck.

Later analysis clarified that the new vehicles were not designed to meet the needs of the field employees. Costly rework was required for each vehicle that had been ordered. The lesson management learned was to involve employees when decisions are made that effect them. This reasoning is also applicable when management determines to help their employees by implementing an Employee Involvement Program.

Guideline 1
Identify the needs of your employees. Find out what will motivate them to participate, then involve them in directing the program to satisfy these needs.

There are two proven effective methods for identifying the needs of a group. First, if the number of people is small, **interview** everyone in the group. Second, if the number of people is large, **survey** a percentage of the population to obtain a statistically accurate picture of the whole population. There are many consultants and firms with the expertise to do this well. Armed with this information, you are better prepared to provide a program that is on target. In addition, there is considerable information available to you regarding what motivates workers. Listed below is a summary of some of these findings.

Maslow[4] determined that human needs can be scaled in terms of importance; how urgently they must be satisfied. *Physiological* needs are first, then *safety* from external threats, *love* - the need to belong, *esteem* - a high sense of personal worth, and finally *self-actualization* - the need to realize our potential. Maslow predicts that it is a quest for the higher order of needs like love, esteem and self-actualization that motivates the behavior of the normal adult person.

---

[4] Maslow, A. (1954) Motivation and Personality, New York, Harper and Bros. p. 92.

Herzberg[5] is famous for his *two-factor theory*. In it he describes a set of factors called "motivators," and a set of factors called "hygienes," which influence behavior on the job. The motivators include pay, competent supervision, the quality of supervision, company policies, working conditions, and the security of the job. The hygiene factors are achievement, recognition, responsibility, and advancement. Herzberg's findings establish that different kinds of needs motivate employees.

Adams[6] and Weick[7] are authors who argue for an *equity theory* which states that employees examine their inputs, costs, and outputs on the job, and compare this information with individuals in similar positions. Any inequities that are identified serve to motivate the employee to restore equity or balance.

Vroom[8] in his widely accepted *expectancy theory* states that motivation is a function of both the expectation that good performance will lead to rewards, and the importance of these outcomes to the person involved. In other words, a worker will put out more effort if he or she feels that performance will likely increase and be followed by desirable rewards.

The literature on motivation is helpful both in pointing out the kinds of worker needs that must be met, and areas where management might begin to assess the culture that exists in their organization. In particular, consider what type of needs the employees have. For example, if the company were tightly held, and the employees given little freedom to act, their needs would be different from employees in an organization where they were encouraged to act and think without fear.

For an Employee Involvement Program to be effective, the needs of the employees must be first understood, then translated into actions that match the employee's needs. Studies[9] have shown that results are optimized when management's actions address the development level (*competence* - skill and knowledge, and *commitment* - motivation and confidence) of the employees.

[5] Herzberg, F. (1966) Work and the Nature of Man, Cleveland, OH, World Publishing Co.

[6] Adams, J.S. (1965) Advances in Experimental Social Psychology, Vol. 2, New York, Academic Press.

[7] Weick, K.E. (1966) "The Concept of Equity in the Perception of Pay," Administrative Science Quarterly, vol. 11, pp. 414-439.

[8] Vroom V.H. (1964) Work and Motivation, New York, John Wiley and Sons.

[9] Blanchard, K.H., Carew, D.K. and Parisi-Carew, E. (1986) "Group Development and Situational Leadership: A Model for Managing Groups," Training and Development Journal, June, pp. 46-50.

Consider this example. You tell an employee to perform a task. Will it get done? Maybe by a highly motivated and competent employee, but an employee who is not motivated requires that you spend more time enlisting their cooperation with supportive statements like, "We need your help. You understand this work better than anyone else."

To optimize employee involvement, listen to your employees. Involve them in planning program changes, and developing implementation strategies.

MEASURE PERFORMANCE

In today's fast tracked business world, where stress is rampant, the norm seems to have become: get something started, then turn to another crisis. The hope is that what was started will do well on its own. Many Employee Involvement Programs are initiated in this hands-off manner. The program may have been well planned out; a top notch idea that worked well elsewhere, and properly positioned to meet the needs of employees in the current organization. Unfortunately, this does not ensure success.

Success is measured in the results achieved over a period of time. The key word being "measured." To measure the effectiveness of employee involvement, establish indicators that communicate how well the program is doing.

Guideline 2
Establish indicators and targets to measure performance, analyze results, and take appropriate action to correct deficiencies.

Indicators and targets should be used to assess the effectiveness of your Employee Involvement Program. First, use **outcome indicators** to monitor performance at the end of the process. Second, use **process indicators** to monitor performance within a process. Third, use **targets** to establish a performance goal for each indicator.

Outcome Indicators provide an overall picture of process performance. Reviewing an outcome indicator yields a quick assessment of the Employee Involvement Program's performance. To develop an outcome indicator, consider why the program is being implemented. What needs is it intended to satisfy? For example, were the need to "improve the capacity for identifying and solving problems," an outcome indicator might be the number of problems solved. In a slightly different example, were the need to improve product quality, everyone must understand how quality is to be defined. Deming[10] refers to this as an operational definition. That is, a definition that allows a reasonable person to make sense of the term. In this example, by defining

---

[10] Deming, W.E. (1982) Out of Crisis, Cambridge, MA, M.I.T.

quality as, "the ability of a product to meet customer needs," an outcome indicator might be the level of external customer satisfaction with the product as measured in a survey taken annually.

Process Indicators are measures within a process used to identify where improvements can be made that will assure a satisfactory outcome. Process indicators enable management to control the Employee Involvement Program; to assess its effectiveness and take action when results are not as anticipated. This approach is the antithesis of the old paradigm of quality inspectors, standing at the end of a production line, throwing imperfect products into a reject pile. Using process indicators, a team made up of employees and management can look upstream of the outcome to control results. Examples of process indicators in an Employee Involvement Program include: how often teams meet, how long teams meet, how many people attend team meetings, the ability of team members to use tools and techniques, and harmony within the team.

Targets establish a measurable performance goal for each indicator. Targets may be based on past performance, industry standards, or other analyses. They are used to clarify whether performance is where it should be, and signal when action must be taken. Actions to resolve problems should involve some form of scientific method, and the use of quality tools[11].

Managing employee involvement using outcome and process indicators with targets, helps to assure that the program is doing what is was intended to do. The next time someone tells you that they have hundreds of active teams in their organization, ask, "What are the teams doing? How many are meeting their potential? What impact are they having? How do they feel about their participation?" Questions like these provide critical information for those who desire to optimize employee involvement.

TREAT EACH OTHER WITH RESPECT

Plans, systems, financial reports, and Employee Involvement Programs are but structures that reflect the work of people who are involved in making things happen. It takes people to achieve results, and people must work together in harmony in order to be effective. Effective employee involvement requires a shared respect for the contribution that each person makes to the whole. In many organizations this means that employees and management must change from an adversarial relationship[12].

---

[11] Kelly, M.R. (1992) Everybody's Problem Solving Handbook, New York, Quality Resources.

[12] Myers, M.S. (1978) Managing With Unions, Reading, MA, Addison-Wesley Publishing Company.

It is management's responsibility to tear down the walls that separate the people who must work together to get the job done. Management must lead the change in culture that is embodied in employee involvement by using the program to open up new channels of communication and cooperation within the organization[13].

Guideline 3
Treat people as you would like to be treated. Be honest about your intentions. Reinforce performance that is directed at the achievement of your stated goals.

Kouzes and Posner[14] have done extensive research concerning the characteristics that workers most admire in their leaders. Figure 1 lists the attributes they have identified that leaders have which cause workers to put forth something extra, to feel motivated and embrace change.

Characteristics That Workers Look for in Their Leaders

Honesty	Someone who can be trusted; whose values are clearly defined and modeled.
Competence	In order to follow someone with confidence, workers need to feel that the leader knows what they are doing; that they are capable and effective.
Forward Looking	Leaders must have a sense of direction; concern for the future; have a destination in mind that is clearly communicated.
Inspiring	Leaders must be enthusiastic, energetic, positive about the future; people who make others feel that what they are doing is important.

Figure 1

Kouzes and Posner see these characteristics not as individual items, but rather as a set of traits that can be summed up with the word *credibility*. When management is perceived to have high credibility, employees have a correspondingly high commitment to the organization. They are proud to tell others that they are part of the organization. They see their values as similar to those of the organization, and they feel a sense of ownership.

---

[13] Tichy, N.M. and Devanna, M.A. (1986) The Transformational Leader, New York, John Wiley & Sons.

[14] Kouzes, J.M. and Posner, B.Z. (1987) The Leadership Challenge, San Francisco, Jossey-Bass.

Credibility must be a characteristic of management in any organization that desires to optimize employee involvement. It creates loyalty and commitment that doesn't emanate from a "program," and causes employee involvement to become a way of doing business. Leaders within the organization must demonstrate credibility in the way they handle employee involvement. They must be honest about their plans and goals, competent in the way the program is administered, forward looking in their vision of what can be accomplished, and inspiring in generating a desire to participate. Leaders with these behaviors demonstrate their personal commitment to employee involvement, and engender a like response in their employees.

Leaders also recognize that effective employee involvement requires that people be recognized for performance that contributes to the achievement of stated targets. A recognized success creates in others the desire to share in the recognition. Recognition and rewards clarify expected behavior and build support. To identify the kinds of recognition that will work best, ask the employees. Employees at one company[15] were asked what they felt were very strong motivators for participation in employee involvement. The employees listed *personal satisfaction* and *a cash bonus based on the solution's impact* as the top two motivators. For other companies, the findings may be different. Identify what form of recognition will work best in your organization and make it part of the Employee Involvement Program.

CONTINUOUSLY IMPROVE

Constant improvement means change, and change is necessary because needs don't remain the same. As referenced earlier in the work of Maslow[16], once needs are satisfied at one level, individuals seek to have them satisfied at another, e.g., after the need to belong is satisfied, people need to feel a sense of personal worth. An effective Employee Involvement Program is administered to anticipate the changing needs of those it is intended to serve.

Guideline 4
Never be satisfied that your Employee Involvement Program is as good as it can be. Constantly seek to make it better.

Founded in the work of Walter A. Shewhart,[17] the concept of continuous improvement is widely supported in today's corporate board rooms. It simply states that a

---

[15] Florida Power & Light Co. (1988) "QIP in a New Light," Sunshine News, vol. 49, no. 7, pp. 7.

[16] Maslow, p. 92.

[17] Shewhart, W.A. (1939) "Statistical Method from the Viewpoint of Quality Control," Washington, Department of Agriculture, p. 45.

competitive advantage, or a program's success, cannot be maintained without the application of a cycle of activities that includes planning, doing, checking and acting on the results.

>Plan. Clarify ideas concerning either the implementation of the program, or the improvements to be made. Ask questions like: What is to be accomplished? What changes are desirable? What data are available? Is additional information needed? Then, plan a change, or identify a way to obtain the necessary information.

>Do. Implement the plans, preferably on a small scale. No need to go company-wide right away. Start with a few teams of workers.

>Check. Observe the effects of your actions. Were the results what you expected? Had you properly identified employee needs? Was the structure of the program appropriate for your employees?

>Act. Study the findings. Determine what can be learned, and how this information can be used to make predictions. Incorporate these ideas into the next plan, thus making each of these four steps part of a *cycle* of activities. Use the information you have obtained to either fully implement a new program, or make changes to an existing one.

The continuous improvement cycle as described above begins with "plan," which is appropriate when implementing a new program. For existing programs, first "check" to determine what actions, if any, are necessary. When applied to an Employee Involvement Program, the four steps of the continuous improvement cycle provide a comprehensive approach for optimizing results over time.

IN SUMMARY

The four guidelines outlined in this paper clarify what is needed to optimize an Employee Involvement Program. They begin with understanding customer needs. The customer in this case being the employees, whose efforts the Employee Involvement Program is intended to enlist. Involving your employees, and satisfying their needs, should be the overall objective of the program. Through the work of your employees, other constituents will be served.

Before implementing a new program, or as an essential modification to an existing one, establish indicators and targets to measure performance. Then, periodically use this data to analyze results, and take appropriate action to correct deficiencies.

Two other ongoing activities are also critical. First, remember that the program is only as good as the people who work to give it life. Treat these people with respect, give them credible management, and provide recognition frequently. Second, never stop working to improve the program. Constantly seek to make it better.

By following these guidelines, you can know that your Employee Involvement Program is achieving optimal results.

BIBLIOGRAPHICAL SKETCH

Currently a management training consultant, Michael R. Kelly served as a Quality Specialist for Florida Power & Light during its successful quest for the prestigious Deming Prize. In addition to the text referenced in this paper, he has another under development, and has written training texts for various companies that enable both management and employees to work together more effectively in identifying and meeting customer needs.

Productivity & Quality Management Frontiers-IV, edited by Sumanth, Edosomwan, Poupart, and Sink. ©1993 Institute of Industrial Engineers.

Quality First, or Productivity First?

L.A.J. Borges
Federal University of Rio Grande do Sul
Porto Alegre, RS BRAZIL

ABSTRACT

This paper deals with productivity and quality management and emphasizes that the quality approach is the starting point of the whole process. Productivity improvements will ensue and, eventually, cost reduction will follow, if it is a new project.

But, if you are in the middle of a running plant, and you need to have better results, you must look inside your company, under a self-discovery point of view and be ready to apply problem-solving methods, while inplementing quality programs and adopting proper production techniques. At this time, you reach the moment you have to determine which comes first: Quality, or Productivity?

When you find the problem area, you get the first point to tackle: It could either be a problem of Productivity, Total Quality Control, or Quality of Work Life, but whatever the problem is, you begin at it. But you cannot miss the opportunity to start, simultaneously, an integrated strategic process involving the three techniques. Basically, they are implemented through the same approach.

In order to get a better interrelation among them, the paper suggests:
1. to get everybody involved in the Strategic Planning, as far as Productivity, Total Quality Control and Quality of Work Life are concerned;
2. to revise the cost accounting management system;
3. to revise present operational methods, with a gradual shift towards new techniques, depending on the company's technological status; and,
4. to establish new productivity and quality measure patterns, to reach the next step, where the productivity and the quality level is first maintenained, and later improved.

The real question, of course, is not WHICH IS THE FIRST?, but WHO IS THE FIRST? - Naturally, the CUSTOMER.

INTRODUCTION

This paper deals with productivity and quality management and there is unique opportunity to get started in an integrated approach, involving a single process concerning the three areas: Quality, Productivity and Quality of Work Life. This derives from the consideration that the three improvement efforts demand the same implementation techniques.

You can reach the answer to the title question: "Quality First, or Productivity First?" through this integrated point of view.

1. QUALITY FIRST IN A NEW PROJECT

The design process has its starting point in Quality Control, a pre-condition to productivity improvement. As a result of both, cost reduction will follow.

As we can see in the Deming's Chain Reaction (see Figure 1), you start with Quality improvement, and after, you improve Productivity, and then, make cost reductions.

Figure 1: Deming's Chain Reaction

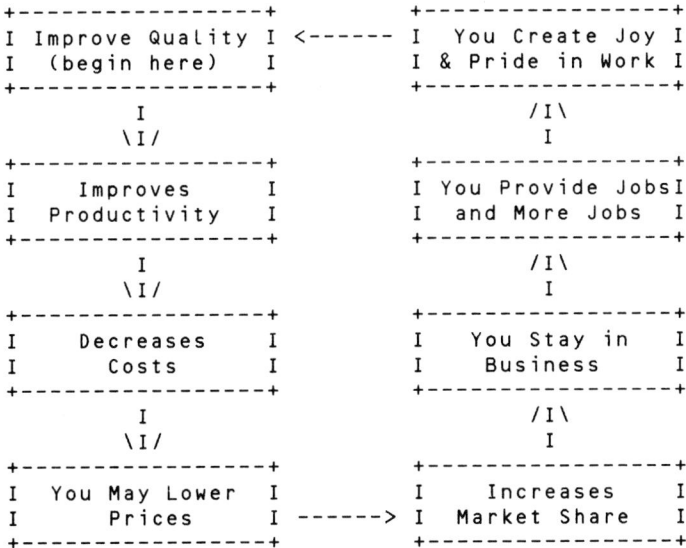

```
+-----------------+           +-----------------+
I Improve Quality I <------ I  You Create Joy I
I  (begin here)   I           I & Pride in Work I
+-----------------+           +-----------------+
        I                            /I\
       \I/                            I
+-----------------+           +-----------------+
I    Improves     I           I You Provide JobsI
I  Productivity   I           I  and More Jobs  I
+-----------------+           +-----------------+
        I                            /I\
       \I/                            I
+-----------------+           +-----------------+
I    Decreases    I           I   You Stay in   I
I      Costs      I           I    Business     I
+-----------------+           +-----------------+
        I                            /I\
       \I/                            I
+-----------------+           +-----------------+
I You May Lower   I           I    Increases    I
I     Prices      I ------> I  Market Share   I
+-----------------+           +-----------------+
```

Source: Boardman Associates, 1991

775

Boardman & Hunter(1991) say that the Leverage Ratios on Improvement of Product Quality are:

        1:1 in Production
        10:1 in Process Design
        100:1 in Product Design

and the Leverage Ratios on Improvement of Service Quality are:

        1:1 in Front-Line Operations
        20:1 in Process Design
        300:1 in Service Design

It is clear that if you agree with the ratios above, you can obviously assume that in a new factory or in a new project, you can start with Quality Assurance in the Product/Service Design. Therefore, Productivity comes later, and Quality is first.

2. WHAT ABOUT A RUNNING PALNT ?

If your problem area is on a running factory/shop, the focus can be changed. You must look into the situation, through problem-solving methods, apply Pareto's principle, to find out which comes first: Productivity, Total Quality Control, or Quality of Work Life. (See Figure 2)

Figure 2: Triangle of Integration

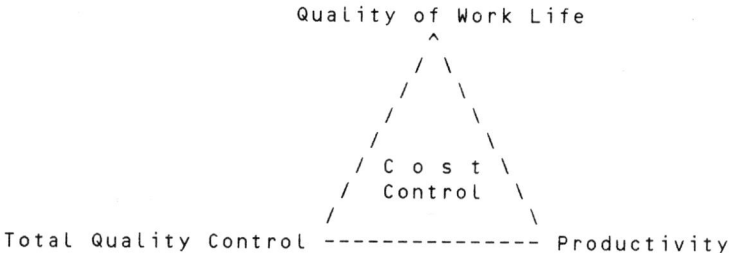

```
                    Quality of Work Life
                            ^
                          / \
                         /    \
                        /      \
                       /        \
                      / C o s t \
                     /  Control  \
                    /             \
      Total Quality Control -------------- Productivity
```

After investigating by means of whatever problem-solving technique you got, like the Effect-Cause Diagram or The Resource Optimization Matrix, you may find that the main problem area is Quality; so, Quality will come first. If the problem area is Productivity, let it be the first. Finally, if the problem area is working conditions or personnel, the first program to engage in will be Quality of Work Life.

Whatever corner you start, you have a target, sited in the triangle's center: "Cost Control". This is the way by which arbitrary cost limitations may be avoided, while a strong vigilance is kept on the way you will spend the money to solve the problem.

3. HOW TO DO IT ?

The best way to proceed is to invite the participation of all people involved in the company's strategic planning. Let the workers submit their suggestions about problems in Quality, Productivity, and Quality of Work Life.

The present trend points to the holistic character of the organization with full interaction of the whole group and a strong commitment from the Board of Directors, to satisfy the customer's needs. On-the-job training and the adoption of the "Apply, then Learn" philosophy, will lead, in fact, to the best results.

The revision of the accounting management system is very important. As Johnson & Kaplan(1987) state: "...the organization's financial reporting system is too late, too aggregated, and too distorted to be relevant for managers' planning and control decisions".

You have to analyse your company to see which of the modern cost accounting system should be selected, whether the ABC (Activity Based Costing) system proposed by Cooper and Kaplan (1988) or the P.E.U. (Production Effort Unit) method introduced in Brazil by Allora(1985). This paper is not discussing these methods.

It has to be considered that we are in a changing world. Therefore, let's have a look at your present operational methods. There are always some good ideas leading to new solutions.

It is mandatory to measure performance and to establish challenging goals. Plossl(1991) states that: "Performance measures are much more than standards to measure people – they are the means to communicate desired objectives. Management must set challenging goals for the right activities if they desire really significant progress."

Schaffer(1988) suggests some ways of getting a set of limited goals whose addition becomes an overall objective. He states: "To assure success, select a goal that:
a. Is urgent and compelling – a real attention-getter.
b. Is a first-step goal achievable in a short period of time – in weeks rather than months.
c. Is a bottom-line result, discrete and measurable.
d. The responsible participants feel ready, willing, and able to accomplish.
e. Can be achieved with available resources and authority."

4. CONCLUSION

This paper shows that quality comes before productivity when we are involved in a new project or a new factory.

When we are in a running plant, the more significant problem should always come first, be it Productivity, Total Quality or Quality of Work Life.

It does not matter which is the first vertex to select in the triangle of Figure 2, above. The whole point is to place the three processes in the company's strategic planning equally ranked, all regulated by cost control.

To sum up, the question is not which is the first, but WHO IS THE FIRST? - Of course, the CUSTOMER.

BIBLIOGRAPHIC REFERENCES

Allora, F. (1985) Engenharia de Custos Técnicos, São Paulo, Editora Pioneira e Fundação Universitária Regional de Blumenau.

Belcher Jr., J. G. (1987) Productivity Plus: How today's best run companies are gaining the competitive edge, Houston, Gulf Publishing Company.

Boardman T. J. and Hunter J. S. (1991) The Role of Statistical Thinking & Technology Improvement of Quality, Washington, Boardman Associates.

Cooper R. and Kaplan R. S. (1988) "Measure costs right: Make the right decisions", Harvard Business Review, Sept.-Oct.:96-103.

Johnson, H. T. and Kaplan, R. S. (1987) Relevance Lost: The Rise and Fall of Management Accounting, Boston, Harvard Business School Press.

Plossl, G. W. (1991) Managing in the New World of Manufacturing, New Jersey, Prentice Hall, Inc.

Schaffer, R. H. (1988) Breakthrough Strategies, New York, Harper & Row.

BIOGRAPHICAL SKETCH OF THE AUTHOR

B.A. in Civil Engineering at Fed. U. of Bahia (69). Advanced Course in Production Methods & Management, at U. of Cambridge, UK (77/78). MSc student in Industrial Enging., af Fed. U. of Rio Grande do Sul, Brazil (91/92 - End in Dec/92). Consultant on Project Planning, Scheduling and Control.

Productivity & Quality Management Frontiers-IV, edited by Sumanth, Edosomwan, Poupart, and Sink. ©1993 Institute of Industrial Engineers.

Quality, Productivity, Cost — Are We Looking at the Right One?

H. Bahari-Kashani
Western Oregon State College
Monmouth, Oregon USA

ABSTRACT

This paper identifies two main areas for improving quality. One is "internal consideration for quality" in which the production process, design, etc., can improve and the net result is both improvement in quality and reduction in cost and therefore reduction in the price. The second way of improving quality is based on "external consideration for quality." Quality can increase only if the cost of production increases and therefore the price. Under this condition, there will be an optimum amount of quality which should be decided upon by using customers utility function. The amount of satisfaction gained by quality should be compared with the added cost of increased quality. This leads to the conclusion that price-quality decisions should be made simultaneously. Since the aim is toward maximizing quality and minimizing cost at the same time, one has to come up with an optimum level of quality-price based on the customer's perception of the trade off between these two factors.

Key words: Quality, Cost

INTRODUCTION

This paper emphasizes the importance of the customer's needs and requirements in decisions concerning quality. Quality may be viewed from two different directions. One is the "internal consideration for quality" and the other one is "external consideration for quality." Internal consideration is from within the firm, where a higher quality product may reduce the cost of rejects, rework and so on. A higher quality unfinished product may improve the process at the later stages of production resulting in higher productivity. The external consideration is the quality of the product from the consumer's point of view. In this case improving the quality is normally associated with higher costs which in turn translates to higher prices for customers. Producers of goods or providers of services should try to identify the optimum point in this trade off between quality and price. The difference between internal and external consideration is that the firms can change and improve the production process and gain quality which in turn reduces the costs (internal consideration). External consideration by the customer is that the firm can not improve the process further, but higher quality will cost more to obtain. An added feature which may be perceived as higher quality by a customer will add to the cost regardless of what the manufacturer does with internal operations. So the decision maker of quality should study and understand the value of quality to the customer and compare it with the price the customer is willing to pay for the gained level of quality. This may require developing a different product for a different group of customers and making sure that within a group there is a balance between quality for various aspects of the product.

INTERNAL CONSIDERATION FOR QUALITY

The effect of quality on internal operations may be very comprehensive since the concept of quality is so broad and can be applied to many parts of an organization. To narrow the scope of the problem, let us consider the quality on, for example, a manufactured product. Higher quality may have the following effects. (Stevenson, 1990).

--Improved image for the brand name
--Improved productivity (higher rate of production)
--Reduction in liability costs

The above factors will reduce the cost. Improved productivity and reduction in liability expenses have a direct cost reduction effect, while the improvement in the image will increase demand and reduce the marketing costs. A higher economy of scale may be realized due to an increased level of production in response to a higher demand. These savings should be compared with the cost of improving quality. The cost for improving quality may include the factors such as the cost of inspection and the statistical quality control charts and tests, cost of capital to invest on new equipment and improving the process, improving the education of employees to be able to achieve higher levels of quality in the production process, etc. The decision concerning the amount of quality from this point of view is direct. If the savings in cost is more than the additional expenses this will result in a simple strategy of improving the quality or putting that process in action. Firms should measure the costs and obtain an optimum level of quality. By quality when we define it as meeting standard the comparison consists of a set of simple decisions such as identifying the optimum level of inspections, by comparing the inspection cost and the cost of passing defective product as depicted in Figure 1.

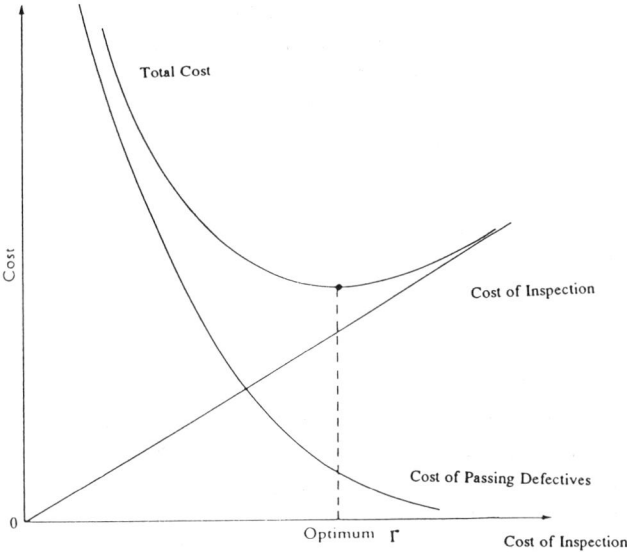

Figure 1.

Figure 1 shows classic economic tradeoffs in quality of conformance. I^* identifies the optimum level of inspections as a function of the cost of defective products passing through the process and the cost of inspection.

The cost related to quality has been classified in four groups: Internal Failure Costs and External Failure Costs which are due to low quality, and Appraisal Costs and Prevention Costs which occur for improving quality. See Ebel (1991), Evans (1989), Deming (1985), and Skecter (1992). Many correctly believe that improvement in quality results in cost reduction. Ronald Reagan (1988) concerning the Malcolm Baldrige National Quality award has indicated, "This Award salutes companies that improve the quality of their goods and services, thus enhancing productivity, lowering costs, and increasing profitability." Also, some believe that emphasize should be only on quality and not productivity. It is indicated by Gitlow, Gitlow, Oppenheim, and Oppenheim (1989) that, "In sum, stressing productivity means sacrificing quality and possibly decreasing output. Employee morale plunges, costs rise, customers are unhappy, and stockholders become concerned. On the other hand, stressing quality can produce all the desired results: less rework, greater productivity, lower unit cost, price flexibility, improved competitive position, increased demand, larger profits, more jobs, ..."

The quality of a product has been recognized as a major factor for success in business. While it is important to recognize the value of quality, there should be a recognition of the costs (cost of having high quality). The issue becomes complicated since the quality may refer to different things in different people's minds. The concept of quality measured by conformance to the standard which is actually a measure of disturbance around a preset standard have a different implication than the concept of quality as a measure of customer satisfaction, and so on.

Skecter (1992) explains that Taguchi, for the cost of not having quality, suggests a loss function which is of the form:

$$L = (Y-t)^2 \qquad\qquad\qquad (1)$$

This is a function of deviation from the targeted standard, which can be modified, Roy (1990), to a more flexible loss function. The measuring cost as a continuous function of deviation from the target, and trying to minimize it seems to be more reasonable than making sure that the product is meeting the pre-specified lower and upper allowable limits. The frequency of being close to the boundaries vs. target can change while the product is produced within pre-specified control limits. This makes a difference in customer satisfaction, as is evident by TV's made by Sony Japan and Sony U.S. and indicated by Roy (1990). "The Sony case demonstrated that quality is more than just producing between upper and lower limits-- quality is achieving the target as much as possible and limiting deviation from the target."

Achieving higher quality in the sense of meeting standard or in other words minimizing the value of quality loss function can be achieved by improving the process. It has been suggested to improve the process rather than inspecting the product to see if it is meeting the minimum requirement or it should be rejected.

This type of improvement through improving the process has been emphasized by Deming (1985). He believes improving the quality will bring the cost down. This is done by a reduction in scrap, rework, etc. since the improved process will reduce defects. So, improving the process for meeting standards may increase productivity and reduce the cost.

The above noted importance of quality for meeting the standard has been around for a long time. The consequences of not conforming with the standard could become high to the producer. Gitlow, Gitlow, Oppenheim, and Oppenheim (1989) have indicated, "An example of a quality issue in ancient times is found in the Code of Hammurabi, dated from 2150 B.C. Item 229 states: 'If a builder has built a house for a man, and his work is not strong, and the house falls in and kills the householder, that builder shall be slain'. Phoenician inspectors eliminated any repeated violations of quality standards by chopping off the hand of the maker of the defective product. Inspectors accepted or rejected products and enforced government specifications."

While the importance of meeting standards have existed for a long time the lessons that we have learned from Taguchi, Deming and others, in recent years, is that improving the quality by improving the process will bring the cost down.

EXTERNAL CONSIDERATION FOR QUALITY

The decision concerning the added features of a product as "higher quality", or higher life expectancy of the product as "higher quality" and so forth, which increases the cost of production and so the price of the product lend itself to studying the effect of quality from the customer's point of view and its value to the customer. Like any forecast or prediction, it is accuracy which is the most important value. The crucial factor is to have a good estimate and understanding of the value of quality to the customer and recognizing customer behavior. The customer should be the main factor in identifying the level of quality. Quality here is referred to as attributes satisfying the customer rather than engineering specifications. Of course, a good engineering specification should be based on customer satisfaction. But understanding the customer behavior is difficult and other considerations by engineers may move them away from final decision makers who are the customers. The satisfaction of the customer has always been a business concern.

The idea of customer satisfaction is nothing new either. Mahatma Gandhi (Q. C. Trends, 1988) has indicated, "A customer is the most important visitor on our premises. He is not dependent on us. We are dependent on him. He is not an interruption on our work. He is the purpose of it. He is not an outsider on our business. He is a part of it. We are not doing him a favor by serving him. He is doing us a favor by giving us an opportunity to do so."

Customers' Preference:

The utility function can explain a customer's preference toward quality. It can be expressed as:

$$u_i = f(X_i) \qquad for\ all \quad i = 1, \ldots, n \qquad (2)$$

where:

i = different features of the product which are considered by the customers

X_i = level of quality for feature i

u_i = the amount of utility obtained from X_i level of quality

A customer is interested in maximizing the total utility that he/she will receive from a product, indicated by:

$$MAX \qquad u = \sum_{i=1}^{m} f(X_i) \qquad (3)$$

S.T.   A fixed amount of budget allocation for this product.

A customer as a rational decision maker is interested in maximizing total utility received from all products consumed. A typical customer constantly adjusts the proportion of the product he/she consumes from total demand. Therefore, the objective is to maximize the overall utility function which can be written as:

$$MAX \ U = \sum_{j=1}^{m} \sum_{i=1}^{n} f(X_{ij})$$

$$s.t. \quad \sum_{j=1}^{m} \sum_{i=1}^{n} C_{ij} X_{ij} \leq B \qquad (4)$$

where:

X_{ij} = the amount of utility obtained from feature i of the product j.

C_{ij} = cost that the customer has to bear for obtaining X_{ij}

B = the budget constraints the customer will operate within.

Using a common assumption that the marginal utility function has negative slope illustrated by Figure 2.

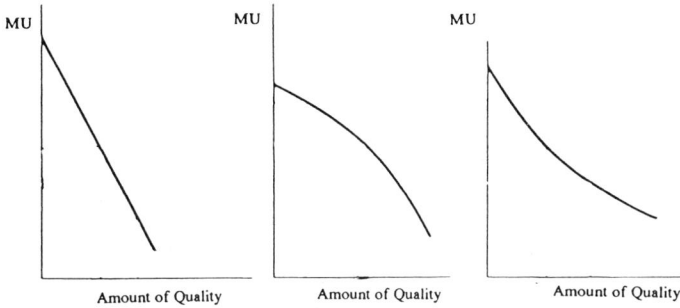

Figure 2.

can result in an theoretical optimum point when:

$$\frac{MU_{X_{ij}}}{P_{X_{ij}}} = \frac{MU_{X_{kl}}}{P_{X_{kl}}} \quad for \quad \begin{array}{l} i=1,\ldots n \\ j=1,\ldots m \\ k=1,\ldots n \\ l=1,\ldots m \end{array} \tag{5}$$

The customers are willing to pay for a higher quality product if the customers are getting higher satisfaction (utility) for each additional dollar they spend on quality compared to the satisfaction they get from other choices available for spending their money on. The customers may prefer a lower quality product to a higher quality product if the price of the lower quality product is reasonably lower than the price of the higher quality product. If the price of the higher quality product is slightly higher than the lower quality product the customers will select the higher quality product. All depends on the utility function of the customers. In the aggregate form for the society as a whole, there will be a relationship between quality and price in which for every combination of quality and price there will be a fixed aggregate demand for the product. These combinations of the quality-price in which the aggregate demand stays unchanged is given for three different

785

levels of demand shown by D_1, D_2, D_3, in bottom of Figure 3.

The top part of Figure 3 shows as the price increases and quality stays the same, the demand decreases. As quality increases and price is unchanged, the demand increases. When both price and quality changes depending on the magnitude of the

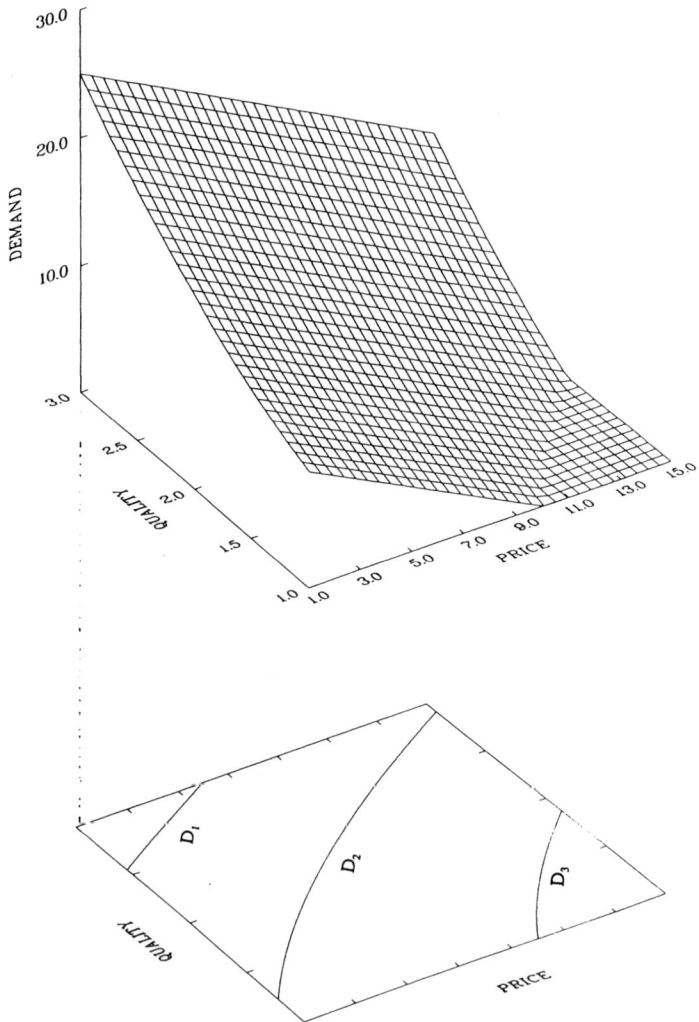

Figure 3.

changes, the other part of the graph is obtained.

CONCLUDING NOTE

Business success depends on the customer's demand for the product. Customer's demand is a function of several variables; those which a firm can influence are price and characteristics of the product which produces satisfaction (utility) for the customer. The firm may be able to reduce the cost through improving the quality of a product to conform with standard via, say, improving the process. as suggested by Deming and others. This will be a net gain and must be done. Given the same improved process, etc., the firm has the opportunity of improving quality (as perceived by customers, such as increase in expected life of product, additional features, etc.) by increasing the cost of production which translates to higher prices for the customers. Understanding the trade off between the price of the product and the value of quality to the customer is essential. After recognizing the customer's preference the decision maker can come up with the level of quality suitable for the market they are operating in. One should not make the decisions concerning the quality independent from the price (in the long run, price depends on the cost of manufacturing) and the decisions concerning the price independent from quality. The decision concerning quality and price should be made together so that the customers will get higher satisfaction for spending their money which results in increase in demand.

REFERENCES

Deming, W. Edwards. (1985) Transformation of American Industries - Video Series.

Ebel, Kenneth E. (1991) Achieving Excellence in Business, American Society for Quality Control, New York, Marcel Dekker, Inc., page 123.

Evans, James R., and William M. Lindsay. (1989) The Management and Control of Quality, St. Paul, West Publishing Company, page 33.

Feigenbaum, A. V. (1961) Total Quality Control, Engineering and Management, New York, McGraw Hill Book Company, Inc., pp. 85-89.

Gitlow, Howard, Shelly Gitlow, Alan Oppenheim, and Rosa Oppenheim, (1989) Tools and Methods for the Improvement of Quality, Boston,

Richard D. Irwin, Inc.

Q. C. Trends, Vol.4, Issue No. 3, February, 1988, Cover page.

Reagan, Ronald, Letter printed in *Q. C. Trend*, May 1988, page 24.

Roy, Ranjit K. (1990) A Primer on the Taguchi Method, New York, Van Nostrand Reinhold.

Ryan, Thomas P. (1989) Statistical Methods for Quality Improvement, New York, John Wiley & Sons, Inc., page 349.

Skecter, Edwin S. (1992) Managing for World-Class Quality, New York, Marcel Dekker, Inc., pp. 63-67.

Stevenson, William J. (1990) Production/Operations Management, Homewood, IL., Richard D. Irwin, Inc., page 809.

Hamid Bahari-Kashani is a Professor of Production Operations Management and the chairman of the Division of Business and Economics at Western Oregon State College. Before moving to Oregon, he has been Assistant Professor of Production Operations Management at Washington State University. His work has been published in such journals as IIE Transaction, and Journal of the Operational Research Society. He has presented many papers in national and international conferences.

Productivity & Quality Management Frontiers-IV, edited by Sumanth, Edosomwan, Poupart, and Sink. ©1993
Institute of Industrial Engineers.

Getting Productivity through Quality

B. Chavarria
Costa Rican Telecommunication Company
San Jose, COSTA RICA

ABSTRACT

This paper will provide an adequate meaning and relationship between Productivity and Quality. Moreover, it will be demonstrated that an important approach in order to increase Productivity is to improve both the quality of the products and services in an organization.

On the other hand, it is important to mention that the organizations require to see the importance of measuring and designing systems in order to know the cost of lack of quality. In other words, the organization must measure in order to know, to know is to control, to control is to manage, to manage is to improve, and improve is to reduce the cost of lack of quality, to reduce the cost of quality is improve quality, to improve quality is to improve productivity.

Furthermore, it is important to find the current cost of lack of quality in order to reduce it. "The cost of lack of quality is the expense of non-conformance". Therefore, the organization should invest in prevention and appraisal activities to reduce external and internal failures.

The following topics will be addressed in the paper: some criteria used to measure the performance of an organization, basic concepts about both Productivity and Quality, the types and cost of lack of quality, and the importance of measuring through a specific example that Productivity is getting by quality.

Productivity & Quality Management Frontiers-IV, edited by Sumanth, Edosomwan, Poupart, and Sink. ©1993
Institute of Industrial Engineers.

Key Factors Affecting the Productivity/Quality Choice

G.A. Vargas
Califorina State University
Fullerton, California USA

ABSTRACT

This paper addresses the key competitive, technological and organizational
factors affecting the managerial decisions involved in determining the
sequence of quality/productivity implementation.

The "quality revolution" of the last decade has sharply challenged long-
standing practices primarily focused on the achievement of productivity, by
asserting that quality and productivity are the same and thus must be
achieved simultaneously. In practice, however, it has also been frequently
found that they cannot be attained at the same time regardless of the amount
of commitment and effort involved.

Four critical factors: product life cycle, competitive strategy, conversion
technology, and location of operations, ultimately determine whether quality-
or productivity-driven programs must be implemented first. Although all firms
will logically want to achieve both objectives in the end, the question of
sequence of implementation is "the" critical issue for operational managers.

The analysis presented here develops the profile of the firms and of their
internal/external environments necessary to establish the implementational
priorities. There are both logical and empirical foundations in this
analysis, as detailed in the summary cases described in this paper. In the
end, the choice is a matter of the proper matching between the challenges a
firm faces, the resources it commands, and the time frame where its actions
take place.

Keywords. Quality Management. Product Life Cycle. Productivity Management.
Competitive Choice. Implementation Sequence. Conversion Technology.

INTRODUCTION

The classical operational priorities of manufacturing firms are currently in a state of upheaval. The "quality revolution" of the last decade has sharply challenged long-standing practices primarily focused on the achievement of productivity, by asserting that quality and productivity are the same and thus must be achieved simultaneously.

In spite of the logical and empirical connection found between quality and productivity, in practice, however, it has also been frequently found that they cannot be attained at the same time regardless of the amount of commitment and effort involved. Firms that experienced this latter type of situations have typically been considered as not allocating enough resources and dedication to the task. Such a view is, to a large extent, reminiscent of the way in which many struggling firms were wrongly dismissed at the time of the "MRP revolution".

This paper attempts to bridge the "implementation gap" by looking into the successful real-life experience of firms that addressed and overcame such challenges, and by characterizing the circumstances internal and external to the firm that determine the implementation priorities.

QUALITY AND TIME INTERFACES

The classical productivity-quality tradeoff states that a firm's productivity, i.e. its ratio of output to inputs, is liable to suffer as a consequence of a greater emphasis on quality, since a firm will have to consume more resources per unit of output. In other words, to make a better widget the firm will have to use more manhours and machine capacity, and thus its output will consequently go down. However, the new and emerging productivity-quality tradeoff states that an emphasis on quality i.e. better output, will ultimately result in increased productivity since both the value of the output will increase (because it commands higher prices) while the costs of the inputs will decrease (because waste is reduced). Figure 1 exemplifies the opposing views of the productivity-quality tradeoffs.

The missing aspect in such statements is the time dynamics of the short- and long-term effects derived from the product-market characteristics and the managerial decisions on competitive strategy, technology and location of operations. Firms, in general, will naturally want to achieve both productivity and quality in the long term. However, firms are also conscious of the fact that the effort required to increase their quality will initially have a negative impact on their productivity, simply because of the time lag between the development/acquisition of better resources and the productive use of such resources. A training program for improvement of, say, production and maintenance personnel will demand additional expenditures and will need some time elapsed before it pays off. Thus, as also shown in Figure 1, as quality increases, productivity will initially take a dip before it also increases over time.

Figure 2 shows that, in economic terms, the firm's profitability will also suffer initially before it rebounds as productivity surges ahead because of greater quality in products and operations. The evolution of the quality-related costs over time explains how quality, profitability and time inter-

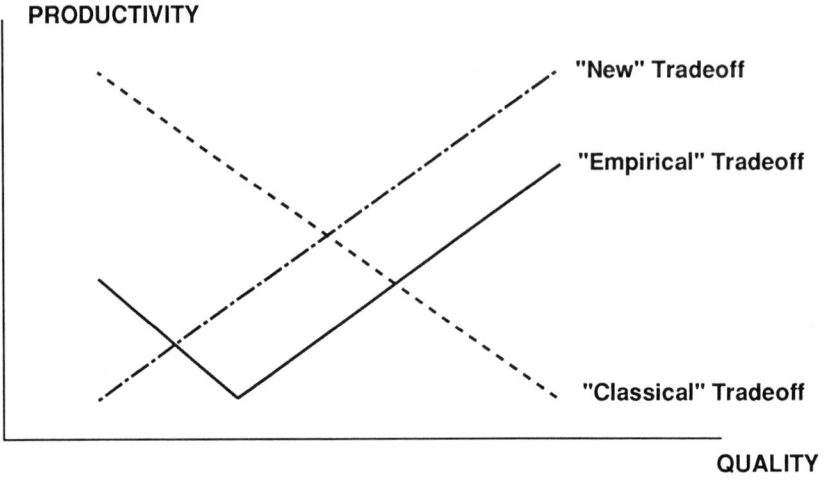

THE QUALITY-PRODUCTIVITY TRADEOFFS

Figure 1

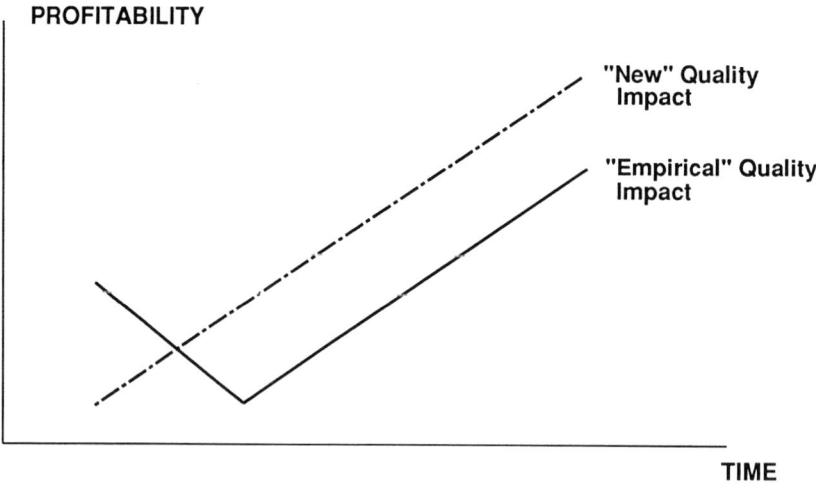

THE QUALITY-PROFITABILITY-TIME INTERFACES

Figure 2

face with each other. Figure 3 displays how such evolution takes place. The internal and external failures (and their costs) are high in the short term, since they take place before a good analysis of the production system exists; these failures serve, however, as warning signals about where the troublesome activities are located and they indicate the types of prevention and appraisal tasks (and their costs) that the firm must undertake to attain greater quality. Over time, failures will progressively decline and become negligible, while prevention and appraisal will become stabilized at relatively low, but critical, levels.

The key question to address within this scenario is whether there will be enough time for the firm to attain the upward swing in profitability provided by a quality emphasis. Clearly, if a product's life cycle is too short vis-a-vis the timing of the quality payoffs, a firm will not be well served by its pursuit of a better product; rather, such a pursuit will be detrimental to a firm's economic objectives.

QUALITY, PRODUCTIVITY AND GROUP TECHNOLOGY

The length of the product life cycle provides the first key parameter to assess whether quality or productivity must be implemented first. This assessment is exemplified in Figure 4, which compares short vs. long single product life cycles. A single product with a long life cycle, such as automobiles, will be well served by a quality-first implementation priority; eventually, quality will cause the firm to attain low costs and command higher prices.

Typically, the conversion technology used in these circumstances will be fairly complex and primarily process-oriented, since most (or all) product models will share common manufacturing requirements. Some flexibility will also be built into the conversion technology to accommodate a variety of alternative end-product configurations, derived from a competitive strategy of differentiation. Intensive use of capital and technical know-how will be necessary to support this implementation priority, thus dictating the physical location of operations.

However, a product with a short life cycle, such as toys, runs the risk of high costs without the offsetting advantage of high prices if a quality-first implementation priority is pursued; by the time quality brings costs down, the product is in the decline stage and the possibility of higher prices is foregone. The logical alternative available to deal with a short life cycle is to pursue a productivity-first priority, linked up with a competitive strategy of cost leadership and immediate accessibility to products by customers. To support this priority, a simple, specialized, product-oriented conversion technology will be appropriate so to accommodate a unique end-product configuration. In turn, the physical location of operations will be dictated by the availability of abundant, low-cost labor and material resources.

The four critical parameters of product life cycle, competitive strategy, conversion technology, and location of operations will thus ultimately determined whether quality- or productivity-driven programs must be implemented first. Since all firms will logically want to achieve both objectives, the quality-productivity dichotomy constitutes a highly troublesome

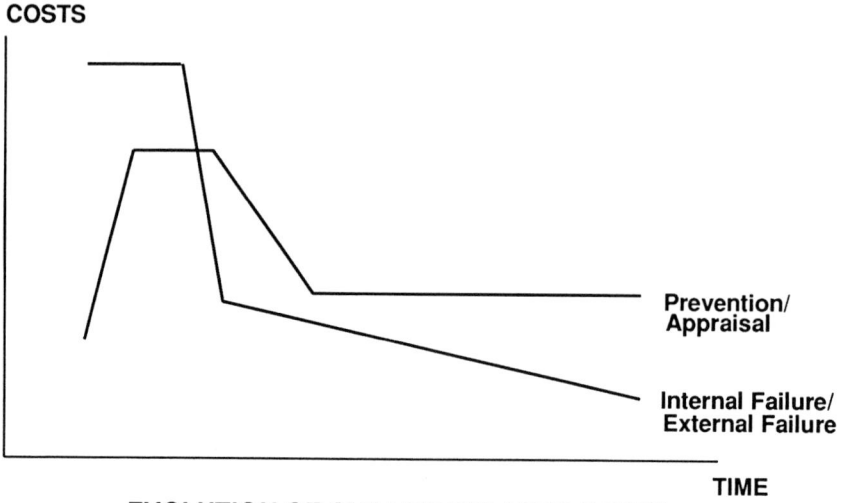

EVOLUTION OF QUALITY-RELATED COSTS

Figure 3

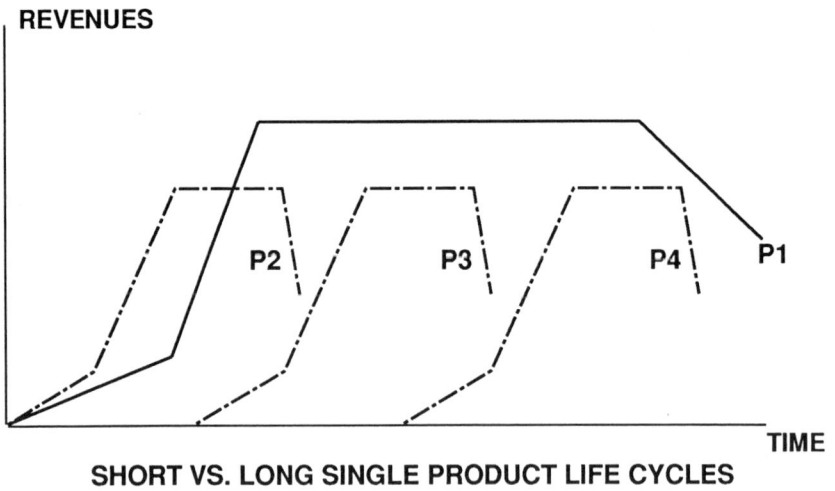

SHORT VS. LONG SINGLE PRODUCT LIFE CYCLES

P1, P2, P3, P4 = Products 1, 2, 3, 4

Figure 4

issue for operational managers.

An effective way to overcome this dichotomy is through the use of Group Technology and/or Group Methodology. Group Technology is used here in its commonly accepted meaning of grouping of end-products or components on the basis of common processing and/or geometry requirements. Group Technology, however, tends to be capital-intensive. For labor-intensive settings, the term Group Methodology is used here, meaning the grouping of end-products or components on the basis of common work methods and/or skill requirements. Conceptually, Group Technology and Group Methodology are identical.

Using Group Technology/Methodology effectively allows for the creation of an "envelope" product group life cycle, as presented in Figure 5. This envelope facilitates the implementation of a quality-first priority, without having to sacrifice the benefits derived from a productivity-first priority. Effectively, Group Technology/Methodology provides a firm with the necessary time span within which to make the quality efforts pay off. At the same time, it enables the firm to compete on the basis of cost leadership and immediate accessibility to products by customers.

The economic effects of Group Technology/Methodology are presented and compared in Figure 6. The envelope process life cycle will be longer than any of its constituent parts, and its lifetime costs will be significantly lower, although it will not lower costs as much as a long-running process based on a single long-cycle product will. Group Technology/Methodology has provided significant economic and competitive advantages to the consumer electronic industry i.e. television sets by achieving simultaneous productivity and quality gains in both the short and long terms. Unfortunately, the applicability of Group Technology/ Methodology is still far from universal.

CASE STUDIES

The empirical foundations for the analysis presented here are exemplified by three case studies, which are briefly described as follows:

Case Study 1: Turbine Fabrication.
The firm in case is based in the Southern California region, and manufactures a variety of turbines and electrical motors for both domestic and international customers. Products have a typical 5-year half-life cycle, and are produced and marketed in 450-500 different final configurations. The conversion technology requires high-precision metal machining and wiring equipment, with workers able to operate different stand-alone Numerical Control machines, to interpret complex engineering drawings, and to gauge dimensional accuracy of parts. The markets are fairly stable, and growing at an annual rate of about 1.0-1.5%. Typical lead times range at 4-6 months, with about 15-20% of features being customized. This firm pursued a quality-first implementation priority, and managed to achieve both quality and productivity gains over a period of 3 years, with an ongoing continuous improvement program currently in place.

Case Study 2: Toys and Games Assembly.
This firm is based in the U.S/Mexico border region, operating under the in-bond "maquiladora" regime. It manufactures a limited number of toys and games for U.S. domestic customers. Products have a typical 3-month half-life cycle,

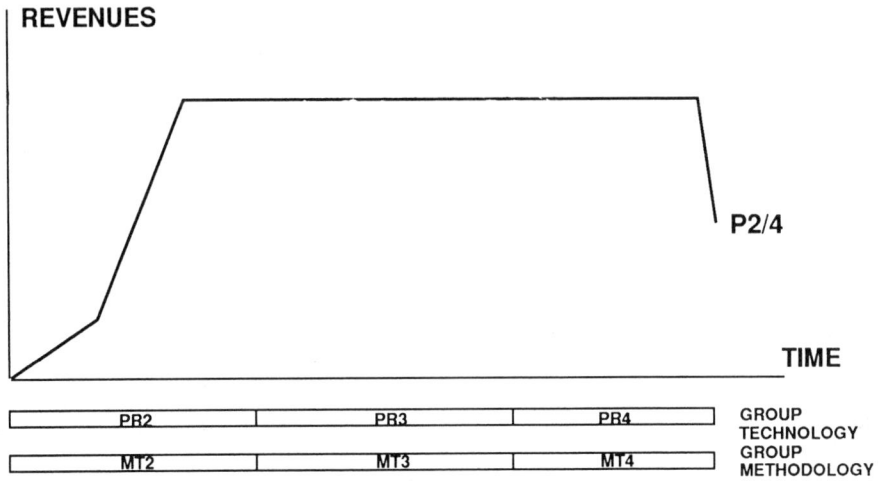

"ENVELOPE" PRODUCT GROUP LIFE CYCLE
EFFECTS OF GROUP TECHNOLOGY/METHODOLOGY

P2/4 = Product Group 2, 3, 4.
PR2, PR3, PR4 = Process 2, 3, 4
MT2, MT3, MT4 = Methodology 2, 3, 4

Figure 5

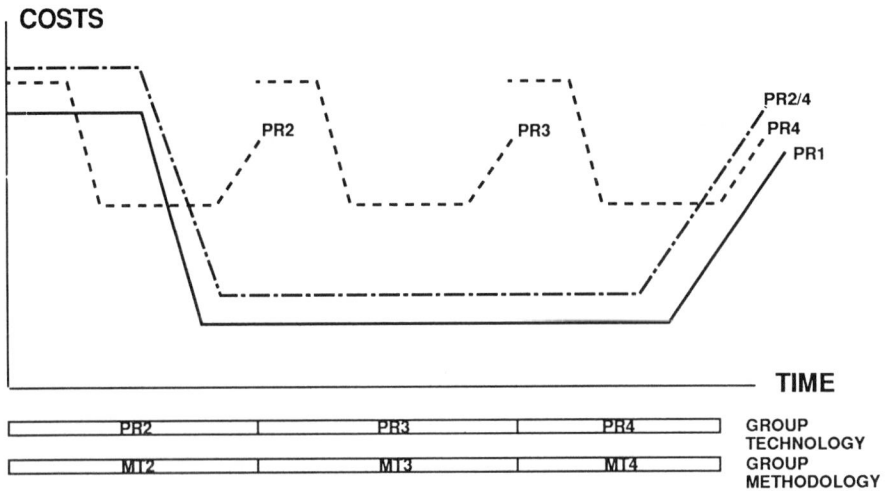

SINGLE VS. "ENVELOPE" PROCESS LIFE CYCLE
EFFECTS OF GROUP TECHNOLOGY/METHODOLOGY

PR2/4 = Process Group 2, 3, 4
PR2, PR3, PR4 = Process 2, 3, 4
MT2, MT3, MT4 = Methodology 2, 3, 4

Figure 6

and are produced and marketed in 15-20 different final configurations. The conversion technology requires simple hand tooling and fastening equipment, with workers able to follow a few well-defined work methods, and to interpret pictorial drawings. Production supervisors and quality inspectors check dimensional accuracy and positioning of parts. The markets are highly volatile with annual rate variations of about 25-50%. Typical lead times range at 3-5 days, with all product features being 100% standardized. In these circumstances, the firm pursued a productivity-first implementation priority, and managed to achieve substantial productivity gains over a period of 6 months, constantly providing its customers with immediate accessibility to its products over time.

Case Study 3: Television Set Manufacturing.
This particular firm has facilities in both the Southern California and U.S./ Mexico border regions, and manufactures a variety of monochrome and color sets for both domestic and international customers. Products have a typical 2-year half-life cycle, and are produced and marketed in 50-80 different final configurations. The conversion technology for components requires high-precision equipment, with workers able to operate in low-pollution environments, follow complex engineering specifications drawings, and maintain high-reliability standards. The conversion technology for sets requires hand tooling and fastening equipment, with workers able to follow repetitive, well-defined work methods, and to interpret pictorials; checking of conformance to product specifications is the responsibility of production supervisors and quality inspectors. Markets are fairly stable, with an annual growth rate of about 3.5-5.5%. Typical lead times are 7-10 days, with about 5% of features being customized. The firm implemented a thorough Group Technology/Methodology program, and achieved combined quality and productivity gains over a period of 18 months, providing its customers with easy accessibility to reliable, inexpensive products in a continuous fashion.

IMPLEMENTATION GUIDELINES

From the analysis presented above, it is possible to define the profile of the firms and of their internal/external environments shaping the productivity-quality implementational priorities. There are both logical and empirical foundations for this analysis, as detailed in the summary cases described in this paper. Table 1 summarizes the implementational guidelines, by focusing in on the four key parameters for selection of implementation priorities. Briefly stated, Table 1 implies that:
    1. the most important criterion is the set of product-market characteristics that a firm faces; neither productivity nor quality are good per se, but, rather, they are highly contingent to the product's life cycle, the degree of product variety, and the market growth rate. Quality becomes competitive and profitable only when long life cycles, high product variety and long-term market growth are present.
    2. a firm's competitive strategy, based on the product-market characteristics, is the second most important criterion for initial selection of either a quality or productivity emphasis; the productivity-caused effects of cost leadership and immediate accessibility will allow a firm to cope with short life cycles and explosive market growth, while reaping the benefits of the innovator's profit in being first to get to the marketplace. Quality-caused effects will initially work along opposite parameters.
    3. a firm's conversion technology is to be attuned with the competitive

797

Table 1

KEY QUALITY/PRODUCTIVITY IMPLEMENTATION PARAMETERS

IMPLEMENTATION PRIORITY	PRODUCT-MARKET CHARACTERISTICS	COMPETITIVE STRATEGY	CONVERSION TECHNOLOGY	LOCATION OF OPERATIONS
Productivity First	- Short Life Cycle - Low Product Variety - Limited/ Explosive Market Growth	- Cost Leadership - Immediate Accessibility - Innovator's Profit	- Simple - Specialized - Product-Oriented - Short Lead Time	- Labor/ Resource-Driven - Under/ Undeveloped Settings
Quality First	- Long Life Cycle - High Product Variety - Extended/ Gradual Market Growth	- Differentiation - Continuous Accessibility - Operator's Profit	- Complex - Flexible - Process-Oriented - Short/Long Lead Time	- Capital/ Knowledge-Driven - Developed/ Emerging Settings

strategy of choice; productivity is clearly achieved through simple, specialized, and product-oriented technology that turned a low-cost product in great
numbers and in a short time, thus providing cost leadership and immediate
accessibility. On the other hand, quality is best achieved through the use
of flexible, relatively complex and process-oriented technology, resulting
in product differentiation and continuous accessibility for the customers,
and in long-term operator's profits for the firm.

4. the conversion technology used by the firm determines the cost
structure of the firm's end-products and the type of inputs needed; this, in
turn, will dictate the physical location of the firm's operations and the
kind of socioeconomic environments most amenable to the firm's activities.
A quality emphasis will be primarily capital- and knowledge-driven resource-
wise, a characteristic of well developed geographical areas. On the other
hand, a productivity emphasis will consume more labor and materials, which
will have to be quite low in cost for the firm to remain profitable, as
commonly encountered in less developed physical settings.

5. the initial emphasis on whether productivity or quality comes first
is just that: initial only; since, by definition, quality is what the customer wants, a better, cheaper, and accessible product is the ultimate goal
of the firm. Given enough time, a firm will strive for quality attainment.
Time, in turn, can be provided by the product-market characteristics or it
can be earned by the firm through the use of Group Technology/Methodology.
Lacking enough time, a firm will be compelled to start out with a productivity emphasis.

In the end, of course, the choice of implementation sequence is a matter of
the proper matching between the market challenges a firm faces, the resources
it commands, and the time frame where its actions take place.

REFERENCES

1. Dobyns, L. and Crawford-Mason, C. (1991) Quality or Else, Boston, Houghton
   Mifflin Company.
2. Garvin, D.A. (1988) Managing Quality, New York, The Free Press.
3. Hauser, J.R. and Clausing, D. (1988) "The House of Quality", Harvard Bus-
   siness Review, vol. 66, no.3, pp. 63-73.
4. Saraph, J.V., Benson, P.G. and Schroeder, R.G., Fall 1989, "An Instrument
   for Measuring the Critical Factors of Quality Management", Decision Sciences, vol. 20, no. 4, pp. 810-825.
5. Sheridan, J.H. (1990) "World Class Manufacturing", Industry Week, vol.
   239, no. 13, pp. 36-46.

BIOGRAPHICAL SKETCH

Gustavo A. Vargas, Ph.D., M.S.I.E., M.B.A., CPIM, is Professor of Management
at California State University, Fullerton. He has been Manager of Industrial
Engineering for Uniroyal-Tires Worldwide, Materials Handling/Automation Project Manager for Sietam-North America and Manager of Industrial and Manufacturing Engineering for B.F.Goodrich-Mexico. He also was Economic and Engineering Consultant with USAID/Latin America, and Operations and Maintenance
Engineer with Exxon-South America. His domestic and international experience
covers the oil, tire/rubber, automotive, metal/mechanic, plastics, electronics, food processing, construction and health care industries.

Productivity & Quality Management Frontiers-IV, edited by Sumanth, Edosomwan, Poupart, and Sink. ©1993 Institute of Industrial Engineers.

Value Focus — Performance, Not Conformance

R.L. Horst
Peak Productivity USA
Lancaster, Pennsylvania USA

G.E. Plecha
Avery Dennison Corporation
Covina, California USA

ABSTRACT

Value enhancement to customers is the best quality improvement objective. Value focus begins with manufacturing performance excellence and leads to minimum loss to society-- the manufacturer, suppliers and customers. In a global economy, focusing on the value of products and performance--rather than conformance--is necessary for sustained competitiveness and perpetuation of a business enterprise.

Practitioners of productivity and quality improvement (PQI) on the factory floor know the key to success lies in meaningful metrics, diligent measurement and astute application of analytical tools. While PQI theorists and strategists stress quality management themes such as culture changes, corporate commitment, conformance to requirements, rewards and celebrations, in the final analysis the enterprise that performs is the winner.

Hierarchical levels of performance and related attributes, compiled in a matrix, provide a value-quality-productivity paradigm. Quality focus at the workplace, customer focus before and after the sale, and value focus from beginning to end and for the lifetime of a product or service are quantifiable. Positive performance is reinforced and product value is increased when PQI tools are used to analyze process and product data and subsequent improvements are implemented. The degree to which we improve our processes, upgrade our products, and analyze and enhance their value to customers is indicative of our level of performance excellence. Measurable objectives and measured results are the proof of our commitment and performance. The Horst productivity equation and Taguchi quality-loss function are tools for analyzing data and providing factual information about process and product quality, inherent inefficiencies and losses, and associated financial risk. Examples are given.

Key Words: Value, Quality, Productivity, Performance, Customer, Manufacturing, Taguchi, Six-Sigma, TQM

RATIONALE FOR VALUE FOCUS

The value of goods and services--products and processes--is their degree of excellence in utility, execution or design as perceived by customers. For a manufacturing or service enterprise, value enhancement is the best quality improvement objective. It is the ultimate indicator of supplier or vendor productivity.

Often, value is difficult to measure and it is sometimes confused with the price paid for a product or service. The value received by a buyer equals the price paid only when the product or service meets customer expectations for performance. An alternative to value measurement is the appraisal of losses experienced by the users of products and services that are designed to, but do not, satisfy customer needs. Products and processes with minimum loss to customers have the greatest value.

A manufacturer's value focus begins with performance excellence throughout all phases of the product creation cycle, and eventually leads to minimum loss to all society--the manufacturer, suppliers, and customers--for the lifetime of the product. In a global economy, focusing on the value of products and on *performance*--rather than on *conformance* to real or imagined benchmarks and requirements--is necessary for sustained competitiveness and perpetuation of a business enterprise.

VALUE FOCUS GOES BEYOND TRADITIONAL QUALITY FOCUS

Value focus is a vital element of, and necessary condition for, "world-class" performance as illustrated in Figure 1. By providing superior value to customers, an enterprise can remain competitive and profitable despite the presence of global economic pressures. A company is not world class if it is not prospering.

Figure 1. Elements of World-Class Performance

801

In addition, the figure indicates that corporate-wide quality training is essential for achieving a quality focus and culture that will score highly in the annual U.S. competition for the Malcolm Baldrige National Quality Award. Along with a manufacturing quality thrust and conformance-to-customer-requirements strategy, teaching and talking the tenets of quality management are all that is required of the nearly 100 companies who annually apply for the prestigious Baldrige Award.

Unfortunately, value focus and competitiveness are not strong elements of the Baldrige criteria. Only 30% of the possible points awarded are for customer focus and satisfaction, fewer than those awarded for administration--management, information and planning (52%). Quality and operational results (i.e. performance) account for only 18% of the score weighting. Creative companies can enroll a quality manager as a Baldrige Award Examiner and learn first hand how to conform to the criteria and prepare a competitive application. Hillkirk (1992) reports that Xerox spent $1 million preparing its Baldrige Award-winning application in 1989!

VALUE FOCUS REQUIRES PERFORMANCE MANAGEMENT

Productivity and quality improvement (PQI) theorists and strategists stress themes such as culture changes, corporate commitment, conformance to requirements, and rewards and celebrations. In the final analysis, however, the enterprise that *performs* is the winner.

Performance management is aptly described as *management by fact*. This term infers that performance measurements are in place for all key processes of a business and for metrics of product value as perceived by customers. Cultivating a management-by-fact, value-focused culture presents a real challenge for American industry because it demands a long-term vision for reaching long-term quality objectives (winning the Baldrige Award is a short-term objective). Although the short-term view is clearer than a longer one, its principal objective usually is to satisfy short-term profit-focused goals.

Baldwin (1992) describes the traditional profit-motivated management philosophy as *management by accounting*. It is characterized by managers who are interested principally in bottom-line numbers. If the numbers are not right, the remedy is to put pressure on the system and on employees. The philosophy is that performance can be improved by direct pressure and fear of consequences if goals are not met. This management style propagates to every level of an enterprise.

Performance management is likewise contagious. Its basic concepts are simple but implementation requires daily discipline (not unlike the regimen of a world-class runner). Practitioners on the factory floor know that value gains at the process level are the result of astute application of scientific method. The key to process performance improvement lies in meaningful metrics, diligent measurement of process variables, data analysis using appropriate statistical tools, synthesis of solution concepts, concept testing and focused implementation. Corrective actions--triggered by variable process data acquired through real-time measurements--lead to continuous process improvement in the factory, reduced product variability, and subsequent value enhancement to customers.

At Marlow Industries, 1991 Baldrige Award winner, an information system consisting of 500 data categories describes all essential elements of company performance--from customer satisfaction to manufacturing process control and supplier quality. This allows Marlow to continually focus on facts and results, and to track progress against performance goals. Regular reviews ensure that the information supports effective management of the company (King 1992).

Performance management begins in the executive suite. It is the methodology for reversing the cycle of low productivity and low quality via tools and discipline.

LEVELS OF QUALITY PERFORMANCE

The performance emphasis of a business entity can be classified as being *quality focused* (manufacturing excellence class), *customer focused* (Baldrige class), or *value focused* (world class). Figure 2 summarizes the activities, objectives, analytical tools and metrics which are essential for driving an organization to higher levels of performance excellence.

PERFORMANCE LEVEL	QUALITY DEFINITION	DEFINING ACTIVITY	QUALITY OBJECTIVE	TOOLS	METRICS
Value Focus (World Class)	Exceed customer expectations	Customer loss analysis (quantitative)	Enhance value to society	•Taguchi quality-loss function	$$ Loss to customer
Customer Focus (Baldrige Class)	Satisfy customer expectations	Customer feed-back analysis (qualitative)	Upgrade product performance vs. price	•Customer survey •Benchmarking	•Product differentiation •Price •Perform. variation
Quality Focus (Mfg. Excellence Class)	Conform to requirements	Non-conformance assessment	Improve mfg./supply processes	•Productivity equation •Statistical anal. & SPC •ISO 9001	•Rate (Cycle time) •Availability •Yield •Process deviation

Figure 2. Levels of Performance Excellence

Quality Focus
The most basic level of quality performance is characterized by a pervasive quality focus in the total workplace. The objective is to conform to customer requirements where, by definition, a customer is any internal or external recipient of work-in-progress, finished goods or services. The requirements to which one must conform, however, are often controlled by management and are not really customer requirements at all. For example, a machine operator is an internal customer who must meet production requirements but may have zero power to influence upstream processing which directly affects the yield at his machine (i.e. garbage in, garbage out).

A genuine quality focus optimizes the value added at every step or subprocess of fabrication and materials handling. It requires the disciplined use of analytical tools which depict process variability and portray the productivity metrics of rate, availability and process yield. These tools include the productivity equation (example given below), statistical analysis methods such as SPC, and the ISO 9001 international quality systems model. All processes must exhibit minimum variability (e.g. Motorola's six-sigma objective (Weisz 1987)), as well as recognized quality system characteristics such as the International Standards Organization (ISO) criteria, in order to achieve the most basic level of performance excellence.

803

Customer Focus

When corporate management commits to the higher performance level of customer focus, the end user or consumer is kept in mind after the sale as well as before. In addition to the tools used at the quality-focus level, customer focus utilizes surveys and comparative process benchmarking studies to provide qualitative information on the shortcomings of conformance-to-requirements performance. The higher quality goal is to "satisfy customer expectations". Consider again the machine operator: he expects to earn his bonus by making good product and expects incoming stock to be perfectly processed upstream. Only management can make that happen.

Genuine customer focus is manifested in differentiated products--product design, utility and pricing to suit targeted markets--and product performance that does not vary from the expectations of the user. As at the quality-focus level, performance excellence is quantifiable. For example, the Baldrige criteria suggest using customer feedback to evaluate and improve customer satisfaction and marketplace competitiveness. This customer feedback comes in the form of complaints, claims, refunds, recalls, returns, repeat services, litigations, replacements, downgrades, repairs, and warranty work. While the Baldrige criteria address customer losses such as these from a qualitative standpoint, a manufacturer or supplier can estimate the cost of such non-conformances and, thus, quantify the organization's level of customer satisfaction.

VALUE FOCUS FOR WORLD-CLASS RESULTS

The best quality performance level is world class, or value focus. The goal of value focus is to "exceed customer expectations" in utility, execution and design. Typically, the product or service surpasses the user's previous experience. Returning again to the earlier example, the machine operator is now flabbergasted because incoming stock has no scrap or defective material--even selvage has been eliminated before the material arrives at his machine. The operator can just start the machine and watch it run!

Genuine value focus demands a quantitative analysis of customer losses at all levels--on the factory floor, during handling and distribution, at the point of sale or service, and in the customer's hands for the lifetime of the product or service. These value losses are quantifiable and must be measured and known because they are indicative of the overall degree of performance excellence.

Without value (or loss) measurement tools and identified value metrics, an enterprise is not world class because the value of its products and services is arguable. *Measured results* demonstrate an organization's commitment and value focus by indicating the achievement of performance and value excellence through minimum loss to customer and producer alike.

Measuring Value to the Customer

Excellence, however, is a matter of individual perception. The perceived value of a good or service relates to the degree of satisfaction it provides according to a customer's own personal value metric. The metric may be quantity received, product uniqueness, price paid, lifetime cost, or some other esoteric combination of metrics.

Figures 3a and 3b are examples of value quantification graphs which indicate perceived value to the customer as a function of product differentiation and customer expectations, respectively.

In Figure 3a, one customer perceives value to be the degree of "excellence of quantity"

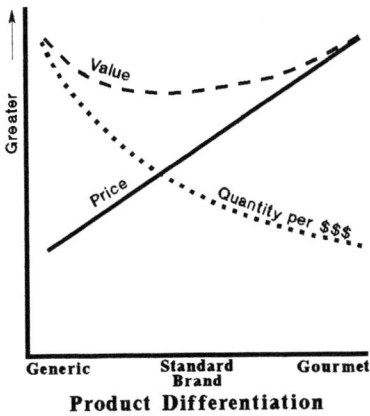

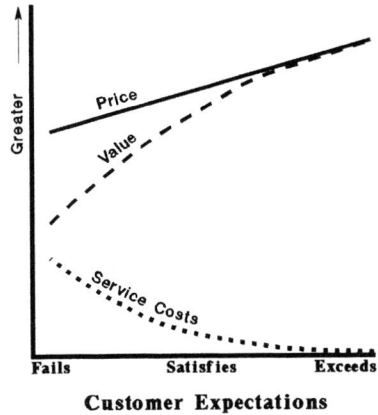

(a) Consumable　　　　　　　　　**(b)** Capital Equipment

Figure 3. Examples of Value Quantification

received of a given consumable (such as coffee or gasoline), while another will say that "gourmet (or high-test) quality" provides the greatest value for the same money.

Figure 3b illustrates a value function for capital equipment (such as a machine or vehicle) when service costs are taken into consideration. A machine with low purchase price but high lifetime service costs provides low financial value to the customer. Although it may conform to the manufacturer's requirements, the machine likely will fail to satisfy the purchaser's expectation.

A similar machine with a long-term warranty will have lower service costs to the owner, thus providing greater customer value (even at a higher purchase price), and may satisfy expectations for the product. The manufacturer and dealer, however, will experience losses when repairs are made. A similar machine with inherent design excellence and no defects provides the greatest value to the customer, and its performance likely exceeds expectations. When there are no service calls, there are no losses to the customer, dealer or manufacturer, and loss to society has been minimized.

The Taguchi (1981) quality-loss function is an ideal tool for quantifying loss to society (example given below). By utilizing this tool as well as the PQI tools applied at quality-focus and customer-focus levels, an organization can achieve the highest level of performance excellence: value focus.

KEY PERFORMANCE MEASUREMENT TOOLS FOR PROCESS, PRODUCT AND PLANT

An organization's level of performance excellence is proportional to the degree to which it improves its processes, upgrades its products, and analyzes and enhances product value to customers. The productivity equation and Taguchi quality-loss function are essential tools for analyzing data and providing factual information about process and product quality, inherent inefficiencies and losses, and associated financial risk.

Productivity Equation

A useful analytical definition for productivity was first described by Horst (1981, 1982) and later adapted by the Japanese (Nakajima 1988) with identical terms and slight changes in terminology. The equation relates productivity to quality performance by characterizing process and plant effectiveness in terms of throughput, availability and yield. The productivity (P) of a manufacturing process is described by the equation

$$P = R \times A \times Y$$

where R = producing rate (throughput per man-unit of time)
A = process availability (ratio of uptime to total scheduled time)
Y = process yield (ratio of non-defectives to total process output).

Since the reciprocal of R is duration or cycle time, the productivity equation can be rewritten as

$$P = \frac{1}{T} \times A \times Y$$

where T = time period (cycle time per unit or activity).

Throughput (R) is a meaningful metric for continuous operations such as web processes as well as for discrete part processes. A traditional approach to productivity improvement is to maximize labor productivity, that is, maximize R with respect to manpower employed. An equivalent approach, which has been popularized by Japanese practice, is to maximize labor productivity by minimizing cycle time ($1/R$) at every stage or step of a manufacturing process.

Availability (A) is primarily a measure of equipment and manufacturing system reliability and, therefore, should be maximized. Production lines can be designed, engineered and constructed for high reliability and low maintenance. In addition, effective preventive and predictive maintenance programs ensure that unscheduled system downtime is held to a minimum.

The remaining variable, yield (Y), while often the most elusive and difficult of the performance variables to control, equally impacts a plant's productivity. If, at a given time, all parts or goods from a production line are defective ($Y = 0$), the effect on P is the same as if employees were on strike ($R = 0$) or a primary machine had failed ($A = 0$). Productivity is zero! Or, more typically, if 10% of total output is defective on the first-pass, the impact on plant productivity is the same as if employees were working at only 90% efficiency ($0.9R$) or the production line was inoperable for mechanical reasons 10% of the time ($A = 0.9$)--productivity is 90% of maximum capability. More significantly, when all these conditions exist simultaneously, productivity is only 73%!

R, A and Y are independent and continuously variable with time in every plant. While a quality-focused objective is to stabilize them at maximum levels, attaining such high-level performance requires continuous improvement. This process involves applying the scientific method in an iterative fashion: measuring the variables at planned intervals, analyzing the data, conceptualizing and implementing upstream improvements, and then repeating the process.

Taguchi Loss Function and Six-Sigma Objective

A method for product quality analysis that measures the loss to society (i.e. manufacturer and customers) due to product variation is the Taguchi loss function. The power of this approach lies in its usefulness for economically justifying process quality improvements in the factory which may not satisfy traditional payback guidelines.

Every product (and process) exhibits variation and has a loss characteristic. This loss function, expressed in financial units, is based upon the variance (σ^2) of a product characteristic which, if out of tolerance, will cause the product to be considered defective. Note that σ is the root-mean-square (rms) deviation or standard deviation.

The loss function is a quality measure. For a two-sided specification of tolerance $\pm\Delta$, Taguchi shows that loss is proportional to variance. Thus, the function does not measure defect rate, but rather, relates loss (or negative value-added) to product variation as shown in Figure 4a.

The continuous nature of the loss characteristic (as opposed to pass/fail) is intuitive when one considers a quality measure for, say, jelly beans which are being manufactured at the limit of an allowable size tolerance (a vending machine requirement). Although the jelly beans are not defective, there is economic risk for the manufacturer since a slight drift in process conditions can quickly lead to 100% defectives, even though intrinsic value did not change (they taste just as good) when size tolerance was exceeded.

Variable product presents economic risk at the point of use because customers (the jelly bean vendor and the little kid) become dissatisfied when the machine jams. Since dissatisfaction leads to service costs and the likelihood of lost sales, the economic consequences of variable product affect manufacturer and consumer alike. The loss function quantifies these consequences in financial units.

The value-focused optimization objective is to minimize *total loss* to the manufacturer and customers. This loss is the sum of:

Cost of product inspection + Loss due to defectives + Loss due to product variation.

Applying this to the hypothetical jelly bean example, assume that the manufacturer's cost for manual inspection (taste) and on-line automatic inspection (color and shape) is $150 per million (pm) jelly beans, and the loss due to taste, color and shape defectives is $50 pm. Assume also that jelly bean size is under control with $\pm 3\sigma$ variation corresponding to a size tolerance of $\pm\Delta$ as illustrated in Figure 4a.

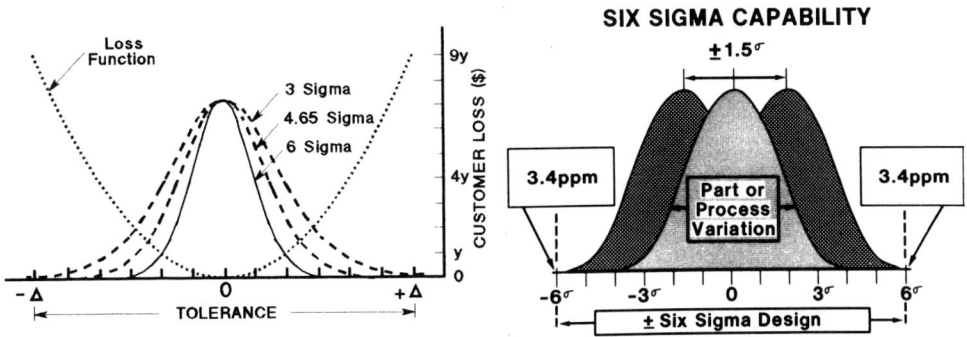

(a) Taguchi Loss Function

(b) Motorola Objective
(Source: Weisz 1987)

Figure 4. Process/Product Variation Illustrations

807

There is a tendency for vending machines to jam with any size variation from the ideal, and a jam-up becomes a certainty whenever at least one jelly bean per 10-bean serving exceeds $\pm\Delta$ in size. Note on the graph that the $-loss is zero when there is no size error. As size varies to $\pm\frac{1}{3}\Delta$ (or $\pm\sigma$) the loss is $y, at $\pm\frac{2}{3}\Delta$ the loss is $4y, and at $\pm\Delta$ the loss is $9y. The value of y is quantity- and process-dependent and can be calculated from the customer loss due to an out-of-spec ($>\Delta$) jelly bean causing a vending machine malfunction.

Horst (1992) shows that the loss function due to size variation for this problem is $L = 100(\sigma/\Delta)^2$ ¢ per 10-bean serving when it is assumed that service time costs 50¢ per jam-up and the lost profit during vending machine downtime averages 50¢; the vendor's total loss per jam-up is $1.00.

When σ is $\Delta/3$ along with the given data, the total loss per million jelly beans produced and sold is as follows:

$$L_{total} = 150 \quad\quad \text{(inspection cost to manufacturer)}$$
$$+ 50 \quad\quad \text{(defectives loss to manufacturer)}$$
$$+ 11,100 \quad\quad \text{(variation loss to customers)}$$
$$= \$11,300 \text{ pm jelly beans.}$$

It is obvious that vendors (customers) bear the brunt of the loss to society due to product variation in this example. One way to reduce the loss without upgrading or replacing thousands of vending machines is to reduce size variation by improving the manufacturing process.

Consider now the "six-sigma" quality improvement objective which was conceived by 1988 Baldrige Award winner Motorola in the mid-80s and continues to be the company's minimum goal. The 6σ objective is to reduce process (and part) variation to such a degree that even when the process mean shifts by as much as $\pm1.5\sigma$, defectives will not exceed 3.4 parts pm as shown in Figure 4b. Such a process is equivalent to one with a centered mean value and broader variability with tolerance limits at $\pm4.65\sigma$. Both processes yield 3.4 defectives pm.

Engineers can devise improved process control methods and automation apparatus that will reduce the range of variation to meet the six-sigma goal. A 35% reduction in deviation from $\pm3\sigma$ will achieve $\pm4.65\sigma$ performance, and a 50% reduction will achieve true $\pm6\sigma$ performance as illustrated in Figure 4a. At these improved levels of process capability, the new values for loss due to size variation are $4600 and $2800, respectively, per million jelly beans produced and sold. For true six-sigma capability, the loss to customers is reduced to ¼ the original loss and the new total loss to manufacturer and customers is now $3000 pm jelly beans instead of $11,300.

Note that no size inspection procedure is required to achieve reduced product variation and savings--process improvement alone will accomplish the desired results. Nor is there additional manufacturing cost for labor or materials. However, there is an annual cost for the capital invested in new and improved process control apparatus to reduce jelly bean size deviation. This investment is justified based on the *value enhancement for customers* which it provides, rather than on traditional *cost reduction* or *income expansion* justifications for the manufacturer. The primary objective of such investment is to increase customer satisfaction which, in the long-term, perpetuates a business enterprise. In view of the business risk that is taken if the investment is not made, such investment--and value focus--can be one of the very best opportunities for employment of company funds.

CONCLUSION

Survival in a global economy requires more than just conformance to perceived customer requirements. The economic well-being of an enterprise or a nation ultimately depends upon productivity growth and value enhancement to purchasers of its products. Both are essential for sustained competitiveness and viability as an economic entity. By focusing on value (i.e. minimum loss to customers) and exceeding customer expectations, an organization can maximize its performance and its profits.

REFERENCES

Baldwin, B.A. (1992) "The Morale of the Story", USAir Magazine, April, vol. XIV, no. 4, p. 14-22.

Hillkirk, J. (1992) "Europe Upstages Quest for Baldrige Awards", USA TODAY, April 27, p. 1B.

Horst, R.L. (1981) "ABCs of Productivity Analysis and Improvement...How Quality Affects Productivity", Production Engineering, April, vol. 28, no. 4, pp. 48-49.

Horst, R.L. (1982) "Factory Productivity Analysis Method", Proceedings of the Third Annual Conference and Exposition of the National Computer Graphics Association, vol. 1, pp. 433-437, June 13-17, Anaheim CA.

Horst, R.L. (1992) "Investing in Automation: Total Quality Management Unlocks the Dollars", Controls & Systems, vol. 39, no. 1, pp. 46-48, January.

King, G. (1992) Avery Dennison TQ Network Newsletter, April, 12th ed., pp. 6-7.

Nakajima, S. (1988) Introduction to TPM, Cambridge MA, Productivity Press Inc., pp. 21-29.

Taguchi, G. (1981) On-Line Quality Control During Production, Tokyo, Japanese Standards Association.

Weisz, W. (1987) "What is Six Sigma?", Motorola University Videotape, Schaumburg IL, Motorola Inc.

BIOGRAPHICAL SKETCHES OF AUTHORS

Robert L. Horst, MSEE, PE, is founder and principal of the technical consultancy Peak Productivity USA, Lancaster, PA. A registered engineer, he holds 23 U.S. and foreign patents in manufacturing methods and apparatus, serves on the U.S. Competitiveness Committee (IEEE) and on the Board of Trustees, The Pennsylvania State University.

Gayle E. Plecha, MBA, BSE, is senior operations analyst at Avery Dennison Corporation, Commercial Products Division, Covina, CA, and has extensive experience in manufacturing. She received highest honors from Anderson Graduate School of Management, University of California Los Angeles, and in Industrial and Operations Engineering, University of Michigan, Ann Arbor.

Productivity & Quality Management Frontiers-IV, edited by Sumanth, Edosomwan, Poupart, and Sink. ©1993 Institute of Industrial Engineers.

Research on the Relationships between Productivity and Technology System's Harmony

W. Wang

Zhejiang University, School of Management

Hangzhou, PEOPLE'S REPUBLIC OF CHINA

To date, despite the increasing studies of technology and productivity, little is known about the relations between productivity and technology system's harmonious degree & level. Under the Chinese National Science Foundation (NSF), this paper first presents a framework of the five components of technology, namely: 1) Coreware (production embodied technology) 2) Techware (object embodied technology) 3) Humanware (person embodied technology) 4) Inforware (document embodied technology) 5) Orgaware (Institution). Each component's contribution to productivity has been described and measured briefly, based on the 108 enterprises in China. Futher, using this framework, a mathematical model according to the Harmony Theory, was established to analysis the mechanics of technology's harmonious effects on productivity. And this model can aslo help the enterprise to diagnose the state of its technology system and find out the non-harmony point mainly affecting the productivity. Morever, the technology strategy model, combining with the business stratgy & innovation capability, was developed for choosing the portfolio of different level of technology progress, to improve the technology harmonious level to develop the productivity.

Keywords: Technology System Harmony, Harmony Degree, Harmony Level, Harmony Theory, Productivity, Technology Strategy Model,

Productivity & Quality Management Frontiers-IV, edited by Sumanth, Edosomwan, Poupart, and Sink. ©1993 Institute of Industrial Engineers.

Is Quality Another Organizational Quick-Fix?
Redefining the Structure of Organization and Management

S. Ozatalay and B.J. Reilly
Widener University
Chester, Pennsylvania USA

ABSTRACT

Quality is not consistent with a primary emphasis on quotas and productivity. Productivity in a competitive environment is an outgrowth of higher quality, not a substitute for it. Therefore, quality is not consistent with an approach that is limited to an engineering constraint of quality systems since product responsibility is not limited to the product design and detection defects alone. Therefore, the real race for competitive success is not the development of new technology and invention but the ability to implement both.

Traditionally, management controlled the process flow of inputs and outputs by the engineering designs of work. Problem solving in the traditional organization was the function of management who imposed definitions on those who implement them. Modern technology and quality require an entirely different set of structural principles of organizations.

This study lists and analyzes the factors which will be most important for the implementation of the new culture necessary for improving quality and productivity dimensions in order to stay competitive into the structure of new organization and management.

Keywords: Quality, management organization, human resources.

1. INTRODUCTION

The meaning and importance of science and technology has become an over-riding ideology which assumes that technology, information systems, technological design, and optimum manufacturing systems will create both quality and productivity. The paradigm of thinking is that strong-form or robust definitions will create optimum product and services.The paradigm of thinking has a critical flaw in bureaucratic organizations. It is the assumption that "better technique" (or doing things better) creates better product. However, it has been observed many times that an organization which utilizes the most advanced technology can create unacceptable products. An advanced technology alone does not create quality.

Changing technology, however, is still one of the leading sources for improving product quality as well as increasing organizational productivity. Since technology is only an instrument and its effectiveness depends on the way it is being utilized, without proper development of human resources it will be impossible to reach higher levels of productivity and quality management. (Ozatalay and Reilly, (1991))

The scientific explanation of reality does not create working reality. The traditional business organization clearly separates organizational decisions from individual decisions. Business decisions are based on "strong form" definitions while people decisions are based on "weak form" definitions. The strong forms are objective and tend to be conclusive, supportable through objective and measurable definitions; the weak for definitions are mainly qualitative and debatable. Strong form definitions "disembody" the production and service reality. The following are examples of strong form and weak form definitions:

Strong Form	Weak Form
Narrow Specialization of Jobs	Functional Integration
Financial Mgt Principles	Skills and Knowledge
Accounting Principles	Commitments and Loyalties
Work Measurements	Motivations
Financial Models	Working Teams (Projects)
Cash-flow Analysis	Subordinate Empowerment
Inventory Control	Participative Mgt Systems
Promotion/Demotion	Continuous Training and Education
Budget Definitions	Reward Structures
Materials Handling	Job Security
Individual Expertise	Project Teams
Clear Authority Lines	Open Communication

Quality is both a strong and a weak form definition that cannot be grafted onto a strong-form organizational system. In the traditional organization, technology produced the value added while people subordinated themselves to the technology-narrow specialization and unskilled or semi-skilled work. (Estime, (1988))

The slow progress of the majority of Total Quality Management programs in the U.S. is directly attributed to the non-integration of quality into the functioning principles of organization. Strong form definitions, the traditional approach of the organization towards decisions, must be modified by the less objective weak form definitions. The problem lies in the fact that the scientific paradigm is based on systems of objective answers to seemingly "objective" questions. The paradigm essentially prefers objective (quantitative, supported conclusions, measurable) over subjective (qualitative, tentative and debatable conclusions, non-measurable) reasoning.(Cotton, et al, (1988))

A good example of this difference is evident in the following statement: Advanced technology together with highly skilled and competent people are the leading source for the improvement of product and service quality. The first part (advanced technology) is defined in terms of "measurable" output. The second part (highly skilled and competent people) is defined in terms of potential quality and productivity as well as the development and implementation of technology. If quality is the essence of good product, then the critical dimension of quality must be defined in terms of the people who invent and develop technology and the people who use and operate the technology. Quality is not the objective (technically sound) separated from the subjective (pleasing and understandable) but rather is a combination of the two.

2. THE SCIENTIFIC AND TECHNICAL PARADIGM

Technical quality alone is not total quality. The mistake of not recognizing this leads to the assumption that technological improvement of process and product leads naturally to a better product or a better service. Quality is a connection between objects and subjects. However, this immediately introduces a problem: one is measurable and the other isn't. Technology is defined and organized by science and scientific principles.

The scientific or technical paradigm is striving for technical mastery of the "total" production process. Technical proficiency is only one part of the definition of quality. It is the objective formulation of research, product design, development, inventory, manufacturing process and procedures. However, technical quality definitions do not create quality. Rather, technique must be combined with people that design, implement and use the technique. In a real sense, an "identity" between people and technique is critical for any ability to approach quality as a goal. The technology will not create quality nor will people create quality separate from technique. (Suzaki, (1987))

The engineering design of work has always assumed that it was the technology which created products. In traditional mass production industries, this was true to a large extent. In this design people were secondary, subservient to this technology and ultimately "accidental" to the process of product flowing among machines. The engineering scientific design of the factory, which had de-skilled manufacturing work through narrow specialization and job segmentation set as its goal the "minimal" interference of human beings in the process of manufacturing which was to be determined by technology and science. This approach discounted the significance of people in favor of the scientific-technological organization of work. The inevitability of scientific-technological progress is to eliminate the source of error and defects, namely people. This is the current stage of technological evolution.

The new stage of technological development is both costly and risky. While the inevitability of this technological stage of development is clear, the intervening time of product-production process is more embedded in the past technologically and is only slowly progressing through this third stage of the industrial revolution.

The pressure of international competition is requiring a new approach to the operation of the factory as a departure from the traditional . People (or the non-scientific factors) have to be given a priority in order to compete in the production of quality products such as machinery, automobiles, machine tools, electrical equipment, instruments, chemical, pharmaceuticals, industrial machinery, fabricated metal products, steel products, etc. Currently, many traditional mass production jobs are being exported to countries with significantly lower costs for supplies, labor and facility development. This is inevitable and translates into the world product with such realities as the American automobiles, the American computer, the American telephone a less relevant and meaningful concept. (Teresko, (1989))

The defects flowing from the "people factor" at all levels become less tolerable in a highly competitive international environment. Therefore, the re-constitution of work, using traditional (and updated) technology requires that success come from a definition of quality which defines both people and technology as critically important productive and product factors.

3. A STEP INTO A QUALITY ENVIRONMENT

The objective and scientific bias gives meaning to the technology, while denying meaning to the people. However, if one steps out of the scientific analytical process approach and begins to treat seriously the working reality, a different picture begins to emerge. For instance, a firm which makes fine china and crystal attempts to cut costs in order to increase the profit margin. The management of the company chooses to use "less expensive' suppliers who provide lesser quality sourcing materials for making the china. Obviously, the grade of china being produced deteriorates. The employees of the firm have previously perceived themselves as craftsmen. As the quality of china deteriorates, they sense a loss of value in the products which they are making. Naturally this affects their work.

It is easy to generalize this illustration to the marketplace. A department store has two departments of glassware-one a fine crystal department and the other, ordinary glasses. Do people treat the crystal glass differently than the kitchen glass? Is there a different feeling towards the importance and value of one over the other? The perceived significance of one's work has long been viewed as a core dimension of a job yet the measurement of such characteristics has frequently been plagued by the efforts of including such qualitative factors in the decision making process concerning task redesign. (Pirsig, (1974))

The sense of value and quality in both the product and the process intuitively have a strong influence on how people feel and therefore how they relate to their work. However, the overwhelming problem is how to incorporate this sense of meaning into the assessment of organizational reality. How can this sense of meaning be portrayed in a framework of decision making which emphasizes the quantitative and ignores the qualitative and the sublime. Such flexibility of thought is rarely possible when considering the social or human components i.e., harmony, broad, personal involvement; long-term employment, a humanistic approach to people; personal loyalty; organizational commitment, and the sense of security and trust. These elements of the organization, by fiat, are excluded from the organizational and decision making realities of the scientific approach and, yet, few would deny that they are extremely critical elements. (Nonaka, (1988))

The social-scientific paradigm of the organization must incorporate into its critical mass of meaning the significance of the subjective, unmeasurable and uncontrolled elements which make an organization function in the concrete. Some of these elements are:

1. The sense of value
2. Pride in work
3. Commitment to quality
4. The place for ability, knowledge and caring
5. A sense of security
6. A culture of trust
7. An environment for learning more and doing it better
8. A respect for people and their capabilities
9. Managerial service to its workforce
10. The development of organizational unit
11. Vision and leadership

It is clear that these elements are hardly objective. However, to state that one can not express reality objectively is not a proof that the reality does not exist. It is merely a proposition that one will only consider as important those things which are measurable and can be verified. This does not prove that the unmeasurable is not important. The traditional scientific paradigm and the basis of the most important business and technological decision disembodies the functioning of both the organization and the technology from their human architects and operators. The ability to integrate total quality within an organization is the basic ability of the management to bring out the "reflective and qualitative" part of the organization in the unfolding of skill, knowledge, competence, commitment, loyalty and the potential "richness" that cannot be arrived it through the scientific analytic process. (Berger and Luckmann, (1986))

4. NON-PARALLEL SYSTEMS

The bias of the objective formulation of reality tends to be built around the belief that the objective business decision, based on numbers or the technology, based on state of the art production facilities will create quality and productivity. However, people must be accounted for in the quality mix. The technical/behavioral must be joined in order to integrate technology and people. While the underlying technologies of computers, microelectronics, flexible manufacturing operations, artificial intelligence, robotic engineering, and alternate advanced technologies will be the hallmarks of the future, the implementation of invention and innovation will determine their success. (Hayes, (1981))

The integrated-quality oriented organization requires not only the controlled process flow of inputs and throughputs by the engineering design of work but the problem solving of an organization of those who implement decisions with various skills, competencies and knowledge. The monopolization of knowledge, traditionally the hands of engineers and managers, is now dispersed throughout the organization at all levels.

Modern technology and quality require an entirely different set of structural principles of organization. First, management does not possess the control of the critical information to implement modern technology or quality control. Second, the requirements of implementation involve the skill and education (training) of the implementors. This education and skill, by its very nature, means an "empowerment" distinct from that of management and administration. Third, the integration of design-purchasing-production and marketing require a relaxing of the principles of hierarchical power and control. Fourth, the "new" function of management shifts to providing service, support, and resources to the skilled, information, and knowledge sources of the implementors who are the new factory workers. This is the radical departure of definition from the old factory to the new and from traditional managerial power and authority theory to participation and partnership. (Taguchi and Clausing, (1990))

The disappointments in the majority of Quality Circle programs and Quality Assurance programs as well as the ineffectiveness of a large number of Total Quality Management Programs has its root cause in the inability of the U.S. firm to place its organizational emphasis on people who possess skills and education since its scientific management principles are still rooted in the traditional organization. Therefore, modern technology, innovation, and invention become irrelevant because of the inability to take advantage of them in systems which are not designed to be able to successfully implement them.

The human resource and its meaning are the critical factors in the modern organization of work. Therefore, skilled and knowledgeable human resources must be served or "empowered" by the management and the organizational system. New technology or innovation will not create quality products. The well-trained "worker" with knowledge and expertise will operate, control, service, and successfully "make valuable" new technologies and innovations. Management, in this setting will be valuable if it understands its function of service to competence and expertise.

5. THE STRATEGIC CHARACTER OF MODERN TECHNOLOGY AND QUALITY

Everything that is required for success in implementing modern technology and quality is negated by the U.S. organization's emphasis and priorities. The emphasis on power, administration, short-term budgets, cost-cutting, quotas, and productivity are distinctly different than the priorities required for implementation of technology-investment, long-term orientation, people-centered relative to skills and training, and structural organizational redesign. Therefore, technology and quality implementation is both a people problem and a structural problem. It is a people problem in the sense that implementation of both technology and quality require a very high value placed on the skills and knowledge of implementors and continual training. It is a structural problem since the traditional emphasis has been on "narrow specialization and division of labor with administration and management controlling and directing the process, and the central role of agency theory.

The strategic character of modern technology and quality implementation require:

1. the integration of quality into the goal structure;

2. the investment in training and skill-upgrading is as significant an investment as that in technology;

3. the information, accounting and financial data gathering for both the costs of improving quality and the costs of a lack of quality must be

expanded;

4. the strategic development of accounting systems that recognize that less than 20% of the defects in products come from workers - 80% come from the structural principles of organization and management; and

5. the mission and goal objectives with the understanding that choices based on price alone negate quality as a critical component of product output.

The self-evident relationship of Cutting Costs = Increase in Productivity = Increase in Profits is a simplistic strategic orientation since an emphasis on cutting costs will limit the perception of the need to invest in quality. The self-evident relationship does not provide a critical path for investment in quality nor for a concern for the critical quality component-people.

The cost cutting-profitability relationship contains an emphasis on the short term. This is not a strategic orientation to the company's products, its people, its technology or its quality. The emphasis is on the short-term. Quality and technology are strategic, long-term concepts. Both are costly, not only in themselves, but in the investments which have to be made in the people who use "modern" technology and "practice" quality.

6. QUALITY-TWO DIMENSIONAL PHENOMENON

The American paradigm of management requires slashing through the objective formulation of scientific certitude and accounting for the Qualitative elements of feeling, the sense of well-being, security, creative and intuitive behavior, high levels of skill and knowledge and the richness potential of committed and loyal people.

An intelligent environment is the mix of objective and subjective, certainty and ambiguity. The serene and objective structure of organization needs to be tensed by the forces chipping away-like a stone cutter, re-shaping and re-constructing the stone into a new reality which blends both the objective and the subjective so that both are united in a productive, quality environment. The science without the people is unusable while the people without the science is unworkable. However, both are different in the conclusion than they were before they came together.

The attempts of the technology manager or the engineer will be to create sound technique, but the people will determine the "meaning" of the technique. The attempt to be objective and scientific while discounting the people meaning will inevitably separate objects and subject from each other and destroy the essence of quality which is the bonding of the two.

Organizations and management, through lay-offs, personnel cost cutting, "lean-and-mean" conceptualizations of reality walk a dangerous path of creating the total reality in the object while discounting the subject (people). Is it possible for the customer to be number one while the "product-maker" or "service-giver" is unimportant? An uninformed and untrained service giver is hardly capable of fulfilling the slogan of customer meaning and importance.

Technology (modern or traditional) has value and meaning only in the people who implement or use it. It is friend or foe depending on people who define it as such. It is invited or hated by people who see it as friendly or unfriendly. Each of these realities are determined by the presence or absence of a bonding of technique and people.

Total Quality or quality itself are usually thought of as "things", "techniques", "means", "forms". However, their realities and meanings will be determined by those who implement decisions and users. The gimmick of total quality is technical. However, the meaning of total quality is in unifying or connecting object and subject, science and non-science, things and people, techniques and meaning, decision making and implementation, the measurable and the unmeasurable. Quality is a "way of life" in which people value and technology value are integrated and united.

In their recent book titled Total Quality Management, Tenner and DeToro (1992) define the quality as "a basic business strategy that provides goods and services that completely satisfy both internal and external customers by meeting their explicit and implicit expectations. Furthermore, this strategy utilizes the talents of all employees, to the benefit of the organization in particular and society in general.." (p:31). Concurrently, Kanji, Kristensen, and Dahlgaard (1992) include the following among essential quality strategies for TQM: "excellence of all managerial, operational, and administrative activity; a culture of continuous quality improvement; the creation of customers' and suppliers' relationships; involvement of all personnel..." (p:6). The striking similarity in these two definitions is the acceptance of the need for a new corporate culture in understanding, defining, and implementing TQM.

The scientific paradigm or the technical paradigm, by its very nature, assumes a "certain" world. Its goal is to eliminate risk. However, creativity, innovation, progress, development and quality do not arise from certitudes but rather risk and uncertainties. Better quality comes from what is not known rather than what is known. Its assumptions challenge existing certainties.

The scientific paradigm tends to narrow the scope of alternatives by suggesting that what is important is that which is measurable while the reality of improving and discovering is, by nature, the commitment to what is not known. It is incorporating the "less tangible" elements into the concept of current accepted objectivities.

The very nature of a social-scientific paradigm is a two dimensional form of reality as it exists, rather than how it is interpreted and analyzed.   Objective quality has little meaning if people who implement "objective quality" or use "objective quality" do not perceive it as quality. On the other hand people perceiving quality where it does not exist generate a declining civilization where things do not work, people and societies begin to decay, and general well being deteriorates.

The anomaly of quality is that it is both objective and subjective. It is both technique and people. It is an event that does not stand by itself as a thing but rather a meeting of object and subject experienced and comprehensive, producing an experience of good, comparable to something else where the experience is less good.

The current environment of laying people off, cutting their salaries or creating insecurity in workers while trying to promote technical quality is a contradiction in an environment which sets as a goal total quality. In reality, it is the assumption that total quality is equal to technical quality. It is the scientific paradigm at work with no advance beyond traditional management. The customer will not be number one in this environment, nor will total quality be anything beyond words.

REFERENCES

Berger, P.L. and Luckmann, T. (1986) The Social Construction of Reality. New York: Anchor Books.

Cotton, J.L., Vollroth, D.A., Froggott, K.L., Lenznick-Hall, M.L. and Jennings, K.R. (1988) "Employee Participation: Forms and Different Outcomes" Academy of Management Review, 13(1), 8-22.

Estime, M. (1988) "Quality: An Imperative for Industry" The O.E.C.D. Observer, Aug.-Sept., 20-32.

Hayes, R.H. (1981) "Why Japanese Factories Work" Harvard Business Review. July-August, 56-66.

Kanji, G.K., Kristensen, K.K, and Dahlgaard, J.J (1992) "Total Quality Management as a Strategic Variable", Total Quality Management, Vol. 3, no. 1, pp. 3-8.

Nomaka, I. (1988) "Toward Middle-Up-Down Management" Sloan Management Review, Spring 9-18.

Ozatalay, S. and Reilly, B.J. (1990) "The Human Aspects of Technological Revolution", Management of Technology II: The Key to Global Competitiveness, (ed. T.M. Khalil and B. Bayraktar), Industrial Engineering and Management Press, Norcross, pp:749-758.

Pirsig, R. (1974) Zen and the Art of Motorcycle Maintenance. New York: William Morrow and Co. Inc.

Suzaki, K. (1987) The New Manufacturing Challenge. New York: The Free Press.

Tazuchi, G. and Clausing, D. (1990) "Robust Quality" Harvard Business Review, (Jan.-Feb.), 65-75.

Tenner, A.R. and DeToro, I.J. (1992) Total Quality Management, Reading, Ma. Addison-Wesley Publishing Company, Inc.

Teresko, J. (1989) "Manufacturing in Japan: Beyond the Stereotype" Industry Week. (Sept.) 35-70.

BIOGRAPHICAL SKETCHES

Savas Ozatalay is a Professor and the Head of the Management Department at Widener University. He has a B.S. degree from the Middle East Technical University, and a M.A. and Ph.D. degrees from Northwestern University. He has published a number of articles in the production management area and is a member of the Institute of Management Science and the American Production and Inventory Control Society.

Bernard J. Reilly is a Professor of Management at Widener University with a Ph.D.

from Georgia State University. Since joining Widener in 1980, Dr. Reilly has published extensively in journals and has presented a large number of papers at professional meetings on organizational behavior, management, and health administration and policy. Currently, he is writing a book on business ethics.

Productivity & Quality Management Frontiers-IV, edited by Sumanth, Edosomwan, Poupart, and Sink. ©1993 Institute of Industrial Engineers.

Productivity and Quality Management by Design of Flexible Manufacturing Systems

S. Arsovski
Mašinski Fakultet
Kragujevac, YUGOSLAVIA

A. Pereira
Universidade, Da Beira Interior
Covilha, PORTUGAL

J. Hodolič
Institut for Production Engineering
Novi Sad, YUGOSLAVIA

ABSTRACT

In this paper are analyzed aspects of productivity and quality management in introduction of FMS (Flexible Production Systems) in certain production conditions. Authors especially emphasize design of FMS from the aspect of necessary level of productivity ("ex ante" approach). Results of simulation point to the fact that the same level of productivity can be achieved by application of different technologies and spent labor at the input. Management analyzes results of simulation, and for certain production conditions, defines appropriate decisions related to elements of FMS.

Productivity & Quality Management Frontiers-IV, edited by Sumanth, Edosomwan, Poupart, and Sink. ©1993 Institute of Industrial Engineers.

Aging and Productivity: Myths and Realities

S.J. Czaja
University of Miami
Coral Gables, Florida USA

Current demographic trends have drawn attention to the importance of understanding the relationship between aging and work performance. Since 1950 the proportion of older males in the labor force has steadily declined; at the same time older people represent the fastest growing segment of the population. Unless strategies are developed to retain older people in the labor force, the issues of economic dependency and inter-generational equity are likely to become formidable in the near future. Another reason that we need to consider the implications of the aging process for work environments is that the age composition of the labor force is changing. In the next few decades the labor force will largely consist of middle-aged people. During the 1980's and 1990's the "baby boom" generation will move into middle age and by the year 2000 the number of middle aged workers will increase by 79% (OTA, 1985).

The effects of age on employee productivity has been a long standing concern of employers. It is a commonly held stereotype that worker productivity declines with age. However, this negative age stereotyping is unwarranted. The available literature regarding occupational performance and age indicates that while some age-related declines in productivity have been observed for certain occupations, in others no significant age differences have been found and in some occupations older workers are more productive than younger workers. Furthermore the relationship between age and productivity is often mediated by factors such as type of productivity measure and experience.

This paper will present a state-of-the-art review of the available literature on aging and occupational performance and will summarize what is known regarding the impacts of the aging process on worker performance. Factors such as experience and job characteristics which impact on the age performance relationship will also be discussed. Finally the implications of emerging workplace technologies for an aging workforce and some preliminary data on age differences in the performance of computer based work will be presented.

Productivity & Quality Management Frontiers-IV, edited by Sumanth, Edosomwan, Poupart, and Sink. ©1993 Institute of Industrial Engineers.

Is "Specialization" Always Effective?

X. Wu

Zhejiang University

Hangzhou, PEOPLE'S REPUBLIC OF CHINA

It is a long-standing viewpoint that the more a work is specialized the higher the productivity of the work will be. Also, it is generally acknowledged that "specialization" is one of the most important marks of modern industry. We are agreed that "specialization" is often effective to improve productivity, and it is especially significant in the industrialization process of less developed countries (LDCs). However, is "specialization" always effective in improving productivity?

It is found that there exist polarized problems in industrial "specialization", especially in LDCs for their dual economy, e.g. P.R. China. On the one hand, "specialization" is very difficult to apply in some traditional sectors; on the other hand, "specialization" is often overemphasized and blindly used in some newly established technology-intensive sectors due to the preconcept of "specialization is always effective" in some well-educated professionals in production management. Focused on the latter problem, this paper analyses the troubles and limits of "specialization" in tech-intensive industries, especially in China, in relation with the rapidly changing technological environment.

The negative effects of overemphasized "specialization", such as highly compartmentalized functions, narrow definition of tasks, over-division of labor, are identified. The importance of creating initiative organizational culture, e.g. to make all players feel equal importance, and accelerating information flows either within an organization or inter-organizations are emphasized. The impacts of technology advance in design and manufacture, e.g. CAD, CAM and CIMS etc., are discussed.

Referring to the industrial innovation model, proposed by Abernathy and Utterback, and the technology development cycle, the relative availability of "specialization" at different stages of development are analyzed dynamically.

It is concluded that "specialization" should be applied flexibly in accordance with the nature of production technology and the stage of organization development dynamically. Finally, some propositions of coordinating the "specialization" and the flexibility of production patterns are offered.

Productivity & Quality Management Frontiers-IV, edited by Sumanth, Edosomwan, Poupart, and Sink. ©1993 Institute of Industrial Engineers.

Development of a Checklist for Self-Assessment of Competitivity in Small and Medium-Size Industrial Firms

E. Oliva-López and E. Hernández-García
National Polytechnic Institute
Iztacalco, MEXICO D.F.

J.J. Flores-Valtierra
Cierres Ideal
Iztacalco, MEXICO D.F.

M. Pérez-Bailón
CONALEP
Iztacalco, MEXICO D.F.

ABSTRACT.

Most small and medium size industrial firms in Mexico need to have a qualitative assessment of their competitivity before they set-up an improvement program or seek external assistance for diagnosing and/or solving their related problems. Tight budgets, lack of knowledgeable-trustworthy consultants and local managerial culture, tend to discourage the utilization of external expertise for the improvement of productivity, quality and commercialization. Because of this, our research group started, three years ago, to develop a productivity self-diagnosing tool, whose progress was reported at the Third International Conference on Productivity & Quality Research (ICPQR'91).

As the signature of the free trade agreement becomes imminent and the effects of the globalization of the Mexican economy are more strongly felt by our industry, it has been realized that the analysis and improvement of productivity alone is not sufficient to ensure an international competitivity level for any firm, therefore, it was decided to develop the original system further and cater also for quality and commercialization aspects, in order to provide its prospective users with a suitable analytical tool for diagnosing their competitiviness, which is now at the very core of their survival and development. This tool has now the form of a checklist and it is planned to develop it further to build an Expert System.

This paper examines the main issues considered throughout the development of this checklist, and reports on its validation process in industry.

KEYWORDS.

Diagnosing, Competitiviness, Industry.

OBJECTIVE

This paper aims to show the progress achieved in the development of an analytical tool, suitable for self-diagnosing the competitiviness of small/medium size manufacturing firms by their own managers. In this context, the competitiveness of a given firm should be attained as a result of a simultaneous improvement of productivity and quality levels, as well as a better commercialization of its products/services.

JUSTIFICATION.

Piecemeal approaches and independent improvement actions have been tried out in industry for many years and, the results yielded have fallen short of the expectations in most cases, leaving behind a sense of frustration, disappointment and pessimism among the majority of participants, thus making the initiation of further development programs very difficult.

As the complexity of interrelations between the components of a Production System has been increasingly realized by industrial managers and consultants, conventional piecemeal approaches to tackle these problems have lost effectiveness and feasibility. Diagnosing the competitiviness of a firm, because of its complexity, usually calls for a well integrated team of specialist who should join their expertise and efforts in order to perform an orderly and thorough examination of all aspects of the organization. However, integrating and affording such a team is seldom within the capability of small and medium-size firms and, because of this, they should look for more accessible alternatives or face the situation of having to settle for an incomplete, probably biased and of doubtful usefulness diagnostic.

BACKGROUND.

For many years, the goals and objectives of most firms involved some kind of growth and progress, in a goods-avid and more or less protected marketplace. However, such a situation has changed radically in the last two decades, to the point that many previously successful firms, find themselves now striving for survival in a global and highly competetive marketplace. In this new world, competitiviness has become a key word and indeed a much sought objective for all conscientious organizations. So much so, that all of them spell out in their targets the continuous improvement of their competitive level.

The awarness of productivity improvement in industry, began in Mexico in the early 60's, and its most representative consequence was the setting up of The National Productivity Center, which aimed to help industrial organizations to train key people and to develop productivity improvement programs. The quality ensuring function was seen (and still is in many instances) as a vigilant of the manufacturing process, and as an independent entity without responsability on the corrective actions aimed to ensure the fulfilment of the established product specifications, thus preventing the realizations of joint improvement efforts by a suitable team of the organization.

The Productivity Autodiagnose System depicted by Carrion-Guerrero (1991) in a precursory paper, made two important things evident to the authors, namely: i) The methodology used looks very promising; ii) The analysis of productivity alone is not sufficient to ensure the firm's competitivity.

Because of this, it was decided to restructure the existing model, in order to:
- Cater also for quality and commercialization aspects.
- Formulate it as a checklist for ease of application.

SYSTEM DEVELOPMENT.

On the basis of some pilot trials in our local industry and in accordance with the authors' experience, a checklist suitable for self-diagnosing of competitiveness by managers of small and medium-size industries in Mexico, should be:
a) Friendly.
- It should be whitten in a common-to-all language.
- It should address unambiguous questions directly.
- It should requiere accessible information.
- It should be applicable by middle and top managers.
b) Objective.
- It should be based on easily observable facts.
- It should begin with general questions and proceed later with increasingly specific aspects.
c) Effective.
- It should provide useful results troughout its various stages of application.
- It should highlight the main problem areas.
- It should provide a good basis for ulterior quantitative analyses.

Apart form this, one should consider that performing this kind of diagnosis may be carried out best, if it is done in three stages of increasing insight and progessive emphasis.

During the first stage, the main problem areas should be pointed out and the basis for the diagnosis should be outlined. A second stage could then be oriented to obtaining a qualitative diagnosis and some general quantitative indicators of the main problem areas. Complementarily the third stage could focused on a detailed analysis of all the problems, working out the appropriate quantitative indicators of their situation.

The checklist described in this paper is aimed to fulfil the first of these stages, thus giving the firms' management a suitable starting point from which they can visualize what needs to be done. More than 40 years of joint experience, involving many types of organizations, have led the authors to believe that the single most important question which managers ought to ask themselves is: which are the things that the firm should carry out in order to ensure the achievement of its goals and objectives?

However, such inquisitive attitude tends to encounter the following problems before it can yield any benefits:
a) The overall goals and objectives tend to become diffuse and misunderstood by people in the lower levels of the organization.
b) Not all managers are equaly able toidentify and take their responsability in the achievement of the firm's goals and objectives, not to mention their translation into feasible, effective and efficient actions.
c) Few managers are mature (willing) enough to risk their power and influence in the organization for the sake of a general achievement.

It must be said, though, that problems a) and b) tend to be more serious in medium and large-size companies, on the other hand, one should consider that:
Managerial activites in small and medium-size firms are not essentially different from those of large organizations, since all functions have to be equally performed in both of them, it is only the way in which they are distributed and carried out that changes from one to the other. On the whole, it is the size of activites which determines the amount of resources required for their performance and, in turn, the adequate management of such resources make evident the complexity and specialization of the activities involved.

A manager of a small/medium size firm has to be more interdisciplinary (versatile) than his/her counterpart in a large one, since a single person has to carry out a number of duties which are usually assigned to several individuals in large firms. To be fair, a numbers of activities call for a rather deep analysis in large companies.

Because of the way in which most small size firms have been born and developed, their managers are not usually able to visualize, on their own, all the problems and barriers which they have to overcome in order to become globally competitive. Generally, small and medium-size industries lack internal capability for successfully facing today's increasingly demanding challenges on technological, social, ergonomical, financial and administrative aspects. Simply, information is changing at a very fast rate on matters such as laws and regulations (tax, labour, import/export) technology, management techniques, workers' needs and expectations, to name a few, and it is impossible for any individual to keep him/her self up-to-date on so many aspects.

On the whole, small and medium-size industries in Mexico lack specialized personnel on productivity, quality and commercialization related aspects; because of this, they need to seek external assistance for tackling this kind of problem.

Under these circumstances, it becomes obvious that the aforementioned managers urgently need external help on:
- Analytical tools which can help them to examine a large variety of situations and to make the best possible decisions.
- Specialized advice on the identification and solution of different types of problems.

As far as we have observed, there is a grave lack of analytical tools for helping managers of small and medium size industries to tackle their competitivity problems. This situation encouraged our research team to develop this tool. Developing this analytical tool has compeled us to place ourselves, alternatively, as industrial consultants and industrial managers, in order to understand fully the situation in which both of them are, in relation with the successful tackling of competitivity problems.

As things stand, one important question that consultants ought to pose to themselves is: what kind of external assistance do small and medium size industries need for identifying and solving their competitivity problems? At the light of the experience gathered, the external assistance needed is one that complements the existing capabilities within the firm, with a minimum of external intrusion and a maximum of effectiveness, allowing the firm's own personnel to yield their best contribution and to grow as problem solvers and individuals, for, it should be understood at the outset that no improvement program will be successful if it is not born together with the people's determination for a better situation.

External consultants and service suppliers should always bear in mind that their help will only be welcomed if:
- It is really needed,
- It abides by the company rules,
- It does not hurt people's feelings and pride,
- It does not diminish the autonomy of the firm, and
- It has the right cost, quality and timing.

It is important to realize that, in our environment, consultancy firms are rather scarce, and those which are knowledgeable and trustworthy in our field of interest are only a few. Considering that the existing deficit of these firms is not likely to be fulfiled in the short term, a supplementary strategy should be developed and implemented. We believe that part of that strategy should be the development of analytical tools like our checklist and, of course, suitable expert systems.

VALIDATION.

An important aspect of the validation process has been the testing of the language employed, so as to ensure that it is accessible to all potential users; so far, only small problems have arisen.

The validation of this checklist is understood as its application in a sufficient number of organizations, with the aim of assessing if all those causes of problems which actually happen in industry, have been included in the checklist and are placed within it in their right place.

Generally, it has been found that:

- Users find difficult to acknowledge that they do have some competitivity problems.
- Existing problems are more easily addressed when they are presented as a multiple-choice statement, rather than as a question.
- The expectations of users exceed the capability of this checklist, i.e. they tend to ask for some quantitative indicators (in spite of the fact that they do not supply any figures) and they want to have some clues about appropriate improvement actions.

From these experiences, a follow-up project to be carried out, once the validation process is finished, will be the development of a corresponding set of recommendations on corrective actions, which will be automatically picked by an appropriate software, in accordance with the information previously keyed-in by the user.

CONCLUSIONS.

It is clear that the compulsory starting point of any improvement program should be a thorough characterization of the existing problems and their root causes.

The analytical tool explained in this paper is believed to be appropriate for application is small and medium-size firms in Mexico, because:
- It does include all possible causes which could affect competitivity.
- It has been thoroughly examined from all pertinent viewpoints.
- It is practically oriented.
- It has been specifically developed for application by actual managers.
- It is not costly.
- It has the backing of a top level academic institution.

An adequate diagnosis of competitivity problems, when it is carried out in a systematic and well-structured way, enables the analyst to delve into the root causes of such problems, as well as their interrelationships; and, additionally, helps to outline a solving methodology. This analytical tool will also enable our students to characterize and develop their industrial case studies in a more complete and objective way.

The widespread availability of software for development of expert systems will soon enable us to take this work a step further and develop an expert system for diagnosing the competitivity of a firm.

BIBLIOGRAPHY.

Carrión - Guerrero, M.A. et al (1991) Productivity autodiagnose system, PRODUCTIVITY AND QUALITY MANAGEMENT FRONTIERS - III, edited by Sumanth, Edosomwan, Sink and Werther. Institute of Industrial Engineers.

ANNEX.

COMPETITIVITY

A. Productivity.

1.   Inventory levels.
2.   Delivery times.
3.   Materials flow and handling. (*)
4.   Purchasing.
5.   Factory Maintenance.
6.   Financing.
7.   Human aspects (industrial relations).

B. Quality.

1.   Product.
            Specification.
            Design.
            Inspection.
            Packaging
2.   Process.
            Specification.
            Design.
            Operation.
3.   Inputs.
            Labour.
            Materials.
            Machinery.
            Services.
4.   Managerial process.
            Planning.
            Organizing.
            Integrating.
            Directing.
            Controlling.

C. Commercialization.

1.   Market information.
2.   Product requirements.
3.   Service level.
4.   Market strategy.
5.   Publicity.
6.   Public relations.

The above listing is shown to the user in order to guide him/her through the various aspects (problem areas) to be examined. For illustration's sake, point A.3 has been marked for further analysis. The listing shown below, depicts the factors affecting the "materials flow and handling"; for each of them, the user should indicate if its current situation within his/her company is a) very satisfactory, b) satisfactory, c) deficient, d) very deficient, or e) does not know.

Owing to space limitations this ANNEX does not show a complementary set of options in which the user comments on the certainty of his/her answer, in six levels, namely: absolutely sure, reasonably sure, slightly sure, slightly uncertain, uncertain, or very uncertain.

(*)

		current situation				
		a	b	c	d	e
3.1	Plant layout (including services).	( )	( )	( )	( )	( )
3.2	Materials handling. (**)	( )	( )	( )	( )	( )
3.3	Products and materials packaging.	( )	( )	( )	( )	( )
3.4	Materials standardization.	( )	( )	( )	( )	( )
3.5	Utilization of handling equipment.	( )	( )	( )	( )	( )
3.6	Working condition of handling equipment.	( )	( )	( )	( )	( )
3.7	Handling loads (batches).	( )	( )	( )	( )	( )
3.8	Materials flow (timing).	( )	( )	( )	( )	( )

```
------------------------
```
(**)   current situation

                                        a   b   c   d   e

3.2.1 Suitability of handling
       equipment.   ( ) ( ) ( ) ( ) ( )

3.2.2 Knowledge of handling
       requirements.   ( ) ( ) ( ) ( ) ( )

3.2.3 Knowledge of handling
       equipment.   ( ) ( ) ( ) ( ) ( )

3.2.4 Knowledge of appropriate
       handling methods.   ( ) ( ) ( ) ( ) ( )

3.2.5 Training of materials
       handling personnel.   ( ) ( ) ( ) ( ) ( )

3.2.6 Morale and motivation
       of materials
       handling personnel.   ( ) ( ) ( ) ( ) ( )

3.2.7 Materials handling
       procedures.   ( ) ( ) ( ) ( ) ( )

3.2.8 Materials classification
       system.   ( ) ( ) ( ) ( ) ( )

3.2.9 Materials identification
       system.   ( ) ( ) ( ) ( ) ( )

BIOGRAPHICAL SKETCHES OF AUTORS.

Dr. Eduardo Oliva - López has 30 years of professional experience in México, covering private industry, descentralized organizations, research institutions, posgraduate teaching and consultancy work. He is currently a professor of Production Management and Ergonomics at UPIICSA (IPN) of which he is a founder.
Mr. José J. Flores - Valtierra is an Industrial Engineer with practical industrial experience on methods and time studies applied to incentives' schemes.
Mr. Enrique Hernández - García is an Industrial Engineer with practical experience on quality control in the manufacture of buses,
Mr. Manuel Pérez - Bailón is an Industrial Engineer with practical experience on plant layout.

Productivity & Quality Management Frontiers-IV, edited by Sumanth, Edosomwan, Poupart, and Sink. ©1993
Institute of Industrial Engineers.

Varied Technology and Agricultural Productivity in Developing Countries

F. Ezeala-Harrison
University of New Brunswick
Saint John, New Brunswick CANADA

ABSTRACT

The Problem Addressed

Technological variation refers to application of innovative inventions to traditional ways of accomplishing production tasks, with a view to embodying more efficient and more productive methods into the production process. As the state of contemporary agriculture in developing countries has continued to be that of inefficient and low-productivity levels under very little or no technological variation, there is the need for an indepth analysis of its prevailing conditions, in search of appropriate policy paths to development.

This paper studies the role of technological variation in augmenting agricultural productivity in developing countries within the context of the earnings-productivity model of production. The objective is to offer important policy guidelines for further research and policy actions aimed at improving agricultural productivity and incomes.

The Methodology

The basic approach is the development and application of a structural model that draws from existing research on agricultural productivity in developing countries, and the analysis of technological variation within the framework of the model. The results are viewed in the light of stylized facts, and based on consistency of these results with the stylized facts, policy recommendations are formulated. The major stylized facts on agricultural productivity and technology in developing countries are set out in Section I, followed by Section II which presents the model in a systematic and rigorous application of comparative static treatments that explain productivity and technology under the positive effort-sensitivity and null effort-sensitivity variants of the model. An empirical dimension of the research is given in Section III in which the results are tested econometrically, while Section IV gives the conclusion and policy recommendations.

I. STYLIZED FACTS ON AGRICULTURAL PRODUCTIVITY AND TECHNOLOGY

The bulk of the studies on agrarian technology and productivity indicate that traditional agriculture can be "efficient" in the standard sense of the term, that is, under existing technology, farmers maximize their output from the available set of inputs, or obtain a given output level with less input use. However, the central characteristic of agricultural technology in developing countries (DCs) is that it changes very slowly, if at all. This means that farmers are not able to constantly respond to changing agricultural methods. Weitz (1971) had indicated that rural farmers tended to experiment with alternative techniques over very long periods of time, for decades or even centuries, until they could stumble upon the right method for a given technology. But they are no doubt willing to change if they clearly perceive imminent benefits from a change, and this is demonstrated by their observed positive respose to changes in prices of their agricultural products.

Before the advent of modern science and its application to farming, there were fundamental advances in all aspects of agricultural technology. The evolution from traditional slash-and-burn tenure methods of shifting cultivation (also referred to as the forest-fallow cultivation) to permanent cultivation in which a crop is grown on a piece of land once every year, represents a gradual, albeit masked technological progress. This evolution was very sluggish -- farmers had to discover ways to restore nutrients in the soil by crop rotation and addition of fertilizers, and ploughs had to be developed. The result has been that productivity growth could not match the rapidly growing need for sustenance. This indicates that technology with little or no variation lacked the potential for requisite productivity growth, and therefore calls for rapid technological variation to be applied to agrarian societies on an ongoing basis.

A major distinction between DCs' agriculture and modern agriculture in developed countries lies in the pace and source of technological change. In the former, technological change is slow and sluggish because it is mostly based on the tinkering of individual farmers and/or accidents of nature that may reveal a high-yield seed variety, for instance, whereas in the latter, it is rapid and varied and based on scientific research which produces most of the new techniques used. As this crucial difference is technological, it implies that the development and modernization of agriculture in DCs borders on technological issues.

Technological variation deals with such issues as the role of irrigation facilities and chemical fertilizer and the impact of these on crop yields, crop and plant varieties, and productivity. Gillis and Perkins (1992) observe that there is no universally best technology for agriculture, as all agricultural techniques must be adjusted to local soil, climatic conditions, and factor endowments. However, a society must clearly innovate in both major aspects of Mechanical package and Biological package of agricultural technology in order to effect a viable technological variation.[1] Thus, the optimal levels of capital-labour substitutability as well as plant variety-chemical fertilizer complementarity, have to be employed and kept in place. The productivity effects of such technological input in DCs' agriculture cannot be over emphasized.

In the model that follows, we develop a framework that demonstrates the fundamental importance of technological variation in this most important economic sector of most DCs, and proceed to verify the empirical evidence there may be in support of these stylized facts and the explanatory models used to analyse them.

II.THE EFFICIENCY WAGE-PRODUCTIVITY MODEL

The productive effort of an agricultural worker is presumed to be a positive function of the wage payment and local unemployment level, in the form

$$e = e(\omega,u) \tag{1}$$

where e = productive effort per hour applied to work,
ω = the real wage rate per hour,
u = the local unemployment rate.[2]

The model would posit productivity as a function of actual work effort derived from labor time employed, where the relationship is characterized by productive-effort sensitivity functions (or simply effort responses)

$$\partial e(\omega,u)/\partial\omega = e_\omega(\omega,u) \geq 0; \quad \partial e(\omega,u)/\partial u = e_u(\omega,u) > 0 ;$$
$$\partial^2 e(\omega,u)/\partial\omega^2 = e_{\omega\omega}(\omega,u) < 0; \quad \partial^2 e(\omega,u)/\partial u^2 = e_{uu}(\omega,u) < 0;$$
$$e_{\omega u}(\omega,u) = e_{u\omega}(\omega,u) = 0.$$

In the model's application of the sensitivity functions, the following explanations are necessary: the research on

---

[1]Gillis and Perkins (1992) applied the terminologies of Mechanical and Biological package in their studies of agricultural development in DCs. The Mechanical package refers to tractors, combines, and other forms of labour-saving machinery which would replace agricultural labor that is lost to the industrial sector. The Biological package refers to improved plant variety use such as hybrid corn, seed stock, and the like (the "Green Revolution").

[2]Unemployment is introduced in this model as a shirking-deterrent, following Shapiro and Stiglitz (1984).

agrarian production[3] posit three crucial production features, namely, (1) the seasonal nature of operations: the busy seasons of planting and harvesting when employment demand is high, and the slack gestation periods when the employer only needs a portion of workers for maintenance (and enters into permanent contractual arrangement with such workers); (2) monopsony employment: a condition where a single employer dominates, such that the wage rate varies with employment levels; (3) the existence of two-tier labor markets, in one of which workers are employed under permanent or semi-permanent contractual arrangements, while the other is casual. We presume that contractual workers have less incentive to shirk, as the employer adopts higher wages to obtain self-enforcing "monitoring" on employees that maximizes his profits, so that effort sensitivity functions are positive under contractual setting, and zero under casual employment as productive-effort is insensitive to wage rate due to the very nature of casual labor with no disincentives to shirking.[4]

The short-run production function is:
$$Q = Q[L.e(\omega,u)], \quad Q'(.)>0, \quad Q''(.)<0, \tag{2}$$
where Q = quantity of output, L = labour employed.

The typical agricultural monopsonist employer operates in the short run with the labor employment demand function
$$\omega = \omega(L), \quad \omega'(L) > 0, \quad \omega''(L) = 0;$$
with objective to maximize profit Π given by
$$\Pi(L,\omega) = p(Q(.))\Omega Q[Le(\omega,u)] - (\omega L + \gamma(u,v)[\alpha L]) \tag{3}$$
where output price p is a function of output Q: $p'(Q(.)) \leq 0$,
$\Omega > 0$ = exogenously determined technological parameter for the production function,
γ = average incidental labor costs that is a negative function of local unemployment level u, and a positive function of quasi-fixed labor costs v; thus γ is such that
  (a) $\gamma(u,v) \geq 0$,
  (b) $\partial(\gamma(u,v))/\partial u = \gamma_1 < 0; \quad \partial(\gamma(u,v))/\partial v = \gamma_2 > 0$;
and $0<\alpha<1$ is the fraction of total labor force employed that is made up of underlined casual labor, which can be viewed here as the proportion of labor turnover per given time period.

---

[3]Notable among these are the works of Osmani (1991), Dreze and Mukherjee (1987), Eswaran and Kotwal (1985), Binswanger and Rosenzweig (1984), and Bardhan and Rudra (1981).

[4]This is the idea expounded in the efficiency-wage model of economic theory which has become a major analytical tool widely applied in studies of productivity and employment. A complete profile of the model can be found in Weiss (1990) and in Akerlof and Yellen (1986).

The employer chooses $(L*, \omega*)$ to maximize (3) under the first-order conditions:

$$p(.)\Omega Q'(.)e(\omega,u)-\{\omega+\omega'(L).L+\alpha\gamma(u,v)\} = 0 \qquad (4a)$$
$$(p(.)\Omega Q'(.)e_\omega(\omega,u)-1)L = 0 \qquad (4b)$$

(4a) yields the optimal wage rate as a function of effort, productivity, and technology:

$$\omega* = p(.)\Omega Q'(.)e(\omega,u)-(\omega'(L).L+\alpha\gamma(u,v)) \qquad (5)$$

However, the employer does not operate a uniform wage rate across the two tiers of workers. $\omega*$ is available to only one of the tiers while not available to the other. The question then is: what factors determine which of the tiers receive $\omega*$?, and more so, what would be the appropriate wage of the other tier? To explore these issues, the following proposition is stated, and then formally proved:

Proposition

A typical agricultural enterprise i operating with state of technology Ω_i and employing L workers of whom αL are under casual employment arrangements (L^0), and $(1-\alpha)L$ are under semi-permanent contractual arrangements $(L*)$, maintains different wage levels for its workers:

$$\omega*_i(p,\Omega*_i,Q'(.),e_i,\gamma_i(u,v)) > \omega^0_i(p,Q'(.)),$$

where $\omega*$ = technologically determined contractual wage paid to $L*$, and is invariant to market conditions,
ω^0 = wage paid to L^0, which is flexible and immune to varied technology.

The proof of this LEMMA:

under assumptions that wage equals marginal productivity, if the wage rate is responsive to technology, then it implies that agricultural productivity across enterprises will differ only according as technology differs (assuming workers are characterised by uniform effort sensitivity to wage), with implication that technological differences are the only factors that would cause productivity differences; and if wage is not responsive to technology, then it must be casual wage, and indicates stagnant technology. We perform these proofs in two stages: the cases respectively of positive effort sensitivity and null effort sensitivity.

Case 1: $e_\omega(\omega,u) > 0$

Differentiating the wage function totally and rearranging yields

$$d\omega*_i[1-pQ'\Omega*_ie_\omega L\{(Q''e/Q')+(1/L)+(p'Q'^2e/p)\}$$
$$= dL\{p\Omega e^2Q''+p'e^2\Omega Q'^2-(\omega'+\omega''.L)\}$$
$$+du[p\Omega*_ie_i(Q''Le_u+Q'e_u^2/e+p'Q'^2\Omega eL/p)\alpha\gamma_1]$$
$$+d\Omega*_i(p(.)Q'(.)e_i(\omega,u) - \alpha\gamma_2dv$$

from which we obtain the wage-distribution effect of technology:

$$\partial\omega*_i/\partial\Omega*_i = \{p(.)Q'(.)e_i(\omega,u)\}/[1-pQ'\Omega*_ie_\omega L\{(Q''e_\omega/Q')$$
$$+(1/L)+(p'Q'^2e_\omega/p)\}]$$

which simplifies to

$$\frac{\partial \omega *_i}{\partial \Omega *_i} = \frac{p(.)Q'(.)e(\omega,u)}{1-p\Omega e_\omega(LQ''e_\omega+Q'+Lp'(Q')^3e_\omega/p)}$$

whose sign is positive if
$$- \{LQ''(.)e_\omega(\omega,u)+ Lp'(.)Q'^3(.)e_\omega(\omega,u)/p(.)\}-Q'(.) > 0 \qquad (6)$$
or
$$- \frac{p(.)LQ''(.)e_\omega(\omega,u)+Lp'(.)(Q')^3e_\omega(\omega,u)}{Q'(.)p(.)} > 1$$

that is
$$-(\frac{LQ''(.)e_\omega(\omega,u)}{Q'(.)} + \frac{\sigma e_\omega(\omega,u)LQ'(.)}{\eta} - 1) > 0$$

where
η = price-elasticity of demand of output such that
$$\eta = p(.)/p'(.)Q < 0,$$
σ = output-elasticity of labor such that
$$\sigma = Q'(.)/Q(.) > 0;$$
and this satisfies (6). This indicates that wage distribution is a function of technology, which in turn is a function of output-elasticity of labor. We suggest that the parameter σ is a good proxy for Mechanical package of technological effects, and verify this empirically in Section III below.
Case 2: $e_\omega(\omega,u) = 0$
In this condition
$$\partial \omega^0_i/\partial \Omega^0_i = (p(.)Q'(.)e_i(\omega,u))/[1-pQ'\Omega *_i eL\{(Q''e_\omega/Q')$$
$$+(1/L)+(p'Q'^2Q''e_\omega/p)\} \qquad (7)$$
giving upon substitution of $e_\omega(\omega,u)$ = 0
$$\partial \omega *_i/\partial \Omega *_i = \{p(.)Q'(.)e_i(\omega,u)\}/(1-pQ'\Omega *_i e(\omega,u).Q'(.)) \qquad (8)$$
which can be positive or negative. This suggests that the casual wage rate is not consistently linked with technology, and defines the current state in most DCs' agriculture.
Finally, we show that in equilibrium, any static change in $\omega *_i$ exceeds a similar change in ω^0_i, and to that extent $\omega *_i$ must exceed ω^0_i in absolute terms, i.e.
$$(d\omega *_i)^e_{\omega>0} >> (d\omega^0_i)^e_{\omega=0}.$$
For simplicity, assume all factors remain unchanged under competitive product market: du=dv=dΩ=0, p'(.) = 0,
then $(d\omega *_i)^e_{\omega>0} - (d\omega^0_i)^e_{\omega=0}$ gives
$$\frac{dL(p\Omega *_i e^2Q''(.)-\omega'(L))}{1-pQ'\Omega *_i eL[Q''e_\omega/Q')+(1/L)]} - \frac{dL(p\Omega *_i e^2Q''(.)-\omega'(L))}{1-pQ'\Omega *_i e} > 0,$$

which yields upon dividing through by the common numerator

(which is a negative value) and inverting
$$1-pQ'\Omega*_ieL\{(Q''e_\omega/Q')+(1/L)\} - (1-pQ'(.)\Omega*_ie) > 0,$$
i.e.
$$-pQ'\Omega*_ieL\{(Q''e_\omega/Q')+(1/L)\} + pQ'(.)\Omega*_ie > 0$$
or

$$pQ'(.)\,\Omega*_i e_i\,[-L(\frac{Q''(.)\,e_\omega}{Q'(.)}+\frac{1}{L})\ +1]\ >\ 0$$

which reduces to
$$pQ'(.)\Omega*_ie(-LQ''(.)e_\omega/Q') \gg 0.$$
   The above results, together, verify that technological variation would necessarily raise productivity and earnings.

III. THE EMPIRICAL ANALYSIS

   To test the results of the model we utilize cross-sectional data collected by this author for rice production in South-Eastern Nigeria in 1989. The wage equations are specified respectively for contractual employment:
$$\omega*_i = \omega*_i(p,\Omega*_i,Q'(.),e_i,\gamma_i(u,v));$$
and for casual employment:
$$\omega^0_i = \omega^0_i(p,Q'(.)).$$
The productivity equations are also specified respectively for contractual employment:
$$Q*_i = Q*(L*,\omega*,p,\Omega*_i,\gamma_i(u,v)),$$
and for casual employment:
$$Q^0_i = Q^0(L^0,\omega^0,p,\gamma_i(u,v)).$$
These equations are tested using a straight-forward regression model of the forms:
$$WGE = INT+\beta_1LND+\beta_2DEP+\beta_3CON+\beta_4BUSY+\beta_5LEAN+\beta_6UNEMP+\beta_7IRR$$
$$+\beta_8PRICE+\beta_9COST+\epsilon_1 \qquad (9)$$
$$logQ = INT+\beta_1log(WGE)+\beta_2log(LND)+\beta_3CON+\beta_4log(L)+\beta_5IRR$$
$$+\beta_6log(COST)+\beta_7log(L)+\epsilon_2 \qquad (10)$$
where
   WGE = daily wage received by the laborer;
   INT = intercept term;
   LND = per capita land cultivated by laborer's family;
   DEP = number of the laborer's dependents;
   CON = dummy variable: 1 if contractual, 0 if casual;
   BUSY = dummy variable: 1 if busy season, 0 if not;
   LEAN = dummy variable: 1 if lean season, 0 if not;
   UNEMP = average unemployment rate in the region;
   IRR = dummy variable: 1 if irrigated land, 0 if not;
   PRICE = general price level of output;
   COST = all other costs, measured in Nigerian Naira;
   Q = yield of rough rice in bushels;
   L = labor input in man-days of 8 hours;
   β_i's = parameter estimates, (i=1,2,...);
   ϵ_j's = error terms, (j=1,2).

Table 1 presents the primary regression results and shows a pattern of parameter estimates that are consistent with the theoretical findings. Use of the t-test indicates that all the estimated coefficients are significant. The values of the F-ratios also confirm an overall significance.

III.1. The Wage Effects

The positive coefficients of IRR and BUSY support the effects of technology implied by changes in the parameter Ω [see inequality (6)], of our model. The estimate for labor demand effects of the contractual wage is not significantly different from zero, implying that this wage is invariant to market forces. For the casual labor wage, while the estimated coefficients of the technology variable is not significantly different from zero, that of the labor market demand is.

Table 1
Regression Estimates of Agricultural-Wage Effects of Labour-Tying and Casual Employment Contract

Variable	ω^*_i	ω^0_i	Log Q
INT	1.4986	1.0625	-1.019
	(.2101)	(.1132)	(.0116)
LND/log LND	-0.9062**	-0.2801**	0.1005***
	(.0811)	(.0521)	(.0163)
PRICE	0.0103***	0.0281***	
	(.004)	(.0186)	
DEP	1.3021**	0.0105**	
	(.0544)	(.009)	
CON	1.6110**		0.5209**
	(.1242)		(.1061)
BUSY	0.9921**	0.5994***	
	(.0254)	(.0332)	
LEAN	-0.8168***	-1.0881***	
	(.015)	(.0112)	
UNEMP	-0.9023	-1.067	
	(.0223)	(.01147)	
IRR	1.8816**	0.0032**	0.9891**
	(0.1013)	(0.0024)	(0.0402)
COST/log COST	-1.5422**	-1.092***	0.3112
	(.4340)	(.3442)	(.1102)
L/log L	0.0018**	1.4811**	0.5722**
	(.1160)	(.1071)	(.0351)
R^2	0.209	0.211	0.180
F	42.1	39.4	33.7

Note: Standard errors in parentheses.
Wages are cross-sectional averages.
** Significant at 5% level
*** Significant at 10% level

These indicate that the contractual wage is influenced by productivity-enhancing technological variation, as well as nutritional level, while not responsive to changes in employment demand. The casual wage rate however exhibited competitive traits, and the effect of technological variation is not evident. This confirms the current situation in the agricultural sector of most DCs.

III.2. Productivity Effects

We use the productivity results to estimate the values of σ (output-elasticity of labor), the value of Q' (marginal productivity of labor), and the technological parameter Ω, which are the central parameters on which the model rests. If we obtain the relevant empirical values for these parameters, then it implies that, given the model's assumptions, inequality (6) is empirically valid.

For a given area of land and a given level of miscellaneous costs, we can write, from the output equation:

$$\log Q = \log k + 0.5722 \log L, \quad k = \text{constant}.$$

From this, the output-elasticity of labor is given as:

$$\sigma = d(\log Q)/d(\log L) = .5722,$$

and further,

$$\log Q = \log (kL^{0.5722}),$$

i.e.

$$Q = kL^{0.5722},$$

giving us the marginal productivity of labor

$$\partial Q/\partial L = k_1 L^{-0.4278} > 0$$

where $k_1 = 0.5722k = \text{constant}$.
This production function yields k as the technological parameter Ω.

IV. SUMMARY AND POLICY CONCLUSIONS

This study has applied the wage-productivity nexus to analyse the issue of technological variation applied to agricultural productivity in developing countries. It reveals significant potential productivity effects of overcoming the constraint of stagnant technology.

The results have wider policy implications for agricultural development engineering and overall long term labor market planning perspectives in DCs, namely that peasant and subsistence level production that have been the force constraining productivity, could be revolutionised through sufficient infusion of varied technology. Also, as rigid wages formed according to efficiency wage behavior characterise a (primary) sector of the labor market in which technology and productivity tend to influence the wage rate, unemployment would not only be consistent with equilibrium in the agricultural labor market, but also would be a permanent condition in the sector, as employers stick to their optimal employment levels at the efficiency wage and only hire from the casual labor pool during the peak seasons. This explains why rural earnings are known to vary widely across localities and between seasons, and why agricultural occupation offers very little attraction to people in these societies.

The outcome of this study leads us to reach policy conclusions which have important implications for researchers and policy makers targeting upon agricultural productivity growth in developing countries. Focusing the requisite varied technological policy drive to agricultural sectors of these countries would entail, not only far-reaching employment effects, but also longer-term productivity enhancement for these societies.

REFERENCES

Akerlof, G.A. and Yellen, J.L.(eds.) (1986):Efficiency wage models of the Labour Market, New York, Cambridge University Press, pp. 1-21.

Ahmed, I.(1983): "Wage Determination in Bangladesh Agriculture", Oxford Economic papers, Vol.33, No.8, pp.299-323.

Bardhan, P.K., and Rudra, A.(1981): "Terms and conditions of Labour contracts in Agriculture: Results of a Survey in West Bengal 1979", Oxford Bulletin of Economics and Statistics, Vol.43, No.1; pp.89-111.

Binswanger,H.P. and Rosenzweig, M.R.(eds.)(1984): Contractual Arrangements, Employment and Wages in Rural Labor Markets in Asia, New Haven, Yale University Press, pp.1-40.

Dreze,J. and Mukherjee,A.(1987): "Labour contracts in rural Asia: Theories and Evidence", Development Research, LSE, London.

Eswaran, M. and Kotwal, A. (1985): "A Theory of Two-Tier Labour Markets in Agrarian Economies", American Economic Review, Vol.75, March; pp.162-177.

Ezeala-Harrison,F.(1988): "An Application of the Efficiency Wage Hypothesis to Modelling LDC Labour Problems", Journal of Economic Development, Vol.13, No.1, pp. 71-94.

Gillis, M., and Perkins, D.H. (1992): Economics of Development, New York, W.W. Norton and Company, pp. 487-522.

Osmani, S.R. (1991): "Wage determination in rural labour markets: The theory of implicit co-operation", Journal of Development Economics, Vol.34, pp. 3-23.

Shapiro, C. and Stiglitz, J.(1984): "Involuntary Unemployment as a Worker Discipline Device", American Economic Review, Vol.74, June, pp.433-444.

Weiss, Andrew (1990): Efficiency Wage Models of Unemployment, Layoffs, and Wage Dispersion", Princeton, New Jersey, Princeton University Press, pp.1-22.

Weitz, Raanan (1971): From Peasant to Farmer: A Revolutionary Strategy for Development, New York, Columbia University Press, p.6-9.

Productivity & Quality Management Frontiers-IV, edited by Sumanth, Edosomwan, Poupart, and Sink. ©1993 Institute of Industrial Engineers.

Management of Technology Education for the 21st Century

T.M. Khalil
University of Miami
Coral Gables, Florida USA

Abstract

This paper addresses the issues associated with technological change and their impact on the econo-socio system of society as we approach the 21st Century. The author takes the position that the speed of change and scope of change of technology represents one of the most distinguishing features of our current and future societies. This requires a corresponding change in educational requirements of engineering and business schools. Existing engineering curricula fail to educate engineers that are sensitive to issues of technological competitiveness in an increasingly global economic system. Likewise, existing business school curricula, by and large, put less emphasis on the vital role of technology and production in creating wealth. The need for injecting an educational component on Management of Technology in existing curricula or totally revamping the curricula is indicated. A diagram is given showing the core subjects covered by the interdisciplinary field of Management of Technology. This is an important prerequisite for the advancement of scholarly pursuits and the development of educational programs in this concentration.

INTRODUCTION

Technology is an indispensable part of society today. It is the heart of the industrial enterprise system and the entire modern lifestyle. Its level of existence in a society is synonymous with the standards of living of that society. These are facts that have been the mainstay of engineering activities since the dawn of civilization.

Technology and science have followed separate paths for millenniums. The connection between both, by and large, is a recent phenomenon. Before the 20th century, technology grew up independently -- a product of mechanical ingenuity. However in recent years, most technologies owe their origin to scientific discovery. Engineering education recognized the importance of science in technological development and proceeded to foster the link between them. It also recognized the importance of creating more rounded engineers and introduced a set of educational requirements in humanities and social sciences. However, in my view, engineering education has yet to fulfill the promise of educating the complete engineer who is capable of serving the changing technological needs of society and industry as the world moves towards the 21st century.

In spite of its pervasive nature many people think of technology in the narrow sense of machines or physical structure. In fact, technology consists of hardware, software and brainware or know-how. It can be defined as "all the products, processes, tools, methods and systems employed in the creation of goods or in providing services". Engineering disciplines have each staked its own niche in technological development and application. The technology base for electrical engineers, civil engineers, chemical engineers, etc. are well defined. Industrial engineering owes its origin and namesake in contributing to management technology, human technology, and process/operation technology. When Frederick Taylor first came up with his principles of scientific management, he essentially linked the scientific approach to develop a management technology. When Taylor suggested that management should design the workers jobs, he was attempting to design the first technological software and know-how to be used by the industrial enterprise. His ideas were good and right for his time and his environment. When Henry Ford developed the assembly line for his Model-T cars, he introduced a new process technology which was good and right for his time and environment. When the Gilbreths introduced principles of motion study it was the right technology for their time and environment. When Shewharat, Deming and Juran introduced principles of quality control it was a technology with far reaching impact on industry and society. Each one of these technologies and the subsequent ones developed and used by engineers and managers were developed with knowledge of the environment and the perceived needs of society. This is still true today, However, our educational programs seem to have lost the link between technological developments and societal needs. In particular, we are not leading the way and sometimes not even keeping pace with the change.

In the 70's and 80's business schools grew at a phenomenal rate. Many business schools prescribed to the notion of educating "the professional manager" who is capable of managing any enterprise regardless of the need to understand the technologies underpinning its operation. The net effect was more emphasis placed on financial transactions and less emphasis placed on technology and productions, where real wealth is created. The emphasis must change to tip the balance more towards technology and its uses.

Probably one of the most distinguishing features of our current environment is the speed of technological change. The pace of change and the scope of change have been unprecedented in human history. The expansion in service industry and the explosion in communication and transportation technology have created new global dimensions in production, innovation, technology transfer and in marketing.

EDUCATION AND GLOBAL COMPETITIVENESS

Issues of competitiveness have dominated discussions associated with the recent downturn of economic growth in the United States. Educational issues seem to consistently top the list of concerns of people dealing with this problem. In a survey conducted in 1990 Berman and Khalil (1992) asked a group of leading experts to rank their views on the change in competitive position of the U.S. industries relative to 11 other countries. Respondents felt that the U.S. competitiveness is declining with respect to all the countries listed with the exception of England where they felt there was slight but not significant improvement in position (Figure 1).

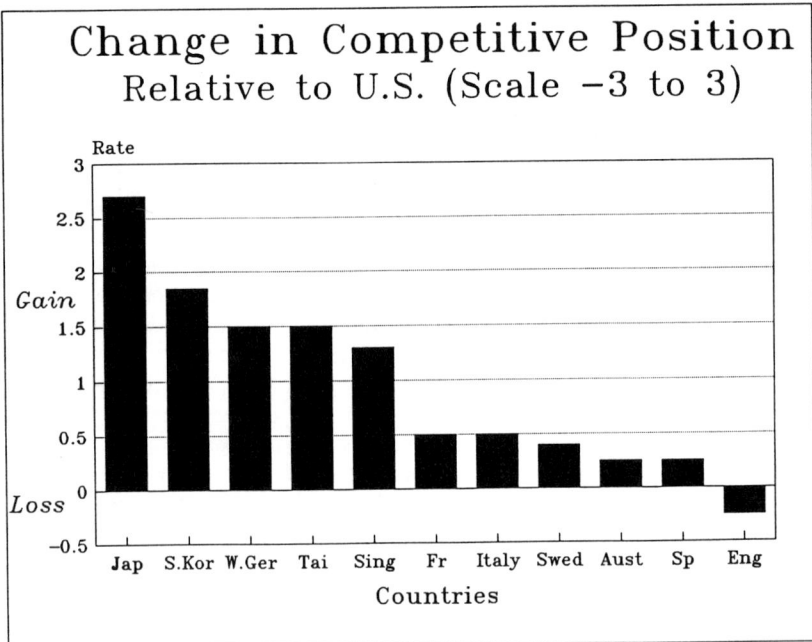

Figure 1

Five Most Important Areas
For U.S.

Percent

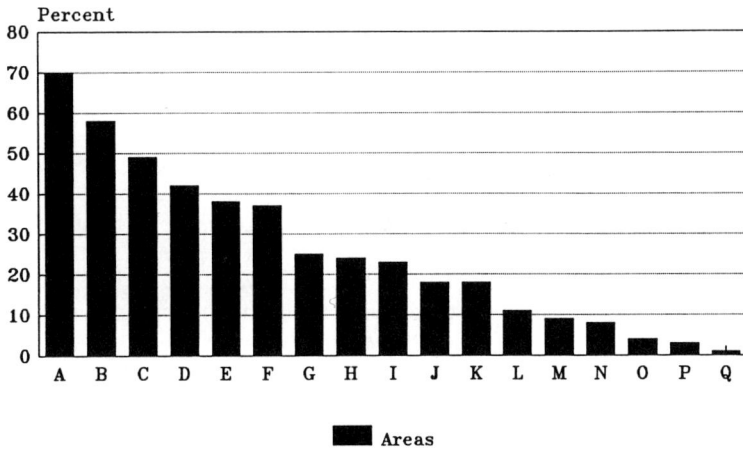

A: improving general education
B: improving technology transfer
C: more engineering education
D: better technology management curricula
E: tax credits for technology
F: helping industry cooperation
G: reducing management-labor conflict
H: monetary policies
I: more university research
J: enforcing fair trade practice
K: increasing venture capital
L: more university-based incubators
M: reducing social regulation
N: export subsidies and aid in marketing
O: gov't procurement performance standards
P: gov't procurement buy-domestic policy
Q: more government purchases

Figure 2

When requested to give their views on the important areas that the U.S. needs to address in order to improve its competitive position, the surveyed experts ranked those areas as shown in Figure 2. General education, more engineering education and better technology management curricula received very high priority ranking. A strong response by educational institutions is needed to address educational needs of engineers and managers.

Educational programs must be able to effectively adjust to meet the challenges of the new world environment. Competitiveness in a global environment is becoming the key to survival in the global economic warfare. Competitiveness will depend not only on the development of new technology but also, on how to respond to technological change and manage the technological enterprise.

We have seen the failure of most current engineering disciplines in developing engineers who can manage in stable technological systems, let alone fast changing global dynamic systems of today and tomorrow. We have also witnessed the failure of business schools in developing the professional manager who has knowledge of the intricacies of technology and technological development. We must develop the engineers and managers who have the potential of filling the gap. With a shift in our emphasis in curriculum we have an opportunity to develop industrial leaders of tomorrow.

We must broaden the horizon of our engineers and change the focus of business education. Make our students aware of the environment, its opportunities and threats. Educate them to have a more strategic outlook as opposed to merely training them on simple operational methodologies, or to work with single gadget or procedure that can become obsolete with a slight change of the technology or the environment. We must be able to relate one subject to another and one notion to another and emphasize the know-how of transferring knowledge to real life situations. The ever popular notion of creating the integrating engineer and the technical manager must be realized. But it can only be realized if those engineers and business students are aware of the environment in which they live and conduct business. They must be sensitized to the characteristics and dynamics of the techno-econo-socio system in which we live.

MANAGEMENT OF TECHNOLOGY AS A NEW FIELD

In 1987 the National Research Council published a report on the deliberation of its sponsored workshop on Management of Technology (NRC 1987). The report recognized Management of Technology as "the hidden competitive advantage" and defined it as a field linking science/engineering and Management. Management of Technology (MOT) was defined as an "Interdisciplinary field concerned with the planning, development and implementation of technological capabilities to shape and accomplish strategic and operational objectives of an organization." The report delineated the existing issues and responsibilities currently under the preview of engineering education on one hand and management education on the other hand. However, the report did not establish a core for the field of Management of Technology as an independent field of study and research. The definitions of such a core is considered an important prerequisite for the advancement of scholarly pursuits and the development of solid educational programs in the concentration. Following a series of international meetings held at the University of Miami (Khalil and Bayraktar 1988, Khalil, et al., 1988, 1990, 1992) a consensus emerged from the deliberations taking place in these meetings as to what constitutes a core for Management

848

MANAGEMENT OF TECHNOLOGY

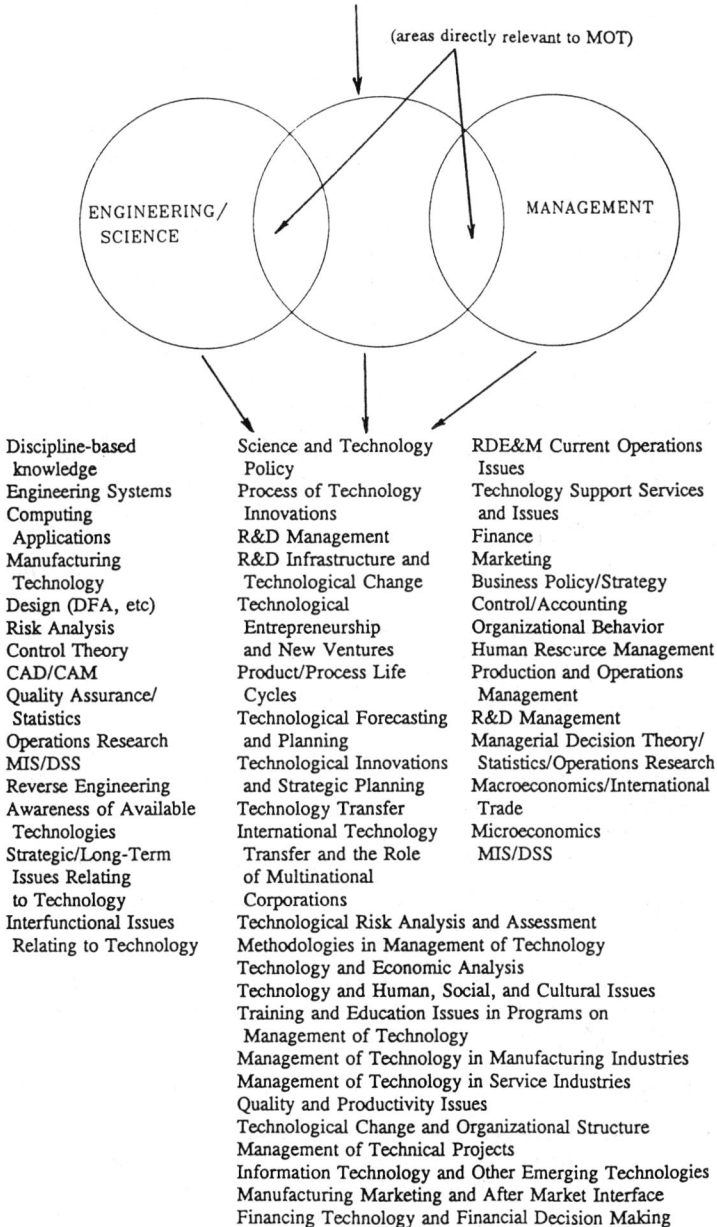

(areas directly relevant to MOT)

ENGINEERING/
SCIENCE

MANAGEMENT

Discipline-based knowledge	Science and Technology Policy	RDE&M Current Operations Issues
Engineering Systems	Process of Technology Innovations	Technology Support Services and Issues
Computing Applications	R&D Management	Finance
Manufacturing Technology	R&D Infrastructure and Technological Change	Marketing
Design (DFA, etc)	Technological Entrepreneurship and New Ventures	Business Policy/Strategy
Risk Analysis	Product/Process Life Cycles	Control/Accounting
Control Theory		Organizational Behavior
CAD/CAM		Human Resource Management
Quality Assurance/ Statistics		Production and Operations Management
Operations Research	Technological Forecasting and Planning	R&D Management
MIS/DSS	Technological Innovations and Strategic Planning	Managerial Decision Theory/ Statistics/Operations Research
Reverse Engineering	Technology Transfer	Macroeconomics/International Trade
Awareness of Available Technologies	International Technology Transfer and the Role of Multinational Corporations	Microeconomics
Strategic/Long-Term Issues Relating to Technology		MIS/DSS
Interfunctional Issues Relating to Technology		

Technological Risk Analysis and Assessment
Methodologies in Management of Technology
Technology and Economic Analysis
Technology and Human, Social, and Cultural Issues
Training and Education Issues in Programs on
Management of Technology
Management of Technology in Manufacturing Industries
Management of Technology in Service Industries
Quality and Productivity Issues
Technological Change and Organizational Structure
Management of Technical Projects
Information Technology and Other Emerging Technologies
Manufacturing Marketing and After Market Interface
Financing Technology and Financial Decision Making

FIGURE 3: Integration of Engineering/Science and Management in
Management of Technology
(Adapted from NRC Report (1987) with modifications)

of Technology as an interdisciplinary field of study and research. This core is shown in Figure 3 superimposed on the concept illustrated by the NRC workshop report.

Based on the concepts illustrated in Figure 3 a more encompassing definition of the field can be given as follows:

"Management of Technology is a field concerned with setting and implementation of policies to deal with technological development and utilization, and the impact of technology on society, organizations, individuals and on nature. It aims to stimulate innovation, and to foster responsible use of technology for the benefit of humankind."

RECOMMENDATIONS

It is proposed that an emphasis on Management of Technology be an integral part of the educational program of engineers. The level of such emphasis can vary from the inclusion of one more course on Management of Technology in existing programs, to a complete overhaul of engineering curriculum with such a theme in mind. Management of Technology is also most pertinent to business school education which needs revamping with the injection of more emphasis on technology, production and globalization issues.

References

Berman, E. and Khalil, T., (1992). "U.S. Technological Competitiveness in the Global Economy: A Survey", International Journal of Technology Management, Vol. 7, No. 415.

Khalil, T.M. (1988). "Management of Technology: An Emerging Field for Industrial Engineers." Proceedings of the 2nd International Congress on Industrial Engineering, Nancy, France, December.

Khalil, T.M. (1991). "Current Issues in Management of Technology". (invited paper) Proceedings of the 3rd International Conference on Industrial Engineering, Tours, France, March. pp. 751-758.

Khalil, T.M. (1992). "Educational Programs in Management of Technology". ORSA-TIMS Spring Meeting, Orlando, Florida.

Khalil, T.M., and B.A. Bayraktar (Eds) (1992). "Management of Technology III". Industrial Engineering and Management Press, Atlanta, Norcross, GA.

National Research Council, (1987). "Management of Technology: The Hidden Competitive Advantage." National Academy Press, Washington, D.C.

American Association of Engineering Societies, (1988). "Management of Technology: The Key to America's Competitive Future." AAES, Washington, D.C.

Khalil, T.M., and B.A. Bayraktar, (1988) "Challenges and Opportunities for Research in the Management of Technology: Report of the NSF/UM Workshop on the Management of Technology." Department of Industrial Engineering, University of Miami.

Productivity & Quality Management Frontiers-IV, edited by Sumanth, Edosomwan, Poupart, and Sink. ©1993 Institute of Industrial Engineers.

Strategic Manufacturing Management Issues in Europe

R. Maull, D.R. Hughes and J.P. Bennett
University of Plymouth
Plymouth, England UNITED KINGDOM

Abstract

This paper will describe the results from a Eureka (Eureka is a major European funding body) definition study entitled Maestro - the management evaluation of strategic options. The project is a joint UK/Swiss proposal and the results contain data from both countries. The results presented here will focus on the user survey part of the Maestro project which is the result of a questionnaire distributed to small and medium sized enterprises (less than 500 employees), both in the UK and Switzerland. The paper will conclude by indicating a number of areas that require methodological developments.

BACKGROUND TO THE MAESTRO PROJECT

The research team at The Centre for Research in World Class Manufacturing and the SIGA management group based in Switzerland have developed a EUREKA proposal entitled Maestro. Maestro has 3 broad areas of research.

- Identify the needs of small and medium sized enterprises (SME's) in the area of strategic manufacturing.
- Identify the availability of strategic manufacturing methodologies, from academia, consultants and vendors (throughout Europe).
- Match needs and methodologies and in so doing identify potential areas for future funding in the development of strategic manufacturing methodologies.

This paper will present the results from each of these 3 areas and conclude by presenting recommendations for future European research projects.

IDENTIFICATION OF USER NEEDS

The methods used to identify user needs fall into 3 categories.

- Postal questionnaire
- Face to face interviews
- Telephone interviews

The data was collected together using a structured question set of 47 questions. This question set was based around a hybrid model of the manufacturing business. The manufacturing part of the model owes its antecedents to the work being carried out on European standards for CIM by CENCENLEC based on CIM-OSA [1] and the subsequent development of that model into the IBM EUROCIM model.

In the model the key activities of a manufacturing business are broken down into three categories, Manage, Operate and Support:

- **Manage** includes management, organisational issues and business planning

- **Operate** includes, product development (including links through to marketing) and process development, Materials Management (which includes purchasing) and Production

- **Support** includes, finance, personnel, information systems and facilities

Most importantly, the identification of appropriate manufacturing systems is irrelevant without an understanding of the strategic context, therefore the questionnaire also asks a series of questions around the strategic context in which manufacturing alternatives and options are considered.

UK RESULTS

The questionnaire was distributed to 2000 manufacturing SMEs having between 19-500 employees and falling into SIC codes 3 and 4 (ie manufacturing). The total UK sample was 160 companies, representing 0.8 of 1% of the 21,000[2] manufacturing legal units that fall into these categories. The results presented here are **weighted** according to the proportion of the total population taken as a sample, this means in practice that a 72% weighting is taken from companies with between 20-150 employees and a 28% weighting from companies with between 150-500 employees. The main results are as follows;

Business Strategy. The greatest area of difficulty for the SME respondents, clearly demonstrated by the results, was the identification of new products. 75% of all respondents had this problem with 45% (50% of mechanical companies) expressing their difficulty as considerable. The next highest strategic difficulty was cost reduction at 72%, just ahead of lead time reduction at 70%, the intensity of the difficulty expressed being marginally greater in the lead time area. The identification of new markets held difficulties for 67% of respondents, with many respondents commenting that they felt they knew of their potential markets but did not have suitable products.

Interestingly, achieving desired quality was only an issue for 58% of respondents, with an intensity level of less than 25%, clearly not a **perceived priority** amongst this sample. The generation of business plans caused the least difficulty at 51%. This somewhat surprising result can be explained by the fact that plans generated by SMEs were generally inadequate, often amounting to no more than a cash flow forecast. In such a situation it is hardly surprising that little difficulty was expressed. If adequate business plans were to be developed it is likely that a greater degree of difficulty would be expressed by respondents.

Product Design. Design was a clear priority for the respondents with 75% expressing difficulty in developing and introducing new products. Of those that responded 70% of Managing Directors (MD's) recognised that they had a problem with design, yet less than 60% of non MD's identified this a problem.

The second greatest area of difficulty was in the generation, evaluation and implementation of a design strategy with 67% of respondents expressing difficulties. To some extent this may explain the difficulties being experienced in developing and introducing new products (75%) and the respondents' difficulties in designing products which are easy to manufacture, 64% and in managing design, 62%.

Further analysis of the data revealed that design was key for electronics firms, with 75% of the respondents having a problem managing design and 70% experiencing difficulty developing a design strategy. Conversely, similar concern was expressed by only 60% of mechanical engineering companies. However, 66% of these companies indicated they had more difficulty in designing products for manufacture as against 61% of electronics companies.

The least difficulty were expressed in assessing the environmental impact of design with fewer than 50% indicating this was an area of any concern, and with less than 20% indicating an intensity of concern.

Process Planning. Developing and introducing new processes was a problem for just over 70% of the sample. The second greatest concern was the simplification of processes with 66% of respondents expressing difficulty. Surprisingly, assessing the environmental impact of processes was regarded with the same degree of concern as deciding which processes to automate at 57%. It is interesting to note that environmental effects are only perceived to be an issue when planning manufacturing processes whereas it could be argued that these problems should be considered much earlier, during the design product design phase.

Respondents reported that they found little difficulty in identifying which process to automate, many claiming that in their particular situation it was almost self evident.

The area causing least difficulty was in deciding the layout of machines and equipment, with 40% of respondents registering concern. As respondents expressed the lowest volume and intensity of concern in any category, this clearly indicated that sufficient information, methods or experience were available.

Control of Manufacturing. With respect to manufacturing, 73% of respondents had a problem in minimising set-ups and reducing WIP, with 30% registering considerable difficulties. Identifying training needs and controlling costs had equal levels of difficulty at 63%. However, respondents expressed a far greater intensity of concern for controlling costs and establishing costs rather than for training. This supported the respondents concern for cost reduction expressed in the "strategic issues" as the respondents second greatest cause of difficulty.

The lowest levels of perceived difficulty were related to rationalisation of suppliers, managing the supplier base and identification of suppliers, all with less than 55% of respondents expressing some difficulty.

Summary of Results. The main difficulty currently being experienced by UK manufacturing SMEs appears to lie in the identification of new products, markets etc, and the attendant development and introduction of new products within a design strategy. Taking these results in conjunction with a recent PA survey[3] we are able to draw some interesting conclusions. The crux of the problem appears to lie with technological innovation, that is to say the creative assembly of science and engineering to meet or create a market need. The PA survey has shown that historically the key source of that innovation was internal R&D. However, over the next five years they anticipate that government and EC funded research will take on a much more important role. PA's survey concludes that, like Japanese and German companies, other European companies need to spend more effort on the up-front part of the development cycle, and to integrate product, process and control systems development within a single framework.

METHODOLOGIES

The research team has also investigated the methodologies that are available to meet the strategic needs of SMEs. We regard a methodology as "a set of principles of method which in any particular situation have to be reduced to a method uniquely suitable to that situation"[4]. This usually takes the form of a workbook. Furthermore, for a methodology to be acceptable for use by SMEs, it must be <u>accessable</u>, <u>affordable</u> and of <u>practical use</u> to maagers who may not have specific manaufacturing systems backgrounds.

<u>Consultant Methodologies</u>. Many respondents initially indicated that "residual company knowledge" and written up case studies were the source and storage method of their "expertise". However, deeper probing demonstrated that this impression was incorrect. The research into methodologies and tools undertaken as part of the Maestro investigation revealed the following results:

- Most of the large companies have well-developed methods, best practice procedures, consultancy services and software tools which they use to "deliver" packaged knowledge and/or methodologies to clients.

- Most of the major consultancy companies are able to provide services in **all** the areas where manufacturing companies have expressed difficulties. Smaller consultancy companies usually offer a more specialised portfolio of services.

- Most of the major consulting companies have developed their own version of public domain best practice methods for many commonly requested areas. Fewer smaller companies have been able to do this, mostly offering standard public domain methodologies, although this situation is now changing.

- Most of the consultancy methodologies identified focused on the solution to a specified problem rather than problem identification, usually providing little diagnostic help.

- Only in situations where the contract specifically calls for it is the client taught the best practice method. It is this expertise that the consultant is selling, and obviously wishes to resell as often as possible.

- Methodologies and tools are usually kept well hidden from the client (except items already in the public domain). Methodologies and tools may well be custom designed and built by the consultancy companies themselves or for themselves by outsiders. This often includes versioned, or tuned common knowledge, public domain techniques.

- The trend revealed by our survey indicates that the more "technical" and complex the topic the more use is made of computer-based methodologies and tools. These tools are not usually supplied to the client but are used by the consultant to carry out his or her assignment. Examples include IT audits, communications network assessment, design simulation, factory layout, risk analysis etc

- Unfortunately, most consultancy services, particularly from the major companies, are based on fee rates related to a consultant's time and, in the main, can not be considered as accessible or affordable by SME's.

Implications. There are a number of key implications that arise from these findings. These include:

- Large consultancies: If such firms wish to address the SME market, they are likely to need new methodologies and new methods of delivery.

- Small consultancies: Potential legal requirements (obtaining licences), or the need to to deliver "best practice" consultancy will need to acquire such best practice knowledge themselves. This is likely to require suitable education/training or tools.

Trends. Expert System (AI) based tools are becoming the norm for delivery of certain types of consultancy. They are used to encapsulate knowledge and then to provide training and user education. Such tools tend to be customer-oriented for on-line use.

Accessability, Affordability and Practicality. Many of the methodologies and tools identified during the survey are not suitable for SMEs for one or more of the following reasons:

- Too expensive, more than £25,000
- Not practical, for example requires an in-house IT team
- Needs specialist staff or facilities eg, mathematicians
- Needs expensive computer hardware or networking capability
- Needs training, education or experience

Even large companies like Lucas Industries which advertise their methodologies do not generally sell them to SMEs. A recent deal between the Lucas company and Coventry University in the UK may bring two methodology products to market and be the first to break this rule.

To some extent the smaller, more specialised consultants do provide useful practical support in certain areas. However, it is clear that the majority of individual consultants and small consultancies in the UK do not have sufficient knowledge of best practice, nor do they have access to kinds of software tools available to the larger companies. This may account for some of the variability in consultancy quality of and the mixed reputation enjoyed by consultants in the UK.

857

Academic Methodologies and Tools. Of the 17 academic projects examined 13 had developed methodologies or tools which qualified for consideration on the basis of their accessability, affordability and practicality. However, there were a number of factors restricting the effective exploitation of the methodologies and tools by potential users:

■   Many of the methodologies developed, although well documented, were not in a form which could easily be applied by SMEs.

■   The majority of the most useful methodologies deal with Computer Aided Production Management (CAPM) as a result of research initiatives funded by the UK Science and Engineering Research Council (SERC).

■   Few of the methodologies and tools had been tested in earnest and therefore their effectiveness was uncertain.

■   Often, the availability of the methodologies was not widely known in the SME community and consequently are unlikely to be used.

European Collaborative Research Projects. Two major collaborative European funding agencies were investigated, ESPRIT and Eureka. ESPRIT tends to focus on pre-competitive work related to Computer Integrated manufacturing (CIM) and few of the 127 projects examined have produced results which are of immediate commercial value to SMEs.

Eureka projects tend to be closer to the market but, until very recently, only focused on Flexible Automated Assembly (FAA). Unfortunately, FAA represents a very small area of interest to SMEs and not one which was accorded a high priority by survey respondents.

IDENTIFICATION OF MISMATCH

The major areas of difficulty identified from the analysis and interpretation of the UK and Swiss results will be examined in detail to identify any mismatches between needs and available methodologies and tools.

■   Identification of new products, new product introduction process
■   Reduction, control and establishment of costs
■   Process design, simplification and management
■   Management of change

Identification of New Products, New Product Introduction Process. In the area of greatest perceived difficulty for both Swiss and UK respondents, the identification of new products, most of the large consultancies have carried out a considerable number of successful assignments and achieved some notable successes. Unfortunately, few were able to offer solutions which satisfied the criteria of accessability and affordability.

There was, however, some evidence that certain smaller consultancies, or specialist consultancies associated with larger companys, were able to provide a number of discrete offerings in a form which satisfies the criteria. For example, P-E's Technology and Marketplace Development activity, based on the expertise of the recently acquired Gosling Associates, in identifying new markets and products addresses part of the problem.

Other methodologies are available for design for manufacture, concurrent engineering, simultaneous engineering etc though these tended to focus too narrowly on this aspect. Lucas Industries' Product into Production methodology was another example of an excellent discrete methodology which could not readily be integrated with other approaches to provide a complete solution.

Reduction, Control and Establishment of Costs. A number of different approaches are available to assist SMEs in discrete areas of cost reduction, for example in stock and WIP reduction and in set up and machine cycle time reduction. However, little or no guidance was available on where best to focus cost reduction efforts in a particular situation.

This factor represents a major area of difficulty. SMEs have little chance of being aware of all the relevant methods and tools available, nor would they know which to use in a particular situation and in any event some of the methods are likely to prove incompatible when used together.

The problem, though appearing to be straightforward on the surface, is likely to prove extremely difficult to resolve. It would entail substantial amount of research to cover the development of diagnostic tools, the development of a framework in which otherwise incompatible approaches could be integrated and not least rules to guide the selection of particular approach or approaches in a particular situation.

Any work to be undertaken in this area should take account of the increasing recognition of the importance of Activity Based Costing.

Process Design, Simplification and Management. Recently, consultants have focused on processes as a means of securing significant improvements in competitive performance and have developed specific methodologies and services in this increasingly important area.

This interest has arisen because of the increasing recognition of the impact of process simplification on cost reduction and lead time. Most of the larger consultancies have well defined offerings on process simplification relying on both proprietary, computer based simulation tools, and public domain approaches to process modelling, IDEF0 [5], value analysis, departmental purpose analysis etc.

Management of Change . In this area consultancy activity is strong with a number of strong methodologies being offered by both large and small consultancies. Unfortunately few of these methodologies are fully documented and those developed within the academic community have not been fully tested in live situation.

Management of change was recognised by suppliers and users as a critical issue. Many large consultants claimed they were really only in the business of selling change management expertise. The difficulties of managing change did not just relate to the introduction of technological change, but all kinds of change, organisational, cultural and methodological.

Not surprisingly, the smaller the user company the less difficulty they had in managing change.

CONCLUSIONS

The Maestro study has produced a number of interesting conclusions, of which only the basic conclusions have been presented here. The research team feel that the key competitive pressure currently being faced by UK companies lies in the identification of new products and markets. Other studies, notably the PA survey support this view. The key source of identification and development of new markets and products is through technological innovation. However, this does need to broken down further into a series of key activities. The research team has identified four key priority areas within the framework of technological innovation:

- The new product introduction cycle
- The management of change
- Process simplification
- The identification and reduction of cost in the manufacturing cycle

Each of these areas will be explored in more detail in the presentation.

REFERENCES

[1] See for further information International Journal of Computer-Integrated Manufacturing, special issue on ESPRIT, Vol.3 Nos.3 and 4, 1991

[2] The Employment Gazette 1990. Published by the Central Stastical Office. UK Government.

[3] "Chief Executives' attitudes to Technological Innovation in UK manufacturing Industry", PA Consulting Group. January 1992.

[4] Waterlow, G. In Computer Aided Production Management,, the report of the research iniative, funded by the ACME Directorate of SERC, 1990.

[5] The ICAM Definition Method, IDEF0. The architects manual, April 1979. Published by CAM-i.

After taking a BA in Economics and an MSc in Management Information Systems, Dr Roger Maull obtained his PhD (using IDEF0 to model Computer Integrated Manufacturing systems) from Bristol Polytechnic in 1986. He then worked on a collaborative project with DuPont Electronics to develop an Integrated Quality System.

In 1987 Dr. Maull joined the Centre for Research in World Class Manufacturing (CRWCM) at the University of Plymouth as a Research Fellow managing a large production management project. Since 1990 he has been a Senior Lecturer within the School of Computing, responsible for manufacturing systems. He has published over 40 papers on a wide number of topics including; CIM, Quality, CAPM, Simulation, Group Technology and Engineering Change Control. He acts as a referee for a number of international journals and is a member of the UK Operations Management Association.

David Hughes is the Professor of Computer Integrated Manufacturing in the CRWCM at the University. He has over 60 international publications, is the UK member of a number of international standards organisations and is the Founding Editor of the International Journal of CIM.

Jan Bennett is a Research Fellow in Electronics Design and Manufacture at the University of Plymouth. He has an Honours Degree in Computing and Informatics and has spent the last three years working on a research project to functionally specify an advanced electronics design tooset for use by small and medium size UK electronics firms. Mr. Bennett has travelled widely in Europe and the Far East on behalf of the UK government investigating the state-of-the-art in electronics product design practice.

Productivity & Quality Management Frontiers-IV, edited by Sumanth, Edosomwan, Poupart, and Sink. ©1993 Institute of Industrial Engineers.

Employee Empowerment-Opportunities and Problems

G.R. McClenaghan
London Public Utilities Commission
London, Ontario CANADA

B. Portis
The University of Western Ontario
London, Ontario CANADA

ABSTRACT

The London Public Utilities Commission (PUC) began its "Journey to Excellence" or total quality management (TQM) five years ago when it adopted a corporate strategy to enhance customer satisfaction through employee involvement. Becoming a new age organization and customer focused requires a significant cultural change.

Overview of the PUC
The London Public Utilities Commission (PUC) was started in 1872 to provide water to the residents of London, Ontario. By 1892 the utility was providing water, electricity, parks and recreational services to the city. In 1992 the PUC had a $250 million annual budget, 96 percent of which came from ratepayers (our customers) with the rest funded by the taxpayers of the city.

The PUC has approximately 560 full-time staff made up of the following: trades, technicians/technologists, engineers, accountants, general labourers, support staff and business graduates. The PUC adds another 1300 staff during the summer months. The workforce is generally very well technically trained and has an excellent safety record. There is an active union for operating employees and there is a good relationship between union and management.

The utility, up until five years ago, operated in a "system driven" manner. It was a traditional autocratic hierarchical organization. The main concern was whether or not the electricity or water was on or not. The PUC did not worry about its relationship with the customers.

Management and staff were normally promoted through the "rank and file" as a result of seniority. They never received any training or orientation as to what was expected of them. They usually learned from their previous experience.

Service Quality
Today companies recognize that their competitiveness depends on service quality or continuous improvement made possible by empowering their workforce. Not many public

agencies considered this five years ago. The PUC "jumped-into" a program of service quality and employee empowerment with no definite plans as to how the program was to be run. The PUC has learned from experience, mostly its own.

Five years ago, senior management of the PUC introduced a program called "Committed to Excellence" with logos and promotional aids, bur without detailed planning. The two main elements of the program have become a customer focus and employee involvement.

A number of meetings were held with supervisors to discuss service quality and to get their commitment to the program. The supervisors felt that employee involvement was needed to improve service to the customer.

The employees were given problem-solving training, much like quality circles, to identify opportunities for improving service to customer. This was done in focus groups since it was intended that the groups would focus on improving service.

The focus groups have had many important consequences. In addition to actual improvements in customer service, focus groups have made changes to improve their own working conditions. The PUC has come to realize that employees are internal customers and must be treated well. The entire employee relations program has been greatly expanded as outlined shortly.

The focus groups behaved much like quality circles and wanted to choose their own problems. Sometimes these problems were clearly inappropriate, such as dealing with personnel or leadership matters, which should be handled in other channels, such as regarding safety or grievances. Some accommodations were made to the focus groups since they identified problems affecting their own performance, such as training needs and troubled relations between departments.

The most surprising aspect of the focus groups was that the groups usually barred their supervisors from attending their problem solving meetings. After many years of working to an agenda set by supervisors the employees had achieved some measure of freedom or empowerment.

Most supervisors did not understand or appreciate being locked out of meeting of focus groups. It was only a few exceptional supervisors that could meet comfortably with leaders of focus groups to help implement their recommendations.

Employee Relations
The program for Service Excellence forged ahead. Management has tried to create a learning culture and respond to requests from focus groups. One common concern of focus groups was whether the PUC cared about its employees as well as its customers. This led to the development of the following comprehensive program for employee relations to go along employee involvement.

EMPLOYEE DEVELOPMENT AND RECOGNITION

- Development activities
  - Recognition
    - long service award
    - safety award
  - Orientation
    - full day for full-time staff
    - half day for part-time staff
    - career planning
    - succession planning
    - performance planning - performance review system with a communication and
      planning tool for managing positive work relationships.

- Leadership training
  - Senior management training
  - Corporate plan
  - Team work - focus groups
  - Leadership development

- Customer relations
  - Customer relations training
  - Review of policies/procedures
  - Customer feedback
  - "I got caught"
  - Leadership training

- Education opportunities
  - Problem solving
  - Team work
  - Tuition program - 100% reimbursement
  - Technical training
  - Wellness program

- Communication
  - Highlight bill insert
  - Link newsletter
  - Retirees's digest
  - Business report
  - Living in London directory
  - Orientation
  - Feedback
  - Performance planning
  - Vision
  - Mission
  - Value
  - Goal statement

Resistance of Supervisors

Everything was going along fine until a major barrier was encountered, resistance of supervisors. Although the supervisors had originally recommended involving employees in the focus groups on service quality, they did not anticipate themselves being excluded from the focus groups. Most supervisors did not know how to handle this turn of events. They either ignored the recommendations of focus groups or made it difficult for the focus groups to meet.

Senior management could not condone the opposition of the supervisors. If the focus groups were not supported then Service Excellence would simply have become history or the program of the month. The alternative has been to provide training to the supervisors.

Part of this training has been to acquaint supervisors with the changing nature of the work force and work should be done in the future.

It is directly related to the changing workforce, i.e. younger, better educated workers who are demanding more involvement in day-to-day operations.

1. To make the P.U.C. a more satisfying place for people to work - increase employee morale.
2. To improve profitability.
3. To satisfy customers' increasing expectations - fewer complaints.
4. To improve the P.U.C. public image.
5. To improve teamwork between departments.

Attention has been given to causes of supervisors resistance.
1. The concept goes against their belief system.
2. They fear losing prestige.
3. They doubt the sincerity and the support of upper management.
4. They feel that they are being bypassed and left out of the program.
5. The program interferes with one-on-one relationships with workers.

Also, attention has been given to the changing role of supervisors.

SUPERVISORY ROLES

Traditional	Supervisory of the 90s
Get results primarily be directing people and by gaining cooperation.	Involve people and help them invest their personal commitment.
Build good followers.	Build good initiators.
Get people to understand good ideas.	Get people to generate good ideas.
Manage people one-on-one.	Build collaborative, interdependent and supportive teams.
Develop strengths within their own work units.	Develop strengths between units and among peers.
Implement direction for above.	Initiate new ideas and directions.
Help people change when directed and help them make the best of it.	Generate positive innovations with people without those changes being imposed from above.
Communicate well.	Be masterful at interpersonal relationships.
Manager Directing Inspecting Controlling	Coach Influencing Communicating

Lessons
However, there are some things you can do that are important to minimize the resistance.

1. Executives have to be solidly behind.
2. Bring managers and supervisors into the process right away. Let them see an attractive future for themselves.
3. Train them more than team members about the value of teams and how to coach them - cascading the training down the ladder.
4. If unionized, get executive/officials on board.
5. Determine what is in it for the supervisor. Let supervisor draw the new blueprint. Kodak did this and involved them in the training.
6. Be honest - tell the truth - if you are phasing out jobs, reassure them. No one should lose their jobs without giving them choices. Most companies are doing it through attrition.

7. Reward behaviours that are consistent with the desired cultural values - reward, both formal and informal.
8. Help them deal with this loss of prestige and other emotional issues. They worry about demotion and have to tell friends, family, etc. Cadillac Motors built a support group for them.
9. Train, train, train - most of it in the interpersonal skills - how to delegate, facilitate meetings, resolve conflicts, encourage consensus decision making, asking a question and so on.
10. Share in the increase of profit.
11. It is relatively easy to describe the role but not so easy to relate the duties. Terms like coach, trainer, facilitator, delegator, educator, strategist, counsellors help to clarify the role a little. But it doesn't tell them what they are doing day-to-day. Training can help clarify duties but, in the end, managers probably still won't have a sharp picture.
12. Organizations send silent, but strong messages, about their readiness for employee involvement, i.e., at one company, the only reserved parking is for the handicapped/customers.

In Summary
The decision to improve service quality of your organization's products or services is important, but will not lead to real quality enhancement unless significant attention and resources are allocated to the process. Continuous improvement is a process. It has no real beginning and no real ending.

In the past, too many E.I. efforts have begun with great hopes only to flounder because of unrealistic expectations or unfulfilled responsibilities. Resistance can be dealt with in a planned manner.

Productivity & Quality Management Frontiers-IV, edited by Sumanth, Edosomwan, Poupart, and Sink. ©1993 Institute of Industrial Engineers.

Techniques for Identification and Optimization in Quality Control

M.A. Durfee

Wyman-Gordon Company

North Grafton, Massachusetts USA

ABSTRACT

A model for the quality control of a production line where items are classified as conforming or nonconforming to specifications is considered. An adaptive algorithm for checking the process performance (identification) and minimizing the total inspection cost (optimal control) is implemented.

The quality control of a production line (i.e., maintaining the average outgoing ratio of defective items below a desired level) leads naturally to the problem of designing a testing procedure where the main objective is to accurately estimate the process parameters while minimizing cost risks associated with sampling. When the process parameters are time dependent, the optimal testing procedure can be achieved only through an adaptive method in which identification and control occurs simultaneously. In this paper, an adaptive method is considered and analyzed. Since the model of interest assumes inspection for attributes (i.e., conforming/nonconforming, pass/fail,), the p-chart and acceptance sampling for attributes may be used for comparison.

The procedure is designed not only to identify the fraction defective, p, but also to detect any change in p. Simultaneously, the average outgoing ratio of defectives must not exceed a desired maximum level, p_d, and total inspection costs of type-I and type-II errors must be minimized.

KEYWORDS

adaptive algorithm, attributes inspection, closed-loop sampling, identification - process performance, optimal control, optimization - sampling frequency, quality control, sampling cost

PROBLEM STATEMENT

The adaptive technique tests the following null and alternative hypotheses:

H_0:   Average ratio of outgoing defectives is less than or equal to p_d (desired maximum level). Operate sampler at frequency $f=1-p_d/\hat{p}$, where $\hat{p}=m+K\sigma$ from beta distribution.

H_a: Not H_0. Update f based on prior and present inspection data. As soon as a change is signaled, inspect at $f=1$ for remainder of the lot. Perform a double test on the next lot to either confirm or not confirm a change in p.

MODEL DESCRIPTION

Since both standard attributes inspection procedures, acceptance sampling and p-chart, do not automatically adapt to changes in the process output stream and to increases in sampling cost risks, other techniques, which facilitate identification and control of process output and sampling costs, should be developed and implemented. An adaptive algorithm, by Runggaldier and Jacur (1973), describes a procedure of simultaneous identification and control. Applied to a problem of quality control of a production line where items are classified as conforming or nonconforming to specifications, the model addresses the following:

1) Verifying the process performance, which is actually an identification problem.

2) Designing a sampling procedure, where the nonconforming items sampled are replaced by conforming items in the output stream (i.e., sampling with replacement). Given requirements to be met include keeping the average outgoing ratio of nonconforming parts below a specified level, p_d, and minimizing the sampling risk costs. This is viewed as an optimal control problem.

From dual control concepts, a unified closed-loop procedure for the simultaneous identification and control is developed and is illustrated in Figure 1.

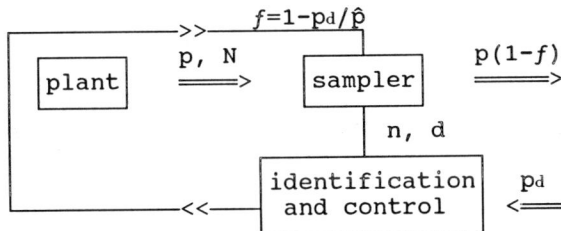

Figure 1 - Unified Closed-Loop Sampling Procedure

The output stream of a production plant - assumed to contain a fixed proportion, p, of nonconforming items - is formally grouped into lots of N items each. A robotic sampler (or inspector), operating at a frequency f, inspects $n=Nf$ items from each lot and removes the d defective items from the output stream, replacing them with conforming items. Thus, sampling with replacement is assumed. The average outgoing ratio of nonconforming becomes $p(1-f)$. The average number of nonconforming items remaining in the lot after sampling is:

$$E_P(d_{tot}-d) = p \cdot N - p \cdot f \cdot N = pN(1-f), \qquad (1)$$
$$d_{tot} = \text{total number of nonconforming items in the lot.}$$

For each lot, the cumulative values of n and d are utilized to obtain refined estimates of p (identification) and to update the optimal sampling frequency f (control).

Objective

The sampling algorithm, depicted in Figure 2, is designed so that it not only identifies the value of p but also signals any change in p - ensuring that the average outgoing ratio of defectives does not exceed a desired level, p_d. While maintaining these objectives, cost of risks is minimized. The value of p is initially assumed to change in only one direction, namely it increases. The production process may only deteriorate. When p is assumed to vary (increase or decrease) with time, a testing procedure is derived and implemented to decide from lot to lot whether p has changed.

From principles of Bayesian statistics, p is assumed to have an a priori beta distribution with parameters α and β.[1] Observing d_i defectives among n_i sampled from the i_{th} lot, an a posteriori beta distribution is obtained, with parameters:

$$\alpha_{i+1} = \alpha_i + d_i$$
$$\beta_{i+1} = \beta_i + (n_i-d_i) \qquad (2)$$

Initially, the absence of information implies a uniform distribution for p with $\alpha_1=\beta_1=1$. Since the variance of the beta distribution is defined by:

$$\sigma^2 = \alpha \cdot \beta / (\alpha + \beta + 1)(\alpha + \beta)^2, \qquad (3)$$

the increasing number of items sampled over time results in a decreasing σ^2. Thus, an increasingly accurate identification of p occurs.

Let p_i equal the ratio of nonconforming items in the i_{th} lot to be sampled. With sampling frequency f, the average outgoing

[1] Durfee, pp. 54-57.
[2] Durfee, pp. 57-58.

ratio of defectives equals $p_i(1-f)$. Since p is a constant, $E(p_i)=p$, and to meet the objective involving p_d, the sampling frequency f must satisfy the constraint:

$$p_i(1-f) \leq p_d. \qquad (4)$$

Simultaneously, sampling cost, assumed as a linear function of f ($A \cdot f$ where A is the cost to sample N items), is minimized.

The value of p_i follows a beta distribution with mean m and standard deviation σ (based on the current parameters, α_i and β_i). By Chebyshev's inequality, the probability of p_i exceeding $\hat{p}=m+K\sigma$ is less than or equal to $1/K^2$. Therefore, with K=3, $\hat{p}$ is substituted for p_i and the objective of keeping the average outgoing ratio of defectives below a desired level, p_d, is satisfied except for a small probability with upper bound $1/K^2=1/9$. Setting $\hat{p}=p_i$, the constraint equation for sampling frequency f is solved for f: [3]

$$f = 1 - p_d/\hat{p}. \qquad (5)$$

Next, the ratio of defectives, p, in the production line is assumed to vary over time. A testing procedure is derived to decide from lot to lot whether p has changed. At the beginning of the ith lot, the ratio of defectives is denoted as p_i. If p has not changed, the beta distribution with updated parameters, α_i and β_i, continues to hold. By Chebyshev's inequality, $p_i<\hat{p}$, except for a small probability.

Since $E(p_i)=p$, the lot's output is assumed as unchanged if $p_i<\hat{p}$. In this instance, identification and control proceeds for p constant. However, if $p_i \geq \hat{p}$, a change in the lot fraction defective has occurred. A new identification is started, and the control procedure requires changes. Since the actual value of p_i is unknown, the testing procedure must be coupled with the sampling to reach a decision about a change in the lot. A value c is determined such that if the number of defective items sampled in the lot reaches the value of c, during sampling of the lot, a change in p is signaled.

In deciding on no change in p, the sampling frequency is selected according to $f=1-p_d/\hat{p}$, which guarantees that the average outgoing ratio of defectives does not exceed p_d only if $E(p_i)<\hat{p}$. The testing procedure must recognize if $E(p_i) \geq \hat{p}$. When $E(p_i) \geq \hat{p}$ and the sampling frequency is f, the average number of defectives found, $E(d)$, exceeds $Nf\hat{p}$. Thus, to guarantee our objective, c must satisfy the constraint:

$$c \leq Nf\hat{p}. \qquad (6)$$

---

[3] Durfee, pp. 59-60.

When a change in the lot is indicated, a control procedure is implemented. Sampling a lot with frequency f, if a number of defectives d is found, the total number of defectives in the lot up to this point is $E(d_i)=d/f$. Therefore, as soon as a change is signaled ($d=c \geq Nf\hat{p}$), the expected number of defectives already passed through inspection is given by:

$$E(d_i-d) = E(d_i)-E(d) = d/f-d = d(1-f)/f \geq N\hat{p}(1-f) = Np_d \quad (7)$$

To guarantee that the average outgoing ratio of defectives will not exceed p_d, from the moment a change is indicated, additional defectives cannot be allowed to pass through the inspection process. Therefore, a sampling frequency $f=1$ (100 percent inspection) is implemented to the end of the lot.

The value of c is determined by the principles of Bayesian testing.[4] Two composite hypotheses to test for a change (8) are substituted by two corresponding simple ones (8a).

$$(8) \quad \begin{aligned} p_i &< \hat{p} \\ p_i &\geq \hat{p} \end{aligned} \qquad\qquad (8a) \quad \begin{aligned} p_i &= m \\ p_i &= \hat{p} \end{aligned}$$

A type-I error occurs when p is assumed to have changed (identification) when, in fact, p has remained the same. The probability of a type-I error, P_I, is based on the binomial distribution. When p is assumed as unchanged but, in reality, has changed, a type-II error occurs with probability P_{II}.

$$P_I = \sum_{d=c}^{n} \binom{n}{d} m^d (1-m)^{n-d} = 1 - \sum_{d=0}^{c-1} \binom{n}{d} m^d (1-m)^{n-d} \quad (9)$$

$$P_{II} = \sum_{d=0}^{c-1} \binom{n}{d} \hat{p}^d (1-\hat{p})^{n-d} \quad (10)$$

where   m is the mean of the updated beta distribution
             n is nearest integer of Nf (i.e., number sampled).

The wrong decision about p_i will accrue additional testing costs. Specifically, let the cost of a type-I error be represented as $C_I = A \cdot n_{(i,t)}/N$ (A: cost of sampling N items; $n_{(i,t)}$: number of items sampled from lot i at time t), and let C_{II} equal the cost of releasing a lot of N items whose average ratio of nonconforming items exceeds p_d (type-II error). When a type-I error occurs, n_t may be large relative to N, implying a large value for C_I. Assuming equal a priori probability for alternative hypotheses (8a), the testing cost equals:

$$C = \tfrac{1}{2}(C_I P_I + C_{II} P_{II}) \quad (11)$$

The value of C which minimizes this cost should be determined. Suppose a minimum c exists and is unique. The minimum of C is found by examining how (11) varies for two successive values,

---

[4] Durfee, pp. 61-64.

c and c+1. This evaluation simplifies to computing:

$$C(c+1)-C(c) = \tfrac{1}{2} \binom{n}{c} [C_{II}\, \hat{p}^c(1-\hat{p})^{n-c} - C_I\, m^c(1-m)^{n-c}] \qquad (12)$$

and examining the sign of the expression within the brackets

$$C_{II}\, \hat{p}^c(1-\hat{p})^{n-c} - C_I\, m^c(1-m)^{n-c}. \qquad (13)$$

When the value of c is increased by one, the first term of (13) is multiplied by $\hat{p}/(1-\hat{p})$ and the second term is multiplied by $m/(1-m)$, where $\hat{p}/(1-\hat{p})>m/(1-m)$. Therefore, (13) and consequently (12) are strictly increasing functions of c, implying the minimum of C, if it exists, is unique.

The minimizing value of c is determined by a sign change (negative to positive) in (13). Since (13) is negative for c=0, this sign change occurs in the range c>0 for reasonable choices of C_I and C_{II}. By (6), c must not exceed $Nf\hat{p}$. Thus, if (13) does not exhibit a sign change over the interval $(0,Nf\hat{p})$, c is set equal to $Nf\hat{p}$.

Instead of determining the value of c at the beginning of each cycle and using it for testing, recursive calculations simplify the testing procedure. Initially, (13) is computed at c=0. For each defective item found during sampling, (13) is computed recursively for the next value of c. As soon as either (13) changes sign or $d \geq Nf\hat{p}$, a change in the lot is assumed, and the sampling continues with $f=1$ to the end of the lot with a new identification of p started. However, if by the end of the lot sampling, neither of the two situations has occurred, no change in the lot is indicated, and identification and control proceeds with $E(p_i)=p$.

If a wrong decision is made about a change in p, the n_t items sampled since the start of the present identification and from which the relevant information is derived are no longer considered since a new identification of p begins. Therefore, to attain the same level of information as before, an additional n_t items require inspection. As aforementioned, when a type-I error occurs, n_t may be large relative to N, implying an elevated cost of a type-I error, C_I.

In order to reduce the costs of type-I and type-II errors and to improve the identification's reliability to detect changes in p, the initial testing procedure is extended to a double testing procedure. With the intent of verifying the change indicated in the previous lot, a second test is performed on the lot that immediately follows. The second test parallels the approach of the normal test, determining a c' such that if $d \geq c'$ by the end of the current lot, the change signaled in the prior lot is confirmed, otherwise rejected. However, the value of c' is not obtained by minimizing a cost function but by setting it equal to $Nf\hat{p}'$, where $\hat{p}'=m+K\sigma'$ (m', σ' refer to the beta distribution from the old identification, including the n_t items sampled from the prior lot at $f=1$). This selection of c' is justified since the previous and present (double test) lots are sampled at a higher frequency, implying increasingly accurate identifications. Also, double test costs are difficult to determine and are partly due to chance.

Minimization of costs or risks, C, related to the entire testing procedure depends upon f. Since C (11) is related to not only the sampling cost, $C_I = A \cdot f$ (for the entire lot) but also the cost of a type-II error, C_{II}, a reduction in the value of f (and thus, C_I) might not compensate for the corresponding increase in C_{II} (and thus, C). Since f depends upon σ which reduces as the lot sampling proceeds, the value of σ should not be decreased further and should be set equal to its last value, denoted σ_{min}, from the moment the savings in sampling costs ($A \cdot \delta f$) is less than the increase in total costs (δC).

The comparison is not performed when a change has been signaled in the previous lot since a new identification of p and a double test are occurring. If δC exceeds $A \cdot \delta f$, σ is maintained as a constant (σ_{min}) for the subsequent lots. If σ has previously been set equal to σ_{min} or if only two lots have been inspected, the comparison is not performed. In the instance of a signaled change that is confirmed, a new identification begins (including a new σ estimate) and the entire procedure starts anew. However, if the signaled change is not confirmed, the comparison of δC with $A \cdot \delta f$ proceeds, excluding the lot where the double test is performed.

CONCLUSIONS

An optimal testing procedure for controlling process output may be achieved only by an adaptive algorithm, depicted in Figure 2, in which identification and control occurs simultaneously. This approach surpasses standard techniques:

1) Since acceptance sampling procedures are not adaptive, only a course of action (accept or reject) is determined for each lot. No automatic feedback for adjusting the sampling frequency and minimizing the costs of risk is provided.

2) Although the p-chart may detect changes in the fraction defective, this Shewhart control chart does not indicate what increase in sampling frequency is necessary and does not utilize a double-testing procedure to verify changes. However, when the output from the adaptive technique is plotted on the p-chart, the sampled process stream is maintained in a state of statistical control even if the average fraction defective is greater than p_d.[5]

[5] Durfee, pp. 70-71, 74.

Figure 2 - Adaptive and Optimal Sampling Algorithm

$N, \; p_d, \; A, C_{II}$ **Input**

$i = 1$ **Initialization**

$f_i = 1 - P_d$

$\alpha_i = 1$

$\beta_i = 1$

$n = d = 0$ **Lot Initialization**

$n_i = \; d_i = n_i' = d_i' = 0$

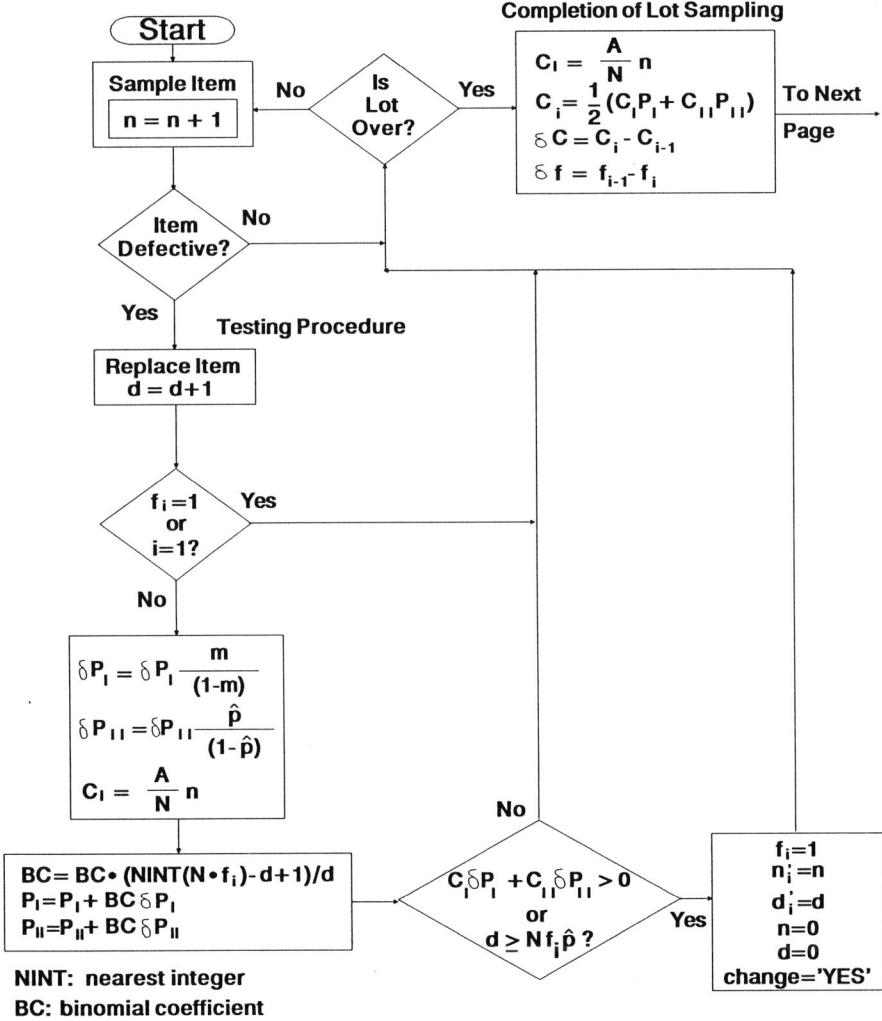

Completion of Lot Sampling

$$C_I = \frac{A}{N} \, n$$

$$C_i = \frac{1}{2}(C_I P_I + C_{II} P_{II})$$

$$\delta C = C_i - C_{i-1}$$

$$\delta f = f_{i-1} - f_i$$

Testing Procedure

$$\delta P_I = \delta P_I \frac{m}{(1-m)}$$

$$\delta P_{II} = \delta P_{II} \frac{\hat{p}}{(1-\hat{p})}$$

$$C_I = \frac{A}{N} \, n$$

$$BC = BC \cdot (NINT(N \cdot f_i) - d + 1)/d$$

$$P_I = P_I + BC \, \delta P_I$$

$$P_{II} = P_{II} + BC \, \delta P_{II}$$

$$C_I \delta P_I + C_{II} \delta P_{II} > 0$$

or

$$d \geq N f_i \hat{p} \; ?$$

$f_i = 1$

$n_i' = n$

$d_i' = d$

$n = 0$

$d = 0$

change = 'YES'

NINT: nearest integer

BC: binomial coefficient

Risk Cost Minimization

Double Testing Procedure

Updating Identification and Sampling Frequency

m: mean
V: variance

876

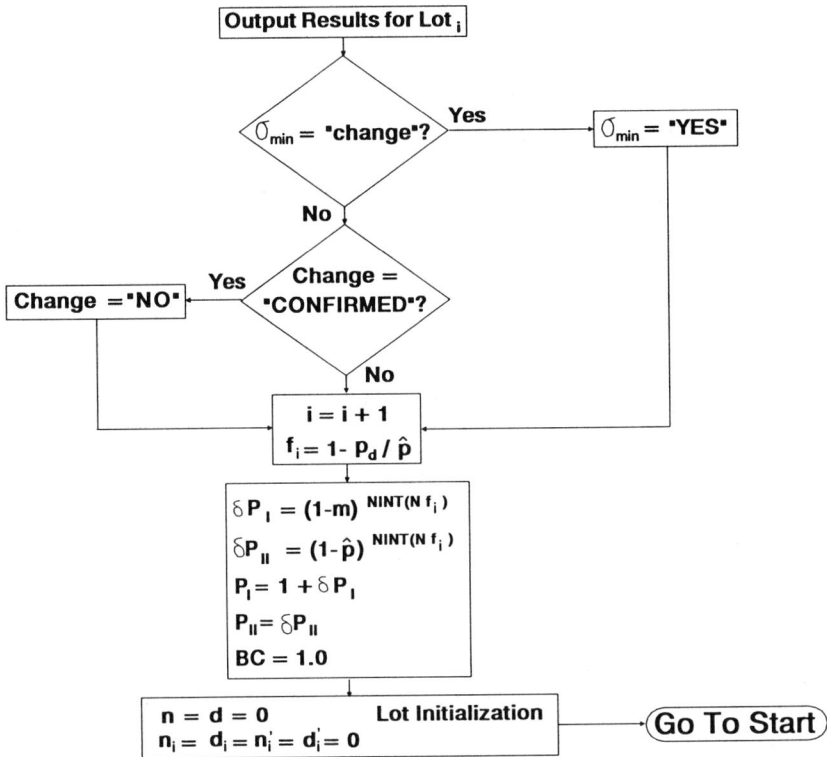

Output Results for Lot $_i$

$\sigma_{min} =$ "change"? — Yes → $\sigma_{min} =$ "YES"

No

Change $=$ "CONFIRMED"? — Yes → Change $=$ "NO"

No

$i = i + 1$
$f_i = 1 - P_d / \hat{p}$

$$\delta P_I = (1-m)^{NINT(N f_i)}$$
$$\delta P_{II} = (1-\hat{p})^{NINT(N f_i)}$$
$$P_I = 1 + \delta P_I$$
$$P_{II} = \delta P_{II}$$
$$BC = 1.0$$

$n = d = 0$ Lot Initialization
$n_i = d_i = n_i' = d_i' = 0$ → Go To Start

REFERENCES

Durfee, Melissa A. (1989) "Techniques for Identification and Optimization in Quality Control", Thesis, Worcester Polytechnic Institute.

Runggaldier, W. and Jacur, G. Romanin. (1973) "An Approach to Identification and Optimization in Quality Control", Lecture Notes in Computer Science, vol. 3, New York, Springer-Verlag.

BIOGRAPHICAL SKETCH

Melissa Durfee has a B.S. in Applied Mathematics from Brown University and a M.S. in Applied Mathematics from Worcester Polytechnic Institute (W.P.I.). She is pursuing a Ph.D. in Manufacturing Engineering at W.P.I and is employed at Wyman-Gordon Company as a Senior SPC Analyst.

Productivity & Quality Management Frontiers-IV, edited by Sumanth, Edosomwan, Poupart, and Sink. ©1993 Institute of Industrial Engineers.

TQM in Modular Housing:
Big Lessons from a Smallish Industry

F. Grobler
USACERL
Champaign, Illinois USA

J. Willenbrock
Pennsylvania State University
State College, Pennsylvania USA

Many large, mature manufacturing industries are well convinced of the benefits of TQM. Sophisticated corporations have evolving techniques for measuring the cause-effect relationships of quality on productivity and prosperity. However, in some smaller industries the questions prevail. Is it worth the effort and cost? Is there a proven relationship between TQM and consumer satisfaction in my industry? If quality in my industry is based purely on subjective consumer satisfaction, how does it affect the bottom line?

The study reported in this paper addressed these and other issues in a small, highly fragmented industry - the modular home manufacturing industry. This industry is characterized by a large number of small companies using labor-intensive manufacturing techniques with minimal automation. Unlike mobile homes, modular homes have to comply with all local building codes. A two-tier distribution system is customary where the manufactured home is sold by the manufacturer to a "builder-dealer", who completed the finishing of the home before it is sold to the consumer. It is typical that very little feedback occurs between these tiers on quality issues.

The paper describes a study conducted in Summer and Fall of 1992. Three manufacturer were selected, each with a different tenure of experience with TQM. These manufacturers were rated on a TQM metric developed for this purpose, to determine how successfully they have assimilated TQM in the organization. The ratings were the result of extended on-site work with the manufacturers. Through extensive questionnaires to the builder-dealers of each manufacturer, and in turn the consumers who purchased homes from the builder dealers, the perceptions of quality throughout the chain were related to TQM programs at the manufacturers. Significant conclusions emerged in this study which have wide ranging implications for TQM in smaller industries.

These lessons are discussed in detail in the paper, and their application to other small industries are suggested.

Productivity & Quality Management Frontiers-IV, edited by Sumanth, Edosomwan, Poupart, and Sink. ©1993
Institute of Industrial Engineers.

Control Dimensional Variation of Stamping Panels

Z. Zhou and X.-R. Cao
The University of Michigan
Ann Arbor, Michigan USA

Abstract

This paper presents a research based case study in stamping operation of automobile industry. The focus of the work is about the dimensional quality of the stamped panel details and its impact on the assembly line.

The stamping panels are made from sheet metal going through blanking, drawing, trimming, piercing, and flanging operations in the press room. The dimensional quality, especially the 6 sigma variations of the panels plays a vitally important role in controlling the dimensional quality of the assembled auto bodies. Variations for stamping panels appear mainly in the form of within run variation and run to run variation. To control and reduce the dimensional variations of the stamping panels, we go in two steps: (1) use optimal control parameters to reduce within run variation, and (2) exercise disciplined repeatable set up each time running the same job to reduce run to run variation. To find the optimal control parameters in (1), a statistical experiment was conducted for a rear right door inner panel. The inner and outer tonnages on the draw press and the shut heights on the re-draw and flanging presses are selected as the key control parameters. An optical coordinate measurement machine (OCMM) called Flexible Measurement System (FMS) was used to measure the dimensional variations of some key characteristic points. It was found that the tonnages and the shut heights (essentially the amount of force hitting the sheet metal) have the direct impact on the dimensional variations of the stamping details. Optimal tonnages and shut heights are found through the experiment. The 6 sigma variations before and after the control of the tonnages and shut heights are compared and show significant reduction.

This work, for the first time, provides a practical useful direction on how to control the dimensional variations of the stamping panels in a real industry environment. The entire work was conducted on the floor of a stamping plant and the approach was adopted by the production process in the stamping plant.

Part IV
PRODUCTIVITY AND QUALITY MANAGEMENT PROCESS

1. Planning and Organizing for Productivity and Quality Management Process

2. Managing the Resistance to Change to Productivity and Quality Thinking

3. Compensation and Productivity Gainsharing Systems

4. Training and Retraining Processes During Periods of Productivity Gains

5. Employee Empowerment and its Impact on Technical, Social, and Financial Aspects of Business

6. Research-Based Case Studies

7. Managing Change-Results on Productivity and Quality

Productivity & Quality Management Frontiers-IV, edited by Sumanth, Edosomwan, Poupart, and Sink. ©1993 Institute of Industrial Engineers.

Planning and Organizing Complex Conceptual Design Process for Productivity and Quality

H. Shen
University of Minnesota
Minneapolis, Minnesota USA

ABSTRACT

It has been widely recognized that both productivity and quality are significantly affected by decisions made during the design phase. So far, productivity and quality research has been concerned more with improvements during the later design phases, such as Taguchi's designs. Much attention has not yet been given to productivity and quality improvements during the conceptual design phase. Errors made during this phase can be among the most elusive.

Design problems usually are complex, and also human activities involved in a specific design are complex. These two complexities relate to both engineering and management functions within a company. Decomposition can reduce such complexities. Conceptual design problems are often non-hierarchical. Planning and organizing the conceptual design process through the organizational hierarchy of management and engineering becomes a very challenging problem.

This paper studies scopes of various decomposition methods and applications during the conceptual design phase. Based on theses studies, conceptual design could be strategically planned and organized. As a result, design problems will be decomposed into several subproblems of hierarchy, and design engineers will be assigned to various tasks. Such planning and organizing provides a good basis for design iteration.

Coordination play an important role during the iteration process of design. After each design team submits its solution, a coordination problem firms up, i.e., how can optimal design of the global design problem be generated from many solutions of subdesign problems? Industrial engineers are supposed to answer such questions within a company. The principles guided further design activities are proposed here. Certain rules are also established for ensuring higher productivity and quality.

Keywords. Conceptual design, design management, decomposition, design engineering, productivity, quality, and industrial engineering.

Productivity & Quality Management Frontiers-IV, edited by Sumanth, Edosomwan, Poupart, and Sink. ©1993 Institute of Industrial Engineers.

Ethics in Productivity and Quality Management

A.I. Stainer
Middlesex University Business School
London, England UNITED KINGDOM

L. Stainer
University of Hertfordshire Business School
Hertfordshire, England UNITED KINGDOM

A B S T R A C T

The paper provides a critique of the present state of the art of the relationship between productivity and quality, including the Deming Chain Reaction and Quality-Productivity Ratios. The Productivity and Customer-Driven Quality Cycles are discussed in economic and social terms, putting forward guidelines for both improved performance and job satisfaction for the individual, leading to more effective management.

Within this framework, ethical issues are analysed. These encompass aspects such as motivation of the work force, stress and health factors, safety, creativity and respect. Conflicts are shown to exist between corporate and individual aspirations and standards of conduct. Other key concerns relate to the social responsibility towards employees, community and other stakeholders. Examples include the professions as well as manufacturing and service industries, from a European perspective.

Ethical behaviour must be integrated within the productivity and quality management process. This ultimately leads to a better understanding of organisations' responsibilities as well as enhance perception of their reputation. The synergy between productivity, quality and morality improves performance in achieving the corporate objectives and goals.

KEY WORDS

Britain	Ethics
Management	Morality
Productivity	Quality

1.   THE PRODUCTIVITY AND QUALITY RELATIONSHIP

Productivity, whether partial or total, and quality are closely related. Managers have always intuitively known this, even though some of their reactions and decisions seem to defy the fact.   Lee Iacocca turned the phrase "Quality and Productivity - they go together" into one of his four measures when he assumed the helm of the troubled Chrysler Corporation.

Unfortunately, many managers believe that quality improvement will result in decreased productivity, as an improved product or service may take more time to produce and cost more.   And, although productivity improvement is frequently associated with improvements in technology, such as automation, these alone cannot be relied upon to solve many productivity problems.   Therefore, the relationship between quality and sales, quality and productivity, quality and profit, quality and competitive position, have never been really understood by most managers.   This is particularly true of much of British and European industry where they are only beginning to comprehend the teachings of Deming.

Aguayo (1990) is correct in assuming that probably the most stimulating part of Deming's approach is his treatment of the relationships between quality, cost, productivity and profit.   As quality is increased, costs decrease, setting in motion a chain reaction.   Better quality leads to lower costs and higher productivity.   Businesses with lower costs can pass along some of the savings to their customers in the form of lower prices.   The businesses' customers get the best of both worlds, better quality and lower prices.   This allows the business to capture markets and increase its market share, which in turn allows it to survive and provide more jobs. The Deming approach, whose adoption by the Japanese is now legend, is of a strategic nature.   Garvin (1992) states that there are three major competitive operations strategies : competing on quality, competing on productivity and competing on new products and processes.   It is felt that it is the synergy between these three strategies that is vital to the future of both manufacturing and service industries.

There have been attempts to make the productivity quality connection at a more operational level.   Adam et al (1981) introduce the concept of quality-productivity ratios, where unit costs of processing and rework are considered separately to account for the quality changes in an organisation.   The basic appeal of quality-productivity ratios is that they clearly illustrate that when quality improves, so will productivity.   However, these ratios can often be misleading when they are dependent on the number of rejected items.   Lawlor (1985) talks about quality productivity, that is where the cost of quality is dependent upon the design specification as well as how effectively the workforce conforms to that specification.   A method he advocates is that cost trends of all rework and scrap should be shown as a percentage of costs on a moving quarterly average.

According to Heap (1992) productivity is the organisation's aim whilst quality is the customer's aim. Any effort to undermine either of these is only addressing part of an overall business success scenario. This concept is supported by Evans et al (1990) who believe that the quality cycle must be customer-driven, the major objective of which is to translate customer needs into product or service specifications. Any quality cycle must link in with its productivity cousin, as expounded by Sumanth (1984), in its four phases of measurement, evaluation, planning and improvement.

Managers are faced with many challenges relating to the improvement of productivity and quality. The four major areas are :

   (1) to effectively manage technology and change

   (2) to provide the workforce with sufficient knowledge and tools

   (3) to motivate the workforce by ensuring understanding for the need for such improvements

   (4) to create an ethical climate within the organisation

In recent years, there has been much talk of business ethics but little has been focussed to quality and productivity management thinking.

2. THE ETHICAL PERSPECTIVE

Ethics is no easy subject. Through time, ethical issues have been discussed theologically and philosophically. There was always concern for morality and, as Ferrell and Fraedrich (1991) advocate, "each religion applied its moral concepts not only to business but also to, government, politics, family, personal life, and all other aspects of life". According to Boone and Kurtz (1987), business ethics "are questions about the right and wrong of actions that arise in a work environment; the business person's standard of conduct and moral values." But, what is good or bad? What is right or wrong? What is acceptable by society and what is not? These are questions that managers, in a business environment, ought to ask themselves when addressing problems and making decisions. Their dilemma is that they need to balance the legal, profitable and ethical issues, where legal is the lowest denominator of acceptable ethical behaviour.

Businesses are comprised of individuals, be they rogues, angels or 'in-between'. It is often their principles and personal values that are crucial in decision making. Furthermore, management's ethical behaviour is dependent upon :
                     - the business situation itself
                     - the task to be performed
                     - the group of peers
                     - the leadership style
                     - past experience

Also, managers must recognise how they intend to continue to operate in the business environment. Whatever the outcome of a decision, they need to focus on its consequences and anticipate whether it would withstand the lapse of time. This is especially relevant because of the greater exposure by the media and more public awareness of ethical issues.

Within the framework of improved productivity and the competitive issue of quality, it is important to consider in great detail the consequential aspects and the ethical issues that may be encountered. As Shetty and Buehler (1988) state, making companies productive and competitive is the ultimate responsibility of the manager. Unfortunately, managers often believe in updating equipment rather than developing and training their employees. However, in Germany and Sweden, as well as Japan, both productivity and quality have been improved through giving more autonomy to the workforce. It is true that industries do not like to admit that employees who work long hours, more meticulously, and too hard, can create long term 'losses' for an organisation. They need to be aware of the reasons for illness, absenteeism, turnover of human resources, with their consequences in both economic and social terms.

In this regard, a key issue relates especially stress with its physical, behavioural and psychological effects. Schermerhorn (1989) suggests that there is a relationship between stress and performance. From low to moderate stress intensity, constructive stress, there is a positive impact on personal productivity, whilst from moderate to high stress intensity, destructive stress, there is a negative impact. In Japan, karoshi, death from overwork, is estimated at 10,000 cases a year. In Britain, the British United Provident Association [BUPA] (1992), a private health care group, carried out a survey which showed that 33% of all stress is job related, rising to 48% for men. In 1991, over 100 million working days were lost in Britain through job stress related illness. Interestingly, blue collar workers were twice as vulnerable to stress as their white collar cousins.

Motivating the workforce to produce products and services more efficiently and of a high calibre quality must be a top priority for a manager. This should enhance loyalty towards the organisation, breed self-respect and respect from peers, as well as encourage creativity and self-development. It can also improve job satisfaction, leading to a more effective management. Mathis and Jackson (1991) state that there are three kinds of individual performances that organisations need to prosper : productivity, innovation and loyalty.

In relation to productivity and quality, conflicts in ethical behaviour often occur, whether between the employee and the organisation, the employee and the consumer or the employee and society. Employees seem to 'sense' whether an organisation is ethical or not. But what constitutes an 'ethical establishment'? Which and whose rules and standards are followed, whether they are communicated verbally or in writing? Are there legal requirements? Are there Codes of Ethics? It is because the basic acceptable moral standards are not adhered to that regulations, and more regulations, are needed. That is why an organisation is only as ethical as the people it employs. As Carmichael and Drummond (1989) advocate, the individual responsibility should equate the corporate responsibility within an ethical framework.

3.   THE PRODUCTIVITY, QUALITY AND ETHICAL SYNERGY

Kurosawa (1991) points out that the ethico-resource dimension is the foundation of corporate capacity in relation to productivity and reflects how effectively the business resources are raised, created, fostered and accumulated.   Frederick et al (1992) believe that organisations must balance competititive pressure with community needs. In other words, the   productivity and quality demands of both business and society must be respected.

Social responsibility in business means that organisations should be held accountable for any actions that may affect people, the community and the environment.   However, in practice, the business is often limited in its social responsibility by decisions that might impair productivity and quality, that are too costly, or that are unrelated to the company goals.   MacShane (1992) argues that the Japanese car industry, by an insular attitude, has created a gap between the companies and society, causing trade conflict and misreading of consumer requirements.

Though there is acceptance of the philosophy of social responsibility, it is not always practised.   This is because it is a voluntary commitment from each individual, who has different values and beliefs. Therefore, it is the synergy between productivity, quality and morality that improves performance, achieving goals both at the operational and strategic levels.

Drucker (1991) believes that, in this century, the productivity improvements in the making and moving industries have been a major factor in wealth creation.   He also advocates that, today, management's first social responsibility is the raising of productivity of knowledge and service workers.   Professionals, such as accountants, lawyers, doctors, engineers and academics, are, to a great extent, bound by the ethics of their profession, that is the conduct, aim and quality which characterise that particular profession.   Over the last decade, professionals have been working in an increasingly competitive environment.   Allied to this, as Albrecht (1992) mentions, increased pressures for recruitment and retention of customers, clients and staff, and a greater strive for operating efficiency, have evolved.

Professionals have often been concentrating their efforts on short-term goals to 'maximise the bottom line' rather than aiming for long-term productivity and quality improvement.   An auditor, who is given an unreasonable time constraint to complete his/her report, would probably achieve it in the long hours of the night, compromising quality.   In Britain,   there have been instances   where engineers,   especially in the construction industry, have ignored health and safety regulations for the purpose of deadline completions. In 1991, over 100,000 major industrial injuries were mostly caused by the laxity of safety and, of these, only 3% lead to prosecution. In the British National Health Service, on average, junior doctors at present work over 80 hours per week, which has an adverse effect on the quality of service they provide.

There are strong arguments 'for' ethical behaviour in organisations. The four most important aspects relating to the productivity and quality scenario are :

    (a) the corporate image, both internally and externally

    (b) a better environment, in and out of the workplace

    (c) the avoidance of stricter government regulation

    (d) the prevention of social problems rather than their cure

Crosby (1992) points out that, in the field of quality, there has been much debate but little direction. He believes that governments and authorities have the illusion that they can make up rules about quality and think that, if their philosophy is adopted, organisations will prosper. But, in reality, this is not so as their implementation is more complicated. For instance, Europeans, exporting the ISO 9000 quality criteria and attempting to 'colonise' from Malaysia to Mexico, may be using methods that are not culturally appropriate. The same could be said with regard to productivity, when it is expected that Japanese methods could be successfully implanted in the West. In implementing quality and productivity change, the ethical issues have often been under-estimated or ignored.

In decision making, managers must appreciate that there is a close link between productivity, quality and ethical concerns. In Europe, there are clear examples of conflict between these elements within the energy debate in relationship to the use of fossil fuels and nuclear energy. Industry, governments and the European Economic Community are discussing the economic and social issues of progress against the environmental consequences globalised, to some extent, in the Earth Summit in Rio de Janeiro in Summer 1992.

4.   THE WAY FORWARD

Separately, Stainer (1989) and Winfield (1990) surveyed over 500 British companies. The former looked at productivity practices and had a response rate of 80%, whilst the latter investigated ethical concerns with just over a 10% response. It is felt that, perhaps, this may demonstrate the reluctance and timidity of the respondents when the subject of ethics is approached.

However, the future is far more encouraging. Today, in Europe, there are several conferences on business ethics and a greater awareness in business education of its importance. More and more organisations are producing and implementing codes of practice and performance standards. Their application has particularly blossomed under public pressure which led to the present British Government's Charter Initiatives to ensure greater responsiveness to society.

In order to develop an ethical climate in business, especially in relation to productivity and quality, there are four basic steps to pursue :

Step 1 - Prepare a statement, or code of ethics, outlining what the organisation expects in the way of ethical behaviour, with clear links with productivity and quality

Step 2 - Give clear guidelines for implementation, enabling employees to understand and participate in an ethical corporate culture

Step 3 - Ensure compliance by establishing mechanisms for violation and for questionable practices

Step 4 - Monitor the ethical policy and revise as necessary

In any organisation, whether in the manufacturing, extractive or service industry, with whatever the mix of stakeholders, a blend can be created by combining productivity and quality improvements with ethical behaviour to give a triadic gain, which is the economic and moral 'gain' in both operational and strategic terms

In the words of John H. Stookey, President and Chairman of Quantum Chemical Corporation, "Ethical issues come down to the fundamental question of how much of today's benefit you are willing to forgo for tomorrow's gain".

5.   REFERENCES

Adam, E.E. Jr., Hershauer, J.C. and Ruch, W.A. (1981) Productivity and Quality, Englewood Cliffs, Prentice-Hall

Aguayo, R. (1990) Dr. Deming, New York, Fireside

Albrecht, W.S. (1992) Ethical Issues in the Practice of Accounting, Cincinnati, South-Western Publishing

Boone, L.E. and Kurtz, D.L. (1987) Contemporary Business, Chicago, The Dryden Press

British United Provident Association [BUPA] (1992) as reported by Fletcher, D. "Jobs Are Chief Cause of Stress", The Daily Telegraph, London, 19 April 1992

Carmichael, S. and Drummond, J. (1989) Good Business, London, Business Books

Crosby, P. (1992) "Viewpoint - Philip Crosby on Quality Leadership in the Global Marketplace", The Quality Observer, May 1992, vol. 1, no. 7, p.2

Drucker, P.F. (1991) "The New Productivity Challenge", Harvard Business Review, November/December 1991, pp.69-79

Evans, J.R., Anderson, D.R., Sweeney, D.J. and Williams, T.A. (1990) Applied Production and Operations Management, St. Paul, West Publishing

Ferrell, O.C. and Fraedrich J. (1991) Business Ethics, Boston, Houghton Mifflin

Frederick, W.C., Post, J.E. and Davis, K. (1992) Business and Society, New York, McGraw-Hill

Garvin, D.A. (1992) Operations Strategy, Englewood Cliffs, Prentice-Hall

Heap, J. (1992) Productivity Management : A Fresh Approach, London, Cassell Educational

Kurosawa, K. (1991) Productivity Measurement and Management at the Company Level : The Japanese Experience, Amsterdam, Elsevier

Lawlor, A. (1985) Productivity Improvement Manual, Aldershot, Gower

MacShane, D. (1992) "Japanese Car Empire is Attacked by its Exhausted Workforce", The Guardian, London, 1 June 1992

Mathis, R.L. and Jackson, J.H. (1991) Personnel/Human Resource Management, St. Paul, West Publishing

Schermerhorn, J.R. Jr. (1989) Management for Productivity, New York, John Wiley

Shetty, Y.K. and Buehler, V.M. (1988) Productivity and Quality Through Science and Technology, New York, Quorum Books

Stainer, A.I. (1989) "Productivity Practices in the United Kingdom", Paper presented at the Xth Internaitonal Conference on Production Research, University of Nottingham, August 1989

Sumanth, D.J. (1984) Productivity Engineering and Management, New York, McGraw-Hill

Winfield, M. (1990) Minding Your Own Business, London, Social Audit

BIOGRAPHICAL NOTES

Alan I. Stainer. Chartered Engineer with over 20 years managerial experience in British and American organisations. MSc in Technological Economics. PhD, on the Productivity in Longwall Mining of Hard Coal. Head of Engineering Management, Middlesex University Business School. Productivity Consultant.

Lorice Stainer. MSc in Decision Making. Senior Lecturer in Business Organisation at the University of Hertfordshire Business School. Teaching and Research specialising in Business Ethics, Risk Perception and Decision Making. Member of the Institute of Management Services.

Productivity & Quality Management Frontiers-IV, edited by Sumanth, Edosomwan, Poupart, and Sink. ©1993 Institute of Industrial Engineers.

Managing the Process of Change in a Productivity Project

K.H.M. Rosander
Chalmers University of Technology
Göteborg, SWEDEN

This paper is based on a case study at the Swedish company Hägglunds Denison Drives. The company is producing large hydraulic motors in small batches. The paper describes a productivity improvement project and how the process of change were managed in the project. The background of the project were problems with high cost per units produced and low security of delivery accuracy. The material flow was disrupted by a limited number of parts and the arrangement of the workshop layout. The planning of the workshop was done with a MRP system, managed by a central planning department. The vision for the change formulated by the senior management for the productivity improvement project were: organise a flow oriented work shop, establish production groups, each production group should have the total responsibility of the entire production and the groups should be managed without supervisors.

Different approaches for change used are mainly, the sociotechnical approach, the organisational development, the bureaucratic model, the *KAIZEN* concept and the "democratic dialogue model" . Previously an action oriented model which is a combination of socio technique and the democratic dialogue model, called the Gothenburg model has been presented. It was decided to use a model called the Gothenburg model for the productivity improvement project, it has earlier been successful at the Swedish companies VOLVO and SKF.

Among the middle and lower management of the company, it was found that the resistance against change was much larger than anyone could believe before the project started. When the workers once where convinced that they had some benefits out of the changes, they where willing to change. Therefore the will for change was to address as an information problem. By following the Gothenburg model it was possible to go through the project with success. It took almost two years to complete the project and the results achieved where:

Measure	Change in %
Break-even level # units sold	- 23
Change in production cost	- 13
Change in distribution cost	- 25
Accuracy of deliveries	+ 20

Key words: manage, change-process, productivity improvement project

INTRODUCTION

When a company needs to change this often occurs when there is economical problem, the competition is increasing or the top management want to make a change by various reasons. Most managers are aware of the fact that there is a growing need for the organisations to be able to handle the process of change. The speed by which the need for changes seems to be occurring is increasing since the the competition is increasing more and more. This has to do with factors such as :

- increased internationalisation of the entire value chain from vendors and producers to end customers
- extended need to monitor and invest in technology and competence development concerning both products and business processes
- increased customer demands on quality, lead times and delivery performance
- national and regional characteristics reflected in changing attitudes
- the competence for change within the companies

described by Beer (1990), Weisbord (1987), Harrington (1991), Björk (1990) and Sarv (1991).

To manage the process of change is not a trend, it is a question of survival. Companies must be developed to be able to remain in business over a period of time. Some companies are very profitable in one business while some are restructured and some dies on the same markets. The differences between the companies are the competence and how they manage the process of change, Sarv (1991).

Almost everyone can agree on the fact that we must be able to handle the process of change and what to do . The question that now arises is how to manage the process of change. This paper describes common approaches to change and shows how a radical productivity improvement project was implemented successfully by using the Gothenburg model.

FRAME OF REFERENCE

The frame of reference is build upon earlier known theories about how to manage the process of change in an organisation. There is mainly two dominating approaches of how to manage the process of change Karlsson (1992). The socio-technical approach is described by Trist (1981), Van Eijnatten (1990) and Pasmore (1988). The organisational development approach is described by Huse and Cummings (1985), French and Bell (1990).
There is although other perspectives existing as the Japanese *KAIZEN* described by Imai (1986), the "democratic dialogue model" described by Gustavsen (1991) and the beraucratic model Tischy (1986). Lately a change model to solve the conflicts which always occur in design oriented research has been introduced by Chalmers University of Technology called the Gothenburg model.

This model has been used with success by large companies like VOLVO and SKF. The Gothenburg model is described in figure 1 below

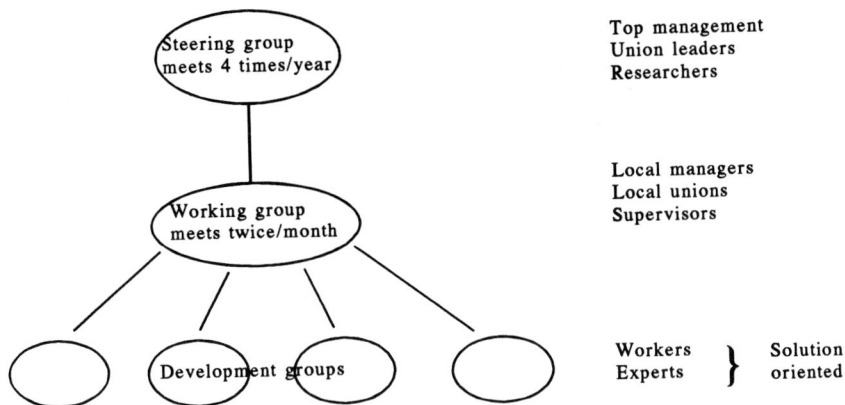

Figure 1. The Gothenburg model

The advantage of the Gothenburg model is that there is a mechanism to handle conflicts in the steering committee and that the development groups will accept the solutions to questions since it has been their responsibility to find them. If the steering committee is changed toward a reference committee there is a risk that the project will collapse since the conflict handling mechanisms are not as powerful as in a steering committee. Varela (1971) describes other way to handle conflicts even if they are more time consuming then the Gothenburg model, Karlsson (1992).

When setting up the guidelines for the project: technical, economical and social goals must be formulated since each production system always is a compromise between different goals, Karlsson (1992). To manage the change is very difficult but it is essential for long term survival. Sarv (1991) has formulated four prerequisites of what must be fulfilled in order to be able to successfully manage the process of change:

- insight of reality, how are we functioning today, what is the demands of the future?
- vision, what does competence of change mean to us
- ideas of what to change in order to increase the overall productivity
- a road to follow and thereby makes ideas and visions to reality

If the above is fulfilled and spread to the entire organisation there will be will to change in the long run according to Sarv (1991).

DESCRIPTION OF THE PROJECT

The project which has been the case in this study has been implemented at Hägglunds Denison Drives, a Swedish company which produces large high torque hydraulic motors and power units. The organisation of the company at the time before the project was to be regarded as functional. The resistance against change had in earlier projects shown to bee high. A psychologist had ranked the resistance to 2 on a scale from 1 - 7, where 7 represents a high will to change. The production consists of a lot of metal cutting with very narrow tolerances. The top management formulated the following vision of how the company should be organised and functioning:

The old centralised way of organisation shall be abandoned, we shall create a number of more or less autonomous production groups where each employee is responsible for the entire workload from input to output within his/hers area.

The social, technical and economical goal was formulated by the steering committee and the management team. Examples of goals that where formulated are:

- the break even level should be decreased by 20%
- the delivery time should be decreased with 50%
- the cost per unit should be decreased by 17%
- the cost of distribution should be decreased by 10%
- the workers shall be able to perform 3 different tasks
- necessary authorities shall be delegated to the production groups

Within the workshop the following main principles where established:

- own and limited area within the workshop
- each part is produced to completation within the production group
- the size of a production group is 4 - 10 members
- each member is able to do 3 or more tasks within the group
- a schedule between tasks within the group, time of rotation is 1 week
- no supervisor within the group
- increased flexibility regarding products and volume

The tasks that each group should be responsible for where the following:

- material transportation
- workshop planning
- machine set-ups and programming
- production
- quality
- maintenance of standard faults

Regarding the arrangement of the workshop it should be arranged according to the material flow and the MRP system should be abandoned and a push-pull system implemented for the high volume value parts instead.

The principal workshop and the material flow is shown in figure 2 below. In this figure the responsibility of the production groups can be seen.

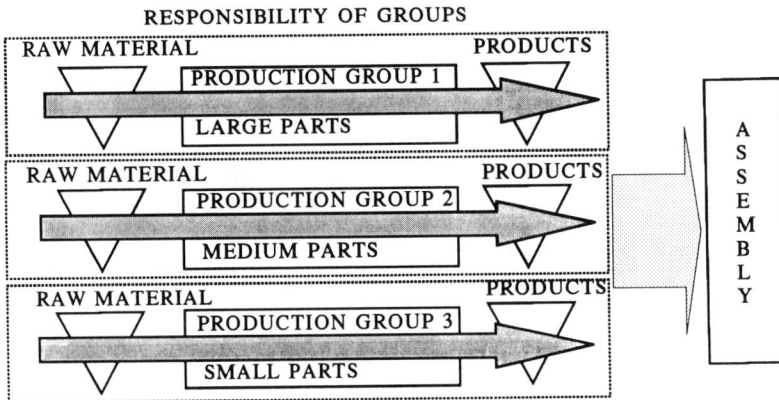

Figure 2. The principal workshop layout and material flow.

DESCRIPTION OF THE PROCESS OF CHANGE

The first step of the study was to create a description of the project based upon a vision formulated by the president of the company. Thereafter the goals to reach in terms of technical, economical and social were set by the management team and the steering committee.

At this time the unions were informed by the company, the description and the goals of the project were presented. The comments from the unions were taken under consideration and some changes were made.

Thereafter it was decided to use the design oriented change strategy together with a variant of the Gothenburg for the conflict handling. The project organisation presented in figure 3 below differs from the Gothenburg model presented in the frame of reference slightly since there is no conflict handling group where for questions that had to be negotiated with the union. Instead questions that could cause conflicts with the union were presented to the reference committee and thereafter negotiated. The reason for this is that the union did not want to give mandate to their members to solve the conflicts together with the company.

The unions requested centralised negotiations between their negotiation groups and the company.

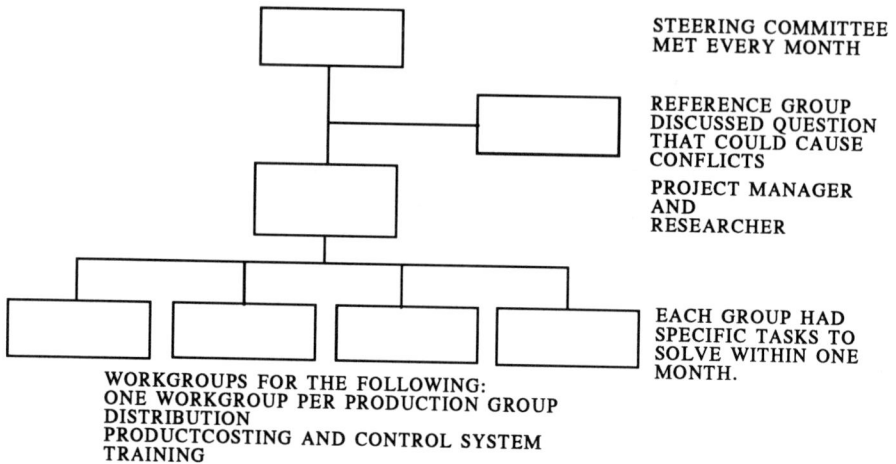

STEERING COMMITTEE MET EVERY MONTH

REFERENCE GROUP DISCUSSED QUESTION THAT COULD CAUSE CONFLICTS

PROJECT MANAGER AND RESEARCHER

EACH GROUP HAD SPECIFIC TASKS TO SOLVE WITHIN ONE MONTH.

WORKGROUPS FOR THE FOLLOWING:
ONE WORKGROUP PER PRODUCTION GROUP
DISTRIBUTION
PRODUCTCOSTING AND CONTROL SYSTEM
TRAINING

Figure 3. The project organisation

To secure that all groups were working in the same direction, the project manager and researcher joined the meetings in the workgroups as often as possible.

The experienced difficulties in the implementation of the productivity improvement project are the following:

- to secure that the employees have valid and reliable information
- to get the middle management to cooperate
- to pursue the blue collar to change their way of work
- to create alternative careers for personnel which were not needed in the changed organisation
- to train the employees about the new way of working and their new tasks

The information to the employees should have been taken care of by the unions and the members in the different workgroups. This was a mistake because the union did not feel the responsibility to inform their employees about the changes. After 1 year there where much criticism against the project since the people had got little information. The project management decided therefore to have a meeting with all employees where the concept where explained and the results this far where presented. Thereafter the grumbling about the project was decreased and the project could be implemented through-out almost on time schedule.

The middle management wanted to protect their territory and their role within the company and there were little incentive to this group to change. Therefore this group was most difficult to cooperate with. The blue collar needed a person which they could rely on as a contact person, the workgroups were not enough. After shown results at the assembly department the magnitude of this problem decreased.

Historically this company do not have successful story of change and the people thought that they where going to get layed off as the project were completed. When the company had showed that people did not get layed off according to this project the resistance against change decreased but it did never disappear totally.

A training program were created and it included 40 - 80 hours of practical training per person involved in the project. To this we must add the time it took to learn the new tasks out in the workshop.

The total time for the completation of the project was 2.5 years. The critical occasions in the projects are shown in figure 4 below.

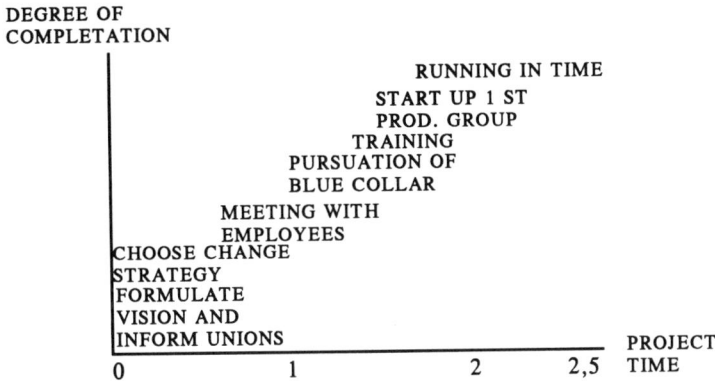

DEGREE OF
COMPLETATION

```
                              RUNNING IN TIME
                         START UP 1 ST
                          PROD. GROUP
                           TRAINING
                        PURSUATION OF
                        BLUE COLLAR
              MEETING WITH
              EMPLOYEES
        CHOOSE CHANGE
        STRATEGY
        FORMULATE
        VISION AND
        INFORM UNIONS                        PROJECT
        0            1           2      2,5   TIME
```

Figure 4 The critical occasions and different happenings in the project

RESULTS OF THE PROJECT

The goal of establishing an organisation with no supervisors has been fulfilled. Twenty percent of them are used in production support, the persons selected are skilled specialists workin with all groups. The production groups are following a rotation schedule with a rotation cycle of 1 week. Each member of the groups have the knowledge of performing 3 tasks or more. The groups are performing the different tasks that where described earlier with few exceptions. It has been possible to delegate the necessary authorities to the groups since a framework of rules have been implemented.

The new organisation is shown in figure 5 below.

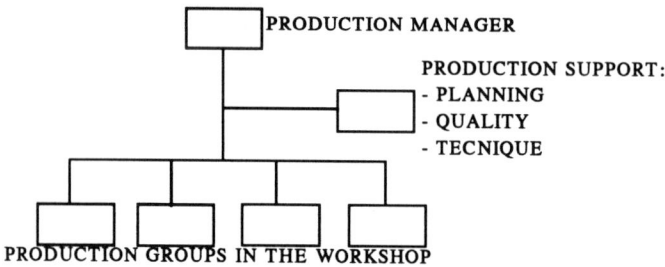

Figure 5. The new organisation with out supervisors

The goal of to decrease the deliverytime from 4 to 2 weeks has been met. This delivery time is for standard products. The deliverytime for non standard has been decreased with 2 weeks. This means that the company now has a substantial advantage to its competitors regarding time.

The economical goals have been met as follows

Measure	Change in %
Break-even level # units sold	- 23
Change in production cost	- 13
Change in distribution cost	- 25
Accuracy of deliveries	+ 20

DISCUSSION AND CONCLUSION

To manage the process of change is very difficult but it is necessary that a company that wants to survive in the future will learn how to handle it. The most important part in creating conditions for change is to establish a culture within the company which stresses change and makes it a natural part of the working life. Therefore the *KAIZEN* is something to strive for since it makes change a part of the working life. But to get from where we are today and against a process that is willing to change there must be something in between. When talking about change it is where important to keep in mind what kind of change that is going to be done.

If the changes are radical and large the *KAIZEN* concept might not be the best concept to use since it can be difficult to require that the personnel sometimes lay-off them self, which in some cases can be the result of a change. Therefore the *KAIZEN* concept would not have been successful in this project.

The bureaucratic model has been used with success by SAAB lately. Although when there is a resistance against change this will sometime lead to conflicts which can be difficult to handle without loosing tempo in the process of change. Also after some time after the implementation things tend to become the same as they were prior the change if there is not a broad acceptance for the change. Since the resistance against change where large this model would not have been functioning well for this project.

The dialogue model is not complete since it lacks the conflict handling mechanism. Since conflicts are common in such a radical change this mechanism is essential for success. Therefore the dialogue model would not have been as good as the model used to implement the changes.

The experience gained from the project is that it is extremely important to be aware of the different types of conflicts that will occur. To solve the conflicts the Gothenburg model or a variant of it is has several advantages. The largest is that it forces people with different objectives within a organisation together in a group where a critical discussion can be held and thereby makes it possibly to within a limited time make decisions in the discussed questions.

The development groups used in the Gothenburg model are responsible for solutions to a lot of problems and questions. Therefore they will have extremely little resistance against the changes. In the project described it would have been better to have a steering group which would have included the unions so that the discussions could have been held and the decisions taken instead of having a reference group and separate negotiations with the unions as we had. One more reflection is that it is very important that the management group (manager) of the project will have high organisational authority. The reason for this is that when an organisation have a lean structure and the area managers want their workload to be performed people tend to priorities their organisational tasks. Therefore it is critical to the success of a project to get high priority within every department were tasks belonging to the project shall be performed.

The three best models for change are the *KAIZEN* , the bureaucratic model and the Gothenburg model. They have all different advantages and can be seen as complementary. The *KAIZEN* concept is where useful in the process of continuous improvement The bureaucratic model is useful where there is little resistance against change and that people tend to accept changes. The model can be used in the range from small to large changes even though the Gothenburg model is better for radical changes.

The Gothenburg model can be used for all types of changes even though its advantages becomes clearer with increasing complexity in the changes.

BIBLIOGRAPHIC REFERENCES

Beer, M., Eisenstat, R. A., Spector, B. (1990) "Why Change Programs Don't produce change" , Harward Business Review, Nov-Dec, pp 158-166.

Björk, L.,Docherty, P., Forsling J., Stjernberg, T. (1990) Att behärska Förändligheten, Stockholm, Arbetsmiljöfonden

Gustavsen, B. (1990) Vägen Till Bättre Arbetsliv-Strategier ocharbetsformer i ett utvecklingsarbete, Stockholm, Arbetslivscentrum

Harrington, J. H (1991) Business Process Improvement, New York, McGraw-Hill Inc.

Imai, K. (1986) KAIZEN-The key to Japan's competetive Success, New York, McGraw-Hill Inc.

Karlsson, U. (1992) "The Development of Design Oriented Research", Göteborg, Chalmers University of Technology, Department of Industrial Management an Economics

Pasmore, W. A (1988) Designing Effective Organisations-The Sociotechnical Systems Perspective, New York, John Wiley & Sons

Sarv, H. (1991) Bakom framsteg-om förändringsarbete i företag, Stockholm, Trygghetsrådet SAF-PTK

Tischy, N.M, Devanna, M.A (1986) The Transformal Leader, New York, John Wiley & Sons

Trist, E. (1981) The evolution of socio-technical systems-a conceptional framework and an action oriented research program, Ontario, Quality of Working Life

Van Eijnatten, F.M. (1990) "Classical socio-technical systems design: the socio-technical design paradigm of an organisation, Eindhoven, Eindhoven Univerity of Technology

BIOGRAPHICAL SKETCH OF AUTHOR

Kurt H.M. Rosander is a member of a research group at Chalmers University of Technology in Gothenburg. He has been working with productivity improvements programs within the Swedish Industry. The changes to achieve increased productivity can be transferred to production organisation and the Activity Based Management area.

Productivity & Quality Management Frontiers-IV, edited by Sumanth, Edosomwan, Poupart, and Sink. ©1993 Institute of Industrial Engineers.

A Methodology for Developing the Quality Management Capabilities of a Manufacturing Organization

K.P. Triantis

Virginia Polytechnic Institute & State University

Falls Church, Virginia USA

ABSTRACT

This research presents a systematic approach that can be used by any manufacturing organization to plan and develop of its Total Quality Management (TQM) capabilities. The first task in this methodology involves TQM <u>assessment</u> where the organization establishes its total quality management capability baseline. A group of existing nationally and internationally recognized TQM criteria and TQM documents were used to provide a comprehensive set of TQM assessment criteria. These criteria integrate two views of the organization. One is a top-down view that focuses on the strategic and corporate management quality criteria and the second is a bottom-up view that emphasizes the operations management, production process and shop floor criteria.

The second task of this methodology involves the <u>strategic planning process</u> for organizational TQM capability development. This task is responsible for strategically planning the development of the organization's TQM capability over the long-run. The third task focuses on the <u>design process</u> of the appropriate TQM system configuration for the next stage of the TQM system development. The fourth and final task involves the <u>implementation planning process</u> which chooses the most profitable process level projects in terms of quality improvement for the short-run.

All of these tasks presuppose a systematic definition of a TQM system exists. The TQM system definition was developed using a systems engineering approach. The TQM system definition incorporates the input/output definition of a number of system "modules" or "building blocks". Each "module" is an important piece of the TQM system. This TQM system definition is based on the current quality management knowledge base. The current knowledge includes the national and international quality standards, the national and international quality awards, the DOD quality management documentation and the teachings of all the current quality management scholars.

In addition, to support the TQM system design and implementation planning tasks appropriate weighting methodologies are proposed. These weighting methodologies help decision makers choose the significant elements of the TQM system that they would want to develop.

Productivity & Quality Management Frontiers-IV, edited by Sumanth, Edosomwan, Poupart, and Sink. ©1993 Institute of Industrial Engineers.

Planning and Implementing Japanese Total Quality Control Systems: The Mexican Experience

J.A. Gomez
Monterrey Institute of Technology
Monterrey N.L., MEXICO

ABSTRACT

This work investigates the issues of how Mexican Manufacturing companies are coping with processes of survival and/or adaptation to new and more competitive markets by Planning and Implementing Dynamic Total Quality Control Systems, PIDTQCS.

Sixty four Mexican plants in major urban areas were visited and evaluated via the Deming Prize and the Malcom Baldrige Award criteria plus the author's particular interest on dynamic intervention/change, organizational stages of maturity, Mexican culture, and multidimensional design.

The research has two objectives: The first is exploratory in nature and investigates the current state of affairs in both the planning and the implementation of Dynamic Total Quality Control Systems. The second objective aims at interpreting the findings in terms of social (Mexican culture), technical (role of technology and know-how), and managerial (intervention process management and control) aspects.

The research, which is the first of its class in Mexico, shows that a lot of work has still to be done to account for 1. cultural dissonance between the Mexican and Japanese values system (underlying assumptions), 2. total quality and its relationship to manufacturing and technology strategy, 3. dynamic versus static conceptualization of the intervention process, 4. organizational stages of maturity , 5. socio-technical design of the whole effort when PIDTQCS, and 6. a whole variety of operative issues concerning education, team work, top management commitment, suppliers, customers, etc.

Key terms: Survival and adaptation, competitive markets, planning and implementing, Dynamic Total Quality Control, dynamic intervention/change, organizational stages of maturity, Mexican culture, socio-technical design.

Mexican manufacturing companies are becoming increasingly interested and involved in developing world class competitiveness as a consequence of a) the difficult economic times experienced in the early 80's, b) the recent opening of borders (Mexico joined GATT in 1986) to all kinds of products and services produced in other countries, c) the de-regulation of government protected/subsidized production sectors, and d) the realization of business people that economic forces are not domestic any more but global.

To develop such world class status, companies are undertaking the notion of Total Quality Control,TQC. Mexican companies, after the Japanese quality and productivity miracle, have tried to reproduce, emulate and/or adapt the use of philosophy, methods, techniques and tools related to "Japanese" TQC, JTQC, in order to improve their competitive position[1].

Since the early 1980s there has been a considerable number of case studies and anecdotes describing the planning and implementation of JTQC, but little in the way of systematic research work to permit the evaluation of the representativeness of case studies and the validity of anecdotic information.

This situation was perceived as an important opportunity area and a strategy was developed to carry out research work to 1.- explore the current state of affairs regarding the Planning and Implementation of JTQC systems, PIJTQCS, in Mexican companies and 2.- interpret the findings in terms of social (Mexican culture), technical (role of technology, manufacturing, and know-how), and managerial aspects (intervention process management and control). The end product of this research work is to design culture-consonant prescriptive planning and implementation TQC strategies to help Mexican companies improve competitive position.

With this purpose in mind, sixty four Mexican plants in major urban

[1] Japanese Total Quality Control is understood in this work as Shigeru Mizuno describes it " ..is integrated quality control in which the whole company, every division at every level, is involved for the achievement of a common corporate goal" (quality).

areas were visited and evaluated via a data collection instrument based on some criteria of the Deming Prize, The Malcom Baldrige Award, and the authors particular interest on strategic organizational variables[2].

Companies in this research were all private and medium-to-large in size and had made a serious commitment regarding a quality improvement process.

Findings.

Major areas of **operational inquiry**[3] were leadership and top management commitment, management of TQC culture, interaction with customers and suppliers, education and training systems, recognition systems, obstacles and/or shortcomings experienced, supporting (administrative) systems, and benefits produced by the quality improvement efforts.

Given the importance of designing generic and strategic elements to help companies plan and implement TQC as well as complement the quality gurus' frameworks [4], this papers concentrates on those quality aspects that are long term oriented, top management level by nature, and have organization-wide impact. For full description of operative findings see Gómez, 1990.

Strategic inquiry was aimed at identifying and analyzing how the following aspects were considered in the quality improvement effort: a) planned change effort and/or intervention process, b)

---

[2] Dynamic versus static process of intervention/change, organizational stages of development, Mexican culture, and multidimensional design (Technological, Managerial and Social) of the quality improvement effort.

[3] Findings have been initially analyzed via the use of basic statistics (means, standard deviations, histograms). Operative findings refer to those aspect inherent to the activities performed by middle and lower organizational levels, to the more focused quality aspects involving part of the organization but not the whole, and to the more short or medium term quality issues.
Strategic findings relate to those quality aspects that tend to be long term, organization-wide, and top management level in nature.

[4] i.e., Deming's 14 tasks for management, Crosby's 14 points, etc.

technology and manufacturing strategy, c) Mexican culture, d) TQC dimensions (social, technical, and managerial), and e) organizational stages of maturity.

1. Static versus Dynamic Intervention.

Most companies in the research work acknowledged that the planning and implementation processes inherent to TQC can be characterized as "one shot" efforts. They recognized that little mobilization, allocation of organizational resources and managerial talent were involved beyond the start-up ceremony and initial activities. Generally speaking, companies concentrated and deployed their efforts only at the beginning of the TQC movement. Energy, enthusiasm, follow-up and assurance activities were noticeably decaying as time went by.

Additionally, this "static" approach to planned change intervention did not include either deliberate evolutionary change of values , behaviors, attitudes, managerial practices, ways of solving problems, etc., beyond cognitive (classroom educational) processes. Companies did not make significant changes to traditional organizational structure, performance evaluation systems, job design, and work measurement. A foreman once said, "it was like management saying to us (middle managers and workers) ....I already gave you the credo and values, now go and multiply yourselves; implement the TQC philosophy".

When asked why this lack of consideration of more dynamic and sustainable-along-the-whole TQC process, companies mostly said that they simply followed the recommendations of one of the gurus, i.e., Deming's 14 tasks for management, Crosby's 14 points, etc., (or a combination of them) and nothing else occurred to them. They assumed that this was sufficient for the planned change effort.

2. Technology and Manufacturing strategy.

The majority of the companies initiated their TQC planning and implementation process without decisively considering their manufacturing strategy as presented by Hayes and Wheelwrigth (1984); nor their type of technology and its degree of complexity.

According to them a company can be positioned in one out of four different stages. Mexican companies seem to understand in their TQC movement only the internally neutral strategy an do not consider any evolution to "more" competitive stages of manufacturing. They tend to think that "fixing" current operations problems will automatically make them competitive; they do not realize that another company with the same manufacturing strategy but more efficient process technology can put them out of the race.

The same situation takes place with the notion of technology. Companies assume that as long as their machinery works well, there will be no problem. Issues of flexibility, process efficiency, machine/tool accuracy, process capability, etc., are simply ignored. No realization of foreign companies with state of the art technology competing in Mexican territory has taken place yet even tough this is already a real possibility.

Probably, this lack of consideration of technology and manufacturing strategy happens because, all quality frameworks[5] emerged in countries where technology and control of manufacturing processes were problems of much lesser magnitude than those in developing countries (i.e., Mexico). The gurus' basic assumptions (implicit in their frameworks) imply a series of manufacturing strategies, technological capabilities, and technology based work habits that did not exist (and do not yet) exist in Mexican manufacturing companies as a whole.

Becoming competitive in industrializing settings is more related to non-hard technology issues (relatively speaking) since equipment, machinery, and instruments are "out there" in the manufacturing area. Becoming competitive in Mexico does imply major capital investment and/or technology modernization.

Finally, for those few companies that do have modern technology, experience has shown that the selection of the tools and techniques to be used in quality improvement depends to a great

---

[5] The four major Gurus (Crosby, Deming, Ishikawa, and Juran in alphabetic order).

extent on the type of technology and manufacturing process; i.e., statistical process control, correlation analysis, process capability studies, are quite adequate for high volume, repetitive, continuous manufacturing. However, Mexican companies did not give consideration to these aspects, they simply followed what the basic quality frameworks specify without thinking for instance about the fit between process/product structure and quality tools and techniques.

It has been mentioned by many writers, Woodward (1958), Emery and Trist (1964), Pasmore (1978), Kleindorfer and Partovi (1988) that both manufacturing strategy and technology do have influence in a company's culture (values, attitudes, behaviors, problem solving methods, working skills, etc.) and a company's competitive position (quality and productivity).

The TQC intervention process simply overlooked these crucial issues; actually no guru gives explicit consideration to these points in their frameworks.

3. Culture.
This third point is a direct consequence of the two previous issues. Companies started their TQC processes, which imply culture change, without defining/evaluating the initial conditions of the fundamental aspects characterizing their current culture as compared to the ones that are inherent to TQC.

For instance, a) TQC assumes and implies that work is a value and that workers can find meaning in it (culturally speaking), b) that workers can be able to plan, do, check, and act to improve their work, c) that supervisors will function as facilitators, guides, etc., d) that there is harmony between the working and the managerial strata, etc. In a country like Mexico, with more than 3000 years of tribal, foreign elite groups, and externally based economic domination, the prior TQC issues are not precisely easy to find nor to develop. The resulting lack of consideration has been a major cause of energy/enthusiasm decay and conflicts in many TQC processes.

In some cases it actually provoked the complete extinction of them.

The four gurus have developed frameworks that emerged from indigenous conditions that are inherent in their cultures. They claim that they are transferable to other cultures, but they do not account explicitly for adaptations to a country's/company's indigenous characteristics.

4. Unidimensional approaches.
TQC processes in Mexican manufacturing companies have been typically initiated by human resources people who have a bias in favor of social issues and generally have no solid incorporation of other aspects of organization life (production, sales, etc.). This narrow/incomplete view of TQC has endangered a sense that people, in general, look at TQC as another "wave", "fad", or "fashion" without recognizing it as a major business variable and a as a strategic weapon to become competitive[6].

5. Organizational maturity.
TQC planning and implementation processes in Mexican plants did not consider, not in a single case, the "organizational age" of the company. What is meant here is that, it did not matter (for all purposes) if the company was in its "infancy", "adolescence", "youth", "adulthood", etc. This stands in contrast to the organizational literature where it is recognized that different stages of organizational maturity require different intervention schema, Adizes (1986), Gomez-Aguirre (1988) a), b),, Hayes, and Wheelwrigth (1988).This issue is not addressed by the quality gurus either.

Concluding comments.
The realization of this research has been a quite enriching and

---

[6] Human resources people in Mexican companies have generally been responsible to a great extent, for the management of the two previous company wide projects" management by objectives and organizational development activities. Both efforts fade out quickly and were considered as "fashionable" but not really contributing to bottom line results. Consequently, human resources people saw their "prestige" affected and were said to "sail with any organizational fad" without serious undertaking of it.

5. In summary, and as a direct result of this research , there is opportunity to complement the frameworks of the quality gurus by considering the following aspects when planning and implementing TQC:

- Dynamic versus static TQC intervention. Allowing for evolutionary change, learning and assuring continuous follow-up activities.
- Technology and Manufacturing strategy
- Consonance with indigenous local culture initial conditions
- Multidimensional approaches to TQC (social/culture, technological and managerial). Not only the culture or human resources approach when doing TQC
- Organizational stages of maturity

The way ahead is challenging and demands commitment. Deming (1986) says: "Long term commitment to new learning and new philosophy is required of any management that seeks transformation, The timid and the fainthearted, and people that expect quick results are doomed to disappointment".

Bibliography

Adizes, I., "Como Evitar la Incompetencia Gerencial"; Editorial Diana, 1980.

Crosby, P., "Quality is Free"; New American Library, 1980.

Deming, W. E., "Out of the Crisis"; MIT Press, 1988.

Díaz-Guerrero, R., "Psicología del Mexicano", Trillas (4 Ed.), 1982.

Gómez-Aguirre, J., "Manufacturing Technology Transfer: A Socio-Technical Study of its Inadequacies"; Social Systems Sciences Working Papers, Univ. of Pennsylvania, April 1988.

Gómez-Aguirre, J., "Las Etapas de Madurez de la Organización y su Relación con el Proceso de Mejoramiento de la Calidad"; Speech given in a conference on Quality Improvement Processes presented to executives of Grupo VISA, Monterrey N.L., México, March 1989.)

Hayes, R., Wheelwright, S., Clark, K., "Dynamic Manufacturing", Free Press, 1988.

Ishikawa, K., "What is Total Quality Control? The Japanese Way"; Prentice Hall, 1985.

Juran, J., "Juran on Planning for Quality"; The Free Press, 1987.

Ramos, S., "Profile of Man and Culture in Mexico", University of Texas Press, 1962.

Dr. Gomez holds academic degrees and diplomas from universities in Mexico, Canada, Japan and the USA. Currently, Dr. Gómez is the Director of the Graduate Programs in Business Administration, Associate Researcher at The USA-Mexico Center for Strategic Studies (both at Monterrey Institute of Technology in Monterrey, Mexico), and Distinguished Visiting Professor in International Business for the College of Business of The University of Houston

Productivity & Quality Management Frontiers-IV, edited by Sumanth, Edosomwan, Poupart, and Sink. ©1993 Institute of Industrial Engineers.

The Customer Needs Analysis:
A Key Tool for Strategic Quality Planning

D.L. Baila and W.C. Hayes
Management Systems International, Inc.
Boca Raton, Florida USA

ABSTRACT

The *Customer Needs Analysis* has proven itself to be an excellent method to apply quality function deployment on an organizational level to create a systematic means of focusing the organization on the most important issues. By using a graphical format to present the information, this vehicle easily identifies the most important areas to address organizationally, based on the leverage each business process has in meeting customer needs.

The graphical display of the information provides significant advantage. Convening an organization's experienced people in a group format to identify the most important customer needs often brings first time agreement on what the customer really desires. This presents a tremendous opportunity to communicate to the entire organization these needs, and push the information down to the lowest levels of the company. Often, these levels are the ones that have the most direct contact with the customers who are purchasing the product or service. These concepts are equally valid in non-profit organizations and government agencies. With the increasing competition that nearly any organization faces, be it market-driven competition or merely a competition for funding, highlighting the needs of the customer will be of critical importance in achieving success in the future.

Productivity & Quality Management Frontiers-IV, edited by Sumanth, Edosomwan, Poupart, and Sink. ©1993 Institute of Industrial Engineers.

Using Implementation Teams to Manage Total Quality

J.K. Somers
Cumberland Group
Houston, Texas USA

ABSTRACT

Planning and organizing for Total Quality (TQ) is essential for successful start up and sustained TQ results. Symptoms of poor TQ planning and organization include inadequately trained teams working on the wrong problems, ineffective measurement and no accountability for results.

A primary root cause of these symptoms is the lack of an implementation process which provides the organizational structure, management systems and employee involvement required to operationalize TQ. An effective solution is the Implementation Team, an employee team empowered to plan, organize and manage TQ, under the auspices of the Quality Council.

The Implementation Team is not a problem-solving team, but the implementation body for TQ in their area. The Team is empowered to "turn on" and manage the quality culture. *The power of the Implementation Team is that it gives employees an ownership and management role in TQ.*

The Team is a "diagonal slice" of the organization. Team members are selected to represent the levels and functions of the organization. The Team designs and operates four TQ management systems: search for opportunities, measurement, corrective action and training. Employee suggestions are collected, evaluated and prioritized by the Team. Measurements and accountabilities are determined. Then, with Quality Council approval, the Team commissions, trains and tracks improvement efforts.

This process allows TQ management decisions to be made at the lowest level, where the employee constituency is best represented. The Implementation Team works under the auspices and leadership of the Quality Council, to create a partnership where employees have an important voice in TQ.

Key Words: **Employee Involvement**   **Implementation Teams**
                Empowerment   **Total Quality Management**

USING IMPLEMENTATION TEAMS TO MANAGE TOTAL QUALITY

Planning and organizing for Total Quality (TQ) is essential for successful start up and sustained TQ results. Symptoms of poor TQ planning and organization include inadequately-trained teams working on the wrong problems, ineffective measurement and no accountability for results.

A primary root cause of these symptoms is the lack of an implementation process which provides the organizational structure, management systems and employee involvement required to operationalize TQ. An effective solution is the Implementation Team (I-Team), an employee team empowered to plan, organize and manage TQ, under the auspices of the Quality Council.

The logic for I-Team TQ management is compelling. The I-Team offers increased degrees of employee participation, involvement and decision-making in the TQ initiative, working in partnership with senior management to design and administer the TQ structure and process.

HOW THE IMPLEMENTATION TEAM MANAGES TQ

The I-Team is not a problem-solving team, but the implementation body for TQ in their area. The I-Team is empowered to "turn on" and manage the quality culture. *The power of the Implementation Team is that it gives employees an ownership and management role in TQ.*

The I-Team is a "diagonal slice" of the organization. Team members are selected to represent the levels and functions of the organization. The I-Team designs and operates four TQ management systems: search for opportunities, measurement, corrective action and training. Employee suggestions are collected, evaluated and prioritized by the I-Team. Measurements and accountabilities are determined. Then, with Quality Council approval, the I-Team commissions and trains Corrective Action Teams (CATs) and tracks improvement efforts.

The I-Team members themselves become responsible for the decisions usually left to management, and management serves a leadership role, steering, guiding and allocating resources to commission corrective action teams. This process allows TQ management decisions to be made at the lowest level, where the employee constituency is best represented. The Implementation Team works under the auspices and leadership of the Quality Council, to create a partnership where employees have an important voice in TQ.

TEAM RESULTS

During the past 10 years, we have helped a number of organizations install Implementation Teams in blue- and white-collar environments. These empowered employee teams realize improved levels of communication, autonomy, problem-solving, involvement, accountability, recognition and team work.

There are many potential benefits. Employees who are closer to the decisions that affect quality feel higher levels of pride and motivation in their work. Many organizations using I-Teams report a sharpened focus on customers, since improvement decisions affecting internal and external customers are jointly shared by workers and managers.

TEAM MEMBERSHIP

I-Team members should be chosen from all parts of the organization, representing employees closest to the daily work. All employees are eligible to volunteer, and nominees are solicited from managers. Team members are appointed by the Quality Council, in conjunction with union leadership where bargaining units exist. Team members are selected so that there is a representative sample of all levels of employees and functions within the I-Team's boundaries. For this reason, it is sometimes necessary to include drafted candidates with volunteers and nominees.

Team membership and time commitments vary by organization. I-Teams generally consist of 6 to 12 members serving periods of 12 to 18 months. Teams average 4 to 6 hours per week on management activities, with greater time commitments in the first two months, as action plans and quality systems are developed, and initial training takes place.

To focus on broad organizational issues and warrant the investment required, I-Teams best serve constituent employee groups of 100 to 500 people. Smaller constituent pools require fewer team members. Often the I-Team duties can be accomplished for smaller groups by a joint management/employee coalition. Multiple I-Teams are recommended in large organizations.

TEAM FUNCTIONS

The I-Team is not a problem-solving team, but the implementation body for TQ in their area. Their initial responsibility is to design the who, what, where, when and how of the TQ management and administration systems.

The I-Team operationalizes Total Quality, and is designed to "turn on" the quality culture. The I-Team has four functions, each critical for TQ success. As their names imply, these functions partner with management and establish systems to identify improvement opportunities, take corrective actions, measure results and train employees. The functions and tasks are:

Search for Opportunity (SFO):
- Design the SFO process, or adapt existing SFO process.
- Collect suggestions and opportunities via the SFO process.
- Clarify opportunities with stakeholders.
- Determine owners.
- Evaluate opportunities for optimum solution paths.
- Pass opportunities to the corrective action, measurement and training functions.
- Close feedback loops with stakeholders, owners and management.

Corrective Action:
- Analyze and classify opportunities.
- Determine management "ownership" of the opportunity.
- Jointly with the Quality Council, commission corrective action teams (CATs), as required, for opportunities within realm of control.
- Monitor CATs and owner support.
- Monitor solution and implementation.
- Close feedback loops with stakeholders, owners and management.

Measurement:
- Work with owners and CATs to develop initial benefit analyses.
- Develop necessary measures.
- Consult with CATs to measure progress.
- Determine ongoing impact.
- Close feedback loops with stakeholders, owners and management.
- Measure and monitor I-Team success.

Training:
- Consult with management and teams to determine training needs.
- Acquire/develop and deliver awareness training to employees.
- Acquire/develop and deliver skills training to CAT members, as required.
- Communicate with the business unit to share TQ improvement status.

ROLES AND RESPONSIBILITIES

To achieve TQ goals through partnering, the I-Team and the organization's executives must clearly understand and meet their respective roles. These roles serve as the checklist for success; failing to meet them results in decreased I-Team performance or failure:

Executives:
- Commit to quality as a prominent part of the business policy.
- Put a quality structure into place and ensure integration.
- Align management behavior with the quality goals.
- Partner with labor to select I-Team members.
- Support start-up by meeting with the Team before and after training.
- Maintain an on-going, active, participative role with the Team.
- Commission improvement teams and provide resources.

I-Team:
- Form a strong partnership with management.
- Develop and practice skills of working together as a team to implement and manage the TQ systems.
- Design, implement and manage systems to surface opportunities.
- Measure opportunities for improvement.
- Support corrective actions on selected opportunities.
- Coordinate their activity with other I-Teams in the organization to synergistically develop systems using the best ideas of all teams.
- Train employees on improvement techniques, and communicate organizational success stories.

TRAINING FOR TEAM WORK

Training is essential for I-Team success. The I-Team must develop a foundation of teamwork during the initial training session. Beyond designing and mastering the technical functions operated by the I-Team, the group must gel as a team if they are to be self-managed and able to grow in team autonomy.

The team begins by examining the stages of team development to gain an awareness of their current state, and the phases they are likely to encounter over the coming weeks as they learn to work together. Next comes basic training on conducting meetings, solving problems, reaching consensus, and group communication dynamics.

During training, the team designs its work processes, setting operational and interpersonal norms. Responsibilities and accountabilities are agreed upon, and commitments are firmed up among team members and with the Quality Council. Weeks after training, I-Teams frequently relate that the time spent on developing their team norms was the most valuable output of the training session. Clear accountabilities and norms established in training facilitate decision making when inevitable problems arise.

The training objectives include:
- Understand the fundamentals of quality.
- Understand the organizational need and objectives for the TQ process.
- Understand the role of the I-Team.
- Design the four TQ management systems:
  - search for opportunities
  - measurement
  - corrective action
  - training
- Develop and practice the team skills required to implement and manage the TQ systems.
- Develop the work plan required to institutionalize the TQ management systems.
- Develop a team action plan jointly with management to direct the improvement process in their organization.

During team training, executives from the Quality Council play a key role. They set the stage for the team during the initial orientation by outlining expectations and establishing the leadership behavior required to support the team in its design process. Near the culmination of the team training, the executives re-join the team to review and reach consensus on team-designed operating norms. This process and interaction begins the cycle of I-Team and management partnership essential for success.

ON-GOING PARTNERSHIP

Management partnership begins during training, when the Quality Council joins the I-Team for a read out on the Team's preliminary design. Council members work with the I-Team members to de-bug the systems as designed, and to ensure that the operational plan can be supported by the organization's leadership team. Conflicts are resolved and the work plan is fine-tuned in concert between leadership and I-Team members.

The I-Team leader, who is elected by the team, serves as the conduit through which the Team's recommendations for corrective actions and resource needs are channeled. Successful teams realize long-term partnerships when the team leader regularly joins the Quality Council sessions to update progress and maintain open communications.

TEAM EVOLUTION: SUCCESSES AND LESSONS LEARNED

What makes successful I-Teams work? I-Teams are successful when the Quality Council, management, and I-Team members understand fully their respective roles and accountabilities, and maintain open channels of communication. Review the section on Roles and Responsibilities for a listing of the critical success factors.

During the past 10 years, we have helped a number of organizations install I-Teams in a variety of blue and white-collar environments. These teams are all custom-designed to meet organizational needs, so their evolutions vary. Some interesting constants exist, however, which reveal lessons learned for organizations thinking of using I-Teams to manage the TQ initiative.

The most common path is for teams to continue, with team norms and operational duties evolving to meet changing organizational cultures. Team membership changes over time, either through rotation or wholesale team replacement. Both techniques offer advantages. Rotating members allows the original culture to continue with the Team, and lets new members come up to speed gradually without disruption. Total replacement of Team members allows the new Team to start from scratch, with the successes and failures of the previous Team to imitate or sunset.

In organizations where teams have continued under either scenario, the results are improved communications, increased levels of worker autonomy in local problem-solving and decision-making, and dramatic culture shifts in employee involvement, communications, accountability, recognition and teamwork.

Not all I-Teams have remained intact, however. Teams are abandoned for two obvious reasons. First the culture can change so that a I-Team structure is no longer necessary. Opportunities are identified and corrective actions are taken without the need to wash them through a formal standing team of employees. In these situations, the I-Team succeeds by shifting the culture to one of "automatic" continual improvement. Indeed, in such cultures, I-Teams are unnecessary. But Teams are also abandoned due to failure. Looking at reasons for failure is equally instructive at successes.

FAILURES AND ROOT CAUSES

I-Teams are not always successful. Our experience points to several key elements which can guarantee Team failure. In organizations where I-Teams fail, the root causes for the failure can usually be traced to several systemic conditions:

Lack of Management Support: If the senior executives do not support the concept, it will not succeed. I-Teams managing the TQ initiative can thrive only in an atmosphere of high employee involvement and participation. If management is not ready for that leap, the I-Team, and TQ in general, will fail.

Inadequate Resource Commitment: Quality is not free, and the cost in person-hours and capital to staff I-Teams to manage the TQ process is significant. The benefits must outweigh the costs, obviously, and the investment must be focused on clear business needs.

No Alignment with Business Vision/Mission: The I-Team and Quality Council are equally accountable for keeping the Team mission aligned with business strategies. Effectiveness is compromised when the larger vision is lost.

Quality of Work Life (QWL) Issues: QWL issues, when accepted by the I-Team, can cloud the business relevance of continual improvement. The Team may choose to accept or reject QWL issues. However, a lack of protocol for dealing with them can hamstring the effectiveness of improving key business processes. Thus, clarity of Team purpose is compromised.

Internalizing the Process too Soon: Some organizations attempt to try a new concept, like the I-Team, and then replicate it without adequate experience. The result is likely to be subsequent I-Teams which set norms and standards too much akin to current, familiar norms. Unfortunately, organizations do not realize that their very comfort with a norm is a danger sign; it signals "business as usual." The concept of using I-Teams to manage the TQ initiative is not usual, and must be handled in unusual fashion.

CONCLUSION

Planning and organizing for Total Quality (TQ) can be truly involving and dynamic with the use of Implementation Teams. By involving employees early on, ownership for TQ is built at all organizational levels, ensuring TQ impact and success.

ORGANIZATIONAL ASSESSMENT

Using I-Teams to design, administer and manage the TQ process is a logical, yet bold move. Use this self-assessment to gauge your readiness for using I-Teams to manage the TQ Process.

Yes No

Management Support Culture

___ ___   1. Does your management staff involve employees in work and continual improvement planning?

___ ___   2. Is communication open and two-way?

___ ___   3. Are employees generally empowered to make decisions that affect their customers without seeking unnecessary approvals?

___ ___   4. Is accountability, for executives as well as employees, a norm?

___ ___   5. Do performance reviews include a focus on continual improvement?

___ ___   6. Is team work recognized and rewarded at the team level?

Organizational Structure:

___ ___   7. Are teams operating successfully in the organization at this time?

___ ___   8. Are people centrally located, versus geographically dispersed?

___ ___   9. Do work processes routinely cross functional boundaries, versus being self-contained by department?

___ ___ 10. Does the organization currently have a mechanism for improving quality of work life needs?

___ ___ 11. Are other suggestion systems formalized and operational at this time?

Organizational Culture:

___ ___ 12. Do managers visibly support employee involvement at this time?

___ ___ 13. Are managers willing to let employees make decisions traditionally made by management?

___ ___ 14. Does your organization follow through on improvement initiatives and associated structure changes, versus reverting back to the "old culture?"

___ ___ 15. Is the management time horizon for culture change long-term and patient?

___ ___ 16. Are employees motivated and enthusiastic about participation and empowerment?

		17.	Is your organization stable and financially secure enough to support I-Team management of the TQ initiative?
___	___	18.	If your organization has bargaining unit representation, will the union leadership view I-Team management of TQ as positive?
___	___	19.	Is there a felt need for organization and focus of the improvement ideas generated around TQ?
___	___	20.	Does your organization have a history of sticking with a culture change long enough to test results before attempting modifications?

Scoring: "Yes" answers indicate a positive climate for I-Team management of the TQ Process. "No" answers indicate opportunities for management, cultural, or structural improvements. If the question does not apply, slide the scoring scale accordingly.

15 - 20 Yes: Your organization is well-positioned to use I-Teams to manage the TQ initiative. Recommend further investigation.

10 - 14 Yes: Proceed with caution. Investigate the root causes of the "No" answers, and focus on improvement at that level before or while instituting I-Teams for TQ management.

< 10 Yes: I-Teams for quality management may be risky, depending on the nature of the "No" answers and management's willingness to focus attention on root causes. Recommend prioritized focus on critical "No" issues before proceeding.

ABOUT THE AUTHOR

James K. (Ken) Somers is a principal with the Cumberland Group, a consulting firm specializing in continual improvement. He practices TQM and general management consulting for service and manufacturing firms, with experience in aerospace, education, R&D, utilities, computers, graphic arts, and transportation. He holds the Ph.D. from Texas A&M University.

Productivity & Quality Management Frontiers-IV, edited by Sumanth, Edosomwan, Poupart, and Sink. ©1993 Institute of Industrial Engineers.

Total Quality Management in Private and Public Sectors

R. Goldstein
Fannie Mae
Washington, D.C. USA

R. Khorramshahgol
The American University
Washington, D.C. USA

ABSTRACT

In an ailing economy like that of the U.S., both the public and private sectors are increasingly under pressure to adopt Total Quality Management (TQM) in the management of their enterprises. This paper provides a comprehensive coverage of TQM and its principles and practices in private and public sectors.

This paper first examines public sector principles and practices as well as measurement systems to determine the degree to which all products and services satisfy customers. Furthermore, it discusses federal internal process improvement procedures. This discussion is followed by an analysis of TQM practices in some industries: how the International Business Machine (IBM) Corporation and some other firms strive to become a genuinely TQM company--i.e., a company in which the customer is the final arbiter. Finally, a comparative analysis of TQM in public and private sectors is presented.

Key Words: Private Sector TQM; Public Sector TQM; Quality Measurement; TQM Implementation; Proactive vs. Reactive.

INTRODUCTION

Pioneered by W. Edwards Deming and J.M. Juran in the early 1950's, Total Quality Management (TQM) theories and techniques have been used by different industries to improve goods and services. The Japanese first gained from Deming's and Juran's teachings in 1951 and have since applied them to all areas of industry. This has resulted in superior Japanese goods and services as defined by fewer defects and better customer treatment. The United States lags behind in its TQM implementation and has only recently begun to play catch-up. To increase competitiveness, both domestic public and private sectors are embracing TQM implementation strategies (Juran, 1991). J.M. Juran recently addressed an audience of Japanese executives and declared that The United States is about to rebound. He estimates that the phrase "Made in the USA" will become a symbol for world-class quality in the 1990's. Juran expects big gains in competitiveness during the next decade and states that, "...during the 1990's we will make great strides toward regaining world quality leadership. The job of scaling up is massive, but the methodology is known" (Juran, 1991).

Others, from the federal government to private industry, expect the same improvement. The federal government has established The Federal Quality Institute (FQI), a resource center designed to market Juran's and Deming's methodologies throughout its agencies. Private industry, including many major U.S. corporations, are establishing quality directives. These companies realize quality simply is not implicit in the way they design and make products or in the way they treat customers. The underlying macro TQM theories are very similar in both the public and private sectors, but the micro implementations are varied.

If government and industry are to work toward a common goal, quality, it is necessary for the two to understand each others rationale for TQM implementation. To this end, TQM methodologies used in both sectors are described in this research and actual and potential applications of TQM are discussed. Also addressed, are similarities and differences between public and private macro/micro TQM strategies and the gaps in the quality movement in both sectors. This research is primarily based on structured interviews with 15 top level managers from both the public and private sectors. The results of this study should be of interest to a wide audience, including: (1) organizations planning to enter a TQM effort, (2) organizations in the embryonic stages of a TQM effort, (3) government contractors, (4) TQM consultants marketing services to both the public and the private sectors, and (5) TQM educators.

TQM IN THE FEDERAL GOVERNMENT

The Federal Quality Institute (FQI) defines the general federal environment in its Federal Total Quality Management Handbook (TQMHB-3): "In general, most federal agencies are managed in a top-down, hierarchical, bureaucratic mode and operate through highly structured administrative rules and procedures. As a result, management styles tend to be non-participative and rigid." When an entity as large as the federal government defines its own managerial practices in such a manner -

change is needed. In fact, some believe that the entire government is a large conglomerate of activities and functions operating under inflexible and outdated management practices and principles.

The main objectives of TQM in the federal government are to break down the rigidity and excess bureaucratic structure and to design ways to enlist the energies and talents of its workforce to meet the nations challenges. Other objectives include rewarding truly exceptional group performance and increasing agency wide cooperation and process improvements. The goal is to increase the quality of products and services provided to the American taxpayer without additional resource allocation. These objectives and goals are difficult enough to carry out across one organization, yet alone the entire federal government and all its agencies. Each individual agency's missions, goals, and objectives vary greatly, and to say that one specific TQM approach will work in the federal government is absurd. In fact, TQM implementation is heralded as a great success in some agencies and viewed as a great disaster in others.

FQI defines TQM as meeting customer requirements the first time and every time. The TQM approach to quality is systematically inquiring of customers what they want, and striving to meet, and even exceed those requirements. That is, instead of the agency specifying what it views as quality, it makes continuous inquires of customer needs and realizes that customers' expectations change over time. This paper examines the federal TQM structure and shows that, while the federal macro TQM strategy remains constant, TQM micro strategies must vary across and even within agencies.

The federal government's TQM macro strategy includes three basic principles: (1) focus on achieving customer satisfaction, where a customer is anyone internal or external who receives a product or service from a federal worker, (2) a continuous and long-term improvement in all processes and outputs, and (3) a full involvement of the entire workforce in improving quality. In addition to the three TQM macro principles, seven micro TQM operating practices exist: (1) top management leadership and support, (2) strategic planning, (3) customer focus, (4) measurement and analysis, (5) commitment to training and recognition, (6) employee empowerment and teamwork, and (7) quality assurance. Even though other government agencies were interviewed in our study, we chose DOC to include in this paper for two reasons (1) The DOC is a good typical example of how TQM is applied in the government, and (2) DOC's Malcolm Baldridge Award, given annually to industry's high TQM achievers, will particularly assist us in this study to link TQM in public and private sectors and to perform an objective analysis of each and what each sector perceives TQM is or ought to be.

TQM at The Department of Commerce

The current TQM campaign was introduced in 1989 by Thomas Murrin, then Department Secretary. TQM in The DOC, unlike many private industry campaigns, is a result of an opportunity. The rationale behind the DOC's TQM is the Malcolm Baldridge Award. Since The DOC administers the Baldridge Award (for private corporations), private industry hinted that DOC adopt the same processes. DOC initiated an internal award, The Secretary of Commerce Quality Award, to parallel the Baldridge in both quality focus and evaluation criteria. This award is designed to recognize DOC organizations who have made "significant and dramatic improvements in Commerce's operations."

All DOC's organizations are eligible to receive the award. The two eligibility categories include: small organizations with 50 to 500 employees and large organizations with over 500 employees. Subunits of large organizations are also eligible to compete as a small organization. Annually, Secretarial Officers nominate organizations achieving excellence over several categories. Also annually, the Secretary of Commerce appoints a Quality Award Board of Judges to review nominees. Commerce officials as well as members of private sector organizations recognized for their accomplishments in quality and productivity provide the board's make-up. It is interesting to note that private organizations play an active role in the awards selection process. This is one example of both the public and the private sectors cooperatively forming a common quality definition.

The DOC views TQM as an overall initiative. The Office of Administration oversees the macro initiative and expects each office (bureau) to carry out its own micro level TQM policies. The Office of Administrations' macro level policy and the individual bureaus' micro level policies appear to parallel IBM's current move toward decentralization. A decentralized strategy allows more flexibility and room to tailor a specific TQM implementation to a specific bureau. As with the private sector, a TQM implementation appropriate for one (company) agency may not be appropriate for another. That is, while macro strategies remain constant, micro strategies should have the flexibility to change.

Top Management Leadership and Support

DOC is currently in the embryonic stages of its most recent implementation, and faces an enormous task implementing TQM to all its 35,000 employees across 600 national and international installations. Top-level political support presently exists. To ensure top managerial commitment, DOC establishes a quality council. The council is comprised of top-level managers and meets regularly to share experiences and learn from each other's successes and failures. By establishing the quality council, top management provides identity, structure and legitimacy to the TQM effort. It is the council's responsibility to publish the agency's vision, goals, and mission statement. It is also the council's responsibility to oversee the agency-wide TQM effort.

Strategic Planning

Besides the Quality Council (macro level), Quality Improvement Teams exist (micro level). Their purpose is to focus on teamwork and processes rather than on individual efforts and tasks. Accordingly, these teams are involved in strategic planning. The Bureau of Census, A DOC member bureau, has over 125 formal quality action teams, each with a specific set of objectives. For example, the objectives for one unit, the Graphics Systems Software Upgrade Team were (1) to reduce time to upgrade software and (2) Reduce
Production Downtime. Consequently, a four stage process was designed which reduced downtime from ten days to three days. Each quality improvement team

is expected to develop its own set of quality objectives, but still adhere with DOC's overall implementation.

Measurements

The DOC's measurement process, like in private organizations, is very difficult. Measurements are still viewed as a public burden, and many agencies shy away from such processes. DOC does conduct focus groups, however, comprised of its management and its main clients. These groups serve as a forum for customers to vent both satisfactions and dissatisfactions. Customer surveys, unlike in private industry, are very complicated as prior managerial approval is needed.

Once top management has made the commitment to TQM, one of the most crucial ingredients to a successful federal implementation is employee empowerment. Employee empowerment efforts often fail because management have not adopted procedures to make employee involvement routine. One quality improvement manager, from another federal agency, states that the employee empowerment process must be real and integrated into every process - it cannot be half hearted. Greater efficiency occurs when the process experts, the workers, are involved. In theory this sounds like a good initiative, but in practice, a manager states that too much empowerment can be very dangerous. If employees are given too much freedom, they may deviate from process improvements to other destructive behaviors. Also, empowering employees may make some insecure managers nervous and feel they have little control. Based on our interviews, TQM seems more threatening to middle management.

Recognition

To support and reinforce the employee empowerment effort, explicit recognition awards exist for both quality improvement teams and individual employees. Besides the previously mentioned Secretary of Commerce Award, several award programs exist. One manager states, "we offer immediate recognition for both groups and individuals. The key here is quick and immediate recognition. You want to immediately reinforce employees for excellent performance. If you wait too long (for praise) incentives for future quality performance may be lost."

An interesting incentive is called the "Pioneer Fund." This incentive is offered three times annually to employees who engineer innovative projects which further quality management. It is interesting to note that there is no penalty for failure. Perhaps more private sector organizations should follow this same "no penalty" incentive structure. Maybe more new and creative ideas will develop. All of these incentives serve to increase employee involvement and foster an atmosphere of creativity (in continuously improving processes).

Training

Training in public sector poses the same problems as it does in the private sector. Most training efforts are currently in their embryonic stages and are not formalized. There is some cross training between bureaus, but more needs to be done in the training arena.

Working With the Private Sector

A luxury of private organizations is that they have the ability to work closely with their suppliers. The DOC, being a public agency, does not have this luxury. One Manager states, "The private sector can do so much more dealing with suppliers. The DOC is locked in with procurement, we cannot work closely with suppliers because it would give them an unfair advantage." The DOC cannot give these suppliers, any outside contractor, its TQM specifications or force these suppliers to adhere with its TQM implementation.

TQM IMPLEMENTATION AT IBM

Even though we interviewed other firms for our study, we include The International Business Machine Corporation (IBM) in this research because it is mature in its TQM, is a winner of The Malcolm Baldridge Award, therefore, a good typical example for TQM in industry. IBM committed itself to providing quality products and services when the company was founded. However, during May 1989, in face of a declining market share and increased global competition, IBM reaffirmed its original commitment via total quality management techniques. IBM calls its TQM implementation strategy Market Driven Quality (MDQ) where the final arbiter is the customer.

A TQM expert in the Federal Quality Institute states that organizations enter quality implementations for one of two reasons: "vision or pain." An IBM official states, "IBM does not have as good of a record as it had in the past, our business base is changing from mainframe to PC based applications...the years of forcing mainframe solutions on customers are over...we must listen to and meet our customers requirements." Listening to customers was in direct conflict with corporate objectives during the 1960's, 1970's and 1980's. The same IBM official states, "We were in a state of paralysis and everything was changing around us...MDQ implementation was needed for sheer corporate survival." Obviously, IBM is implementing MDQ due to a problem - corporate pain.

In a recent reorganization in March 1992, IBM created a more autonomous corporate structure in which IBM classifies some, but not all, of its former corporate divisions as "companies." IBM expects each autonomous company to adhere with its total MDQ implementation strategy, but also encourages each company to define its own MDQ goals and objectives. A review of every company within IBM is beyond the scope of this paper. This study examines IBM's Macro TQM strategy as well as the TQM strategy in one company within IBM, The Federal Systems Company (FSC) and its relationships to government clients.

TQM in Federal Systems Company

FSC, formerly the Federal Sector Division (FSD), primarily serves the federal aerospace industry and has contracts with The National Aeronautics and Space Administration (NASA) and The Department of Defense (DOD). NASA and DOD both deem approximately 50 percent of these contracts classified. FSC is in Gaithersburg, Maryland, employs over 2,000 people, and is an example of an autonomous company within The IBM corporate structure. Most employees view the entire MDQ idea as a problem. MDQ implementation seems too global and goals are not realistic. IBM intends the creation of FSC from FSD to foster a local environment where local objectives can be set. These objectives should nail down tough, specific, realistic, and realizable goals.

Employee Participation

To meet TQM goals, an organization needs to increase employee participation (TQMHB-1, 1991). An IBM employee states that subordinates easily realize this initiative as management pushes down the decision making process to employees. These employees, in turn, feel they have more authority and a feeling of job ownership soon develops. In essence, they feel empowered. "My people are now thinking about processes and customer satisfaction, previously, they were only concerned about the final product - not about the process," states a manager.

Quality Measurement and Benchmarking

IBM literature states that measurements are essential to help establish and meet MDQ goals. To accomplish a successful measurement criteria, IBM ensures continuous feedback and improvement in every work process. Every unit accepts its own process measurement responsibility. As with other MDQ concepts, benchmarking at IBM is specific to the process at hand. IBM uses benchmarking techniques on a company by company, unit by unit, process by process basis. An FSC manager states, "benchmarking at FSC is conducted on a process by process basis not on a project by project basis...the reason being the focus of MDQ: continual process improvement."

Another IBM manager states, "Finding the gaps between yourself and your competitors is only half the benchmarking activity...you also need to look at noncompeting organizations. When you start talking to them, you not only find out how well they're doing, but often they're willing to share why, and to talk about how they reached their admirable levels of achievement." Talking with competitors is also important...we talk about personnel activities and processes, rather than about products, which are our competitive edge. (Commitment Plus Magazine, 1991)." As an additional benchmarking technique, IBM uses The Malcolm Baldridge Award.

The Need For Realizable Objectives

The paramount issue uncovered during the interview process is the need for better objectives. An IBM Manager suggests that there is still a need for better local and short-term objectives that "nail down" specific realizable goals and help in measuring progress. Particularly, the first short-term objective should have a very high probability of success. "You have to let employees see that it works," states one manager. After realization of this first short-term objective, you can set other tough, realistic, short-term objectives. In other words, employees need to see the quality effort working before the buy in process occurs.

ANALYSIS OF RESULTS

More similarities than differences are noted between private TQM and public TQM. However, We found two major differences between public and private TQM efforts: (1) there are more private sector TQM quantitative measurement systems in place than in the public sector; and (2) TQM efforts in the private sector always affects the bottom line whereas TQM efforts in the public sector often does not affect the bottom line where the bottom line is defined as job security.

Our first finding, more private sector measurement systems, is exemplified through IBM as well as other private sector organizations we studied. By contrast, The DOC sets standards for private sector quality implementations (Malcolm Baldridge Award), but does not implement a standard quantitative quality measurement system throughout its own agencies. The interviewed DOC managers freely admit that quantitative measurement systems are needed. We suggest that more research is needed on quantitative measurement in both the public and private sectors and that TQM researchers and practitioners should begin to develop new measurement techniques. Our second finding, bottom line affect, is also exemplified through IBM and other organizations we surveyed. If private TQM efforts fail, usually implemented in a retroactive manner due to corporate pain, corporate death is likely to occur. If public TQM efforts fail, on the other hand, agency death is highly unlikely. Therefore, a public agency has the luxury of learning from its mistakes whereas a private organization may not have another chance. If a public TQM effort fails, the agency is presented with three options: (1) terminate the implementation and, at most, lose face, (2) give the TQM effort more time to develop, or (3) terminate the implementation and begin a new campaign. Furthermore, the agency's management and subordinates are highly unlikely to lose their jobs.

Therefore, it is important that more private organizations implement proactive TQM efforts before corporate pain occurs. This way, proper time can be allocated to achieve both top management buy-in and employee commitment without the retroactive force that usually is the main characteristic of many abortive TQM efforts. Furthermore, it is also crucial that private organizations implement proactive incentives modeled after The DOC "Pioneer Fund." This will not only further their quality efforts but serve to attain employee involvement. Careful attention must be given to ensure that, like in The DOC, there will not be any penalty for failure. This may be a difficult concept for many private organizations to digest because success or failure usually affects the bottom line, and many jobs! However, if employees are no longer fearful of losing their jobs, they will be able to show more creativity in a less restrictive environment where success is not the bottom line, at least not in the short term. Moreover, a comprehensive and well defined TQM implementation plan is very crucial to its success.

Proper safety valves must also be developed. To ensure that a project has legitimate potential and that no project deviates from corporate objectives, a quality council comprised of both top management and subordinates should carefully scrutinize all proposals. To ensure that no favoritism exists, proposals should be submitted blindly. Based on our research, a timely feedback (acceptance or rejection) should be offered (in less than two weeks time) to retain employee enthusiasm. This is viewed as a proactive approach to employee involvement rather than the common retroactive reward for accomplishment. However, a retroactive reward for accomplishment should not be considered as unimportant.

Throughout our research and as a consequence of interviewing many TQM experts in the public and the private sectors, we feel that there is a need for greater public/private educational cooperation across TQM planes. For example, private organizations are presently allocating funds to universities that teach TQM in their classrooms. Also, many private organizations (IBM, Motorola, and Milliken for example) are currently training university level business and engineering faculty in TQM practices. This educational program should be taken even one step further in that universities train both public and private sector organizations. Furthermore, more universities should get involved in TQM training. The organizations, in turn, should allocate more educational funds to further the study of quality management. This would create a "cycle of continuous improvement" in which both the education and public/private sectors gain from the others expertise and/or experience.

Finally, every TQM manager interviewed in our study stressed the need for better benchmarking alternatives. Presently, it is not difficult to benchmark non-competing organizations. However, what an organization really needs is to benchmark its main competitors. This is difficult for obvious reasons. First, why would your competition give up confidential information and risk its competitive edge? Second, a firm may offer false information to trick its competitors. We recommend the establishment of private benchmarking warehouses. These warehouses could survey organizations involved with TQM implementations for relevant information. The information could be stored in a central database. Other organizations wishing to benchmark could access this database, for a fee, and obtain needed information. This would save endless visits and phone calls to other organizations and pinpoint only relevant implementation information.

CONCLUSION

This review of TQM applications and strategies in public and private sectors suggests that there are more similarities than differences between them. Regardless of the sector, it is evident that there are several common factors that contribute to a successful TQM implementation and its practice--namely, top management support, employee involvement, customer satisfaction, TQM education. Nevertheless, a few major differences have to be kept in view: (1) there are more TQM quantitative measurement systems in place in the private sector than in the public sector and (2) while TQM initiative in both private and public sectors result in quality improvement, in the private sector it may affect job security whereas in the public sector its impact on job security is not evident.

One of the conclusions that stands out is that more systematic measurement techniques and benchmarking practices as a standard way of doing business are imperative in both sectors. Therefore, the establishment of private benchmarking warehouses, whose function is to provide reliable industry-wide data on TQM implementation goals and performance is essential for success. Furthermore, there is an enhanced need for which closer collaboration between TQM planes and universities is called for. Such a collaboration demands the allocation of more educational funds by both private and public sectors to universities.

BIBLIOGRAPHY

Camp, R.C. (1990) "Benchmarking: The Search for Industry Best Practices that Lead to Superior Performance," American Productivity and Quality Center Magazine, pp. 1-6.

Crosby, P. B. (1989) Let's Talk Quality,New York,McGraw-Hill.

Deming, W. E. (1986) Out of the Crisis,M.I.T.,Center for Advanced Engineering Study.

Juran, J.M. (1978) "Japanese and Western Quality: A contrast in Methods and Results," Management Review, Vol. 67, No. 11, pp. 19-24.

Juran, J.M. (1991) "Made in USA - A Quality Resurgence," Journal for Quality and Participation, Juran Institute, Inc., pp. 6-8.

McGovern, J.P. (1990) "The Evolution of Total Quality Management," Program Manager, pp. 16-22.

TQMHB-1 (1991) Federal Quality Institute, How to Get Started Implementing Total Quality Management, Washington, D.C., Government Printing Office.

TQMHB-3 (1991) Federal Quality Institute, Introduction to Total Quality Management In the Federal Government, Washington, D.C., Government Printing Office.

ABOUT THE AUTHORS

Robert Goldstein is a Business Analyst with Fannie Mae. He received a B.A. in Business Management and Psychology from Mary Washington College in Fredericksburg, Virginia in 1989. He is currently pursuing a M.Sc. degree in Information Systems at The American University, Washington, D.C.

Reza Khorramshahgol received a B.Sc. in Mathematics from Tehran University and, from the George Washington University, an M.Sc. in Engineering Management and a D.Sc. in systems analysis. He is currently with the Department of Computer Science and Information Systems at the American University, Washington D.C. He is a senior member of the IEEE and serves on the editorial board of the IEEE Transactions on Engineering Management.

Productivity & Quality Management Frontiers-IV, edited by Sumanth, Edosomwan, Poupart, and Sink. ©1993 Institute of Industrial Engineers.

Creating the Research of Excellence

Y. Sato
ACON Co. Ltd.
Tokyo, JAPAN

Y. Katori
Mitsubishi Research Institute
Tokyo, JAPAN

ABSTRACT

This paper explores key factors and conditions for the Research of Excellence.

The Issue is one of the most important mission in the Japanese scientific and technological society.

Research of Excellence is defined as follows :

1. To undertake basic research
2. To provide top level scientists
3. To create the best environment and facility
4. To provide sufficient support and service for research
5. To develop superior management for both academy and administration
6. To make it well-known with high prestige

In order to find solution for creating excellence, Author made a field survey in existing superior research organizations and found key factors and conditions for breeding, incubating, and fostering excellence which are as follows : 1. role of government, university, establishment and international organization, 2. research environment, 3. source of fund, 4. management structure, 5. management and budgeting, 6. research strategy, objective and programme, 7. research function, 8.physical functions, 9. supports and services, 10. evaluation of research, 11. incentive, 12. optimum researcher, 13. recruit, 14. outcome.

INTRODUCTION

①   With the growing interdependence among all nations, there is an increasing need for the recognition of new common values and standards in the field of science and technology. Namely, the paradigm is now changing.

②   The research activities of various countries are summarized in Table 1.

③   The priority and proportion of research differ in each country. This survey is intended to determine the problems and issues involved in the realization and the implementation of excellence in scientific and technological research.

④   Nations are ever eager in the search for scientific and technological breakthroughs, placing greater importance on " excellence " in research.

Table 1: INTERNATIONAL COMPARISON OF RESEARCH

COUNTRY	PERCENTAGE OF RESEARCH EXPENDITURE AGAINST GNP		ANNUAL RESEARCH EXPENDITURE PER RESEARCH SCIENTIST	BASIC RESEARCH RATIO %
	TOTAL % (1989)	UNIVERSITY % (1987)		
U.S.A.	2.73	0.40	$ 142,468 (1988)	14.3 (1990)
U.K.	2.19	0.33	£ 100,917 (1988)	16.1 (1975)*
GERMANY	2.89	0.41	DM 136,544 (1987)	20.5 (1983)
FRANCE	2.33	0.34	FF1,134,314 (1988)	20.9 (1979)
JAPAN	2.91	0.30	¥21,089,000 (1989)	14.3 (1987)

SOURCE : OECD
* only Natural Science

RESEARCH INSTITUTIONS AND THEIR EXCELLENCE

According to the statement of Mr. Hickman and others, the number of Nobel prize laureates from a research institution is to be used as an indicator of research excellence. Therefore, this study focused on necessary and sufficient conditions for excellent institutions and how these institutions which has produced some researchers of distinguished talent as Nobel prize laureates were formed, developed and maintained.

Accordingly the following institutions are known as the best existing samples of excellence. In the U.S., the National Institute of Health, the IBM Laboratories and the AT&T Bell Laboratories ; in Germany, the Max Planck Institutes ; in France, the Centre National de la Recherche Scientifique and the Institute Pasteur ; in the U.K., the Science & Engineering Research Council and the Associated Universities ; in Switzerland, the Basel Institute for Immunology and IBM Laboratory.

To maintain high prestige of excellency in research, the research institutions must satisfying the following conditions.

Conditions Necessary for Research Excellence
   (1) Undertaking basic research
   (2) Providing top level scientists
   (3) Creating the best research environment and facilities
   (4) Providing sufficient support and services for research
   (5) Developing superior management for both academic and administrative branches
   (6) Gaining wide recognition and high prestige

And examples of research institutions satisfying these conditions are listed in Table 2:

Table 2: TYPICAL RESEARCH INSTITUTION OF EXCELLENCE IN THE WORLD

	FIELD OF RESEARCH	MISSION	FOUND-ED IN	BUDGET (1990) 1)RESEARCH BUDGET 2)GRANT 3)OTHERS	INTRA-MURAL STAFF 1)SCIEN-TIST 2)OTHERS	NOBEL LAUREATES INTRA-MURAL	NOBEL LAUREATES PAST RECORD
A U.S. INSTI-TUTION	BIO-MEDICAL	INTRA-MURAL RESEARCH, AND AWARD GRANTS AND CONTRACTS	1887	MILLION DOLLARS 7,581 1) 1,259 2) 5,215 3) 1,107	15,315 1) 7,186 2) 8,129	78 (1939~ 1990)	BEFORE 1939 4
A U.K. INSTI-TUTION	COMPRE-HENSIVE EXCEPT MEDICAL, AGRICUL-TURAL, FOOD, SOCIAL AND ECONOMICS	INTRA-MURAL RESEARCH, AND AWARD GRANTS AND CONTRACTS	1965	MILLION POUNDS 478 1) 172 2) 105 3) 201	2,730 1) 700 2) 2,030	10 (1965~ 1990)	BEFORE 1965 23
A GERMAN INSTI-TUTION	COMPRE-HENSIVE	INTRA-MURAL RESEARCH	1911	MILLION MARKS 1) 1,080 2) -	8,718 1) 3,195 2) 5,523	20 (1911~ 1990)	BEFORE 1911 8
A FRENCH INSTI-TUTION	COMPREH ENSIVE EXCEPT MEDICAL	INTRA-MURAL RESEARCH, AND AWARD PROJECT TO ASSOCIATED LABORATO-RIES	1939	MILLION FRANCS 11,144 1) 11,144 2) -	26,457 1) 11,193 2) 15,264	9 (1939~ 1990)	BEFORE 1939 16

SOURCE : ANNUAL REPORTS OF INSTITUTIONS

METHODOLOGY

Directors, Nobel prize laureates and R&D opinion leaders at research institutions recognized worldwide for their excellence were interviewed to obtain their views on the conditions required for breeding, incubating and fostering research excellence. For a greater clarity of the intent of the interview, the interviewees were supplied, in advance, with a list of possible qualifications for excellence, and were asked to select and express views on those qualifications they thought particularly important. Also, the interviewees were asked to specify and explain additional qualifications they considered necessary and important.

Qualifications selected by the interviewees were compared by percentage of selection, and it was assumed that a higher percentage indicated a greater importance of those qualifications for excellence. It was also assumed that, in the semantic sphere of the factors of questions, there was no significant perception gap among (a) institutions receiving national basic research grants, (b) government offices for the promotion of basic research, (c) private non-profit institutions with a 90% or higher dependency on national grants, (d) international institutions with a 100% dependency on international funds, (e) private institutions with a 100% dependency on private funds, and (f) private institutions with a 50% dependency on national grants. Further, it was assumed that there was no significant perception gap among the individual interviewees (i.e. directors, R&D opinion leaders and Nobel prize laureates), since the first two groups of interviewees were all former research scientists.

DISCUSSION AND CONCLUSION

The items selected as " important" for the research of excellence by the interviewees are shown in Table 3. The survey results indicate that strong support from the government is important for the maintenance of excellence. All of the interviewed research institutions widely acclaimed excellence depend on public support for at least 80% of their necessary funds.

Table 3: RESULT OF SURVEY

ITEM	KEY FACTORS & CONDITIONS
EXTERIOR RELATIONS	GOVERNMENT, UNIVERSITY, OTHER INSTITUTIONS, INTERNATIONAL ORGANIZATIONS
DIRECTION & SUPPORT	COMMITTEE, BOARD
FINANCIAL SOURCE	PUBLIC FUNDS, GRANT, CONTRIBUTION
MANAGEMENT	ADMINISTRATION OF TOP DIRECTOR, PLANNING BUDGET ALLOCATION, RECRUIT STANDARD, MAINTAIN PRESTIGE
STRATEGY	OBJECTIVE, PROGRAMME
RESEARCH	AUTONOMY, COLLABORATION, COOPERATION, ACCESS TO OTHER SCIENTIST & INFORMATION, SUPPORT & SERVICE, EPONYMY
PHYSICAL FUNCTION	FACILITY, BUILDING
STANDARD CAPACITY & ABILITY OF CORE SCIENTIST	QUALIFICATION, DIPLOMA, CULTURE, CHALLENGE, CREATIVITY, VISION, SELF ASSERTION, RESPONSIBILITY, SELF DEVELOPMENT
ASSESSMENT	PEER REVIEW, EVALUATION BY SCIENTIFIC COMMITTEE, APPRAISAL
INCENTIVE	AWARD, CONTRIBUTION, PRIZE, RECOGNITION, PUBLICATION IN THE BEST SCIENTIFIC JOURNAL
CONDITION	SALARY, JOB SAFETY SECURITY, LABOUR UNION, VACATION

Other important factors are policy directions and support from a scientific committee composed of the institution's board and authorities from the outside. Regarding the management of the institution, management ability of the top administrator (president) is very important, especially for the

939

acquisition and budgetary allocation of research funds are regarded important. In addition, importance is placed on the recruitment of outstanding scientists.

Another vital factor in the maintenance of research excellence, as pointed out by the interviewees, is the preservation of autonomy both for the institution and the scientists. In the area of research assessment, a proper examination of projects and grants are selected as important, together with an evaluation of research results by peers and a scientific committee consisting of members from within and outside the institution.

It is also considered necessary that the research findings be widely disseminated through active utilization of prestigious journals and conferences. The average number of printed papers is 1.5 to 5.7 per year for a scientist at the prestigious institutions of excellence, compared to 0.15 for a scientist at large in the U.S., 0.25 in the U.K., 0.15 in Germany, and 0.18 in France on the national average.

The salaries of core scientists at the renowned institutions are found to be relatively low, since they are employed as public servants, but it is found that this level of salaries do not affect excellence in research. The reasons why distinguished scientists have chosen their research institutions are found to be the prestige of institutions in specific research fields, greater autonomy given to the scientists, sufficient services and support available at the institution, the best access to scientific information and knowledge, and other factors for the improvement of the research environment. And this survey concludes that these are the important factors and conditions for such renowned institutions as to produce many Nobel prize laureates and/or to maintain their high prestige for the research of excellence.

REFERENCES

Craig R. Hickman & Michael A. Silva (1984) Creating Excellence, New American Library, page 21.

Japan Science Technology Agency (1992) White Paper, pp. 319~327.

MIRI (1992) International COE Forum, MIRI & JRIA, pp. 1~128.

Y.Sato (1992) The Survey Report of European COE, MIRI, pp. H1~H76.

BIOGRAPHICAL SKETCHES

Yoshio Sato is Counselor of the board and former Director of Overseas Planning Division, Mitsubishi Research Institute.
He served at the Battelle Memorial Institute Geneva Research Center, Mitsubishi Research Institute as Manager of the Techno-Economic Department and Manager of the Overseas Department. He has also served at the Institute of Business Administration and Management as a visiting faculty member, and at the Japan Productivity Center.
He is the author of Technological Forecasting, as well as other books. He has been appointed a member of various governmental committees.

Yoshishige Katori is Manager of New Science Department and Micro Machine Research Center of Mitsubishi Research Institute.
He graduated from Control Engineering Department, Tokyo Institute of Technology in 1973.
He has served for Engineering Research Institute, Kawasaki Heavy Industries from 1973 to 1979.
He has been appointed a member of Committee for the Center of Excellence, Japanese Government.

Productivity & Quality Management Frontiers-IV, edited by Sumanth, Edosomwan, Poupart, and Sink. ©1993 Institute of Industrial Engineers.

A Model for Managing and Measuring the Performance of a Training Function: Applying TQM Principles

S.L. Coleman, G.D. Coleman, and C.S. Johnston
Virginia Polytechnic Institute & State University
Blacksburg, Virginia USA

ABSTRACT

Juran (1988) and Ishikawa (1985) have said quality management begins and ends with training. Many organizations are devoting significant resources to training as a way to increase their skill base and improve organizational performance. Managing and improving these training services is increasingly important.

A common problem for training functions is measuring the quality and productivity of their services (Kusy, 1988). Not only must training functions measure quality and productivity for the purpose of supporting improvement, but also to justify their resource requirements (Schneider, Monetta, & Wright, 1992). Upper level management must often be convinced of the value added by the training function.

A current review of relevant literature revealed no comprehensive research-based model for managing and measuring the performance of a training function. However, the components of such a model have been discussed by different authors, for example, managing information retrieval from subject-matter experts (Ford and Wood, 1992), and determining the cost effectiveness of a training program (Hawley, 1991; Schneider, Monetta, & Wright, 1992). Given the increased emphasis placed on total quality management and related training, why not apply those concepts to the training function?

The modified Management Systems Model (created by Kurstedt, 1986 and modified by Sink & Tuttle, 1989) provides a framework for applying total quality management concepts to the training function. An input/output analysis technique is used to define the managerial system components of a typical training function operating as a cost center within a larger corporation. The result is a literature-based systems view of a training function. Current managers of training functions were interviewed to validate the literature-based model.

The modified Management Systems Model contains five checkpoints for the management and measurement of quality: customers, outputs, value-adding processes, inputs, and suppliers. Applying this model to a training function provides a basis for a prescription for managing and measuring the five quality checkpoints. The authors discuss how the training function can be managed, measured, and improved using the information from the systems view of a training function. Suggested next steps include the testing of recommended interventions on a small scale using a PDSA (Shewhart Cycle, or plan-do-study-act) approach.

Key Words: measuring quality and productivity, Management Systems Model, training, input/output analysis, total quality management

This paper was prepared, in part, with funds from a Department of Energy/New Production Reactors Grant studying Program Management and Grand Strategy Systems. Grant No. DE-FG02-91NP00119.

INTRODUCTION

"There is no substitute for knowledge," says Dr. W. Edwards Deming, the man who led the transformation of Japan from a second class nation to a major force in the global marketplace. "Best efforts are not enough, you must know what to do." (Deming 1986). In today's increasingly complex organizational environment, where continuous improvement is an economic imperative, knowing what to do requires that sufficient resources be expended on training and education of the workforce (Thurow, 1992).

It is widely acknowledged that education and training is a key element in an organization's Total Quality Management effort. For example, Juran and Ishikawa have said that quality begins and ends with training. (Juran, 1988; Ishikawa, 1985) Two of Deming's 14 Points for Management address training: #6--Institute modern methods of training on the job; and #13--Institute a vigorous program of education and retraining. (Deming, 1986) Further, education and training is incorporated into the criteria of all major quality and productivity awards, including the Malcolm Baldrige National Quality Award; the Deming Prize; the President's Award and the Quality Improvement Prototype Award; the Institute of Industrial Engineers Award; the George M. Low Trophy--NASA's Quality and Excellence Award; and the U. S. Senate Productivity Award for Virginia (1991 Guide, 1991)

Heeding the direction of the quality gurus and the example set by world class companies, American organizations are devoting a significant amount of resources to education and training. However, a paradox exists in that training function managers are finding it increasingly difficult to justify these resources (Kusy, 1988, Schneider, Monetta, and Wright, 1992).

We contend that by applying a TQM orientation to the training function, managers will become better able to utilize resources to optimize the organizational system, thus gaining greater visibility and support for their efforts. The importance of education and training, the cost of education and training, and the continuous improvement paradigm make the training function a logical place to apply TQM principles. Yet, it is interesting to note that a review of the literature found no comprehensive applications of TQM to the training function. Although limited applications of specific tools and techniques were found, an overall framework for applying TQM principles was conspicuously absent. This paper attempts to provide training function managers with a such a framework.

A MODEL FOR VIEWING AN ORGANIZATION AS A SYSTEM

A system is a group of interrelated parts which, when working together, make up a complex whole (Kurstedt, 1986). When one component is affected by some force internal or external to the system all other components are affected, due to the interconnectedness of the system. Because of the interdependence of each component, actions taken upon the system must be planned carefully in order to achieve the overall desired effect. In order to predict how the system will respond to one action, the system must be understood thoroughly.

An organization is a system and should be managed as such. Actions taken in one part of the organization will affect other parts of the system as well. To manage the system effectively, each component must be understood thoroughly and the critical indicators of the health of the organization identified so they can be measured and monitored (Sink, 1989; Dobyns & Crawford-Mason, 1991). Understanding the organization as a system is the first step in planning for a TQM effort (Sink, 1989). The Management Systems Model (Kurstedt, 1986 and Sink & Tuttle, 1989) can be used to understand an organization as a system so that it can be better measured and managed. This paper will use the Management Systems Model to examine a typical training function within a larger organization. The result will be a systems understanding of a training function. This understanding along, with the concept of managing and measuring quality at five checkpoints (Sink & Tuttle, 1989), will facilitate the identification of indicators or measures of the training function's performance.

The Management Systems Model Described

The Management Systems Model (MSM) helps to define and portray the manager's domain of responsibility as a management *system*, resulting in a better understanding of this system (Kurstedt, 1986). Kurstedt describes the MSM as having three parts: "who manages", "what is managed", and "what is used to manage". Who manages is the individual or team responsible for the organization, what is managed is the organizational system, and what is used to manage are the tools of management (Kurstedt, 1986). The interfaces between the three parts show the interdependency of the system (Figure 1). First, the tools used to manage (what is used to manage) portray information to managers (i.e., who manages). The portrayal of this information and the characteristics of the manager influence the perception of the information, affecting the manager's subsequent decisions. These decisions become actions directed toward the organizational system (what is managed). The effects of these actions are measured and the data are cycled back using management tools, to the manager in the form of information. This management cycle functions continuously.

Sink and Tuttle (1989) modified the MSM by expanding the what is managed component, facilitating the identification of key performance indicators of the organization (Figure 2). What is managed is now defined by providers of input, their inputs (e.g., labor, energy, information), value-adding processes (which turn the inputs into outputs), outputs (a product or service of the organization), and customers. By identifying these system components, managers have a total systems view of their organization. The input/output analysis technique is used to develop this system view. In addition to identifying the five components of the organizational system, the input/output analysis also identifies the customers' desired outcomes. Understanding these desired outcomes is key to identifying the critical indicators of an organization's performance.

Sink and Tuttle (1989) also describe five quality checkpoints necessary to manage quality totally (see Figure 2). These quality checkpoints coincide with the five components of what is managed in the modified MSM. The quality of the upstream systems (providers), inputs, value-added processes, outputs, and downstream systems (customers) is managed at these checkpoints. The first quality checkpoint (Q1) is the management or selection of upstream systems or the providers of input. The second quality checkpoint (Q2) is the assurance that the inputs meet the organization's requirements (i.e., incoming quality control). The third quality checkpoint (Q3) is the management of the key processes which transform the inputs into outputs, ensuring quality is built into the product or service. The fourth quality checkpoint (Q4) is assuring the output meets established requirements or specifications (outgoing quality control). The fifth quality checkpoint (Q5) is the proactive understanding of the customers' desired outcomes and their reaction to the organization's product or service. If performance is managed at each of the five key checkpoints, the manager will succeed in managing quality totally (Sink & Tuttle, 1989).

The research presented in this paper focuses on what is managed in a training function. Our research produced a systems view of a training function in terms of the Sink and Tuttle (1986) expansion of what is managed. This model was reviewed by practicing training managers to assure its applicability to practitioners.

METHOD

Parameters for the training function were defined to narrow the scope of our model. For the purpose of this study, the training function is defined as a one-person cost center within a larger organization. This one-person training function is responsible for the training programs only within the company; no course development is performed for outside customers. At times, the training manager finds it is necessary to hire outside trainers or purchase ready-made training programs.

The organization in which this training function exists is structured such that the training manager reports to a member of top-level management, an increasingly popular organizational option (Camp, Blanchard, and Huszczo, 1986). Often, this top level manager functions as the Chief Staffing Officer, responsible for the all staffing functions of the organization (Laird, 1985).

Once the parameters were defined, the literature-based model was developed using an input/output analysis to organize and portray information from the literature review. Once the literature-based model was established, the results were shared with training managers in order to validate the model. The "Systems Model Of A Training Function" (see Figure 3 - the literature-based model is shown in non-italicized text) and a list of the interview questions were distributed to each subject. Structured telephone and face-to-face interviews were conducted and consisted of six questions, plus demographic information. The interviewer asked the practitioner to examine the contents under each of the six columns of the model and make recommendations for changes, additions, or deletions.

The interview data was analyzed by comparing responses of the training managers, question by question (and column by column on the model). The changes, additions, and deletions as suggested by the training managers are included in the final model (see Figure 3; practitioner's comments are portrayed by the italicized text).

Current training managers from four organizations participated in the interviews. The managers represent training functions serving as cost centers within their respective organizations. Two organizations are in the public sector (one federal government, and one state government) and two are private manufacturing firms. The size of the organizations served by each training function ranges from 152 to 10,000 (152, 350, 900, and 10,000). The size of the training functions ranges from 1 to 3 employees, consistent with established parameters (see above). All four training functions utilize outside training services, as well as design some of their own courses.

RESULTS AND DISCUSSION

The Literature-Based Systems Model of a Training Function

This section describes the literature-based systems model of a training function. The six components of the input/output analysis are grouped by providers and inputs, value-adding processes and outputs, and customers and desired outcomes to enhance readability.

Providers and Inputs. The suppliers who provide the training function with inputs include: the organization's personnel department (or industrial/organizational psychologists), top-level management, individual employees and their supervisors, outside training vendors, bookkeepers, and subject matter experts.

The personnel department supplies input to the training function in the form of job analyses for each job in the organization. The job analysis identifies the knowledge, skills, and attitudes (KSAs) necessary for the incumbent to perform a particular job adequately (Cascio, 1987). The job analysis also can be used as a gauge for identifying employees who lack the necessary KSAs (Goldstein, 1986). In this case, the job analysis can be used in conjunction with past employee evaluations, an input also provided by the personnel office. The training manager can match performance problems with the KSAs identified in the job analysis to detect gaps.

Determining if the gap can be closed by training requires input from the personnel department regarding the background of the employee. This information can be gathered from employment applications or resumes. Specifically, the training manager would want to know the educational background and experience of individual employees. An employee possessing the KSAs to do the job will not benefit from training. Other solutions will have to be explored by the employee's supervisor, such as performance incentives (Goldstein, 1986).

Input regarding employee performance can also come from supervisors. Supervisors have first line of sight for individual employees and can identify individual strengths and weaknesses (Camp, Blanchard, Huszczo, 1986). The training manager can gather data about performance problems or perceived training needs from a supervisor through a questionnaire or interview (Camp et al.,1986). Also, supervisors will have to be consulted when a training program is being planned so that arrangements can be made for employees to be away from their jobs.

One of the primary purposes of the training function is to help the organization meet its strategic goals (Camp et al., 1986; Spitzer, 1991). Training managers cannot contribute to the organizational effort if they do not understand the organization's goals. Thus, top-level management is also a provider of input to training managers. This input is usually in the form of a written strategic plan (or report) for the organization. Communication between training managers and top-level management must be maintained so that the training function is not at cross purposes with the organization.

Smaller training functions often purchase training materials from external sources. Outside training vendors supply training managers with information regarding their own products and services (e.g., outside instructors) which may be solicited or unsolicited.

Bookkeepers provide training managers information regarding the expenses incurred by the training function. Specific inputs include instructor and subject matter expert salaries, cost of instructional materials development and/or acquisition (e.g., photocopying, audiovisual equipment, and books), facility fees, and developmental costs.

Participants of training programs provide input during the course evaluation through a variety of data collection procedures. For example, to evaluate a training program, the training manager may want to design a questionnaire for the participants to determine their perceptions of the program. The training manager may also choose to conduct interviews before or after the training session. There are several other providers of input for course evaluation data - instructors, participant supervisors, subject matter experts, and even some top-level managers.

SMEs provide additional input into the training function. Often, the content of the training program is unfamiliar to the course designer and an SME is hired to provide technical content. The SME is not only a provider of input but also a customer of the training function (e.g., when receiving specific information about the course from the training function).

Value-adding processes and outputs. The value-adding processes are the sets of actions which convert the inputs of the organization into outputs (Sink & Tuttle, 1989). Identification of training needs is a process that typically rests with the training function. The mechanisms used by the training function to identify the organization's training needs have many names (Renard & Sinnock, 1990) but accomplish the same goals. This mechanism will be called needs analysis for the purposes of this paper. Basically, a needs analysis leads to the identification of performance problems, the determination of the root of the problem, and suggestions for solutions to the problems (training or otherwise). The needs analysis includes examination of personnel abilities, the work environment, organizational goals, and prioritization of the organization needs. Details of these processes will not be elaborated upon here but can be found in Mager (1988), Camp et al.(1986), Goldstein (1986), and Rossett (1987). The training manager uses input from top-level management, the personnel office, supervisors, and individual employees to produce recommendations regarding current training needs and to describe how the training function can contribute to organization goals. An output from a needs analysis is a report or presentation to top-level management regarding how the training function can help the organization meet current needs and begin to prepare for projected needs.

A second value-adding process of the training function, systematic instructional design, consists of several smaller processes, which guide the development of an effective and efficient instructional program. A popular description of these processes is the Gagne, Briggs, and Wager model presented in *Principles of Instructional Design* (1992). Some of the sub processes included in instructional design include audience assessment, objective writing, task analyses (i.e., ordering the objectives hierarchically), media selection, lesson design, and student performance assessment. The output from the process of systematic instructional design is the documented course(s) or training program(s) and train the trainer programs.

A third value-adding process, which occurs prior to instructional design, involves interactions with the SMEs. The output of this process is information regarding the content contained in the training program. Accurate objectives can be written and placed hierarchically when the instructional designer is familiar with the structure of the knowledge behind the subject matter. Ford and Wood (1992) describe a computer program called SNOWMAN (System for Knowledge Management) which guides the instructional designer in gathering and analyzing SME knowledge. A more popular process for gathering this information is through formal SME interviews.

A fourth value-adding process, logistical planning, must be addressed once the course has been developed. The process of logistical planning ensures that an appropriate meeting room is scheduled, supervisors and employees have been consulted to determine a convenient time for the training to take place, the required audio-visual materials are secured (e.g., student notebooks, video tapes and VCR, a course agenda, and computer equipment), and refreshments are ordered, if appropriate. The output from this process is a smooth-running course.

A fifth value-adding process, evaluation, is composed of several sub-processes, including evaluation planning (i.e., what you want to learn from the evaluation and how you will get the data to answer your questions), data collection, and data analysis. The output from the evaluation process is recommendations for improving future training programs leading to improved training function services.

A final value-adding process, cost/benefit analysis, enables the training manager to determine the overall benefits of training to the organization, including cost savings (Heneman, Schwab, Fossum, & Dyer, 1989). During the cost/benefit analysis, the training manager considers all the resources allotted to training, and the results of the training effort. The output from the cost/benefit analysis is an indication of the performance of the training function. This is information the training manager can share with top-level management to document the training function's contribution to organizational efforts.

Customers and Desired Outcomes. Davidove (1991) points out two important tasks in a successful systems approach to instructional design - identifying the customers, and understanding their desired outcomes. The following is a description of some of the customers of the training function and the associated desired outcomes.

Top-level management is a less-obvious customer of the training function. They receive the results of the needs analysis, cost/benefit analysis, and even the program evaluation from the training manager. Also, the improved performance of employees as a result of training is less tangible, but an important outcome for this customer.

Understanding this customer's (i.e., top-level management) desired outcomes will help the training manager demonstrate how the training function can contribute to the organization's goals. First, management desires a workforce that is qualified and prepared to help the company meet its strategic goals (Camp et al. 1986). For example, if an insurance company plans to link all agents to the company's mainframe computer within the next five years, the transition will be smoother if employees possess some level of computer literacy. Understanding this desired outcome enables the training manager to demonstrate how current courses will support this effort, as well as to suggest the implementation of future courses to ensure employees are prepared for change.

Another desired outcome of top-level management is to reduce costs by increasing worker productivity. A well-trained workforce can do just that for the organization. For example, secretarial staff trained to write routine business letters enable their managers to spend time on higher-value-adding tasks. Also, safety training not only contributes to individual employee well-being, but decreases shut-down time due to accidents and can reduce healthcare costs. These kinds of data may be included in the output from the cost/benefit analysis.

Top-level management also desires satisfied employees. The training function can enhance employee satisfaction by providing developmental opportunities. By providing these opportunities, employees feel they have a future with the organization (Heneman et al., 1987; Goldstein, 1986) and are less likely to quit. Decreased turnover reduces the cost of recruiting and training new employees.

A shared body of knowledge can also be a desired outcome of top-level management. In any organization, there is a common language or knowledge base essential to all or a group of employees. For example, a company may want all managers to understand and implement TQM principles and may call upon the training function to provide TQM training programs to management.

Another customer of the training function is employees' supervisors. Supervisors expect improved employee performance as an outcome of training. Other desired outcomes will be specific to employees' jobs. For example, a supervisor of coal miners may want the workers to perform their jobs more safely.

Individual employees are also customers of the training function. The desired outcomes of this customer include qualification for promotion, ability to perform their job better, and/or increased income. This is another instance where the desired outcomes will vary from person to person.

The training function can be its own customer, with a desired outcome of improved services. This is accomplished through the process of evaluation. Understanding the training function's desired outcomes will contribute to a more comprehensive evaluation.

The instructors hired by the training function are customers of the training function (note that instructors can also be suppliers of services). These customers desire a well-designed course so that the session runs smoothly. They also desire the instructional strategies used during the course to be in line with their personal teaching styles. For example, a particular instructor may be uncomfortable leading large group discussions and prefer small group discussions instead. If small group instruction is appropriate for the situation, the training function should strive to meet the instructor's need.

The results of this literature review are summarized in Figure 3. To produce a model which more accurately reflects what actually occurs in a training function, practicing training function managers were asked to review the model. The practitioners' responses to the model are summarized in the next section.

Practitioner Response to the Literature-Based Model

Feedback from training practitioners adds an important dimension to the model (Figure 3). Their responses to interview questions enable the model to reflect a more practical systems view of the training function. In some cases, the training managers suggested deletions to reflect their own organizational practices; however, these items were not removed from the model in order to maintain its applicability to a wide range of training functions.

The training managers responded similarly in two areas. First, practitioners suggested that providers, inputs, value-adding processes, outputs, and desired outcomes are shared among the customers, making it difficult and sometimes misleading to portray them separately as is done in the model. The practitioners pointed out that information contained in each component for individual customers could actually be shared among the customers. This is not reflected in the revised model to reduce redundancy, but should be considered when applying the model. Second, the terminology will vary among training functions, depending on the culture of the organization. For example, an organization taking a team approach to management may not have supervisors, but team leaders. The model can, of course, be changed to reflect specific needs of any training function.

The remainder of the suggested changes are specific to individual components of the model and are identified in Figure 3 by the italicized text.

Using the Model to Apply TQM Principles to a Training Function

The systems model of a training function introduced in this paper provides a framework to operationally define the quality checkpoints for a training function. It also facilitates identification of appropriate interventions and tools for each checkpoint. The following discussion, organized by quality checkpoint, provides specific examples of how the model can be used to spark systems thinking and guide the training manager's efforts to apply TQM principles.

Quality Checkpoint 1. An important tenet of TQM is that suppliers are vital partners. Partnering activities for the training function might include collaborating with a local college or university, and guaranteeing long term relationships with suppliers as a part of a formal certification process. Systematic analysis of instructor evaluations is an example of a measurement activity applicable to quality checkpoint one. Loosmore (1991) describes a tool for maintaining information about instructors called a presenters' information book. General information about the instructor/presenter as well as information regarding the instructor's effectiveness (on pre-developed forms) are kept in this book. The information is used by the training manager to make decisions regarding the selection of instructors. Similar data could also be kept for facilities used during training to justify future selections of preferred sites.

Quality Checkpoint 2. With respect to the training function, management of quality checkpoint two (incoming quality assurance) might include activities such as reviewing detailed course descriptions and lesson plans to ensure instructional soundness (e.g., ensuring performance-based objectives have been identified). Instruction provided by presenters is also an input and can be managed and measured using a check sheet or other type of form. Clark, Steele, Niemiec and Walberg (1992) provide an instructor observation form to be filled out by the training manager. Noted on this form are the instructional methodology and the frequency with which the instructor demonstrates appropriate instructional behaviors (e.g., relating key points to practical situations). When the data are analyzed, they yield information such as the number and types of behaviors exhibited by the instructor, which can be used to measure performance. Additionally, worksheets can be used to ensure that all logistical data necessary to conduct the course has been provided.

Quality Checkpoint 3. Documenting and establishing procedures for key processes is one of the basics of TQM. The act of documenting key processes and sharing documentation with stakeholders often leads to the identification of areas for continual improvement. Once a process has been documented, data on the time and cost required to complete the steps can be collected. For example, it is often useful to measure the amount of time it takes from when a training request is received to when the request is filled. Flowcharting is another mechanism for managing quality checkpoint three. Kastigar (1991) provides a flowchart for tracking a performance analysis project which a training manager can use to assure all performance analysis projects follow a prescribed progression of activities. The value-adding process can be measured by the degree to which the process portrayed in the flowchart is followed, or time taken to complete the steps. Check sheets are valuable tools for managing the myriad of logistical details that accompany training program delivery. Templates and graphical specifications for guidance in developing training materials are other examples of a management effort aimed at this checkpoint.

Quality Checkpoint 4. Numerous approaches can be taken to manage and measure outgoing quality assurance. For example, the training manager might attend selected course offerings to review and ultimately provide feedback to the instructor. Here, it is important to note that the training function manager must ensure evaluation reports are more than just compilations of data. Data should be compiled, analyzed, and converted to information that can be used by the manager. This might include tracking evaluation data across time to provide a longitudinal data base for a given course or instructor.

The training manager can test recent training course attendees to measure the knowledge and skills they have gained. Simple output measures, such as number of courses offered within a given time frame might be another measure. Review/inspection of training materials to identify or even count mistakes can provide data on the quality of training materials, as well as provide feedback that can be used to improve the next iteration of those materials. If the training function issues payment to its instructors, tracking the time between course delivery and instructor payment is a measure of how well an important customer is being treated.

Schneider, Monetta, and Wright (1992) describe a return on investment model that can be used to manage training function outputs. The model uses data concerning the dollar value of tasks, employee proficiency, and employee salary to calculate the dollar value of employee performance improvement as a result of training.

Quality Checkpoint 5. The proactive assurance that customer needs and expectations are being met and exceeded is crucial to long-term success and survival. Clearly, it is important for the training manager to spend time with customers to understand how they are affected by training function services. Measuring data that indicate how effectively customers' outcomes are being achieved is called for at this checkpoint. As an example, one indicator might be the number of employees qualifying for promotion based on training completed. Tracking the performance of training program participants can also be useful, and might be accomplished by interviewing the participants' supervisors at specific post-training intervals to assess the impact of training on employee behavior/performance. A regular meeting with top management to show how the training function's activities support the organization's goals and to receive feedback on performance is also advised.

The ideas discussed here offer only a partial list of what could be done to manage and measure quality at each of the Five Quality Checkpoints. By referring to the systems model, Fig 3, while re-reading the above discussion, one can see how the structure of the model assists in the identification of interventions and performance indicators.

CONCLUSION

The model described in this paper can be a useful tool for managing and measuring the performance of a training function. The Systems View of a Training Function helps training managers to not only bound their own management domain, but view their domain as a total system. Understanding the training function as a system and identifying the components of the system is the first important step in managing quality totally. We recommend additional education and training on how to apply this model to individual organizations to take full advantage of the model.

Our systems view of a training function should be considered a starting point to be improved upon rather than a final product. Feedback from additional practitioners will be collected to continue the validation of our model. We hope this research will lead to further modifications, producing a more comprehensive model for training managers.

REFERENCES

1991 Guide to awards. (1992). *QPM: Quality and Productivity Management*, 9(2). 5-13.
Camp, R. R., Blanchard, P. N., & Huszczo, G. E. (1986). *Toward a more organizationally effective training strategy and practice.* Englewood Cliff, NJ: Prentice Hall.
Cascio, W. F. (1987). *Applied psychology in personnel management, 3rd edition.* Englewood Cliffs, NJ: Prentice-Hall.
Clark, G., Steele, R., Niemiec, R. P., & Walberg, H. J. (1992). Promoting teacher behaviors that promote student learning. *Performance & Instruction, 31* (4), 22-24.

Davidove, E. (1991). The most important lessons I've learned as a consultant about the systems approach to instructional design. *Performance & Instruction 30* (10), 11-13.

Deming, W E. (1986). *Out of the crisis.* Cambridge, MA: MIT Center for Advanced Engineering Study.

Dobyns, L. & Crawford-Mason, C. (1991), *Quality or else: The revolution in world business.* Boston: Houghton Mifflin.

Ford, J. M., & Wood, L. W. (1992). Structuring and documenting interactions with subject matter experts. *Performance Improvement Quarterly, 5* (1), 2-24.

Gagne, R. M., Briggs, L. J., & Wager, W. W. (1992). *Principles of instructional design..* New York: Holt, Rinehart & Winston.

Goldstein, I. L. (1986). *Training in organization: Needs assessment, development, and evaluation, 2nd edition.* Pacific Grove, CA: Brooks/Cole Publishing.

Hawley, J. K. (1991). A practical methodology for determining cost-effective instructional programs. *Performance and Instruction, 30* (5), 17-23.

Heneman, H. G. III, Schwab, D. P., Fossum, J. A., & Dyer, L. D. (1989). *Personnel/Human Resource Management.* Homewood, IL: Irwin.

Ishikawa, K. (1985) *What is total quality control.* Edgewood Cliffs, NJ: Prentice Hall

Juran, J. M. (1988). *On planning for quality.* New York: The Free Press.

Kastigar, G. J. (1991). Aligning and tracking a performance analysis project. *Performance & Instruction, 30* (4), 5-7.

Kurstedt, H. A. (1986). The management system model helps your tools work for you. MSL Working Draft Articles and Responsive Systems Article. Management Systems Laboratories. Virginia Tech, Blacksburg, VA.

Kusy, M. E. Jr. (1988). The effects of types of training on support of training among corporate managers. *Performance Improvement Quarterly, 1* (2), 23-30.

Laird, D. (1985). *Approaches to training and development, 2nd edition.* Reading, MA: Addison-Wesley.

Loosmore, J. (1991). Keeping track of your presenters with a presenters information book. *Performance & Instruction, 30* (2), 34-37.

Mager, R. F. (1988). *Making instruction work.* Belmont, CA: Lake Books.

Renard, P. G. & Sinnock, P. (1990). Training needs assessment: Fact or Fiction? *Performance & Instruction, 29* (8), 12-15.

Rossett, A. (1987). *Training needs assessment.* Englewood Cliffs, NJ: Educational Technology.

Schneider, H., Monetta, D. J., & Wright, C. C. (1992). Training function accountability: How to really measure return on investment. *Performance and Instruction, 31* (3), 12-17.

Sink, D. S. (1989). TQM: The next frontier or just another bandwagon to jump on? *Quality and Productivity Management, 7* (2).

Sink, D. S. & Tuttle, T. C. (1989). *Planning and measurement in your organization of the future.* Norcross, GA: Industrial Engineering and Management Press.

Spitzer, D. (1991). Training: What it is and how to use it appropriately. *Performance & Instruction, 30* (3), 20-23.

Thurow, L. (1992). *Head to head.* New York, NY: William Morrow & Co.

BIOGRAPHICAL SKETCHES OF AUTHORS

Susan L. Coleman is a Research Associate in the Technology Transfer Group at Management Systems Laboratories and specializes in instructional technology.

Garry D. Coleman is the Director of Business Development at the Virginia Productivity Center and specializes in quality and productivity management.

Cynthia S. Johnston is a Research Associate at the Virginia Productivity Center and specializes in quality and productivity education and training.

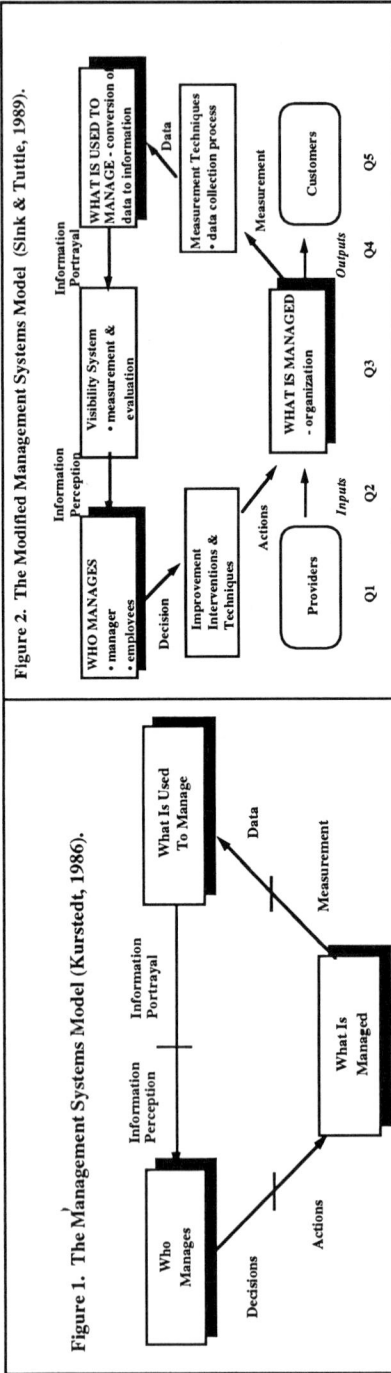

Figure 1. The Management Systems Model (Kurstedt, 1986).

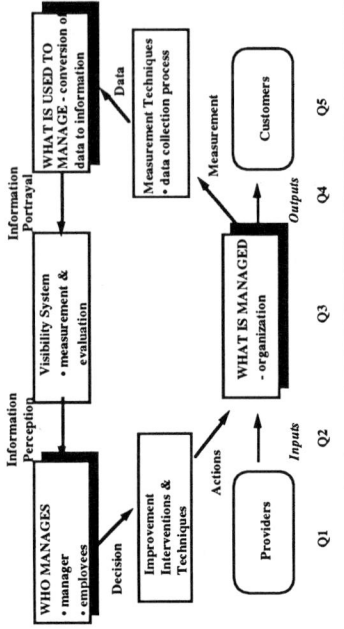

Figure 2. The Modified Management Systems Model (Sink & Tuttle, 1989).

Figure 3. A Systems Model of a Training Function.

Providers	Inputs	Value-Adding Processes	Outputs	Customer	Desired Outcomes
Subject-matter experts Supervisors Top-level mgt Outside vendors Employees Supervisors Training records *Contractors*	Detailed content information. Course offering suggestions. Previous program evaluations. Information regarding vendors products/services.	Systematic Instructional Design Evaluation & acquisition of vendor products and services. *Matching individual training needs to courses.*	Courses/Training Programs	Individual Employees	Qualify for promotion. Perform current job better. Qualify for a different job. Increase income. *Resolve deficiencies. Application of training content.*
Supervisors *(team leaders)* Training facility managers	Logistical data affecting the delivery of the course (e.g. room size and availability).	Logistical planning. Conducting planned or purchased programs.	Employees with improved knowledge skills, and/or attitudes	Supervisors *(team leaders)*	Improved employee performance. Minimal interruptions due to employee training *Better supervisory skills Application of training content. Improved team performance.*

Figure 3 Continued.

Providers	Inputs	Value-Adding Processes	Outputs	Customer	Desired Outcomes
Personnel office Top-level mgt Bookkeepers	Job analyses Employee information Employee evaluations Employee salary info Strategic plan/goals for the organization	Organizational needs assessment. Cost/benefit analysis. Designing and conducting training programs.	Report to top-level mgt. re: how the training function can contribute to the organization's long-term goals. Return on investment report (i.e. money saved due to training). Identification of organization's current training needs. Skilled employees.	Top-level mgt *Dept. Heads (i.e. mid-level management.)*	Productive employees. Employees prepared to help the organization meet future goals. Save money. Have a common body of knowledge shared among a group or all company employees. Satisfied employees. *Application of training content. Recognition for progressive training practices.*
Training program participants Supervisors Trainers/ Instructors	Interview and/or questionnaire data.	Program/course evaluation (i.e. data analysis)	Program/course evaluation report	Training function	Improved services to the organization. *Application of training content. Justify the training function existence. Bring recognition as "leading edge."*
Instructors	Instructor's presentation strengths/weakness/ preferences *Logistical data and requirements Proposals/quotes from instructors.*	Course materials development *Logistical planning Contract management*	Well documented instructor materials Train-the-trainer program *Instructor payment order (paperwork to pay instructor). Facilities arranged and ready*	Instructors	Successful and smooth running session. *Application of training content. Compensation for services*

Productivity & Quality Management Frontiers-IV, edited by Sumanth, Edosomwan, Poupart, and Sink. ©1993 Institute of Industrial Engineers.

The Production Game

D.K. Denton
Southwest Missouri State University
Springfield, Missouri USA

ABSTRACT

This classroom simulation called The Production Game has been used in basic or advanced Production/Operations Management university courses, and it is designed to simulate real-life productivity and quality problems and solutions.

It is not a computer simulation nor a "board" game. Instead, students actually form their own companies, divide managerial duties and produce a product. All of this occurs within a classroom setting. Once students have formed their team, they are given instructions for how to run the simulation. Materials used in the simulation include one-half sheets of construction paper (raw material), product specification, and production equipment (scissors, glue, rules, etc.)

In its simplest form, students have 30 minutes to make as many products as they can while trying to control inventory, quality, labor and financial matters. The remaining 20 minutes is used to evaluate the team's performance. These comments and suggestions can be used by the participants to improve their operation before the next "production run."

Productivity & Quality Management Frontiers-IV, edited by Sumanth, Edosomwan, Poupart, and Sink. ©1993 Institute of Industrial Engineers.

How to Reduce Total Cycle Time in Your Company

R.G. Ligus
Rockford Consulting Group, Ltd.
Rockford, Illinois USA

ABSTRACT

Use time-based competition as one of your most powerful strategic weapons! Drive down the time it takes to develop and deliver new products, dramatically reduce inventory and manufacturing time, slash the cost of quality, and win back market share. This article tells you how you can do it, and become a fierce competitor.

Substantial market share has been lost over the years to foreign competitors. No industry is immune. The pressure is on to be nothing less than the best. Reducing cycle times in your company is a new way of tackling the problem. It's a new world-class manufacturing strategy that is making companies fiercely competitive. Companies who are doing it are cutting out 50% of the time to develop and introduce new products. They have already reduced factory throughput time by 98%.

But being the best takes radical change and it's no easy matter. Becoming a time-based high performance company requires overcoming organizational inertia. Often overlooked are outdated cultures, ineffective management skills, bureaucratic red tape, and a reward system that doesn't fit .

You have to streamline factories, systems, and organizations and open up lines of communications. You have to break down barriers between departments and put an end to the "we've always done it that way" argument. You have to get your employees highly involved in assuming new responsibilities if you're going to compete in the tough global markets of the 1990's. None of these is an easy task.

Managing large scale change requires a comprehensive plan as well as accountabilities for getting work accomplished.The integrated change model provides a way to do it. It's the shell of a master plan for reducing cycle times in your company. It utilizes social and technical application tools. It emphasizes a continuous improvement approach, with high involvement of people. This cycle time reduction program guides and facilitates you. It takes you through the steps in reducing the total cycle time in your company. This broad approach covers all parts of the organization: marketing, manufacturing, engineering, accounting, etc. It includes the full service chain from customer through warehousing, distribution, assembly, production, and supply.

In summary, the integrated change model provides a systematic methodology for large scale change and implementation of time-based strategy. It gives you the means of becoming world class, and provides a new approach to competing in the 1990's.

Time-based competition is one of the most powerful strategic weapons to emerge in the last twenty years! It allows you to drive down the time it takes to develop and deliver new products, dramatically reduce inventory and manufacturing time, slash the cost of quality, and win back market share. Today, and for the next five years, **speed kills the competition.** Time compression can result in consistently producing happy customers: a great formula for success. Why? When given a situation where costs and quality are similar, customers will choose delivery as the deciding factor.

Compressing time has a cascading affect on quality and cost. As cycle times are reduced, productivity increases proportionally. Stalk(1) concludes that a fifty percent reduction in cycle time and a doubling in work-in-process inventory turns causes productivity to increase from 20-70%. As productivity increases, resource capacity is freed. Two things happen: Costs decline, and the organization becomes capable of producing significantly more output with less resources: a winning combination.

Why do anything?

What about survival and growth for starters? If you value your business and your job, there are a few things that you may want to consider. First it's no secret that in 15 years, the U.S. lost significant world market share in key industries: wide-bodied aircraft, semi-conductors, automobiles, electronics, and steel. The U.S. manufacturing base has eroded to our offshore competitors, losing our edge--in price, delivery, and quality. Our foreign competitors are delivering high quality products with one pass through the factory, while we're impeded by mistakes.

There are almost no VCR's, camcorders, tape players and recorders, radios, phonographs, or compact disc players produced in the U.S. Imports in other industries continue to increase. Industries under intense foreign competition include farm machinery, lawn and garden equipment, machine tools, bicycles, and process controls.

Secondly, competing is taking on new proportions. A global resegmentation of markets emerging is changing the world economy: the U.S./Canada/Mexico trade agreement, EC-92, the democratization of Eastern Europe, the recent rising growth of Latin America: Mexico, Venezuela, Brazil, Chile, and Argentina, and the accelerated growth of the Pacific Rim countries: Korea, Taiwan, Singapore, Thailand, Hong Kong, and Japan.

U.S. manufacturers face stiff offshore competition in most markets. Companies failing to respond to the challenge will find themselves left behind in the dust. It doesn't matter whether you're large or small in size. The new expectations of fast delivery and top quality by the end-user is working its way back through the service chain, from retail to distribution, from assembly to production, and in the process, to you.

What's wrong?

The way we have organized ourselves over decades works against us. Our current organizational structure is stifling. Functional departments result in colloquial thinking and narrow points of view. Natural and functional conflicts create internal adversarial rela-

(1) Competing Against Time, George Stalk, Jr. and Thomas M. Hout

tionships that prevent sharing of ideas. Classes in the business environment cause an "us and them" syndrome. Politics prevail. Worse, operations are physically separated from headquarters, component plants from assembly, assembly from the market.

Factory floors are organized by process, creating poor product flow. Poor part flows through a factory, caused by process layouts or haphazardous growth, consume enormous amounts of time. The results are excessive routings, parts in queue, material handling, expeditors, computer tracking, production scheduling, manufacturing orders, work center updates, and forklift trucks, among others.

In the office people are separated by departments and physical walls creating poor communications and information flow. The results are sequential processing of customer orders, slow product development, poor communications, and excessive paper handling, among others. The net result is a dramatic and strategic loss of time in the entire organization. Most manufacturing companies spend anywhere from 5-10% total time actually adding value to the product, i.e., transforming the part or moving it closer to the customer. The rest of the time is waste, resulting in higher costs occurring with loss of time.

But we also have a serious problem with our tendency to court the fads in search of a panacea or quick fix: automation, material requirements planning, computer integrated manufacturing, flexible machining systems, just-in-time, etc. Forget the easy path, if it were there we would all be fast cycle companies. You have to change the basic infrastructure to get at the roots and the causes of slow business cycles.

What can we do about it?

Crush cycle times and total throughput time within the complete service chain of events: distribution, assembly, manufacture, and supply. Be fast and flexible to change with market dynamics. All of the physical events must be enacted swiftly, accurately, and effectively. Extending velocity through the service chain of events insures fast responsiveness in the demand cycle, without the added costs of inventory. **The faster that parts, information, and decisions flow through an organization, the faster the response to customer needs. The keys are flow and time.**

Start with streamlining the physical flow of parts. Physically couple successive operations in the chain of work, remove nonvalue-adding functions, and induce velocity. Integrate processes and reduce setups using a zero-based goal. Focus on core products and physically close the distance between supply points, production, assembly, and the customer.

Implement physical changes to place facilities close to sources of supply. Form partnerships with fewer suppliers such that components can be delivered to quickly satisfy real demand. **Deep organizational changes cannot be effective until problems in the factory flow and cycle times are removed.**

Locate final assembly points close to major end-customers. Create short, direct lines of distribution to make it very easy for customers to place an order and receive fast delivery. Streamline and electronically link the information chain so that flow is direct--without interruptions and delays--eliminating queues.

Reduce business cycle times to the time it actually takes to efficiently process information, supporting the fast movement of physical parts. It makes little sense to move a part through the factory in a day, when it takes two weeks to enter an order.

Design information systems to support business objectives. Technically advanced computer architectures mean nothing if the supporting systems force people to structure their work inefficiently, slowing the business cycle. Induce fast communications and decisions throughout the organization by physically clustering functions needed to complete business cycles quickly. Physical walls that stand in the way of communications have to come down.

Replace large centralized organizations with smaller business units, focused by market or by product, with not more than three management layers. Test each corporate function as to whether or not it adds value in serving the market.

Recompose operational organizations with cells that address logical separations of business cycles, containing multiskilled members, trained to do everything within the cell. Allow cell leaders to be periodically chosen by cell members; give the members the responsibility for making 90 percent of the decisions needed to maintain velocity in the business cycles. Physically collocate them to accomplish this.

Permeate the organization with this structure in the office and the shop. Measure performance simply the same way the customer does: time, quality, and cost. Employ judicious and effective use of automation, technology, and techniques to accomplish objectives.

Inducing velocity throughout a business has a profound effect on time and cost. The need for non-value adding functions disappears, and the functions designed to accomodate exceptional circumstances fall out. The organization chart becomes flatter. Following this is a dramatic reduction of overhead.

How to Reduce Total Cycle Time

Every business has basic cycles that govern the way that paper is processed, product is manufactured, and decisions are made. They may be documented in the form of procedures or routings. Examples of business cycles are customer order, product development, production, and procurement.

A customer order cycle begins with the placement of an order by a customer. It ends when you are finally paid for goods or services rendered. But there are activities in between the two events that consume time. Some add value, such as packing and shipping, and some are non-value adding and delay time, such as moving the order around the building from mailbox to mailbox, sitting on a desk, or repetitive motions.

When a cycle ends, a lot of non-value adding time has been consumed that may constitute 90-95% of total time. Some of the time is lost in travel, some is lost in the processing backlog, and some may be lost diverting a customer's order to a credit department for release. If you can identify the non-value added time in the cycle, you can devise ways to eliminate the causes. The basic business cycles in a manufacturing company are as follows:

Marketing

The definition of the size, scope, nature, and location of markets. It includes predicting future potential, analysis of current developments, sales forecasts, product life cycles, market movements, geographics, segmentation, sales planning, selling strategy, product pricing, advertising, promotion, and sales.

Customer order servicing

The processing of a customer order from inquiry through delivery. It includes quotations, applications engineering, order processing, inventory picking, shipping, invoicing, and receivables.

Engineering and design

The conception, design, and testing of a product. This includes product definition, conception of the operating principle, functional analysis, product definition, value analysis, design, drafting, prototyping, field testing, part classification, engineering change control, and product costing.

Manufacturing process planning

The definition of the operations and resources required to manufacture a product. It includes machining operations, assembly procedures, machine tool selection, process sequences, tooling, and fixturing.

Production planning and scheduling

The conversion of a sales forecast to a master schedule of finished products. It includes capacity planning, inventory levels, production schedules, and material requirements.

Procurement

The acquisition of parts and materials to supply production. It includes supplier selection, order placement, supplier evaluation and certification, receiving, and payables.

Production

The manufacture of parts and assemblies. It includes shop schedules, material movement, production operations, assembly, and inspection.

These long sequential strings of cycles make up the mainstream order flow and contribute to long throughput times. Geographics worsen the time delays; i.e. when distribution is physically separated from the main assembly plant, or engineering is separated from sales, etc. Component plants located overseas add even more to the overall throughput time of the service chain of events.

Mainstream value-add activities are identified on flow process charts. Flow process charts are analyzed for activities that delay mainstream activities. Delays can be moves, slow operations, inspections, as well as waiting time. Cutting cycle times fifty percent per established period of time is a good goal. The process is continuous.

It is not uncommon for the manufacturing time to only consume 40% of the total time a customer has to wait. Yet the value-add time in the plant is generally 5-8% of the manufacturing throughput time. The way to identify the activities is to use process mapping.

Mapping process flow is a fundamental step in reducing total cycle times. Mapping the flow and tracking time for each of the events provides a basis for analysis. The process is not difficult, however it is time consuming. It provides a step by step image of work flow, systems, procedures, and volumes. It reveals the relationships between the tasks.

A process is any series or combination of tasks or activities which produce a result. The result could be a machined part, a drawing, or a requisition for materials. Cycles are sequences of recurring successions of processes or events. The cycle time is the time from the beginning of the first step until the end of the last step. Processes can be decomposed into smaller activities. Traditionally those activities may be performed in a sequential manner, as shown in Figure 1. In this situation each step is completed before the next one begins.

Once cycles are mapped, the opportunities to compress time can be pursued. The goal in compressing time is not to devise the best way to perform a task, but rather to either eliminate the task altogether or perform it parallel with other tasks so that the overall system response time is reduced. A basic premise of reducing total cycle times is to separate activities between in-line and off-line. Extending this approach to the entire service chain and focusing in on the mainstream activities that add value is key. Each of the steps can be further decomposed into smaller activities. By providing the output, such as transferring information, from smaller activities much sooner to the subsequent smaller activities, time can be compressed as in Figure 2.

No sacred cows exist. Functions, tasks, jobs, and parts of organizations that stand in the way of value-add are removed from the mainstream to off-line positions. Off-line functions and positions perform preparatory work for in-line activities. Examples of off-line work are pre-engineering, pricing, credit-checks, and purchasing's negotiations for just-in-time supplier contracts. Credit and accounting are not allowed to delay orders.

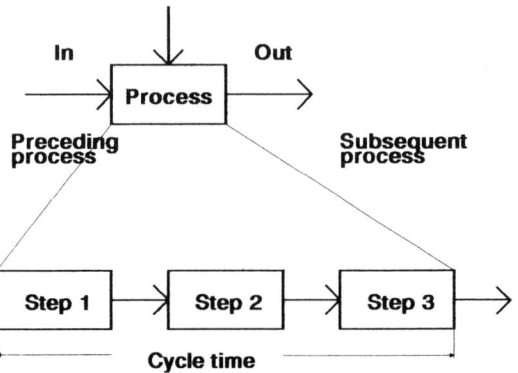

Figure 1. Sequential strings of activities

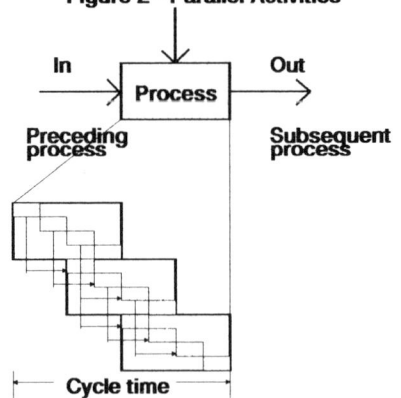

Figure 2 - Parallel Activities

But totally compressing time throughout a company is no easy matter. You have to streamline factories, systems and organizations, and open up lines of communications. You have to break down barriers between departments and put an end to the "we've always done it that way" argument. You have to get your employees highly involved in assuming new responsibilities if you're going to compete in the tough global markets of the 1990's.

Becoming a time-based, world class company requires overcoming organizational inertia. Often overlooked are outdated cultures, ineffective management skills, bureaucratic red tape, and a reward system that doesn't fit. How do you get your arms around such a mammoth effort to make it happen?

The integrated change model provides a way to do it. It utilizes social and technical application tools. It emphasizes a continuous improvement approach, with high involvement of people. This exclusive cycle time reduction program guides and facilitates you. It provides you with a masterplan that takes you through the steps in reducing the total cycle time in your company. This broad approach covers all parts of the organization: marketing, manufacturing, engineering, accounting, etc. It encompasses the full service chain from customer through warehousing, distribution, assembly, production, and supply.

The Integrated Change Model

At the heart of the program is the integrated change model. Managing large scale change requires a comprehensive master plan as well as accountabilities for getting work accomplished. The integrated model provides that plus more. It's the shell of a master plan for reducing cycle times in your company. It consists of three dimensions.

Figure 3 - Integrated Change Model

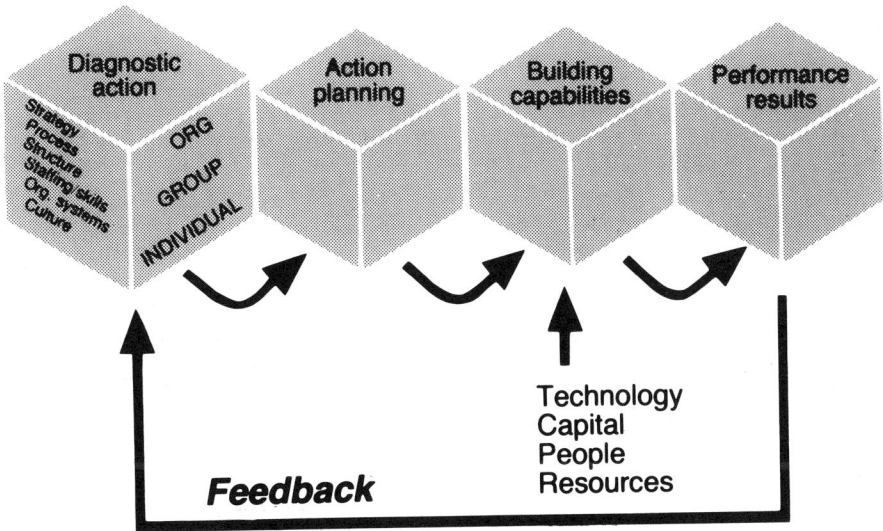

961

First Dimension: The Closed Loop

Large scale change requires managing in phases or stages to control the effort. The first dimension consists of four stages, looped as a continuous process: diagnosis, action planning, building capabilities, and performance results.

Stage 1, Diagnostic Action, is preparation and discovery. You begin with awareness raising and data gathering to discover problems and build a case for change.

Stage 2, Action Planning, guides you in the development of a vision, processes, structure and a master plan with executable steps.

Stage 3, Building Capabilities, guides you in implementing the master plan through team building and high involvement activity.

Stage 4, Performance Results, guides you in measuring the results of the plan to close the loop. The loop is a continuous process that returns to stage 1.

Second Dimension: Six Keyholes

Total cycle time reduction utilizes social and technical application tools. It emphasizes a continuous improvement approach, with high involvement of people throughout the organization. It also requires large scale changes in the way we operate in the office and the factory. This program links the six keyholes into a cohesive approach to managing change. To implement large scale change, there must be a balance in six key areas: Strategy, Process, Structure, Staffing/Skills, Culture, and Organizational systems.

Most companies work intensely with one or two of these, and miss the others. Single approaches amount to knee-jerk reactions, quick-fixes, and band-aid solutions that tend to be applied to symptoms. No efforts are made to find out how other interrelated aspects such as outdated cultures, ineffective management skills, poorly functioning work groups, and bureaucratic red tape contribute to the problem.

Strategy

Strategy is a plan of action defining how an organization will use its resources to gain a competitive edge. It conveys a vision of what the company will look like in the future. The vision focuses and energizes the organization. Efforts that are not linked vertically with the vision are suboptimal.

The strategy track develops a new plan for the firm, then aligns divisions, departments, work groups, jobs and resources with the new strategic direction. Working through the strategy keyhole, you build a fast cycle company vision that provides direction. You develop a new plan for the firm, then align divisions, departments, work groups, jobs, and resources with the new strategic direction. You define where you want to be in terms of market share, people issues, profit, product lines, etc., by setting goals in terms of specific outcomes.

Process

In the process keyhole you define new methods of converting materials and data into products and services. The focus in this keyhole is the reduction of cycle times using state-of-the-art innovative methods and techniques. You revise production methods, work flow, and equipment. You simplify flow, integrate processes, reduce set-ups, and use automation. You remove delays and interruptions in the factory and office and reduce overall throughput time.

Structure

Understanding the way an organization functions is key to the redesign for time-based competition. The structure dictates how labor is divided and how power is allocated. Physical proximity normally follows structure, both of which have a direct impact on ease of information sharing and time.

In a traditional functional organization, communication walls begin to build as the organization grows. Over time, functional entities develop and become self-serving, losing sight of the mission of serving the customer.

Sequential decision-making becomes prevalent, coupled with poor or non-existent communications. The organization develops functional empires, fraught with politics and narrow points of view. The result is an organization slow in decision-making, heavy with vertical layers of management, bureaucratic in nature, low in productivity, and generally ineffective. Through the structure keyhole, you design the logical and physical architecture to support the new direction. You define how you can physically or logically organize to produce fast cycle products or services. You revise the way your organization is designed and define relationships between groups. You revise job structures and determine where power is allocated. You specify rules, procedures, and policies to control operations and direct organizational behavior.

Staffing/Skills

A large-scale effort inadequately staffed or skilled burns out people. Using the staffing/skills keyhole, you define the mix and quality of human resources required to develop a fast cycle company. You determine the skills needed to cope with complex problems. You define the mechanisms for selecting, training and developing employees.

Culture

Any large scale effort that doesn't address culture and people's needs meets stiff resistance. Culture is to the organization as personality is to the individual. Working through the culture keyhole, you facilitate the measuring of climate, organizational behavior, attitudes, and management style. You define the character of the organization, and the new norms, values and beliefs that drive behavior. You devise the new principles that guide human actions for the fast cycle company and cascade them throughout the organization.

Organizational Systems

The organizational systems keyhole defines performance measurements and rewards. In this segment you close the loop, sanctioning the new culture, and you devise new rewards for cooperative efforts and new behavior. You reward adherence to new principles and achievement of new objectives.

Third Dimension: Levels of Focus

The third dimension consists of three levels of focus for change strategy: organization, group and individual. They are used in the four stages and must all be addressed for organizational effectiveness. They include responsibility and accountability. Using team building techniques, you faciitate the process of diagnosis at each level, and develop technical and organizational strategies. Using high involvement, you transform them into executable and measureable short-term actions. This is the way work gets accomplished.

You develop concise objectives for all managers that focus on cycle time reduction. Each manager has a short range action plan for which he or she is accountable. You measure the successes and link them with the performance system.

Summary

Time based competition is a powerful strategic weapon to counter stiff foreign and domestic competition. Reducing total cycle time in your company can make you fast, flexible and a fierce competitor. Its implementation requires an attack on the basic company infrastructure. Focusing on streamlining physical flow of parts and information and compressing time in the basic business cycles can make it happen. But it's not easy, and requires a comprehesive approach that integrates all six keyholes: strategy, process, structure, staffing/skills, culture and organizational systems. The integrated change model provides a systematic methodology for large scale change and implementation of time-based strategy. It gives you the means of becoming world class, and provides a new approach to competing in the 1990's.

Bibliography

Harrington, J., Jr. (1984) Understanding the Manufacturing Process, - Key to Successful CAD/CAM Implementation, New York, Marcel Dekker.

Huse, E.F., and Cummings, T.G. (1985) Organization Development and Change, 3rd ed., St. Paul, MN., West Publishing Company.

Kilmann, R.H. (1989) Managing Beyond the Quick Fix - A Completely Integrated Program for Creating and Maintaining Organization Success, San Francisco, Jossey-Bass.

Stalk, G., Jr., and Hout, T.M. (1990) Competing Against Time: How Time Based Competition Is Reshaping Global Markets. New York, Free Press.

Thomas, Philip R., and Martin, Kenneth R. (1990) Getting Competitive: Middle Managers and the Cycle Time Ethic, New York; McGraw-Hill, 1991.

Biography

Rich Ligus is a certified manufacturing management consultant, with over 20 years experience in engineering, manufacturing and distribution. He specializes in time-based consulting and facilitation. Mr. Ligus holds a bachelor of science degree in mechanical engineering from the New Jersey Institute of Technology, and a master of business administration degree from Rutgers University. He is a speaker and author.

Productivity & Quality Management Frontiers-IV, edited by Sumanth, Edosomwan, Poupart, and Sink. ©1993 Institute of Industrial Engineers.

Cycle Time Reduction

T. Dorsey and A. Fasano
CINTAS Corporation
Cincinnati, Ohio USA

This paper presents the methodology for cycle time reduction of processes to be followed by an organization working to continually reduce costs while simultaneously improving the quality of services to both internal and external customers.

Implementation of the methodology is broken down into seven (7) phases. A brief outline of the strategy for each phase is provided. Phases include:

1. Process Mapping

2. Extraction of Weaknesses

3. Recommended Changes

4. Trial and Error

5. Recovery Plan

6. Implementation (Backward Quality)

7. Future Plans (Forward Quality)

A case study of a company, a leader in their industry, details the implementation of the seven (7) phases.

Key words: Cross-functional Communication, Quality Improvement, Brainstorming, Big Picture Optimization, Teamwork, Continuous Improvement, Cycle time, Employee Involvement, Cost Reduction, Productivity.

Productivity & Quality Management Frontiers-IV, edited by Sumanth, Edosomwan, Poupart, and Sink. ©1993
Institute of Industrial Engineers.

Planning and Organizing for Farm Productivity: Concepts & Strategies

J.S. Babu
J.N.T. University
Mehidipatnam, Hyderabad INDIA

G.J.P. Prakash David
J.N.T. University
Anantapur, INDIA

ABSTRACT

Driven by rapid technological breakthroughs in high-yielding and hybrid seeds, chemical fertilisers, pesticides coupled with extension and training measures, the Indian agriculture, especially over the last two decades, has witnessed unprecedented growth and development. Despite such spectacular technological strides, the hiatus between the demand and supply of agricultural inputs, implements etc. is too glaring. Ineffective logistics, inadequate extension and training measures at the grass-root level and improper usage and application of various inputs at field level have stifled the agricultural productivity in the country. This necessiates proper planning and organising on various aspects of the agricultural management.

Of late, efforts have, ofcourse, been initiated to tone up the system through the concept of Agro-Service Centres, which were created to provide various inputs and services including extension and training support to the farmers under one roof. But, the concept was a short-lived one and many agro-service centres, within no time, have ended up as sale counters for undertaking the distribution of products manufactured or procured with tie-up arrangements by most of these agencies. Consequently, there is the need for conceptual restructuring of the modalities and strategies on empirical premises to ensure optimal operational efficiency in agriculture.

The present paper is an attempt to rebuild the concept of Agro-Service Centres on scientific premises and accordingly evolve imaginative strategies aimed at enhancing productivity levels in agriculture.

Productivity & Quality Management Frontiers-IV, edited by Sumanth, Edosomwan, Poupart, and Sink. ©1993 Institute of Industrial Engineers.

Implementing a Strategic Architecture for TQM

S.A. Levin
Strategic Solutions
St. Charles, Illinois USA

IMPLEMENTING A STRATEGIC ARCHITECTURE FOR TQM

Creating and implementing a quality strategic architecture to ensure the achievement of the organization's vision and mission is the essential task of management. A quality organization is one that "continually understands, anticipates, meets and exceeds their customer's requirements." A total quality management system is one that allows the organization to flawlessly execute their strategic plans, continually improve their processes and develop their employees.

Implementing a strategic architecture involves three phases:

- Creating the Architecture
- Establishing a Performance Support System
- Managing the Change Process

This paper will describe the strategic architecture and the nine performance variables required to successfully implement TQM in an organization.

Productivity & Quality Management Frontiers-IV, edited by Sumanth, Edosomwan, Poupart, and Sink. ©1993 Institute of Industrial Engineers.

Total Quality Management and the Employment Service in Scotland

W.N. Shaw
Heriot-Watt University Business School
Edinburgh, Scotland UNITED KINGDOM

M.J. Lowrey
Nature Conservancy Council
Edinburgh, Scotland UNITED KINGDOM

ABSTRACT

The aim of this paper is to discuss how Total Quality Management (TQM) can be used to focus the efforts of the Employment Service in Scotland on delivering high quality services that meet the needs of its customers, the unemployed. The paper starts by briefly describing the Employment Service, a government run agency that plays a positive role in the functioning of the labour market and aims to help alleviate the worst effects of unemployment. The Service operates through a network of Job Centres and Unemployment Benefit Offices. The Employment Service is a hierarchical bureaucracy, exhibiting features typical of this form of organisational structure. It lacks the incentive of profit and as its dominant customer is not the end-user but the Government of the day, political considerations often outweigh market forces. The main part of the paper outlines the most significant of the quality programmes, initiatives and experiments already taking place throughout the Employment Service. In the absence of a core quality programme driven from the top, initiatives have appeared in various forms and at various levels of the organisation. These are discussed under the headings of quality initiatives, cost of quality and human resource development. The final part of the paper specifies a TQM implementation strategy for the Employment Service in Scotland that not only places the accent on cultural change but builds on the gains already made. The paper ends with some suggestions as to how Total Quality Disillusionment can best be avoided.

KEY WORDS: TQM, Services, Public Sector

INTRODUCTION

This paper discusses how Total Quality Management(TQM) can be used to focus the efforts of the Employment Service in Scotland in delivering high quality services that meet the needs of its customers, the unemployed. The paper starts by briefly describing the Employment Service (ES). This is followed by an overview of TQM in the public service sector. The major part of the paper then deals with the most significant of the quality programmes, initiatives and experiments already taking place throughout the Employment Service. This analysis leads to the concluding section which specifies a TQM implementation strategy for the Employment Service in Scotland.

THE EMPLOYMENT SERVICE

The first UK national system of Government-run employment offices was established in 1910. Since these early days, the organisation has seen various peripheral responsibilities come and go. The core concerns of Employment Offices however have always remained the same - to play a positive role in the functioning of the labour market and to help alleviate the worst effects of unemployment. The first Jobcentre was opened in the South of England in 1974. At that time, with unemployment in the UK at "only" 600 000, many employers were experiencing difficulties in filling vacancies. It was felt that a more accessible, specialist public Employment Service was necessary. Accordingly, a network of around 1000 Jobcentres was established. The majority of these were in high profile, main street locations. An interventionist job broking role was quickly assumed, leading to an estimated market share in terms of vacancies filled of around 30%. This figure has been roughly maintained ever since. It compares with, for example, a market share of 7% for the equivalent United States agency. [1] By 1987, the UK jobless total had risen to nearly 3 million. Of particular concern was the rise in the numbers of long-term unemployed[2] as a proportion of the whole register. This reflected the trend in many parts of the country towards structural as opposed to frictional or cyclical unemployment. The scaling down of traditional heavy industries meant that by May 1991 for example, 55% of unemployed men in Scotland had been without work for longer than 6 months[3]. As a result, a further revision of corporate strategy took place. The main priority is now to help the long-term unemployed back to work. In an attempt to bring services for the jobless closer to this priority client group, the Employment Service was formed in 1988.

Employing some 36,000 people in the UK, with 4,500 in Scotland, the ES now operates through a network of 1,600 Jobcentres and Unemployment Benefit Offices. Some 250 of these offices are located in Scotland. In a major restructuring due to finish in early 1994, these are being progressively integrated in order to provide clients with a full range of services under one roof.

In 1990, the Employment Service became an Executive Agency of the Employment

---

[1] Source: Employment Intelligence Unit, Employment Services Office for Scotland (ES OS)
[2] Defined as those out of work for longer than six months
[3] Source: Employment Intelligence Unit, ES OS

Department Group as part of the Government's "Next Steps" initiative. The aim of the initiative is to

"rebuild the shape of central Government and improve the quality of its services" (Holland 1990).

Within a policy framework determined by the Secretary of State for Employment, the ES now works to performance targets set as part of an Annual Performance Agreement. The Employment Service in Scotland is one of nine regions for the whole of the United Kingdom.

The Employment Service aims to help to promote a competitive and efficient labour market, particularly by giving positive help unemployed people through its job placement service and other programmes and by the payment of benefits and allowances to those who are entitled to receive them.

In pursuit of its aims the Employment Service offers a diverse range of services which includes helping people find jobs; helping people who become unemployed; additional help for long-term clients (LTC's); help for people with special needs; extra help for people with disabilities.

TQM IN THE PUBLIC SERVICE SECTOR

"In establishing their quality of design, the service industries are bound by the same considerations as are the manufacturing companies: identification of what constitutes fitness for use, choice of a design concept which is responsive to the identified needs of the user, translation of this concept into specifications" (Juran, 1984).

The service sector does however feature characteristics not normally present in manufacturing industry:

. The workforce is often dispersed around a network of locations, as in the retail sector and indeed the Employment Services.

. Service standards vary. Ensuring predictability and consistency of performance when the product is delivered by human beings of varying levels of skill, application and commitment is difficult.

. The volume of customer contacts is very high. As a result, service products have to be kept simple, and a wide range of tastes has to be catered for. Customer contact skills are of great importance.

TQM is an attractive proposition to service sector managers because of these features. Wythe (1990) sees the key issue as *"standards of performance"*. Because of the difficulties of imposing these in the service sector, it is better,

"for people in the 'front line' to do their own thinking, taking into account their particular circumstances, and setting their own standards". He concludes, *"TQM in the service sector uses the same concepts found elsewhere. What varies is how the message is communicated and the activities controlled" (Wythe,1990) .*

The public sector has been slow to accept the challenge of managing for Total Quality:

"As was the case with British companies in 1984, there is a growing awareness amongst these public services that their customers are becoming more and more demanding. But, like industry in 1984, few fully understand what Total Quality

encompasses, and few have had the vision and determination to implement it properly" (English, 1990).

A number of public sector organisations have already introduced short-term, "motivational" quality improvement programmes. These have been particularly prevalent in the Health Service and in local government. However,

"although they bring benefits, they will not bring about the required fundamental change in culture and attitudes" (Walsh, 1990) .

These fundamental changes are often rejected on the grounds that public sector organisations are "different" from commercial companies. Indeed they are, but

"there are far more similarities than differences....every organisation is a collection of people, providing products or services for customers. The problems incurred are to do with utilising fully the abilities of the people in the organisation to meet the requirements of their customers" (English, 1990).

English then concludes,

"public sector organisations start with a significant advantage over their opposite numbers in the private sector. Employees....have a far stronger desire to serve their customers than those who join industrial companies. The challenge is to turn this enthusiasm into the effective satisfaction of customer requirements".

QUALITY INITIATIVES IN THE EMPLOYMENT SERVICE

This section outlines the most significant of the quality programmes, initiatives and experiments already taking place throughout the Employment Service. In the absence of a core quality programme driven from the top, initiatives have appeared in various forms at various levels of the organisation. They will be discussed under five main headings:

  . TQM programmes
  . Quality initiatives aimed directly at external customers
  . Quality initiatives aimed directly at internal customers
  . Measuring the Cost of Quality
  . Human Resource Development

TQM Programmes in the Employment Services

The UK Treasury supports the introduction of TQM programmes into Civil Service departments. It sees its role becoming that of a central clearing house for good practices, and intends to publish material aimed at creating

"a commonality of development around a set of basic principles" (Laing, 1991).

The developing Treasury model emphasises the importance of identifying and reducing the cost of non-conformity to design within administrative processes. The leading role of senior management and the need to empower employees to contribute are stressed. They see the use of external consultants as inevitable. The Treasury's acquiescence is of considerable significance. It adds weight to the drive for better quality of public services emanating from the top ranks of Government. Secondly, vigorous Treasury opposition would have presented serious obstacles to Departments seeking to adopt the TQM philosophy. Its policy of fairly passive endorsement and quiet encouragement is probably strategically correct. The Treasury is firm and proactive in seeking value-for-money improvements. The way in which departments ultimately achieve this is best left to them. Current Employment Service Head Office thinking mirrors that of the Treasury. Quality improvements must be achieved. TQM is endorsed as a valid means of bringing these about. TQM programmes must however be driven from Regional rather than Head Office level. Two forces impose a degree of caution. The ES Internal Audit Branch and the independent and powerful National Audit Office are charged with ensuring that public monies are used appropriately and effectively. They are reluctant to see the abandonment of traditional quality control systems in favour of radical quality improvement programmes unless assurances as to the effectiveness of the new approach can be given. Secondly, Ministers and senior officials set out targets which they expect to be met. Radical programmes which are thought to threaten levels of performance as currently measured will attract suspicion. The current approach is cautiously to endorse rather than to champion the concept.

Of the nine Employment Service regions in the UK, to date only one has implemented a full scale TQM programme. This was introduced some three years ago based on the approach of W E Deming (1986). Four of the other Employment Service regions, including ES Scotland, have experimented with aspects of TQM.

Quality Initiatives - External Customers

National Customer Satisfaction Surveys which were introduced by the Employment Service in 1989 are essentially internally oriented. They elicit client views on the quality of existing services measured against criteria established by the organisation itself. They cannot replace surveys of customer needs as a means of achieving a customer orientation.

The Employment Service decided in 1987 to bring its job broking and benefit payment functions under one roof. One-stop shopping allows easier targeting of the priority client group, the long-term unemployed, to whom the full range of services can now be exposed as they attend each fortnight to claim benefit. The quality of service seems to have improved as a result:

> "the highest proportions of claimants saying they were satisfied with the service were among those that attended a fully integrated Employment Service Office" (Social Survey Division, 1991) .

A cohesive service offered in pleasant, civilised surroundings does not guarantee customer satisfaction. It is however a significant step forward, not least in terms of the working conditions of employees.

A Jobseeker's Charter which was launched in December 1991, is being presented within the ES as a continuation of the organisation's drive for improved quality of service, rather than as a "new beginning". There are three main themes to the Charter:

.   Published performance targets - local and national
.   Publication of information on standards achieved
.   More effective complaints procedures.

Clear messages are now being sent by senior management regarding the relationship with

clients that ES employees should be developing. For example, a customer care package has recently been distributed to all Employment Service locations. Its stated purpose is to
"sharpen up awareness and to build consideration of service and its continued improvement into our basic thinking as an organisation" *(Employment Service, 1991a).*
The development of an Area Accuracy of Payments Indicator represents an attempt to introduce more scientific quality measurement systems into the benefit payments process. Quality Assurance, as distinct from TQM programmes, have been implemented in a number of Employment Service Regions. Such a programme is, for example, currently being designed for ES Scotland. Its aims are to assure senior management that a quality service is being delivered, and to further increase the awareness of all ES Scotland staff of their customers' needs and how these should be met.

Quality Initiatives - Internal Customers
Parts of the organisation are beginning to move towards the practice of Departmental Purpose Analysis (DPA). The approach, originally developed within IBM, helps to define clearly the real purpose of each organisational unit with the objective of improving its performance.
Internal customer satisfaction surveys are being used more frequently throughout the Employment Service. Such surveys present opportunities for full and frank discussions of strengths and weaknesses. It is essential that the true feelings of respondents are gauged. In addition annual staff attitude surveys, which are designed to inform senior management of employee's views on a range of key organisational issues, have been introduced.

Cost of Quality (COQ) in the Employment Service
The cost of quality in the ES can at present only be guessed at. It will be enormous however, given the resources devoted to quality control. The cost of the benefit payment internal inspection system alone has been estimated at just over ten million pounds sterling, which equates to 1.9% of the total ES salaries budget (Employment Service, 1991b). This takes no account of costs associated with other functional areas, no account of rework and prevention costs, and of course no account of external costs, those borne by the end-user. The ES has much to gain from efforts to identify and reduce its COQ.

Human Resource Development
The Employment Service established in 1988,a national staff development programme known as "HRD". The programme recognises that
"people are the most important resource in the Employment Service" .
It aims *"to create a well-managed organisation; this means ensuring that efforts are appreciated and that everyone is given the chance to develop personally within their job" (Fogden, 1988).*
During the early years of HRD, the focus tended to be on setting up as many "events" as possible. These were often glamorous and expensive affairs which benefited relatively

few people. The emphasis has now shifted towards encouraging employees at all levels to accept responsibility for their own self-development. The programme is now seen by management as a long-term cultural change process, relevant to all and offering a menu of flexible, practical development tools with wide appeal. Employee perceptions of the programme may well change accordingly.

HRD will not on its own create a quality organisation. It cannot, for example, take the place of a full-scale TQM programme. It remains however an effective vehicle for cultural change, a means of addressing the "soft", "people" issues. Such a programme must be a key element of any attempt to manage for total quality.

CONCLUSIONS

The Employment Service is a hierarchical bureaucracy, exhibiting features typical of this form of organisational structure. It lacks the incentive of profit. Its dominant customer is not the end-user but the Government of the day. Political considerations often outweigh market forces. These factors have bred an organisational culture that frequently puts the needs of internal systems before those of end-users.

There are signs however that the ES is beginning to break free from the constraints traditionally imposed by its structure. Parts of the organisation have demonstrated a growing awareness of the need to justify its existence solely on the basis of its ability to provide a quality service to internal and external customers. This has manifested itself in the wide range of initiatives and experiments reviewed in the previous section.

At the corporate level the organisation is beginning to develop a coherent quality strategy. In addition, a more participative senior management style is perceptible. The results of Staff Attitude Surveys however indicate that, at the level at which services are delivered and where the vast majority of staff actually work, there is little evidence of cultural change and little sense of vision. In order to bridge this gap, a cultural change programme is required that encompasses all levels and all employees within the organisation, that ensures that concern for quality is everyone's common goal and a natural and ingrained part of everyday work.

Cultural change strategies do not just happen - they have to be systematically managed, implemented and monitored.

> *"You do not change values much by talking about them. The abstractions and rhetoric are not driving forces, not agents for change. You have to start with the tasks and jobs people do, with what is done and how it is done. That is what builds the culture and sends the* signals" *(Psychology Branch, 1991)* .

The Way Forward

This then leads us to two conclusions:

- . There is evidence that the ES is ready to develop a new strategy based on a vision of quality of service. In effect it has begun to do so in the form of various initiatives and a changing style of senior management.
- . Because of its size and dispersed network, its cultural legacy and the need to address cultural issues in the language of practitioners, the new ES strategy needs

to be managed and implemented by way of structured, systematic and functional mechanisms to ensure it reaches everyone in the organisation. Customer care packages and similar materials are important, but more is required.

It is clear that the ES is both ready to accept the challenge of TQM and *needs* to do so if the drive for quality is to succeed.

A TQM Implementation Strategy for ES Scotland

There is no TQM blueprint that can be applied to any and every organisation. Off-the-shelf implementation strategies are offered by consultants. However, these will only be effective if they are tailored to the particular needs, structural characteristics and cultural climate of the customer organisation.

Policy and commitment.. ES Scotland must have a clear quality policy, formulated and driven by senior management.

Roles and responsibilities. TQM must be driven from the top. A senior management Quality Council should therefore be formed. Its functions will be to demonstrate commitment and vision, and to coordinate and oversee quality policy matters. A quality champion must be appointed at middle-management level to drive the programme forward on a day-to-day basis.

Cost of Quality. A cost of quality exercise would be a useful selling point. If repeated over time, it would be a valid means of evaluating the programme.

Documentation. TQM in Scotland should initially focus on cultural issues.

Tools and Techniques. To become a quality organisation, the ES must at some stage critically reassess the systems and processes on which it relies. Many are poorly designed and in need of overhaul.

Teamwork. In a quality organisation, inter-departmental rivalry is subsumed and people work together for a common purpose. That purpose will be to meet the needs of the customer.

Evaluation. An ES Scotland programme could be evaluated through Customer Satisfaction Surveys, Staff Attitude Surveys and through limited COQ exercises. Ultimately, improvements will show in standard performance indicators.

Total Quality Disillusionment

TQM will not succeed by itself, but must be carefully managed. To avoid disillusionment, all those involved must:

Avoid overstating the benefits of TQM. Expectations, particularly at the outset, must not be too high.

Avoid understating the commitment required for TQM.

Emphasise the long, slow journey to TQM to avoid the "flavour of the month" tag.

Avoid creating the impression that quality is a finite task, that once installed will last forever, with only minimum maintenance.

Prevent TQM being used as an instant solution to a particular problem.

Emphasise that quality improvement requires an on-going, never-ending commitment in order to reap the benefits (DTI, undated).

REFERENCES

Deming, W. E. (1986) 'Out of the Crisis', MIT Cambridge

Department of Trade and Industry (DTI), (undated) 'Adapted from Total Quality Management' booklet.

Employment Service Head Office (ESHO) (1991a) 'Customer Care Pack'

Employment Service Head Office (ESHO) (1991b) 'Costing of Quality Control of Benefit Work', April.

English, G. (1990) 'Total Quality in the Public Services', Total Quality Management, June.

Fogden, M. (1988) 'From the foreword to Success Through People: Human Resource Development in the Employment Service: A Framework for Action', Employment Service Head Office, July.

Holland, Sir Geoffrey (1990), 'From the foreward to A Guide to the Employment Department Group', Employment Deparatment Group.

Juran, J. M. (1984) 'Quality Control Handbook' 3rd Ed, McGraw-Hill.

Laing, A. (1991) 'Head of Consultancy and Inspection Services Division', HM Treasury, Interview 17 July.

Psychology Branch (ESHO) (1991), 'Changing the Culture and what Managers in Local Offices do' Presentation to Senior Management.

Social Survey Division, Office of Population Censuses and Surveys (1991) 'Customer Satisfaction with the Employment Services 1990.

Walsh K. (1990) 'Managing Quality in the Public Services', Management Education and Development Vol 21, Part 5 pp 394-400.

Wythe, R. (1990) 'Agenda for Change', TQM Magazine, August.

BIOGRAPHICAL SKETCH OF THE AUTHORS

Prior to joining the Business School at Heriot-Watt University, Nigel Shaw held management positions in industry. He teaches and researches in production/ operations and technology management. He has been or is currently involved with several highly innovative and successful Teaching Company Programmes, has published extensively and undertaken a number of consultancy assignments in both private and public sector organisations. He is on the board of management of two companies.

A graduate of Aberdeen University, Malcolm Lowrey joined the Scottish Employment Service in 1984. Various field managements posts led to a place in the Management Services Team where he completed several quality management projects. Having gained his MBA at Heriot-Watt University, he is now Senior Auditor with Scottish Natural Heritage, a new Government agency concerned with protecting and enhancing the Scottish environment. SNH is actively considering a TQM programme on its own.

Productivity & Quality Management Frontiers-IV, edited by Sumanth, Edosomwan, Poupart, and Sink. ©1993
Institute of Industrial Engineers.

A Comparison of Japanese Total Quality Control and Dr. Deming's Theory of Management

H.S. Gitlow
University of Miami
Coral Gables, Florida USA

ABSTRACT

This paper critically contrasts two schools of thought on Total
Quality Management; Japanese Total Quality Control and Dr.
Deming's theory of management. An overview of each school of
thought is presented in respect to definition of quality,
purpose, structure, and intrinsic value. Structure refers to
the logical, physical and emotional systems which form the body
of each school of thought. Intrinsic value refers to the use
of each school of thought beyond the improvement of quality.

The differences between the two schools of thought are
discussed in respect to five issues; they are: (1) the purpose
and structure of Total Quality Management, (2) the role of
competition to individuals and organizations, (3) the use of
fear as a managerial tool, (4) the use of numeric targets as a
tool of management, and (5) the use of performance appraisal as
a tool of management.

KEYWORDS

Total Quality Management, Japanese Total Quality Control

Productivity & Quality Management Frontiers-IV, edited by Sumanth, Edosomwan, Poupart, and Sink. ©1993 Institute of Industrial Engineers.

Psychological Considerations for Productivity and TQM Programs

S.F. Hennigan
Marathon Oil Company
Lafayette, Lousiana USA

J. Lee
University of Southwestern Louisiana
Lafayette, Louisiana USA

Abstract

Total Quality Management (TQM) is an application of quantitative methods and human resources in business management to design, control, and improve productivity and quality management process with a focus on meeting the needs of the customers. Procedures for implementing TQM have been discussed in recent literatures. However, implicitly omitted in many of the existing TQM programs is how and what is involved in successfully implementing TQM, psychologically. That is, the subjective criteria must also be considered in the management process. The psychology is an integral part of the entire productivity and quality program.

A psychological view of total quality management that emphasizes subjectivity and relies on objective criteria for establishing and validation of a productivity and quality improvement process is summarized in this study. A review of existing implementation procedures and evaluation procedures for TQM programs will be given first. The potential pitfalls will then be discussed. Finally, an outline of a servo-system TQM program where the psychological aspects are included is presented. In safety, for example, after the physical safety is taken care of, the psychological needs of employees are prominent. One needs security in the mind. Permanence of job, consistency of product, stability of expectations and others contribute to the psychological safety.

Understanding of psychological needs can help set up the productivity and quality program using quality tools and keep it continuous. The psychological needs of the customer, employee, management, and others involved in the quality relationships must be met. Using the psychology of change, behavior can be positively altered whether it be customers' perceptions, education and training, and/or culture change. Once the psychology of all aspects involved in a TQM program is understood and addressed, then the "Total" Quality Management program is complete.

Productivity & Quality Management Frontiers-IV, edited by Sumanth, Edosomwan, Poupart, and Sink. ©1993 Institute of Industrial Engineers.

A North American Reflection on Sociotechnical Systems Design in White Collar and Professional Knowledge Work Settings

R.E. Purser and J.A. Fixler
Loyola University
Chicago, Illinois USA

R.V. Tenkasi
Case Western Reserve University
Cleveland, Ohio USA

Abstract

Classical sociotechnical systems (STS) perspective views organizations as open systems, comprised of both social and technical subsystems, which must be jointly optimized in order to achieve and sustain high performance. This paper identifies, evaluates and reviews STS interventions that have been implemented in white collar/knowledge work settings. Interviews with consultants and management experienced in the application of STS principles resulted in a sample of 24 unpublished cases. This study evaluates: (1) the approaches and processes that characterize successful nonroutine organization redesigns; (2) the redesign features associated with nonroutine office settings; and (3) the outcomes resulting from the redesign efforts.

Keywords: Sociotechnical systems, knowledge work, organization design.

One of the most significant challenges for the 1990s and beyond lies in designing organizations to effectively manage and organize knowledge-based work. Quality and productivity improvements in both white collar and knowledge-based work are not derived solely from installations of new technology, but also require substantial changes in business processes and organizational arrangements (Pava, 1983). Further, as work centered around production processes shifts to work that is dependent on people to generate ideas, as well as to think systemically about the design and delivery of products and services, new methods are needed for unleashing and tapping this creative potential.

This research study examines organizational redesign efforts in non-manufacturing settings which utilized sociotechnical systems theory and methods for improving the performance of white collar and professional knowledge work. Sociotechnical systems (STS) theory emerged in England at the Tavistock Institute in the 1950s. The classical STS perspective views organizations as open systems comprised of both social and technical subsystems which must be jointly optimized in order to achieve and sustain high performance (Emery, 1959). Over the course of the last thirty years, classical STS design has been applied extensively and successfully in manufacturing settings in a variety of industries--ranging from complex refining operations to food processing--both in North America and abroad.

In contrast, applications of STS design in white collar and professional knowledge work settings have been fewer and are not well understood. Thus, it is not surprising that the literature on STS applications in non-manufacturing settings has been limited to a few case studies (Pasmore and Gurley, 1991; Purser, 1991; Shani and Elliott, 1988; Taylor, 1986), or is more theoretical in orientation (Pava, 1983; Pava, 1986). Lacking a more systematic reflection and empirical analysis of such applications, this study reviews and evaluates 24 recent unpublished cases where STS theory and methods were applied to redesign white collar/knowledge work organizations.

METHOD

Data Sources and Procedures

The initial contacts for this study were drawn from a pool of 100 internal and external STS consultants who were members of a peer-based professional network known as the "STS Roundtable". Those consultants who had acknowledged experience in applying STS in white collar/knowledge work settings, and who also indicated that they would be willing to participate in a telephone interview were contacted. In addition, each consultant interviewed was asked to discuss one assignment where he/she was most extensively involved. At the conclusion of the interview, each was asked to provide the names of their clients, which allowed us to conduct additional interviews with those personnel actually involved in the organizational redesign projects. In total, telephone interviews were conducted with 20 external consultants, 5 internal consultants, and 9 clients.

981

Based on these interviews, 24 organizations which had recently used STS theory and methods for redesigning white collar/knowledge work were identified and included as research cases for this study. Table 1 below shows the type of non-manufacturing setting and industry for all the cases.

TABLE 1
Information on Cases Included in the Study

Case #	Type of Setting	Industry
1	R&D	Electronics
2	R&D	Corn Products
3	R&D	Glass
4	R&D	Chemicals
5	R&D	Petrochemicals
6	Engineering	Oil
7	Energy Support	Oil
8	Distribution	Oil
9	Accounting	Paper
10	Accounting	Tile
11	Accounting	Electronics
12	Corporate Office	Financial Services
13	Regional Office	Trade Union
14	Administration	Electronics
15	Adminsistration	Brewery
16	Administration	Chemicals
17	Senior Management	Chemicals
18	Information Systems	Oil
19	Legal Department	Chemicals
20	Claims Processing	Healthcare Insurance
21	Claims Processing	Insurance
22	Customer Service	Paper
23	Real Estate	Computer
24	Distribution	Consumer Goods

Interview questions for both consultants and clients focused on identifying, exploring and understanding: (1) the business rationale and precipitating circumstances that justified the redesign effort in the case under study; (2) the analytic methods and change strategy employed; (3) the features and configurations associated with the redesign; and (4) significant financial and behavioral performance improvements. The average interview lasted 45 minutes. Nearly all of the interviews were tape-recorded and transcribed verbatim totalling over 175 pages of data.

Data Analysis

The data analysis was guided by the main questions of the study. In the first phase of the analysis, the responses to each question from the interview transcripts were collated. The first and second author read through the collated transcripts of the interview participants and categorized the responses items. The second author then coded the question categorized response items into themes. For the next phase, the second author counted and tallied the themes. Finally, the third author read the transcripts and evaluated each collated question set in terms of the thematic coding schemes that emerged from the earlier analysis. No significant disagreements were noted.

FINDINGS

Business Rationale for Redesign

When asked the business rationale for engaging in the redesign effort, respondents most often cited curing the usual organizational ills; namely, to reduce costs and improve business performance. The general need to reduce costs overall was mentioned, as well as the need to redesign due to downsizing. Equally frequent was the need to improve organizational response time capability, time-to-market performance and the general need to better meet deadlines/schedules. Performance issues focused on improving quality, service, flexibility of the workforce, competitiveness and customer satisfaction. The social aspects of employees' work was also mentioned regularly, such as the need to improve people's working relationships and their overall quality-of-work life.

Among other reasons given for engaging in the change effort were that it was part of a larger organizational redesign or Total Quality Management change effort, that new technology was being implemented, that the organization in question had a desire to create a "new kind of future", or be on the "cutting edge."

STS as an Organization Design Philosophy

The majority of those interviewed emphasized the importance of viewing STS as a philosophy--or new organizational paradigm--rather than as a set of tools and techniques. This is an interesting theme given that the initial question asked of the participants was to describe the types of methods and tools that were used for during the analysis phase of the redesign process. In total, six participants stated that if STS is understood as a philosophy and set of organization design principles, then it is just as applicable to white collar/knowledge work as it is in manufacturing settings. However, a number of consultants were of the opinion that STS in the majority of cases has mistakenly been viewed as a set of tools, which has thus limited its application and diffusion into non-manufacturing work settings.

The cases in which STS was viewed as a set of principles for organization design also emphasized that, in knowledge work settings, a great deal of attention must be given to understanding the overall *business process* and *organizational purpose*. In these cases, the unit of analysis was decidedly more focused on the total business, strategic issues, and probable future demands. Further, these cases showed that their members invested considerable time during the early stages of the redesign process in understanding and scanning the business environment. Several consultants referred to using an "outside in" approach which identifies current and anticipated demands from both internal and external customers. It is clear that the theme of *defining business outcomes* is more critical in knowledge work settings which consist of highly discretionary and specialized tasks, and which produce information rather than a tangible product. Thus, in many of the cases, the strategic emphasis is on designing a *purpose-driven* rather than a *task-driven* organization. In sum, this theme suggests that the redesign of white collar/knowledge work settings first requires developing a macro-orientation that allows the target organization to develop a clear understanding of the business purpose and environmental demands before more detailed analyses of the technical and social subsystems are conducted.

Wide Variation in Analytic Methods

The STS perspective is both a theory and a methodology for designing effective organizations (Pasmore, 1988). In brief, the classic STS approach is defined by three analytical phases that involve the application of various tools and diagnostic methods. Specifically, the classic STS methodology proceeds through a series of steps that involves a considerable amount of detailed data gathering on the effectiveness and requirements of the environmental, technical and social subsystems of the organization under study. The environmental analysis identifies current and future stakeholder demands and assesses how effectively such demands are being met.

Reference to the methods used in the interviews revealed that the classic STS approach was used in only two of the cases. Why? Many of the participants stated the classic STS methodology was too rigid and needed considerable adaptation for it to be of benefit in the office environment. Others noted that the classic STS method tends to focus too much on details and tactics, and lacks the macro-strategic perspective which is needed when redesigning knowledge-based organizations. Still others found that the classic, step-by-step, "workbook" methodology simply takes too long in project-oriented organizations characterized by rapid and frequent environmental changes. Similarly, an internal consultant who was involved in the redesign of an information systems division at a large oil company pointed out the limitations of the classic STS method in professional settings where career mobility often precludes the use of an isolated task force or design team.

Thus, many different variations on the classic STS methodology were encountered in the data base. However, the variety of methods were classified into three generic types, namely: the classic-adapted, the deliberation analysis, and the customized methods.

The classic-adapted method still consisted of three analytic phases (albeit, in highly abbreviated forms), but with alterations to the technical analysis method. For example, in the technical analysis of one R&D center the design team spent an extensive amount of time interviewing customers in order to determine their requirements. Customer requirements were then factored into work process specifications which in turn became control standards for the detection of variances. This is one example where TQM tools were used synergistically with the STS technical analysis method. Several other cases expanded the classic technical analysis method--which mainly has been used to detect variances in the work flow--by including an analysis of non-value added work steps. In the financial services case this method innovation was extended even further through the addition of a step which calculated the economic cost of each non-value added work activity. Thus, this method variation allowed design team members to build strong cases based on quantifiable data for restructuring or eliminating work steps. When applied to the redesign of management systems and support areas at a large chemical manufacturer, the technical analysis method was adjusted to focus on variances that occur in using the knowledge base to produce business-specific outcomes. Similarly, other cases adapted the classic technical analysis method by simply reframing its focus to identifying variances in the flow of information.

Three sites (cases 1,4,23) used Pava's (1983) deliberation analysis methodology. Unlike the classic technical analysis method--with the deliberation method--the analysis shifts to identifying the key topics and forums for necessary information exchanges which must occur between different parties in order for them to make informed decisions and negotiate trade-offs. For example, the new product development process at a chemical company was analyzed using the deliberation analysis method as a means for identifying the key topics which nesseciated information exchanges between divergent but highly interdependent disciplines (e.g., marketing, R&D, manufacturing).

The customized approach did not follow any prescribed methodology; instead, they relied upon local invention, "participative redesign" (Emery, 1988), and customized methods derived from the "local theory" (Elden, 1983) of the site. In these cases, it was clear that time was spent on the front end of the project educating members on STS design principles. With the help of either internal or external consultants, organizational members created, invented and customized their own tools, methods, and processes for the redesign effort. One external consultant summarized the essence of this do-it-yourself methodology approach:

> Professionals don't need to and will not tolerate sitting
> down through a rigorous, drawn out, step-by-step method,
> that looks like a cookbook process which STS has traditionally
> been. The main task is an educational one, where we get
> professionals thinking about STS principles. After that,
> we simply just let them go at it. From there, they are
> guided by the question of: What do we need to do, and how do

we need to be organized to meet the needs of the environment?

There are several reasons that could explain why the customized approach was used in these settings. As we mentioned earlier, some settings were faced with rapidly changing environments and short-product life-cycles that necessiated a speedier and more compressed approach. A mechanistic, step-by-step methodology may be of little value in non-linear technical systems. In these cases, the methodology itself needs to be somewhat experimental and evolutionary. Further, autonomous and creative professionals in knowledge work settings often resist methods and ideas which are invented elsewhere or originate from external sources. In sum, a more organic and self-designing approach may have been necessary for engaging the commitment of professionals and for understanding the complexity of the technical system in these white collar/knowledge work settings.

Common and Uncommon Design Features

Respondents at each site were asked to describe the organization design features which were implemented as a result of the white collar/knowledge work redesign effort. An analysis of the data base yielded 14 specific design features, some that were commonly implemented across many of the cases, while others were fairly uncommon and unique to a particular site (see Table 2). Using criteria developed by Macy et al. (1991), each of the design features were classified as whether they were representative of a structural, human resource, or process interventions.

Table 2
Common and Uncommon Design Features of Cases

Design Features	Case Numbers
Teams	1,2,3,4,5,6,7,8,9,10,12,14,15,16,17,18,19,21,22,23,24
Self-managed teams	2,5,9,12,14,16,17
Cross-functional teams	2,3,6,8,16,18,20
Customer-focused teams	3,10,12,17,24
Regionally-based teams	12,22,24
Technology-based teams	1,18
Multi-skilling	5,6,9,12,13,14,15,16,21,22
Redesigned rewards/recognition	1,2,6,9,10,12,14,16,18,23,24
Peer/group review	6,18
Reduced levels of hierarchy	3,6,7,12,14,18
Role of manager changed	2,6,7,9,11,12,14,15,17,18,19
Organized by deliberations	4
Teams designed own processes	1,2,5,6
Project integrator role	4

Note 1: Refer to Table 1 for case descriptions

Structural Design Features. Clearly, and perhaps not surprisingly, the most common design feature implemented was a team-based work system (n=21 cases). Similarly, "autonomous work groups" were also found to be the most common design feature implemented in 53% of the 134 STS manufacturing cases reviewed (Pasmore et al., 1982). While the use of "teams" could be considered a generic design feature common to both STS manufacturing and knowledge work settings, our data shows that different types of teams were created for specific organizational purposes. Table 2 shows that five different types of teams were implemented. These five are: self-managing teams (n=7), cross-functional teams (n=7), customer-focused teams (n=5), regionally-based teams (n=3), and technology-based project teams (n=2).

As a design feature, the implementation of self-managing teams often resulted in the redrawing of organizational boundaries so that a department could manage itself as a small business. This also often included significant changes in decision-making processes, but as a rule, the team itself became accountable for all business outcomes. For team members to become self-managing and accountable for their outcomes, a significant amount of cross-training was required. Thus, multi-skilling was a common design feature when associated with self-managing teams. One striking example of this increased accountability was noted in the financial services case. During a major flood in Southern United States customers wanted immediate access to their mutual funds but had lost the necessary documentation for processing the transaction. Unbeknownst to the Vice President of that division, teams who had responsibility for that region of the country made an instantaneous policy decision that allowed people access to their funds without back-up documentation.

In the cases which implemented cross-functional, customer-focused, and regionally-based teams, the structural design features were used to refocus the efforts of professionals towards serving either internal or external customers more effectively. An electronics manufacturer and information systems group implemented technology-based project teams. Technology-based teams were used primarily as a means to speed up the development process or product delivery. The social architecture of the teams was based on the interdependencies between components of the technology.

Another significant structural change in five of the cases where teams were implemented were reductions in the levels of the management hierarchy. This structural intervention represents a significant change in the traditional power structure. For example, in the information systems division of a large oil company, two levels of management were eliminated which resulted in large spans of control. As a result of this change, some managers had up to 40 people reporting to them. This structural design change was often accompanied by significant redesign of human resources systems, the next design feature category.

Human Resources Design Features. The redesign of rewards and recognition systems was a common design feature across 11 of the cases. Three of the white collar work settings (accounting, financial services) and a chemical pilot plant implemented pay-for-knowledge compensation systems. While pay-for-knowledge compensation schemes are not uncommon in STS designed manufacturing plants, implementing them in salaried areas presents new challenges. For example, it took over two years for the corporate HR department of the acoustical tile company to approve the pay-for-knowledge scheme for a plant accounting department. Other cases altered their recognition and performance review procedures to support the new team structures. Rather than assigning supreme value to individual contributions (which traditionally has been the sacred cow in white collar/knowledge work settings), performance criteria shifted to recognizing team contributions. One uncommon design feature in this category, which was implemented in the information systems division case, was the use of peer reviews. Managers who typically had 30-40 direct reports were too far removed from the actual work activities of professionals to be able to realistically assess their performance. A considerable amount of training is required for professionals to be comfortable and skillful in assessing their peers. Thus, it is not surprising that peer reviews were an uncommon design feature.

Process Design Features. Process design features are those which resulted in institutionalized changes in role behaviors and social interactions. The most common process design feature is the change in management's role. Eleven cases indicated that management's role changed from the traditional directing and controlling function to becoming more of a coach and facilitator. This role change is a common feature of STS designed sites.

Within the limited sample of sites and firms studied here, it cannot be said that the following design features were in actuality uncommon. For example, the creation of a project integrator role was reported in only one of the cases. However, the process design feature of organizing by deliberations did appear to be unique. Rather than actually changing the formal structure of the organization, the process for developing new products was institutionalized. Coalitions of business and technical people were organized around key deliberations in the development process. For each deliberation, the roles and information contributions of each participant were clearly defined and made more explicit. Another unique process design feature is that some teams were given tremendous amounts of autonomy in designing their own work processes. These self-designing teams had high degrees of autonomy in organizing their own reward systems, information technology process, work design, and goal-setting practices. In the cases where self-designing team processes were operative, time-to-market and speedier technology development were key drivers.

Performance Improvements

Respondents were asked if attitudinal, behavioral and/or financial improvements resulted from the STS intervention. Most respondents reported significant attitudinal and behavioral improvements, but few had "hard" data on financial results. "Hard" data includes the more measurable short-term cost savings, which can have real staying power and are not necessarily one-time hits. "Soft" results are the long-term, harder-to-measure competitive and strategic advantages gained due to the shift in employee's attitudes towards their work and the accompanying behavioral changes.

While a number of respondents merely explained that the financial results were "reduced costs," others gave more explicit examples of how the organization/division/department was able to do more work with fewer people. One described how a financial transactions processing operation was processing 20-40% more with 25% less employees. Another said productivity was up 20-25% although staffing was down. Other "hard" financial changes were that turnover had reduced, departments had downsized, employees were making more money and overtime costs were reduced.

STS redesign efforts may not provide short-term, quick hit cost savings, but, ultimately, should lead to long-term competitive and strategic advantages. Thus, financial results are often difficult to evaluate and quantify in the short-term.

CONCLUSION

Our findings suggest that white-collar/knowledge work settings are being redesigned using STS theory and methods. However, when applied to white-collar/knowledge work settings, there is much more emphasis on STS as a philosophy and set of organizational design principles, whereas in the manufacturing arena the emphasis has been on the application of the classical STS tools and methods. Further, the structural design features in knowledge work settings serve as an integrative function to focus professionals on the total business system. Clearly, the generalizability of our findings is limited by the small sample size. Overall, more empirical research is needed to determine the causal relationships between various design features and performance outcomes.

BIBLIOGRAPHIC REFERENCES

Elden, M. (1983). Democratization and participative research in developing local theory. Journal of Occupational Behavior, Spring, 136-147.

Emery, F. (1959). Characteristics of socio-technical systems. London: Tavistock Institute Document no. 527.

Emery, M. (1988). Participative Design for Participative Democracy. Canberra: Australian National Univeristy.

Macy, B., Bliese, P, & Norton, J. (1991). Organizational change and Work innovation: A meta-analysis of 131 North American field experiments--1961-1990. Paper presented at the National Academy of Management Meeting, Organization DEvelopment Division: Miami, Florida.

Pasmore, W., Francis, C., Haldeman, J., & Shani, A. (1982). Sociotechnical Systems:

A North American Reflection on Empirical Studies of the Seventies. Human Relations, 35(12), 1179-1204.

Pasmore, W. Designing Effective Organizations: The Sociotechnical Systems Perspective. New York, NY: John Wiley & Sons.

Pasmore, W., & Gurley, K. (1991). Enhancing R&D across functional areas. In R. Kilmann & I. Kilmann (Eds.), Making Organizations More Competitive (pp. 368-396). San Francisco, CA: Jossey-Bass.

Pava, C. (1983). Managing New Office Technology. New York: Free Press.

Pava, C. (1986). Redesigning sociotechnical systems design: Concepts and methods for the 1990s. Journal of Applied Behavioral Science, 22(3), 201-222.

Purser, R. (1991). Redesigning the knowledge-based product development organization: A case study in sociotechnical systems change. Technovation, 11(7), 403-416.

Shani, A., & Elliott, O. (1988). Applying sociotechnical system design at the strategic apex: An illustration. Organization Development Journal, 6(2), 53-66.

Taylor, J. (1986). Long-term sociotechnical systems change in a computer operations department. Journal of Applied Behavioral Science, 22(3), 303-313.

BIOGRAPHICAL SKETCHES OF THE AUTHORS

Ronald E. Purser is an Assistant Professor of Organization Development at Loyola University in Chicago. He received his PhD in Organizational Behavior from Case Western Reserve University.

Jessica A. Fixler is completing her Masters Degree in Organization Development at Loyola University in Chicago. She received her BA degree from Tufts University in Social Psychology.

Ramkrishnan V. Tenkasi is completing his PhD in Organizational Behavior at Case Western Reserve University in Cleveland, Ohio. He is currently a research associate on a NSF funded study on distributed group decision making.

Productivity & Quality Management Frontiers-IV, edited by Sumanth, Edosomwan, Poupart, and Sink. ©1993 Institute of Industrial Engineers.

New Directions: Productivity and Shift Work

S. Whitworth
Headquarters, Department of the Army
Washington, D.C. USA

ABSTRACT

Approximately 20 million workers are on the evening, night, rotating, or split shifts, and more will be needed in the future. Demographers report that the workers who are willing to work non-traditional shifts are declining and being replaced by those who prefer traditional day hours. Companies that want to attract and retain tomorrow's most productive shift workers will need to apply new management directions in three key areas: work hour schedules, employees self management, and assistance in balancing work and family life.

KEY WORDS:

Family, productivity, schedules, shift, work

THE PREVALENCE OF SHIFT WORK: TODAY AND TOMORROW

Of the 125 million people in the American work force, the majority prefer to work the standard Monday through Friday day schedule. Most workers have those hours, but 16% (or approximately 20 million) work the less preferred evening, night, rotating, or split shifts that often fall on weekends or holidays (figures include all full, part-time, and contingency positions).

Certain occupations have a higher prevalence of shift work. These include protective agencies, food services, health services, and manufacturing companies that require continuous operation. But soon there will be more shift workers needed in these and other occupational fields because companies are adopting the twenty-four hour operation schedule as a way to stay competitive in the new global economy.[1] The extended operation trend is presently most evident in the service industry.

All categories of people can be found among shift workers: men, women; young, old; single, married, separated or divorced with or without children; and all ethnic and cultural groups. Within this diversity the profile of the "average" shift worker of today is a young, single, male. By ethnic group, African American men are more likely to work these hours, and Hispanic women the least likely.

About 28% of all shift workers prefer non-traditional hours for one or more of the following reasons: The hours allow them to attend school during the day; it solves a child or elder care problem; they believe it may lead to a better job; or they need the extra hourly wage often offered to work these hours (shift pay differential). The other 72% of all shift workers do not prefer these hours but work them involuntarily generally because they either could not find another job and the hours are required by their employer.[2]

---

[1] Stam, Jim and Soano, Andrea. (1991) "A Productive and Human Approach to Shiftwork Operations", National Productivity Review, Vol. 10, Issue 4, pp. 465-479.

[2] Mellor, Earl F. (1986) "Shift Work and Flexitime: How Prevalent Are They?", Monthly Labor Review, Vol. 109, Issue 11, pp.14-21.

The limited job market and recessionary environment of the early 1990's have allowed employers to require employees to take shifts they do not like. However, this is unlikely to continue in the future. Demographic forces are working against long term easy access to shift workers. The young, single, white male who now makes up 47% of new entrants to the total work force will drop to 15% by the end of the 1990's. He will be replaced by workers who are less inclined towards shift work.

Demographers assert that 62% of the work force will be between the ages of 35 to 55+ by the beginning of the next century, and nearly half of all the future work force will be women.

Most female workers prefer the day shift because it is most compatible with their second job as a homemaker. It is an established fact that even when the husband is present and working too, the wife still does most of the homemaking and child raising chores. Older workers also prefer the day shift because it is compatible with their life stage and style. Shift work, as it is usually managed today, is not in concert with older workers' needs. Both of these groups have valued commitments inside and outside the work place and, for that reason, place a high value on how their time is scheduled.[3]

The new challenge for employers will be how to attract and retain the shift workers of the future, and increase their productivity. Given the likely demographic profile of available workers in the near future, employers must be prepared to convince workers to choose shift work, rather than being able to count on a pool of workers with few choices. Successful employers of the future work force will master the challenge by applying new directions in key areas of human resources management. Innovative methods will be needed in scheduling work hours, involving employees in management decisions, and assisting workers to achieve an appropriate balance between work and family life.

Companies requiring shift workers in the future will be wise to offer new management directions with enticing policies, programs and tools that assist employees in overcoming real or perceived barriers to the shift work.

NEW MANAGEMENT DIRECTIONS IN THREE FUNCTIONAL AREAS

Scheduling
Unique shift schedules and rotational patterns targeted to capture worker interest and sustain productivity will be a key new direction in successful shift work management.

---

[3] Barton, Jane and Folk, Simon. (1991) "The Response of Day and Night Nurses to Their Work Schedules", Journal of Occupational Psychology, Vol. 64, Issue 3, pp. 207-218.

Each position in a continuous, or 24 hour, operation requires 168 hours of coverage per week. A manager may choose from many combinations of workers and number of hours per shift to provide the needed coverage. The decision is somewhat governed in part by the type of work to be done. For instance, to increase productivity and reduce the risk of accidents or injuries, physically demanding work is best done on an eight hour shift. Also, work that is mentally demanding or stressful is best done in eight or less hour shifts.

Emergency response workers often work 24 hour shifts (for about three days per week) because it fits best with their fluctuating periods of light and heavy activity. The rotational pattern of the shift schedule is also best matched with the type of work to be performed.

One rule is necessary for every shift rotational pattern: It must be charted on a clockwise rotation to accommodate the basic physiology of the workers' circadian rhythms. Within that guideline there are many choices of hours and shift patterns managers may select. Employees from numerous occupational fields seem to prefer twelve hour shifts as these allow for more consecutive days off.[4] Researchers have found that twelve hour shifts demonstrate no increased safety problems; no change in absenteeism; no change in turnover; and result in more applicants for non-traditional shift work[5]. The manager of future shift workers will want to explore new directions in shift patterns to find the most alluring fit between the needs of the company and workers who are attracted to blocks of time off for personal and social business. Table 1 gives examples of common twelve hour shift schedule variations.

Table 1: Common Variations of 12 Hour Shift Patterns

	S	M	T	W	T	F	S	S	M	T	W	T	F	S
4/4	X	X	X	X	O	O	O	O	X	X	X	X	O	O
3/3	X	X	X	O	O	O	X	X	X	O	O	O	X	X
3/2/2	X	X	X	O	O	X	X	O	O	O	X	X	O	O

(Note: 4/4 shift is 4 twelve hour shifts on followed by 4 days off. 3/3 is 3 twelve hour shifts on followed by

---

[4] Burnes, R. N. and Koop, G. J. (1987) "A Modular Approach to Optimal Multiple-Shift Manpower Scheduling", Operations Research, Vol., 35, Issue 1, pp. 100-110.

[5] Stafford, Edward F.; Sherman, J. Daniel; and McCollum, James K. (1988) Streamlining 12-Hour Work Shifts, Personnel Administrator, Vol. 73, Issue 12, pp. 52-57.

3 days off. 3/2/2 is 3 twelve hour shifts on--off for 2
days--on for 2 twelve hour shifts--off for 3 days, then
again 2 days of twelve hour shifts and 2 days off. The
3/2/2 is also called the EOWEO or every other weekend off
shift.)

It takes a worker several days to physically and psychologically
adjust to a shift change (e.g. moving from day to night shifts or
going from a 4/4 to straight night shift). Short span adjustments leave the worker feeling tired, physically stressed and
unable to perform at optimum levels. The employee preferred
length for a shift rotations is once every six to twelve weeks.[6]

Higher productivity and employee satisfaction with shift schedules are related. Employees are most satisfied with schedules
that a) they have been involved in choosing, and b) allow them to
give their best to the company, themselves, and their family
and/or community.

Increased worker age and the potential stress of shift work can
be difficult to blend successfully. Shift workers must constantly readjust sleeping and eating patterns. Older workers generally lack the physical and psychological resiliency to do this well
for long periods of time.[7] Also, the older worker most likely
had some shift work experience when young. If that is the case,
they will probably feel they earned their way to the more preferred hours and view returning to the non-traditional hours as
losing ground in their career development. Their families are
more established, as is their standing in the community, and
therefore, it is likely that their family and community commitments are higher.

New management directions will call for combinations of creative
shift work patterns with seniority differential and job sharing
opportunities, coupled with benefits that have previously been
associated with traditional day-time employees. Some examples of
these benefits are: child or elder care, on-site adult education
opportunities, transportation subsidies, and opportunities for
occupational training.

Employee Self-Management Teams
Another new direction that will be taken by companies that
successfully recruit and retain shift workers will be the utilization of self-management teams. Industry has almost 20 years of
experience and research to show that these teams are successful

[6] Krantz, Marianne. (1990) "Management in Practice: Twelve
Hours at Manville", Management Review, Vol., 79, Issue 1, pp. 8-
10.

[7] Moretz, Sandy. (1987) "Rotational Shifts: Are They
Harmful to Workers' Health?", Occupational Hazards, Vol. 49,
Issue 10, pp. 54-57.

in producing and retaining highly motivated and productive employees. Their success centers on three elements:

o Early involvement of employees in the development of the teams purpose and goals
o Ensuring there is strong team leadership
o Having a supervisor who is willing to delegate daily decisions appropriate for the team to make

Work/Family Balance
Successful companies of the future will assist all workers achieve a balance between work and family life. Focusing extra attention in this area for shift-workers will be necessary because their hours are more likely to result in imbalance. Successful companies will understand that increased work/family imbalance can lead to conflicts that can negatively affect productivity, and they will take action to:

o Provide a supportive environment
o Train managers in work/family awareness, sensitivity and flexibility
o Provide workers with information and tools to achieve a work/family balance
o Define the parameters of the organization's and employees roles and responsibilities in the balancing process

A company will benefit by developing a comprehensive affordable system of programs, policies and benefits that are responsive to work/family issues. The self-management teams can provide valuable in-put to the system design. When a company builds its human resource system based on the information generated by the self-management teams, it adds greatly to increased worker satisfaction and productivity. A fully developed system will (at a minimum) focus on work schedules, leave options, comprehensive health care, employee education, and information and assistance programs.

Presently, child care is the most widely accepted and implemented segment of work/family balance programs.[8] Companies are already beginning to provide on/or near site day care for pre-school and school age children. Shift workers have an even greater need for resources and referral services for well and sick child care, peer support groups, and information on how to fit traditional family living with non-traditional work hours.

Arrangement of how and where work is done can be varied and beneficial to both the company and the employee. Arrangements can include part-time, flexitime, flexiplace, job sharing, phased retirement, and gradual returns to work. Nearly all plans for work scheduling and location can be creatively applied to the

---

[8] "The Emerging Role of the Work/Family Manager", (1992) Conference Board Report, Report Number 987, pp. 1-28.

shift work population. They can also be combined with leave options to promote a better work/family balance. Leave options can include the accepted sick and annual leave, as well as family illness days, bereavement leave, leave sharing, leave banks, respite and sabbatical leave, or combinations of both compensated and uncompensated leaves of absence.

Benefit programs can be tailored to make acceptance of shift work a more attractive option to workers. Pay differential has already been mentioned, but progressive companies will also enhance shift workers' medical care benefits to offset their known shift work health risks (predominately heart and gastrointestinal problems). A specialized package of cafeteria or flexible benefits, specifically designed for shift workers, will be a new direction applied to attract and retain these employees.

Conclusion

Shift workers will be in high demand in the near future. The companies that are successful in recruiting and retaining the best of them will: a) offer creative shift schedules and rotational patterns; b) empower employee management teams; and c) provide information and assistance for shift workers that will help them achieve a effective balance between their unique work and family demands.

BIBLIOGRAPHY

Koonce, Richard. (1991) "The People Side of Organizational Change", Credit, Vol. 17, Issue 6, pp. 22-25

Krantz, Marianne. (1990) "Management in Practice: Twelve Hours at Manville", Management Review, Vol. 79, Issue 1, pp.8-10.

Mellor, Ear F. (1986) "Shift Work and Flexitime: How Prevalent Are They?", Monthly Labor Review, Vol 109, Issue 11, pp. 14-21.

Moretz, Sandy. (1987) "Rotational Shifts: Are They Harmful to Workers' Health?", Occupational Hazards, Vol. 49, Issue 10, pp. 54-57.

Stafford, Edward F.; Sherman, J. Daniel; and McCollum, James K. (1988)Streamlining 12-hour Work Shifts, Personnel Administrator, Vol. 73, Issue 12, pp. 52-57.

Stam, Jim and Soano, Andrea. (1991) "A Productive-and-Human Approach to Shiftwork Operations", National Productivity Review, Vol. 10, Issue 4, pp. 465-479.

"The Emerging Role of the Work-Family Manager", (1992) Conference Board Report, Report Number 987, pp. 1-28.

Towers Perrin and Hudson Institute, (1990) "Workforce 2000: Competing in a Seller's Market: Is Corporate America Prepared?", pp. 31.

Productivity & Quality Management Frontiers-IV, edited by Sumanth, Edosomwan, Poupart, and Sink. ©1993 Institute of Industrial Engineers.

Benchmarking Successful Quality Programs

J.A. Edosomwan
Johnson & Johnson Associates, Inc.
Morgan Hill, California USA

ABSTRACT

Benchmarking for continuous quality improvement has evolved to be a strategy and process of comparing performance measures of an organization to the best in any industry. This paper focuses on how organizations can use benchmarking as a tool to search for industry best practices that improve overall performance and effectiveness. The various types of benchmarking are discussed. A step-by-step methodology is provided to assist organizations interested in benchmarking. The focus is on comparing all activities being done, all results being obtained, all forms of strategic planning, means and processes for doing work against that of competitors. Case studies of organizations that have used benchmarking to improve performance are presented.

INTRODUCTION

Worldwide competition is driving many organizations to search for industry best practices that could be used to improve performance, quality, productivity and total customer satisfaction. Benchmarking has evolved as the right tool to help organizations compare products, services, and processes to those of the "world class" and "best of breed" organizations. In recent years, benchmarking has received tremendous attention because it replaces other traditional methods such as competitive analysis and functional approaches for improving performance. Organizations are now using benchmarking as a strategy for sharing information on performance improvement strategies and techniques.

BENCHMARKING DEFINED

Benchmarking is the continuous process of searching for the best industry practices to improve performance. The benchmarking process include continuous measurement, evaluation, and research of new ideas, methods, practices and processes; adapting the good features; and implementing them to become the best or world-class organizations. The definition is consistent with the works of Edosomwan (1992a), (1992b), Camp (1989), Geber (1990), and Xerox (1987). Benchmarking has no value unless the best practices sought are implemented. It should be used as a tool for short-term and long-term planning as well as for achieving operational performance. Benchmarking tool and concepts are applicable to manufacturing, service, academe, government, and professional organizations. Benchmarking cuts across industry boundaries and helps organizations analyze the gap between present level of performance and the best that exists.

TYPES OF BENCHMARKING

Edosomwan (1991, 1992) identified six types of benchmarking that are prevalent in modern organizations today. Some of the types of benchmarking presented here are also supported by the works of Camp (1989).

Competitive Benchmarking: This involves comparing a company's performance against its toughest competitors. This is one of the toughest benchmarking activities to perform because competitors are not always willing to share information.

Generic Benchmarking: This involves comparing a company's performance to a world-class organization that is not in the same industry, but has some similarities in work processes. The world-class companies may not be easy to identify, but they are more likely to share information because there is not direct competition and conflict of interest.

Professional Benchmarking: This involves comparing a company's performance to any other world-class company by utilizing the contracted services of a professional or consultant. This approach can bring quick results because the contracted professional is viewed as a neutral third-party without conflict of interest and, as such, sensitive information can be obtained to help the requesting company. In order to get the most from this approach, the professional expert or consultant must be informed in what is needed and also be willing to assist with implementation of findings.

Functional Benchmarking: This involves comparing a company's performance against other world-class companies that perform similar activities. The companies involved are often in the same industry providing similar products and services.

Internal Operation Benchmarking: This involves comparing a company's performance against a similar process, product or service within the same organization or a subsidiary of the same company. This is usually easy to perform because there is not perceived conflict of interest.

Self-Unit Benchmarking: This involves a process where an individual or a group compares their own performances against that of competitors or world-class companies either in the same industry or outside the same line of business. The focus of this effort is usually on management practices and individual performance measures.

BENEFITS OF BENCHMARKING

Benchmarking enables an organization to: 1) identify strengths and weaknesses compared to industry best practices 2) learn more efficient techniques, methods, and tools 3) implement them to stay ahead of the competition. Benchmarking when used for strategic planning enables organizations to identify the keys to success in each business area, provides specific quantitative targets to shoot for, creates an awareness of state-of-the-art approaches, and helps business units cultivate a culture where change, adaptation and continuous quality improvement are actively sought out. Good benchmarking analysis produces two types of information: quantitative data that are used to measure performance by and to set future targets, and qualitative information on the key success factors that explain how other companies became best-in-class in that function.

BENCHMARKING IMPLEMENTATION STEPS

The following ten step approach shown in Figure 1 is recommended for performing benchmarking:

Step One: In order to benchmark performance improvement of products, services, and work processes, it is very important to understand the market and the customer. This requires one-on-one contact with the customer and data collection on market trends. This also involves knowing what is happening in the global market-place by industry, sub-industry, customer size, needs, desires and resource base. It is equally important to understand how world-class companies are responding to the risks and opportunities in the market place. The understanding of the customer's outputs and markets provide the basis for effectively setting the benchmarking goals.

Step Two: Specific goals should be set based on the products, services, and work processes of the company. These goals can be established in a number of different ways, such as by customer base, divisions within the organization, or work units within the organization. Management should form a cross-functional team with people having expertise in benchmarking and this team should be responsible for establishing the benchmarking goals.

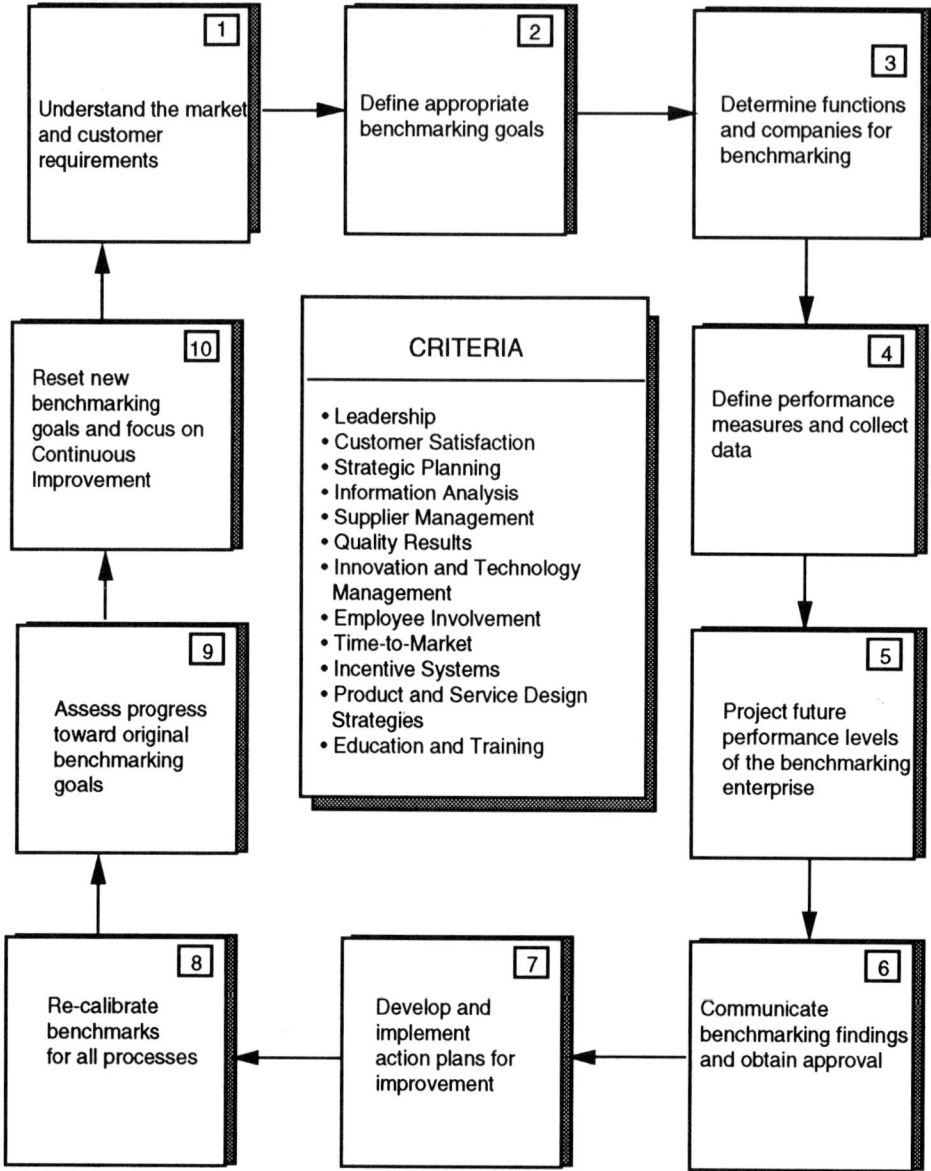

FIGURE 1: EDOSOMWAN BENCHMARKING MODEL (EBM)

The boxes in the figure contain the following text:

1. Understand the market and customer requirements

2. Define appropriate benchmarking goals

3. Determine functions and companies for benchmarking

4. Define performance measures and collect data

5. Project future performance levels of the benchmarking enterprise

6. Communicate benchmarking findings and obtain approval

7. Develop and implement action plans for improvement

8. Re-calibrate benchmarks for all processes

9. Assess progress toward original benchmarking goals

10. Reset new benchmarking goals and focus on Continuous Improvement

CRITERIA

- Leadership
- Customer Satisfaction
- Strategic Planning
- Information Analysis
- Supplier Management
- Quality Results
- Innovation and Technology Management
- Employee Involvement
- Time-to-Market
- Incentive Systems
- Product and Service Design Strategies
- Education and Training

Step Three: Identify the continuous improvement functions or categories: management, technology, quality, productivity, process steps, cost, delivery and schedule, strategic planning, customer satisfaction indices, supplier process and information system. Also identify the companies that are best-in-class in the selected areas for benchmarking. This may require national and international competitive analysis depending on the type, size, products and services offered by the enterprise.

Step Four: Identify and collect data on key performance measures. Review industry trends and select key measures that can be compared with other enterprises. Collect data on key measures. In addition to collecting data, describe key management approaches that differ between enterprises and identify the key success factors.

Step Five: Project future performance levels of the benchmarked enterprise. In this step, establish projections on what the enterprise's performance level will be over the short-term (two years) and long-term (five to ten years). Develop a plan to match or exceed the competitors' or industry best-in-class' performance level. Establish specific functional goals to reach the desired levels of performance.

Step Six: Communicate benchmarking findings to management and obtain approval. The benchmarking analysis and recommendations should be communicated first to management. The recommendations should identify specific areas for suggested improvements and strengths, and strategies to achieve excellence by functional area. After senior management review, the recommendations should also be communicated to employees, to build enthusiasm and support for the new continuous improvement goals.

Step Seven: Develop and implement action plans for improvement. For each specific objective defined, the continuous improvement team develops a step-by-step implementation plan. Data should be collected after a period of time to determine new performance levels. Adjustments to the continuous improvement plans should be made if the goals are not met. The implementation steps should also include a specific work plan with schedule dates, resources, expected benefits and measures of performance.

1003

Step Eight: Re-calibrate benchmarks for all processes. Since the right focus for success is on continuous improvement of all work processes to improve value and excellence, the enterprise continuous improvement team should continue to re-evaluate and update the benchmarks to ensure that they are based on the latest data and accurate current information. While this re-calibration process for benchmarks might seem expensive, it is well worth the effort for any enterprise that aspires to be best-in-class in providing products and services.

Step Nine: Assess progress toward original benchmarking goals. Periodic assessments should be performed to determine how the organization is progressing toward original benchmarking goal. The intervals for the assessments should be based on both the size of the organization as well as the number of benchmarking goals.

Step Ten: Reset new benchmarking goals and focus on continuous improvement. The entire emphasis on benchmarking cannot be achieved at one time. With the dynamic nature of business today and continuous changes in products, services, and customers, there is a need to continually reassess established goals and focus on those that will result in long-term improvement for the organization.

BENCHMARKING CASE STUDIES

Several companies have benefited from benchmarking. A few examples are cited.

Dulaphi (1991) reported how Motorola experienced severe drops in sales in the electric pagers business. The company employed continuous quality improvement techniques and benchmarking and then implemented best practices in areas ranging from accounting to robots. Motorola learned that benchmarking was a source of continued improvement. The result was a "data driven assembly line in which computers translated customer orders into robotic motion". The "Bandit" pager assembly line was capable of making pagers in less than three hours after the sales personnel entered an order. Through the effort, Motorola regained market share in its pager division and spurred numerous technology advances throughout the company.

Biesada (1991) reported how AMP benchmarked for six years in developing its supplier management program and then implemented a supplier certification program. Today, standards are being tightened, suppliers are asked to participate early in the product design phase, and AMP held engineering seminars for 200 of its suppliers during a two-year period. The results from these efforts include improvement in incoming quality up to 98% from 92% in 1984, on-time delivery is up from 70% to 90% today, cycle time has been reduced by 50%, and AMP's supplier based has been reduced by one-third.

Biesada also reported how MBNA America, the credit card subsidiary of Maryland Bank of North America learned a hard lesson in 1982. Its rate of customer retention was slipping, customer complaints were increasing, and profits were down significantly. The company benchmarked customer service practices at Bean, Xerox, L.L. and U.S. Sprint. They learned to listen to their customers - let the customers define service quality. MBNA identified key service points for their customer, isolated profitable accounts, and began to serve them well. Through the application of the benchmarking process and lessons learned from it, MBNA's profitability rose 16 fold, its industry ranking improved from 38th to 3rd, and MBNA now provides the fastest line of credit increase approval in the industry, averaging only one hour instead of the industry standard of seven days.

CalComp, a California manufacturer of plotters and other electronic devices, faced stiff competition in the 1980's. The company employed several quality improvement strategies including the process of benchmarking. In 1986, CalComp introduced design for manufacturability. In 1988, the plotter products division developed a concurrent design methodology with three phases: (1) product definition, in which the product is specified using Quality Functional Deployment, (2) product development, during which the feasibility is determined and prototypes are created, and (3) product qualification, in which the system is verified and both the product and process variability are assessed. CalComp was able to reduce the average time to market from 36 to 22 months, productivity improved 50%, inventory decreased 65%, manufacturing space decreased by 50%, quality increased by 50%, factory operating expenses decreased by 15%, the supplier base went down by 60%, customer shipments improved by 2 months over the original plan.

PRIORITIZING WHAT TO BENCHMARK

There are certainly lots of world-class companies to benchmark. The obvious problems that seem to exist include accessibility and confidentiality of information.

There is always a tendency to benchmark every product, service, and process in order to achieve the goals set forth in continuous quality improvement. Everything done cannot be a target for benchmarking. The best of what is done should be the target for benchmarking. The criteria specified in Figure 1 provides some important areas to focus on when benchmarking.

Benchmarking prioritization should be done using the following criteria: 1) impact of work product on competitors, 2) impact of improvement strategy on customer satisfaction, 3) cost of project, 4) improvement project benefits, and 5) organizational workload.

CONCLUSION

Benchmarking is a process of comparing methods, tools, techniques, processes, practices, outputs, and results in a systematic manner. A benchmark is a standard of quality excellence against which other similar things must be measured. Benchmarking for continuous quality improvement can help organizations understand what to benchmark, what the benchmark is, how benchmarking is achieved and how to use benchmarking data and information to improve performance. Benchmarking is the way to spot emerging competitors and mirror test to see where an organization's performance is headed compared to industry-best practices.

REFERENCES AND BIBLIOGRAPHY FOR FURTHER READING

"A National Benchmark Study On The Attitudes Of The American Work Force" (1989) Wyatt Work America, 25 pp.

Band, W. (1990) "Benchmark Your Performance For Continuous Improvement," Sales & Marketing Management In Canada, May, pp.36-38.

Bemowski, K. (1991) "The Benchmarking Bandwagon," Quality Progress, January, pp. 19-24.

Biesada, A. (1991) "Benchmarking", Financial World, September.

Camp, R. (1989) "Benchmarking: The Search For Industry Best Practices That Lead To Superior Performance", Quality Progress, April, pp. 62-69.

Caulkin, S. (1990) "Best Factories", Management Today, November, pp. 60-89.

"Competitive Benchmarking: What It Is And What It Can Do For You", Xerox Corporate Quality Office, (1987) pp. 1-22.

Dulaphi, J. (1991) "The Bandit Standoff", Financial World, September, pp. 48-49.

Edosomwan, J. A. (1992) Benchmarking Baldrige Award Winners, Johnson & Johnson Associates, Inc., Technical Paper 92-016.

Edosomwan, J. A. (1992) Customer and Market-Driven Quality Management, Excellence Publications, Fairfax, Va.

Edosomwan, J. A. (1991) Continuous Improvement Tools and Techniques, Excellence Publications, Fairfax, Va.

Edosomwan, J. A. (1991a) Benchmarking World-Class Quality Companies, Johnson & Johnson Associates, Inc. Training Guide.

Geber, B. (1990) "Benchmarking: Measuring Yourself Against The Best", Training, November, pp. 36-44.

BIOGRAPHICAL SKETCH OF THE AUTHOR

Johnson A. Edosomwan is President and CEO of Johnson & Johnson Associates, Inc., an international continuous improvement consulting firm. Dr. Edosomwan is author/editor of 24 books and training manuals and has received 43 awards for his contributions to various fields. He is a Senior Member of IIE and ASQC, serves on the Board of Examiners for Malcolm Baldrige National Quality Award, is the Chairman of the Editorial Advisory Board of the Quality Observer, and serves as Executive Editor of Managing Technology Today magazine.

Productivity & Quality Management Frontiers-IV, edited by Sumanth, Edosomwan, Poupart, and Sink. ©1993
Institute of Industrial Engineers.

Towards a Methodology for Quality Software Development

R.T. Plant and P. Tsoumpas
University of Miami
Coral Gables, Florida USA

ABSTRACT

The aim of this paper is to illustrate how the development life cycle of software systems
can be improved through the utilization of quality assurance techniques. The approach
we advocate is novel in that it utilizes a multi-faceted approach to quality assurance in
the software process, placing emphasis upon integrating quality development principles
throughout the process. The underlying principle is to move the emphasis of the software
developers' efforts from the testing phase to the initial specification phase; and to make
this the primary cost center for the quality assurance process.

The methodology we are proposing is novel in that it places a set of measurement tools
at the disposal of the management team from which management can monitor the
development process. These software metrics allow an increased management awareness
of the process to be achieved and ensure the system is created within parameters that
ensure quality development. Having moved our emphasis towards specifications; we then
integrate this with a rigorous development philosophy that advocates formalized
techniques wherever appropriate or possible. We supplement current software
development management techniques with quality management techniques such as those
proposed by Deming, thus creating an integrated and unified approach to software
development, that increases the quality of management's ability to control this process.

Introduction

The aim of this paper is to illustrate how the development life cycle of software systems can be improved through the utilization of quality assurance techniques. Previous methodologies have emphasized inspection as a mechanism for system acceptance; however, this testing approach is prone to error creation and can be wasteful of scarce resources, since error detection occurs after the development of the software system.

In order to illustrate the approach which we advocate, we will first briefly outline three popular life-cycle models, before proceeding to discuss our Quality Development Life Cycle Methodology.

An Overview of Existing Software Life-Cycles

There are many different life-cycle models in use today, including the traditional waterfall based model of Royce (1970), the Spiral Model, the use of CASE environments, prototyping; and formal methods having mathematical specification techniques. These models are utilized in conjunction with the procurers' requirements and standards such as those proposed by ANSI, IEEE, DoD, and American Institute of Aeronautics and Astronautics (AIAA).

Royce proposed a stage-based model, the waterfall model, to facilitate the development of large scale software systems. This approach was an attempt to characterize the various phases of a software development project and to assist in the management of such projects. This model assumed that the various stages were discrete and that each stage's output represents an input for the next one. However, as development can now be seen as a continuous function; new models of development have been suggested:

Exploratory programming and prototyping are two development models which utilize the iterative approach of developing a prototype (which will be acceptable by the user.) In the exploratory programming approach, the process ends with the development of a system which adequately addresses the needs of the users. The prototyping approach utilizes the prototype as a definition of the user requirements. A system design can then be based on this prototype.

The formal transformation model utilizes formal methods for requirement specifications and then transforms these specifications to programs.

In addition to the development paradigm followed for the creation of a software system, there is a managerial aspect to be addressed. Management requires a mechanism for controlling the development process. This can be achieved through a model, based on the development paradigm followed for the specific project, and which specifies certain documents as outputs of each phase. These documents can then be reviewed and assessed for conformance to requirements, a verification process. When it has been established that they conform with what was expected from that specific phase, they are noted as being complete. Sommerville (1992) criticized such systems for making the development process less flexible towards the adoption of changes since employees are reluctant to recreate "finalized"documents and he argues that such systems increase the project cost since they require a great number of reports to be created without helping the effectiveness of the process. The Department of Defense Standard STD-2167A (DOD-STD-2167A, 1988) and the "V diagram" (McManus, 1987) are examples of such a model-based development philosophy. Both of these methodologies describe the developmental process in detail and require documents to be produced for every phase and subsequent reviews to be performed.

These methods of software development, that were briefly described above, have a common shortfall, the absence of process control. These models clearly defined what should be done in every phase and what the resultant of that phase is; however, they did not mention how each phase's performance should be controlled in order to increase quality through measurement and management. The methodology which we present aims at addressing this issue. It is our proposition that the incorporation of rigorous techniques in performing software development as well as changes in management practices inspired from the quality management theories will be a benefit to both software developers and managers.

Proposed methodology

The aim of the methodology we propose is to blend formality, metrics and process control together into a development life-cycle model that is robust, pragmatic and which meets the needs of industrial developers(Tsoumpas, 1992.) The focus of the methodology is upon the early phases of software development, since the cost-function for system changes is much lower than in the later phases (Boehm, 1980) where already a great amount of time, effort, and money have been committed. As Dobbins pointed out:

> *"Quality is free provided that a continuous effort is made to perform failure reduction tasks and to seek ways and means to move the failure prevention, detection, and removal activity closer to the front end of the development process."* (Dobbins, 1987)

The methodology we propose suggests the incorporation of rigorous techniques in the areas that provided the most problems in software development: requirements specifications and process control. The methodology addresses the core of the problem, the reluctance to change management practices. By incorporating techniques from quality management we suggest that the total software development process can be controlled, which in turn, will steadily improve the quality of the end product.

In the following sections we will consider the individual aspects of the development methodology and identify their strengths as they contribute to our new philosophy of development.

1010

System Cost Model Adoption

The first step in development of a system within an organization is a managerial one, in that whilst the requirements for a system are being formulated the system should be endorsed and backed by the top management of that organization. This necessitates that the system perform a useful function, be revenue producing and be developed in a cost effective manner. Thus, it is necessary for the development team to adopt a software cost estimation model such as COCOMO (Boehm, 1980) or SOFTCOST (Tausworthe, 1981) prior to system development. This is necessary for many reasons, in that it will identify cost centers that may occur, special system development needs, such as training or equipment, and that these needs will be met prior to development, ensuring management commitment to the project from the conception of the system.

Requirements Formulation

A Natural Language Approach
The initial phase in the software development life cycle is the system requirements phase. This phase is of great importance, since by describing what a software system is expected to do, determines the success of that system.

Traditional industry practice has been to use natural language as a medium to express the functionality of the system. However, there are many problems with the use of natural language that cannot be overcome. Ince (1990) states that some of the reasons that system specifications are inherently weak when expressed in natural language are that natural language does little to reduce contradictions, ambiguity, incompleteness, and a has a tendency to mix the various levels of functionality within the descriptions. Furthermore, large and complex business or scientific systems require very large documents for their description, thereby making the size of the document an important aspect of the problem specification. This is especially true when combined with the differences in linguistic semantics between the user and the software developer, which may induce new error conditions through incorrect requirements definitions and interpretations.

The inherent problems of natural language have been commented upon by Sommerville (1992), who notes that unstructured natural language specifications are unable to express the functional architecture of the design, and that requirement specifications expressed in natural language are over-flexible since they allow related requirements to be expressed in completely different ways. These abilities, or shortcomings, of natural language force the software developer to distinguish and separate system requirements from the requirements text based on his personal experience, a situation that has led to incorrect, incomplete and inconsistent system specifications. This has therefore led software engineers towards the adoption of a more formal approach to system specification.

A Rigorous Approach

The weakness of natural language specifications has led researchers such as Hoare (1986) to investigate the use of formal mathematical systems in specification. The early work of the formalists was on proving programs correct. This was done by describing, through mathematics, the function of a piece of program code, implementing the function and then using an axiomatic approach to prove the program matched the algorithm specified. Ideally the code would match the algorithm and meet its correctness obligation without the necessity of resorting to exhaustive traditional testing techniques.

The formal approach was thought to be attractive, since it did not require any testing effort; however, problems were faced since the proof of complex systems is tedious and were often longer than the program itself (Ince, 1989). Additionally, the heavy requirements in mathematics made the methods unattractive to the software developers who lacked these skills.

The traditionalist software industry also did not embrace formal methods as they required higher skill levels, a disciplined approach to development and were perceived as lacking software support tools. However, as problems with software development continued, and as the systems grew in size, complexity and consequently in cost, the need to utilize the strengths of the formalist approach has become indispensable. However, the state of formalist research was now focused upon the specification process as opposed to the earlier work on program proving. This more complete approach encompasses many areas as noted by Hall (1990) who notes that formal methods can be used in areas such as specifications, program development and construction.

The use of formal methods through set theory and predicate calculus, can provide the right medium for recording customer's requirements in a form that is unambiguous and understood by software engineers and sophisticated users. This has a positive impact on the whole software development process. However, problems with the usage of formal methods still exist. As Ince (1989) points out, these problems are in the areas of training, lack of supporting tools, and the requirement of a major investment by the company in changing the managerial practices. The adoption of a quality theory will mean the adoption of ideas that solve these problems. In all quality theories, training and education have a pivotal position. The Japanese say that "Quality Control starts with training and ends in training" (Imai, 1987). The implementation of formal methods clearly benefits the software development company by providing explicit, unambiguous specifications. These specifications result in higher quality software products, which can attract more customers and increase software companies' sales. In order for the advantages of formal methods to become apparent within an organization, a significant time period must elapse, in which employees can be trained and become familiar with the theories and their applications while getting used to quickly and routinely developing fast formal specifications.

The opportunities for companies to improve their software development process through rigorous techniques is clear; however, there is still significantly strong resistance to using them. Companies are unwilling to invest the time and effort in introducing formal methods. Associated with companies' reluctance to invest in training of their employee, is high voluntary turnover. Some employees who become trained in certain areas get recruited by competitors, which negates the opportunity for the company to recover its investment in the employees' training. The high turnover problem is one faced by most of the Western companies, and it could be argued that it has its roots in the aggressiveness of skilled employees in pursuing a career. This problem impairs companies' efforts to improve their workforce, and will necessitate action in order to successfully implement a new direction in software management and development. The way the Japanese have faced this problem is by offering lifetime employment, family-like atmosphere in the workplace, and enjoyment of the work (or fulfillment of the employees). The only obstacle for a quality management program in a software development company is management's commitment to it. If management pays only lip service to the quality cause and in the first difficulty or pressure forgets everything and goes back to the old management way of pressing the employees to produce without any consideration for the quality of the product, i.e. defects (bugs) in the code, then the whole investment in a quality program will be jeopardized.

Standards

As Hall (1990) suggested; formal methods could be used to guide the software developers in the design and programming phases, and additionally serve as a clarifier of the requirement specifications document for the customer. A practice which enhances the robustness of the requirement specifications document is the use of standards that assist for uniform understanding of terms, techniques and approaches. These standards are aimed at providing unambiguous definitions and act as a base line document. Participation in this is a practice that can be adopted by all software development companies, and thus establish industry-wide standards. This removes the ambiguity of such terms as: "user friendly" , "easily maintainable" or "reliable".Terms such as these often have different meaning for developers and customers, and both parties rely on their own personal judgement for translating them, resulting in a conflict over the final product.

By introducing these standardization practices, in conjunction with formal methods, management will be able to improvement of the communication between customers and developers. The employment of a quality management program will guarantee that such effort will not be static, but it will get improved by any newly acquired information.

Quality Management

The quality management principal "each process is the customer of the previous process and the supplier of the subsequent one" should become a tenet for the software company's process management. This can be seen when the specification of the system is passed from the team comprising the software engineer and customer to the software designer. The specification has to possess the ability to improve the communication between analysts and designers. Thus the key to achieving this process pipeline is *communication*.

It can be foreseen that one approach to achieving this level of communication and interaction is through quality circles, where professionals from both sides can come together and discuss methods of improving the current practice by introducing new documents, changes in currently used documents, and additions in the utilized tools. On the other side of the design process, the communication between programmers and designers will be improved by using techniques such as the Taguchi methods (Roy, 1990) By utilizing Quality Function Deployment (QFD) tables, customer requirements can be translated in guidelines for programming practices. For example, "user friendliness" means on-line help in every step, pull-down menus, mouse driven menus etc., "reliable" means fault-proof input inquiries, which is that inputs will be rejected if they don't conform with previously defined standards, or that aspects such as existence of a file or a file's size will not be reasons for system crashes etc. This process will be continuously improved as new data become available from the customer support and testing teams.

Measurement and Metrics

In order to assess the impact of differing methodologies upon development, software engineers utilize measurement theory and software metrics. These metrics are intended to enable developers determine the impact and effect one parameter of a design has upon another. Research is active in this area, and workers consider such design issues as module length, optimal number of modules, and criteria of module separation (Conte, 1986).

The aim of software metrics is to assist the developer understand the relationship between the parameters of software design and creation. These parameters are however, not always easy to determine or measure, in addition to the difficulty in determining the consequences of the results. For example, a software engineer may use the whole-function criterion or an optimum-length criterion to decide when to split a program in modules, or determine the optimum length of a module, but other human-based parameters such as measurement of a programmers experience, or suitability of the programming language used are not so easily measured.

This state of flux in software measurement necessitates that companies utilize a software metrics measurement program that will help each specific company to understand their own development parameters and their inter-relations. Grady et al.(1987) has pointed out that a program like this is difficult to implement and serious commitment of all interested parties should be obtained before the implementation. Successful implementation lies on the following two aspects:

- training courses that will help programmers, analysts, and project managers alike to understand the importance of such tools, and

- the reassurance of the top management that this tool will be used only for the improvement of the product and the process and not as an evaluation instrument.

In addition, Grady et al. (1987) points out the importance of automated data collection. The lower the degree of human intervention in the collection process the higher the degree of accuracy in those measurements. However, some data will still necessitate manual collection and this can be done through standardized forms, after a training course has been undertaken to reinforce their validity. Results from the metrics and data can then be used for improving subsequent projects and in establishing standards for every task. These standards can then be regularly evaluated and altered accordingly.

The literature describes a great number of software metrics gauging various attributes of the software development product. A comprehensive review of such metrics as well as predictive models is presented by Conte et al. (1986) and Zuse (1992). They present various metrics in categories such as size, data structure, logic structure, effort and cost, defect, and design metrics.

The testing phase is the last in-house phase for a software product. Schulmeyer (1990) has suggested that an independent team should perform the acceptance tests. The relationship between the of number of problems (errors) detected after delivery and the testing practice used has not yet been proven by research, but the idea of an independent testing entity is intuitively appealing. However, software development companies have not yet widely use this practice since it is costly and requires redundant personnel. Two factors that should however be used in the testing process, are i) the representation of the customer and ii) the type and number of tests that will be performed should be agreed with the customer in the requirement specifications phase.

System operation could be considered the extended testing phase of the real life performance of the system. Even though operation should be without problems, any discovered errors or problems should be utilized to pinpoint areas requiring improvement as well as actions required to improve the robustness of the end-product. Maintenance is the activity which will benefitted the most from a developmental process like the one described above.

Summary & Conclusions

Some of the advantages of the proposed methodology are:

i. Clearer communication between customer and supplier (in all phases)
ii. Measurement of existing process' attributes and establishment of standards
iii. Continuous improvement effort
iv. Shift of focus from testing to requirement specifications and design
v. Shift from an artistic belief about software development to an engineering one.

The proposed methodology is one which recognizes the importance of communication between customer and software developer as well as between professionals with different skills. We believe that by establishing formal procedures for communication the performance will be enhanced and problems will diminish. Furthermore, the establishment of informal meetings, in the context of quality circles, will enhance the understanding between professionals with different educational background, as well as help in the dissemination of information which would not happen otherwise. In addition, such informal meetings will foster the team spirit between members of an organization.

The establishment of a software metrics program will provide the necessary insight in the process and product attributes. It will also become the foundation of an improvement program. The proposed methodology is the only one which facilitates a formal mechanism for continuous improvement. The advantage of such a mechanism is that the need for the process to be always considered as under evaluation is recognized and thus the performance is never allowed to deteriorate.

The aim of our approach is to move the emphasis of the development from being an artistic expression to one of engineering. However, research (Couger et al. 1978), (Couger, 1988) shows that the single most important motivator for data processing professionals is the *job itself*. Thus a shift or perceived removal of the creative aspect from the software developers work function could lead to decrease of performance. Our argument is that such action will benefit the quality of the product as well as the maintenance of it. Furthermore, the cost of the product will decrease since the waste of resources will decrease. A second argument is that we shift the creativity of data processing professionals from the software product to the software development process. With the improvement mechanism in place and the formal and informal activities the interest will focus on ideas for improving the process and the final product as well.

REFERENCES

Boehm, B. (1980) Software Engineering Economics, Prentice Hall, Englewood Cliffs, NJ.

Conte, S.D., Dunsmore, H.E., and Shen, V.Y. (1986) Software Engineering Metrics and Models, The Benjamin/Cummings Publ. Co., Inc., Menlo Park Ca.

Couger, J.D. (1988) "Motivating IS Personnel", Datamation, September 15 1988, p.59-64

Couger, J.D. and Zawacki, R.A. (1978) "What Motivates DP Professionals", Datamation, September 1978, p. 116-123

DOD-STD-2167A (1988) Military Standard Defense System Software Development, Department of Defense, SPAWAR 3212, Washington, D.C. 20363-5100

Dobbins, J.H. and Buck, R.D. (1987) The Cost of Software Quality, in Handbook of Software Quality Assurance, ed. Schulmeyer, G.G., and McManus, J.I., Van Nostrand Reinhold Co. Inc., NY.

Grady, R.B., and Caswell, D.L. (1987) Software Metrics: Establishing A Company-Wide

Program, Prentice-Hall, Inc., Englewood Cliffs NJ

Hall, A. (1990) "Seven Myths of Formal Methods", IEEE Software, September 1990, pp.11-19

Hoare, C.A.R. (1981), The Emperor's Old Clothes, CACM Vol. 24, No. 2, pp 75-81.

Imai, M. (1987) Kaizen, The Free Press

Ince, D. (1989), "Set Piece", Datalink, VNU Business Publications BV., January 23, 1989

McManus,J.I. (1987) The Heart of SQA Management: Negotiation, Compliance, Regression, in Handbook of Software Quality Assurance, ed. Schulmeyer, G.G., and McManus, J.I., Van Nostrand Reinhold Co. Inc., NY.

Roy, R.K. (1990) A primer on the Taguchi methods, Van Nostrand Reinhold Co. Inc., NY.

Royce, W.W. (1970), "Managing the development of large software systems", Proc. WESTCON, Ca. USA.

Schulmeyer, G.G. (1990) Zero Defect Software, McGraw-Hill, Inc. New York, NY USA

Sommerville, I. (1992) Software Engineering, 4rd edition Addison-Wesley Publ. Co., Wokingham, England

Tsoumpas, P. (1992) Towards a Methodology for Quality Software Development dissertation (in preparation)

Tausworthe, R.C. (1981), Deep space network cost estimation model. Publication 81-7, Jet Propulsion Laboratory, Pasadena, Ca.

Zuse, H. (1992) Software Complexity: Measures and Methods, de Gruyter.

Productivity & Quality Management Frontiers-IV, edited by Sumanth, Edosomwan, Poupart, and Sink. ©1993 Institute of Industrial Engineers.

Company-Wide Deployment of Project Management Methodologies

G.T. Troskey

IBM Corporation

Boca Raton, Florida USA

ABSTRACT

Companies can improve quality, productivity and competitiveness by deploying advanced project management methodologies. Benefits include better schedule integrity, reduced schedule and cost overruns, improved resource effectiveness and shorter cycle times. Products and services can be introduced earlier in the window of opportunity. This means that there is less risk of losing current revenue and less risk of inroads by competitors.

In today's dynamic business environment, companies survive by aggressively pursuing business transformation. This should include a focus on integrating project management philosophy into business practices. This paper begins by explaining why a company would want to invest in better project management and what the relationship is to total quality and productivity management. It asserts that rigorous project management can raise a product development process from an initial, immature stage that is unstable and unrepeatable to an optimized maturity level characterized by continuous improvement and innovation.

After discussing the advantages of project management, the paper discusses important deployment initiatives and critical success factors. It focuses on the importance of a shared organizational vision in changing company culture and in overcoming resistance to process reengineering. The company needs to document a project management process that covers the creation and execution of project plans, change management, quality management, risk management, plan recovery and status reporting. It must also emphasize team work and empowerment so that synergistic, creative project management teams succeed in delighting customers with fast delivery of innovative products and services. The company also needs to provide practical education in the technical and human aspects of project management and the use of project management tools and software designed to support group work and decision making. The creation of a project management career path and the role of certification are also highlighted.

The paper analyzes the challenges to traditional hierarchical and matrix management organizations that can be addressed by a project-like organization. Companies are moving toward global project management strategies to handle alliances, joint ventures and the increasingly complex international relationships with vendors and customers. Team work and employee empowerment make organizations more responsive, flexible and creative. Project management is one of the few management disciplines that is well equiped to master the challenges of tomorrow.

Keywords: Project Management, Self-Directed Teams, Reengineering Processes, Transformational Leadership, Resistance to Change, Assessment, Career Path, Certification

INTRODUCTION

Product development companies can improve productivity by deploying advanced project management methodologies. Among the benefits are better schedule integrity and resource effectiveness, and anticipative rather than reactive program management. This shortens product development cycle times and reduces or eliminates schedule and cost overruns. This paper describes a game plan for instituting wider usage of project management techniques and tools in a company.

Most companies can benefit from strengthening the project management infrastructure already in place. Individuals in a company may use different kinds of computer-based scheduling programs already, but usage may be spotty and uncoordinated. Although organization and coordination could grow through the grass-roots collaboration of project managers, centralized direction at the headquarters level is usually needed. The reason for this is that one of the common inhibitors to company-wide exploitation of project management is lack of senior management awareness that improvements to the infrastructure are needed.

Once a centralized project management deployment office is operating at the headquarters level, it can begin implementing project management methodologies. Part of this effort is educating and overcoming resistance among senior management and employees in the company and its divisions. Executives should be encouraged to require the use of project management charts in project reviews and to review progress in deploying project management. Common tools should be recommended for scheduling and dependency management so that data can be easily internetworked or shared by organizations working on a project. The same data can be presented graphically for convenient review by interested managers at their own computer terminals.

The headquarters office can write a project management process to be used at the corporate level with guidelines for implementation by lower levels of management. Each division or location can have its own center of competence to customize the company's project management processes for local needs. The company may wish to write a project management job description outlining the skills and experience required for new project managers. The job requirements may include certification for project managers by an outside association or internally by the company's own certification board.

At the project manager level, better communication between peers is very helpful in promoting better project management. Company-wide symposia can assist in communicating ideas, tools and techniques. Larger companies may be able to disseminate the proceedings book or even broadcast the symposium live by internal television to reach a wider audience in the company. Communication can also occur on computer-based conferencing disks dedicated to use by project managers between formal meetings. In this way, committees working on specific goals can work together even if the members are at different locations. Local project management councils can improve communication at a location. Professional concerns that are identified in the local councils can then be brought to the company-wide symposia as needed to be addressed on a wider basis for a globally-optimized solution.

Companies that identify project management as a desirable productivity enhancement need a well-organized, coordinated plan to achieve good deployment. This paper addresses the components of an effective deployment plan. It explains how the project management discipline integrates other management processes to achieve the defined objectives in developing a product. It addresses the critical success factors of management participation, an introduction plan, a hierarchical process structure and support skills, in addition to the facilitators of a common tool strategy and education.

WHY FOCUS ON PROJECT MANAGEMENT?

What motivates a company to invest in better project management? Consider the following questions:

Why Focus on Project Management?

1. *Question*: What percentage of the company's projects are completed on time?
   Answer: Many firms answer "less than 50%".

2. *Question*: What percentage of the company's projects systematically implement project management practices?
   Answer: Many firms answer "less than 15%".

3. *Question*: What is the maturity level of the product development process?
   Answer: Many firms answer "immature, unstable, unrepeatable, with costs and schedules out of control".

Figure 1. **Why Focus on Project Management?**. Few companies can give satisfying answers to these questions. When a company begins to measure and track its missed commitments and late deliveries, the usual outcome is more attention to the project management discipline.

These answers are typical, not just of bad companies, but of many well-managed companies. Most companies can benefit from a realistic assessment of the company's project management capabilities.

Examples of poor project management abound, from cost and schedule overruns on public works projects and military weapons procurement projects, to examples from industry literature. In the United States, Lauffer (1990) found that the mean schedule variance between actual and planned construction time was 2.5 weeks and average man-hour variance was 8.4% for projects averaging 18 months in duration and $20 million in average cost. The National Economic Development Office in England (NEDO, 1983) found that 50% of projects overrun their schedules by one month or more (Figure 1, Question 1). Keeping a project on schedule and on budget is not easy.

Even in a high technology field, companies frequently have immature product development processes lacking disciplined project management. The Software Engineering Institute (SEI) at Carnegie Mellon University defined five levels of maturity for the software product development process:

Product Development Process Maturity Levels

Initial	Few stable processes. Performance cannot be predicted by organizational capability.
Repeatable	Process is stable for planning and tracking projects because of **disciplined use of project management techniques**.
Defined	Cost, schedule, performance and quality are under control and being tracked.
Managed	The process is operating within measurable limits. Quality can be predicted.
Optimizing	Focus is on continuous improvement which occurs incrementally and by innovation.

Figure 2. **Product Development Process Maturity Levels**. These five levels can be used to assess the maturity of a product development process. The most immature level does not use project management, but the more mature levels depend on it extensively (SEI, 1990).

In 150 project assessments, SEI (1990) found that 85% were at the Initial Level, where rigorous project management techniques were not understood or practiced (See Figure 2, Initial Level).

Only 14% were at the Repeatable Level and 1% at the more advanced levels, where project management was used extensively (See Figure 1, Questions 2 and 3). This study indicates that although project management may seem to be a simple and fundamental part of management science, there is still considerable need for improvement in practice.

It is hard to imagine a company that has embraced a Total Quality and Productivity Management (TQPM) discipline (QPMA, 1991) that is not focusing on project management. To reach higher levels of quality and productivity, a firm first documents its processes. A process is a series of definable, repeatable tasks. Project management is the planning, tracking and control of a series of tasks. Therefore, project management practices are needed to provide stability and control for most processes (SEI 1990). In the later TQPM phases, benchmarking leads to action plans to change processes. Balm (1992) says, "If the changes are broad, multifunctional or even multisite, they should be managed by project management techniques. Keep the project on schedule and on cost. Detect problems early (anticipate them if possible) and resolve them quickly (pg. 122)." Consider how project management is involved in the typical TQPM implementation steps:

The Relationship Between Project Management and TQPM Implementation Phases

Assess To find out what needs to be done, a firm conducts surveys and does benchmarking to compare itself to the competition. It finds that it needs to implement TQPM and that world-class companies are producing products in much shorter development cycles.

Organize To get ready to begin TQPM, the company's executive steering group chooses a quality strategy. Project management tools and techniques must be deployed to reduce product development cycle times.

Plan Project management is at the heart of this planning and scheduling step. It should be used in planning TQPM deployment and in product development.

Educate The company explains to everyone the importance of pleasing the customer with timely delivery of new products and improving productivity by reducing cycle times.

Involve To get employees to buy in to TQPM, it is desirable to have them work on cross functional teams. This is an important element in successful project management.

Improve This is the implementation step, where project management and other quality management processes are put into action. Project management teams focus on the customer and continuous improvement.

Review Once project management methodologies are deployed, check cycle and delivery times against the plan and do benchmarking to identify best practices to improve the process.

Figure 3. **The Relationship Between Project Management and TQPM Implementation Phases.** Project management is important in all seven phases of the implementation of Total Quality and Productivity Management.

Figure 3 shows that companies that are focusing on the quality and productivity of their business processes and product development processes also need to focus on cycle time and schedule commitment integrity, which is the science and art of project management. The use of project management also assists with other TQPM initiatives, such as defect elimination, employee participation and measurements. Defects are less likely to be injected by poor time/resource management. Since employees working on a project jointly develop the project plan, they feel a sense of ownership. The employees execute the plan better because of the knowledge shared during team meetings in the plan development and implementation phases of the project. Finally, measurements are easier because data is captured by project management tools as the project is tracked.

1021

Companies also need to focus on new ways of organizing. The familiar, hierarchical structures are not bearing up; they were designed for more placid settings than today's dynamic business and economic circumstances (Peters, 1988). A new management style is emerging at the leading TQPM organizations. The traditional Plan-Organize-Direct-Control style is changing to a Lead-Empower-Assess-Partner (LEAP) style (QPMA, 1991). Project management meshes perfectly with today's TQPM processes and the LEAP style. It is intrinsically involved with leadership by empowered partners working together in cross-functional teams to improve cycle/delivery times, quality, productivity and customer satisfaction. For these reasons, most companies today need to establish initiatives for deploying world-class project management methodologies.

DEPLOYING PROJECT MANAGEMENT METHODOLOGIES

Deploying project management methodologies usually requires direction at the headquarters level because reengineering processes can lead to resistance from middle management and operational personnel. Research has shown that 85% of Americans are reactive (Rogers 1989); pro-active leaders are needed to change the status quo. To successfully overhaul a process, there is a need for paradigm pioneers to lead the paradigm settlers into the new territory (Barker 1984). The company should select transformational leaders, capable of transforming organizations by creating a vision and generating commitment, to initiate the process changes (Ulrich 1989).

Implementation of advanced project management practices can be expected to be slow until employees are educated and *sold* on their benefits. Employee buy-in is a critical success factor; this can be accomplished more effectively when Barker's explanation of the psychological elements of paradigm shifting is taken into account. When senior management understands the project management discipline and "walks the talk" by asking to see project management charts in project reviews, this encourages employees to value the discipline and schedule charts also. Line management involvement in setting style, culture and expectation levels is another critical success factor. Management must follow up with regular deployment progress reviews.

Showing employees the gap between current reality in project management and a desirable vision for future project management can engender enthusiasm for the proposed new practices.

Table 1. Establish a Project Management Vision. Getting employees to share a clear project management vision enhances the chances for successful project management deployment.	
CURRENT REALITY	FUTURE VISION
Short-term focus, problem driven	Optimum management, long-term focus
Unstructured approach	Structured, disciplined approach
Reactive problem management	Risk management, anticipative, proactive
Plan churn	Approved plan changes
Various individual goals	Aligned goals, teamwork
No feedback	Continuous status and control

A shared organizational vision is vital because it motivates workers to develop and implement action plans to change from the current state to the desired state.

Document a Project Management Process

To bring the company closer to its future vision, several project management initiatives should be deployed (See Figure 4). The headquarters office should first write a project management process that describes the plan creation stage and the plan tracking and control stage. Each division or location can have its own center of competence to customize the company's project management processes for local needs. The center can also assist with education and improvement of processes and tools.

The process document describes the suppliers, customers, inputs and outputs of the process. It describes the steps in compiling the resources, tasks, schedules, issues, dependencies and work breakdown for the creation of a plan. It also explains the steps for tracking and directing the execution phase of the plan, including methods for risk management and plan recovery. This document also explains the equally important roles of the lead project manager and the project management team members. Modern project management recognizes the synergy and fast, decisive work of an enthusiastic team led by a competent project manager (Kezsbom, 1991).

Define a Project Management Career Path

The company may wish to write a project management job description describing the skills and knowledge required for project managers. This could include standard, pre-approved job descriptions for each of the job position classifications and a project profile complexity matrix to aid in determining the correct salary grade for a particular project. A clear, attractive project management career path is beneficial because it builds the status and the morale of project managers.

The Upjohn Company established a line organization for career project managers in 1985. Because the successful execution of the project management process depends to a large extent on the expertise of the project manager, Upjohn has constructed an appraisal instrument to measure leadership, expertise, and human skills to complement the job description (Ploughman 1990).

Project Management Deployment Initiatives

- Document a Project Management Process
- Define a Project Management Career Path
- Develop a Multiphased Introduction Plan
- Provide a Practical, Relevant Educational Program
- Establish a Consistent Tools Base

Figure 4. Project Management Deployment Initiatives. These initiatives are needed to deploy project management methodologies effectively in a company. Added to this list is another critical success factor: management support and participation.

IBM established its career path for expert professional project managers in 1991. This position is for project managers who sell their consulting services expertise to outside companies. IBM uses its own internal certification board for certifying the competence of these professionals.

Frame (1990) says that AT&T assessed its project management capabilities in 1988:

AT&T had almost no formal organizational structure, professional standards, or support system for project management. Project managers were hampered by:

- Unclear and inconsistent levels of authority over project resources.
- Lack of established performance standards and tools.
- Lack of familiarity with sophisticated principles and practices.
- Lack of a defined career path and formal standards for progression.
- Lack of comprehensive educational and career training programs.
- A growing perception that the status and financial rewards of project management were not commensurate with the overwhelming responsibility, difficulty, and risk associated with the position.

Because project management at AT&T exposes managers to the broadest variety of responsibilities in virtually all aspects of corporate business, employees should consider it a superior development assignment.

As a result of its findings, AT&T made many changes, including the establishment of a project management career path. It considered its own internal certification program, but chose certification by the Project Management Institute as a Project Management Professional for "two reasons: (1) PMI is the recognized leader among nonprofit organizations for promoting project management; and (2) outside accreditation would ensure customers' recognition of AT&T value-added project management expertise (Frame 1990)."

Provide a Practical, Relevant Educational Program

Because the effectiveness of a company's project management methodologies lies with its practitioners, it makes sense to train them adequately. Courses should be made available to train the lead project manager and to train the project management team (Rogers, 1990). Some colleges and universities now offer courses and even masters degree programs in project management and also in the related fields of engineering management and the management of technology.

There is a need for additional emphasis on educating line managers. Strong project management practices revolve around the project management process and teamwork. This requires a new line management style and a shift in company culture. The traditional approach used management commitment to a tops down schedule, as contrasted to the preferred approach: team development and ownership of the schedule using shared problem solving. In the old management style, projects were tracked between major checkpoints only. Management reacted to missed dates that had already occurred and managed on a crisis to crisis basis. Line managers were unable to react quickly to change in complex, dynamic projects spanning many organizations and locations.

In the new project management paradigm, the project management team understands the critical path, predicts schedule problems, assesses alternatives and implements recovery plans before the missed dates begin to cascade. Line managers are asked to trust the project management team which is empowered to take quick action on its own to solve problems and satisfy customers. This new way of thinking is one of the reasons that deployment of project management methodologies may meet resistance from line management. Education is needed to overcome the resistance to change.

At the project manager level, better communication between peers is very helpful in promoting better project management. This grass-roots education is achieved by one-on-one personal interaction at the initiative of the individual, rather than the centralized education department. Company-wide symposia are one way to facilitate an exchange of ideas and techniques. A wider exchange is possible when the proceedings book is made available company-wide. A recent development is the live broadcast of the symposium to project managers at remote sites who can ask questions of the speakers by telephone.

Project managers can also communicate with each other and answer each others' questions through computer-based conferences. These conferencing disks can have forums on various topics, such as different tools, processes and measurements, and organizational and professional concerns. Local project management councils can improve communication between project managers and team members at a location. A final means of informal education can occur through the national conferences and the local chapters of the Project Management Institute.

Establish a Consistent Tools Base

A company's deployment strategy should include initiatives that integrate the project management process with methodology and tools. The process's recommended methodology should be network based project management using critical path analysis. A consistent tool base across all projects involved in a product development program is very advantageous. An example of such a tool is the IBM Application System Project Management program product. It allows data to be easily internetworked or shared by organizations working on a project. Because it is a mainframe-based tool, it can update a high-level, master schedule by receiving the detailed schedules from organizations around the world that automatically report the latest data. It is more difficult to share data using project management tools that run on personal computers.

With additional effort, it is possible to present the product definition and objectives and the project schedule and status information graphically for convenient review by managers and employees at their own computer terminals. Without a consistent set of tools, this would not be possible.

Another desirable tool is a dependency manager application tool. The tool should run on a mainframe or on personal computers that are linked by a network. The tool is used by one person to open a dependency against a second person. The dependency is sent to the second person who answers or rejects the requirement being placed on him. This response is returned to the first person who can accept the response or close the dependency. This tools makes it easy to keep track of all of the dependencies and deliverables in a project. It is not a burden for the lead project manager because the promised delivery dates are negotiated by the supplier and customer directly.

It is also important to note the emergence of new software designed especially to support group work. In some cases, a special "knowledge mining center" room with interlinked personal computers is used by the team for brainstorming solutions to problems. Various programs are now available to aid communications, decision making and consensus reaching.

Finally, expert systems can be expected in the near future to assist project management teams. All of these existing and new tools require training. The investment in advancing the skills of the employees are payed back by greater productivity, innovation and competitiveness for the firm.

SUMMARY

Project management can make the difference between the success or failure of a project to proceed from conception to the achievement of its goals. Most companies can benefit from a greater penetration of project management methodologies in their processes and organizations.

Companies that identify project management as a desirable productivity enhancement need a well-organized, coordinated plan to achieve good deployment. This paper addresses the components of an effective deployment plan, with attention to overcoming resistance to change. It also explains the key operational and strategic role of the project management process in relation to a total quality and productivity management process.

In the 1990's, the corporate environment will change radically. Because circumstances in the future will change even faster than they do now, no two situations will be exactly alike or call for the same set of experts or procedures. Teams of people will form and responsibilities will be turned over to project managers. The goal in using project management concepts is to give organizations more speed and flexibility, and to unleash the creative power inherent in a team.

Traditional hierarchical management and matrix management will both be challenged by new technologies, and changing political, social and economic conditions. The corporate environment is becoming increasingly projectized. Many companies are adopting a global project management team strategy. There is increasing globalization of business and a move from the traditional bureaucratic corporate structures to more flexible project-like organizations. Project management is one of the few management disciplines that is well equiped to master the challenges of tomorrow.

BIBLIOGRAPHY

Balm, J. (1992) Benchmarking: A Practitioner's Guide for Becoming and Staying Best of the Best, Schaumburg, IL, Quality and Productivity Management Association.

Barker, J.A. (1984) Discovering the Future: The Business of Paradigms, St. Paul, MN, ILI Press.

Frame J.D. (1990) "Issues and Future Directions of Project Management Certification", Proceedings of the 1990 PMI Annual Seminar/Symposium, The Project Management Institute, Drexel Hill, Pennsylvania, pp. 557-560.

Kezsbom, D.S. (1991) "Strengthening Project Team Productivity Through the Integrated Planning Process", Productivity and Quality Management Frontiers - III, Norcross, Georgia, Industrial Engineering and Management Press, pp. 217-222.

Laufer, A. (1990) "Factors Affecting Construction Planning Outcomes", Journal of Construction Engineering and Management, vol. 116, no. 1, pp. 87-99.

NEDO (1983) "Faster Building for Industry", NEDO Building EDC, National Economic Development Office, England.

Peters, T. (1988) "Restoring American Competitiveness: Looking for New Models of Organizations", The Academy of Management EXECUTIVE, vol. II, no. 2, pp. 103-109.

Ploughman, T.L. and Assenzo, J.R. (1990) "Appraisal of Project Manager Performance in a Pharmaceutical R&D Organization", Proceedings of the 1990 PMI Annual Seminar/Symposium, The Project Management Institute, Drexel Hill, Pennsylvania, pp. 287-290.

QPMA (1991) "TQM 101: The Basics of Total Quality Management", Commitment-Plus, vol. 7, no. 1, Schaumburg, Illinois, Quality & Productivity Management Association, pp. 1-4.

Rogers, D.J. (1989) "Fight To Win -- Why Business Leaders Study War", Success, pp. 52-53.

Rogers, L.A. (1990) "Project Team Training: A Proven Key to Organizational Teamwork and a Breakthrough in Planning Performance", Project Management Journal, vol. XXI, no. 2, pp. 9-18.

SEI (1991) "Key Practices of the Capability Maturity Model", Software Engineering Institute (SEI), Carnegie Mellon University, Pittsburgh, Pennsylvania 15213, CMU/SEI-91-TR-25.

Troskey, G.T. and Gibson, G.F. (1991) "Quality Management Processes in the IBM Entry Systems Division", Productivity and Quality Management Frontiers - III, Norcross, Georgia, Industrial Engineering and Management Press, pp. 550-555.

Ulrich, D. (1989) "Gaining Strategic and Organizational Capability in a Turbulent Business Environment", The Academy of Management EXECUTIVE, vol. III, no. 2, pp.115-122.

Ward, D.; Hart, N.; Phelps, E. and Bush, L. (1990) "Innovation in Education: ATC Masters Certificate Programs in Project Management", Proceedings of the 1990 PMI Annual Seminar/Symposium, The Project Management Institute, Drexel Hill, Pennsylvania, pp. 601-608.

PROFESSIONAL PROFILE

Gene Troskey is a project manager for the development of new personal systems in the IBM Entry Systems Division. He earned a BA degree in physics from the University of California and an MSEE from UCLA. He is a registered Professional Engineer and the author of many articles. He has presented papers at the Second International Conference on the Management of Technology and the Third International Conference on Productivity and Quality Research.

Productivity & Quality Management Frontiers-IV, edited by Sumanth, Edosomwan, Poupart, and Sink. ©1993 Institute of Industrial Engineers.

A Conceptual Framework for Overcoming Resistance to the Measurement of Productivity and Quality

W.B. Werther, Jr. and E. Berman
University of Miami
Coral Gables, Florida USA

ABSTRACT

The continuous improvement of productivity and quality assumes the use of measures. However, measures often encounter resistance for a variety of psychological and technical reasons. While much of the performance measurement literature focuses on the nature of these measures, the proposed paper addresses the measurement setting process and necessary maintenance activities needed to ensure the effectiveness of productivity and quality measurements.

The paper proposes a minimum, interconnected framework that consists of four parts: measurement, maintenance, acceptance, and participation (M-MAP). This four-part model places measurement in a behavioral context that makes the inauguration and continued use of productivity and quality measurement more readily acceptable to those who are being measured. The model assumes that those responsible for productivity and quality have limited awareness of the need for measurement and may even be hostile to its introduction, believing that measurement is impossible or inappropriate for their situation, as is sometimes the case with white collar, professional, or knowledge workers.

To increase acceptance and overcome resistance, the process incorporates the participation of those who are to be measured. Participation is used to identify areas in need of measurement and the actual measurements to be used, often relying on group approaches. Maintenance of the system depends on specific, periodic feedback about productivity and quality.

The M-MAP framework is interconnected because the timely performance feedback maintains employee acceptance and awareness of the measures and their importance. And, since the measures monitor elements of actual performance, employees participate through their day-to-day efforts in the shaping the feedback they receive. Thus, the participation in their jobs and the timely use of feedback serve to maintain acceptance.

Growing global competition places a premium on the need for a sustainable competitive advantage among for-profit firms (Werther, 1991a). Although that advantage can be achieved in a variety of ways (Porter, 1989), ultimately firms find themselves competing in mature markets, characterized by an excess of potential supply compared with actual demand. These mature markets are further characterized by competition on a price and non-price differences. When price competition ensues, industry leaders survive this competition through some combination of superior productivity and/or superior quality. Superior productivity affords the advantage of being able to meet price competition and margin compressions with a low cost structure. Superior quality--if recognized and desired by customers--allows the firm to charge premium prices and thus minimize its margin compression (Miller, 1984). Combinations of superior quality and productivity suggest a powerful strategic advantage for those firms able to achieve this desirable combination (Judson, 1984).

The pathway to superior productivity and quality depends on continuous improvement of both. Continuous improvement is needed regardless of whether a competitor is an industry leader or follower. Leaders need on-going improvement to maintain their advantage (and margins) because competitors with lower levels of productivity and quality are likely to face even more severe margin compression, causing them to focus their attentions on productivity and quality variables as a means of survival (Miller, 1984). Beyond these straightforward economic arguments are behavioral ones (Werther, 1991b).

Behaviorally, continuous improvements create an expectation of change in the processes and procedures of the company. When productivity and quality improvements are periodic in nature, as when a short-lived productivity or quality program is initiated in the firm, periodic programs challenge employee expectations about "how things are done" in the organization because these programs represent a new source of change in the work environment. Change from well established procedures and thinking is generally resisted, further delaying the needed productivity or quality improvements.

MEASUREMENTS AS A TOOL

Productivity and quality measures are not ends. They are but a part of a successful effort to continuously improve productivity and quality. As this paper will argue in more detail, however, measures are a pivotal component, without which productivity and quality improvements are unlikely to occur and if they occur they are unlikely to continue.

Applying a systems view of the organization, labor, capital, materials, energy, and ideas are inputs. The organization itself serves as a transformational entity that turns these resource inputs into valued goods or services, called outputs. Although financial measures serve as a feedback element to the productive system, they often lack both precision and timeliness. This is not to argue against financial measures; they are needed, even required by tax laws (Shetty, 1986). However, these economic sources of feedback, important as they are, provide, at best, only limited feedback of use to managers. Economic declines or advances in the firm's fortunes may be attributable to economic cycles, inflation, competitors, productivity, quality, or a host of other business or economic-related variables. However, productivity and quality measures offer a tighter focus, enabling management to identify and, presumably correct, deviations with greater precision and confidence. Nevertheless, productivity and quality measures are just tools. As such, they must be created, used, and evaluated within the organizational context in which they are applied.

THE M-MAP FRAMEWORK

The measurement map, or "M-MAP" framework proposed here identifies the key variables to successfully designing, implementing, and maintaining a productivity or quality measurement system. This measurement framework stresses the need for measurements to include consideration of the maintenance, acceptance, and participation (M-MAP) among those impacted by the metrics. These variables form an interconnected framework. This four-part model places measurement in a behavioral context that makes the inauguration and continued use of productivity and quality measurement more readily acceptable to those who are being measured. The model assumes that those responsible for productivity and quality have limited awareness of the need for measurement and may even be hostile to its introduction, believing that measurement is impossible or inappropriate for their situation, as is sometimes the case with white collar, professional, or knowledge workers.

In practice, the measurement-MAP focuses on maintenance to maintain acceptance through participation. The first-time initiation of the M-MAP framework, however, begins with acceptance and participation to ensure the successful introduction of measures, which are then followed with maintenance efforts. The remainder of this paper, therefore, follows the acceptance-participation-maintenance sequence encountered when first applying the M-MAP framework.

Acceptance
It is axiomatic that thinking people cannot accept what they do not understand. And, the first step toward understanding is an awareness of the need for continuous productivity and quality improvement. Awareness of the need for continuous productivity and quality improvement is well understood by senior managers in mature industries who search for ways to differentiate their outputs from competitors. As they face increased competition, often on a global scale, margin compression demands greater efficiency and the need to stay up with competition (or even better, to differentiate the firm's outputs) demands greater quality.

Either or both approaches often lead senior managers to find better ways to track these important variables. In the name of efficiency, some companies develop metrics by creating a task force to study the measurement issue and make recommendations. In turn, these recommendations are approved by senior management and the implementation process begins. Among senior managers and those who designed the metrics, their need is obvious. With little consultation or education, the measures are implemented, often complete with resource- and time-consuming demands on lower levels of management and the workers. These measures are then combined with organizational pressures for improvements in quality and productivity. Lower level managers and workers often see the time and resources devoted to the measurement process as an impediment to achieving the very improvements the measures track. Under these circumstances, workers and lower level managers either see the metrics as unimportant, leading to incomplete or inaccurate reporting, or they see the measures as important, causing them to focus their attention on the improvement of the metrics, sometimes with consequences for other areas (such as maintenance, safety, or tradeoffs between productivity and quality) unintended by senior managers. Although senior management may subscribe to the axiom that "people do what is inspected, not expected," the new focus on productivity and quality metrics may overlook expected, but unmeasured, areas of performance leading to no net improvement in the organization's performance (Werther, 1991b).

To overcome the limited awareness about the importance of productivity and quality metrics, some organizations institute massive education or training efforts, as happened at Bell Canada or Hewlett Packard and TRW in the United States (Ruch and Werther,1989). Although these efforts may raise the awareness of the role played by productivity and quality in organization success, awareness efforts by themselves do little to build acceptance, let alone commitment and ownership to productivity and quality improvement.

Participation

Although awareness efforts do serve the purpose of alerting organizational members to the need for productivity and quality improvement, it may still be seen as "not my job" by many. Responsibility for improvements may be mentally assigned to specialized quality control departments, management, or others in the organization. Even when improvement is accepted by employees and lower-level managers, middle-level managers may resist simply because their remoteness from the actual performance may make them feel that they have little control over the actual performance outcomes but will be measured (and evaluated) by the new metrics. In short, what is needed is "ownership" of both the measures and the underlying performance the measures track. Simply stated, people do not resist their own ideas (Werther, 1988).

Participation has two dimension: The creation process and the on-going maintenance of the measurement system. Participation should extend not only to workers and their immediate supervisors, but should embrace middle-level managers as well. Using participative approaches these middle-level managers can work with first-level supervisors to develop aggregate measures that "roll up" the measures at lower levels. Although such metrics may be little more that weighted averages of supervisor/worker measures, the process of their creation sends a powerful messages to first- and middle-level mangers. Without regard to which level of measurement is being addressed (supervisor/worker or middle manager/supervisor) the process of participating in the creation of measures underscores their importance. And, at least among those who are actively involved in the discussion of what and how to measure the various elements of their work, and understanding of the measures and their intent is fostered. When dealing with employees who have jobs that are particularly difficult to measure--such as research scientists, lawyers, and other staff professionals or white collar workers--achieving "buy-in" to the measures is essential.

Maintenance

Many companies with successful productivity measures, such as American Express, give employees weekly, even daily, feedback on their quality and productivity efforts. By posting productivity and quality metrics as they become available several powerful messages are communicated. First, management is saying that the "program" is still alive. Second, it suggests that management remains interested in the results tracked by the measures. Third, the implication exists that this information would not be provided if those receiving it were helpless to do something to change the results. Fourth, the feedback can be a springboard for managers to question how further improvements can be attained. Fifth, the measures increases awareness of the importance of productivity and quality among those involved in collecting, posting, and reviewing the data. Simply put, the feedback about the measured results provides a form of on-going "psychological" maintenance to those involved measurement process by renewing their awareness of the productivity and quality issues that underlie the metrics.

Maintenance of the measurement system is also furthered by allowing employees to participate in discussions of productivity and quality improvements. Whether through employee participation groups, multi-functional project teams, quality circles or other approaches, employees who can impact the work environment through their ideas and then receive feedback in the form of productivity or quality measurements gain an increased sense of autonomy and control over their work environment along with greater ownership of the measures and their underlying performance. Similarly, such employees are likely to be more receptive to training in work methods that improve productivity and quality. Then performance evaluations based upon these measures are less likely to be seen as arbitrary since employees have received on-going feedback about their performance combined with opportunities to improve their abilities and results.

INCENTIVES: GOING BEYOND THE M-MAP MINIMUMS

Although maintenance, acceptance, and participation form the minimum conditions for a successful measurement system, the systems' responsiveness can be enhanced through the use of incentives. Though incentives are not a minimum necessary condition for a successful measurement system, by connecting rewards to measurement goals, the organization can achieve productivity and quality goals more quickly, because incentives can induce greater effort among employees to attain the productivity or quality goals. This assertion assumes, of course, that the organization leaders can identify rewards that are widely seen as incentives to employees--incentives that can overcome past practices, peer pressure, and other human-imposed constraints on performance.

The central issue with installing an incentive system is whether are rewards to be based on individual or group performance. Rewards set on an individual basis do not encourage group performance and may even lead to intra-group competition. In jobs where teamwork and cooperation are relatively unimportant, perhaps in the job of salespeople with well-defined territories, for example, individual incentives are preferable. However, in organizational settings where teamwork is necessary to high performance and quality, incentives are typically established on a group basis. Here, the group receives the reward if an overall target is reached, such as a measurable gain in productivity or quality. The "all-or-none" effect of group rewards puts a premium on intra-group cooperation and, if the reward is seen as meaningful, peer pressure will be focused on those who are not contributing to the goal. Whether individual or group rewards are used, the reward is an incentive to better performance. When interdependence among workers is crucial to success, group rewards not only act as an incentive but may enlist the use of peer pressure to further ensure that the goal is attained.

INTERACTION EFFECTS OF M-MAP

Measurements are part of the organization's overall system of management; they do not operate in isolation. Measures must be clear and address those productivity and quality elements that are within the control of those being measured. For example, overall indexes that incorporate items such as customer satisfaction with design or delivery should not be applied to production workers who are not allowed input on these elements. Besides perceived relevance to those affected, measures should be timely and make visible both objective and subjective factors over which employees have control. These straightforward prescriptions must also consider the emotional needs of employees and the informational needs of the organization.

The human side of the organization and the fears that measures sometimes create are effected by how the measures are used by management. Emphasis on recognition, incentives, and other rewards for good performance should be stressed in favor of punitive sanctions for those who perform poorly. Though sanctions may be needed, many organizations fall into the trap of expecting improved performance so that when it occurs, it goes unrecognized. But when poor performance occurs, it is acted upon. The result often creates an organizational mentality that stresses "not being last" rather than finding ways to improve. In time, measures are seen as a source of pressure and criticism that fosters non-productive behaviors, such as blame placing and excuse creation, instead of creative productivity and quality improvement ideas.

To be effective, measures also must appropriately fit the organization's information systems. The development and tracking of measures creates additional work in the organization. Measures that draw on existing information minimize the time, effort, resources, and resentment that measures can create. The result can be more elegant measures, which are defined as providing maximum insight with minimum data requirements, and measures that are managerial appropriate. That is, they must provide management with information that can be used to better guide the organization to higher levels of productivity and quality. However, for measures to be effective managerial tools, their design and implementation must strike a balance between the measures and the organizational systems used to introduce and maintain them.

CONCLUSIONS

The objective of measures is to track improvements in the performance being tracked. The measures are surrogates for the performance. If the measurement creating process and the subsequent use of measures does not foster improvements in actual performance, they are a waste of organizational resources. The M-MAP approach seeks to create not just measures but to do so in a way that acceptance and maintenance are reinforced through participation. Participation reinforces acceptance because the process of involvement in the design of measures leads to questions about the purpose, nature, scope, cost, timeliness, and other dimensions of measures. The search for answers to these questions expands the awareness of those involved in the process. And, as this awareness grows to understanding of the importance of productivity and quality issues, acceptance of measures can be based on the employees' self-interest of job security and advancement opportunities, not just faith that management's measures are needed.

The on-going maintenance of the measurement system is furthered through feedback on the results. Since those who designed the measures also produce the results tracked by the measures, the measures become a source of feedback. Workers learn about he connection between their efforts and the results attained. The feedback helps to maintain the measurement process because it allows the employees to see that they are part of an integrated system. It appears that the combination of objective, appropriate, and timely feedback empowers employees to better understand their role and contribution to the systems' levels of productivity and quality. Additionally, this information is usually charted and posted so employees can determine how well they are performing. This simple posting process appears to help shift the burden of improvement from the supervisor to the chart. Instead of the supervisor serving the role of providing feedback (often by being critical of poor performance), the posted feedback sends the message in a more neutral and less personally threatening manner.

The minimum critical conditions for a successful measurement system stated at the beginning of this paper argued that any successful system must address the acceptance of the system by those affected by it. This acceptance begins with an awareness of the underlying importance of the issues being measured. Although awareness is a necessary condition, it is unlikely to be a sufficient one. Needed is an understanding of the need for measurements that leads to an acceptance of the measurement system. At the same time, to overcome entropy the measurement system needs on-going maintenance in a way that reinforces awareness of the performance underlying the measures. Participation in the design of the measures address the initial awareness and acceptance issues; and feedback about performance serves a maintenance function of maintaining that awareness. To withdraw any element of this measurement framework--maintenance, acceptance, or participation--suggests that the minimum conditions for a successful, on-going measurement system would be missing.

The question that this paper sought to address is what are the minimum conditions for a successful productivity and quality measurement system. Proposed was a Measurement-MAP framework that addresses the critical elements of maintenance, acceptance, and participation as keys to a viable measurement system. The development of a productivity or quality measure systems that does not consider these three elements is not likely to succeed and if it does initially succeed it is unlikely to continue as employee and supervisory support wane. This system can be enhanced through the use of individual or group rewards to motivate those responsible for the actual performance.

BIBLIOGRAPHIC REFERENCES

Judson, A. S. (1984) "Productivity Strategy and Business Strategy: Two Sides of the Same Coin,"Interfaces, January-February, pp. 103-115.

Miller, D.M. (1984) "Productivity =Productivity + Price Recovery," Harvard Business Review, vol. 62, no.3, pp. 145-153.

Porter, M. E. (1989), "From Competitive Advantage to Corporate Strategy," Harvard Business Review, vol. 67, no. 3, pp. 63-76.

Ruch, W. A. and Werther,Jr., W.B. (1989) "In-House Productivity and Quality Colleges," Productivity Management Frontiers-II (D. Sumanth et al, Editors) Geneva, Switzerland: Elsevier, 1989, pp. 468-473.

Shetty, Y.K. (1986), "Quality, Productivity, and Profit Performance: Learning from Research and Practice," National Productivity Review Spring, pp. 168-178.

Werther, Jr., W. B. (1988), "Productivity Through People: The Decision Making Process," Management Decisions, Volume 26, No. 5, pp. 37-41.

Werther, Jr., W.B. (1991a) "Strategic Foundations of Productivity Improvement," Canadian Journal of Administrative Sciences Vol. 8 No. 1, pp. 3-8.

Werther, Jr., W.B. (1991b) "Management Resistance to Productivity and Quality Efforts," in D. Sumanth, J. Edosomwan, D. Scott Sink, and W. Werther, (Editors), Productivity and Quality Management Frontiers-III. Norcross, GA.: Industrial Engineering and Management Press of Institute of Industrial Engineers, 1991 (pp. 507-512).

BIOGRAPHICAL SKETCHES

William B. Werther, Jr., Ph.D., is the Samuel N. Friedland Professor of Executive Management at the University of Miami's School of Business Administration. He has published more than eight books and seventy articles in addition to work on a variety of in-house productivity and quality efforts at such companies as AT&T, Bell Canada, NASA, TRW, and others.

Evan M. Berman, Ph.D., is an Assistant Professor at the University of Miami's School of Business Administration. He has worked for the National Science Foundation, the Office of Technological Assessment, and other organizations. His recent research focuses on technology strategy and R&D planning.

Productivity & Quality Management Frontiers-IV, edited by Sumanth, Edosomwan, Poupart, and Sink. ©1993 Institute of Industrial Engineers.

Currents and Undercurrents of Organizational Resistance to Change

M.B. Sokol
AT&T Bell Laboratories
Short Hills, New Jersey USA

C. Harris
Rath and Strong
Lexington, Massachusetts USA

In recent years the leadership of American organizations have been called upon to implement broad workplace innovations such as total quality management. "Resistance" is often treated as one of those necessary evils of the change process, an unfortunate constraint to the brighter future that presumably accompanies the innovation. Whether it is to be cut out like a cancer, or talked through like a neurotic anxiety, resistance is often treated as something that can be removed from the body and spirit of the organization. In this paper we take issue with the assumption that resistance to is be removed from the change process. Rather we propose it be harnessed in a way that provides a window to the history of successful and unsuccessful change efforts of the past. Some of the topics discussed in this presentation include:

- Assumptions and myths about resistance to change in the workplace
- Resistance to change by individuals and by groups: how is this similar, how is this different?
- Variations in the patterns of resistance within the workplace
- Conscious and unconscious forms of resistance
- The effects of organizational fads over time
- How senior levels of management foster resistance
- The positive dimensions of resistance.

Finally we discuss some strategies to access organizational resistance, to give it a legitimate voice in the change process, to calibrate change effectiveness as an awareness of resistance (present and past), and to incorporate resistance to change as a vehicle for organizational learning over time.

Productivity & Quality Management Frontiers-IV, edited by Sumanth, Edosomwan, Poupart, and Sink. ©1993 Institute of Industrial Engineers.

Phases in a Turnaround: Managing Resistance to Change

M.J. Mestre
Trinity Western University
Langley, British Columbia CANADA

ABSTRACT

Resistance to change may have several causes, among which are the momentum of the past, the vested interests of those involved, the tendency to implement processes poorly, and the possible lack of integrity in the system. When engaged in the change process, the effective manager must recognize and carefully handle each of these points of resistance.

Four distinct phases are repeatedly present no matter the causes of the problems or the combinations of the variables.
I. Breaking with the past
  A.   Preparing the employees
  B.   Exposing the folklore--a catharsis
  C.   Building a new vista
  D.   Instituting new organizational values
II.   Nurturing the new process management
  A.   Implementing with top management
  B.   Recognizing early successes
  C.   Involving all subunits
  D.   Training of lower and middle management
  E.   Recognizing the problems and reinforcing the solutions
III.   Making a Quantum leap
  A.   Avoiding the rut of any system
  B.   Encouraging creativity
  C.   Removing walls
IV.   Monitoring the process
  A.   Maintaining accountability at each level
  B.   Noting un- or counter-productive practices
  C.   Assuring self-evaluation
  D.   Guaranteeing recognition
The above are the minimum requirements, for the process has no short cuts. Furthermore, the timing is crucial.

Because the initial stages of the process are most important and because of space constraints, I have concentrated on section I. I have referred briefly to the remaining steps, however, since only a complete system will yield the desired results.

Managers list a variety of variables to support their claim for the uniqueness of their business. These variables include such things as the nature of the industry, the differences in culture, and the variety of the product. In spite of this complexity, however, one can identify recurring principles that supersede any of the differences.

The following are the common realities:

1. Every organization has a folklore that is a composite of past events--both facts and fiction--and that is colored by the role one assumes in the organization.
2. Each party is reluctant to face its situation objectively.
3. No common reference point exists by which to initiate dialogue between individuals, functions, and levels of management.
4. No ongoing management processes exist on an organization-wide basis by which to tackle the above three items.

Resistance to change comes from a variety of sources; one of them is management. In "Demand Better Results and Get Them," Robert H. Schaffer gives several reasons why management resists change. For example, if the newly installed manager asserts that major gains are possible, he may unwittingly threaten both his predecessor and his current supervisor. "[Managers] fail," Schaffer argues, "because imposing heavy demands entails risks and threatens subordinates. So it is safer to ask for less" (91). Schaffer uses the example of a vice president of a manufacturing operation who queries: "'What would happen if we set specific targets and my people didn't meet them? I'd have to do something . . .'" (92). Schaffer also observes that high demands increase the risk that subordinates will resist change and that management will be embarrassed because it fails to reach ambitious goals (93).

These factors combine to create a momentum that may hinder the progress of the organization. Both workers and managers--previous or present--own the situation and may or may not be pleased with the proposed changes. The leader who decides that change is needed must face this obviously major risk. The risk of a poor response may be offset somewhat, however, by careful implementation.

We could divide an organization into two parts: the technical system and the social system. The technical system includes the technologies, the physical layout of the plant, and the overall approach to operations; and the social system includes the organizational structure, the job roles, the performance measurements, the decision making, the problem solving, and the overall communication (King and Wood 60). Too frequently, management focuses only on the technical system. Robert King and G. Christopher Wood point out that ". . . time, effort, and resources spent on designing the appropriate social system to support and complement the technical system could significantly shorten implementation and accelerate the achievement of intended benefits" (60).

Quality or productivity or both are fertile grounds for such an approach. Schaffer suggests that "[a] manager may avoid the necessity of demand making by putting his chips on a variety of management programs, procedures, mechanisms, and innovations which he hopes will produce better results" (93). One must recognize, therefore, that solutions to problems are rarely technical in nature. A perfect solution may provide poor results when it is poorly implemented.

Once we equate productivity and quality with the performance of people instead of with statistical procedures, we will recognize that the field contains a lot of usable research. Locke and Latham, for example, provide an excellent recap of applicable research; they combine a series of separate studies to form a single model.

Using Locke and Latham's model of the High Performance Cycle, we see that performance is contingent on a variety of factors that have little to do with ability. While ability, which should include both training and proficiency, is a necessary ingredient, it is neither the starting point nor the stumbling block. As an example, Locke uses the "work to rule" practice whereby employees can snarl productivity by working "by the book." He explains: ". . . peer pressure has long been known to induce commitment to low goals in the form of restriction of output. Strong group norms may also produce commitment in the form of low variance production among group members. Commitment to high goals occurs when the group norms are high . . . when there are peer models performing at a high level. . . . Assigning both individual and group goals for a group task produces higher commitment to the individual goals than assigning individual goals alone. . . . Another peer factor is the degree to which the commitment was made publicly . . ." (8).

We must recognize, therefore, that the problems are a combination of such elements as demands, standards of performance, recognition, communication, and expectations, a composite that is probably best labelled "culture." Most people want to do a job well, and a manager must provide the proper environment. Ronald Grey and Ted Thone argue that ". . . to harness this driving force for success, companies must first define the culture they require for competitive advantage, assess their existing culture and then manage the changes needed to close the gap" (26-27).

BREAKING WITH THE PAST

Several papers on turnarounds suggest that the first step involves confronting the reality as it exists in the company or the department. Confrontation, however, need not connote conflict between antagonists but rather comparison between the desired and the actual. The end point should be the agreement to remove hindrances.

The most crucial step in a turnaround is diagnostic analysis. Because human nature impels us to act without reflection, the diagnosis of the problem itself is very often inaccurate. Anthony DiPrimio suggests that the diagnostic phase should begin with individual meetings among senior officers and should be followed by interviews with all levels of lower management. By considering the perceptions of the receivers, the manager, as part of the diagnostic phase, might even rethink his or her initial objective.

Preparing the Employees

Because one element affects all the others, the manager must consider combinations of the message, the medium, and the originator. Long points out that "[c]hanging the normal medium can send a message in itself which may not be the intent of the decision-maker" (70).

To break with the past the manager must get the attention of the people by finding a different setting. For example, when management at Campbell's Soup, recognizing that the business was in jeopardy, used a location apart from the work environment, they brought the message home forcefully that change was imminent (Trueman 31). Acuity of vision and a willingness to articulate the reality that the organization is facing are two essential ingredients of the solution. The whole company, therefore, must be aroused. John F. Akers, the chairman of IBM, notes: "'The tension level is not high enough in the business--everyone is too damn comfortable at a time when the business is in crisis'" (Carroll B1). Relying on past performance will lead to complacency and failure. "'No company,'" Akers argues, "'is going to survive in tomorrow's global marketplace by virtue of its history'" (Loomis 44). All involved must feel the uneasiness, the tension, the need for change. Some companies have used television satellite hook-ups to reach all of the employees at the same time. Both the actual "kick-off message," then, and the medium used are critical.

Because cultural consistency is a significant ingredient in the change process, all decisions must be assimilated into the corporate culture itself. "If there is a discrepancy between the culture and the change," Leathem argues, "culture will always win" (42). Management, therefore, must either modify the change or modify the culture. Bombardier, for example, acknowledged the world that we live in. In other cases, the company got the attention of its people by acknowledging past errors in leadership.

Raymond Royer, president and CEO of Bombardier, speaking about the need for complete awareness, remembers that the employees ". . . had to understand by themselves what was happening abroad [and] who and what our competition was. . . . [T]o win contracts . . . we needed to work very closely together. . . . [T]o beat competition . . . we needed to be individually and collectively fully accountable for our roles and responsibilities" (29-30). "To make everybody 'sing from the same songsheet,'" Royer continues, "I decided to convene all our 1,350 Division employees at all levels to group sessions. . . . These sessions were extremely productive to unite our thinking and actions. They also became a strong vehicle to fully explain . . . fundamental values, beliefs and principles" (30).

On the same lines, William Sandy writes that "ideas shaped with clarity must have the power to ignite action. Whoever conveys the most compelling vision of the future has the best chance of earning involvement of the people who must carry it out" (7). These excerpts from the work of Royer and Sandy demonstrate the start of a frequently repeated process in turnaround situations. The first step in the process is to break with the past by confronting the present. All involved need an indicator to show that times are changing; they need a clear send off, a kick off that will demonstrate that from this point on things will be different. Ralph Stayers, the president of Johnsonville's Sausage, gives a good example of this: instead of testing the sausage himself he allowed his employees to do it (Stayer 76). In each case, the person in charge--the division president, the production manager, the person in charge of the unit that is taking ownership of the need for change-- must initiate the action.

Exposing the Folklore: A Catharsis

While workers know what needs to be done, or have helpful ideas, they frequently do not act. Management must discover, therefore, how it can remedy this paralysis, how, in other words, it can acknowledge the folklore and effect a catharsis. The following steps embrace the process of change: one, recognizing new horizons; two, acknowledging past sins; three, accepting responsibility; and four, expressing new values.
If the leader has personally initiated the process by articulating the problems, identifying sacred cows, and recognizing the mistakes of management, then the employees will be ready for the catharsis. All concerned must recognize the causes of their behaviour and the reasons for their not acting. This process, however, must take place in a productive meeting, not a gripe session.

Complaints and excuses must all be channelled so that action will resolve the issue. This can be done with the use of a flip chart, a pen, and masking tape. Five benefits result from making a visible list of all the problems people believe hinder their performance:
1. It allows the person an opportunity to express his or her concerns and promises freedom from retribution.
2. It acknowledges the concerns and guarantees action.
3. It demonstrates an eagerness to address all concerns.
4. It permits priorities to be established and ensures that the problems will eventually be resolved.
5. It enables the group to review the list in the future and to ascertain whether the problem has been solved.
In many instances, those complaining will later acknowledge

that the problems were a matter of perception or were crutches and excuses for an unwillingness to act. This last step is most important because the group environment creates a forum for the members to acknowledge that they are making progress and that they are the ones who must make the changes. This same process should begin with the senior management and should continue all the way down to the first supervisors. As progress meetings are held, old problems that have been solved will be removed from the list and new ones will be added. The manager should expect that the first few months will serve only to get the house in order.

Building the New Culture

The purpose of the new culture, Grey and Thone suggest, is ". . . to provide employees with a greater say in how company operations are run and to ensure employees are treated as partners, not 'disposable resource'" (29). The new culture requires new things of management. First, they must show they are committed to performance. Communications consultant Richard Bevan of Towers Perrin argues: "'It's nuts if you don't involve employees; they are the only people who can fix the business'" (Rice 112). We see another example in Mattel Company, which has undergone radical change since John Amerman took the position as CEO in 1989. His second day on the job, "he told employees he was letting in some 'fresh air' and that the new watchword at Mattel was to be 'fun'" (Rice 112). Amerman followed up on his commitment to the new processes and his belief in them by wandering around the plant and meeting and chatting with the employees in their cafeteria (Rice 112). Second, the management must provide visible signs that are constant reminders of the new spirit. Such mundane things as attention to the cafeteria, the restrooms, and the lockers are good examples of commitment to people and problems.

All these actions presuppose that the leaders have firsthand knowledge of the situation and are sufficiently aware to openly mention specifics that call for action. The leaders' credibility does not come from saying "Change!" to the troops, but by making decisions and taking action in situations that do not make sense or have been long ignored. If the leaders were part of the mess, they must admit it. The leaders' subordinates will grant them instant credibility if they acknowledge: "Because of so and so, I was part of the problem and this is my remedy." Actions such as these build a solid foundations of new values and new attitudes.

Instituting New Organizational Values

New values will not come about through such things as slogans and programs. Instead, they will be in use when the process is implemented, for the process must be characterized by credibility and integrity. Naturally, some areas of risk exist. The "wait and see" attitude is a typical example. As Xerox's

CEO, Paul Allaire, explains: "When people know some order or memo is eventually going to come down from above and demand something different from what they want to do, it's easy to say, 'Hell, I've been burned enough times. I'm not going to do anything until I'm told to do it'" (Dumaine 37-8). Another attitude, again expressed by a person in leadership, is "I will wait and see how it develops. If it works, I'll join right in." The problem with this fallacy is that by not being involved, the leader will be unable to contribute his or her ideas. Furthermore, he or she will cast a shadow of nonconfidence and confuse their subordinates or peers.

A second area of risk is inherent in different ways of record keeping. The attitude "we have our set of books; you have your set of books" will also divide the organization. Self aggrandizement replaces corporate glory.

Distinguishing between union and management is a third area of risk. "You are not supposed to participate," the International Union leadership commented who had come to "visit" (that is, to "chew out") the local representatives. Needless to say, they went back empty handed. Only one team can exist, not two, nor three. If all fully understand what is going on and agree on direction, they will realize that there can be only one camp.

To minimize these risks, the manager must maintain control of the process and obtain early successes, preferably with a pilot group. This action permits the requisite intensive care and allows all levels of management to grow into the new expectations. It also acts as a beacon, a hope for others in distress. For example, on one trouble shooting assignment the plant manager told me that some of the employees felt neglected. He asked: "What is wrong with the other groups that you don't work with them?" We were only three weeks into the project and already the employees were very eager. Needless to say, the rest of the workers did not need to be persuaded of the project's desirability.

Initially, the manager should expect chaos. When communication begins, Anna Veerstag warns, areas of conflict will probably surface (12). Here again, the manager should begin with a small group and wait before including the entire organization. It is imperative, however, that the manager maintain integrity within the system. Those who refuse to participate or who obstruct the process must be confronted, first privately and then within the group in which they operate. If this is not done, the system will lose its integrity.

Early successes are critical. Words without action will soon kill interest, but short-term payoffs will result in long-term benefits. Michael Barrier points out that by uncovering ways to make immediate and constructive changes, management will achieve two things:
1. It will demonstrate to the employees that it is serious about making changes.

2. It will remind everyone that results are paramount (25).
Although the practical transitions to a quality system may come
in stages, Barrier notes that the actual philosophical change
must be total (24).

INSTITUTING A MANAGERIAL PROCESS

Instituting a managerial process requires that the process of
catharsis be repeated many times at each level of management and
in each functional area until all areas have adopted the same
values and the same philosophy. Stayer observes that top
management must become coaches; they must present the vision in
such a way that the employees will eagerly pursue it (72). He
writes: "I mean communicating a vision and then getting people
to see their own behavior, harness their own frustrations, and
own their own problems" (72).

"Don't tell people what to do, or how to do it," Larry Wilson
suggests, "but give them the map, the destination, and sometimes
the general direction in which to start" (38R). Eventually,
each person must own both the problems and the solutions that
are peculiar to his or her own area. Those involved in the
process must make demands of themselves and of others if the
problems are to be solved. Moreover, they must realize that
they are "working for themselves." Instead of giving "official
answers" to employee problems, Stayer points out, the
troubleshooter must make them repossess their problems and ask
the proper questions (80).

By getting the group to prioritize, categorize, and organize
at the outset, the manager creates a somewhat neutral exercise
that will cause the people to see that they have an active part
to play in the solution. Each person, as a part of the group,
must have an active voice in ascertaining whether the solution
or solutions will result in solving the problem or in creating
more problems. They must also together seek the best solution.

Next, the manager must establish several premises if the
people are to play a part in the solution:
1. Each person is an expert (Stayer explains: ". . . we asked
   ourselves who was in the best position to own the problem and
   came to the obvious conclusion that the people on the shop
   floor knew more about shop-floor performance than we did, so
   they were the best ones to make these decisions" [73-4].)
2. Because they are experts they probably know best where the
   opportunities lie.
3. Management's job is to help them secure the resources and
   talents they need.
4. Solutions should be sought with the cooperation of the entire
   team so that any ramifications can be dealt with on the spot.
5. All must voice their opinions. (Rice observes that the
   employees should be encouraged to ask tough questions and be
   prepared for tough answers [116].)
6. A flip chart should record the commitments and the actions

and should also keep track of the time factors and the participants.
7. Periodic reviews, usually weekly at the start, will ensure action toward solving both old and new problems.

Action plans further permit the group to work as a team. If each manager is a leader of a team and is at the same time a part of his or her superior's team, accountability will permeate the organization. Ideally, the person closest to the problem should both describe it and suggest a means of solving it. The group, in the spirit of helping, will either agree or disagree with the suggestions and will voice their concerns as individuals. The continuous focus is, obviously, to resolve the problem in the best way possible.

At all levels, each person must review frequently and regularly to ensure that his or her area is either on target, in need of assistance, or finished. The role of the leader is not that of inquisitor, which will remove accountability from the subordinates, but rather that of facilitator, assuring the integrity of the process.

Peer pressure and managerial power interact to create evaluation and recognition. My experience is that peer pressure is a powerful tool among both strong and weak performers. Initially, people will close ranks around the weak performer. Within three months, however, if that person has not improved, his or her poor performance will affect the whole team and will demonstrate that he or she is part of the problem. The group will see that the lower performer affects production, and it will expect the leader to take action. This condition is ideal for all motivational theories, for it provides reinforcement, creates expectancy, builds on the Herzberg satisfiers, minimizes the dissatisfiers, grants a self-fulfilling prophecy of success, and assures equity.

The ideal consultant is best sought outside of the company. The issue is not whether capable people exist within the organization, but rather whether the facilitator is, or has been, part of the culture and part of the problem. We cannot be prophets to our own people.

CONCLUSION

The key to the whole process is to travel with as little luggage as possible, an attitude made possible by the leader's insistence on treating the problem with openness, honesty, excitement, and confidence. If the employees are encouraged to articulate their problems, the group will be free from personal resentments, excuses, and rationalizations. The key tools of the action plan are acknowledging the problem, formalizing the solutions, specifying the ownership, and ensuring accountability by following up.

BIBLIOGRAPHIC REFERENCES

Barrier, Michael (1992) "Small Firms Put Quality First" Nation's Business, vol.80, no.5, pp. 22-32.

Carroll, Paul B. (1991) "Akers to IBM Employees: Wake Up!" Wall Street Journal, May 29,1991, pp. B1,B4

DiPrimio, Anthony (1988) "When Turnaround Management Works" The Journal of Business Strategy, vol.9, no.1, pp.61-64.

Dumaine, Brian (1991) "The Bureaucracy Busters", Fortune, vol. 123. no.13, pp 36-50.

Grey, Ronald J. and Ted J.F. Thone (1990) "Differences Between North America and European Corporate Cultures", Canadian Business Review, vol.17, no.3, pp. 26-30.

King, Robert a. and G. Christopher Wood (1989) "Overcome Cultural Barriers to Manufacturing Improvement", The Journal of Business Strategy, vol.10, no.3, pp. 59-60.

Leathem, J. Trevor (1989) "Managing Organizational Change", Business Quarterly, vol.54, no.1, pp 39-43.

Locke, Edwin A. and Gary P. Latham (1990) Work Motivation: The High Performance Cycle. In Uwe Kleinbeck and others (Eds.). Work Motivation. (pp 3-23). Hillsdale, NJ: Lawrence Erlbaum Assoc.

Long, Stephen (1988) "The Manager's Role in Communicating for Results" Business Quarterly, vol.52, no.4, pp 67-71.

Loomis, Carol J. (1991) "Can John Akers Save IBM?" Fortune, vol.124, no.2, pp 41-56.

Rice, Faye (1991) "Champions of Communication", Fortune, vol.123, no.11, pp 111-120.

Royer, Raymond, (1991) "Managing By Commitment" Business Quarterly, vol.55, no.6, pp 29-32.

Sandy, William. (1990) "Link Your Business Plan to a Performance Plan" The Journal of Business Strategy, vol.11, no.6, pp 4-8.

Schaffer, Robert H. (1974) "Demand Better Results - and Get Them", Harvard Business Review, vol.52, no.6, pp 91-98.

Stayer, Ralph. (1990) "How I Learned to Let My Workers Lead", Harvard Business Review, vol.68, no.6, pp 66-83.

Trueman, Wendy (1991) "Alternate Visions", Canadian Business, vol.64, no.3, pp 29-33.

Versteeg, Anna. (1990) "Self-Directed Work Teams Yield Long-Term Benefits", The Journal of Business Strategy, vol.11, no.6, pp 9-12.

Wilson, Larry (1989) "Creating the Best Work Culture", Nation's Business, vol.77, no.4, pp 38R.

Acknowledgements

A special word of appreciation to Stephanie Hawes who has been working as a research assistant and to Andrew Gutteridge who has been most helpful in editing the manuscript.

Biographical Sketch of the Author

Michel Mestre has held a variety of positions in industry and in an international management consulting firm. His own consulting firm specializes in turn around situations. For the last three years he has been teaching at Trinity Western University as an Associate Professor of Business.

Productivity & Quality Management Frontiers-IV, edited by Sumanth, Edosomwan, Poupart, and Sink. ©1993 Institute of Industrial Engineers.

From Resistance to Commitment: The Rest of the Journey

R.D. Smith
The LEADS Corporation
Englewood, Colorado USA

ABSTRACT

The principal thesis of this paper is that those who would create change within an organization must understand the impact of that change on the day-to-day working lives of those who are called upon to implement it if the change is to be acted upon with genuine commitment. In many instances top management embarks on a well-intended journey of systematic change to enhance quality, improve productivity, and/or increase competitiveness only to find the program mired in apathy, half-hearted compliance, or outright recalcitrance. A review of the processes by which change is directed can provide insight into the natural tendency for others to resist externally imposed change. More than a dozen specific reasons why people tend to resist change are discussed.

Building commitment among employees beyond mere compliance requires time and planning. While there are resistance issues common to most organizational changes, quality initiatives (particularly when applied to the white collar sector) present a unique set of challenges. The paper explores these problems and discusses the pitfalls of paying insufficient attention to the dynamics of resistance. Categories of resistance are examined to gain a better understanding of the underlying issues associated with them.

The central theme of the recommended approach is to not focus on overcoming resistance per se, but rather to understand, anticipate, and take preventive measures in order to avoid the negative impact of the manifestations of resistance to change in the work place. Key stages to change implementation are identified and discussed as well as possible causes for resistance at each point. This approach treats resistance to change as a natural human phenomenon, rather than as an evil entity that must be wrestled into submission. The methods presented emphasize two complementary themes of management leadership: maintaining constancy of purpose and dealing with underlying causes instead of symptomatic behaviors.

A progressive American manufacturing firm once recognized the need to introduce more advanced technology in order to increase productivity. Despite management's strong record of maintaining open communication with its employees, the proposed changes met significant resistance from the hourly work force. A subsequent case study of the firm focused on two major issues: First, why people tend to resist change so strongly and, secondly, what can be done to overcome this resistance. Among the recommended actions items was the suggestion that group meetings be held between labor and management to better communicate the need for change and to stimulate group participation in planning the changes. While this scenario may have a familiar ring to managers of the 1990's, the year was actually 1948, the company manufactured pajamas, and the issues were not new even then (Coch, Lester, and French:512-533). Forty-four years later the subject of dealing with human resistance to change remains a central theme in planning systematic organizational change.

In an era in which businesses are increasingly focused on building or maintaining their status as world-class competitors and as productivity and quality methodologies, which have been used successfully in manufacturing, begin to find application in the white collar service sector, the pressure to re-evaluate processes and practices is intense. The concept of continuous improvement requires an unprecedented commitment to perpetual change. Developing such commitment involves working with resistance in all its various aspects and at all levels of the organization. Fundamentally, management involves bringing people together to achieve a common purpose. Contending with resistance to change and building commitment from it involve aspects of management that are more art than science.

THE NATURE OF RESISTANCE

Understanding resistance

It is a popular notion that resistance to change within organizations, while to be expected, is an evil entity which must be overcome. Effective management sometimes is assumed to be that which successfully wrestles this beast into submission. It is perhaps more useful to consider resistance to change as a natural mechanism which can actually maintain organizational health. Taken to a logical extreme, the hypothetical absence of resistance to change within an organization can easily result in complete chaos as each management suggestion is acted upon with total commitment. There is clearly a place for loyal opposition and healthy skepticism. And rather than learn techniques to control resistance, it is perhaps more important to understand it and to find ways to anticipate and manage its manifestations.

It is paradoxical that while change is an inevitable occurrence in the lives of people and organizations, the first response to the recognition that change is necessary (or that it is already occurring) is frequently denial. The next most common reaction to change is a quick mental assessment of two factors: To what extent will the change affect me personally and to what extent can I exercise control over it. The answers to these questions play a significant part in the degree to which and the manner in which an individual may exhibit resistance to the change. Senior and mid-level managers go through this process as much as do junior supervisors and rank and file employees. Resistance to change is more a matter of human status than it is one of positional status. If managers would recall their own initial reactions to an organizational change and recount not only the process, but the time it took to convince themselves that the change was a proper one, they would be well on the way to understanding and anticipating resistance in others.

One's perspective on change often depends on whether one is the initiator or the subject of a change. A change initiator is more likely to perceive as obstinate resisters those who do not share the initiator's view of a proposed change; those opposed are apt to regard themselves as preservers of the present system and to see their doubt as a line of defense maintaining the status quo from the threat of an ill-conceived idea (Fine:20).

Resistance to imposed organizational change takes many forms and an attempt at categorization may suggest a mutual exclusivity between types; in practice resistance tends to range along continuums of type, motive, and intensity. In its simplest form resistance is most commonly based on a need for more information. It is unrealistic to expect a rational person to support an idea he or she does not understand. A more complex type of resistance is that of intellectual skepticism where the merits of the change are examined and weighed. The most severe form of resistance is resistance for its own sake. This can be particularly difficult to contend with, because it frequently has a non-rational basis.

While there can be as many motives for resisting change as there are people and proposed changes, motives tend to range along a continuum from an expression of annoyance to a genuine disagreement with the nature of the change and its consequences to resisting in order to gain an advantage from the change process to a resistance based simply upon the ability to do so. Resistance to organizational change can range in intensity from mild carping to strenuous argument to outright refusal to subversive compliance. Given that all change is stressful, resistance may reflect personal coping mechanisms related less to the merit of the change itself, but connected more to the degree to which individuals perceive to have control over a particular change and the perceived personal effect of the change. The result is one of the most complex human dynamics facing the management of any organization.

Anticipating resistance

Since resistance to organizational change is such an intricate reaction, it is not always clear when and in what manner it will manifest itself. Some situations in which resistance can be expected are obvious: If the change involves a loss of prestige, status, or position; if people learn of change without adequate and accurate information to understand it; if the change will require skills currently not possessed; or if there is a perception that the resources necessary to make the change will not be made available.

Other situations are not so obvious, but should not be unexpected: if there is a perceived lack of commitment for the change from key people within the organization; if there are inconsistencies between the change and the existing organizational framework; if there appears to be no incentive to make the change; and if similar changes have been attempted unsuccessfully within the organization in the past.

Still other situations are more subtle and may mask the true nature of resistance: if there is a perception that those initiating change lack a clear vision of the impact the change will have on the organization or its members; or, if there is a perception that the culture of the organization will not support the change.

Unexpected resistance may be simply an indicator that the organization is overloaded with change and needs time to absorb what it is currently contending with. Or the timing of the change may be bad in terms of conditions within the organization for reasons that may be totally unrelated to the change itself.

STAGES OF SYSTEMATIC CHANGE

Planning

At the outset of a planned organizational change, managers should be aware of the fallacious assumption that the decision to make a change equates to causing the change. Frequently, dynamics of a change process are already underway and producing outcomes, prompting management to have some reaction. For example, elements of employee involvement and a general recognition of the need to become more competitive often precede a decision to begin a total quality improvement program. Change is normally more incremental in nature than comprehensive; not everything changes at once. Therefore, before announcing a significant change, it is important to view the change from the perspective of the employees. An excellent method for doing this is to consider the following questions (Conner & Lake:131):

> Why must the organization change?
> What is being changed?
> How will the change be accomplished?
> Who is involved in the change?

The difference between the answers to these questions from the perspective of senior management, middle management, and the other categories of employees can be useful to anticipate potential resistance. In responding to why the organization must change, it is important to convey the appropriate degree of urgency. Unless dire consequences are truly anticipated, however, histrionic predictions are quickly detected and can undermine credibility. Yet, without a perceived compelling need to change, developing commitment to the change process will be hampered.

At the heart of the change process is the matter of what is being changed. Again, it is important to consider the perceptions of the change from the perspective of those involved. In a service organization embarked on a quality improvement change process, senior management may see the focus of the change as customer satisfaction; an employee may see the change as a restructuring of his or her department. The degree of difference between such perceptions can be the source for lingering resistance.

The answer to how the change will be accomplished also is critical. If management has developed a specific solution and seeks only to impose it, the approach will be significantly different from the situation in which the change involves employee participation in developing new solutions. Each can be perceived favorably by various segments of the organization; each may produce various types and degrees of resistance.

The answer to who will be involved is equally important, for timing and sequencing of systematic change within an organization are crucial to its success. Senior management also needs to assess such matters as contractual agreements, either with labor, suppliers, or customers which may inhibit a change process.

A clear timetable is indispensable to provide a time perspective of what has been done so far and about how long it is expected to accomplish what needs to be done. It has been the author's experience that this step is often not taken out of concern that since management may not be able to accurately predict the time it will take to make a change that they will lose credibility if the timetable isn't met. However, without some estimate the difference between what management expects and what employees expect can vary by orders of magnitude.

Transition

The use of pilot projects can be an effective means to "shake-down" a new process or organizational change (Hodge:382). In large organizations, pilots can be conducted in one functional area throughout the organization (e.g. accounting), cross-functionally in a geographically separated section (e.g. the Denver office), or in one product line but not in others. In the author's experience with pilots there are at least two potential traps associated with them. The first is a tendency for pilots to undergo a metamorphosis from something with the nature of an examination of alternatives to a purely demonstration project in which the operative goal is to "make it work". This is usually accompanied by a fair amount of cynicism and loss of enthusiasm for participating in future change process evaluations. The second trap, which is particularly prevalent when there are multiple pilots, is the tendency for the emergence of internecine competition. These alterations of a pilot project's original objectives can cause significant confusion as to what senior management actually intended to change.

An important aspect of the transitional phase is the need to convey a clear "migration path" (Belasco:24) from the present state to the desired, changed state. Modeling new behaviors, especially by respected members of the organization is a particularly effective method of demonstrating what is expected. For example, an organization may adopt the policy of delegating authority for routine decision making to those closest to the issue. Senior management might model this new behavior by providing more autonomy to department heads. Such a clear signal is important, because if mid-level managers do not see such action by those senior to themselves, they are unlikely to practice it with those subordinate to themselves.

Implementation

Throughout the period of initial change implementation, managers need to scrutinize their own beliefs, values, and commitment to the change process. Managers' actions may, in themselves, be a source of resistance in others. The implementation phase is the crucible in which resistance, both of the loyal opposition and of the dysfunctional variety, can be most intense. Several alternative strategies can be used, but it is imperative that management exhibit leadership and maintain a constancy of purpose to whatever paradigm has been selected. For example, if a total quality management approach is taken to improve processes in an area of an organization which has traditionally worked under a stovepipe management structure, a likely central dynamic of change will be empowerment. Assuming that everyone involved understands the process and appears willing to give it a go, employee commitment to the new order may depend more on management's response to the subtle issue of delegated responsibility than to overt resistance on any individual's part. Empowerment will succeed only if management is successful in maintaining the delegation of decision making within pre-set parameters. An action as benign as requesting management to choose an alternative can be perceived as shifting responsibility for the outcome back to management.

People tend to lose confidence and raise resistance mechanisms when they are faced with the tension of cognitive dissonance: an incompatibility between what they are told to expect and what they experience. An announced policy shift to build more teamwork within the organization is unlikely to win commitment if the appraisal and promotion system continue to favor individual effort.

BUILDING COMMITMENT

Commitment versus compliance

There is a tendency in both individuals as well as organizations to revert to previous behavior patterns if a firm commitment has not been made to a specific change. Thus, one of the primary goals of change management should be to build commitment to an appropriate change in order to ensure its continuation. Change often involves moving from the familiar to the unfamiliar. Those being asked to make such a journey need assurance that senior management knows where they are going and how they are going to get there. Organizations in which there is a shared vision of the future, articulated in terms consistent with the culture of the organization, are in a better position to build commitment among their members. In organizations where change is perceived to be imposed with an imperial attitude the more likely outcome is compliance.

Commitment involves a willingness to incorporate a change into the natural work routine and occurs when resistance has been replaced with agreement. Compliance, on the other hand, is little more than acquiescence to a superior force, obedience. Compliance to change is the more likely result of simply overcoming resistance. Compliance can be obtained by fiat; commitment must be earned. It can be a serious error to mistake one for the other.

From resistance to commitment

A recurring theme among employees in organizations undergoing systematic change, is the issue of management leadership. Resistance to change seems to focus less on the fact that change is being made as much as it does on the manner in which it is being implemented. There are no magic rules or cookbook solutions to successfully implementing change. However, success is associated with more of some activities and less of others.

In organizations where continuous change processes appear to be running smoothly, managers tend to be seen by employees as coaches and facilitators who understand their employees perceptions and who have a clear vision of where the organization is going. In organizations where the systematic change process has bogged down, there is generally a marked absence of shared vision and an uncertainty on the part of employees that management truly understands the impact of change on their day-to-day work lives. Whether either situation accurately represents reality is almost irrelevant; perception is reality when it comes to opinions.

Successful change implementation is frequently assisted by an attitude of humility toward the complexities of human interactions and a recognition that no one may have all the answers. It is useful for management to ask open-ended questions about the process or change at hand. Asking questions rather than providing pat answers helps develop people and increases their sense of ownership for the change.

This is particularly useful if combined with the willingness to listen carefully to the answers. And few management actions defuse unproductive resistance and help build commitment better than a frank acknowledgment of imperfection and a willingness to learn from mistakes.

It is also important to allow enough time for change to occur. Minor set backs do not necessarily indicate that the change process has failed, but neither do short-term successes indicate that the change has been completely adopted.

Building commitment entails keeping the change process in a rational perspective as well. If a change or sub-change is judged by all involved to be relatively simple, it should not receive the same attention and time as more complex issues. This may appear to be absurdly self-evident, but many organizations find themselves the victims of "paralysis by analysis" from giving all change items equal weight and importance. Organizations most vulnerable to this phenomenon are those which have adopted a rote change process through which all changes must be evaluated.

A key factor in building commitment is the willingness to focus on root causes, rather than simply responding to symptomatic issues. This is particularly true when dealing with resistance. It was Nietzsche who noted that ideas are often not accepted merely because the tone of voice in which they were expressed was unsympathetic. If employee resistance is based not on the merit of the change itself, but rather on a perception that management acted in a cavalier manner, then responding to the resistance from an intellectual basis will deal only with the symptom and never reveal the root cause.

Building commitment from resistance frequently involves the concept of giving away a good idea; planting the seed for change and letting someone else develop it as their own idea. Good managers have the ability to do this on a regular basis, projecting the confidence that there is virtually no limit to what can be accomplished if one isn't overly concerned with who gets credit for it.

BIBLIOGRAPHIC REFERENCES

Beer, Michael and Eisenstat, Russel (1990) "Why Change Programs Don't Produce Change", Harvard Business Review, Nov-Dec, pp. 158-166.

Belasco, James A. (1990) Teaching the Elephant to Dance, New York, Crown Publishers, Inc.

Benton, Peter (1990) Riding the Whirlwind, Oxford, Basil Blackwell, Ltd.

Coch, Lester and French, John (1948) "Overcoming Resistance to Change", Human Relations, vol. 1, no. 4, pp. 512-533.

Connor, Patrick E. and Lake, Linda K. (1988) Managing Organizational Change, New York, Praeger Publishers.

Drucker, Peter F. (1989) The New Realities, New York, Harper and Row, Publishers.

Fine, Sara, (1991) "Change and Resistance to Change: The Cost-Benefit Factor", The Bottom Line, vol. 5, no. 1, pp. 18-23.

Hodge, B.J. and Anthony, William P. (1979) Organization Theory: An Environmental Approach, Boston, Allyn and Bacon.

Hultman, Ken (1979) The Path of Least Resistance, Austin, Learning Concepts.

Saraph, Jayant V., PhD. and Sebastian, Richard J., PhD. (1992) "Human Resource Strategies for Effective Introduction of Advanced Manufacturing Technologies (AMT)", Production and Inventory Management Journal, vol. 33, no. 1, pp. 64-70.

Warrick, D. D. and Zawacki, Robert A. (1987) High Performance Management, Colorado Springs, Eagle Publishing Company.

Zuboff, Shoshana (1988) In the Age of the Smart Machine, New York, Basic Books, Inc.

BIOGRAPHICAL SKETCH OF AUTHOR

R. Dennis Smith is Associate Vice-President of the LEADS Corporation, an international management consulting firm specializing in productivity and quality improvement. He has been directly involved in successfully implementing systematic organizational change for more than 20 years in a variety of executive leadership positions. Mr. Smith resides in Englewood, Colorado.

Productivity & Quality Management Frontiers-IV, edited by Sumanth, Edosomwan, Poupart, and Sink. ©1993
Institute of Industrial Engineers.

Perceptions of Roadblocks and Change Management Strategies during Implementation of Organizational Productivity Improvement Projects

R.C. Preziosi
Nova University
Ft. Lauderdale, Florida USA

ABSTRACT

The success of or lack thereof in organizational productivity improvement efforts is influenced by barriers which surface during implementation. A literature review identified seventeen (17) such barriers. Survey respondents validated the presence of these barriers.

Use of change management strategies increases the likelihood that the barriers can be overcome and productivity improvement projects can attain higher levels of success. A literature review identified fourteen (14) strategies. Survey results suggest that there were discrepancies between what change management strategies were actually used and what change management strategies could have been utilized.

Mean scores were analyzed and discussed. Conclusions were drawn. Implications for further study were suggested.

KEY WORDS: Change management, productivity improvement, productivity management.

INTRODUCTION

Organizations have been attempting for decades to become more productive. These attempts have been organization-wide in nature or have focused on something less, such as a level or two in the hierarchy or a few specific departments. The purpose of activity has been to increase competitiveness, except in the case of government agencies. The focus of such government efforts is to use resources better because of taxpayer unwillingness to provide what is perceived as inefficient government with more resources. Whether business or government, the task has been to find ways to increas efficiency.

A wide variety of strategies and tools have been utilized to increase efficiency. Efforts have been directed toward improving technology, making changes in products or services, utilizing human resources more effectively, simplifying tasks and work methods, or a combination of these. The general strategy has always been based upon the fundamental need to improve the ratio of outputs over inputs. These options have included; 1) increasing outputs while decreasing inputs, 2) increasing outputs while stabilizing inputs, 3) decreasing inputs while stabilizing outputs, 4) decreasing both but inputs at a faster rate, or 5) increasing both but outputs at a faster rate.

All of the resources that organizations have expended to increase efficiency have produced mixed results. There has been no rhyme or reason to the level of success attained. It has not been possible to identify trends for a particular industry or type of government agency. Each productivity improvement project has brought about a measure of success, influenced by organizational culture, project type and size, expertise brought to bear on the project, resources committed, and top management support.

Perhaps, the major influence on productivity improvement is the existence of organizational barriers and the capability to overcome those barriers. Werther (1991) and Sink (1989) have both identified the existence of such inhibiting factors. Both suggest indirectly the need to manage change processes if productivity improvement is going to have the impact on an organization's competitiveness that is currently required for organizational survival.

PURPOSES OF THE STUDY

An opportunity exists to understand roadblocks that inhibit successful implementation of productivity improvement projects. At the same time, knowing what change management strategies are available and being used will increase our understanding about how to successfully change manage productivity improvement projects. Thus, the study has two purposes. First, roadblocks will be identified as will the extent to which they are evident during such projects. Second, change management strategies will be identified along with their actual utilization and proposed utilization.

METHODOLOGY

The first task was review of the literature on change management. The literature focused on two different considerations. An identification of the roadblocks to successful change implementation was the first consideration. This was followed by the identification of change management strategies that when used lead to success. Seventeen (17) roadblocks were identified as were fourteen (14) change management strategies after a reveiw of the following; Campbell and Campbell (1988) Productivity in Organizations, Bell and Burnham (1991), Managing Productivity and Change, Kopelman, (1986) Managing Productivity in Organizations, Werther, Ruch, and McClure (1986) Productivity Through People.

The development of a survey instrument using the roadblocks and strategies occurred next. The instrument was given to a convenience sample of one hundred and thirty (130). Respondents were attendees at a five-day productivity improvement workshop. A total of one hundred and twenty-four (124) usable questionnaires were returned from a sample that averaged 9.2 years of professional and managerial experience in private, public, and not-for-profit organizations. Thus, the response rate was 95%.

The following roadblocks were identified from the literature review and incroporated in the questionnaire;

1. People given new (more) responsibilities,
2. Project outcome goals were not clear,
3. The emergence of new communication patterns,
4. The establishment of new work relationships,
5. A temporary drop in productivity,
6. The cost of the project in budget terms,
7. Changes in policy and/or procedure,
8. The reorganization of task flows,
9. Working with departments in new ways,
10. Not knowing who is in charge of the project,
11. Things taking longer than expected,
12. People having to learn new skills,
13. Different people expecting different results,
14. The pace at which the change proceeded,
15. Recognition of employee efforts to change,
16. Moving work stations around, and
17. General information about the progress of the change.

The following change management strategies were identified from the literature review and became part of the question-naire;

1. Building commitment by managers to the desired results,
2. Encouraging a team effort,
3. Rewarding behaviors that supported the change,
4. Having a well respected project leader,
5. Negotiating to maintain cooperation,
6. Communicating constantly and consistently,
7. Cheerleading by managers for the change,
8. Obtaining everyone's voluntary involvement,
9. Asking for feedback about the process,
10. Redirecting resources to bring about the change,
11. Sticking to the schedule and timetables,
12. Creating excitement about the new-opportunities,
13. Engaging in ongoing project evaluation, and
14. Updating the project plan as required.

Survey participants were asked to evaluate three things. First, they were asked to evaluate the extent to which each of the seventten (17) roadblocks occurred during recent organizational productivity improvement projects. A four-point Likert scale was used with the following values; 1 = Not at all, 2 = Infrequently, 3 = Frequently, and 4 = Constantly. Next, they were asked to assess the extent to which the change management strategies were actually utilized to enhance organizational productivity improvement projects. The exact same scale as described above was used. A third assessment measured the extent to which productivity improvements would have been enhanced if the change management strategies had been utilized. A four-point Likert-scale was used with the following values; 1 = Disagree strongly, 2 = Disagree somewhat, 3 = Agree some-what, and 4 = Agree strongly.

RESULTS

Table 1 reports the means for each of the seventeen (17) Roadblocks. Analysis of the mean scores revealed that 10 out of 17 roadblocks had means above the 2.5 level on the interval data scale. This suggests that over one-half of the roadblocks did indeed exhibit themselves somewhat frequently during the implementation of organizational productivity improvement projects. This is true since the higher the score on the four-point Likert scale, the more likely the roadblock was encountered.

TABLE 1

ROADBLOCKS TO PRODUCTIVITY IMPROVEMENT

Roadblock	Mean Score
A. New Responsibilities	2.56
B. Clarity of Outcome Goals	2.53

C.	New Communication Patterns	2.40
D.	New Work Relationships	2.58
E.	Drop in Productivity	2.36
F.	Project Costs	2.58
G.	Policy/Procedure Changes	2.56
H.	Reorganization of Task Flows	2.52
I.	Working in New Ways	2.34
J.	Project Manager Unknown	2.30
K.	Longer Time Than Expected	3.00
L.	Learning New Skills	2.66
M.	Differing Expectations	2.95
N.	The Pace of Change	2.64
O.	Employee Recognition	2.49
P.	Moving Work Stations	2.11
Q.	General Information About Progress	2.39

Mean scores were also calculated for the extent to which change management strategies were actually utilized to enhance the outcomes of productivity imporvement projects. Analysis of the mean scores revealed that 11 out of 15 strategies received scores below the mid-point of 2.5. This indicates not very frequent use of almost three-fourths of the strategies. Table 2 reports the means as well as inter-item reliability co-efficients.

TABLE 2

Change Management Strategies - Reported Use

	Strategy	Mean	Co-efficient
A.	Building Commitment	2.38	.850
B.	Team Effort	2.77	.875
C.	Reward Behavior Support	2.37	.866
D.	Respected Project Leader	2.41	.915
E.	Maintaining Cooperation	2.35	.781
F.	Communication	2.57	.897
G.	Cheerleading for Change	2.27	.854
H.	Voluntary Involvement	2.32	.877
I.	Asking for Feedback	2.27	.890
J.	Redirecting Resources	2.42	.773
K.	Sticking to the Schedule	2.57	.826
L.	Creating Excitement	2.41	.861
M.	Ongoing Project Evaluation	2.33	.836
N.	Project Plan Updating	2.44	.880

Table 3 reports mean scores that were calculated for the extent to which productivity improvements would be enhanced if the strategies had been utilized. The means ranged from 3.05 to 3.62. Means for this set of responses except for one item are at least three-quarters of a point higher than the corresponding mean for the previous set of responses. Table 3 reports the inter-item reliability coefficients along with the means.

TABLE 3

Change Management Strategies - Suggested Use

	Strategy	Mean	Co-efficient
A.	Building Commitment	3.49	.692
B.	Team Effort	3.62	.691
C.	Reward Behavior Support	3.44	.791
D.	Respected Project Leader	3.39	.736
E.	Maintaining Cooperation	3.09	.769
F.	Communication	3.56	.757
G.	Cheerleading for Change	3.05	.884
H.	Voluntary Involvement	3.22	.849
I.	Asking for Feedback	3.49	.715
J.	Redirecting Resources	3.22	.817
K.	Sticking to the Schedule	3.20	.787
L.	Creating Excitement	3.39	.748
M.	Ongoing Project Evaluation	3.42	.810
N.	Project Plan Updating	3.47	.774

DISCUSSION

The study focused on 1) the identification of roadblocks that interfere with the implementation of productivity improvement projects, 2) the actual existence of those roadblocks in such projects, 3) the identification of change management strategies to enhance productivity improvement projects, 4) the extent to which such strategies were actually used, and 5) if used, would those strategies have enhanced the projects.

Only 7 out of 17 roadblocks showed any indication of not being problematic. Of those, 7 only "moving the work station around" showed a very low indication of not being a problem. It seems safe to suggest that 16 out of 17 roadblocks are present to a fairly common extent during the implementation of productivity improvement projects.

The change management strategies are all used to some extent, though only 3 of them seem to be used fairly frequently. The 3 were encouraging a team effort, communicating constantly and consistently, and sticking to the schedules and timetables. These were the only 3 with mean scores above 2.5. The other scores ranged from only 2.27 to 2.44.

The range of scores for suggesting the use of the change management strategies to enhance productivity improvement projects was 3.05 to 3.62. More importantly, though, was that only 1 of the strategies produced a discrepancy of less than .74 between actual use and the corresponding item under suggested use. Such discrepancies on a 4-point scale can certainly be indicative of a general need for the strategies to be utilized if productivity improvement projects are to be more successful.

CONCLUSION

This study certainly suggests that there are a variety of roadblocks to productivity improvement. It also points out that there are change management strategies that can be used to enhance the success of productivity improvement projects. Caution should be noted in that each project must be considered individually on an organization by organization basis. The respondents represented a wide variety of organizations, so it would be impossible to draw any conclusions about the data that could be applied to the larger universe. The roadblocks and the change management strategies, though, represent a fairly valid and reliable group of variables that could be used as a basis for further research.

REFERENCES

Bell, R. and Burnham, J. Managing Change and Productivity, South-Western, Cincinnati, 1991.

Campbell, J. and Campbell, R., Productivity in Organizations, Josey-Bass, San Francisco, 1988.

Kopelman, R., Managing Productivity in Organizations, McGraw-Hill, New York, 1986.

Sink, D., "Performance Action Teams: Case Study" in Sumanth, D. (ed.), Productivity Management Frontiers - I, Elsevier, Amsterdam, 1987.

Werther, W., "Management Resistance to Productivity and Quality Efforts", in Sumanth, D. et.al. (eds.), Productivity and Quality Management Frontiers - III, Industrial Engineering and Management Press, Norcross, GA, 1991.

Werther, W., Ruch, W. and McClure, L., Productivity Through People, West, St. Paul, MN, 1986.

BIOGRAPHICAL SKETCH

Dr. Robert C. Preziosi is Associate Dean of Academic Affairs and an Assistant Professor of Management Education at the School of Business and Entrepreneurship at Nova University in Ft. Lauderdale, Florida. He has been teaching a graduate level course in productivity for ten years. He has published on the topics of productivity and quality in the National Productivity Review and the Training and Development Journal. He has also edited a sixteen page piece on Improving White Collar Productivity and has published a

Productivity Assessment Questionnaire and a Productivity Audit. His other interests are in the theory and practice of adult learning. He is an accomplished business executive, having been in academia only since 1987. He has been in the consulting business since 1979.

Productivity & Quality Management Frontiers-IV, edited by Sumanth, Edosomwan, Poupart, and Sink. ©1993 Institute of Industrial Engineers.

Overcoming Resistance to TQM in a Government Research Laboratory

D.W. Tomlinson and G. Brown
USACERL/FST
Champaign, Illinois USA

Abstract

How do you tell a recognized authority in a scientific area that he or she needs to begin thinking quality? This paper examines the need for quality thinking, ways to implement quality thinking, managing the personalities in a highly educated workforce, and taking the R&D organization through the change cycle. The US Army's Construction Engineering Research Laboratories (USACERL) in Champaign, Illinois is the lead Department of Defense (DOD) laboratory in infrastructure and environmental sustainment research. Although commanded by an Army Colonel, USACERL's workforce is virtually all civilian. TQM was introduced to USACERL in 1990 when a new commander was assigned. TQM was introduced to top management and then initialized through the various organizational levels.

Creating a quality culture in any organization is becoming a necessity for survival in the increasingly competitive global arena. In times of ever declining budgets, especially research budgets, the need for a quality-minded R&D organization is clear. The competition for research dollars is keen, especially in DOD. For example, a $200,000 Knowledge Worker research project is in direct competition with a $200 million dollar weapons research program. Creating a quality culture that serves both the internal and the external customer is mandatory for survival.

Managing the diverse psyche of the personnel involved in research and having the researcher be customer driven are two very important issues which are addressed. For government functions, overcoming the stigma attached to TQM is the biggest obstacle. Many middle manager's and employees believe TQM is just another new commander's agenda or Government "program".

The need for an innovative laboratory to have TQM applied, how TQM principles have been introduced, the reaction to these TQM ideals from various levels of employees, and how the change process has been and is being managed will be explored in depth.

Productivity & Quality Management Frontiers-IV, edited by Sumanth, Edosomwan, Poupart, and Sink. ©1993 Institute of Industrial Engineers.

Personality Traits: Could They Be Hurdles in Productivity and Competitiveness

D.P.S. Arora
Florida International University
Miami, Florida USA

Abstract

Managers in the organizational environment are faced with ambiguous situations everyday. Individual personality traits and management styles can affect both managers' and organizations' productivity and competitiveness. Personality variables, like Locus of Control and Intolerance of Ambiguity, may affect the management styles of managers. The hypothesis were developed in this regard and tested on the students from the management class. Rotter's (1964) scale was used to assess the respondents' internal-external Locus of Control orientations. Budner's (1962) scale was used to assess the respondents' Intolerance of Ambiguity. The respondents were also administered the MSI survey (Taggart and Valenzi, 1990) to assess their management style. The results are discussed with their implications.

Key Words: Locus of Control, Intolerance of Ambiguity, Innovativeness, Competitiveness, productivity

Finding new and better ways to perform a job continuously is very crucial for being competitive and productive. Crandall and Wooton (1978) proposed a step-by-step productivity improvement program in which the key ingredient were the "re-development strategies." According to Crandall and Wooton (1978) re-development strategies concentrate on doing things in a different and a better way at each stage of the "organizational growth stage." To implement such a program organizations need managers who can take charge and deal with uncertainties, especially, when more than ever before, organizations are faced with competitive and hostile environment (Chittipeddi and Wallet, 1991). Managers in this environment are faced with ambiguous situations everyday. Individual personality traits can affect the way managers perceive such situations (Budner, 1962; Rotter, 1964). Managers' perceptions and confidence in decisions made in such situations can mean a difference between a firm's success or failure. Personality attributes like "locus of control" (Rotter, 1964) and "intolerance of ambiguity" (Budner, 1962) are crucial for managers in dealing with such uncontrollable situations, especially in small businesses (Duchesneau and Gartener, 1990; Brockhaus, 1980; Brockhaus and Horwitz, 1986; and Fredrickson and Mitchell, 1984). These personality attributes may be manifested in the management styles, through which managers deal with their professional responsibilities. Management styles may help/prevent managers to effectively respond to environmental contingencies. Attributes of management styles such as innovativeness (Gartener, 1990), creativity (Kao,1989; Gartener, 1990), planning (Duchesneau and Gartener, 1990), and participative decision making (Duchesneau and Gartener, 1990) may contribute a great deal in managers' success to cope with constraints and still be effective. Managers' perceptions and management styles can transform threats into opportunities. Though personality variables like locus of control and intolerance of ambiguity have been associated with various behavioral characteristics of the managers, little is known about their effects on management styles. In this study, the hypothesis were developed in this regard and tested on the graduating students from the management class. The results are discussed with their implications.

Managers prefer individual management styles to perform their duties in organizations. The wide array of individual preferences may make generalizations about management styles very complex. Researchers have tried to cope with this problem using different ways. Some researchers have attempted to classify the management styles on two point continua, others have attempted to study the issue more minutely. The following section reviews some of the diverse approaches used by researchers in such attempts.

ASSESSMENT OF MANAGEMENT STYLES
Two-point-continua approaches

Researchers with different orientations have attempted to analyze management styles. Kirton and McArthy (1988) believe that task orientations of organizations often demand predominantly adaptive or predominantly innovative management styles. Previously, Kirton (1976) developed an instrument (the Kirton Adaptation Inventory, or KAI) for locating individuals on a continuum of adaptiveness - innovativeness. KAI has been used for a variety of research purposes including cross cultural analysis (Thomson, 1980; Kirton, 1977, 1980; and Keller and Holland, 1978), associating management styles with attitudinal traits (Kirton and Sean, 1980; Kirton, 1978; Isaksen and Kaufmann, 1990; and Elder, 1989) and consumer behavior (Foxall and Goldsmith, 1988). However, Glenn and William (1980) reported lack of face validity of the KAI.

Kauffman (1979) in the same vein identified two management styles for problem solving as "assimilators and explorers." Assimilators displayed a tendency to follow established principles in attacking a problem and explorers tended to seek out novel solutions even when established solutions were adequate. Goldsmith and Matherly (1986) include some of the proponents of this approach.

Another approach to analyze management styles includes a research piece by Posner and Kouzes (1988). Posner and Kouzes (1988) assessed the extent of innovativeness in management styles of the managers in developing their "Leadership Practices Inventory (LPI)."

A further refinement was attempted by Agor (1984), who designed an instrument using the Torrance and Taggart Human Information Processing Survey (Torrance and Taggart, 1984), the Myers - Briggs Type indicator (Briggs and Myres, 1962) and the Mobius Psi - Q test (1981). Based on this instrument he identified management styles in managers as "left brain-right brain."

Taggart and Robey (1981) in the same vein proposed neurological, psychological, and philosophical foundation for the "Human Information Processing" (HIP) metaphor for management style. The neurological discussion provided the rationale for left brain/right brain differences in human information processing. Further, using the split brain metaphor, Taggart and Robey (1981) presented a concept of "dual human information processing." They summarized a theory of a two-mode HIP metaphor for management style for the complementary "rational-intuitive" style.

The works cited discussed basically categorized the management styles on two point continua. Escoffier, Arora, and Taggart (1992) argued that dimensions of management styles may be too complex to be represented by bi-polar continua. Some researchers have made concerted efforts to study the complexity of management style microscopically, that is on multiple dimensions. The following section reviews such attempts.

Multiple-dimensions approaches

The Torrance and Taggart Human Information Processing Survey (1984), categorizes management style into one of four types of information processing: rational-dominant (left-brain), intuitive-dominant (right-brain), mixed (either rational or intuitive), or integrated (both rational and intuitive). Following on their previous research, in a recent article, Taggart and Valenzi (1990) went a step further and presented a conceptual model that elaborates the rational-intuitive HIP metaphor for management style into two broad groupings of three modes each: planning, analysis, and control for the rational style grouping and vision, insight, and sharing for the intuitive style grouping. As a basis for their model, they reviewed innovative management studies, and Eastern and Western philosophical perspectives as a background for synthesizing three lines of neurophysiological research to formulate the six mode HIP management metaphor. Taggart and Valenzi (1990) developed <u>Management Style Inventory (MSI)</u> survey on the basis of their conceptual framework. This assessment tool contains a scale for each of the six modes of HIP metaphor for management style. The MSI is a second generation assessment tool based on a broader neuro-psychological model than first generation instruments, which were designed around the left-brain/ right-brain construct.

The HIP metaphor views management style as a planning versus vision way of preparing for the future, an analysis versus insight way of solving problems, and a control versus sharing way of approaching tasks. The following sections describe the typical management behavior associated with each of six modes or scales of the MSI Survey.

How do managers prepare for the future?

<u>Planning</u> - In planning mode, the managers want to know what will be done and when. To help meet this need, they seek the desired information and prefer to set priorities for things to do and stick to them as best as they can. They arrange events well in advance and organize everything from the start. As a part of this preparation, they organize the relevant information and carefully outline what is needed to get the job done.

<u>Vision</u> - Using a visionary approach, managers prefer to find better ways of doing things based on the information of present ways and better available alternatives. They prefer to devise imaginative ways of getting things done, and to do this they like to work with people who are imaginative. In communicating their preparations for future, they develop recommendations that show ingenuity.

How do managers solve problems?

<u>Analysis</u> - In analysis approach, managers prefer to use accepted approaches to solving problems. They like instructions that are explicit about details. This enables them to follow a prescribed, step-by-step method for solving problems in which they focus on problem details. In arranging their work, they prefer to have a place for everything and everything in its place.

<u>Insight</u> - Following insight mode, managers rely on hunches and first impressions in solving problems. They prefer to follow general instructions and leave the details open. It is important for them to look at a problem as a whole, while approaching it from all sides. They prefer working with general ideas and discovering things through free exploration.

How do managers approach work?

<u>Control</u> - A control oriented manager prefers to work on the tasks alone since they reward the individual, and personal work. In making decisions, they rely on rules and procedures. To help ensure the success of their work, they carry out procedures.

<u>Sharing</u> - In the sharing mode, managers prefer working on tasks in a team, sharing information and resources. They find satisfaction in collective and group work. They want to work on activities that involve cooperation.

They make sure that concerns of others are considered in the work group. To ensure success, they also try to get along with people.

This study, using MSI survey, attempts to answer: how do management style dimensions, discussed above, relate to personality dimensions, such as locus of control and intolerance of ambiguity? The following sections develop hypotheses in this regard.

INTERNAL-EXTERNAL LOCUS OF CONTROL (LOC)

The locus of control (LOC) construct is derived from Rotter's social learning theory (Rotter, 1954). Locus of control has gained considerable amount of attention by behavioral scientists (McGee and Crandall, 1968; Harrison, 1968; Nowicki and Roundtree, 1971; and Bartell, 1969). The popularity of this construct is attributed to its social relevance (Robinson and Shaver, 1985). Internal-external locus of control refers to the extent to which persons perceive contingency relationships between their actions and their outcomes. People believing that they have control over their destinies are called "internals." "Externals," on the other hand, believe that their outcomes are determined by factors extrinsic to themselves (Robinson and Shaver, 1985).

Robinson and Shaver (1985), after reviewing previous locus of control research argued that: "people are handicapped by external locus of control orientation." Their conclusions from the vast research on the locus of control construct were that "externals and internals occupy different positions on the instrumental-expressive behavior dimension." Robinson and Shaver (1985) argued that internals engage in more instrumental-goal oriented activities, whereas externals more often manifest emotional-non-goal directed responses.

Phares (1968), from an information processing orientation, argued that locus of control (being external versus being internal) affects the person's acquisition of information, information-seeking, retention of information, and effectiveness of influencing others. His study specifically addressed the hypothesis that internals are more effective in utilization of the information. Later, Davis and Phares (1967) tested and confirmed Phares (1969) hypothesis and reported that internals are more active in seeking information.

When locus of control research (Robinson and Shaver, 1985; Phares, 1968; and Davis and Phares, 1967) are interpreted in the light of human information processing theory (HIP metaphor) (Taggart and Valenzi, 1990), it can be argued that: mangement style dimensions on MSI survey most closely associated with seeking, and utilizing information will be prefered more by internals (as the scores on the locus of control test rise, so should the scores on the information utilization dimensions of the HIP). As discussed earlier, the management style dimensions most closely associated with information utilization are: planning, vision, and sharing. Based on above arguements it was expected that:

H_1: Managers with highest locus of control (internals) will have highest preference for planning, vision and sharing dimensions of management style.

INTOLERANCE OF AMBIGUITY (IOA)

Intolerance of ambiguity (IOA), as defined by Budner (1962) is "the tendency to perceive (or, interpret) ambiguous situations as sources of threat; and "tolerance of ambiguity" as the tendency to perceive ambiguous situations as desirable." Ambiguity may arise in situations characterized by novelty, complexity, or insolubility.

The IOA construct has been associated with many behavioral constructs like occupational stress (Frone, 1990), role conflict, and prejudice (Norcross, 1988). Kirton (1985) related IOA to adaptation-innovation continuum. According to Kirton (1985), adapters are more concerned with consistency than innovators. Kirton (1985), further argued that adapters are likely to choose strategies and stick with them to achieve high consistency, whereas innovators are more likely to switch between the strategies.

Following on Budner's (1962) theory, managers high in IOA will strive to make situations as unambiguous as possible in order to feel in control and to regain a sense of security. They may perceive ambiguous situations as sources of threat and may prefer planning, analysis, and control dimensions in their effort to reduce ambiguity. Managers with high IOA may rely on these dimensions to maintain control of situations which they may perceive as sources of threat due to ambiguity. Based on above arguements, it was expected that:

H_2: Managers with highest IOA will have highest preference for analysis, control, and planning dimensions of management style.

Furthermore, managers with high IOA will have a tendency to avoid management styles that have a potential of making the situation more ambiguous. Such styles can give managers a perception of lack of control and make them feel threatened in certain situations. In other words, managers with high IOA scores will tend to avoid the management style dimensions like: vision, sharing, and insight, all of which can be perceived as potential sources of ambiguity. Thus, it was expected that:

H_3: Managers with highest IOA will have least preference for vision, sharing, and insight dimensions of management style.

METHODOLOGY

Instruments

The Management Style Inventory (MSI) Survey (Taggart and Valenzi, 1990) was used to measure dimensions of management styles of the subjects. The MSI survey consisted of 30 items: six scales with five items each. The items were answered based on a six-point Likert type scale ranging from "never" to "always." Subject scores were assigned values "1" for never through "6" for "always." Each scale, therefore, had a possible range of responses from 5 to 30.

Subjects' intolerance of ambiguity (IOA) was measured using the Budner's (1962) Intolerance of ambiguity scale. The IOA scale consisted of a total of 16 items. 8 items are positive and the other 8 items are negative items. The items were answered based on a seven point Likert-type scale ranging from "strongly disagree" to "strongly agree." Scoring was accomplished by assigning 7 to strong agreement and 1 to strong disagreement, and adding across items. Negative worded items were scored in the reverse direction. A maximum score of 112 and a minimum score of 16 was possible on this scale.

Finally, subjects' locus of control (LOC) was measured using Rotter's Internal-External Locus of Control scale (Rotter, 1964). The LOC scale consisted of ten sets of statements. Each set consisted of two statements each, one indicating towards the internal and the other towards the external orientation. Internal orientation was scored as "1" and the external orientation as "0." The total score was for an individual was calculated by adding scores on each set of items. A maximum score of 10

1070

and a minimum score of 0 was possible on this scale.

Sample

The questionnaire consisting of three instruments (as discussed in the section above) and questions pertaining to demographic information was administered to soon-to-graduate under-graduate students, in their final year, from a Management class. These students were used as surrogates for working managers. In all 147 students completed questionnaires, but 132 cases were found usable for the study. There were 54 males and 78 females. The average age of the subjects was about 31 years. 101 of them were employed in management related jobs. Both, dependent (management style dimensions) and independent (LOC and IOA) variables were tested for sex, age, and employement status effects using ANOVA. No significant confounding effects due to sex, age, and employement status were found.

Analysis

Means, standard deviations, and inter-correlations between the variables are shown in Table 1. Internal-consistency-reliabilites, which were computed by Cronbach's alpha formula (Guilford, 1954) are also shown in Table 1.

Table 1.

Means & Reliabilties			Correlation Coefficients						
	M	SD	alpha	AN	IN	PL	CL	VI	SH	LOC
AN	19.38	4.01	.73							
IN	18.40	4.19	.72	-.24*						
PL	19.90	4.81	.86	.56**	.12					
CL	18.56	3.56	.61	.36**	.21*	.39**				
VI	21.72	3.71	.69	-.07	.54**	.18*	.30*			
SH	19.43	3.06	.71	.10	.20*	.07	-.14	.28*		
LOC	7.73	1.70	.73	.14	.12	.28*	.11	.26*	.26*	
IOA	54.73	9.75	.80	.39**	-.32**	.15	.12	-.28*	-.13	-.18*

n = 132
*   Significant at .05 level
**   Significant at .001 level
Alpha: Internal consistency Reliability (Cronbach's Alpha)

Since relationship between sets of multiple predictor (independent) and multiple criterion (dependent) variables was required, canonical correlation, a multi variate technique was considered appropriate for analysis (Hair, Anderson, and Tatham, 1987).

RESULTS
    The maximum number of canonical functions theoretically possible are
equal to the minimum number of the variables in either of the two sets
(Hair, Anderson, and Tatham, 1987). There were two variables [IOA and
LOC] in one set; and six [management style dimensions] variables in the
other. Thus, two sets of canonical functions were obtained. The canonical
correlation analysis tests the series of hypotheses that each canonical
correlation is zero.

Table 2. Canonical loadings of Personality
         variables (Variate 1) in Functions 1 & 2

Variable	Function 1	Function 2
Int. of Ambiguity	1.01	0.05
Locus of Control	0.11	1.00

Table 3. Canonical loadings of Management
          Style dimensions (Variate 2)
          in Functions 1 & 2

VARIABLE	FUNCTION 1	FUNCTION 2
ANALYSIS	0.64	-0.01
CONTROL	0.19	0.04
PLANNING	0.06	0.62
VISION	- 0.33	0.42
SHARING	- 0.09	0.52
INSIGHT	- 0.33	- 0.15

    The canonical correlation for the first function was 0.49 (p <
0.0001) and the canonical correlation was 0.40 (p < 0.0087) for the second
function. This suggested that there were significant correlations between
the canonical variates in both the functions. Each side of the function
represents a canonical variate. The canonical variates are interpreted on
the basis of the set of correlation coefficients or canonical loadings.
    In canonical functions, one side (variate) of the functions
represents personality variables and the other set represents dimensions
of management style. As shown in Table 2, the variate that represents
personality variables in first function, had correlation coefficient or
canonical loadings of 1.01 and .11 for IOA and LOC respectively. For a
sample size of around 100 the minimum acceptable value is +/- .19 (Hair,
Anderson and Tatham, 1987). In other words, variate 1 (personality
variables) in the first function represented IOA variable. In second
function, variate 1 (personality variables) had canonical loadings of .05
and 1.00 for IOA and LOC respectively. Thus variate 1 (personality
variables) in the second function represented LOC variable.
    On similar standards, variate 2 (management style dimensions) in
first function, represented: Analysis (0.64), Control (0.19), vision
(-0.33), and insight (- 0.33) dimensions, as shown in Table 3. Planning

(0.06) and sharing (- 0.09) did not represent variate 2 in the first function.

Similarly, variate 2 (management style dimensions) in function 2 was represented by Planning (0.62), Vision (0.42), and Sharing (0.52). Other three dimensions: Analysis (- 0.01), Control (0.04), and Insight (- 0.15), did not have significant canonical loadings.

To put everything in perspective, function 1 represented relationship between IOA (variate1) variable and management style dimensions: analysis, control, vision, and insight (variate 2). Whereas, function 2 represented the relationship between LOC (variate 1) and management style dimensions: planning, vision, and sharing (variate 2).

DISCUSSION

It was expected in Hypothesis 1 that managers with highest LOC scores (internals) will score highest scores on planning, vision, and sharing dimensions of MSI. All three, planning, vision, and sharing dimensions had both positive and significant loadings. Thus hypothesis 1 was supported.

The second hypothesis expected that managers with highest intolerance of ambiguity will score highest in planning, control and analysis dimensions. The loadings for analysis and control dimensions were both positive and significant. Whereas, loading for the planning dimension, although not significant, was in the expected direction. This indicates that, although the managers with high intolerance of ambiguity had a tendency of planning in advance, setting priorities and sticking to them, this preference was not strongly shared among them. Thus hypothesis 2 was supported in part.

The third hypothesis expected that managers with highest intolerance of ambiguity will score lowest in vision, sharing, and insight dimensions of management style. The loadings for vision and insight dimensions were both negative and significant. The loading for the sharing dimension was negative but not significant. This indicates that although the managers with high intolerance of ambiguity had a tendency of not sharing responsibilities and work in teams but this preference was not very strong. One way to explain this may be that, sharing jobs with others induces ambiguity, but the responsibilities are also divided at the same time.

CONCLUSIONS

The results of this research have important implications. Organizations need managers who can deal with environmental uncertainties as business environment in 1990's undergoes macroscopic changes (Chittipeddi and Wallet, 1991). It may be very difficult to analyze and predict the ever-changing- trends in 1990's. Managers, who can tolerate ambiguity; are flexible in their management styles by being both analytical and visionary; and are sharing with their employees are better poised to adopt strategic changes in order to respond to these dynamic changes (Chittipeddi and Wallet, 1991). High IOA and external LOC orientation may pose hurdles and prevent managers successfully deal with these changes and be competitive and productive.

Robinson and Shaver (1985) argued that, "people are handicapped by their external locus of control orientation." The prevailing belief in the literature is that it is desirable to change people in the direction of internality (Robinson and Shaver, 1985). Many internal-external locus of control (IE) change techniques have been proposed by researchers (Dua, 1970; Reimanis and Schaefer, 1970; and Coven, 1970). If IE change techniques are successful in changing the managers' directionality of locus of control towards internality, as claimed by their proponents, this change may be manifested in their management styles. Change of direction towards internality may help managers to plan for future strategic moves, with a broader vision and participatory (sharing) management styles. Furthermore, the negative and significant correlation between IOA and LOC, as shown in Table 1, implies that change in LOC orientation towards internality may help reduce managers' IOA too.

Chittipeddi and Wallet (1991) argued that the model for organizational structure in the 1990's will be that of "symphonic orchestra, as layers of management continue to be thinned out, and hierarchies are replaced by networks." Peters (1988) in the same vein, argued that organizations in 1990's and beyond will resemble "Fleet-of-Foot" organization, which is characterized by "flexibility, adaptiveness, and action." Chittipeddi and Wallet (1991) also emphasized the necessity of "information bases" for employees to share responsibilities with the managers. Organizations, while adopting such structures need managers, especially members of their top-management-team (TMT) who are receptive to sharing information and responsibility with their employees without feeling threatened of ambiguity that may arise as a result.

Finally, discussion of one caveat is in order. The use of students as a surrogate for managers might reduce the external validity of the study. But, playing as devil's advocate, one can argue, as believed by many trait theorists (Phares, 1984; and Pervin, 1984), that personality traits like LOC and IOA are quite stable over time. Alternatively said, the soon-to-graduate, students might go to work for organizations with same personality traits as they demonstrated while they were students. Furthermore, majority of the students were employed in management related jobs. Thus, it can also be argued that the subjects may have already acquired their preferred management styles while working in their jobs or while they are being trained to be managers. To conclude, we hope that above arguements may have convinced readers that the external validity of the study may not have suffered severely. Dobbins, Lane, and Steiner (1988) in the same vein argued that, all the research with student subjects should not be categorized as externally invalid as it may "seem comparable to throwing out the baby with the bath water."

REFERENCES*

Agor, W. H., (1984). Intuitive Management: Integrating Left and Right Brain Management Skill, Englewood, New Jersey, Prentice Hall, Inc.

Bartel, N. R. (1969). "Locus of Control and Acheivement in Middle Class and Lower Class Children," Dissertation Abstracts International, 29, 2991.

Briggs, K. C., and Myers, I. B., 1962, Myers-Briggs Type Indicator, Palo Alto, California, Consulting Psychologists Press.

Brockhaus, R. H., and Horwitz, P. S. (1986). "The Psychology of Entrepreneur," in D. L. Sexton and R. W. Smilor, eds., The Art and Science of Entrepreneurship. Cambridge, MA: Ballinger.

_____
* Selected list of references. Complete list is available from the author on request.

Brockhaus, R. H. (1982). "The Psychology of the Entrepreuner," in C. A. Kent, D. L. Sexton, and K. H. Vesper, eds., Encyclopedia of Entrepreneurship. Englewood Cliffs, NJ: Prentice-Hall, 39-56.

Budner, S., 1962, "Intolerance of Ambiguity as a Personality Variable," Journal of Personality, 30, 29-50.

Chittipeddi, K., and Wallet, T. A. (1991). "Entrepreneurship and Competitive Strategy for the 1990's," Journal of Small Business Management, January, 94-98.

Coven, A. B., 1970, "The Effects of Counselling and Verbal Reinforcement on the Internal - External Control of the Disabled," Dissertation Abstracts International, 31, 1006.

Crandall, N. F., and Wooton, L. M. (1978). Development Strategies of Organizational Productivity," California Management Review., vol. 21, no. 2, 37-46.

Davis, W. L., and Phares, E. J., 1967, "Internal - external control as a determinate of Information - seeking in a social influence situation," Journal of Personality, 35, 547-561.

Dobbins, G. H., Lane, I. M., and Steiner, D. D. (1988). "A Note on the Role of Laboratory Methodologies in Applied Behavioral Research: Don't Throw Out the Baby with the Bath Water," Journal of Organizational Behavior, vol. 9, 281-286.

BIOGRAPHICAL SKETCH

Davinder Pal Singh Arora is doctoral student in the Department of Management and International Business, School of Business Administration, Florida International University, Miami, Florida. He earned his Master of Science in Industrial Engineering from University of Miami, Florida. His undergraduate degree is in Mechanical Engineering from India. Davinder has a practical experience of 5 years in engineering field. His present research interest are in the areas of Strategic Management, Small business administration, quality and productivity issues.

Productivity & Quality Management Frontiers-IV, edited by Sumanth, Edosomwan, Poupart, and Sink. ©1993 Institute of Industrial Engineers.

The Theory of Grand Strategy Systems: Quality and Productivity Improvement and Large-Scale Organizational Change

D.S. Sink
Virginia Polytechnic Institute & State University
Blacksburg, Virginia USA

D.J. Monetta
Department of Defense
Washington, D.C. USA

ABSTRACT

Managing organizational performance and success has become increasingly challenging and difficult. Just improving is no longer enough; today, an organization's rate of improvement is a deciding factor. It is particularly difficult to implement continuous improvement efforts in the "permanent white water" most organizations are encountering, Vaill (1989). Top management teams must possess profound knowledge in order to lead the positive change necessary to perform competitively.

The requirement for systems thinking has spurred the development of theories and methods for managing large-scale organizational change, Kilmann (1989) and Mohrman (1989). Total Quality Management, Total Quality Leadership, Total Quality, Corporate Wide Quality Control, "Big Q", and Continuous Improvement are the cutting edge themes of the '90s. They integrate some twenty years of experience, acquired knowledge and lessons learned about what does not work, and perhaps a few lessons regarding what does work.

This paper is an attempt to portray, both conceptually and operationally, theory and methods for completing the transformation espoused by Deming and others, Deming (1986) and Deming (1991). Although our theory and methods were developed as a result of over twenty years of research, teaching, consulting and practice, we prescribe hesitantly, since complex socio-technical systems are inherently varied and dynamic. However, what we describe is working for us, and we hope it provides insights to you.

Table 1
Summary of Characteristics of Interview Subjects, Employing Organizations, and Quality/Productivity Programs

Company A: **Financial services company, $100 million annual sales, 350 employees.**
Employee interviewee: Services representative, female, 25 years old, 4 years with company.

Manager interviewee: Director of quality management, male, 35 years old, supervises 15 people, 2 years with company.

Quality/productivity program: 9 months old. Includes TQM orientation, problem solving and process management teams, team building training.

Company B: **Paper, packaging and supplies distributor, $30 million annual sales, 41 employees.**
Employee interviewee: Sales representative, female, 25 years old, 4 years with company.

Manager interviewee: Delivery supervisor, female, 26 years old, supervises over 20 employees, 5 years with company.

Quality/productivity program: 5 months old at employee level; 1 year old at management level. Includes problem solving training, use of cross-functional teams, branch steering team, and work group teams.

Company C: **Hospital (over 500 beds), over 3,000 employees.**
Employee interviewee: Registered nurse, female, 28 years old, 6 years with company.

Manager interviewee: Director of health education services, female, 40 years old, supervises 57 employees, 15 years with the company.

Quality/productivity program: 6 years old. Utilizes a companywide committee with a representative from each department.

Company D: **Medical diagnostic instrument manufacturer, $1.2 billion annual sales, 1500 employees.**
Employee interviewee: Scientist, male, 30 years old, 7 years with the company.

Manager interviewee: Technical support group manager, female, 39 years old, supervises 7 employees, 15 years with the company.

Quality/productivity program: 7 years old. Includes employee training, TQM orientation, and quality improvement teams.

Table 2
Interview Questions

1. Does a quality improvement program provide any advantages to you as an employee (for manager interviewees: and as a manager)? If so, what are these advantages?

2. Can you rank these advantages in terms of their importance to you?

3. Does a quality improvement program provide any disadvantages to you? If so, what are these disadvantages?

4. Can you rank these disadvantages in terms of their importance to you?

5. Sometimes quality improvement programs encounter problems which must be dealt with before the program can succeed. Do you see any problems which must be addressed?

6. (For each problem): Can you describe the problem?

7. (For each problem): Do you have any ideas for solving the problem?

8. Which of these problems are the most difficult to solve?

9. What do you see as the goals of the quality improvement program?

10. What must you have (for manager interviewees: as a manager) to work toward achieving these goals?

11. What must your work unit (for manager interviewees: your employees) have to work toward achieving these goals?

Productivity & Quality Management Frontiers-IV, edited by Sumanth, Edosomwan, Poupart, and Sink. ©1993 Institute of Industrial Engineers.

TQM in the Public Sector: Initiating the Revolution

E. West
Portland State University
Portland, Oregon USA

ABSTRACT

Is it possible for a quality program to succeed in an organization where support is mixed for this new program? What are the strategies necessary to overcome criticisms like:

--   This "quality thing" is just another excuse for downsizing.

--   Quality takes too much time. How can we do this in addition to everything else we're expected to do?

--   It will never work in a university setting. Ever.

This article describes the experiences of one quality team known as "FASST," which is an acronym for "Faculty and Student Services Team." The team is comprised of staff members within the School of Business Administration at Portland State University.

The push for quality is occurring while resources are diminishing primarily as a consequence of Measure 5, a property tax limitation bill which the voters of Oregon passed in 1990. As a result of Measure 5, Portland State is experiencing a 20 percent cutback in state funding. The passage of the bill has fostered an urgent need to reexamine the university system in order to identify more efficient and effective ways of delivering its services.

Enter quality.

What sorts of strategies can an initial quality team use to ensure success of its projects? This article answers that question.

Key words: university, quality, change, support staff.

INTRODUCTION

In his book, <u>Managing as a Performing Art</u>, Peter Vaill (1989) writes the following:

> A manager who attended a seminar I was conducting . . . supplied me with the
> metaphor that in various ways runs all through this book. It is the metaphor of
> "permanent white water." "Most managers are taught to think of themselves as
> paddling their canoes on calm, still lakes," he said. "They're led to believe that
> they should be pretty much able to go where they want, when they want, using
> means that are under their control. Sure there will be temporary disruptions during
> changes of various sorts--periods when they'll have to shoot the rapids in their
> canoes--but the disruptions will be temporary, and when things settle back down,
> they'll be back in the calm, still lake mode. But is has been my experience," he
> concluded, "that you never get out of the rapids! No sooner do you begin to digest
> one change than another one comes along to keep things unstuck. In fact, there are
> usually lots of changes going on at once. The feeling is one of continuous upset and
> chaos" (p. 2).

The quality revolution has catapulted American businesses into "permanent white water."
And public organizations are not immune from this experience. "Continuous upset and
chaos" is also characteristic of the environment which organizational support staff face as
a consequence of the emphasis on quality. This paper discusses the impact of the quality
movement in the School of Business at Portland State University with particular emphasis
on the support staff, the Faculty and Student Services Team (FASST). This group of staff
members have managed to gain control of their wildly rocking boat buffeted by the white
water of the quality revolution.

THE SETTING

Portland State University is an urban university situated in downtown Portland, the major
population, business, and high technology center in the state of Oregon. Founded in 1946
in response to returning World War II veterans, Portland State became a degree-granting
college in 1955 and a university in 1969.

Almost 60 percent of Oregon's population lives within commuting distance of the campus.
Current enrollment is more than 16,000 students with close to 40,000 individuals in credit
or noncredit classes each year.

External Pressure Toward Change
In 1990, the voters of Oregon passed a property tax limitation bill, known as Measure 5,
which will siphon off hundreds of millions of state dollars to replace property tax revenue
lost to local school districts and in the process necessitate massive cutbacks in spending
for public institutions, including higher education. This event has created stress and great
concern for the future of higher education. However, it has also fostered an even more

urgent need to reexamine the university system in order to identify more efficient and effective ways of delivering its services. Enter quality.

QUALITY AND THE UNIVERSITY

The commitment by the University to Total Quality Management (TQM) has been substantial. The President of the University, Judith Ramaley, and her administrative team have made plans to infuse the quality management philosophy into University administrative operations. The University has committed half of the time of one Assistant Vice President to the implementation of TQM and additional support and training staff. During 1990-1991, $50,000 was budgeted for quality concerns, and during the next biennium more than $40,000 has been budgeted per year. The administration has agreed to provide support for TQM training for the various academic units that populate the campus. Additionally, the President has been very vocal in her support of the quality approach championed by the School of Business in the face of internal University concern, resistance, and opposition.

The School of Business
The School of Business has nearly 2,500 enrolled students, of whom 700 are engaged in graduate-level study. At the undergraduate level, students may choose from options in accounting, finance, general business, management, human resources, MIS/quantitative methods, marketing, and advertising.

Critics of business education have suggested the following: business curricula and faculty research are so focused on functional specialties (so-called "silos") that students learn and are evaluated on their knowledge of functional competencies rather than their comprehension of managing the total business operation successfully. Responding to the needs and criticism of local and national industry leaders, the School of Business (SBA) made a determined effort beginning in the spring of 1991 to integrate quality concepts into its curriculum and administration.

Initial efforts to adopt quality centered around faculty development. Activities included the following: plant tours to Oregon Cutting Systems Division of Blount, Precision Castparts, Boeing, NEC, Tektronix, and others; company presentations from Xerox, Hewlett-Packard, Cadillac, US West Communications, and Pacific Telesis; company partnerships including faculty working with Northwest Natural Gas; and off-site training. An important component of the training has been a series of lectures by a number of well-known quality experts including Richard Schonberger and Jinichiro Nakane.

Embracing quality has changed many aspects of the School of Business. Functional departments (finance, marketing, etc.) were disbanded both to eliminate the divisions between silos and respond to cutbacks necessitated by Measure 5. Staff and faculty formed a number of teams and were empowered to make decisions on such matters as computer resources, annual review and merit, and services for faculty.

The FASST

The decision to move in the direction of TQM in the School of Business led to the establishment of the Faculty and Student Services Team (FASST) whose main function involved managing the School's basic service functions: Student Services, Faculty Services, and the Deans' Office. The FASST, consisting of administrative assistants, clerical specialists, and faculty has been involved in significant training, process mapping, process improvement, and surveys of customer needs.

The first meeting of the FASST occurred one hot July afternoon in 1991. There were a dozen people in attendance, including the Dean of the School of Business. People were unclear why the meeting had been called, but one thing was certain--there were no more separate departments in the Business School and life was never going to be the same. Things were changing. There was much talk about quality and continuous improvement and team building and empowerment. People were nervous and wondered how this was going to affect the operation of the School.

The Dean made a few introductory remarks and then the facilitator took over, urging everyone to remember that somehow, some way the group would get organized and would be ready for all 55 returning professors on September 16. There was much to be done. Silence greeted most of her words. People remained unconvinced. She picked up the green dry-erase marker and wrote "mission" on the board and then posed the question-- "What do you think our mission ought to be?"

More silence. Slowly people began to contribute and the words went up on the board to reflect their thoughts. About thirty minutes later, the group seemed energized and pleased with the mission statement they had created: "To facilitate faculty performance in teaching, research and service through efficient teamwork." And so the FASST was born and life was never the same again in the School of Business.

The next order of business was a major one--what were the tasks that had to be done in order to facilitate this "faculty performance"? Dolores Timmins, the former finance department secretary, had brought her list and the facilitator began to write her ideas on the board. Gradually people began to add to those already listed and the board began to fill up with terms like: faculty, sick leave reports, debit cards, travel information forms, and petitions. Before the meeting ended the group decided that prior to the next meeting each person in the group would write tasks needing to be done on separate 3" x 5" index cards and then would attempt to group them according to functional similarity.

Between July and the middle of September the energies of the group were directed toward work redesign issues. The major elements of this consisted of identification of tasks as they were being currently done and discussion of the most appropriate work unit in the SBA that should be responsible for them. What the group spent 16 meetings doing over the course of the eight weeks was threefold: (1) identification of 167 discrete tasks that the members identified as being central to the functioning of the school; (2) grouping those into categories that made sense functionally in terms of similarity of function; and then (3) deciding which office unit would have primary responsibility for the delivery of those services. There were many stormy meetings as the group struggled to build the team, resolve conflict in as humane a way as possible, deal with faculty who were even more disturbed than the staff about all the changes going on and generally try to remain calm in the face of tumultuous changes occurring on a daily basis.

What emerged by the middle of September from the group was the following:

1. The "Team Activity Report" which identified the office in the SBA having primary responsibility for delivery of each service.

2. A primer on often-used services and processes designed to alert faculty to changes in such areas as book orders and debit cards.

3. A new telephone and office directory for the SBA.

What additionally had developed over the two months was a team sensitive to delivering quality services that had worked through its "forming stage" and struggled through its "storming" (Tuckman & Jensen, 1977). Kanter has written that "most people want and need to feel in control of the events around them" (1985). The FASST confronted tumultuous changes in their work environment in an organized fashion, thereby reducing the loss of control they were experiencing. These activities also built consensus for the changes happening in the SBA, an important element in any change process.

TRAINING IN THE TOOLS OF QUALITY

Once the challenge of reorganizing in order to be ready for fall quarter was met, the FASST turned its attention to the issues of becoming skilled in some of the tools of quality. Quality training during 1991-1992 took the form of instruction in the following areas: creative problem solving, a brainstorming technique; designing and interpreting customer survey data, complete with histogram construction; understanding the relationship between customer satisfaction and quality issues; and the rudiments of process mapping.

A unifying theme throughout the training was that of learning to problem solve by taking on the perspective of the customer--by looking at the problem through the customers' eyes. "Customers," as defined by the FASST, were primarily students and faculty and other staff members within the SBA and PSU community.

Creative Problem Solving

It became apparent in the early weeks of fall quarter that without the presence of the now defunct departments, dissemination of information from the Deans' Office and University community was creating problems for the group. How could they be responsive to customers' questions when they didn't know the answers? Because the group had identified learning creative problem solving (CPS) as their number one priority in an earlier survey of training needs conducted by their facilitator, it was the group's decision that CPS would be used in order to solve their communication problems.

Over the course of the next six meetings, the facilitator led the group through a variety of problem-solving steps. The group identified the problem as: "How might we identify what we need to know and establish an accurate and timely network of communication within the FASST and the School of Business?" In response to this problem, the FASST generated 56 solutions, of which 6 were implemented in the form of an action plan.

It was the consensus of the team that the frustration, conflict, and isolation that followed reorganization and interrupted communication flow was reduced due to a variety of solutions implemented including: the publication of an internal newsletter, regular meetings of the Deans' Office, and tours of the various offices represented by the FASST to facilitate understanding of their contributions to the overall goals of the SBA.

The group made a formal presentation of their findings and an update on their progress to the Dean of the Business School, members of his executive team, and the Vice President of Finance and Administration and several of her associates. After a discussion following their formal presentation, the Vice President invited several members of the FASST as quality resource experts to a meeting she was chairing concerning the Quality Initiative at PSU.

Surveying the Customers
In an effort to improve the quality of service provided to the SBA faculty through the newly reorganized Faculty Services office, a customer survey was distributed to 60 faculty. Twenty-five responses (42 percent) were received and the results were summarized and histograms created. Several issues were targeted for improvement based upon the results. Some of the improvements that have occurred as a consequence of the survey include the following: a new photocopy machine was added to Faculty Services to improve turnaround time and the quality of in-house copying; the front work area was redesigned to utilize the phone jack for the newly installed fax machine and to access the electrical outlet for a computer; and a bulletin board was installed to post information of interest to faculty members. Members of Faculty Services agreed that improvements in targeted areas have increased their quality and efficiency and relieved frustration for both faculty and staff.

This office undertook a second survey of faculty needs during the spring of 1992 which resulted in their work order form being redesigned in order to be more responsive to faculty specifications. In the spirit of continuous improvement, Faculty Services staff will be meeting with some of their customers in a focus group to gather further information in order to improve the quality of their services.

Survey Interpretation, Customer Satisfaction, and Process Mapping
The FASST expanded its understanding of the tools of quality by utilizing the expertise of several professors in the SBA. Professor Alan Raedels kicked off the quality series with a

discussion and explanation of interpretation issues relating to the customer survey that Faculty Services had conducted during fall quarter. Raedels explained how to figure both the mean and the median, and the session required team members to determine the median based on the information presented in response to one of the survey questions.

Professor Scott Dawson discussed the idea of customer satisfaction as it related to quality issues. Professor Ellen West, who was also the facilitator of the group, explained the basics of process mapping at a subsequent meeting after which the group embarked on mapping significant processes relevant to each office represented in the FASST. The group will continue to map processes in order to better understand each office's functions as well as continue to streamline and improve efficiencies within the SBA. It has proved to be a useful way of communicating the intricacies of what each office does and thus enhance the communication level within the FASST.

Portland Quality Days
Team members took an active role in Portland Quality Days which were held on April 14 and 15, 1992. The Quality Days was a two-day educational program sponsored by the School of Business and Xerox Corporation. The objective of the program was to provide educational opportunities for those interested in Total Quality Management. Further, the program was designed to facilitate networking of those involved with quality efforts in order to share success strategies.

The TQM Team User Fair was held as part of the Quality Days. The User Fair was similar to a high school science fair, where those who have completed successful TQM-related projects shared their experiences with those from other firms who were interested in how TQM was applied and what results had been achieved. Members of the FASST took an active role in the Quality Days and were responsible for telling the FASST story at the User Fair booth. Team members also had the opportunity to visit other booths representing area firms and learn about successful quality projects from the team members.

CRITICAL SUCCESS FACTORS

In retrospect a variety of significant learnings dealing with change based upon the experiences of the FASST this year are appropriate to mention.

1. Capitalize/build upon your successes. Because the group experienced a very stressful beginning, it seemed necessary to take every opportunity to celebrate in order to sustain the momentum for change. This approach has become part of the FASST culture, and, for example, they celebrate everyone's birthday complete with cake at their regular meetings. In February the team initiated its "Friday Night at the Flicks" series, gathering in one of the seminar rooms to watch "Thelma and Louise," relax, and nibble tasty edibles. Halloween, Christmas, and St. Patrick's Day with green popcorn were also recognized by the team with special efforts. In August the group will celebrate its first anniversary with a buffet luncheon,

distribution of award certificates for the first year's service by the Dean, and entertainment in the form of the first annual "FASST Follies." Although this fun may seem excessive to some, it is much like an emotional bank account (Covey, 1989) which the group may draw upon during more tense and stressful times. Since the University is having to absorb a 20 percent cutback in its operating budget due to the impact of Measure 5, a few festivities go a long way toward easing the tension.

The report that the group made to key decision makers in the SBA and University relative to its progress concerning quality issues during the spring of 1992 was an important step in the group's growth process. It resulted in increased visibility and exposure of group members and accomplishments of the team and was an important element in building the cohesion of the team. It also led to a variety of invitations from around the campus to individual team members for help in quality-related problems.

2. Communicate, communicate, communicate. Harvey has written that "creating a climate where everyone involved in the change program feels free and not threatened to communicate with others can minimize resistance in the long run" (Harvey & Brown, 1992). It was critical from the start that the group inform other members of the SBA regarding its activities. Since the group began in 1991, 43 meeting times ago, the minutes have appeared subsequent to every meeting for approval by the group. A copy of these have been placed in a notebook in the staff and faculty lounge of the Business School building so that anyone interested can read about the activities that occurred during one of the weekly meetings. The presentation to decision makers within the University community was also an effective method of sharing the FASST story. In an effort to provide a more formal means of communicating within the SBA and "manage" the PR side of the change (Pokras, 1989), a newsletter written and edited by members of the FASST was created during winter quarter of 1992. It has proven to be an effective and useful way to communicate news to faculty and staff within the SBA. All team members volunteered their services at the TQM User Fair and were able to share their story with interested fair goers. A videotape depicting the progress the group has made using the tools of quality is being designed and filmed this summer with the help of the campus TV Services unit. As indicated earlier, several members of the FASST have been asked by other campus units to share their expertise on teams and quality and in the process become change agents for the rest of the University. The customer surveys and follow-up letters were another important way of keeping in touch with those the FASST was serving.

3. Network. Since the FASST was the first quality-related team on the campus, it seemed important to be able to establish linkages with key groups which might impact the success of the team. Internally, members of the FASST who worked in the office of the Dean did an effective job of keeping these important resources informed of the team's progress. Additionally, the Dean or his representative

attended meetings occasionally in order to answer questions, clarify expectations, etc. External to the School of Business, establishing a working relationship with Finance and Administration, the unit on the campus charged with initiating the Quality Initiative, was a critical step in building credibility for the work the group had been doing.

4.   Train, train, train. Critical to the success of their team was the decision by the members of the FASST to continue meeting in order to improve their skill set, specifically in the area of quality. Fortunately, this decision was supported by the administration of the SBA in terms of resources. Early during fall quarter, their facilitator surveyed the team members in order to assess their needs and interests in the area of training. A training plan was presented to the group in October which the group approved. Both Schonberger (1990) and Aguayo (1991) among others have written about the need for appropriate training to support a quality effort. The commitment of School resources dedicated to training the FASST in quality methods was a significant indication of top management's belief in the importance of this training.

5.   Light many fires. Shepard (1975) in his article "Rules of Thumb for Change Agents," described the importance of using multiple interventions--"lighting many fires"--in creating change in organizations. He said, "If many interdependent subsystems are catalyzed . . ., the entire system can begin to move" (p. 296). Besides the move toward quality that the School of Business has initiated during 1991-1992, the administration of Portland State has selected the Office of Finance and Administration (FADM) to implement the University's "Quality Initiative." This unit represents the "service side" of the University and is comprised of seven separate areas including: Business Affairs, the Budget Office, Auxiliary Services, Campus Safety and Security, Computing and Information Systems, Personnel Services, and the Physical Plant. The various units represented in FADM have surveyed their customers in order to identify critical processes that would be useful to examine and an advisory group has been selected to help guide this quality effort.

CONCLUSION

Although the University is in the process of layoffs and downsizing as a consequence of the impact of Measure 5, plans regarding the Quality Initiative continue to move forward on the campus and within the SBA. The FASST will be examining its critical processes during 1992-1993 in order to continue to improve its services. The team has played a central role in the efforts of the SBA to move toward a quality method of management. It will continue to do so in the future.

REFERENCES

Aguayo, Rafael (1991) <u>Dr. Deming</u>, New York, Simon & Schuster.

Covey, Stephen R. (1989) <u>The Seven Habits of Highly Effective People</u>, New York, Simon & Schuster.

Harvey, Donald and Brown, Donald R. (1992) <u>An Experiential Approach to Organization Development</u>, Englewood Cliffs, New Jersey, Prentice Hall.

Kanter, Rosabeth (1985) "Managing the Human Side of Change," <u>Management Review</u>, April 1985, pp. 52-56.

Pokras, Sandy (1989) <u>Systematic Problem Solving and Decision-Making</u>, Los Altos, California, Crisp Publications, Inc.

Shepard, H.A. (1975) "Rules of Thumb for Change Agents," <u>OD Practitioner</u>, vol. 7, no. 3, pp. 1-5.

Schonberger, Richard (1990) <u>Building a Chain of Customers</u>, New York, The Free Press.

Tuckman, B.W. and Jensen, M.C. (1977) "Stages of Small-Group Development Revisited," <u>Group and Organizational Studies</u>, pp. 419-427.

Vaill, Peter b. (1989) <u>Managing as a Performing Art</u>, San Francisco, California, Jossey-Bass Publishers.

BIOGRAPHICAL SKETCH

Ellen West is an Assistant Professor in the School of Business Administration at Portland State University, Portland, Oregon, USA. She teaches in the areas of organizational development and organizational behavior. For the past year she has been the facilitator for the Faculty and Student Services Team (FASST).

Productivity & Quality Management Frontiers-IV, edited by Sumanth, Edosomwan, Poupart, and Sink. ©1993 Institute of Industrial Engineers.

"Time-Based" Gainsharing Plans

E.M. Dar-El and I. Meshoulam
Technion, Israel Institute of Technology
Technion City, Haifa ISRAEL

ABSTRACT

Gainsharing plans are traditionally associated with monetary rewards. But it is also well known that earning "free time" can be an effective motivator. For example, we know that employee groups are able to complete their respective missions in greatly reduced times in order to achieve some time-based benefit, such as, holding a Christmas party in company time.

Time-based reward plans have the distinct advantage of being applicable to both private and public service organizations, whereas monetary-based reward plans, for various reasons, are generally not available for employees in public utilities (e.g., postal services, IRS, city council services, military facilities, non-profit organizations, and so on).

The paper discusses the equivalence between performance improvements (using regular money-based bonuses) and earned time-based hours. This is a complex problem, since an employee's working time at high performance, also contributes to the lowering of the company's unit overhead costs. Discussions are dichotomized in two dimensions - between the private and public sectors, and between 'payments' of the rewards ('earned free time', or, EFT) in the long term and short term.

Earning free time could operate in a manner similer to companies that offer 'long service leave' to employees of long standing, such as in Australia, after ten to fifteen years of continuous service. It has the advantage of ensuring the long term interest and loyalty to the company, while providing the means for a long paid vacation which could be of great physical and psychological benefit to the employee and indirectly, to the company. It also provides an opportunity for organizational changes to be introduced while most workers in a department are away on extended leave.

Key Words: Earned Free Time; Gainsharing; Long Service Leave.

INTRODUCTION

Production-based bonus plans are typically used for encouraging superior performances, and are always associated with monetary rewards. It is well known that earning "free time", though not used as a basis for bonus plans, can also be an effective motivator. For example, we know that employee groups are able to complete their respective missions in greatly reduced times in order to achieve some time-based benefit, such as, holding a Christmas party in company time, or, getting several hours off work (as an add-on to the weekend). However, thus far, the literature has generally not formally dealt with utilizing "free time" as a means for achieving higher plant performances.

Time-based reward plans has the distinct advantage of being applicable to both private and public service organizations, whereas monetary-based reward plans, for various reasons, are generally not available for employees in public utilities (e.g., postal services, IRS, city council services, military facilities, non-profit organizations, and so on). This aspect will be discussed at length in the paper.

It would be necessary to determine an equivalence between performance improvements (using regular money-based bonuses) and earned time-based hours. This is a complex problem, since an employee's working time at high performance, also contributes to the lowering of the company's unit overhead costs. Also to be addressed, is how the 'Earned Free Time' (abbreviated to 'EFT') should be utilized so as not to disrupt production. This aspect too will be discussed in some detail.

This paper considers the problem as being dichotomized in two dimensions - between the private and public sectors, and between 'payments' of the rewards ('free days') in the long term or short term. Discussion will begin with 'long term' reward systems for both sectors, followed by an analysis for the 'short term' case.

THE REWARD PLAN

Our assumption is that the reward plan, in order to attract and motivate, must be both performance-based and global in its application. Without question, performance based 'Gainsharing' plans are the only type of reward plan that could meet these requirements, since it is the only productivity-based reward system compatible with organizationally based improvement programs such as Total Quality Management (TQM) - the current rage in most organizations, whether in the private or public sector. The implication with gainsharing, is that one can always define some appropriate 'surrogate' measure(s) for determining the performance of the organization.

Industrial companies, currently using gainsharing plans, reward their employees with cash bonuses. We will consider how a part, or, all of this bonus, can be utilized for generating EFT (Earned Free Time). Most, if not all public utilities do not have this choice. They simply do not operate performance-based reward plans because of budgetary, or, regulatory restrictions. Gainsharing plans created for public utilities would be designed specifically as a means for rewarding superior performances through EFT.

THE 'LONG TERM' REWARD PLAN

By long term, we mean that employees may utilize their EFT bonuses, at least one year after the bonuses were earned. Employers on the other hand, may prefer that the bonuses accumulate for a minimum of three years - for instance, to coincide with some planned organizational changes.

The practice of allowing employees to have extra long paid leave is not new. For instance, labor laws in Australia, mandates that an employee may take a 3-month 'Long Service' paid leave after serving ten years, or, a 6-month paid leave after serving fifteen years with a company. Examples exist in other companies operating with similar plans, as with the Intel Corp. (USA), without being obliged to do so through labor laws.

Two propriety production-based gainsharing plans exist - IMPROSHARE [Fien (1981)] and SHRED COST [Dar-El)]. Both are 50:50 sharing plans - i.e., between the company owners and the employee group covered by the plan. Once the appropriate surrogate performance measure(s) are defined, we are able to set up the **monetary** bonus to employees. Our task then, is to determine an equivalent conversion from 'monetary units' to 'free time', or EFT.

A major consideration for implementing such plans would be its potential cost to the overall system. Let us consider the cost to the company, when an employee utilizes a paid free hour at some time in the future. The basis for these calculations is that the employer must replace the absent employee by another employee, in order that the benefits of production are not lost. The most likely replacement procedure is to allow other employees to work overtime, but this is very costly and could discourage the adoption of the plan. Instead, we assume that a replacement employee is employed to stand in for the employee during the time he utilizes his EFTs. The justification for this action is based on the assumption that at times, neither overtime, nor additional workers may be needed, and the company would consequently benefit financially.

The following cost items apply:
- a) The gross wages of the employee - let this be $w per hour.
- b) The social benefits that the employee must set aside - estimated at $w per hr.
- c) The cost of the replacement employee - estimated at $ w per hour.
- d) The social benefits of the replacement employee - estimated at $ w per hr.

The following cost items are neglected:
- i) The increased wage rate of the employee over and above 'cost-of-living' increases, between the point at which the bonus was earned and the time at when the free time is utilized.
- ii) Additional training needed for the replacement employee and the consequential loss of production. Else, the overtime expenses incurred on utilizing existing employees for doing the extra work.

Application To The Private Sector.

Adding the cost items a) to d), gives a total of $4w per hour. Since we operate the reward plan on a 50:50 sharing deal, then overall, a total productivity gain of $8w would be needed in order to justify an EFT of $w. We can say the same thing with percentages - an employee can get a 1% EFT in lieu of an 4% cash bonus (the employee share of the overall productivity gain).

Let us illustrate this category with an example in which an employee considers converting **all** his cash bonuses into EFT. Assume that the gainsharing bonus rate hovers around the 24% mark for some months (the 'Target Bonus' [Dar-El (1986)] is obviously above the 24%. The Target Bonus used in SHRED COST, represents the **long term** average bonus that could be earned by employees). Let the employee's gross wage be $16 per hour, and let us assume that he works an average of 180 hours per month.

On the one hand, his monthly cash bonus would average at about -
$$24_{/2} \cdot 180 \cdot 16 \cdot 1_{/100} = \$ 345.6$$

Converting this cash bonus into EFT makes it equivalent to -
$$\$ 345.6_{/4} = \$ 86.4$$
or, $$86.4_{/16} = 5.4 \text{ hours of EFT}.$$

The employee must decide between, either receiving $345.6 in cash, or, accumulating 5.4 hours of paid 'free time' to be enjoyed sometime in the future.

A year of 'earning' at this rate, means an accumulation of $12 \cdot 5.4 = 64.8$ hours per year (equivalent to 8.1 days), or:
> over three years, this amounts to 24.3 days (nearly 5 weeks)
> over five years, this amounts to 40.5 days (over eight weeks)
> over ten years, this amounts to 81 days (over sixteen weeks - nearly four months).

How Would it Operate? Operation of the plan is quite straightforward. The employee should determine his own goals, for example, to have a 2-month vacation in Florida, or, to utilize the time to learn new skills, or write a book, etc. Adding his regular vacations to his earned free days, could accumulate to three months. The employee then negotiates with the employer some months ahead of the time that he wishes to to utilize his EFTs and vacations.

The process should be reversible in the sense that an employee may decide at some time later, that he would prefer the cash bonus instead of the accumulated free time. This request should be acceptable to the company, who after all, received the money in the first place. However, the employee would be paid at the rate at which the bonuses were earned, together with some nominal interest since this money should be considered as if it was 'invested' in the company.

Advantages to the Employee:
> i) The means for planning and taking a long vacation (e.g.,with his family).
> ii) The opportunity to coordinate the vacation timing with a working spouse.
> iii) The ability to cancel the EFT plan and receive the accumulated cash bonus.
> iv) Savings in Income tax (since cash bonuses are taxed at a higher marginal rate).
> v) Free time for renewal, gaining new skills, development, etc.

Advantages to the Company:
> i)   The possibility of increased savings by not utilizing the 'replacement' employee.
> ii) The availability of cash loans to the company at no interest and 'no cover'.
> iii) To utilize the vacation timing for introducing organizational changes in the dept.
> iv) To benefit by having 'healthier' employees after these prolonged vacations.
> v)   Encouraging employees to take their vacations during difficult economic times.

Disadvantages to the Company:
   i) Paying a higher salary rate (than from the COL) at the time of the vacations.
   ii) The vacation timing turns out to be 'inconvenient'.
   iii) The cost for maintaining bonus and EFT records for each employee.
   v) Added benefit for attracting potential employees.

Application To The Public Sector.

Budgets in the public sector are generally fixed for a particular year. However, in the subsequent year, the budgets are invariably increased - more often, at a higher rate than inflation. Gainsharing plans in public services simply do not work since there is generally no budget for rewarding superior performances - except in cases where the equivalent of hard cash is actually saved (as in reduced energy expenses, etc.).

From where should the money come from which will enable employees to take EFTs? The following items are given as the possible sources:
   i) Accumulated savings on operating budgets.
   ii) Increases in subsequent budgets.

Budget requests for a subsequent year should include the total value of the EFT amount earned (by all employees) in the current year, if item ii) is to be the **sole** method used for covering the employees going on future vacations. We would suggest that this method typifies an extreme case, it being more usual to rely on items i) - the accumulated savings, and by simply requiring other employees to do the work of the person on vacation, but without overtime (the usual inflated manpower status in most public services would support this argument).

Budget requests may also need to include the the cost of hiring temporary workers for covering the periods employees are expected to be on EFT vacations. Consequently, in spite of the reliance on items i) and ii) above, it is nevertheless recommended that the system operate as if hiring temporary workers applies. This makes the calculations **identical** to that used in the "private company" case, meaning that the sharing ratio for an EFT is 1: 8 on overall performance. Employees in public services are assumed to not have the opportunity for earning cash bonuses, consequently, they have no choice but to enter an EFT gainsharing plan.

   The key, of course, is to define a performance measure that is both meaningful and which could be influenced by employees. In some cases, a monetary value must be given for improving the performance measure by 1% in order to relate performance improvement to fictitious cash bonuses, which are then converted into EFTs. However, in many instances, we only need to look at percentage improvements.

As an example, let us consider a typical postal service office. For simplicity, let there be only one performance measure expressing the quality of service:-

   "total daily customer waiting time (in mins) per postal sales clerk",

or, $$\frac{\text{total customer waiting time (mins per day)}}{\text{total number of postal sales clerks}}$$

What is the monetary worth for improving the performance measure by 1% ? Let a particular office have three postal sales clerks serving the public. Records taken over the past six months show that an average of 1800 customers are served each day, with an average waiting time measured at 3.85 mins per customer. The clerks work an average of 185 hours per month, and are paid an average wage of $11 per hour.

The Standard Performance is: 1800 . $(3.85)/_3$ = 2310 mins. per clerk per day.

Let the gainsharing 'Target Bonus' be set at 20% , and let us assume that each percentage point improvement be equivalent to a 1% improvement in a fictitious cash bonus gainsharing plan.

In a particular month, the clerks succeed in improving the performance measure to 1860 min. per clerk per day. This represents a $[(2310 - 1860)/2310]$. 100 = 19.5 % overall reduction from the Standard Performance, and is equivalent to a fictitious $19.5\%/_2$ = 9.7% bonus to the employees. The average monthly fictitious bonus is, $9.7/_{100}$. 185 . 11 = $197. Using the same formula as before, this bonus earns an equivalent $197/_{(11.4)}$ hours of EFTs, i.e., 4.5 hrs.

> Over a year, this amounts to 54 hrs, or, nearly 7 days.
> Over 3 years, this amounts to 20 $1/_4$ days, or, over 4 weeks.
> Over 5 years, this amounts to 33 $3/_4$ days, or, nearly 7 weeks.
> Over 10 years, this amounts to 67 $1/_2$ days, or, about 3 months.

(Note: we see from the two examples that the wage rate does not affect the outcome).

Buy-Back (BB) Considerations.

The Buy-Back (BB), according to SHRED COST, is a process whereby a consecutive 3-month performance above the Target Bonus, automatically triggers the 'purchase' of employees excess time, for which a 12-month compensation is paid [2]. Buy-Backs present no problem for either of the cases considered. The calculations for determining the EFTs would be done as explained earlier.

As an illustration, consider the last worked example with the postal clerks. Recall, the Standard Performance was determined at '2310 min. per clerk per day'. The Target Bonus is set at 20%, meaning at 1848 min per clerk per day.

Consider a three month performance by the clerks of - 1826, 1818 and 1801 which are all improvements on the Target Bonus. SHRED COST would then trigger a Buy-Back equal to :

$$2 . [1848 - 1/_3 (1826 + 1818 + 1801)] = 66 \text{ min.}$$

i.e., the new Standard becomes 2310 - 66 = 2244 , and the employees receive a compensatory bonus of $(66/_2)$. $100/_{2310}$, about 1 $1/_2$ % for the next 12 months. The Target Bonus is reduced proportionately by 66. $1848/2310$ = 52.8 min. to 1795.2 min.

If, in a subsequent month the clerks perform at 1799 min, then their fictitious bonus would be $100/_2$. (2244 - 1799)$1/_{2244}$ = 9.9% . Add to this their BB compensation of 1.5% gives a total bonus of 11.4% for that month - this is equivalent to:

$$11.4/_{100} . 185/_4 = 5.3 \text{ hrs EFT (for that month).}$$

THE 'SHORT TERM' REWARD PLAN

Under short term reward plans, we consider employees receiving short paid leaves of a half, or full day in order to cater for some pressing personal need. Ordinarily, with most companies, employees do have some limited allowance for paid leave for personal business. Our assumption is that an employee may require time off over and beyond this allowance. The assumption here is that with the employee being away, no attempt is made to replace him (if he works as a member of a team, he may be replaced by another employee from outside the team, but then the new person's regular job is not replaced).

The following cost items apply:
a) The gross wages of the employee - let this be \$w per hour.
b) The social benefits that the employee must set aside - estimated at \$w per hr.
c) The cost of overheads lost to the company by the absence of the operator - estimated at $\$w/_2$ per hr.

Adding the cost items a) to c), gives $\$2 \, 1/_2 \, w$, which, on a 50:50 plan comes to \$5w. This means that for every 5% overall improvement, the employee can receive a 1% EFT for short term leave. This is a higher rate than for long term leave, so an upper limit on the number of hours to be received in this way, may be appropriate. The method for calculating the short term leave is identical to that for long term leave and there is little point in going through another example of the calculations involved.

The main problem we see, is to maintain 'clean' records for each employee in the system - but there is also the possibility of abuse, and the additional administrative costs for maintaining controls. The above remarks apply for both the private and public sectors.

CONCLUSIONS.

This paper presents arguments for linking productivity performance with EFT, or, Earned Free Time, which, in the opinion of the authors, can provide a strong level of motivation since it taps a need that is ever present but rarely satisfied. The approach is based on productivity-based gainsharing plans such as Improshare and SHRED COST. Discussion is split between applications to the private and public sectors, and between long and short term usage.

In private industry applications, employees have the choice between receiving their bonuses either as cash, or, as 'earned free time' (EFT) to be accumulated and utilized sometime in the future at a time determined by negotiations between the employee and the company.

Employees in the public services, as a rule, do not have this choice; their only option is to swap superior performances for EFT. The Buy-Back (BB) aspect applies in the usual manner as with typical productivity-based gainsharing plans.

The EFT outcomes could operate in a similar manner as with companies that offer 'long service leave' to employees of long standing, such as ten to fifteen years of continuous service (the practice in Australia). It has the advantage of ensuring the long term interest and loyalty to the company, while providing the means for a long paid vacation which could be of great physical and psychological benefit to the employee. and indirectly, to the company. It also provides an opportunity for organizational changes to be introduced while most workers in a department are away on extended leave.

REFERENCES.

Dar-El, E.M. (1986), **Productivity Improvement: Employee Involvement and Gainsharing Plans**, Elsevier, Amsterdam, 1986.

Fein, M. (1981), **IMPROSHARE: An Alternative to Traditional Managing**, Mitchall Fein, Hillsdale, NJ.

BIOGRAPHICAL SKETCHES OF THE AUTHORS

Ezey Dar-El is the Harry Lebensfeld Chairholder in Industrial Engineering at the Technion. He has published extensively on the design of production systems, assembly line balancing, project scheduling, R&D productivity and on productivity development issues. He is an internationally known consultant; has worked in several countries covering some fifty companies.

Ilan Meshoulam is Professor in the Faculty of Industrial Engineering and Management at the Technion. He has worked in top managerial positions with US-based international hi-tech companies, such as Intel, Digital Equipment, Control Data Corp., and in Israel, with the Elscint and Elbit Companies. His specific research interests are in managerial and strategic development of human resources.

Productivity & Quality Management Frontiers-IV, edited by Sumanth, Edosomwan, Poupart, and Sink. ©1993 Institute of Industrial Engineers.

Field Experience with the "Shred-Cost" Gainsharing System

I. Yogev

Yissum Applied Management Systems

Ramat-Gan, ISRAEL

ABSTRACT

Israeli industry is currently exposed to a massive drive towards Total Quality Management fueled by external demands (D.O.D, ISO 9000) and the urgent need to compete in the global marketplace.

One of the typical changes made in a plant adopting the T.Q.M philosophy is in the area of productivity incentives, where a majority of companies move from individual incentives schemes, to gainsharing reward plans.

"Shred - Cost" is the leading gainsharing system in the Israeli industry. By December 91, 40 gainsharing plans were operating in 15 companies, yielding results that far exceed the average productivity levels of the appropriate industry.

This paper will present the results and achievements reported by "Shred - Cost" users, and will focus on two main topics:
1. Characteristics for the successfull application of gainsharing reward plans: "External" factors relating to the companies' characteristics, and "internal" factors that reflect the structure and the implementation process of the gainsharing reward system.
2. The integration of "Shred - Cost" with T.Q.M programs.

KEY WORDS

Productivity and quality improvement, gainsharing, incentive system, T.Q.M, "Shred - Cost".

1. BACKGROUND - "SHRED-COST" PRINCIPLES

    "SHRED-COST" (SHaring REDuction in COSTs) is a Total Productivity and
    Quality system, containing two basic components:
    1.1 A Productivity and Quality improvement plan.
    1.2 A Gainsharing incentive plan.

1.1 The Productivity and Quality Improvement Plan (P.Q.I)
    The P.Q.I plan aims at creating the culture, environment, procedures,
    means and knowledge needed to sustain a long term continuous
    improvement process in productivity and quality.
    "Shred - Cost" implements P.Q.I plans in one of two possible modes:
    - a: In a "T.Q.M" mode, where the gainsharing reward plan is
         integrated with an existing T.Q.M program.
    - b: In a "T.P.Q.M" mode, in which the full "Shred - Cost" is applied.
         It differs from the T.Q.M mode in the following manner:
         - T.P.Q.M introduces task-oriented cross functional
           productivity improvement teams, in parallel with the first
           stages of the T.Q.M program.
         - Training focuses on productivity based issues such as:
           ergonomics, safety, scheduling, in addition to the typical
           quality, statistics and teamwork issues.
         - There is a formal and close-loop feedback system between
           improvement efforts and their monitary returns.

1.2 The Gainsharing Plan
    The "SHRED-COST" gainsharing plan is based on the follwing
    principles:
    - a: Group definition is based on "saleable" products, and on the
         integration of direct and indirect workers (including managers).
    - b: Performance measures reflect group performance in non-monitary
         values and in areas that are influenced by workers.
       - c: Improvements are measured in relation to past perfomance
              (base ratio).
       - d: Performance improvement originates from almost all possible
         sources, enhancing partnership between workers and the plant
         owners.
       - e: Bonuses are paid when performance exceeds the basic level.
              "Shred-Cost" shares the productivity gains between workers
         and plant, usually on a 50:50 basis.
    - f: Three elements control the incentive levels:
         - An unique Buy-Back procedure which operate when performance
           consistently exceeds a target bonus. The procedure enables
           standards to be tightened in a manner that minimizes the
           sensitivity to product-mix changes.

- Updating of standards or of base ratio when investment in production equipment exceeds an agreed upon level.
- Updating the base ratio when major organizational changes, that affect the productivity measure, occur.

2. CHARACTERISTICS OF THE SURVEYED POPULATION: PLANTS AND SYSTEMS

By December 1991, forty applications of "Shred - Cost" plans were in operation in various plants whose composition and characteristics are presented in the following tables:

2.1 Plant Characteristics

Table 1 - Type of Industry

Industry	%
Food	46.5
Metal	26.5
Aviation	13.5
Chemical	13.5

Table 2 - Plant Size

Number of workers	%
- 50	16.5
51 - 100	33.5
101 - 250	25.0
251 +	25.0

The plant population represents a typical distribution of Israeli Industry according to size.

1107

Table 3 - Producion Type

Production Type	%
Job shop	28.5
Process	21.5
Mixed *	43.5
Service center	6.5

* Parts of the plants - process, other parts - Jobshop.

Table 4 - Business Status

Business Status	%
Growing *	20.0
Steady	64.5
Declining **	15.5

* annual growth in sales exceeds 20%.
** annual decline in sales is more than 10%.

2.2 "Shred - Cost" Plans Characteristics

Table 5 - System Mode

System Mode	%
T.P.Q.M	22.5
T.Q.M	68.5
Gainsharing only	9.0

Table 6 - Group Size

Nr. of Workers in a Group	%
1 - 25	27
26 - 50	23
51 +	50

Table 7 - System Complexity

Nr. of Performance Meusures	%	comments
1	40	productivity
2	30	productivity and Yield
3	30	additions: process uptime operatinal costs.

Table 8 - System Implementation Age

System Age - Years	%
<- 1	42
1 - 2	31
2 - 3	23
3 - 4	4

The figures indicate that the rate of "Shred - Cost" System applications is accelerating as experience is gained.

3. RESULTS - PRESENTATION AND ANALYSIS

    "Shred - Cost" users reported results should be compared with the
    figures for Israeli Industry, which state a 2% average increase in
    productivity for the 1985 - 1990 period.

3.1 Reported Results
    a. Productivity
    - Average productivity improvement accumulated from the
      respective base line periods until the end of December 1991 is
      17.1%.
    - Average annual improvement from 1990 to 1991 is 12.5%, ranging
      from -1.5% to 40%.
    - First year average annual improvement a mounts to 15.1%, while
      more "vetearn" systems report an average annual improvement of
      8.1%.
    b. Quality
    Quality is generally not used directly as a "Shred - Cost"
    performance measure, though all companies report a significant
    improvement in both product unity and process conformance.
    c. Material Usage (Yield)
    Material (raw, packaging) usage is measured in 60% of the
    applications. Results indicate a 18% reduction in material waste
    (waste due to defects, reprocessing, overweight etc).

3.2 Analysis of Results
    Productivity outputs were analyzed in an attempt at locating and
    defining the factors that determine the level and rate of
    improvements. Results show that only one parameter - company's
    status - appears to have a significant effect on the improvement
    rate, as seen in Table 9:

            Table 9 - Annual Improvement by Business Status

Business Status	Average Annual Improvement: %	Range of Improvement Min - Max: %
growing	16.0	11.5 to 20.4
steady	14.6	1.6 to 40.0
declining	1.3	1.5 to 7.5

Results show a significant reduction in the rate of improvement
associated with declining envinroment: though it is still
positive, the rate of improvement is usually influenced by the
need to reduce the workforce (which invariably occurs "late") and
by the difficulty to effectively maintain the improvement
effort when the company business shrinks, and employees morale is
low.
The fact, that no other factors are determined, is an indication
of the complexity of the organizational changes that occur during
implementation of "Shred - Cost". The Multi dimensional
organizational changes involve managerial culture, style and
methods, basic values of working life, employees - management
relationship, and a shift in the power equation within the
company.
The conclusion, then, is that there is probably no readymade
"menu" for the successfull implementation of "Shred - Cost". Its
success is dependant on several cultural, managerial and
systematic issues, in a different mix, in each application.

4. THE EFFECT OF NON-MEASURED FACTORS

4.1 Process Plants
It is customery to view process plants as having a relatively low
potential for productivity improvement. Indeed, most process
plants report a 1.6 to 5.6% annual improvement rate, but
surprisingly, the system reporting the highest achievement (40%)
is in a process plant, which challenges the conventional view.
A closer look at process plants reveals the following:
- wages account for a relatively low percent of production costs
(compared to materials used).
- middle management has little authority.
- the process is generally not under full control.
These characteristics lead to a concept of employing excess
manpower in order to eliminate damages of "downtime".
In the particular example achieving the 40% improvement, the
manager showed strong leadership, enjoyed relatively wide
authority and the organization encouraged initiative, thus
enabling significant changes in operational procedures to be
introduced. The example shows that there is usually a huge
potential of improvement in process plants, but it requires
strong leadership and a supporting culture to capitalize on.

4.2 Rate of Improvement
Analysis of results in relation to the time dimention shows a
significant difference between systems whose middle management
enjoy's a relative wide range of authority compared to to those
that don't.
The difference is reflected in first year's level of improvement
which averages 22% in such systems, while those where middle
management's "hands are tied", reported only a 6.8% improvement.

These sharp differences are likely to originate from removing
operational constraints, that are typical to an individual wage
incentive plans, when moving into gainsharing plans, and from
tying together both performance measures and incentive of middle
management and workers.

4.3 Use of the Systems'Information as a Management Tool
Companies differ in the way they make use of the information that
emerges from system measurment.
A formal, well planned data presentation and distribution,
usually is comprised of:
- public graphic presentation of monthly and accumulated data.
- quatterly and annual meetings discussing the current
  achievements and goals setting.
- presentation of improvement suggestions and their impact on
  incentive levels.
Results imply that these features tend to strengthen the effects
of the system.

5. T.Q.M AND "SHRED - COST"

Some managers interpret Dr. Deming's T.Q.M philosophy as totally
contradicting any form of wage incentives, but they also find it
difficult to abandon incentives entirely, mainly because of
flexibility in wage structure and power balance with the unions.
Companies moving into "Shred - Cost" as a substitute for individual
wage incentives, integrating it with an existing T.Q.M program, find
that the combination of the two has a positive influence on the pace
of improvements taking place.
It seems that the focus of "Shred - Cost" on both short and long term
results, balances the pitfalls of overextended long term plans, that
are generally associated with T.Q.M programs. Tangible returns from
T.Q.M programs are often reported within three to five years from
program initiation, which many companies find difficult to live with.
Our claim is that "Shred - Cost" caters to immediate returns via the
improvement process, while at the same time supporting
the development of the long-term T.Q.M implementation.

BIBLIOGRAPHY

(1) Dar-El, E.M., PRODUCTIVITY IMPROVEMENT: EMPLOYEE INVOLVEMENT AND
GAINSHARING PLANS. (1986), Elsevier, Amsterdam.

(2) Hatcher, L. and Ross, T.L., (1991). "From individual incentives to an
organization - wide gainsharing plan: effects on teamwork and product
quality." Journal of Organizational Behavior Vol. 12, pp. 169-183.

(3) Israeli Institute of Productivity. Productivity in Israel - An
International Comparison. (1992), Tel-Aviv.

AUTHOR'S BIOGRAPHY

The author is a senior management consultant, age 39, partner and co-manager of "YISSUM APPLIED MANAGEMENT SYSTEMS" in Israel. An industrial engineer, graduate of Tel-Aviv University, Suma Cum Lauda.

He has an extensive experiance in planning and implementing wage incentive plans and reward systems, including active participation in the above mentioned forty applications of "Shred - Cost" in Israel.

Productivity & Quality Management Frontiers-IV, edited by Sumanth, Edosomwan, Poupart, and Sink. ©1993 Institute of Industrial Engineers.

The Flexible Bonus System (FBS)

S. Globerson
Tel-Aviv University
Tel-Aviv, ISRAEL

R. Parsons
Northeastern University
Boston, Massachusetts USA

Abstract

Recently Flexible Bonus Systems or Cafeteria Plans have come into vogue. Although widely adopted, there is a void in the literature regarding the experience of firms with Flexible Bonus Plans as compared to traditional bonus systems. This paper summarizes the findings from a questionnaire administered to thirty manufacturing and service organizations regarding their experience and attitudes with regard to Flexible Bonus Systems (FBS). Use was found to be widespread, not only among the firms participating in the study, but also across departments within the firms. Over 90 percent of the respondents had experience with FBS although the degree of formality varied from firm to firm. There was general agreement as to the low cost of administering an FBS as compared to traditional bonus systems but varied opinion on the issue of application complexity. The study explores common reasons for introducing an FBS, the nature of the reward structures employed, company expectations, extent of employee participation, and organizational differences in the administration of an FBS among participating firms.

Keywords: Motivation, Flexible Bonus System, Cafeteria Plans

INTRODUCTION

Willingness of an individual to invest energy in productive activities is affected by motivation. The underlying assumption behind any kind of incentive system is that an additional amount paid as a function of individual or group performance is a strong motivator. Work motivation, however, is a complex issue. This complexity has spawned an array of theories and a rich toolbox of techniques designed to assist the practioner when confronted with the challenge of motivational issues. Motivational theories play a pivotal role in the design and structure of bonus, or incentive systems. Familiarity with the strategic differences of alternative motivational theories is critical to the successful design and implementation of a bonus system. A brief summary of the different theories and their practical implementation may be found in Eden and Globerson (1992).

Three major motivational approaches will be explored in this paper. The first two, Management By Objectives (MBO) and Goal Setting are management techniques employed to motivate employees to improve and to attain high performance (Locke et al, 1981). Employees have been found to be more responsive where objectives were defined with employee involvement than when objectives were managerially imposed (Erez and Kanfer, 1983). Additional research supports the contention that a combination of goal setting and financial bonuses will result in higher motivation than just participative goal setting alone (Locke et al, 1980: Pritchard and Kurtz, 1979).

Expectancy theory, first formulated by Vroom (1964), is the third theory to be explored. Widely accepted by behavioral scientists, expectancy theory is a process-oriented theory that differentiates between first and second level outcomes. A first level outcome is directly impacted by an individual's efforts, for example, an individual's daily production. A second level outcome is influenced by a first level outcome, but not directly by the individual's efforts. To illustrate, a promotion is a second level outcome influenced by the individual's performance (daily production), which is a first level outcome directly influenced by the individual's efforts. The expectancy theory model states that the individual's motivation to improve performance (i.e. first level outcome) is a function of the following two factors:
1. The value assigned by the individual to the second level outcome; that is, the value assigned to the potential reward to be received.
2. The individual's expectancy concerning the relationship between effort expended and the first level outcome, and the relationship between first level outcome (performance) and the realization of second level outcome (reward).
According to expectancy theory, a bonus system will not be

attractive to an individual unless it satisfies the individual's expectations as expressed by the above two factors.

The degree of success of a bonus system, regardless of its form can often be traced to the degree of adherence, or lack thereof, to established motivational theory. For example, an inherent weakness in many of the established conventional financial bonus systems is the lack of employee confidence in the relationship between performance and compensation. Schneir (1989) discovered that one out of every five employees did not believe that there is a distinct relationship between first level outcome (performance) and second level outcome (reward). Moreover, the perception exists that the rigid structure of the conventional financial incentive system may allow low performers who do not achieve the desired goal(s) to nevertheless be compensated (Cissell, 1987). This is particularly evident in the case of executive compensation where the periodic bonus may masquerade as a bonus for improved performance but in fact be a guarantee as part of the financial package and in no way be contingent on performance (Tharp, 1985).

A number of variations of financial incentive systems exist. These include one time bonus systems, fringe benefits such as additional insurance, and periodic bonuses on a monthly or quarterly basis with a level of payment based upon selected performance measures. The periodic bonus systems may take the shape of conventional incentive systems or gainsharing systems, with some evidence that the latter may be the preferred model (Eden and Globerson, 1992). Recently, Flexible Benefits, or Cafeteria Plans have come into common usage McCaffrey, 1988; Tane, 1985). According to this approach, an employee may create a customized benefit package from a pool of benefits made available by the organization. The employee performs the tradeoffs to maximize the value of their benefit package to them within the constraints of total package size established by the organization. This places a cap on company expense yet provides the employee the flexibility to create a customized benefits package from an array of possible benefits provided by the organization. For example, an employee may choose to decrease the life insurance benefit in favor of increased tuition reimbursement. In a Flexible Bonus System, or "Point Based Reward System", the company agrees to pay a one time reward if a specific one time performance is achieved (Eden and Globerson, 1992). For example, the company may declare that a one time bonus will be paid for early completion of a project with the magnitude of the bonus tied to the savings associated with early completion or that an entire unit will have a paid weekend vacation if end of the month inventory is below a certain level. Adopting the FBS approach provides the company with the ability to move from one objective to another with a minimum of upheaval. This is in contrast with a conventional bonus system which is established for an extended period of time, is characterized by rigidity, and is expected to follow certain rules. Under the FBS approach, the specific rules are adjusted as organizational needs change.

Although the FBS approach seems to be widely adopted, very little appears in the literature as compared with other bonus systems. For example, IBM rewards its employees for exceptional performance in many areas such as innovation and technical performance (Turner, 1979; Henderson, 1982). The FBS approach is particularly appropriate in a project environment with bonuses being paid upon achievement of certain milestones.

Eden and Globerson (1992) refers to the following key tasks in establishing a Flexible Bonus System:
1. Identification of situations where the introduction of a Flexible Bonus System would be appropriate. These situations will have either a performance or an effort dimension. Examples of performance related dimensions are achievement of a certain production rate in a specified period, the completion of a job in a predetermined period of time, or achievement of a specified reduction in customers returns. Effort related examples are long working hours, overtime hours, or working odd hours.
2. Establishment of measurement criteria. These criteria should be situation specific, that is, dependent on the specific circumstance in which the Flexible Bonus System is being applied.
3. The type of reward, or rewards, should be established. Different types of financial related awards exist including actual cash and valuable products and services. The flexible strategy approach may be implemented to allow employees to select the reward that best fits their needs.
4. Determination of the size of the organizational unit to be compensated. Depending on the situation, the relevant organizational boundary may be as narrow as an individual or as wide as a large department.
5. Specification of the magnitude of the reward. The size of the reward must be established prior to implementation of a Flexible Bonus System and be of sufficient magnitude to be perceived by the employees as significant.

In order to gather additional information on Flexible Bonus Systems, a questionnaire was developed and sent to a sample of companies. The study and the findings are described in the paragraphs that follow.

DESCRIPTION OF THE STUDY

Data were collected from thirty manufacturing and service organizations. Companies were not differentiated on the basis of manufacturing or service due to the fact that the majority of employees in manufacturing companies have a service component as part of their job resonsibilities. We have reached an era in which relatively few individuals find themselves working on the line. The number of employees in the participating organizations ranged from as few as 10 up to 18,000, with an average of 1,650 employees. Although the range in number of employees among the participating organizations is wide, 85 percent of the firms employed 3,000 employees or less.

The majority of the companies (90%) indicated experience with the use of FBS, although only 40% had a formal policy regarding their use. Those with a formal policy in place usually required documentation of the reward decision. Documentation was much less prevalent among organizations with no formal policy. Interestingly, no formal recognition regarding the existence of FBS existed in around 20% of the companies that had previous experience with FBS. All participants agreed that the maintenance of a Flexible Bonus System is significantly cheaper in comparison to other reward systems, including conventional incentive systems as well as gainsharing plans. Although there was general agreement as to the low cost of administering an FBS, there was difference of opinion when it came to the issue of application complexity. The trend was toward FBS being simpler to apply, but a few respondents thought the opposite.

The use of FBS was not limited to specific departments. It was practiced in a variety of departmental settings including research and development, marketing, production, and support functions such as human resources. Although applied in a variety of settings, the underlying rationale for utilizing FBS displayed some commonalities. Common reasons given included:
1. To encourage exceptional performance during a crisis
2. To meet schedule commitments
3. To encourage working odd hours
4. To encourage working under difficult conditions
5. To speed up development of a new product
6. To speed up development of a new process
7. To encourage submission of suggestions for improvement
8. To encourage meeting project completion deadlines
9. To encourage performance of an exceptional task not included in the regular job
10. To encourage expending extra efforts
11. To encourage good performance over a long period of time.
12. To acknowledge completion of project milestones
13. To acknowledge special creativity
14. To acknowledge outstanding profitability

The most common reason for using an FBS was "to encourage expending special efforts", which was mentioned by 50 % of the respondents, followed by reasons 8 and 9 each being mentioned by around 20 % of the companies. Companies could, and did, specify more than one reason for the implementation of a FBS in their organization.

A variety of rewards were used. The most common was the one time cash payment, which was used by about 40 percent of the responding companies. The complete list of the types of rewards employed includes:
1. One time cash payment
2. Special trip
3. gifts
4. A special certificate
5. Paid vacation
6. Dinner for two
7. Letter of acknowledgement
8. Shortened waiting period for promotion
9. Praise in company publications

The cash award ranged widely from as little as equivalent $20 up to $8000 equivalent dollars. The average range as reported by the respondents was between $250 (equivalent $) to $1500 (equivalent $) with the specific level of payment being established by the relative importance of the contribution. Companies used a very wide range of high to low payment with a ratios ranging from 1 to 110. A ratio of 110 means that the highest cash award was 110 times higher than the lowest cash award.

The budget assigned to such bonuses was considerably low with an average value below a half a percent of employee's salaries. 30 % of the companies reported a budget that exceeded half a percent, with a maximum of 5 % reported by one company.

The highest annual percentage of employees receiving a reward reported was 375 %. That is, in this specific company, employees received an average of 3.75 rewards per year. The next highest value was 58 % and the rest of the values were less than 5 %. The two highest values belonged to small companies, which may suggest that FBS is particularly useful in small companies.

Rewards were given either to an individual or to a team of employees performing a joint task. The majority of the respondents used FBS for both individual employees and for teams, although 30 % used the FBS to only reward individuals. The decision is impacted by both the nature of the job and by the philosophy of the management of the organization.

Although the reward budget is established by upper level management, the criteria used in each department for the selection process of the rewarded party were primarily determined by the immediate manager. In most of the cases, the reward was given to the rewarded party by the immediate manager, the supervisor of the immediate manager, or the general manager. In a few instances, the reward was given by the human resources manager or a manager of a special unit assigned for tasks of such nature.

Companies keep the frequency of use of a FBS to a relatively
low level. The highest number of annual rewards reported by
a company was 50, the lowest number reported was a single
award, and the average number of awards was 4.

Companies expect something in return when they implement an
FBS. The returns expected by the respondents included the
following:
1. increased morale
2. Improved productivity
3. Increased profit
4. Technical improvement
5. Improved safety
6. Increased motivation to work
7. Increased commitment to and identification with the
   organization
8. Increased employee cooperation
9. Improved quality of performance
10. Employee's rotation
11. Technical knowhow
12. Reduced employee turnover

To evaluate the overall impact of the program, participants
were asked to rank the success of FBS by using a scale from 1
to 5, with 5 being a very successful program. The results are
summarized below:

Category	Responses
Unsuccessful	1
Partially satisfactory	5
Satisfactory	5
Moderately successful	8
Very successful	3
Insufficient data	6

One can conclude that there is general satisfaction with
regard to the use of FBS, in spite of the fact that a few
users feel that they do not have sufficient data to make a
judgement. Forty percent of the respondents indicated an
intention to expand the use of FBS in their organizations.

CONCLUSION

Use of an FBS was widespread, not only among the firms
participating in the study, but also across departments within
the firms as well. Over 90 percent of the respondents had
experience with Flexible Bonus Systems, although the degree of
formality varied from firm to firm. Only 40 percent had a
formal policy in place. General agreement existed as to the
low cost of administering an FBS as compared to traditional
bonus systems, but opinion varied on the issue of application

complexity. The most common reason for employing an FBS, mentioned by 50 percent of the respondents, was to encourage expending special efforts. About 20 percent of the companies mentioned providing encouragement to meet project deadlines and to encourage performance of an exceptional task as major influences. A variety of rewards were used with the most common being a one time cash payment, with the specific level being determined by the importance of the contribution. On average, budgeted one time cash bonuses were below half a percent of employee's salaries. With two excetions, both of which were small companies, less than 5 percent of the employees received an annual award. Recipients consisted of teams as well as individuals although 30 percent of the respondents restricted the FBS to individual awards. The criteria for selection of recipients were typically determined by the immediate manager of the affected group. The average frequency of rewards tended to be low with an average of about 4 annually. Companies were generally satisfied with the results of FBS as a motivational tool. Forty percent of the respondents indicated an intention to expand the use of FBS in their organizations.

REFERENCES

1. Cissell M. J. "Designing Effective Reward Systems."
   Compensation and Benefits Review. Vol. 19, 1987. 45-55.

2. Eden D. & Globerson S. "Financial and Nonfinancial
   Motivation." Industrial Engineering Handbook, 2nd ed.
   Salvendy G. (ed.). New York. John Wiley, 1992.

3. Erez E. M., & Kanfer F. H. "The Role of Goal Acceptance in
   Goal Setting and Task Performance." Academy of Management
   Review. Vol. 18, 1983, 454-463.

4. Henderson R. I., Compensation Management Rewarding
   Performance. Virginia. Reston Publishing Company, 1982.

5. Locke E. A., Fern D. B., McCaleb V. M., Shaw K. N., & Denny
   A. T. " The Relative Effectiveness of Four Methods of
   Motivating Employee Performance." Changes in Working Life.
   In Duncan K., Gruneberg M., & Wallis D. (ed.). New York.
   John Wiley, 1980.

6. Locke E. H., & Latham G. P. A Theory of Goal Setting Task
   Performance. Englewood Cliffs, N. J. Prentice Hall, 1990.

7. McCaffery R. M. Employee Benefit Programs: A Total
   Compensation Perspective. Boston. Kent Publishing
   Company, 1988.

8. Pritchard R. D. & Curtz M. I. "The Influence of Goal
   Setting and Financial Incentives on Task Performance."
   Compensation and Reward Perspectives. Mahoney T. A. (ed.).
   Illinois. Richard D. Irwin, 1979.

9. Schneier C. E., "Capitalizing on Performance Management,
   Recognition, and Reward Systems." Compensation and Benefits
   Vol. 21, 1989, 20-30.

10. Tane L. D. "Guidelines to Successful Flex Plans: Four
    Companies Experiences." Compensation and Benefits
    Review. Vol. 17, 1985, 38-45.

11. Tharp C. G. "Linking Annual Incentive Awards to
    Individual Performance." Compensation and Benefits
    Review. Vol. 17, 1985, 28-33.

12. Turner W. J. "How the IBM Awards Program Works." Research
    Management. July 1979, 24-27.

13. Vroom V.W., Work and Motivation, Wiley, New York, 1984.

Productivity & Quality Management Frontiers-IV, edited by Sumanth, Edosomwan, Poupart, and Sink. ©1993
Institute of Industrial Engineers.

Fiction, Facts, and Friction...
Making Sure the Cart Is behind the Horse:
Are You Sure Your Company Wants a Gainshare System?

R.R. Kegerreis
A.O. Smith Automotive Products Co.
Milwaukee, Wisconsin USA

The question is...which came first: Meeting the company's profit needs or meeting the needs of the employees who generate the profits? Does your company really understand the basics of employee empowerment, and why it is required to make a gainshare system work? Is your management organization set up in the traditional "functional" arrangement (Finance, Sales, Marketing, Human Resources, Manufacturing, Engineering) or is it positioned to focus on Customer Service, Quality and Productivity? Which is needed to make employee empowerment and gainshare work?

"Partnerships and Cooperation" do not just happen—especially in a business environment where for years union chieftains and management have negotiated with "win-lose" vintage. Those who tell you that most employees are eager to join right in and participate in activities traditionally regarded as management prerogatives (such as quality assurance, manpower planning, overtime scheduling and gainshare compensation) may be dealing you a hand of **Fiction**. This paper explores the real **factors** which management (and Union) should consider before entering into a new productivity system. It examines those elements which professional, technical and supervisory staff need to fully understand before "co-management" can become a reality.

There are many factors to consider when changing a business environment. It has to be done in such a way where (all) employees change from the old culture to that of a new participative environment. The new way has to be "user friendly". It has to be designed such that employees feel secure enough to want to motivate themselves toward making it happen. What is the magic "carrot"? How does gainshare enter into this equation when dealing with compensation?

Let's assume everything above happens the correct way. What could cause **Friction**...or in today's real industrial settings, "What happens when the wheels hit the runway....How does a company set up a two-way communication system to facilitate employee empowerment? What happens when the economy fluctuates? How do you handle reductions in work load, reduce inventory, and increase throughput when a Gainshare system is in place? How do you build a esprit de corps of "world class" competitiveness? Do you really understand the hidden agendas of gainshare?

Productivity & Quality Management Frontiers-IV, edited by Sumanth, Edosomwan, Poupart, and Sink. ©1993 Institute of Industrial Engineers.

Hospital Productivity Gain Sharing

A.R. Ganti
MECON Associates
Mesa, Arizona USA

E.J. Nagy
Grace Hospital
Cleveland, Ohio USA

HOSPITAL PRODUCTIVITY GAIN SHARING

Hospitals have been making productivity improvements utilizing the proven industrial engineering techniques. Although some hospitals shared the resulting cost savings with the employees in the past, gain sharing has not been practiced as commonly as in other service or manufacturing sectors. One of the problems faced by hospitals in the past is lack of an equitable methodology that is tied to the existing productivity systems. In the last decade, more and more hospitals are facing strong competition, increased costs and dwindling operating margins on one hand. On the other hand, productivity improvements are reaching a plateau. This is not because there are no productivity gains to be realized but due to lack of incentives to the employees. As a result, hospitals are considering gain sharing as a way to motivate the employees to improve productivity.

impact*REWARD, a gain sharing program, was developed using OPTIMIS, the productivity system as the main platform to reward staff for their contributions to productivity gains. It helps to calculate the dollar amount to be paid out for each department in the hospital on a quarterly basis. Over 70 hospitals from all over the USA are utilizing OPTIMIS and several of those are seriously evaluating some type of gain sharing program.

The criteria for determining the payout includes productivity gain made relative to the peer hospitals, absolute bottom line productivity improvement for the hospital in question and the productivity gains made by the individual departments.

The significant benefits of impact*REWARD program are quantifiable productivity improvements that generated significant cost savings through cost reduction and cost avoidance.

Productivity & Quality Management Frontiers-IV, edited by Sumanth, Edosomwan, Poupart, and Sink. ©1993 Institute of Industrial Engineers.

Experiences with Gainsharing in a Knowledge Worker Environment

D.S. Sink

Virginia Polytechnic Institute & State University

Blacksburg, Virginia USA

We have been experimenting with gainsharing in the Virginia Productivity Center at Virginia Tech. for approximately four years. We begin with a head full of theories on motivation, compensation management and creative ideas on how we thought gainsharing should be done in the 1990's. Four years later we are battle damaged; our theories had holes in them, our creative ideas were naive, our notions on motivation in an organization like VPC has been altered dramatically. This paper is a lessons learned paper. I will present what we have done over time along with critical incidents we have ecountered along the way. I will discuss other interventions that were made along the way that may have confounded the effect of our gainsharing system. And, I will conclude with prescriptions, based on lessons learned, for others to follow if they choose to develop gainsharing as a component of their continuous improvement efforts.

Our gainsharing system has the following efforts:

(1) The amount shared is a function of the financial performance of the VPC for a given period of time;

(2) We share quarterly, but do calculations monthly and share that information freely;

(3) The top management team, with Director approval, determines how much is shared in any given period on the basis of some pre-established guidelines. There is a limit of 30% of base pay for the year for any VPC employee.

(4) The participants in gainsharing determine how the total amount of gainsharing is distributed. We have four categories at present: Equal, Equitable, Team, and Seniority. These categories and the percent allocation to each have changed over time and I will discuss those changes.

(5) Our overall aim is to rely less on base pay and more on variable pay so as maintain competitive position and avoid layoffs during downturns in business.

The paper will briefly introduce the theory of motivation and gainsharing as I understand it, describe what we have done, describe my perceptions of positive impact as well as dysfunctional consequences, and conclude with analysis and interpretation leading to some prescriptions.

Productivity & Quality Management Frontiers-IV, edited by Sumanth, Edosomwan, Poupart, and Sink. ©1993
Institute of Industrial Engineers.

The Human Capital Crisis and Productivity in Florida

R. Cassady
University of Central Florida
Orlando, Florida USA

D. Hosni
University of Central Florida
Orlando, Florida USA

ABSTRACT

The lagging rate of productivity growth in the US is tied
to the need to remain competitive. Competitiveness
necessitates a highly skilled and educated work force. High
productivity in the use of labor and capital in the production
process translates directly into high levels of real wages and
returns on capital which, in turn, provide for the high
standards of living enjoyed by the American people. There is
concern, however that given the skills of the new labor force
entrants, particularly minorities, it will be difficult to
match employment opportunities with the skills of the future
work force resulting in a human capital crisis. This paper
capitalizes on the dimensions of the human capital crisis as it
applies to Florida by assessing the occupational shifts in
demand, the demographic changes and labor supply as well as the
quality of education and training. Appropriate policy
recommendations are offered to circumvent the human capital
crisis and improve the bleak prospects for labor productivity
in Florida.

INTRODUCTION

Labor productivity growth is determined, among other things, by the quality of the labor force. Other things equal, a better educated and more trained work force should produce a higher output per hour than a less educated and poorly trained one. As of the mid-1980s, the United States enjoyed an overall advantage in productivity levels relative to the other industrial economies. However, its position is being threatened as the productivity growth of its major trading partners has consistently outstripped it over the last two decades. America's productivity problems are, in large part, attributed to the educational deterioration of its work force. In 1988, America's functional literacy rate was only 80 percent compared to a better than 95 percent for Japan (12). As America's literacy has dropped, so has its economic growth and productivity. This will be further complicated by the projected demographic shifts which would change the composition of the future labor supply where minorities, women and immigrants will account for 85 percent of the net additions (14). Thus, the ability to build and maintain a quality work force represents a major challenge to the American economy in the face of the rapid technological changes and the globalization of world markets. To many experts the US is indeed facing a human capital crisis posing a serious threat to its future productivity and, ultimately, to the standard of living of its citizens. This paper evaluates the case of Florida and the quality of its human capital which holds the key to the success of its economy in the twenty-first century.

BACKGROUND

The Florida case study is of special interest because the state is expected to undergo several changes that stand to rewrite the geographical landscape of its economic structure. First, Florida is projected to become the third largest state in the US by the year 2000 (7). Second, Florida's job creation potential is ranked third in the nation. Third, Florida ranked sixth in the Southeast region for states with the highest technology employment (11). But, by 1990 its high-tech employment grew minimally due to the lack of qualified personnel. Fourth, Florida, as outlined in its Comprehensive Plan of 1990, is committed to upgrade the quality of its education system and to achieve excellence in mathematics, science and computer education. Fifth, while the work force will be made up of more older workers, the majority of new entrants will be females and minorities projecting a more diversified manpower configuration. The paper evaluates the state manpower profile in the context of its emerging economy by reviewing occupational shifts, demographic changes and the quality of its education and training and comparing them to the U.S.

OCCUPATIONAL SHIFTS IN DEMAND

The transformation of Florida's economy from an agricultural to a more service-oriented one will impact its occupational structure. By year 2000, Florida's service sector employment as a percentage of total employment (81.6%) is expected to exceed that of the US (80.2%). Florida's economy is projected to generate approximately eight million jobs by the year 2000 (8). The occupational shifts will represent a movement toward high-skilled occupations. Changes in technology and job organization will require workers to have greater mathematical literacy and reasoning skills. Based on a skill scale, where six is the highest and one is the lowest, managerial, professional, sales and service occupations (ranging in skill levels from 4.4 to 2.6) will experience the greatest employment growth. On the other hand, occupations with lower skill rating (production, operation and maintenance) will decline as a proportion of total employment. Those projected to have the greatest percentage growth between 1987 and 2000 include medical assistant (7.7%), computer systems analyst (7.1%), registered nurse (6.9%, and data processor (6.4%) (8). According to the Hudson Institute jobs in nursing will require post-high school education and a skill level of 4 or better; but only 5 percent of the nation's new entrants will be able to perform at this level (9). In Florida, it is projected that by year 2000 over 60 percent of the entry level jobs will require at least a high school diploma (10). But, demographic changes may complicate the picture further increasing the likelihood that the required types of workers will be in short supply.

DEMOGRAPHIC CHANGES AND LABOR SUPPLY

A review of the state population dynamics reveals interesting changes (table 1). Florida will experience gains through the year 2000. However, its growth rate is projected to decrease from 55 percent (1972-86) to 33 percent (1986-2000). Nonetheless, Florida's population growth rate has equalled or even surpassed the national rate in every decade since 1900. Such growth rates had moved it from the twentieth most populous state in 1950 to possibly become the third by year 2000 (2). During the 1980s approximately 90 percent of Florida's population growth was attributed to migration (4). But, net migration is expected to decline over the next years as the gradual economic recovery of the oil and midwest states reduces the migrants' incentives to move (5). Migrants always represented an important element in Florida's labor market with a large proportion working in high-skilled jobs (47%). In 1989, 34 percent of the migrants held professional and managerial positions (10). The composition of Florida's population is also changing. The population pyramid is squaring with an increase in the older population and a decrease in the younger population. By year 2000, Florida will have a higher share of the graying population (19.1%) than the US (13%)(6). Florida will also experience gains in the non-white population to reach 17.3 percent by 2000. As of 1990, Florida had the largest Hispanic population in the US (2).

Changing demographics will bring widespread diversification into the future work force. Florida's labor force growth rate has always exceeded that of the US and the projected rates are expected to decline to 49 and 18 percent, respectively, for 1986-2000 due to a slowdown in population gains (7). Florida's labor force is expected to reach 8.1 million by year 2000. Florida's labor force participation rate is expected to increase from 62.9 percent in 1990 to reach 67 percent by year 2000 and catch up with the US projected rate. In Florida greater participation rates for blacks and minorities are noted and these trends are expected to continue (7). The state participation rate for women (55.2%), however, was below the national figure (57.5%) in 1990 (7). Based on past data, a 12 percent growth rate for the period 1990-2000 was assumed. This will increase the state female labor force participation rate to 67 percent in year 2000. This will trigger a corresponding increase in women's share of the labor force to reach 52.5 percent and to continue exceeding the US share (51.6%).

A tight labor market is envisaged for year 2000 with approximately 8 million jobs expected to be generated to match a projected 8.1 million labor force participants. The implications are clear. Labor market shortages may develop which will induce the influx of more women, minorities and older persons into the labor force. Are these workers qualitatively prepared for the world of work?

QUALITY OF EDUCATION AND TRAINING

Labor market demands for higher levels of skills and literacy have increased the pressure on an already beaten-up educational system. First, Florida has one of the most serious drop-out problems in the nation (16). High school graduation rates have steadily declined to be the lowest in the Southeast (58.6%) and alarmingly below the national rate (71.1%). Second, in a recent survey of 37 states, Florida was ranked low (33rd) in the math proficiency of its eighth graders (15). Third, the projected public education expenditures for 1999-2000 will be 11.3 percent less than those for 1990-91 (13). In addition, current and projected state educational spending cuts should greatly impair the prospects of the quality of education. Education has become a subject of major concern as evidenced by the move to establish partnerships between schools and industry to enhance mathematics, science and computer education recognizing that educational reform is critical because today's students are tomorrow's workers.

Training will remain to be a very effective means to upgrade individual skills and industrial productivity in year 2000. Trends indicate that more and more private employers are providing training for their employees. But, Florida is unique in that over three quarters of its employers hire only nine employees or less and, thus, lack the necessary resources to invest in human capital (14). It would require concerted action on the part of the employers to offer extensive training both to new entrants and experienced workers as rapid technological change necessitates job retraining every 3 to 5 years. The success of Florida Power's comprehensive training program represents a case in point, and prompted its marketing to other employers. It included not only a skill - based training but a computer tracking system to automatically audit employees' progress in terms of skill retention. The program is credited with decreasing annual transmission distribution turnover from 48.5 percent in 1982 to 9.5 percent in 1989 (3). The company estimated a saving of 1.2 million dollars in five years. Furthermore, added burden should be placed on the public sector to extend training to the critical masses of the future work force as witnessed by the promises of both presidential candidates.

CONCLUDING REMARKS

It is clear that to meet the labor requirements, employers will have to increasingly rely on the historically disadvantaged segments of the population. This review points that Florida is headed to face a human capital crisis, possibly even more intense that the US one. Florida can no longer only respond to changes. It must intervene now to thwart the human capital crisis. Otherwise, lower productivity, inferior product quality, labor shortages and higher wages would undermine the state competitiveness and possibly transfer jobs elsewhere.

Florida should as its first priority, develop an effective human capital investment strategy with close cooperation between the state, industry and education. Education reform should be directed at revitalizing the school curriculum, fostering school accountability, attracting females and minorities into technical fields, and developing an incentive plan aimed at reducing high school drop-outs. The state should collaborate with the private sector to extend training to the economically disadvantaged and oversee their integration into productive employment. The state should also adopt a statewide child care policy with incentives to firms to offer employer-supported child care. Finally, ensuring a future balance between jobs and workers requires a close monitoring of the state's occupational needs and its manpower configuration through the establishment of a centralized data collection mechanism.

REFERENCES

1. Bureau of Economic and Business Research. (1989) <u>Long-Term Forecast for Florida</u>. Gainesville: University of Florida.

2. Bureau of Economic and Business Research. (1990) <u>Population Estimates and Projections by Age, Sex and Race for Florida and Its Counties 1989-2000</u>, June, Vol 23, 93-94.

3. Filipowksi, D. (1991) "Florida Power Turns Dollars Into Dollars". <u>Personnel Journal</u>, 70, May, 47-50.

4. Fishkind, H. (1990) "Population Growth Takes a New Path". <u>Florida Trends</u>, August, 11-12.

5. Fishkind, H. (1991) "The Population Engine Begins to Stall". <u>Florida Trends</u>, November, 7-9.

6. Florida Consensus Conference (1989, 1990). <u>State of Florida Executive Summary</u>, 6, Spring.

7. Florida Department of Labor and Employment Security. (1988) <u>Florida Work Force 2000: A Governor's Initiative</u>. Florida: Division of Labor, Employment, and Training.

8. Florida Department of Labor and Employment Security (1990). <u>Florida Industry and Occupational Employment Projections 1987 - 2000</u>. Florida Division of Labor, Employment and Training.

9. Hudson Institute (1987). <u>Work Force 2000: Work and Workers for the 21st Century</u>.

10. Jacksonville Community Council. (1990) <u>Future Workforce Needs Study</u>. Jacksonville: Jacksonville Community Council, Inc.

11. Koening, J. (1991) "Making Florida High-Tech". <u>Florida Trends</u>, February, 33-37.

12. Nussbaum, B. (1988) "Needed: Human Capital". <u>Business Week</u>, September 19, 100-103.

13. O'Neal, D. (1991) "Chiles Weigh Appeal Versus A Special Session." <u>Orlando Sentinel</u>, 19 October, 1(A).

14. Salamon, L. and Hornbeck, D. (1991) <u>Human Capital and America's Future: An Economic Strategy for the 90s</u>. Baltimore: John Hopkins University Press.

15. Salzer, J. (1991) "Math Tallies Low but High for Region". The Florida Times Union, 7, June, 1 (B).

16. West, C. (1990) "Economic Growth Hinges on Education". Florida Trends, November, 13-14.

BIBLIOGRAPHICAL NOTE

R. Cassady is a graduate of the University of Central Florida with a Masters in Applied Economics (1991). She wrote her thesis on "The US Human Capital Crisis: Is Florida a State at Risk?"

D. Hosni is an Associate Professor in Economics at the University of Central Florida specializing in human resources and the third world.

Table 1
LABOR SUPPLY: U.S. AND FLORIDA

	U. S.		Florida	
Population Growth Rate	1990-2000		1986-2000	
	14.6%		33.0%	
Graying of Population	1990	2000	1990	2000
(65+ years)	11.5	13.0	17.6	19.1
Labor Force				
Participation Rate	1990	2000	1990	2000
Total	66.6	66.7	62.9	67.0
Female	57.5	–	55.2	–
Black	63.3	–	66.0	–
Non-white	63.7	–	66.6	–
Labor Force Growth Rate				
1972-1986	35.0		90.0	
1986-2000	18.0		49.0	
Labor Force Shares	1990	2000	1990	2000
Female	45.0	51.6	46.4	52.5
Black	11.0	–	14.5	–
Hispanics	7.6	–	13.3	–
Non-white	14.1	–	16.4	–
Graduation Rates	1982	1987	1982	1987
	69.5	71.1	60.2	58.6

Productivity & Quality Management Frontiers-IV, edited by Sumanth, Edosomwan, Poupart, and Sink. ©1993 Institute of Industrial Engineers.

Employee Empowerment and Its Impact on Technical, Social, and Financial Aspects of Business

T.D. Cairns
WTVJ Channel 4 - NBC
Miami, Florida USA

ABSTRACT

The competitive challenges facing organizations today, combined with a demand by employees to have a say in what goes on, has compelled organizations to provide ways for employees to share in problem-solving or the decision-making process. Many organizations have attempted to do this through employee involvement programs such as small groups, quality circles, task force meetings, self-directed work teams, etc. Many organizations try to justify the existence of such programs by measuring their outcomes based on hard facts or objective data. The "real" value of such programs is the contribution they make towards "empowering" employees but evaluation of such programs is difficult. This researcher contends that employee empowerment can be determined and measured. An evaluation of empowerment can be realized by using Frederick W. Herzberg's Two-Factor Theory of Motivation. This hypothesis is based on an analysis of work-related issues or problems accumulated by an employee problem-solving process from 1989 to 1991 within the researchers' organization. The organization is a local television station with about 200 employees. The research confirmed that employee empowerment was achieved when Herzberg's hygiene factors were satisfied. Empowerment resulted when employees participated in a problem-solving process where the organization took action based on employee recommendations. This paper shows the value of such programs and the impact they have on the social, technical and financial aspects of the business.

KEY WORDS

"productivity", "motivation", "empowerment"

BACKGROUND

In October, 1989 WTVJ Channel 4, a National Broadcasting Company (NBC), Owned and Operated Television Station in Miami, Florida began meeting during regular working hours with groups of employees to examine work practices that needed improvement. All work activities were open to scrutiny: reports, paperwork, approvals, procedures, policies, etc. Employees from all levels and departments within the organization were encouraged to identify unproductive practices and offer ideas on how to replace them with more valuable activities. Every issue raised was discussed openly, candidly and without fear of reprisal. Nearly 40% of the workforce participated in these initial sessions and the outcomes were then summarized and published to all employees, along with an action plan that was agreed to by Senior management.

In the Winter of 1990, a follow-up session was conducted with the initial participants and the status of the action items was reviewed. The feedback received from this session suggested certain work-related concerns were resolved and it was decided to continue the problem-solving meetings.

Future meetings were held with small groups of 10 to 15 employees who met bi-monthly with the Station President and General Manager. These sessions were referred to as WTVJ Employee Team Meetings. Employees were selected randomly from all departments to participate in the sessions. Each group meeting began with a review of the open items that were pending before proceeding to new items.

The results of each session were summarized to include: a brief statement of the problem or concern, the names of the individuals responsible for taking action and the action that was taken. Responsibilities for action items were assigned to the appropriate supervisory personnel and the employee relations department assured commitments were fulfilled. A status report was distributed, following every meeting, to all employees in the organization.

During the remainder of 1990, an additional 20% of the workforce participated in the Employee Team meetings for a total of 125 employees in a twelve month period. Although Team meetings were scheduled through December, 1990 the last meeting was conducted in September, 1990 and there were no more meetings until August, 1991.

There are several explanations that could be offered to account for the long interruption, such as the Persian

Gulf War and other "breaking" news events but, this is the nature of the broadcast business which must be accepted to maintain a healthy organization. Thus, the problem-solving sessions were resumed in August, 1991 except with a revised meeting format.

In the previous Team Meetings, employees throughout the organization attended the meetings and presented issues they prepared in advance. However, in 1991, only employees who worked together on a day to day basis went to the meetings. They also went without prepared issues. The President and General Manager presented an overview of the state of the business and challenged employees to delve into ways to improve the organization's operation. A facilitator from the employee relations department introduced the group to brainstorming. These techniques helped the group generate issues they believed needed to be improved. There were 15 employees in the August, 1991 session and in less than 4 hours they generated 72 issues that were later combined into 30 items. Later that day the group's managers went to the meeting to review the recommendations. The managers communicated their pleasure with the many quality issues the group had generated. The group, along with their managers, were unable to solve all the problems that day and met an additional day to complete the process.

The effect the 1990 and 1991 employee problem-solving meetings had on employee motivation, productivity and empowerment was measured by applying Frederick W. Herzberg's Two-Factor Theory of Motivation. Herzberg's theory provides an excellent frame-work with which managers and organizations' actions can be evaluated (Herzberg, 1987).

REVIEW OF HERZBERG THEORY

According to Herzberg, there are two separate and distinct factors that either produce job satisfaction or job dissatisfaction (Herzberg, 1987). The one he refers to as hygiene or maintenance factor needs and the other as growth or motivator factors (Table 1), both represent independent needs and affect behavior in different ways (Herzberg, 1987). Hygiene factors could be considered as those things that influence the work environment and motivators as those things that influence the work itself (Berl, 1984).

When employee hygiene needs are satisfied it does not result in motivated, empowered or more productive employees. For example, good pay and benefits, a clean

Table 1 Herzberg's Two-Factor Theory of Motivation

Hygiene factors	Motivational factors
1. Quality of supervision 2. Company policy and administration 3. Working Conditions 4. Salary 5. Interpersonal relations with peers, supervisors and subordinates 6. Fringe Benefits	1. Achievement 2. Recognition for achievement 3. Work Itself 4. Responsibility 5. Advancement 6. Personal growth and development

shop and a friendly boss do not motivate an employee to become more productive. However, when hygiene factors are not satisfied they result in de-motivation of employees for instance; poor pay and benefits, a dirty shop and an autocratic boss would cause employees to be dissatisfied. The motivator factors, on the otherhand, if satisfied will generate positive feelings and the result is employee motivation (Berl, 1984). Consequently focusing on job content should result in motivated employees. Several research studies of Herzberg's principles have shown that increased worker satisfaction has resulted when employees have more input into job content and business objectives (Paul, 1968; Testerman, 1980).

However, hygiene factors cannot be ignored. According to Herzberg when hygiene factors are satisfied they cause a person to be willing to be motivated. If hygiene factors are not satisfied they will be analogous to a ships' anchor that weighs the organization down and keeps it from breaking out into new territory.

This researcher contends hygiene needs must initially be met before employees can become motivated, productive and empowered. This hypothesis is supported by a study of Borg-Warner employees that showed employees were more concerned about motivator factors when their hygiene needs were satisfied (Kendall, 1975). If motivator factors are to be considered the gateway to employee empowerment then hygiene factors are the gatekeepers.

When you examine Herzberg's list of hygiene factors they are straightforward and do not represent a problem for many organizations. At least not until the mid-1980's, when the changing marketplace (globalization) caused such issues as reward systems, job security and interpersonal relationships to be thrown into confusion at a time when organizations demanded more motivated, productive and empowered employees. The key to employee empowerment is in satisfying hygiene needs. This is demonstrated by the following research analysis using Herzberg's Two-Factor Theory of Motivation.

ANALYSIS

About 125 employees or 62% of the researcher's organization participated in at least 1 of the 10 problem-solving meetings conducted from October, 1990 to August, 1991. During those meetings about 65 different issues were presented, about 35 in 1990 and 30 in 1991. Since nearly a year had passed between the last meeting in September, 1990 and the first meeting in August, 1991 the researcher determined to compare the results of all the 1990 meetings against those of the 1991 meetings. The researcher used Herzberg's Theory of Motivation to classify the 1990 and 1991 issues as either a hygiene or motivator need based on Herzberg's definitions. Tables 2 and 3 are examples of the items and their classification as either a hygiene or motivator needs.

In addition to the social and technical benefits of empowerment there are likewise financial benefits that should not be forgotten by the organization. For example, the hygiene need listed in Table 2 was the computer printer wasting paper. When this issue was resolved it resulted in a $16,000 cost savings to the company.

Table 2 List of 1990 Hygiene and Motivation Issues

Hygiene Needs	Motivators Needs
*Problems with cleaning crew *Explain Paycheck stubs *Security Badge System *Parking for afternoon shift *Ineffective staff meetings *Telephone orientation *Computer printer wastes paper	*Work deadlines *Cross training personnel *Reporter/Story ideas

Table 3 List of 1991 Hygiene and Motivation Issues

Hygiene Needs	Motivators Needs

*Staffing for Cable show
*Better proofing of spelling
*Too Many Special Reports
*More respect for work
  environment
	*Lack of accountability
	*Report stories in-depth
	*Greater participation
	*Identify philosophy
	*More Community
	  involvement

After all the issues were classified, according to hygiene or motivator needs, they were then tallied and the total percentages calculated. Table 4 displays the percentage of hygiene and motivator needs for 1990 and 1991.

Table 4 Percentage of 1990 and 1991 Issues According to Hygiene and Motivator Needs

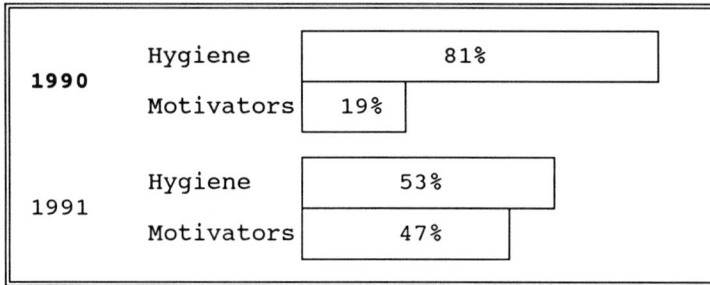

1990	Hygiene	81%
	Motivators	19%
1991	Hygiene	53%
	Motivators	47%

Since there was a significant difference between the percentage of hygiene and motivator issues raised in 1990 and those in 1991 the researcher questioned the variance. To ascertain the reasons for the difference the researcher more closely examined the hygiene issues raised in 1990.

Harvard business school professor J. Richard Hackman says "if you want me to care, then I want to be treated like an owner and have some real voice in where we are going." (Main, 1988) One way to show employees that you care is to listen and then act based on their input. Since hygiene factors are key to unlocking motivator needs, then resolving them can affect behavior in a positive manner. Unsatisfied hygiene needs results in dissatisfied employees while satisfied hygiene needs can result in employee willingness to be motivated.

Employees who attended the 1990 meetings presented mainly hygiene concerns. Senior management responded with commitment to action. Senior management communicated in writing; the planned actions, the names of individuals responsible for acting and a statement whether the action was pending or completed. This report was published and distributed to all employees after each and every Team meeting. Table 5 cites a few examples.

Table 5 Examples of 1990 Issues and Actions Taken

Hygiene Needs	Actions Taken
*Parking for afternoon shift	*Parking decals issued and only authorized employees could park
*Telephone orientation	*Classes conducted for all phone users
*Security Badge System	*Building Services to be notified of visitors in advance
*Computer printer wastes paper	*Employees trained in proper use
*Coordinating "live" shots	*Included in News Operating procedure
*Ineffective meetings	*Prepared agendas
*Lights left on	*Area safety representative responsible
*Releasing Lottery and Fantasy Five Numbers	*Numbers could be released by anyone

A closer review of Table 5 shows a large percentage of the workforce were affected by many of the hygiene issues raised. As long as management was communicating and executing their plan of action employees witnessed in a real and tangible way that their input was valued. Hygiene needs do not remain resolved indefinitely and that meant senior management had to make sure follow-up was a part of the process. Additionally since most of the solutions were the result of employee suggestions, this further reinforced the idea of "empowerment."

The satisfaction of hygiene needs created a work environment where employees in 1991 started focusing on the more intrinsic aspects of their work. However, the separation was about 50-50.

CONCLUSION

Based on this analysis, problem-solving programs do provide management a means of building stronger constructive ties with their employees. Because of these initiatives management can achieve greater employee involvement on issues that can move an organization forward at a faster pace. According to Ken Macher "people feel significant when they have the power to make a difference." According to Herzberg this desire is true for everyone at every level in the organization.

Herzberg's hygiene and motivator factors can be used to measure the impact of the social, technical and financial aspects of employee empowerment on the business. As evidenced by this research the satisfaction of employee hygiene needs improved by 28% from 1990 to 1991 and the resultant effect was a marked increase in motivator factors by the same percentage. The level of employee satisfaction with the process was also high as feedback from the sessions was favorable. The organization also experienced cost savings as a result of resolving items raised.

The findings in this research suggest that empowerment comes when the basics are fulfilled; taking time to listen, communicate candidly, be action-oriented and relentless with follow-up. Addressing Herzberg's hygiene factors will move an organization farther ahead than any complicated management "fad" for employee participation.

How can employees be convinced the organization wants increased productivity if they cannot understand their paycheck stub or find a parking space? Satisfaction of hygiene needs will permit individuals to concentrate on ways to develop and grow in a mature way.

REFERENCES

Berl, Robert L., Powell, Terry E. and Nicholas C. Williamson (1984) "Industrial Salesforce Satisfaction and Performance with Herzberg's Theory" Industrial Marketing Management v13 n1 pgs. 11-19

Herzberg, Frederick (1987). "One More Time: How Do You Motivate Employees?" Harvard Business Review September-October pgs. 109-120

Kendall, Edward L. and Clyde C. Robinson (1975) "Motivation and Productivity of the Technical Employee" Industrial Management June pgs. 1-8

Macher, Ken (1988) "Empowerment and the Bureaucracy" Training & Development Journal September

Main, Jeremy (1988) "The Winning Organization" Fortune, September 26

Paul Jr., William J., Robertson, Keith B. and Frederick Herzberg (1968) "Job Enrichment Pays Off" Harvard Business Review January-February pgs. 61-78

Testerman, Michael B. (1980) "Job Enrichment: Concepts and Consequences" Industrial Management v22 n3 pgs. 9-11

BIOGRAPHICAL SKETCH
   Mr. Cairns is the Director, Employee Relations for NBC's Owned and Operated Television Station in Miami, Florida, WTVJ Channel 4. He has over fifteen years of progressive human resource experience in various businesses. Mr. Cairns holds a B.S. in Commerce from Rider College and an M.S. from Nova University. He is currently pursuing a DBA in Human Resource Management with Nova University.

Productivity & Quality Management Frontiers-IV, edited by Sumanth, Edosomwan, Poupart, and Sink. ©1993 Institute of Industrial Engineers.

Effective Communication in the Working Environment

R.R. Bell
Boeing Commercial Airplane Group
Seattle, Washington USA

Abstract

Never before has the need for effective communication in the workplace been greater than it is today. In our quest to stay on the competitive edge in the marketplace we are failing miserably in effectively communicating with one another on the job. Our high-tech age has provided us with high-tech methods and tools to communicate with one another which includes voice-mail, electronic mail, and oh yes...the fax. While many of these tools have enabled us to become much more efficient in our business they have also to an certain extent caused us to become more and more distant in the "human" side of communication, thus diluting our effectiveness. When the "human" side of communication breaks down we begin to see morale problems as a result which lead to increased attrition and a potentially semi-productive workforce...all of which equate to increased costs. People who leave need to be replaced, their replacements need to be trained and the associated costs continue to grow. In order to be more efficient we need to be more effective. In an effort to initiate that process this paper summarizes a variety of research conducted addressing the perception, types, challenges, and benefits associated with effective communication. Two models are also discussed which when combined with the research provide some useful tools to stimulate the communication process. Our productivity and quality will excel in direct proportion to our ability to effectively communicate with our people. We must begin today.....our future depends on it.

Productivity & Quality Management Frontiers-IV, edited by Sumanth, Edosomwan, Poupart, and Sink. ©1993 Institute of Industrial Engineers.

An Integrated New Product Development Process Utilizing Cross Functional Design-Build Teams

T.M. McClung
Allied-Signal Aerospace Canada
Rexdale, Ontario CANADA

ABSTRACT

Central to success in today's marketplace is the ability to develop a product that meets or exceeds the customer's needs and to deliver that product in the shortest possible time and at the lowest possible cost.

In the Aerospace Electronic Control System marketplace, our products have a high technical content, and development leadtimes frequently are measured in years, both of which imply large cost investments.

The traditional product development process beginning with the creation of a customer's product specifications through a sequential series of design stages with information passing from various functional groups creates avoidable costs, schedule delays, product design changes and ultimately customer dissatisfaction.

The principles of Concurrent Product Engineering are widely known and are based upon integrating the collective effort and knowledge of all involved design disciplines in a parallel and highly interactive manner in order to eliminate the wasted efforts and iterations inherent in the traditional process.

The challenge is to create and implement an integrated product development process embodying these principles, which incorporates internal and external stakeholders, creates the tools and knowledge set, and encourages positive team dynamics which are required to achieve the full potential of the approach.

At Garrett Canada we have implemented an integrated product development process founded upon multi-functional Design-Build Teams which include members from involved internal departments, suppliers and customers. The process was started in 1990 with results to date showing reductions in both nonrecurring effort and product costs approaching 25%.

This paper describes the Design-Build process, how the teams were formed, trained, operate and evolved. Also discussed are the lessons we have learned, what worked well, what didn't, and what we plan to do next.

KEYWORDS

Integrated Product Development Process
Concurrent Engineering
Design-Build Teams
Productivity

INTRODUCTION

Garrett Canada is an operating division of Allied-Signal Aerospace Canada, one of the aerospace companies of Allied-Signal Incorporated, a Fortune 100 Company. Garrett Canada is located near Toronto, Ontario Canada, and employs approximately 1000 people engaged in the design, development, manufacture and support of high technology aerospace communication, thermal, environmental and related electronic sensing and control systems for the global market.

We have excellent long standing relationships with our principal commercial, military and government customers, enjoy a reputation for delivering quality products and service, and a culture that is customer and team focused.

In the late 1980's it became evident that our customers' expectations were increasing and our competitors were redoubling their efforts to displace us from our market leading positions. Driven by these market pressures and a commitment to continuous improvement we began to re-examine our fundamental business processes. We chose to concentrate on cycle time reduction as the key to improvement in quality and customer satisfaction. Employee involvement teams utilizing statistical process control techniques were soon achieving startling improvements in the factory arena. It became increasingly evident that continuing cost and quality improvement would become limited by the inherent product design features, which lead us to include our processes for designing, developing and introducing our products.

THE NEED DEFINED

From mid 1990 to mid 1991 we were introducing two major new products to the factory and were in the middle of flight test validation. In support of these activities we found ourselves undergoing a sequence of product design changes. These product changes were driven from three principal sources: a) changes to correct engineering design errors and performance test deficiencies, b) changes to improve factory producibility discovered during the fabrication of the first production certified articles and c) customer directed changes to improve or better match the product performance to the airline operators needs. Besides adding to non-recurring product development costs, the change cycle required months of engineering development, and placed additional burdens on the airplane development program.

At about this point in time we were awarded another major new product development program. Due to intense competition we had taken product and engineering cost targets reduced by 25%, from our already aggressive plans. Working harder may have achieved a 5-10% savings but we had to find a way to work smarter. To reduce cycle time and corresponding costs we decided we would have to eliminate most of the sequential releases and builds of development hardware configurations. Each version of equipment would have to be as close to right as we could make it. We could not tolerate the several rounds of downstream changes caused by factory inputs and misunderstood customer requirements. Our approach was to form teams to address each major area of engineering development, with members from all of the engineering disciplines involved in the design and definition of the new product. As well as project, design manufacturing, quality assurance, test and customer service engineers, we also incorporated program management, contracts and sales members as appropriate. Our customer and key suppliers were also included in this process. This is the essence of concurrent or simultaneous engineering. We call these teams Design-Build Teams or DBT's. Cost targets for all major system components were established, and cost versus time criteria developed to provide the teams a more objective tool for design review product cost decision making.

GETTING STARTED

We were fortunate as our customer was also deploying their own integrated development process and as a major supplier we were invited to attend training courses at their facilities. We sent a small group of our key people to participate. This group became the core of our own project Design-Build Team and training facilitators for subsequent lower level Design-Build Teams.

Although a smaller project could operate with a single project DBT, the project we addressed involved a significant number of contributors. We divided the project into seven subsidiary DBT's for significant design activities, and assigned appropriate members from cross-functional disciplines. Core members would serve more-or-less full time on these teams, and support members would serve on several DBT's on a part time basis (See Figure 1). Once formed, the teams (both core and support members) were given eight (8) hours of training in two sessions. All teams were trained as a group in the overall process and underlying principles. These included DBT structure, team synergy, building consensus, and project goals. Subsequent to this, each individual team had separate training to help develop their own operating norms and goals (eg. meeting processes, roles and responsibilities, and setting detailed time-phased team goals and objectives).

In this mode of operation, Design-Build Team members operate in a matrix organization. We are a medium size division which is called upon to support 10 to 20 new product development projects at various stages of completion, and provide continuing support for ongoing production products. This approach provides flexibility and optimum use of our engineering resources. Key to success in this process is the balancing of program and functional responsibilities by the DBT members. The program goals are focused on Cost, Schedule and Customer Specification Compliance. DBT members must also incorporate home department functional initiatives focused on departmental resource planning and strategic directions which address preferred technologies, automation, standardization and reuse (See Figure 2). Success in this approach is founded upon training, individual accountability, enlightened, supportive functional managers and an overriding commitment to customer satisfaction.

EVOLUTION OF THE PROCESS

The Design-Build Teams have been operating for approximately eighteen (18) months. The project is on schedule with all major customer milestones met. Development non-recurring costs are tracking the 25% reduction line and the current manufacturing product costs estimate is at 74% of its original value (See Figure 3). Both our customer and suppliers participated jointly in design studies and technical reviews. The program Critical Design Review was successfully

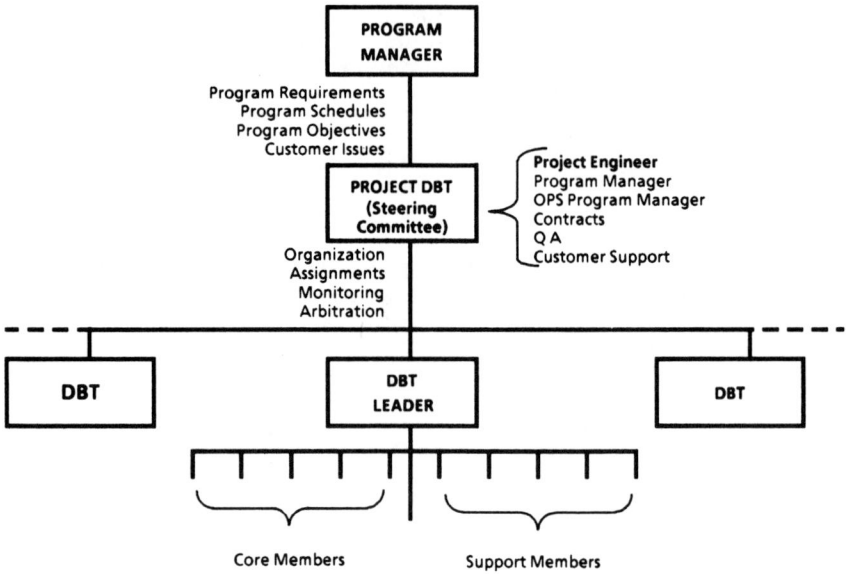

Figure 1 Design-Build Team Structure

FUNCTIONAL FOCUS

- **Departmental Budgets**
- **Resource Planning**
- **Strategic Direction**

  – Technical
  – Commonality / Reuse
  – Standardization
  – Automation

PROGRAM FOCUS

- **Cost Goals**
- **Schedule Goals**
- **Customer Specification**

		MECH. ENG.	ELEC. ENG.	QA	OPS MAT	OPS PROD.	CUST. SUPP.
P R O G R A M	A	X	X	X	X		X
	B	X	X	X	X	X	
	C	X		X	X		X

Figure 2 DBT Members have Matrix Responsibilities

completed this spring and the first production prototype units are being fabricated in our manufacturing new product cell. Several other projects have also benefited from the manufacturing process and test procedure development and reviews conducted in this dedicated facility.

One of the early significant results of the approach was achieved by a sub-team which tackled the design of the Power Converter Module and involved the design engineer, a component engineer and purchasing representative as principals. They evolved a power converter design that eliminated one complete printed wiring board assembly, reduced the types and numbers of components required by 76% and manufacturing operations by 56% (See Figure 4). This design approach offered such significant savings that it has been back designed into several other existing products.

As the individual DBT's addressed their tasks, the only common process procedures they had to work with stemmed from their individual basic training. Each group evolved their own operating procedures and design review approaches. The project Design-Build Team Steering Committee provided a level of consistency and forum for the migration of best practices across the several subsidiary DBT's. Not all of the DBT's were equally successful. One team leader and team members changed at their own request due to dissatisfaction with their results and the process, and two other teams merged into a single team. The process was deemed to be of substantial benefit, due to the cost savings indicated by the pilot project, and perhaps more importantly by the fact that ad-hoc "Design-Build Teams" were beginning to perceive benefits and form themselves spontaneously on other development projects.

The evolution of the design-build process was planned following the Deming/Shewart Plan-Do-Check-Act (PDCA) improvement cycle outlined in Figure 5. As described in the preceding paragraphs the "check" portion of the cycle was indicating that the process was beneficial and the "act" portion of the

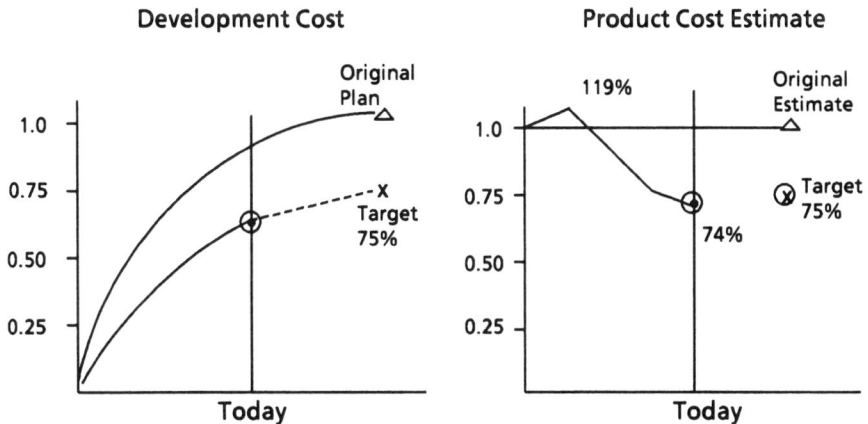

Figure 3 Project Cost Status

Early Results are Positive

LINE CONDITIONER & POWER CONVERTER

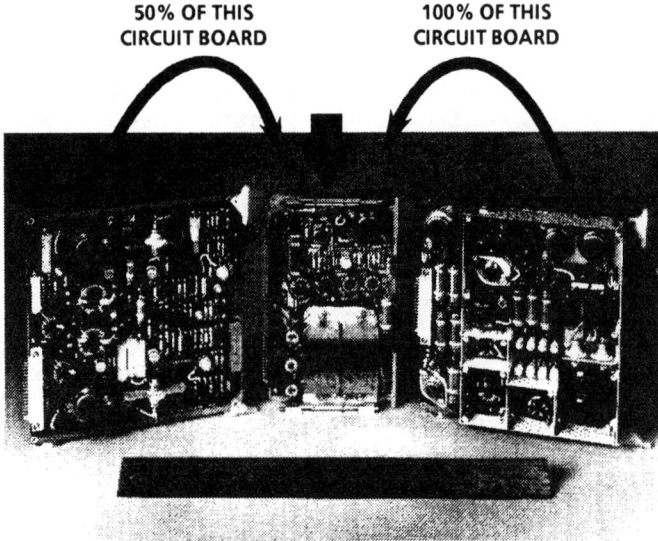

50% OF THIS
CIRCUIT BOARD

100% OF THIS
CIRCUIT BOARD

COMPONENT COUNT

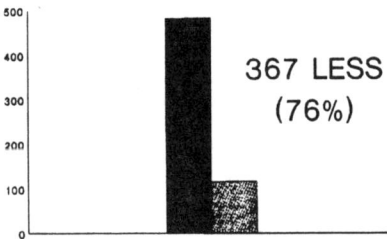

367 LESS
(76%)

NUMBER OF PROCESS STEPS

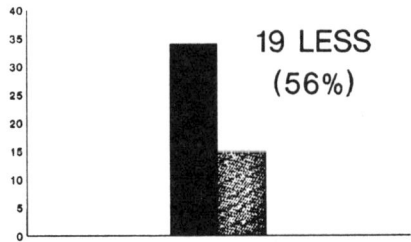

19 LESS
(56%)

Figure 4 Power Converter Module

cycle would require a review of lessons learned, development of formalized process procedures, training and deployment of the process on a division-wide basis.

As we began to develop the formal design-build procedures we identified four (4) key components of the process that required specific proceduralization at the division level (See Figure 6). First was an overriding policy statement (P&P 6.7) that clearly states and acknowledges Management's Commitment to a team oriented, disciplined approach to new product development. The myth that engineering is an art that cannot be defined by an underlying cooperative process cannot be allowed to persist. Second, the definition, composition, roles and responsibilities of Design-Build Teams (P&P 6.8) are defined, as well as consensus and appeal procedures to prevent deadlock. Third, Management Roles and Responsibilities in the review process are defined and checklists provided (P&P 6.9). The key here is to make these periodic reviews a non-threatening and value-added process. They serve to keep a direct management involvement in the product development process and provide opportunity for recognition of the project team for goals successfully achieved. Finally, the methods for conducting detailed design reviews incorporating lessons learned checklists, and action closure logs were defined (P&P 6.10). These technical reviews are to ensure that product performance and product safety requirements are met, as well as functional department initiatives for design practices, standardization and reuse.

LESSONS LEARNED

During the pilot project and evolution of the Design-Build Teams, a Management Process Committee was formed and chaired by the Vice President, Engineering. Members included the pilot project Engineering Team Leader, the Program Manager, the Manufacturing Manager of the New Product Module, a Quality Assurance Engineer, and the Director of Design Engineering. This committee met approximately bi-weekly for a period of six (6) months to track the pilot project, interview DBT members, develop policies, procedures, training materials and process deployment plans. The Division President and Executive Staff were briefed periodically on project status, participated in two Management Program Reviews, and key members reviewed and commented upon the policies and procedures as they were developed. The Management Process Committee conducted two half day training sessions on the Design-Build Team process for division mid-management and functional supervisors who would become involved in the DBT approach to new product development.

Prior to division wide deployment of the process, a summary of the Key DBT Lessons Learned at that point was as follows:
- Set Stretch Goals
- Supervisor Support Required
- Follow Up Training Required
- Process Needs formalizing
- Displined Adherence To Process Essential
- Strive for Real Consensus
- Rigorous, Critical Reviews Necessary
- Physical Co-Location Helps Mental Co-Location

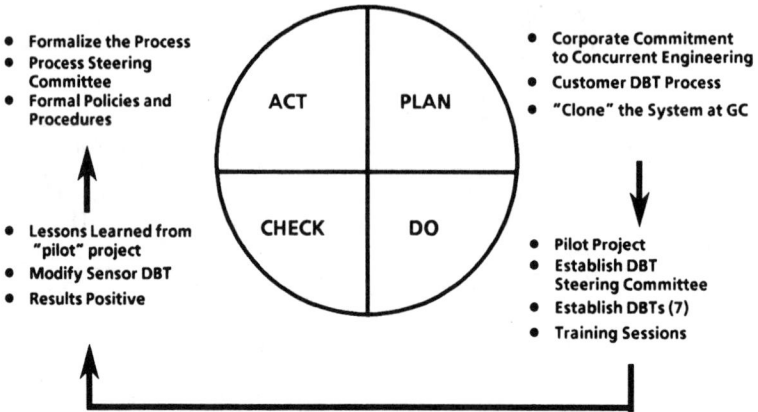

ACT
- Formalize the Process
- Process Steering Committee
- Formal Policies and Procedures

PLAN
- Corporate Commitment to Concurrent Engineering
- Customer DBT Process
- "Clone" the System at GC

CHECK
- Lessons Learned from "pilot" project
- Modify Sensor DBT
- Results Positive

DO
- Pilot Project
- Establish DBT Steering Committee
- Establish DBTs (7)
- Training Sessions

Figure 5 Evolution of the Design-Build Team/Process

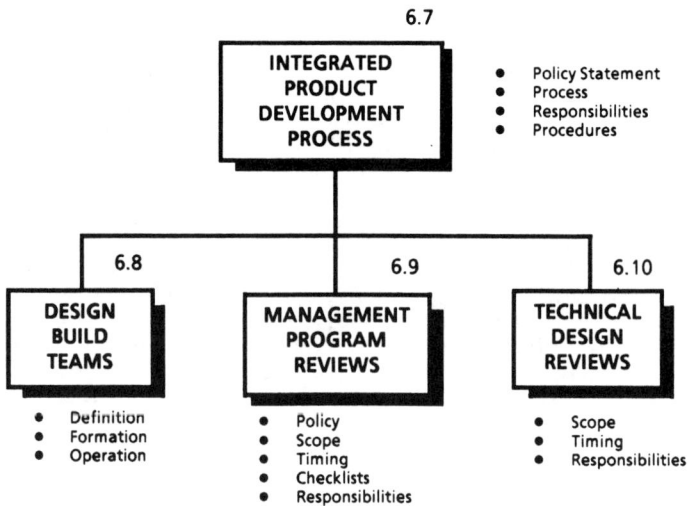

6.7

INTEGRATED PRODUCT DEVELOPMENT PROCESS
- Policy Statement
- Process
- Responsibilities
- Procedures

6.8
DESIGN BUILD TEAMS
- Definition
- Formation
- Operation

6.9
MANAGEMENT PROGRAM REVIEWS
- Policy
- Scope
- Timing
- Checklists
- Responsibilities

6.10
TECHNICAL DESIGN REVIEWS
- Scope
- Timing
- Responsibilities

Figure 6 Integrated Product Development Process

1150

First is a clear project goal, which represents enough stretch to displace the "Let's work a little harder" paradigm and an openness for new approaches to develop. Support from first line supervisors and middle managers from the functional departments is essential. They feel the most threatened by this process and communication, training and re-enforcement of their importance to the process is critical.

A one-time training effort is not sufficient. The new process requires continuous reinforcement in its early stages. As DBT members change due to employee turnover, reassignments or as the project moves into later stages, this initial training will help refamiliarization. More focused training to address specific team needs must also be provided.

The process must be formalized, documented and deployed across all affected departments. It was useful to solicit input and comments from key department managers during development of the top level command media to assure widespread "Buy-In" to the process.

Once established, a disciplined adherence to the process must be enforced. Automated tools, routine use of the review process with Lesson-Learned checklists and closed-loop action tracking are important to success. We are maintaining an active process overview committee, and process changes with upgrades are planned so that improvements may be incorporated and a method of removing areas of discontent is available. Real, not apparent consensus is the foundation of the team approach to the design process. The initial fear of "Design by Committee" must be displaced early. A norm of open, honest dialogue with fact based decision making must be established.

Role playing and consensus building exercises during initial training were found to be helpful and also the more successful teams were comfortable with rigorous open and critical technical reviews. Shifting the focus to customer satisfaction tends to disarm the inherent defense mechanisms and sets up a common goal for all team members.

Finally, team members who were located together benefited from the improved communications. Although it is not possible for all resources to be dedicated and co-located, team meetings and program/technical reviews served to reinforce the "mental" co-location.

WHAT'S NEXT

Teams have been formed to automate and standardize the Lessons Learned data base and a review discrepancy tracking system. Members of the original pilot project DBT's have been retrained, the next several projects to use the process are scheduled for training and by the end of the year all new product development projects will use the process. Additional training modules to provide improved team dynamics, leadership skills, and support tool introductions are planned.

Better process metrics are being developed. Better tools to help the teams make more informed cost decisions during the design cycle and another PDCA cycle to implement automated "Design for Manufacturability and Assembly" analysis tools has been initiated.

A simplified process guidebook to serve as a reference document in support of the policies and procedures is scheduled to be released in the next few months. Finally a preplanned process review and command media upgrade will be conducted.

SUMMARY

At Garrett Canada an integrated new product development process has been implemented which captures the power inherent in multi-functional Design-Build Teams. Customer and supplier representatives have also participated and relationships have been strengthened. Results to date are showing specific reductions in product and development costs approaching 25%. Additionally, design and test approaches have evolved from these teams which have offered additional savings for non-related projects. During the development of this new process a Deming/Shewart PDCA cycle was followed which is now serving as a model as we address other division critical operating processes.

BIOGRAPHICAL SKETCH OF AUTHOR

Tim McClung holds a BSc in Electrical Engineering from UCLA and an MSc in Control Systems from The University of Southern California. In his 24 year career with Allied-Signal Aerospace, he has held various engineering and management positions at three divisions, including $2\frac{1}{2}$ years as Director of Quality Assurance, prior to joining Garrett Canada as Vice President, Engineering.

Productivity & Quality Management Frontiers-IV, edited by Sumanth, Edosomwan, Poupart, and Sink. ©1993 Institute of Industrial Engineers.

Insights on Employee Empowerment and its Effects on Productivity

E. Witt and K. Graebner
The Boeing Company
Wichita, Kansas USA

ABSTRACT: As awareness of America's lack of competitiveness increases, the need to improve employee productivity and provide for the effective use of resources is becoming an increasingly critical concern for American businesses. Since the 1930's, experts such as Scanlon, Deming, and Juran have fostered concepts of employee empowerment and quality improvement. Now, upper level managers are directing the use of these concepts to improve their companies' positions both domestically and internationally. Unfortunately, these programs are frequently misunderstood by managers and employees alike. In this paper, the concepts of an early promoter of employee empowerment will be discussed along with successes resulting from his concepts. Also discussed will be attributes of employee empowerment, modern cases of employee empowerment, and pitfalls in the use of employee empowerment programs.

Key Words:
Quality
Productivity
Scanlon Plan
Employee Empowerment
Delegation of Responsibility
Goals
Training

Productivity & Quality Management Frontiers-IV, edited by Sumanth, Edosomwan, Poupart, and Sink. ©1993 Institute of Industrial Engineers.

The Impact of Assertive Communication on Quality

M.K. Owens
IBM Corporation
Boca Raton, Florida USA

ABSTRACT

In our corporate environment, assertive communication is one of the key elements needed for a team to be productive. In our microcode or firmware testing environment, the engineers, programmers, and analysts' assertive or non-assertive behaviors have had a significant impact on the entire team's quality and productivity results.

This article refers to team members who perform a particular role of function testing microcode. Enhanced technical, organizational, debugging and communication skills are required. The objective of finding all problems, then reporting them to engineers and developers, requires that the engineers, programmers, or analysts with this responsibility need assertive communication skills. These skills enable them to firmly state the problems and openly discuss them. They are able to stand up for themselves in a way that also considers the basic rights of the other person. Conversely, the non-assertive activities of passive, passive aggressive and aggressive employees negatively affect the quality of the code and break down the synergistic team environment; thus, reducing their creativity needed for problem solving.

In today's competitive, ever changing environment, assertive communication skills have allowed this group to become their own best selves, continually growing, continually improving their personal effectiveness and continually finding creative solutions for their customers. By improving the process with assertive communication, they have improved the quality of their microcode so that it is 20 times greater than it was in 1989. Their personal effectiveness and their positive reputation as a team has predictably mirrored the enhanced quality and productivity of the products.

Keywords - Assertive Communication, Productivity, Quality

INTRODUCTION

In our corporate environment, assertive communication is one of the key elements needed for a team to be productive. In our microcode or firmware testing environment, the engineers, programmers, and analysts' assertive or non-assertive behaviors have a significant impact on the entire team's quality and productivity results.

For example, team members who perform a particular role for the organization by function verification testing the microcode require enhanced technical, organizational, debugging and communication skills. The objective of finding all problems, then reporting them to engineers and developers, requires that the engineers, programmers, or analysts with this responsibility need assertive communication skills. These skills enable them to firmly state the problems and openly discuss them. They are able to stand up for themselves in a way that also considers the basic rights of the other person. Conversely, the non-assertive activities of passive, passive aggressive and aggressive employees affect the quality of the code and break down the synergistic team environment; thus, reducing their creativity needed for problem solving. It is noticed that aggressive and passive aggressive team members obstruct progress. By introducing their slow, deliberate obstacles or roadblocks into the team's communication process, they make it especially difficult for others to manage or work with them.

By introducing this team to assertiveness training, listening skills, empowerment and effective leadership habits, they are able to enhance their ability to communicate and produce more effective and efficient results in a corporate culture.

Infante, Rancer, Womack (1990) note the connection of organization and group communication, with the Hawthorne effect on productivity:

The Hawthorne studies (Roethlisberger & Dickson, 1939) led the way for researchers to consider the effect of communication and human relations upon productivity. Likert (1971) stressed open communication and participative decision-making as a means of increasing employees' satisfaction and productivity. (p. 305)

The concepts of assertive communication, quality and productivity are discussed in this paper with emphasis on this team's positive results achieved and their growth in an organization.

ASSERTIVE COMMUNICATION

The assertiveness training of Smith (1975), Alberti & Emmons (1975), and Career Track (1986) was shared with the team along with the correlation of that training to their work responsibility. Smith (1975) sets the base for assertive communication with each person owning and judging their own behavior, thoughts and emotions and being responsible for them. Alberti & Emmons (1975) expands the definition with spontaneity, conversation tone, eye contact, openly expressing feelings and opinions and valuing yourself equal to others. Career Track (1986) shows the progression of training people to treat you differently, increasing your self-respect, and letting people know your needs.

NON-ASSERTIVE COMMUNICATION

As important as knowing assertive communication skills, a team requires a basic understanding of non-assertive communication; such as: aggressive, passive and passive aggressive. Therefore, this information was also introduced to all team members.

Aggressive communication is standing up for yourself by putting down others (Career Track, 1986). Alberti & Emmons (1975) expanded this definition also with speaking loudly and abusively, speaking before the other person is through, accusing, blaming, demeaning, valuing yourself above others and hurting others to avoid hurting yourself.

Passive communication is failing to stand up for yourself or ineffectively standing up for yourself (Career Track, 1986). Alberti & Emmons (1975) expanded on this definition with speaking softly, looking away, avoiding issues, agreeing regardless, not expressing your feelings and valuing yourself below others.

Passive aggressive communication is being dishonest with yourself and others. On the surface it looks and sounds good, but is sarcastic underneath. It is an indirect expression of anger or frustration (CareerTrack, 1986). Again, you are not expressing your feelings and you are valuing yourself below others.

QUALITY AND PRODUCTIVITY

This team develops and tests new technology and new products for the latest state-of-the-art equipment. The environment is fast-paced, competitive and constantly changing with the latest computer designs. The process must be continuously improved with team members identifying, speaking up, and changing the process as well as the product for the best quality. Quality in this environment is best described by Lorinc (1990): "According to Deming's teachings, quality is the predictable absence of error." He further states "Quality must be built in at the design stage" (p. 38).

In this fast-paced, competitive industry, productivity is most important. This team views productivity as the ability to complete a quality product in the shortest amount of time possible. This requires synergistic, clear assertive communication by the team's members. Persico (1990) states employee motivation is best when they have the information to do a job and know what is expected of them. Mann (1992) states, "Research shows that productivity is maximized when three factors work together: ability, opportunity and motivation" (p. 7). He further states that included in the top 10 abilities needed to maximize productivity is the "ability to accurately perceive other's points of view, needs, and interests" (p. 8). Knapp & Vangelisti (1992) agree with this idea where effective communication is adopting to another's primary communication style.

NON-ASSERTIVE COMMUNICATION IMPACT

Now that we have defined the assertive and non-assertive communication, quality and productivity that this team learned, let's look at the impact of assertive and non-assertive communication on quality and productivity.

Team members with aggressive communication are like "tanks," continually needing to get their own way. They instill fear to push their own ideas. They are rude. They do not take the time to view the needs and interests of the entire team. Team members with aggressive communication do not listen. Sypher, Bostrom & Seibert (1989) showed that:

> Inefficient listening is costly to corporations -- costly in wasted money, misused time, deflated morale, reduced productivity, and alienated relationships. (p. 301)

They do not cooperate, which interferes with accomplishing tasks, as indicated by Infante, Rancer & Womack (1990):

> verbal aggressiveness is defined as a trait of attacking the self-concepts of people instead of, or in addition to, their positions on topics of communication (Infante & Wigley, 1986). (p. 159)

Aggressive people hurry the process, verbally put others down, and take shortcuts to quickly get tasks done. In the long run, it takes longer to undo the damage to the team, which affects their team's productivity. The shortcuts in bypassing the process impact quality and require more testing and validation at the end of the cycle. Further, the team members lose the valuable creative and synergistic environment needed for problem solving. Blanchard (1990) states "a real team is committed to open communication that allows its members to state their opinions, thoughts and feelings without fear" (p. 45).

Team members with passive communication are like "wimps" continually having "sand" kicked on their ideas. These timid, shy, quiet people are not convincing and can easily be overrun by a person with aggressive communication. Buckham (1990) says that many employees are not assertive enough to speak up. They do not speak up easily or share their thoughts quickly with the team, so productivity is affected. They avoid telephone calls, avoid pushy people, procrastinate, and do not like to "rock the boat." If they find problems in the design or the code, their passive communication affects the quality if they must negotiate the problem with a particularly aggressive person.

Passive aggressive communication is the most difficult and causes the greatest negative impact to the quality of the product and the team's productivity, because it is dishonest. Therefore, passive aggressive team members obstruct progress. They appear passive and pleasant saying the right thing at the right time, but their productivity and quality does not reflect it. Connor (1991) shares some of the problems in managing passive aggressive people:

> The person might deliberately work slowly or avoid specific deadlines by claiming to have "forgotten." Another might find reason after reason to explain why the effort won't work rather than creativity tackling the sticking points. Yet another may seem resentful of suggestions, sulky, irritable or argumentative. They have passive behavior that slows things down or stonewalls them. (p. 74)

1158

They put obstacles or roadblocks into the teams' progress, and they make it especially difficult for others to manage or work with their immature and unhealthy communication.

Poor self-esteem or exaggerated self-esteem is related to these non-assertive communications. Demarco (1987) tells how "we all tend to tie our self-esteem strongly to the quality of the product we produce" (p. 19).

In 1989, the impact of these non-assertive communication skills included problems found in the field, test escapes, longer cycle times to complete products, and constant holes in the process.

ASSERTIVE COMMUNICATION IMPACT

Assertive communication positively affects the quality and productivity of the products. Assertive communication is thought to increase the likelihood of achieving goals (Er, 1989). Mitchell (1988) shows that from vision to action "one needs to be purposeful, positive and assertive with high confidence and self-esteem" (p. i). Team members with assertive communication are confident and have a high self-esteem.

Managers, too, must assertively communicate to have high productivity. Petit (1990) says that "by teaching managers how to communicate more effectively, employee development programs will have a better chance of enhancing the performance of organization members as well as the organization itself" (p. 8).

Assertive communication skills enable team members to firmly state problems and openly discuss them. They can discuss the new designs and technology in an open, free manner. They are able to stand up for themselves in a way that also considers the basic rights of the other person.

Assertive communication enables empathic listening and empowerment by the team. Covey (1989) teaches the growth process that enables interdependent synergistic teams. This maturity movement from dependent to independent to interdependent has assertive communication as its first habit of being proactive. Being proactive means that each team member is responsible for their own lives. They are truly empowered. Covey (1989) says:

> The difference between people who exercise initiative
> and those who don't is literally the difference

between night and day. I'm not talking about a
25 or 50 percent difference in effectiveness; I'm
talking about a 5000 plus percent difference,
particularly if they are smart, aware, and
sensitive to others. (p. 76)

He refers to proactivity as private victories on our
journey to effectiveness. With proactive, assertive team
members who also acquire technical and debugging skills,
the objective of finding all problems is greatly enhanced.
Covey continues with public victories, and shows how to
truly be assertive with Habit 5, the ultimate assertive
communication--Seek First to Understand and Then to Be
Understood. This enables both sides of the assertive
equation to fully be addressed --to speak up and do it in a
way that considers the other person. Thus, the team's
effectiveness is enhanced by integrating active listening
with assertive communication. The team benefits by
achieving the highest quality products along with optimal
productivity.

Covey (1991) states that total quality is rooted in
timeless principles:

- Faith, hope, humility
- Works, industry, research, testing
- Constancy, consistency, predictability
- Continuous improvement and progression
- Feedback based on both measurement and discernment
- Virtue and truth in human relations. (p. 260)

He further says "without the roots, we don't get the
fruits." That "communication, after all, is not so
much a matter of intellect as it is of trust and
acceptance of others, of their ideas and feelings,
acceptance of the fact that they're different and that
from their point of view they are right" (p. 117).

SUMMARY

Today, the team has improved the quality of their microcode
20 times greater than in 1989. They handle more products
with reduced cycle time. They creatively and openly
discuss problems and propose solutions, and they write
technical disclosures on their inventions.

The productivity and quality of our products improved as
this team embraced the skills of assertiveness,

listening, empowerment and effectiveness. Each of these skills is based on proactive habits and ownership for their part of the team. This is an ongoing improvement process. As new members join this team, they, too, must make the journey to a higher state of maturity including assertive communication skills, and continue to enhance the quality and productivity of the team.

In today's competitive, ever-changing environment, assertive communication skills have enabled this group to become their own best selves, continually growing, continually improving their personal effectiveness and continually finding creative solutions for their customers. Their personal effectiveness and their positive reputation as a team have predictably mirrored the highest levels of quality and productivity.

BIOGRAPHICAL REFERENCES

Alberti, R.E. and Emmons, M.L. (1975) <u>Stand Up Speak Talk Back</u>, New York, Pocket Books.

Blanchard, K. (1990) "Molding a Staff into a Team", <u>Today's Office</u>, vol. 125, no. 4, pp. 44-46.

Buckham, R.H. (1990) "Appraisal training: Not Just for Managers", <u>Training and Development Journal</u>, vol. 44, no. 6, pp. 18, 21.

Careertrack (1986) <u>Assertiveness Training for Professionals</u>, Boulder, CareerTrack.

Connor, J.C. (1991) "Managing Passive-aggressive People", <u>HRMagazine</u>, vol. 11, pp. 74-78.

Covey, S.R. (1989) <u>The 7 Habits of Highly Effective People</u>, New York, Simon & Schuster, Inc.

Covey, S.R. (1991) <u>Principle-Centered Leadership</u>, New York, Summit Books.

Demarco, T. and Lister. (1987) <u>Peopleware</u>, New York, Dorset House Publishing Co.

Er, M.C. (1989) "Assertive Behavior and Stress", <u>Advanced Management Journal</u>, vol. 54, no. 4, pp. 4-8.

Infante, D.A. and Rancer, A.S. and Womack, D.R. (1990) Building Communication Theory, Illinois, Waveland Press, Inc.

Knapp, M.L. and Vangelisti, A.L. (1992) Interpersonal Communication and Human Relationships, Boston, Allyn and Bacon.

Lorinc, J. (1990) "Dr. Deming's Traveling Quality Show", Canadian Business, vol. 63, no. 9, pp. 38-42.

Mann, N. (1992) "Raising Productivity", Managers Magazine, vol. 67, no. 2, pp. 7-8.

Mitchell, E. (1988) "From Vision to Action: The Seven P Process", Leadership & Organizational Development Journal (UK), vol. 19, no. 6, pp. i-ii.

Persico, Jr., J. (1990) "Employee Motivation: Belief vs. Reality", Quality, vol. 29, no. 3, pp. 51-53.

Petit, Jr., J.D. and Vaught, B.C. and Trewatha, R. (1990) "Interpersonal skill training: a prerequisite for success", Business, vol. 40, no. 2, pp. 8-14.

Smith, M.J. (1975) When I Say No, I Feel Guilty, New York, Bantam Books.

Sypher, B.D. and Bostrom, R.N. and Seibert, J.H. (1989) "Listening, Communication Abilities and Success at Work", Journal of Business Communication, vol. 26, no. 4, pp. 293-303.

BIOGRAPHICAL SKETCH OF AUTHOR

Mary K. Owens (Mame) has been an IBM manager for 10 years. Currently, she is managing an Engineering Software development area. Her interest is Industrial Psychology and she is attending The New York Institute of Technology on the Lynn University campus in Boca Raton, Florida.

Productivity & Quality Management Frontiers-IV, edited by Sumanth, Edosomwan, Poupart, and Sink. ©1993 Institute of Industrial Engineers.

Work Humanization: An Essential Requirement for Achieving Competitive Levels of Productivity and Quality

E. Oliva-López
National Polytechnic Institute - UPIICSA
Iztacalco, D.F. MEXICO

Productivity and quality improvement programs are usually resorted to when the organization is facing some kind some competitiveness related problems. In such a situation, most firms tend to experience a noticeable deterioration of their organizational climate, and some degree of frustration, anger and lack of interest can be observed amongst their personnel. Apart from this, one should acknowledge that the improvement of productivity and quality levels has never been an easy task for, right from the beginning, making all people aware of its meaning for the survival and development of the firm and its implications for each individual's duties and responsibilities, does entail a considerable effort by the program promoters and leaders.

This is why the firm's management is advised to show, as early as possible, an authentic concern for work humanization, so that when the discussion and planning of the aforementioned programs take place, they can be performed in a favourable climate with the participation of all areas of the firm. Consequently, all people within the organization should have the opportunity to appreciate some results of good managerial practices, before they are asked to commit themselves to the improvement programs.

This paper examines the way in which work humanization is likely to promote productivity and quality improvement in the Mexican industry.

Productivity & Quality Management Frontiers-IV, edited by Sumanth, Edosomwan, Poupart, and Sink. ©1993 Institute of Industrial Engineers.

Results and Conclusions from Applying TQM to Research

A.C. Endres
Juran Institute, Inc.
Wilton, Connecticut USA

ABSTRACT

Organizations have begun to share their strategies for implementing Total Quality Management (TQM) within research and development (R&D) environments. This paper summarizes the common strategies, some pitfalls and initial results. The summary is based upon both reported results and the author's consulting experience with R&D organizations.

INTRODUCTION

The application of quality concepts, processes, and tools, has been progressing "up stream" from the factory floor to the research lab. The rate of progress, particularly over the last few years, has been accelerating. It is the author's opinion that there now exists a critical mass of organizations that have begun to implement TQM within their research organizations. Several of these organizations have reported their strategies, successes and "lessons learned." Reviewing these reports and participating in some of the initial efforts has provided some conclusions on how to think about quality within a research environment, and how to introduce TQM into research and development environments.

TEXT

Proof of The Need

Within most research organizations there is increasing pressure to produce more results with less budget in less time. Therefore it is imperative that research organizations ensure that their critical resources, the research staff, are focused on projects that address the strategic needs of the organization and the needs are being met efficiently. TQM should not be sold as a means for promoting flashes of brilliant insight. It should be sold as a means of removing chronic impediments that have kept researchers from doing research. For example, one large international corporation has started to introduce TQM into several of its research labs by asking the researchers to identify the policies, procedures, and systems which are preventing them from doing more and better research. This hit list has then been used to prioritize the first round of pilot projects within the labs. The projects are recognized as beneficial, not a threat to creativity, and have resulted in some visible benefits to the research community. Darby (1990) of Dupont has reported that among the primary objectives for introducing TQM to R&D has been "the elimination/reduction of barriers to translating laboratory discoveries to commercialization." Therefore another means of "selling" TQM to researchers is to demonstrate that TQM concepts and tools can help them do their research more efficiently. Sprinz (1991) of Eastman Kodak has reported on specific strategies used to introduce researchers to the concept that statistical concepts and tools can be used "throughout the project starting with the definition of the problem and ending with the interpretation and presentation of the results."

Defining Research Products And Quality

Research quality has been defined by Darby (1990) of Dupont as

Creating, anticipating, and meeting customer requirements

with an associated responsibility to focus both on technology push and market pull. There is an emerging consensus that the product of industrial research is information on technology. With that definition of "product", we can make additional progress in defining research quality from the perspective of the required features of the information it provides. More specifically the information must be timely, accurate, understandable, useful, and affordable to the user/customer/recipient. These requirements therefore necessitate the need to identify the customers of a particular research project, as well as work with them to develop a concise understanding and **agreement** on specific quality indicators and goals for each feature. Shipley (1991) of Dow has discussed the importance of this agreement to promote "Customer Buy-In" through the use of a joint initiation letter signed by research and the customer. The letter, used "for projects passing

1165

initial screening criteria" describes the products technical
needs, pricing objectives, and is "signed by the authorized
decision-makers at both Dow and the customer." Shipley (1991)
has reported that this joint initiation letter "holds great
potential in opening up communication between all parties in the
project."

TQM Implementation Strategies

After demonstrating proof of the need, there remains the
question of implementation. To date there is strong evidence
that the implementation strategy for TQM within R&D does not
differ from that used for other areas of the organization. The
author has used the following implementation process:

1. Train the senior management of the research function
2. Assign a team to develop an implementation plan
3. Identify pilot projects
4. Train facilitators and teams for the pilot projects
5. Develop the infrastructure required to identify,
   prioritize, and support follow-on projects
6. Develop quality goals for the research organization
   and identify specific quality projects for inclusion
   with the organization's overall business plan.

While this implementation strategy is generic, the examples
used for training and the pilot projects must be seen as
relevant to R&D. For example, the author uses quality
improvement examples from product development for organizations
which are "small R and big D." Furthermore, the specific
projects identified must focus on improving the processes
identified as being critical to completing the mission of the
research organization. Specific examples of pilot projects
identified by research organizations include:

Improving lab space utilization
Improving the lab's information data base
Improving the process to identify customer requirements
Improving cost estimates for project test plans
Improving the documentation quality of research reports
Improving hood fan ventilation
Improving hydroprocessing pilot plant data quality
Improving turnaround time on Kinematic Viscosity Analysis
Improving turnaround time for stockroom materials requests
Improving on time delivery of design packages to Lab Shop
Developing a process for benchmarking R&D Effectiveness

Some Initial Results

Among some initially reported results of R&D project teams
have been:

Reduced product development cycles by 12 months by
improving project requirements process (Morgan:Shell, 1990)

1166

Improved percentage of design packages on time to Lab
Shop from 65% to 95% (Yoest: Sverdrup Technology, 1991)

Reduced engineering parts redesign by 45% and write-offs
by 55% (Rocca: IBM, 1991)

Reduced number of single use electrical parts by "order of
magnitude," reduced the number of part types by a factor of
3 and the number of hand inserted parts by a factor of 20
(Waddoups: Motorola, 1991)

Lessons Learned

Reviewing these results with other reports of strategies
and conclusions provides the following list of lessons learned:

The use of cross functional/organizational teams is a
valuable means of improving communication between R&D and
its internal and external customers, which results in
reduced project cycle time.

It is important for R&D organizations to identify, and
manage the quality of key processes, e.g., Stewardship of
Emerging Technologies.

R&D must identify the vital few needs of both external and
internal customers through focus groups, surveys, and
placing researchers in direct contact with customers.

Benchmarking is a valuable tool for not only identifying
best practices, e.g., technology transfer to commercialization, but is also a driver for improving R&D practices
by providing specific goals for improvement.

Compiling Lessons Learned across R&D projects can provide
invaluable insight for improving future project
performance.

BIBLIOGRAPHY

Cole, Roger (1990), "Quality in the Management of R&D,"
Managing For Quality In Research & Development, Symposium
Proceedings, Juran Institute, Wilton, CT.

Darby, Robert (1990), "R&D Quality in a Diversified
Company," **Managing For Quality In Research & Development**,
Symposium Proceedings, Juran Institute, Wilton, CT.

Juran, Joseph (1990, 1991), Closing Remarks at 1990 and
1991 Symposia of Managing for Quality in Research &
Development (Unpublished).

Morgan, Martha (1990), "Quality in R&D - Fit or Folly,"
Managing For Quality In Research & Development, Symposium
Proceedings, Juran Institute, Wilton, CT.

Rocca, Joseph (1991), "IBM Rochester Excellence, Customer Satisfaction; The Quality Journey Continues," **Managing For Quality In Research & Development**, Symposium Proceedings, Juran Institute, Wilton, CT.

Shipley, Randall (1991), "Quality Improvements In The Research And Development Process," **Managing For Quality In Research & Development**, Symposium Proceedings, Juran Institute, Wilton, CT.

Sprinz, Peter (1991), "Implementation of a Quality and Statistics Initiative Based on Management for Quality Principles," **Managing For Quality In Research & Development**, Symposium Proceedings, Juran Institute, Wilton, CT.

Waddoups, Ray (1991), "R&D Engineering in the 1990s," **Managing For Quality In Research & Development,** Symposium Proceedings, Juran Institute, Wilton, CT.

Yoest, David (1991), "Comparison of Quality Improvement Team Training Methods and Results in a Research and Development Organization," **Managing For Quality In Research & Development,** Symposium Proceedings, Juran Institute, Wilton, CT.

As Published in 1992's AQC's Transactions.

Productivity & Quality Management Frontiers-IV, edited by Sumanth, Edosomwan, Poupart, and Sink. ©1993
Institute of Industrial Engineers.

Factors Affecting Value-Based Purchasing and Their Status in Industry

E.J. Dumond
California State University at Fullerton
Fullerton, California USA

ABSTRACT

As the marketplace continues to become more competitive, the concept of "value" is receiving increasing attention. Firms are attempting to increase the value of their products and services and reduce the number of non value-added activities. One function which can have a tremendous effect on these efforts is the purchasing function; hence, the philosophy of value-based purchasing was developed.

Value-based purchasing focuses the efforts of purchasing individuals on the creation of value, as opposed to traditional areas of cost and efficiency. However, the function's internal operating environment must support and enhance efforts in this direction. The performance measurement system, extent of functional interaction, and access to external information can affect the effectiveness of value-based purchasing. Through the empirical data from twenty-one firms in diverse industries, this paper examines the current status of these variables in purchasing functions and attempts to determine whether these variables are inhibiting or enhancing the performance of value-based purchasing. Based upon the findings, recommendations for managers are provided.

Key Words: Value, value-based purchasing, purchasing, management.

INTRODUCTION

Manufacturing firms continue to face an increasingly complex environment. Raw material shortages, price volatility, new technologies, globalization of business activities, currency shifts, supply/demand fluctuations, and other such factors are combining to create a dynamic, challenging operating environment. As these firms seek to improve productivity and quality, more emphasis is being placed upon increasing the "value" of an organization's product or service.

The term "value" has many meanings, but one approach is to view it in terms of the amount that a buyer is willing to pay for a particular product or service. This approach reflects the fact that the value of an item may change given the particular situation, buyer, or time period. The primary way that a firm creates or increases the value of its products or services is through its interrelationships: upstream (with suppliers), internally, and downstream (with customers). Each of these relationships are in effect, an important link in the "value chain" and the extent to which a firm manages these relationships determines its ability to create a competitive advantage.

Each individual and function within the firm plays a role in increasing the value of the firm's products and services; however, one function which may have more impact than others is the purchasing function. Because purchasing interacts within two major links of the chain--internally and with suppliers--the opportunity for this function to impact the value of the firm's products/services is tremendous.

This paper discusses the concept of value chain management and the role of the purchasing function in increasing the value of the firm's products and services. In particular, the paper will 1) describe the concept of the value chain and value-based purchasing; 2) identify the factors that impact value-based purchasing; 3) through the presentation of empirical data, present an indication of the current status of purchasing with regard to value-based purchasing; and 4) provide suggestions which may help purchasing and materials managers effectively manage within the value chain to create a competitive advantage.

VALUE CHAIN MANAGEMENT

In today's competitive environment, a firm can no longer afford to perform activities or incur costs which do not increase the value of the product or service being produced. System redundancies, inadequacies, or inconsistencies must be identified and eliminated. One method by which to focus on value and identify those non value-added processes is to use the concept of the value chain based on the model put forth by Michael Porter (1985). Porter's value chain presents the organization, and the entire economy, as a series of links in a chain. The chain consists of three primary links: upstream--the suppliers value chains, internal--the firm's value chains, and downstream--the customer's value chains. Another link, the distribution or channel link can also be included if appropriate.

Within the concept, not only must each chain be strong but the linkages must also be well-established to prevent the loss of value or productivity in the gaps. The goal in managing within the value chain (creating and maintaining value) is then one of establishing a system which effectively links all portions of the value chain and eliminates redundancies or activities which do not add value to the product or service. Activities such as JIT, EDI, supplier partnerships, and joint product development serve to link the firm to its suppliers; while activities such as DRP, customer development, and market research link the firm to its customers.

This concept is also used within the firm itself because as one might guess, each of these macro links possesses a number of internal links. For example, within the firm, functional integration between purchasing, marketing, manufacturing, and accounting; or between manufacturing workcenters, must be achieved. To develop tighter linkages among the functions, firms can take actions like moving from a traditional commodity structure to one of commodity/product teams or buyer/planner differentiation; developing strategic planning teams; establishing formal, regularly scheduled internal meetings/activities for all functions; or developing functional rotational programs. Whether viewed in a macro or micro perspective, managing within the value chain focuses on developing or increasing the value of the firm's products or services, and each link of the chain must operate with this objective.

"VALUE-BASED" PURCHASING

Purchasing is often viewed as a balancing act between total system cost and value, value being material availability and quality, where increased cost is often seen as a necessity to increase value. This view of purchasing is helpful in that it reflects the need to make trade-offs when making purchasing decisions. In effect, it illustrates that purchasing individuals can't optimize performance on all criteria simultaneously. However, it is also a rather narrow viewpoint in that it implies that increased value is always at the expense of total system cost. In actuality, this relationship is not always true. Purchasing individuals often have the opportunity to increase product value while also decreasing total cost. For example, in working with production, they may elect to purchase raw materials or component parts which cost more but which also provide higher quality, reliability; or perhaps enable the production process to operate more consistently, with less scrap. In another instance, by working with marketing, purchasing individuals may be able to purchase materials which increase the product's value in the eyes of the consumer--thereby increasing demand and sales for the firm. In each of these cases, the additional cost may be more than offset by reduced costs or greater benefits occurring elsewhere in the firm. Purchasing has then provided a net gain in product value. With this perspective, the goal of "value-based purchasing" becomes one of increasing the difference between the value of a product/service and the cost to create it. It is this difference which creates a competitive advantage for a firm.

In the above examples, in which purchasing is able to increase the value of the firm's products or services, it can be noted that each of these ways involve the internal linkages of the firm. Through functional interaction, information is exchanged and product value is enhanced. Similarly, if purchasing works to develop a supplier partnership, it is through a tightening of the linkages that value has been increased. The essence of value-based purchasing is interrelationships and it is the internal operating environment which establishes the means and motivation by which the quality of interrelationships will or will not be improved.

1171

FACTORS AFFECTING VALUE-BASED PURCHASING

The nature of the internal operating environment is critical to effective implementation of value-based purchasing. An operating environment and philosophy must be developed which supports and enhances managing and operating within the value chain. Based upon a review of the literature, it was found that the organizational variables most frequently mentioned as potentially affecting the goals of value-based purchasing include the nature of the goals and objectives, type of performance measures, reporting level, organizational structure, extent of education and training, supplier relations, and amount of supply market planning. These variables are related; thus, the variables were grouped into three primary categories: performance measurement system, functional interaction, and external information.

The performance measurement system, consisting of objectives, performance measures, and feedback, has been shown to have a significant effect an individual's decisions and perceptions. The positive effects of specific, challenging goals on an individual's performance is well-documented (Huber 1989; Locke et. al 1981). As indicated by Locke et. al (1981), goals are thought to enhance performance by increasing the individual's effort and persistence; by focusing attention; and by improving overall strategy formulation. Performance measures are provided with the intent to provide guidelines in decision-making; and the research indicates that these measures do impact both an individual's decisions and perceptions (Dumond 1991). Additionally, a considerable number of studies have been conducted which illustrate that, performance feedback, whether outcome oriented (Kim 1984; Henry and Redmon 1990) or of a behavioral or process nature (Earley et. al 1990), can interact with outcome performance measures to enhance performance.

Communication processes provide information to all parts of the organization, allowing for decision-making and task accomplishment. Horizontal communication (often viewed as interaction) is the flow of information that occurs both within and between departments. Research in horizontal communication shows that job-related, or required, interaction can positively impact an individual's task performance (Hackman and Oldham 1976; Pegels 1991).

An organization is an open system; consequently, to survive, it must interact with its environment. The amount of external information required is generally positively related to the amount of complexity and change occurring in the environment (Schwab et. al 1985). For example, it was found that procurement became more involved with planning and the external environment in times of material shortages, and as it evolved into a strategic function within the organization (Reck and Long 1988).

STATUS IN INDUSTRY

Based upon research results and existing theory, the nature of managerial elements within the operating environment can potentially inhibit or enhance effective performance in the value chain. To develop a sense of the nature of the current purchasing operating environment and its ability to support the concept of value-based purchasing, data was collected from twenty-one firms in diverse industries. Since the general status of these variables in purchasing organizations was of interest, it was felt that a diverse sample of environments would be most useful. The firms consist of three firms producing consumer goods, two in the food industry, four in paper products, one producing business machines, three in computers, four in electronics, and four in aerospace. Extensive on-site interviews were conducted with upper-level managers in each firm.

Within the selected organizations, information was collected on the performance measurement system, functional interaction, and external information. The intent was to determine, based upon the literature and existing theory, whether these variables are perhaps inhibiting or enhancing the development of effective performance in the value chain. Both qualitative and quantitative data was collected with regard to each variable. The primary variables investigated are illustrated in Table 1.

Selected Results

There was a high level of diversity among the firms in terms of demographics. Facility sales ranged from $35 million to $1 billion and the percent of sales accounted for by the purchasing function ranged from 20 percent to 80 percent. All types of production systems were included, with two firms primarily using group technology; six using job production; one using large batch; six using continuous production; and five using a mix of production processes. Nine of the firms were primarily using MRP to control their inventory; only one was primarily using JIT; eleven were using a mix of either MRP and JIT or MRP and ROP. It was interesting to note that three of the interviewees could not identify the method being used to control inventory (later, through other sources, it was determined to be a combination of MRP and ROP). There was a wide range in the position titles of these individuals who were responsible for purchasing performance. Four of the individuals were Material Managers; six were Directors; three held the title of Vice-President; five were Purchasing Managers; two were Purchasing Agents; and one was a Manager of Supplier Management. Nine of these individuals had previously held positions in the purchasing area. However, only two of their bosses had any experience in purchasing.

The infrastructure of the firms was investigated in three areas: the performance measurement system, functional interaction, and access to outside information. The performance measurement system was investigated in terms of three elements: the existence and type of objectives, existence and type of

Field Studies
Areas of Investigation

Demographics
  Industry
  Size
  Production system
  Inventory control system
  Position title

Environment—External
  Complexity of materials
  Rate of technical change
  Market stability
  Availability of materials

Environment—Internal
  Work conditions
  Management style
  Responsibilities
  Computer availability
  Flexibility

Infrastructure
  Performance Meas System
  Objectives
  Performance measures
  Feedback

Functional Interaction
  Reporting level
  Organization structure
  Communication

Outside Information
  Professional organizations
  Professional certification
  Training/education
  Forecasts

Table 1

performance measures, and the extent of performance feedback. All but two of the firms receive objectives from higher in the organization. Of the 18 receiving these objectives, in seventeen of them, the objectives are written. Eighteen of the firms have established objectives for the purchasing function. It is interesting to note that the three firms which do not have purchasing objectives are not the same firms which do not receive objectives from above. Of the eighteen firms with purchasing objectives, five of them do not provide specific, quantitative objectives; rather, they are generally stated. The areas in which objectives were provided are provided in Table 2.

As is indicated in the table, the areas of cost savings, quality, and delivery are the primary areas in which objectives are established. Firms seem to have moved from the tradition of focusing on paper flow or processing times (as illustrated in the lack of efficiency objectives); however, the areas receiving much recent attention in the literature (improving customer service, reducing the supply base, and focusing on continuous improvement) have not yet become areas for objectives in these firms.

Nature of Objectives

Area	Number of Firms
Customer service	7
Automation	6
Cost savings	14
Efficiency	2
Quality	14
Delivery	10
Supplier base	3
Continuous improvement	6

Table 2

In terms of the performance measures, all of the firms quantitatively measure purchasing performance. All of them also measure the performance of purchasing individuals, some more formally than others. The nature of the performance measures varies, as shown in Table 3, but there were also some common areas of measurement.

As is indicated in the table, areas in which performance is most frequently measured include cost savings, efficiency, productivity, customer service, and delivery. In comparing Tables 2 and 3, it can be noted that the firms do not necessarily establish objectives in the areas which are measured. For example, only 14 firms have objectives in cost savings yet 20 firms measure performance in that area. No firm establishes an objective in productivity, yet ten firms measure it (generally in terms of labor productivity).

Nature of Performance Measures

Area	Number of Firms
Customer service	9
Automation	0
Cost savings	20
Efficiency	12
Quality	9
Delivery	7
Supplier base	3
Continuous improvement	4
Value	1
Inventory	3
Supplier certification	1
Innovation	1
Productivity	10

Table 3

In terms of performance feedback, 20 of the managers receive feedback about purchasing performance; however, the frequency, formality, and

1174

extent of detail vary across the firms. Some of the variation may be due to the fact that some of the firms did not have computer systems and/or software which could efficiently track performance. For example, a few of the firms were not able to track incoming delivery and quality at all, while several firms did not have the ability to track delivery and quality as it related to each buyer or supplier. All of the managers indicated that they provided formal, quarterly reports to upper management. Generally, the feedback received by the managers was quantitative and outcome-based, as opposed to process-based.

The area of functional interaction reflects the extent to which the purchasing function is involved with, or has the ability to effectively interact with the other functions. The investigated elements include the reporting level, the organization of the purchasing function, and the degree and type of internal communication.

The reporting level in some ways reflects the importance placed on the purchasing function. The lower reporting level tends to indicate that the purchasing contribution is not valued as much as those that report higher within the organization. The reporting level was viewed much like the levels in a bill-of-material in that the CEO was level zero, with the numbers becoming larger as one progresses down the organization chart. The level in the organization to which purchasing reported ranged from level two to level four, with most firms (15) reporting to an individual at level three (implying that purchasing itself existed at level four in these firms). Within eight of the firms, purchasing existed at a level lower than did operations or manufacturing.

The organization structure was first examined in terms of the extent to which purchasing was centralized or decentralized within these firms. All of the firms had a decentralized/centralized approach in which the individual plants were responsible for particular items, especially those unique to their process, but a centralized staff handled common materials and generally, capital equipment. In terms of organization within the purchasing function, the most common method was the traditional approach in which buyers are organized by commodity (14 firms). Two firms use a buyer/planner organization in which the buying process is divided into strategic and tactical activities. The buyer is responsible for the strategic activities, such as supplier selection, partnering, certification, negotiation; while the planner is responsible for the tactical activities like the daily interactions with the suppliers and production, expediting, order releases, order quantities, and inventory control. Four firms are organized into commodity teams in which purchasing is an integral member of several teams; and one firm is in the process of moving from a traditional commodity approach to commodity teams.

Communication was investigated in terms of its formality and frequency. Overall, communication with management tended to be more formal than was purchasing's communication with other functions. Purchasing tended to have the most interaction with marketing and production and the least with accounting and finance. Interfunctional meetings were not regularly scheduled; rather, they were convened when required. Only the performance reviews were regularly scheduled in terms of meeting with upper management. Two communication problems were frequently mentioned: bad timing of information and lack of understanding and/or cooperation by the other functions. It was indicated that purchasing often received needed information too late to be able to use it. Examples mentioned included materials being designed into future products which were in short supply or materials which were being so tightly specified that there would be only one source. Additionally, the managers felt that other functions, and often, upper management, not understanding the role or importance of purchasing, often did not provide adequate cooperation or support. At times, the professionalism or capabilities of purchasing individuals were questioned.

The area of outside information reflects the extent to which purchasing is able to obtain information from the supply market or about new techniques or trends in purchasing or other fields. The elements investigated include involvement in and/or support for professional organization activities, extent of certification in purchasing, training and educational opportunities, existence of supply forecasting, and the size and nature of the supply base.

In terms of professional involvement and/or support, in twelve of the firms, some of the purchasing individuals belong to the National Association of Purchasing Management (NAPM). The extent of membership ranged from less than one percent to 100 percent. Seven managers indicated that they encourage the workers to become involved in a professional organization. Only eight of the managers are members of NAPM; of these, four regularly attend NAPM meetings. Sixteen of the organizations cover the cost of attending the meetings. Seven of the firms have purchasing individuals who belong to a professional organization other than NAPM (primarily APICS and IIE).

All of the firms indicated that they cover the cost of taking the exams for purchasing certification; however, only four of the managers encourage purchasing individuals to become certified. Of the managers, five are certified in purchasing management. Eight of the firms have some certified purchasing individuals in the function, with the percent of certified individuals ranging from three percent to 100 percent.

In the area of training and education, overall, the average education level for the managers is a bachelor's degree while the purchasing individuals have, on the average, some college education. All of the firms cover the cost of attending college courses which are related to the individual's job. The managers were extremely supportive of training for purchasing individuals; however, they felt their boss was somewhat less supportive of training. Nineteen of the firms have a budget for purchasing training. This budget, as a percent of the purchasing budget, ranged from .2% to fifteen percent, but all but two of the managers indicated that this part of the budget is among the first to be cut in tough times. Fourteen firms possess a corporate training center and nine firms develop formal training schedules for the purchasing individuals. In terms of types of training, it was interesting to find that in eleven of the firms, the purchasing individuals do not know statistical process control techniques.

With regard to obtaining information from the external environment using forecasting techniques, there were a range of responses. Nine firms regularly perform material forecasts; four firms do a little forecasting; two are beginning to do some forecasting; five don't do any forecasting; and one firm only does a forecast when a supply problem has arisen. Only one of these firms tracks the subsequent accuracy of these forecasts.

DISCUSSION AND RECOMMENDATIONS

The research results tend to suggest that the operating environment for the purchasing function may not provide the support or motivation which is needed by the purchasing individuals if they are to increase the value of the firm's products/services. In terms of the performance measurement system, a number of the firms (eight) either do not provide purchasing objectives or the objectives are non-specific. Such a situation creates a lack of focus; thereby reducing the benefit which is provided by the purchasing function. A related factor is the existence of conflicting objectives and performance measures. Such a situation can create both frustration and poor performance. Further, areas of emphases, like customer service, continuous improvement, and supply base issues, which would improve performance in the value chain are not prevalent in the objectives or performance measures. Rather, in a majority of firms, measures of cost and efficiency are common, measures which tend to create or encourage a narrow, internal focus. Additionally, in providing feedback, the provision of process-oriented feedback, as well as outcome-oriented feedback, would be helpful for the purchasing individuals in improving their performance.

In terms of functional interaction, management may wish to elevate purchasing to a level equal to its counterparts. The process of interaction is easier if the involved parties are at an equal level of authority. The internal organization structure of the purchasing function may also need evaluation if value-based purchasing is to be supported. A traditional commodity organization was highly prevalent in the firms. This organization, although providing some benefits, tends to create an internal focus, making interfunctional interaction more difficult. A commodity team approach appears to be the best organization to facilitate, encourage, and even require the flow of information among the functions. The buyer/planner organization serves as an intermediate step.

The establishment of regularly scheduled interfunctional meetings might also enhance the communication process because the functions may then have the opportunity to discuss issues and ideas that will improve the process; rather than simply the crisis of the moment.

The ability to obtain and diffuse information from the external environment allows for improved performance and the opportunity for continuous improvement. The research results indicate that more efforts are needed to involve purchasing with the external environment. There is relatively little involvement in professional organizations and even less in obtaining professional certification. Involvement in professional organizations allows for the development of contacts and transfer of information among fellow professionals on common problems; while the certification process enhances continuous improvement.

A similar argument can be put forth for education and training. Education and training provide a foundation and opportunity for new learning. The purchasing individual in many firms do not have a college education. Nor do they receive a schedule of formal training that they will receive. These individuals have a significant impact on the firm's performance; consequently, upgrading the education level of purchasing individuals might allow them to provide a greater contribution to the firm.

The establishment of formal training schedules often increases the probability that the training will be received.

In summary, in many firms, the operating environment may not adequately support value-based purchasing. Management may wish to evaluate the elements of performance measurement system, functional interaction, and external information and modify them to provide the necessary support and motivation for the purchasing professionals as they try to increase the value of the firm's products and services.

REFERENCES

Dumond, E.J. (1991) "Performance Measurement and Decision Making in a Purchasing Environment," International Journal of Purchasing and Materials Management, V27, No. 2, 21-31.

Earley, P.C., Northcraft, G.B., Lee, C., and Lituchy, T.R. 1990 "Impact of Process and Outcome Feedback on the Relation of Goal Setting to Task Performance," Academy of Management Journal, V33, 87-105.

Hackman, J.R. and Oldham, G.R. (1976) "Motivation Through the Design of Work: Test of a Theory," Organizational Behavior and Human Performance, V16, 250-279.

Henry, G.O. and Redmon, W.K. (1990) "The Effects of Performance Feedback on the Implementation of a Statistical Process Control (SPC) Program," Journal of Organizational Behavior Management, V11, 23-46.

Huber, V.L. (1989) "Comparison of the Effects of Specific and General Performance Standards on Performance Appraisal Decisions," Decision Sciences, V20, 545-557.

Kim, J.S. (1984) "Effect of Behavior Plus Outcome Goal Setting and Feedback on Employee Satisfaction and Performance," Academy of Management Journal, V27, 139-149.

Locke, E.A., Saari, L.M., Shaw, K.N., and Latham, G.P. (1981) "Goal Setting and Task Performance: 1969-1980." Psychological Bulletin, Vol. 90, No. 1, 125-152.

Pegels, C.C. (1991) "Integrating Functional Areas for Improved Productivity and Quality," International Journal of Operations & Production Management, V11, 27-40.

Porter, M.E. (1985) Competitive Advantage, New York, Free Press.

Reck, R.F. and Long, B.G. (1988) "Purchasing: A Competitive Weapon." Journal of Purchasing and Materials Management, Fall, 2-8.

Schwab, R.C., Ungson, G.R., and Brown, W.B. (1985) "Redefining the Boundary-Spanning Environment Relationship," Journal of Management, 75-86.

BIOGRAPHICAL NOTE

Ellen J. Dumond is an Associate Professor of Operations Management at Cal State University, Fullerton. Prior to this position, she was on the faculty at Miami University. She received her Ph.D. from Indiana University and is currently conducting research in areas of productivity and quality improvement in materials management.

Productivity & Quality Management Frontiers-IV, edited by Sumanth, Edosomwan, Poupart, and Sink. ©1993 Institute of Industrial Engineers.

Quality Means Market —
A Case Study in Quality Management

Z.Z. Chen
East China University of Chemical Technology
Shanghai, PEOPLE'S REPUBLIC OF CHINA

It has been the prevailing phenomenon in Shanghai's toy manufacturing sector that for achieving scale economies, more emphasis is placed on quantity of products than quality. However, with the upgrading of products and the change of customers' demands, the traditional philosophy of quality control and inspecting methods cannot meet the requirements of toy manufacturers for survival or growth. For the purpose of improving quality management in toy manufacturing enterprises, this paper intends to expound the success experience of Shanghai Shingli Manufacturing Company Ltd. (SSMC) in organizing quality management.

SSMC is a joint venture with total investment of 2.7 million RMB, mainly producing middle and high level electronic remote-controlled toys. Within five years since its establishment, SSMC has achieved accumulative total profits of 14.0 million, 5 times that of the initial investment.

Its success has a large bearing on the Company's philosophy: "Quality means market" and effective measures adopted under this philosophy. SSMC emphasizes "quality" with respect to three aspects: (1) work quality, (2) product quality, and (3) service quality. Firstly, the quality management has been planned and organized according to the philosophical sequence: ensuring work quality with worker quality, ensuring process quality with work quality, and ensuring product quality with process quality. Secondly, three main measures have been adopted in the control of product quality. The Company establishes a department of product quality management, which has the top authority to deal with the conflicts between quality and quantity. In addition, the management of preventing defects has been strictly exercised, which starts from the entry of raw materials. Moreover, ISO has been introduced in measurement. Thirdly, "service" is regarded in the Company as related to three phases, i.e. before-sales which starts from before the design of new products, in selling products, and after-sales. The improvement of service quality is practiced through these three phases.

From SSMC's experience of obtaining its markets and profits by the competitive advantage of quality, it can be found that to improve the product quality, it is necessary to pay close attention to work quality and service quality which are the basis of ensuring product quality. Moreover, in order to manage quality effectively, the enterprise needs to develop new measures with respect to organization, system, techniques and workers, compatible with the company's objectives and internal culture.

Productivity & Quality Management Frontiers-IV, edited by Sumanth, Edosomwan, Poupart, and Sink. ©1993 Institute of Industrial Engineers.

Use of Value Engineering to Improve Industrial Productivity: A Case Study

R.D. Crowley
TG(USA) Corporation
Perryville, Missouri USA

I.C. Ehie
Southeast Missouri State University
Cape Girardeau, Missouri USA

ABSTRACT

This paper reports on the use of value engineering to improve plant productivity by reducing idle time during shift change at TG(USA) Corporation, a Japanese manufacturing company. The company works a 5-day week with three shifts per day and originally had a thirty-minute overlap between shift changes. This study was focused on developing a plan, appropriately named 30PLAN, aimed at reducing the idle time during shift change. The plan assigns specific duties to both off-going and in-coming factory technicians, as well as establish time limits for each duty to ensure completion during the overlap period. The plan reduced the shift-change time by about 50% and resulted to significant cost savings to the company.

INTRODUCTION

Value Engineering (VE) has different meanings to different people, and is known by such names as; value analysis, value improvement, value assurance, value technology, or value control. Whatever the name, few people will disagree that the main objective of VE is to obtain optimum value for every dollar spent. VE focuses on the function of a process by analyzing that process and relating it to cost. Finding a better way to accomplish something for less is the goal of VE's problem-solving methodology (Dorris & Cosgrove, 1990). VE is the systematic study of the function of a material or product to find how to achieve the desired function at the lowest cost without lowering quality (Dhir, 1987).

VE was originally called value analysis and today the terms are used interchangeably. The methodology was developed by Lawrence Miles of General Electric during World War II in an effort to improve quality and reduce labor cost. Since its introduction, the United States Navy's Bureau of Ships started using the procedures and today it is required that every military project use the techniques (Evers, 1986). Since those early days of VE, the basic approach has been successfully applied to project management (Evers, 1986; Sievert, Jr., 1991), design of industrial water distribution system (Garvin, 1992), plant layouts, materials handling, and organizational analysis (Coffield, Herr & Streahle, 1988).

VALUE ENGINEERING ANALYSIS

There are five phases to VE and they are as follows: Information Phase, Analytic Phase, Creative Phase, Evaluation Phase, and the Implementation Phase. During the Information Phase, information is gathered on the project in order to isolate the components with the greatest potential for improving the value of the project. In the Analytic Phase, each alternative course of action is analyzed and cost estimates developed. In analyzing the alternatives, the advantages and disadvantages of each option is reviewed. In the Creative Phase, common techniques such as "brainstorming" are used to try to develop better methods for performing the primary function. The most promising ideas are then compared in the Evaluation Phase on the basis of cost and ability to meet the required function. Finally, in the Implementation Phase the project is monitored using Gantt charts or some other scheduling technique (Reuter, 1983).

The purpose of the study is to develop a procedure that would ensure a smoother and more productive transition between shifts in an industrial production plant. Toyoda Gosei {TG(USA)} is an automobiles parts producer that is owned and operated by a Japanese giant corporation. The company produces steering wheels, steering wheel air bag covers, interior injection molded parts and trim items for GM, Ford, Chrysler, DSM, Mazda, and Toyota. The plant currently employs over 500 people and operates on a 3-shifts per day and 5 days a week schedule. Between each shift change, there is a 30 minute time overlap at which time non-productive duties such as general housecleaning, preventive maintenance checks and preparation of daily production reports are being conducted. During this period, both the incoming and the outgoing shifts are engaged in those non-productive tasks and the production lines are shut down. Consequently, the productivity of the factory technicians was reduced as a result of the non-productive tasks performed during the shift change.

Value engineering methodology was used to develop a program in the plant that ensures continuing production of parts while at the same time completing the necessary non-productive tasks required by the company between shifts. Such an approach allowed the company to thoroughly assess the situation and develop a plan that was eventually adopted by every production department within the company. The five phases of VE described earlier were used to develop the program know as 30PLAN. With the use of this methodology, the company is experiencing smoother shift changes as well as an increase in plant-wide productivity.

A CASE STUDY: 30PLAN

Information Phase

At TG(USA) the day is divided into three shifts. Each shift is 8 1/2 hours long, as a result of this there is a 30 minute overlap between shifts. The extra one half hour is allotted for lunch. During this overlap, there are two shifts present at the workstation. The problem with this arrangement was that in the past there was no production during this overlap. Most of the factory technicians would shut the press down in order to clean-up. The presses have to be cleaned from time to time, but it was very costly to the company to have this cleaning take place while two work-shifts were present.

In many cases, good parts were being produced before shutting down to clean. After spending 30 to 45 minutes cleaning, a bad part would be produced upon re-starting the press. It was as if the cleaning served no purpose, except to maybe give the technicians a little playing time. In fact, in some cases, it was observed that some of the technicians were merely sitting idle during the shift change. On average, each press would be down from 30 to 45 minutes at every shift change. This amounted to a substantial amount of lost production. The company was also experiencing non-productive labor cost associated with other habits of the factory technicians. Two work-shifts were being paid to work and in reality no one was working. Money was being lost from the lack of production, as well as from non-productive employees.

Analytic Phase

The main objective of this project was to ensure that the factory technicians produced parts during the shift-change time and still be able to perform the required non-productive tasks. Since there was a total of thirty minutes overlap time, the program was named 30PLAN. The concept behind the 30PLAN was to keep production running while at the same time perform several other non-productive jobs during the time overlap. The process was started by talking to the team-leaders to determine what had to be done before production could begin. Every

position required some type of paperwork to be filled out and Total
Preventive Maintenance (TPM) checks be taken. The length of time
required to perform each of the non-productive tasks was recorded.

Creative Phase

A Startup and Shutdown Duty Sheet was then constructed. This chart was
used to fill in the responsibilities of each factory technician present
at shift change. A sheet was designed for each work station and the
factory technicians on all three shifts would follow the same schedule.

One area of one department was used as a pilot group for the project.
The Startup and Shutdown Duty Sheets were constructed for each work
station in that area. The schedules instructed the out-going
technician to continue production until approximately six minutes after
the hour. This allows the in-coming technician enough time to fill out
the required paperwork before taking over the responsibilities of
running production. Furthermore, the off-going technician is assigned
specific duties that must be performed before the end of the shift.
Time limits were also set on these duties in order to ensure their
timely completion. As a result, production does not stop during shift
changes, and other jobs are being accomplished that were not in the
past.

At the bottom of the schedule is a list of non-productive jobs that
must be completed throughout the shift. The time to complete these
jobs is designated as well as the maximum time that should be spent on
each job. An example of a Startup and Shutdown Duty Sheet is shown in
Figure 1. There was still some downtime during the shift, however, the
downtime does not take place while there are two work-shifts present as
was previously practiced.

Evaluation Phase

TG(USA) would experience more production time as a result of the
30PLAN. The plan will not eliminate all downtime, because it is
required that the mold and the walls of the booth be cleaned from time
to time. However, the plan help ensures that the presses will be down
only when they are being cleaned. The plan specifies that cleaning be
done at various times throughout the shift and not at shift changes
when two shifts are present on the floor. It is estimated that the
loss of production could be reduced from 45 minutes per day to 30
minutes per day. The amount of lost production hours was reduced from
367.5 hours per week to 245 hours per week as a result of the 30PLAN.
The cost of developing the 30PLAN for the company was very minimal
since they did not hire any outside help. Data for the study was
gathered by team-leaders and foremen with close supervision by the Vice
President/Plant Manager.

Implementation Phase

At this time, a schedule was made that designated the various steps of
implementing the 30PLAN throughout the department (Figure 2). Two
teamleaders were assigned to work on developing Startup and Shutdown

STARTUP AND SHUTDOWN DUTY SHEET

THE PURPOSE OF THIS SCHEDULE IS TO ELIMINATE ANY LOSS OF PRODUCTION AT SHIFT CHANGE.

30PLAN XX

STARTUP OVERLAP 30 MINUTES

Job To Do	Comments
1 TECHNICIAN SHOULD PREPARE PAPERWORK	(IF DAILY PRODUCTION PAPERS ETC. ARE GETTING LOW NOTIFY TEAMLEADER)
2	
3	
4 CHECK SUPPLIES AND CONFIRM THAT	IF SUPPLIES ARE LOW THE TECHNICIAN WILL FILL
5 SUPPLIES ARE ADEQUATE	SUPPLY RACK ON LINE. THIS SHOULD BE DONE AT 1ST AND 2ND BREAK.
RELIVE TECHNICIAN AND BEGIN PRODUCTION	A SHIFT TECHNICIAN WILL COMPLETLY CHANGE
9 AND CONFIRM PROPER DATE STAMP	DATE STAMP B AND C SHIFT TECHNICIAN WILL
10 AND CONFIRM PROPER DATE CODE	CHANGE SHIFT ON DATE STAMP AT THE BEGINNING OF EACH SHIFT
13 PLACE FIRST ARMATURE PRODUCED ON	THE TEAMLEADER WILL CHECK THE ARMATURE
14 FIRST PART APPROVAL BOARD FOR THE	TO ASSURE QUALITY
15 TEAMLEADER TO CHECK	
18	NOTE: B SHIFT MORNING MEETING WILL TAKE AWAY START UP TIME DO YOUR BEST TO KEEP TURNOVER TIME SHORT SO YOUR START UP SCHEDULE

SHUTDOWN OVERLAP 30 MINUTES

Job To Do	Comments
1 DO NOT STOP PRODUCTION UNTIL RELIEF	
2 TECHNICIAN IS READY TO TAKE OVER	
7 TURN OVER THE RESPONSIBILITIES OF	NOTE: B SHIFT TURN OVER TIME WILL BE LONGER TO ACCOMADATE THE MORNING MEETING TIME. TIME
8 RUNNING TO THE RELIEF TECHNICIAN	LOST IN THE MORNING MTG WILL TAKE AWAY FROM
9 PLACE LAST ARMATURE PRODUCED ON	CLEANING TIME OF MOLDER GOING OFF
10 BOARD FO T.L. CHECK	
11	MAKE SURE THE PAPERWORK IS COMPLETE AND ALL
12 FINISH PRODUCTION PAPERWORK	PRODUCTION PROBLEMS MUST BE RECORDED
13 COMPARE REJECTS ON STAND WITH	THESE MUST MATCH TO ASSURE NO REJECTS
14 NUMBER OF REJECTS ON DAILY REPORT	WERE FILTERED IN THE PROCESS T.L. WILL ALSO
15	CHECK AT END OF THE SHIFT AND THROW THE
16 DO FIRST AND LAST ARMATURE BEND	PARTS AWAY
17 AND IMPACT TEST	THE TEAMLEADER WILL CHECK TO ASSURE QUALITY
18 AND PLACE IN DESIGNATED AREA	IF ANY ABNORMAL CONDITION OCCURS FOLLOW THE
19 ALL TESTS RESULTS SHOULD BE	PROCEDURE PROVIDED ON THE SAFETY PRODUCT
20 RECORDED ON THE APPROPRIATE	REJECT CONTROL BOARD
21 SHEETS	
23 CLEAN AROUND ENTIRE ARMATURE	EMPTY ALL TRASH, SWEEP FLOOR, WIPE MACHINES
24 AREA	STRAIGHTEN ENTIRE AREA
29 RECORD DAILY INFORMATION ON	THIS SHOULD INCLUDE PRODUCTION NUMBERS AND
30 MONTHLY CHARTS	REJECT PRESENT THIS SHOULD TAKE 2 MIN.

Other non-productive jobs which must be done and instructions for doing them.

Job	When	Where, How, Who, Why
PRY BAR CHECK	AT EVERY TIP CHANGE	THIS IS DONE TO ASSURE QUALITY CONTACT TEAMLEADER IF THE TEST IS ABNORMAL
STOP PRODUCTION		
RECORD MATERIAL USAGE		RECORD ON MATERIAL USAGE AND TURN IN AT THE END OF C SHIFT THIS SHOULD TAKE 5 MIN
STOCK LINE WITH SUPPLIES	1ST & 2ND BREAK	TECHNICIAN WILL FILL SUPPLY RACK THIS SHOULD TAKE 5 MIN.
CHECK MATERIAL SHORTAGE	AS NEED	REPORT SHORTAGE TO T.L AS SOON AS POSSIBLE SO CORRECTIVE MEASURES CAN BE TAKEN
ALL REJECTS AND QUESTIONABLES SHOULD BE MARKED WITH RED TAPE AND PLACED ON A STAND IN A DESIGNATED AREA	AS REQUIRED	THE TECHNICIAN SHOULD MARK AND PLACE IN DESIGNATED AREA TO ASSURE REJECTS DO NOT FILTER IN THE PROCESS
CLEANING THE TIP OF THE ROBOT	EVERY 15 ARMATURES	THIS IS TO BE DONE WHEN THE MACHINE CLEANING ALARM GOES OUT

Job	When	Where, How, Who, Why
REPORT ANY MACHINE TROUBLE ANY 3 REJECTS IN A ROW OR DOWN TIME TO T.L	A.S.A.P	CONTACT T.L
ANY PROCESS ADJUSTMENT OR CHANGE MUST HAVE A BEND TEST PERFORMED	AS REQUIRED	TECHNICIAN SHOULD DO THIS WHEN THERE IS ANY PROCESS CHANGE OCCURS
WIRE CHANGE ON ROBOT	AS NEEDED	THIS NORMALLY SHOULD TAKE 15 MIN
TIP CHANGE	AS NEEDED	THIS SHOULD BE DONE WHEN THE TIP CHANGE LIGHT GOES OFF OR A WIRF STICK OR TIP WELDS ITS SELF TO ARM
WELDING GAS SHOULD BE GOTTEN WHEN THE LAST TANK IS TAKEN FROM THE PACK	AS REQUIRED	THE TECHNICIAN SHOULD FILL THE STAND WHEN THE LAST FULL TANK IS TAKEN
CLEANING OF ROBOT BOOTH	DURING DOWN TIME	TECHNICIAN SHOULD CLEAN INSIDE OF BOOTH

FIGURE 1: STARTUP AND SHUTDOWN DUTY SHEET

SCHEDULE

JOB DESCRIPTION: ELIMINATE LOST PRODUCTION TIME AT 8HIFT CHANGE

| DATE ISSUED: | XX–XX–XX |
| COORDINATOR: | |

#	STEPS TO TAKE:	RESPONSIBLE PERSONS	Schedule (SEPT – OCT – NOV)	REMARKS
1	MAKE TRIAL ON C/RO SYSTEM 4	TEAM LEADERS		COMPLETE
2	REVIEW RESULTS	TEAM LEADERS & PLT MGR.		COMPLETE
3	REVISE WORK CHART AS RESULT OF REVIEW	TEAM LEADERS & PLT MGR.		COMPLETE
4	EXPAND 30 PLAN TO ALL C/RO PRESSES PRESS # 4,5,6,7,8,9,10,11,12,13,14.	TEAM LEADERS		TEAM LEADERS WILL TAKE THE CONTROL
5	IDENTIFY SPECIFIC JOB DUTIES BY PRESS AND REVISE WORK CHART.	TEAM LEADERS & F.T.'s		ASK FOR HELP IF YOU NEED.
6	MAKE WORK CHARTS FOR PRESSES 1,2,3 24,25,26,27,28,29,30,31,32,17.	TEAM LEADERS		
7	EXPAND 30 PLAN TO PRESSES IN #6 ABOVE.	TEAM LEADERS & FOREMAN		
8	MAKE WORK CHARTS FOR PRESSES 15,16, 18,19,20,21,22,23,33,34,35.	TEAM LEADERS & FOREMAN		
9	EXPAND 30 PLAN TO PRESSES IN #8 ABOVE.	TEAM LEADERS & FOREMAN		
10	MAKE WORK CHARTS FOR ALL OTHER AREAS INCLUDING MIXING, SEWING, S/W ASSY, ETC	TEAM LEADERS & FOREMAN		
11	EXPAND 30 PLAN TO JOBS IN #10 ABOVE	TEAM LEADERS & FOREMAN		
12	EVALUATE AND PREPAR REPORT TO SHOW RESULT VS. ORIGINAL CONDITION.	FOREMAN		
13	CONTINUE TO USE THIS METHOD TO DELEGATE MORE RESPONSIBILITY TO FAC. TECH.	TEAM LEADERS & FOREMAN		
14	EXPLAIN 30 PLAN TO EVERYONE AT MORNING MEETING. SHOW RESULTS (KAIZEN)	TEAM LEADERS & FOREMAN		
15	SELECT TWO TEAM LEADERS TO CO – LEAD THIS PROJECT	FOREMAN		

NOTES TO CO – LEADERS:
1. PLEASE USE THE HELP FROM INTERN. HE IS ASSIGNED TO HELP YOU WITH THIS PROJECT.
2. KEEP PROJECT BOOK UP TO DATE.
3. KEEP RECORDS TO SHOW QTY PRODUCED AND DEFECTS COMPARED TO THE TIME PERIOD OF THIS PROJECT.

APPROVED BY: PLANT MANAGER
APPROVED BY: COMPANY PRESIDENT

FIGURE 2: IMPLEMENTATION SCHEDULE FOR THE PILOT DEPARTMENT

1185

Duty Sheets for every station in the department. The program was implemented in different stages so as to avoid alienating the factory technicians who have enjoyed the shift-change idle time in the past. The company therefore received less resistance from the factory technicians this way than if the entire department had started this new procedure at once.

Next came the task of implementing 30PLAN throughout the entire plant. Again, it was decided to take it a step at a time in order to minimize the resistance to change from the factory technicians. Teamleaders were assigned from each department to be responsible for developing Startup and Shutdown Sheets for every work station in their department. They worked with the foremen as well as the factory technicians in developing these schedules. A goal was set to have schedules for 5 new work stations every two weeks. These schedules were reviewed by the foremen before they were posted on the factory floor. Once posted, every factory technician received training on the purpose of 30PLAN. Over the course of a two month period, Startup and Shutdown Duty Sheets were designed for every work station throughout the entire plant.

RESULTS

With the use of 30PLAN, the company has experienced substantial savings in every department. In the pilot department alone, there has been an estimated savings of $75,000 in the first year. These savings were achieved by reducing the amount of downtime from seven hours a week to 3.5 hours. The previous seven hours of downtime was due to the thirty minute overlap occurring fourteen times a week during shift changes. The estimated savings was arrived at in the following manner. The average salary for production workers at TG(USA) is $9.80 per hour, this amount includes a 1.4% benefit premium. This figure was then multiplied by the forty-four presses in the department and the 3.5 hours of downtime saved by 30PLAN. The reason there are still 3.5 hours of downtime during the week is that the technicians still have to stop production for fifteen minutes per shift in order to clean their press but this cleaning is no longer taking place while there are two shifts present.

Another department within the company has saved more than $8000 during the same time period. There are three different areas in this department and the savings for each one was calculated in a similar manner as described above. In the past, this department completely shut down during the thirty minute overlap for cleaning purposes. Now the entire department runs continuously throughout the day and the necessary cleaning is done by the shift preparing to leave at the end of the day while the new shift continues with production.

In the remaining two production departments within the plant, production did not stop in the past during the thirty minute overlap because of the nature of the process. However, both departments experienced better organization during shift changes and as a result there is more cleaning taking place. By having a standardized schedule for shift changes, both departments have been able to enjoy less chaos during these times because every employee knows exactly what they are suppose to be doing. In the past, the technicians did what cleaning they wanted to and many areas where overlooked.

Looking at the company as a whole, it has enjoyed savings in excess of $80,000 in the first year alone by using 30PLAN, and the savings are expected to grow each year as the company adds more employees to the production lines. The productivity of the work-shift has increased significantly since the factory technicians now produce parts during the shift change.

CONCLUSION

With the development of the 30PLAN, TG(USA) has accomplished the most basic goal of VE which is to improve upon the productivity of its workforce without sacrificing function or quality, while generating a cost savings for the company. Schedules were prepared for each job plantwide, showing a detailed breakdown for both the startup and shutdown times experienced during the overlap period. Next, a work schedule for each job during the overlap period was posted at each station so that the factory technician in charge will know exactly what tasks need to be done, and the expected completion time. The off-going employees continue producing parts for approximately one-half of the overlap period (roughly 15 minutes). This allows the incoming employees enough time to complete his or her assigned duties which include preparing necessary paperwork and making routine maintenance checks, before taking over the responsibilities of producing parts. At this time, the off-going employees complete their assigned duties, which includes completing the shift's production report and general housekeeping.

The initial study began with one department in the plant serving as a pilot case, and since then the plan has been implemented throughout the plant. With the use of 30PLAN, there is a reduction in lost production hours of more than 8000 hours per year in the pilot department. This translates into an annual savings of over $80,000 in the first year. The cost savings generated by the 30PLAN is expected to grow for several years to come because the company has plans to double in size within the next five years. That will mean that more people will adhere to the 30PLAN at shift change instead of standing around doing practically nothing because they really are not sure what they should be doing. This plan takes all the guess work out of shift changes by telling the employees exactly what to do.

REFERENCES

Coffield, D. H., Herr, R. H. and Streahle, Y. (1988) "Value Engineering: A No Risk Investment", ACEE Transaction, pp. 1-7.

Dorris, V. K., and Cosgrove, T. (1990) "Value Engineering: Search for a Better Buy", ENR, vol. 224, no. 11, pp. 32-36.

Dhir, K. S. (1987) "Formulating Management Policies for Value Engineering/Value Analysis", IEEE Transactions on Engineering Management, vol. 34, no. 3, pp. 161-171.

Sievert, R. W. (1991) "A Review of Value Engineering as an Effective System for Planning Building Projects" Project Management Journal, vol. 22, no. 1, pp. 31-38.

Evers, R. (1986) "Value Engineering", Cost Engineering, vol. 28, no. 12, pp. 32-36.

Garvin, D. A. (1992) "A Note on Value Analysis: Its History and Methodology, in Operations Strategy: Text and Cases, Prentice Hall, Inc. New Jersey, pp. 408-412.

Reuter, V. G. (1983) "Value Engineering/Value Analysis: Valuable Management Techniques", Industrial Management, vol. 25, no. 6, pp. 1-4.

BIOGRAPHIC SKETCH

Ike C. Ehie is an Assistant Professor of Management at Southeast Missouri State University. He received his Ph.D. in Engineering Management from the University of Missouri - Rolla, Missouri. His research areas are in manufacturing/production strategies, multiobjective programming and management information systems.

Richard D. Crowley is a Production Analyst at TG(USA) Corporation, Perryville, Missouri. He received a B.S. (magna cum laude) in Business Administration with a major in Production/Operations management from Southeast Missouri State University in Cape Girardeau, Missouri. His research interest is in the use of computer applications in production systems.

Productivity & Quality Management Frontiers-IV, edited by Sumanth, Edosomwan, Poupart, and Sink. ©1993 Institute of Industrial Engineers.

The Long-Term Target of Japanese Manufacturing Enterprises on Productivity and Investment through MSS Approach

K. Abe
Kyushu Tokai University
Kumamoto-shi, JAPAN

K. Kurosawa
The University of the Air
Chiba-shi, JAPAN

Abstract

International competitiveness of Japanese manufactures has recently promoted dramatically. This paper attempts to find the distinctive reasons from their counterparts abroad from the standpoint of administrative planning. For this, the functional approach to added value productivity analysis is used. It is named multi-purpose theory with satisfactory standards (MSS). Under the restrictive conditions of (1) the rate of profit on gross capital at the necessary and lowest limit, (2) the rate of profit on equity capital at the necessary and lowest limit, and (3) according to the rate of growth, the market share and other concrete strategic and tactical requirements, the size of invested capital should be determined to enhance the total productivity of added value and the amount of added value as much as possible so that the administration can be improved. The MSS analysis presents the target standard of the profit rate on equity capital and the profit rate on total investment in the permitted limits to choice through productivity function between added value labor productivity and capital intensity of labor. It does not hold stick to one-sided arguments of profit maximization principle, creating and maximizing added value, productivity maximization principle, and so on, but involves the cyclic and realistic behavioral pattern of business organization. We show how Japanese manufacturing enterprises have set their targets of those in the long-term management planning.

Productivity & Quality Management Frontiers-IV, edited by Sumanth, Edosomwan, Poupart, and Sink. ©1993 Institute of Industrial Engineers.

Quality and Productivity in Business Education: An Empirical Investigation

G.H. Saad and S. Ozatalay
Widener University
Chester, Pennsylvania USA

ABSTRACT

This paper addresses issues of productivity and quality in business education. The dynamics of quality and productivity are examined from both conceptual and practical points of view.

An empirical study is conducted which comprises views of a sample of MBA students, alumni, and corporate executives. This study indicates some intuitive, as well as, counter intuitive conclusions on: students' expectations, the educational factors affecting career goals, and the market needs as perceived by the students vis-a-vis the employers.

The plan of the study consists of four parts. Part I addresses the problem of interest, the scope of the study and the methodology used. Relevant background and conceptual discussion of the issues are introduced in Part II. The empirical analysis and results are discussed in Part III. The main conclusions are presented in Part IV.

Keywords: Business Education, Productivity, and Quality.

I.   INTRODUCTION

This paper addresses the issue of productivity and quality of graduate Business education from conceptual as well as practical perspectives. Its main objective is to identify factors which will help to improve the quality and productivity of such education with a special emphasis on the Master of Business Administration (MBA) programs.

As a result of rapid changes in the business world towards globalization, a new corporate culture, and applied research; MBA education the most popular graduate business degree program, is increasingly becoming a topic of discussion in both academia and industry. The majority of MBA students are already in middle level management positions and are expected to assume higher leadership positions after graduation. Since the expectations from these graduates are changing together with the business world, there is a serious gap between what industry expects and what graduate business schools are offering. Many MBA graduates, including those from top Business Schools, realize that their career expectations are not satisfied. Furthermore, there are serious claims that Business Schools are not giving their MBA students such skills as leadership, creative thinking, and communication skills that employers expect. In many cases, employers have to retrain or send these graduates to further development programs. Thus, if companies are doing so much on their own in management training, some legitimately question the purpose of the MBA degree (Deutschman (1991)).

Many MBA programs are facing declining applications and many are experiencing financial difficulties. Some top Business schools including Chicago, Columbia, and Wharton have recently engaged in serious market research to determine what their customers want, what they need, and whether they are delivering these. It is now believed that the top talent at universities is often reicher in skills and long-term potential than the top talent in the Graduate Business Schools. In response, drastic changes in MBA programs are taking place in all Business Schools for a more balanced curricula that will help to develop both soft and hard management skills and problem solving techniques. This of course raises the question of how to enhance quality and productivity of MBA education such that market needs and student expectations are fulfilled with reasonable costs.

To be able to answer this broad question, one has to understand first the meaning and dynamics of productivity and quality of business education. This paper seeks to enhance this understanding using conceptual and empirical analyses. The research methodology used comprises conceptual analysis of the issues ; followed by an empirical investigation. The empirical analysis is based on responses to questionnaires given to three parties: corporate executives, MBA alumni, and MBA students at Widener University. The main goal of these questionnaires was to help delineating the market needs and customers perceptions and expectations from MBA programs.

In an earlier study, the authors have focused only on the student's perceptions, Saad and Ozatalay (1991a). This paper extends the empirical investigation by including the expectations, and perceptions of corporate executives and MBA alumni. The productivity quality relationships, in business education are now discussed, and then the empirical findings follow.

II.   PRODUCTIVITY AND QUALITY OF BUSINESS EDUCATION

Education, because of its unique nature, is substantially different than any other service or product.   Furthermore, business education in general and MBA programs in particular are characterized by highly diversified student backgrounds, needs, and career goals as well as the educational philosophies of the offering institutions. Therefore, measuring and improving quality are quite different in education than other service operations.   Such diffreneces will be now illustraded in more detail.

1)   The Output and The Outcome

Applying the traditional definition of productivity as being the ratio of outputs to inputs is misleading in the educational context.   If the output is measured as number of graduating students as suggested by Baker and Cassell (1988), then this quantitative measure of output neglects both the quality achieved and the educational outcome, especially the long range outcome of the educational experience.   One may claim logically, that such outcome is affected by many other noneducational factors which make it impossible to measure.   Nonetheless, the difficulty of measurement should not be an excuse for overlooking this important and real yardstick of productivity.

Measuring higher education quality by the degree of success which participants completing the programs achieve, as suggested by Baker and Cassell (1988), is a very short range focus and incomplete at best.   Such success is measured by exams, class projects and assignments which are not sufficient, nor they are objective indicators for career success particularly in business.   Furthermore, the degree of participants' success in completing the programs, does not reflect the quality of those programs as well, nor their career outcome.

2)   Customer's Role

Education is quite different from other services in the fact that the outcome achieved, and the quality of the output received depend not only on the curricula and program's contents, but to a great extent on the quality, efforts, dedication and motivation of the customers.   The customers as expressed by Higgins, et.al. (1991), comprise: the students in the classroom, the faculty teaching courses which have prerequisites, and the employers of the graduates.

In the same degree program, participants with comparable backgrounds and abilities may have quite different degrees of success in their careers.

3)   Customer's Perceptions, and Expectations

In industrial products and most services, customers' needs and wants are rather similar if not identical.   In business education, this is quite different.   What the students, i.e., customers, want and demand is not necessarily what they need as perceived by the market needs.   This is even more complicated by the fact that market needs are continuously changing.   The average time to complete a part-time MBA degree program which is very popular for those who work full time while completing their degree is beyond five years.   During this period, the skills required and the type of positions that are in shortage in the market may change.   Thus, market needs are not stable.   This imposes a challenge for the students, the educators, and those who design these programs.   Therefore, a measure which focuses only on the students' perceptions and wants overlooks the main mission of the programs - to respond to the market needs and demands.   Hence, an objective measure for productivity and quality of the program should reflect this fact, by measuring the extent to which programs have achieved their mission.

4)   Driving Factors and Dominant Relationships

As indicated above, to measure the quality of a program, mission accomplishment is the most important driving factor. It represents the degree of the program effectiveness. Yet, a program may achieve its mission at higher cost, by using more resources than another program with the same mission. Certainly, the one accomplishing the same mission with less resources is more efficient.

Based on the above discussion, one can easily identify the following driving factors and dominant relationships in understanding business education productivity and quality:

a) the outcome, not only the outputs;
b) the students' motivation, commitment, backgrounds and abilities;
c) the market needs;
d) the program's mission and objectives. The emphasis here should be on the delivered not stated objectives;
e) the cost and resources used;
f) the relationship between d and e above.

5)   The Meaning and Measurement of Quality

Many definitions have been used in the literature for quality (see for example Cole (1992), Garvin (1988), Heskett, et. al. (1990), Zeithaml, et. al. (1990)). These definitions describe quality as:

a) "conformance to specifications."
b) "what is neither mind nor matter, but a third entity independent of the two."
c) "differences in quality amount to differences in the quantity of some desired ingredient or attribute."
d) "the unpriced attributes contained in each unit of the price attributes."
e) "the capacity to satisfy wants."
f) "fitness for use."
g) "the degree of excellence at an acceptable price and the control of variability at an acceptable cost."
h) "the difference between what is perceived and what is received."

Clearly, definitions: `a' is producer-based; `b' is transcendent; `c' and `d' are product-based; `e' and `f' are user-based; `g' and `h' are value-based.

In relating each of these definitions to business education quality, the last two 'g' and 'h' which are value based seem to be more relevant than the others. Yet, if one wants to measure both productivity and quality simultaneously, none of the above definitions will fulfill this goal. More on this point follows.

6)   Productivity and Quality Measurement

Productivity as the ratio of outputs to inputs is inappropriate and may be misleading in education. Quality and productivity are inseparable issues in education. An objective measure should comprise both issues simultaneously, and should not only

1193

account for goals to be achieved but also for the means of achieving them. Efficiency and effectiveness should be considered simultaneously in both the short and the long runs. We suggest the following two measures:

A) Ratio of Effectiveness/Efficiency; where: effectiveness represents goal attainment and mission realization; and efficiency is cost per graduate participant.

B) The Value Added; as perceived by students, alumni, and employers; in terms of fulfillment of market needs and development of skills required to fulfill those needs, i.e. the actual outcome of the educational programs.

7) Quality and Productivity Improvement

Key to Total Quality Improvement (TQI) is a focus on the customer, McMillen (1991). The theme is providing the best education possible at minimum cost. The following are suggested guidelines for effective TQI:

a) Find out exactly what each of the three customer categories want and need.
b) Continuous coordination and cooperation among the faculty. This will minimize overlaps and redundant curricula.
c) Continuous feedback from students and faculty teaching courses which have prerequisites.

d) Interdisciplinary courses and discussion panels.
e) Feedback from employers to specify areas of educational deficiency, improvements needed, and recent technologies.
f) Inclusion of Total Quality Management concepts, and real world practices, as repeatedly expressed by Business leaders, (e.g., Robinson et.al. (1992), Bechtell (1990)).
g) Adopting diversified curricula which integrate both the hard and soft skills needed for business success in global markets.
h) Involvement of all customer categories in the different stages of the education process.
e) Recognition and encouragement of individual differences.

III. EMPIRICAL RESULTS

To be able to assess the students perceptions, as well as the market needs 400 questionnaires were distributed, where 330 responses were received from three categories: 200 from current MBA students who are employed full-time and attend evening MBA program, 86 from MBA alumni, and 44 from corporate executives.

The following is a summary of questionnaires results:

1. The most needed outcome from MBA education comprised ten attributes that were ranked by the executives and MBA alumni as illustrated in Figure 1. Strong similarity existed between the responses of these two categories on this question. It is noticed however that, the students response to this issue differed slightly from the employers, i.e., both the executives and MBA alumni.

The ranking of the students' response was as follows:

	MBA-ALUM RANK	EXEC RANK
Obtaining communication skills	3.5	4.5
Obtaining quantitative skills for objective decision making	1	1
Have a better understanding of the business world & recent developments	3.5	2
Negotiation skills	7	7.5
Understanding the behavioral and human aspects of business	2	4.5
Understanding economic aspects and theories	5	6
Understanding the challenges of international business & how to deal with them	8	7.5
Computer Usage Skills	9	10
Understanding concepts & skills of information processing & statistical methods for information analysis and inference	6	3
Other	10	9

Figure 1 - MOST NEEDED OUTCOME FROM MBA EDUCATION

1st. A better understanding of the current
Business world

2nd. Quantitative skills for making decisions.

3rd. Obtaining a graduate degree in Business.

4th. Obtaining better communication skills.

2.   Concerning the skills needed to be developed, a consensus between the executive responses and those of the MBA alumni was noticed. Both categories whether working in service, industry, and other sectors, stressed the need for developing conceptual, communication, and technical skills, respectively.

3.   A difference in response however, was noticed among the different areas of expertise. Those in Production, Information systems, and Accounting, emphasized more the need for technical skills development; while those in Purchasing, Marketing, and Health Care fields, emphasized more communication skills. This was predictable.

4.   Although 100% of the executives, and 95% of the alumni reported satisfaction with the performance of their MBA subordinates, neither the executives nor the MBA alumni felt that those with MBA perform better on the job than those without an MBA. This result raises a serious question about the actual contribution of MBA education to career success.

5.   The students' rank of the educational factors affecting the achievement of their career goals reflected some intuitive, counter intuitive, as well as some apparently counter intuitive results as illustrated in Figure 2.

IV.   CONCLUSIONS

The above analysis has revealed different conclusions including the following:

1.   Fulfillment of the customers' needs is a main determinant of quality and productivity in Business education. This comprises the needs of:
- The employers in the market place.
- The students in the classroom.
- The faculty teaching courses which have prerequisites.

2.   Since inconsistency and/or diversity may exist among the needs of the above three customer categories, the market needs as specified by the employers should supercede the others.

3.   In addition to fulfillment of the market needs, special attention should be given to:
- The long range outcome and value added, not only the outputs measured by the number of graduates completing their degree.
- The students' motivation, backgrounds, and individual differences in their abilities and career goals.
- The program mission and its compatibility with the above factors.
- The costs and resources used to accomplish the mission.

FACTORS	MODE
Instructors' motivation to students	1 **
Applied Courses	2
Course Content (syllabi)	1 *
Courses with mixed focus (Blend of theory and application)	2
The variety of courses offered	2
Teaching methods and pedagogy	2
Support services (computers, library etc.)	2
Class scheduling (time)	2 *
Conceptual and theoretical courses	3 *
The student background	3 ***
The student motivation	1 *
Research papers and projects	3 **
Consistency between student background and major field	3 **
Homework assignment	3

KEY: *   Intuitive
           **   Counter Intuitive
           ***   Apparently Counter Intuitive

Figure 2 -.EDUCATIONAL FACTORS CONTRIBUTING
TO ACHIEVEMENT OF CAREER GOALS

(1 Extremely Important, ... 5 Least Important)

4. Quality and productivity are inseperable issues in Business education. Hence, they should be looked at simultanuously, in development and improvement of the programs.

5. Two indicators are proposed, to measure such quality and productivity:

   - The Ratio of Effectiveness/Efficiency.
   This reflects the degree of mission accomplishment, and the cost of doing so.
   - The Value Added as a result of a specific education program; as perceived by all the parties of interest. These include: the students, employers, educators, and administrators of the programs.

6. Perhaps the most suddle conclusion of our empirical study is that all executives and MBA alumni confirmed that MBA graduates do not necessary perform better on the job than their collegues who do not have an MBA degree.

   This implies serious doubt about the validity of MBA education for improving job performance, as well as the need for such degree to get the job. This also confirms a current gap between the skills that the market needs, and those developed through MBA programs.

7. Some differences were noted between the students and the employers as to the educational needs that MBA programs should meet, and help fulfill; as well as the ranking of those needs.

8. Establishment of comprehensive TQI and TQM programs, as well as effective management of change, are essential ingredients for simultanuous enhancement of quality and productivity in Business education.

REFERENCES

Baker, M., and Cassell, D. (1988) "A methodology for measuring productivity in higher education". In *Productivity Management Frontiers II*, Sumanth, Edosomwan, Sink and Werther (eds.). Geneva, Switzerland: Enderscience Enterprises Ltd, pp. 22-31.

Bechtell, M.(1990) "Teaching management for quality improvement", *The Journal for Quality and Participation*, vol. 13, June, pp. 92-95.

Cole, R. (1992) "The quality revolution", *Production and Operations Management*, vol. 1, no. 4, pp. 118-120.

Deutschman, A. (1991) "The trouble with MBA's", *Fortune*, July, pp. 67-77.

Garvin, D. (1988), *Managing Quality*, New York: The Free Press.

Haertel, G.D., Walberg, H.J., and Weinstein, T. (1983) "Psychological performance models of educational performance" *Review of Educational Research*, vol. 53, pp. 75-91.

Heskett, J.L., Sasser, W.E., and Hart, C.W. (1990), *Service Breakthroughs*, New York: The Free Press.

Higgins, R.C., Jenkins, D.L. and Lewis, R.P. (1991) "Total quality management in the classroom: listen to your customers", *Engineering Education*, vol. 81, no. 1, pp. 12-14.

McMillen, L. (1991) "To boost quality and cut costs, Oregon State U. adopts a customer oriented approach", *Chronical of Higher Education*, vol. 37, no. 21, pp. 27-28.

Robinson, J., Poling, H., Akers, J., Galvin, R., Artzt, E. and Allaire, P. (1992) "An open letter:TQM on campus", *Production and Operations Management*, vol. 1, no. 4, pp. 121-123.

Saad, G.H., and Ozatalay, S. (1991), "Productivity outcome of MBA education: perspectives and measurement", in *Productivity and Quality Management Frontiers-III*, Sumanth, et al. editors, Norcross, Georgia: Institute of Industrial Engineers, pp. 774-779.

Saad, G., and Ozatalay, S. (1991) "Improving productivity of MBA Education: a 'pull-push' approach", paper presented at the ORSA/TIMS National Meeting, Anaheim, CA.

Taylor, A.R. (1991) "How we practice what we teach", *Journal of Quality and Participation*, March, pp. 78-81.

Zeithaml, U.A., Parasuraman, A., and Berry, L. L. (1990). *Delivering Quality Service*, New York: The Free Press.

BIOGRAPHY:

Germaine Saad is an Associate Professor at Widener University. She has a Ph.D. and M.A. degrees from the Wharton School, University of Pennsylvania; and an MBA and B. Comm. degrees from Cairo University. She has published in the Journal of Operational Research Society, the International Journal of Production Research, Journal of Administrative Research, Journal of Resource Management and Technology, The Public Productivity Review, Technology Management, Journal of Advances in Management Studies, the National Productivity Review, among others. She is author/coauthor of five books.

Savas Ozatalay is a professor and the Head of the Management Department at Widener University. He has a B.S. degree from the Middle East Technical University, an M.A. and a Ph.D. degrees from Northwestern University. Some of his publications have appeared in the American Economic Review, Journal of Higher Education, Business Economics, Journal of Medical System,and Technology Management.

Productivity & Quality Management Frontiers-IV, edited by Sumanth, Edosomwan, Poupart, and Sink. ©1993
Institute of Industrial Engineers.

Productivity Improvements in a Make to Order Company

S.J. Childe, G. de la Pascua, A.J. Hallihan, R.S. Maull, and P.D. Pearce
University of Plymouth
Plymouth, England UNITED KINGDOM

This paper describes some of the results of a collaboration between the University and a
capital goods manufacturing company. The company was experiencing problems of
increasing competition in a field where most products are unique. The paper describes the
use of Group Technology to solve problems of shop floor complexity due to the one-of-a-
kind nature of the products. The selection and operation of a control system designed for
this application is outlined together with some of the benefits which have begun to appear.

Productivity & Quality Management Frontiers-IV, edited by Sumanth, Edosomwan, Poupart, and Sink. ©1993 Institute of Industrial Engineers.

Change Management: The Human Side of Change and Its Relationship to Quality and Productivity

C.A. Stevens and S. Gambrell
Science Application International Corporation
Oak Ridge, Tennessee USA

ABSTRACT:

Change, progress, innovation, continuous improvement, task alignment, reorganization, corporate renewal, programmatic change . . . No matter how you define it, organizations are changing. Change is inevitable and will increase in response to corporate downsizing, the changing economic climate, a fluctuating marketplace, and the ever-changing landscape of our work force. As managers, we must learn to understand the nature of change and take an active role in communicating before, during, and after the change. The more we understand the human side of change the better positioned we will be to compete and provide a positive work environment. In this paper we will investigate change management -- a term used to explain the processes designed to provide order to the human side of change.

Key Words: change, Change Management, maintain quality, maintain productivity.

Productivity & Quality Management Frontiers-IV, edited by Sumanth, Edosomwan, Poupart, and Sink. ©1993 Institute of Industrial Engineers.

Team Communications in the 21st Century: Maintaining Quality and Productivity in a Changing World by Communication

C.A. Stevens and S. Gambrell
Science Application International Corporation
Oak Ridge, Tennessee USA

C. Pepper
Oak Ridge National Laboratory
Oak Ridge, Tennessee USA

ABSTRACT

A major part of managing change is maintaining good communications with all parties involved. In fact, communications is the common thread that weaves our change planning, actions, and results together. Communications before, during, and after the change is critical. Results-oriented communications does not just stop at dispensing information routinely; it requires a proactive commitment from managers to find new ways to understand what employees are experiencing.

As employee demographics change, so do some of the requirements of communicating with the work force. In the future, technical teams will be comprised of higher percentages of women, minorities, and immigrants. Project teams will also require people with different technical backgrounds to work together. In each case these differences can increase the potential for communications problems or can help make the team stronger and more creative. To ensure internal cooperation, productivity, and quality we are going to have to communicate effectively. This is not a luxury - it will become competitive survival.

Key Words: Change Management, communications, communicating.

INTRODUCTION:

Before we talk about change management let's paint a picture of the work place in the 21st century.

During the "3rd International Conference on Productivity and Quality Research," in Miami, D. Hosni made some interesting observations. To summarize, the United States (U.S.) technical work force is beginning a dramatic evolution, the effects of which will not be totally realized until well into the next century. A number of labor studies have concluded that recent demographic changes in the U.S. population indicate a growing racial and ethnic presence. This evolution, sometimes referred to as "the browning of America," is starting to result in reducing the white population's percentage of the work force.

The U.S. Department of Commerce estimated that the White population will be reduced to 50% or less by the year 2080. The rest of the population probably will be predominantly Hispanic at 20% and Black at 19%, mixed with Asians and others.

In addition, the number of White women in the work force have also had an impact by moving into technical and managerial positions previously dominated by White males. But women (at times) continue to experience some social and cultural conflicts from people who are not ready for their leadership roles.

Hosni explained that, of 360,000 foreign students in the U.S., nearly one-half were enrolled in engineering and science degree programs and most of them were South and East Asian. Of 3,376 Doctoral degrees awarded in engineering by U.S. universities, 1,715 recipients were foreign. Many of these people will have returned to their countries of origin to fulfill obligations associated with the support provided by their governments, but many others will remain in the U.S. to become part of its technological work force.

What does this mean to technical project managers? Scientists, engineers and technicians of the next century will be more diverse in language and background, as well as socioeconomic origins. The pursuit of quality will not only require close attention to classic areas of documentation and change management, but also communicating among diversified groups.

Language problems that were earlier attributed to multinational projects can be found in the U.S. today. Employees may have difficulty in understanding the language used to express the change as well as other technical principles. This problem will continue to grow.

In order for our country to compete, we will need a larger number of technical workers. This means women, Hispanics, Blacks and Asians will have to move into technical fields, where White males used to dominate. The new diverse work force will push management teams to respond more quickly to more changes at a rate that has never been seen. Preparing for these changes now can present an opportunity for the companies to bring together teams that will do a better job at competing and delivering quality in the future.

COMPLICATING FACTORS:

The communication issues are complicated by other factors being introduced into the work force. The expansion of federal, state and local government regulations relating to environmental, safety, and health have had a dramatic impact on project management in recent years. Also, litigation has skyrocketed. These issues have affected organizations in ways that contradict good quality and productivity improvement programs. As an example, consider the following:

- Avoiding litigation motivates companies to centralize protective resources and restrict management power, employee flexibility, and decision-making authority. But this contradicts quality initiatives that advise companies to decentralize and empower lower levels of employees. So companies are moving to more closely regulated decisions while wanting to (or at least being advised to) empower the employees.

- Regulations and litigation require more documentation, increasing red tape. So companies are increasing documentation while wanting to limit non-value-added tasks, like paper work.

- Changes are risky, so companies are motivated not to change at a time when change is required to stay competitive. Related to this, the methods of controlling technical changes (like Configuration Management) to lower risk if improperly implemented can become unworkable.

Other complicating factors related to change also contribute to communication problems. As new programs are introduced, we find that some may only be activity based with no meaningful way to measure results. At the same time, project teams are becoming more professionally diversified and results are harder to measure because of this diversity.

This professional diversity can be caused by several factors, two of which are:

1. highly technical projects require specialized professionals with different background to work together in teams, and

2. engineers, scientists, and technicians from one depressed segment of the economy moving to another segment which is more vigorous.

This was realized during the early 1970s with the aerospace industry and the 1980s with the energy industry. Each released thousands of employees who had to move to other regions and search for new employment.

All of these issues are compounded by the fact that the volume of information is reaching a critical mass. And, there seems to be no time for assimilating the most vital information into useable pieces that can be digested by our organizations.

PROBLEM SUMMARY:

So many problems and so little time. The same communicating problems that exist in the U.S. will be multiplied in Europe as entire countries learn to relate to each other.

Communication issues could be summarized as follows:

Gender -- men and women are different and they usually communicate, act, react, and see things differently.

Race -- different races sometimes have problems interacting and understanding one another.

Culture -- native languages, sub-cultural language, slang, and regional dialects color the English language with terms and phrasing that can be confusing.

Organization -- organizational culture and politics add different communicating styles and meanings to terms.

Education -- technical training and education provide different meanings to the same words.

Social -- social behavior and norms complicate the way people perceive one another.

Personal -- personality types, personal problems, and handicaps can add another layer of communication issues in the work environment.

SOLUTIONS:

A major part of managing change is maintaining good communications with all parties involved. In fact, communications is the common thread that weaves our change planning, actions, and results together. As explained in "Managing Change, Part 1 - Change Management," communications before, during, and after the change is critical. Of course, there may be times when ideas should not yet be expressed openly. But in-house communications must be a part of the change process for your team to make the desired results materialize.

Results-oriented communication does not stop at just dispensing information routinely. It requires a proactive commitment from managers in finding new ways to understand what employees are experiencing.

Some possible solutions are as follows:

Promote Understanding
As project managers, we need to understand that people are complicated by their personality types, desires, beliefs, strengths, and weaknesses. Even these traits change based on a countless number of variables.

Different does not mean inherently better or worse, smarter or not. Differences are reflected in ranges that overlap and change. For example, some typical "male" personality traits (like aggression) are present in some women and vice versa.

Be Patient
Be patient when a person fails to understand what you are saying. The ability to receive a message, at times, may be directly proportional to your ability to transmit it. In the biblical sense, don't worry about the speck in your neighbor's eye until you remove the log from your own eye first. Withhold judgement and treat individuals with respect -- realize that people communicate differently.

Simplify
Practice good simple, communication skills when writing and speaking. Someone once said, "the objective is to express, not impress."

Provide Education/Training
At times, words and concepts may have to be defined. Simple words like "system" have many meanings.

Example: To a manager "systems" may refer to scheduling charts and procedures and to a marketeer, promotional layouts. In the computer environment, it may refer to hardware or software. Mechanical engineers may see a piece of machinery, while an industrial engineer may think of people-machine interfaces.

Build For The Future

Encourage your company's involvement in educational outreach at the high school and college levels. Providing summer intern opportunities for culturally diverse students will ease the transition which ultimately must come.

Create leadership incubators. Seek opportunities for cultural exchange, seminars, and training programs dealing with these topics not only for project managers, but future leaders as well.

Be Honest and Fair

Treat people fairly but do not over compensate. Favors in the office place can cause a teachers-pet-syndrome, which may backlash. A history of fairness will go a long way in smoothing the problems that occasionally surface.

Be Optimistic

Finally, approach change with an eye toward the benefits to be gained rather than problems to be experienced.

SUMMARY:

"The times they are a-changing." Without strong lines of communication we can not introduce primary principles related to high technology. Without good communication, friendly relationships are difficult, and without friendly relationships and trust, team building is impossible.

It all points to a critical need for fundamental changes in training and education with an emphasis on effective communications.

Successful managers will be the ones who recognize the need to change with the times and implement new project initiatives that will benefit their companies. Be proactive, be positive, be fair, be patient.

REFERENCES:

1.   Hosni, D., (1991). "Productivity Prospects of the Browning of America," Productivity and Quality Management Frontiers - III, Institute of Industrial Engineers, pp. 695-701.

2.   U.S. Department of Commerce (1986). Bureau of the Census. Projection of the Hispanic Population: 1983 to 2080. Series P-25, No. 995.

3.   Finkbeiner, A.K., (1987). "Demographic or Market Forces?" Mosaic, Vol. 18, No. 1, Spring pp. 10-17.

4.   Pepper, C., C.A. Stevens, "Project Management - Maintaining Quality by Communicating," The Third International Waste Management Conference, Sponsored by The American Society for Quality Control, Energy Division, Las Vegas, Nevada, May 4, 1992.

BIOGRAPHICAL SKETCHES OF AUTHORS

Craig A. Stevens works for Science Applications International Corporation (SAIC) in Oak Ridge Tennessee. He was the 1991-92 president and 1990 IIE Engineer of the Year of the Institute of Industrial Engineers (IIE), East Tennessee Chapter 11. He has provided services for over 60 different companies and organizations and has a B.S. in IE and M.S. in Engineering Management/IE.

Calvin Pepper Works for Martin Marietta Energy Systems at the Oak Ridge National Laboratory, Oak Ridge, Tennessee. He has over twenty years of experience in Quality Control and Quality Assurance related to project management and detail design. He has a B.S. in Nuclear Science and a M.S. in Nuclear Engineering. Mr. Pepper is presently preparing a textbook (The Welding Inspection Handbook).

Steven Gambrell has ten years experience in technical and corporate communication planning and management consulting. He has a B.S. in Corporate/Business Communications and a M.S. in Corporate & Public Affairs Management and Market Planning. He is a consultant for Science Applications International Corporation (SAIC) and Martin Marietta Energy Systems in Oak Ridge.

Productivity & Quality Management Frontiers-IV, edited by Sumanth, Edosomwan, Poupart, and Sink. ©1993 Institute of Industrial Engineers.

Facilitating and Controlling Change: Improving Competitiveness, Quality, and Productivity

C.A. Stevens and S. Gambrell
Science Application International Corporation
Oak Ridge, Tennessee USA

C. Pepper
Oak Ridge National Laboratory
Oak Ridge, Tennessee USA

ABSTRACT

Historically, changing economic environments have contributed to the prosperity or poverty of nations. Innovations in product design and manufacturing have changed the way we conduct business, leisure, war, and life in general. Companies that have forecasted trends or initiated them have grown and successfully competed in the world economy. These companies have anticipated the needs and wants of customers and have changed directions to meet those needs.

Facilitating good changes is essential to improve competitiveness. Our goals for managing change should be results-oriented. These could include the improvement of the present situation (quality, profits, productivity, motivation, etc.) or a solution to a specific problem.

Key Words: Change Management, Change, Facilitating Change, Maintaining Productivity, Maintaining Quality.

MANAGING CHANGE

As explained in the paper "Managing Change, Part 1," changes cause a natural drop in productivity, motivation, and quality. This can be compared to the metamorphose of a butterfly where the drop is similar to the "cocoon stage." During this cocoon stage, things seem to be worse than before the change. But, like the butterfly, our vision (of the desired results) should emerge and bring with it improvements.

The good news is, we can minimize these drops by taking the right actions before, during, and after the change. These actions include communicating a vision, minimizing resistance, providing incentives, and building the team.

LONG BEFORE THE CHANGE

The process of successful change management starts before an organizational change is visualized. The "long-before-the-fact" attributes that mark a successful change are:

(1)   a history of company commitment,

(2)   the presents of good leadership,

(3)   good organizational lines of communication,

(4)   an innovative atmosphere accented by open-mindedness and creativity, and

(5)   good screening and change control techniques.

History of Commitment
Effective Change Management requires a history of commitment long before a change is required.

Companies build respect and employee/customer goodwill over time. If you haven't established a reputation of honesty, sensitivity, and persistence, don't expect cooperation. As someone once said, "cheat me once, shame on you; cheat me twice, shame on me." If honesty is half of the picture, persistence is a large part of the other half. Don't give up too soon.

Leadership
Like a history of commitment, leadership starts long before a change is required. Leadership is built over time as seen in figure 1. It requires many building blocks. Over time, managers progressively lay down this multi-layered foundation.

Leadership, during all stages of change, is expected and demanded by the employees. The reasoning here is, "You have something you want done!? . . . show us your vision and lead us there."

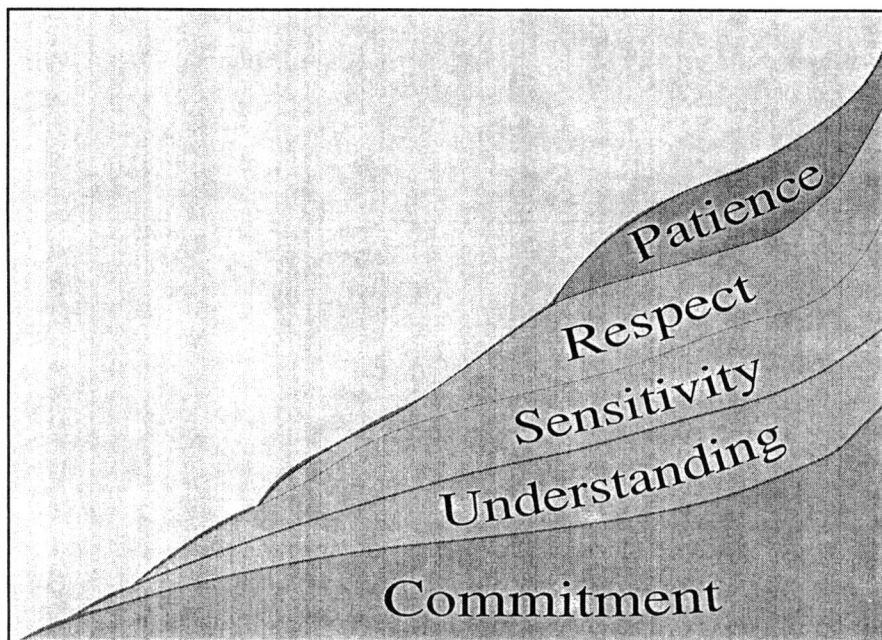

Leadership (y-axis) / Time (x-axis)

Patience
Respect
Sensitivity
Understanding
Commitment

Time   FIGURE 1

Communications

The lines of communication should be designed into our organizations long before a change is required. The paper "Managing Change, Part 2," focuses on some of these issues. Later, as change is required, the resulting atmosphere of trust will help to facilitate the change.

Innovation

Innovation is a broad subject and could take us on a journey too long to do justice in this paper. The following are just a few points that seem appropriate:

- **Open-mindedness:** Ideas come to us from many different sources. We must learn how to be receptive to the ideas in order to benefit from them. However, open-mindedness is a two edged sword - it requires us to listen to points we may disagree with. There is a trend in this country to place less value on conservative and traditional points of view - that "liberal bias" should also be eliminated.

  Once we have studied a problem with an open mind we are in a better position to solve it. The goal is to make decisions on steps to follow in order to obtain the desired results.

- **Creativity:** When managing change, a mechanism to solicit ideas from every available source could provide a competitive edge. Ideas for improvement often come directly from the employees responsible for the systems used or with in the organization where they work. Employees from other work areas may also provide insight to new ways of doing old business.

  Likewise, customers or users sometimes modify existing products to better meet their needs. The general public (non-customers and/or non-users) can help make a company more competitive through scholarship programs or external competitions designed to generate ideas.

- **Value-adding-tools:** Tools like "Value Engineering" (a systematic method of adding value) could be put into place. The real strength in value engineering is the team dynamic approach. Working together, a team uses the concept that two people talking create the equivalent of a third person; therefore, ideas and concepts are generated that are greater than the sum of each individual's creativity.

- **Incentives:** Incentives help encourage innovation. Ask yourself and your team, "What incentives can be used to persuade employees (contractors, etc.) to offer creative ideas for the benefit of the company? What about customers and others?" Find out!

Screening changes

Screening unnecessary changes should be done as early as possible. Change for change sake should be avoided. Ask yourself: what would happen if the change did not occur? Change must be the result of a demonstrated (and usually a documented) need. Constant improvement should be the goal rather than constant change.

Improvements may be accomplished without change. Maybe the answer is to learn to use systems more effectively rather than change them. A system that reviews ideas should be in place. Review all ideas before they are disregarded or used. Even inappropriate ideas may spark other, more appropriate, ideas.

In today's technical often hazardous environments, negative changes to systems critical to safety and health should be screened. All out-of-specification changes to critical systems should have been researched appropriately. For example, if one million dollars has been spent on the initial designs of a process, how much sense does it make to then change that process without the appropriate research and design review?

BEFORE THE CHANGE

Once the groundwork has been laid and an organizational change is in process, we must make the change work. The following factors are important before we implement:

1. a communicated vision;

2. set goals;

3. good planning; and

4. (as explained above) a history of commitment, good leadership, and communication.

Vision
Before you express the organizational change you have in mind, create a vision that can be shared with your group. Concentrate on the results and benefits that will be achieved and the problems to be avoided. Share this vision and encourage suggestions to make it work.

Goals
Develop goals that will allow your group to reach this vision. Break them down into definable and assignable pieces. Discuss the pieces.

Good Planning
A good change plan is based on a vision of desired results and goals to achieve it. The plan should move employees through the change process as smoothly as possible. The intent is to align people with new roles, responsibilities, and expectations early in the process.

A fundamental flaw in many change programs is an attempt by management to "work the change in" to the existing status-quo environment. This is especially true of programs initiated by technical or industrial managers. The managers may think this will create a minimal amount of instability and disturbance to the company. They may realize that their employees' response will likely result in some resistance and decreases in morale or productivity. However, as a result, too many organizational change programs fall short of the goals for three key reasons:

1. The steps identified to make the change are too abstract and mostly adaptive or involvement-oriented, instead of focusing on desired results (like lowering cost).

2. The planning of the transitional phase-in is often fundamentally flawed in design. Management allows the status-quo of the organization to guide the implementation of the change instead of letting the change guide employee adjustment.

3. Management fails to fully understand and apply pre-change, during change, and post-change methods that stress leadership, commitment, good communication, team acknowledgement, and involvement.

History of Commitment, Leadership, and Communications
This is where the groundwork already discussed starts to pay off. Before the change is made we should have:

1. a history of company commitment,

2. the communication links established (to explain the vision of the results wanted and the goals to achieve it), and

3. the leadership in place to guide the company to the results desired.

DURING THE CHANGE

During an organizational change, expect the cocoon stage. However, the dips in quality, productivity, and moral can be minimized by:

1. valid reasoning for the change,

2. acknowledgement of the team for previous work,

3. the reassignment of team members,

4. a reasonable time frame for the change,

5. good communication during the change, and

6. good leadership throughout the change.

Valid Reasoning
Most managers are quick in responding to why change is necessary. Typical reasons may include:

• continuous improvements,

• innovations or "lessons learned,"

• responding to a more fluid marketplace,

• remaining competitive and re-positioning,

• adapting to cultural diversity within the work place, and/or

• other related macro-environmental and industrial forces.

Equally important to most technical managers is a new focus on quality programs like Total Quality Management (TQM). This approach to customer satisfaction, value delivery, teamwork, and continuous improvement, has helped managers approach the change hurdle more easily. However, when it's time for a change, it many still fall short of implementing a planned program based on tangible and measurable results (like cost savings).

Team Acknowledgement and Reassignment
How would you feel if you were asked to change a process that you had been working on for years? What if your previous work was ignored or criticized? How would you feel if during the entire time you did the best possible job with the available resources, knowledge, and skills - only to have your efforts "shelved?" The answers are obvious.

Despite the necessity for change, employees have a strong need to have their previous work acknowledged.

Communicating reasons for the change to employees promptly and clearly will prevent possible misinterpretations of their failure to deliver quality. Communicate the transferability of their previous skills, methods, or management styles. Of course, new skills and commitments will be expected.

If employees see team acknowledgement and acceptance for their efforts, the change will be easier to accept. Celebrate the efforts given and advancements that are coming as a result of the change. Your team will respond.

Time Frame
Effective change programs do not take place over night. A well-managed and implemented change program requires a phase-in plan that progressively gains employee acceptance.

Be realistic but not slow. Drop the change in, encourage involvement and acceptance, but don't overwhelm the team. Again, pre-change planning will smooth out the potential rough edges.

We tend to forget that there will be a "cocoon stage," because management wants to change as quickly and efficiently as possible. This forgetfulness can result in a poorly-implemented change that can both fail to communicate the vision clearly to employees and get the results expected. Again, looking at nature, a caterpillar that is rushed or cut out of the cocoon stage early may result in a dysfunctional butterfly.

Communications
During the change, rumors will be high. Step in early and whenever necessary. Kill the rumors! Answer and resolve the questions. If you don't, someone else will, often with incorrect information. Expose all assumptions, clarify mixed messages, and reduce irrational barriers.

Open, consistent communication is the key during this cocoon stage. Time-conscious, results-oriented managers will clearly communicate new expectations of the employees, including cooperation, new skills, and focused commitment. During this period, it is also critical for managers to provide training to help train people for new tasks.

Provide a communications program that will best meet the needs of your team. Scheduling a weekly round table question and answer session or your team may be more comfortable with access to management "one-on-one" at designated times.

Whatever method you choose, make sure your employees clearly understand the intentions. Your efforts should be to inform and serve as a listener who is receptive and responsive to concerns. You may choose to enroll yourself in a communications workshop to better understand your employees' personality types and work styles.

After the Change

Once the change has been implemented, the organization should see increased productivity and morale. However, it may be a lengthy period between incorporation and increased productivity.

After the change we should:

1. continue planning and providing good leadership,

2. involve the team,

3. think about people, and

4. conduct Post-Change Follow-Ups:

Continue Planning, Communicating, and Leading
It is important to continue to plan and forecast for the future. Any fully implemented change may affect people's productivity in a positive way for a time (Similar to the Hawthorn experiments). However, these increases may fade.

Continued planning, communications, and leadership will allow for the fine tuning of the process. It will help the organization to adjust to the "after the change" environment and prevent a loss of motivation.

Team Participation
Bring the team into the adjustment period. Make sure that the team has ownership in the change and is empowered to fine tune it.

Results

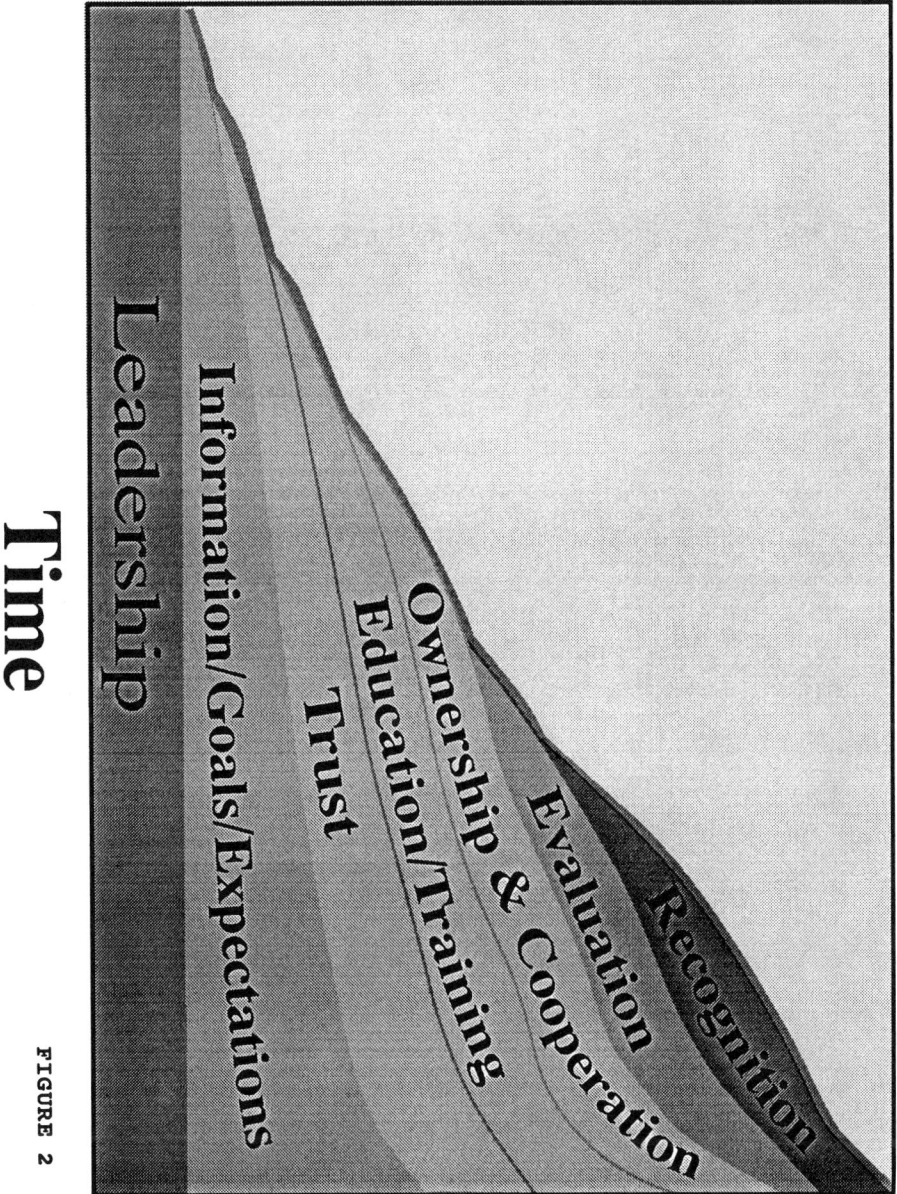

Time

Leadership

Information/Goals/Expectations

Trust

Education/Training

Ownership & Cooperation

Evaluation

Recognition

FIGURE 2

Think People

The Tennessee Valley Authority (TVA) did a study that revealed -- more money is spent on people in the form of salaries, training, sick leave, etc. than all the other life-cycle cost combined. People are important!

Maintain the mechanisms put in place to address the people issues. Continue to enhance the process of dealing with people. The result will be less stress on everyone. Consistent results can be traced back to how you treat your people. Figure 2 slows some of the building blocks related to people, results, and time.

Conduct Post-Change Follow-Ups

Conduct performance evaluations and audits at predetermined time intervals. This will help to (1) determine if the change was effective and (2) "close the loop".

"Closing the Loop" can be used in a variety of contexts when discussing change. During the change, it could be used to ensure that change documentation is understood and executed -- after the change to describe the communications which reveal its effectiveness.

SUMMARY

Everything is changing. It is either growing or deteriorating. We can witness it in nature, our selves, and our organizations. In a competitive environment, to stand sill is to deteriorate. Learn how to facilitate growth and positive changes.

During the process of change, things sometime appear to be worse than before. This is natural and temporary. If we acknowledge this point and become proactive in our approach to change, we can minimize the negative side-effects. However, this requires action before, during, and after the change.

REFERENCES

Bommer, M. and Victor Pease, "Mitigating the Impact of Project Cancellation on Productivity," National Productivity Review 10, No. 4, Autumn 1991.

Bramson, R.N. 1989. The Corporate Wonderland. Personnel Administrator, 72-79

Bridges, W. 1991. Managing Transitions: Making the Most of Change. William Bridges and Associates, Inc.

Kane, J., as reported by Kleiman, M. 1989, September. "Ease the Stress of Change." Personnel Journal, 106-112

Gambrell, S. and C.A. Stevens, 1992, "Change Management," Paper submitted to Industrial Management Magazine.

Stevens C.A., S. Gambrell, L. McCartney, and F. Jordan, 1992, "Managing Change," Presentation - WATTec'92 19th Annual Technical Conference and Exhibition, February 20, 1992.

Stevens, C.A., K. Wright, "Managing Change with Configuration Management, What are the issues related to Quality and Productivity?," National Productivity Review, page 509, Executive Enterprises Publications Co., New York, NY, Fall 1991.

Stevens, C.A., R.F. Brown [P.E.], M. Owens, P. Thompson, R. Best, L. Stevens, "Managing Change with Configuration-Value Management; The Integration of Configuration Management, Value Engineering, and Incentive Programs for Innovation," 1991 Design Productivity Institute and International Conference, Honolulu, HI, February 3-9, 1991.

BIOGRAPHICAL SKETCHES OF AUTHORS

Craig A. Stevens works for Science Applications International Corporation (SAIC) in Oak Ridge, Tennessee. He was the 1991-92 President and 1990 IIE Engineer of the Year of the Institute of Industrial Engineers (IIE), East Tennessee Chapter 11. He has provided services for over 60 different companies and organizations. He has a B.S. in IE and a M.S. in Engineering Management/IE from the University of Tennessee.

Steven Gambrell has ten years experience in technical and corporate communication planning and management consulting. He has a B.S. in Corporate/Business Communications and a M.S. in Corporate & Public Affairs Management and Market Planning. He is a consultant for SAIC and Martin Marietta Energy Systems in Oak Ridge.

Calvin Pepper Works for Martin Marietta Energy Systems at the Oak Ridge National Laboratory, Oak Ridge, Tennessee. He has over twenty years of experience in Quality Control and Quality Assurance related to project management and detail design. He has a B.S. in Nuclear Science and a M.S. in Nuclear Engineering. Mr. Pepper is presently preparing a textbook (The Welding Inspection Handbook).

Part V
TRANSFER OF KNOWLEDGE IN PRODUCTIVITY AND QUALITY RESEARCH

1. From Manufacturing to Service Sectors

2. Highly-Democratized to Newly-Democratized Countries

3. Factors Affecting the Transfer: Challenges and Opportunities

4. Formal Mechanisms, Methodologies, and Processes to Achieve the Transfer

5. Research-Based Case Studies

Productivity & Quality Management Frontiers-IV, edited by Sumanth, Edosomwan, Poupart, and Sink. ©1993
Institute of Industrial Engineers.

Quality Assurance: From Manufacturing to Tertiary and Industrial Services

C.P. Lacaze	J.P. Gazerian and F. Rigaud	J.-M. Ruiz
TERSUD - Buroparc	Université de Droit	Aix-Marseille III University
Marseille, FRANCE	Marseille, FRANCE	Marseille, FRANCE

ABSTRACT :

In simplified terms, **quality control** concerns the operational means to fulfil the quality requirements, while **quality assurance** aims at providing confidence in this fulfilment. Quality assurance is demonstrated through :
- the quality manual : a document stating out the general policies, procedures and practises used to achieve quality
- the procedures manuals : comprehensive documented procedures and instructions that define the execution of work.

Since the early 1950's quality assurance has been growing mainly in the industrial field and four norms (ISO 9004, 9003,9002,9001) describe the different areas of application in process, mass or job shop production. By the end of 1991 the second part of the ISO 9004 intitled "Guidelines for Services" (first edition) was published.

Today the demand for quality assurance in services is increasing rapidly. From consultancy experiences, a specific scheme to organize quality assurance in services has been developed and sucessfully applied in many instances. It is explained in this paper and three examples illustrate some specific details of the method.

Key words :
Service Design and delivery process - Quality assurance in services - Customer's satisfaction - Quality manual for services

INTRODUCTION

The international standard ISO* 8402 defines quality as "the totality of features and characteristics of product or service that bears on its ability to satisfy stated or implied needs". To deliver customers with product or service of "good quality" we were used to operational techniques in the sense of quality control. But it appeared to be unsatisfactory to guarantee a great chance of success.

Quality assurance defined (ISO 8402) as "all activities and functions concerned with the attainment of quality" gives a better answer : it allows a wider scope to provide
- that product or service meet continually the customer's stated or implied needs
- confidence to the management that the required quality is being achieved and sustained
- confidence to the customer that the required quality is or will be achieved.

Quality assurance is demonstrated through :
- the quality manual : a document stating out the general policies, procedures and pratices used to achieve quality
- the procedures manuals : comprehensive documented procedures and instructions that define the execution and the control of work.

Since the early 1950's quality assurance has been growing in the industrial field and today four main norms (ISO 9004, 9003, 9002, 9001) describe the different areas of application in process, mass or job shop production.
ISO 9004 is a guide line for building up a quality assurance system.
ISO 9003 describes the quality assurance requirements for final inspection and tests.
ISO 9002 gives the quality assurance requirements for production and installation.
ISO 9001 is the most comprehensive standard and describes the quality assurance requirements for design and development, production, installation and servicing.
ISO 9000 is a guideline for selection and use of ISO 9001 to 9004
ISO 9001 to 9003 subdivide a quality system into up to 20 distinct elements such as :
- Responsibility of management
- Employee's qualification
- Organizational structure
- Documentation
- Corrective action
- Quality records,
- ...
These norms do not fit well to help construct quality assurance for service processes even with the help of the second part of the ISO 9004 intitled "guidelines for services" published by the end of 1991.

The purpose of this paper is to propose from consultancy experiences a scheme to organize quality assurance in services and show how it can fit the norms.

ISO : The International Organization for Standardization ; Case Postale 58 ; CH 1211 GENEVA 20
    SWITZERLAND

THE QUALITY LOOP : MODEL FOR SERVICES

Figure 1 presents a life cycle for services in two distinct parts. A static part which imagines how a service should be delivered and a dynamic part which effectively answers the customer's demand.

The first part (static part) starts with the SERVICE NEEDS phase based on a marketing process to determine and promote the need and demand for a service. This phase leads to the DESIGN PROCESS which includes service specification, service delivery specification and quality control specification.

Figure 1 : Quality process life cycle

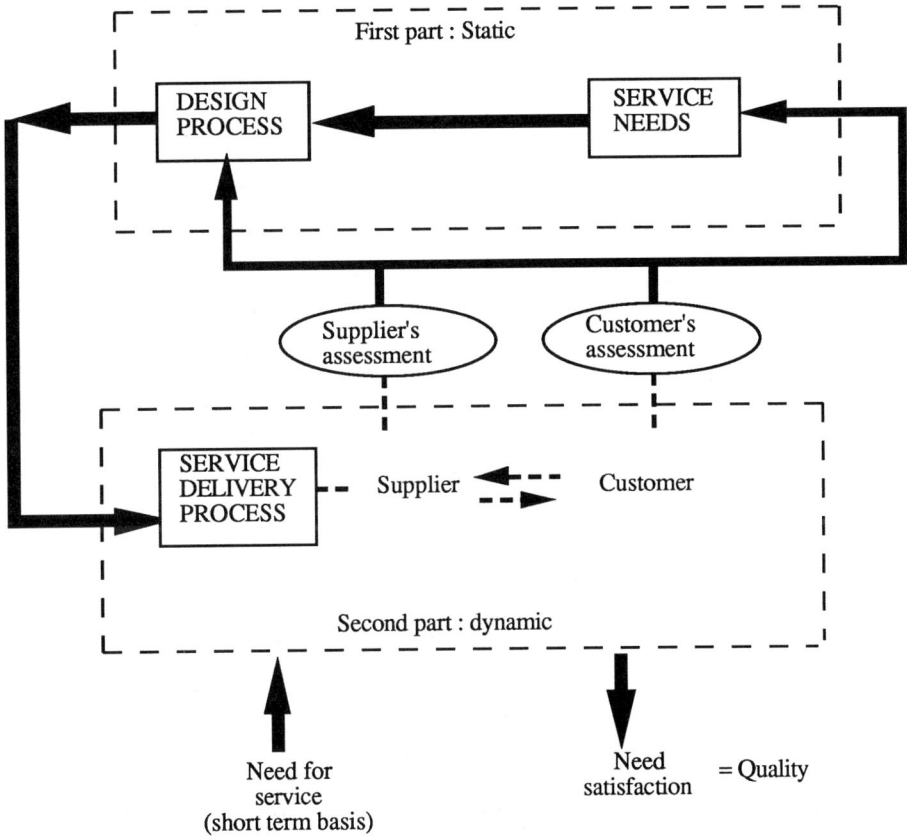

The second part (dynamic part) deals with the SERVICE DELIVERY PROCESS which applies in a dynamic way the DESIGN PROCESS. A supplier's assessment provides a perspective of the quality of service delivered and the customer's assessment is the ultimate measure of the quality of the service.

METHODOLOGY FOR QUALITY ASSURANCE IN SERVICES

Quality assurance can be considered as a way to organize a service process in order to satisfy the customer.

Very often, the SERVICE DELIVERY PROCESS phase exists without a well structured DESIGN PROCESS phase. Through the study of the process of delivering a service, the adequate design process can be created. In other words we start from the dynamic phase to construct the corresponding static model.

How to analyse the process of delivering the service ? Three different logics help describe it.

The Service Process logic : In this logic, traceability of the service to be delivered has to be searched.

Figure 2 illustrates the **cycle approach** from the "implied or stated needs" to the answer that the organization is able to generate and figure 3 illustrates the **spider's web approach**.

Figure 2 : Cycle approach

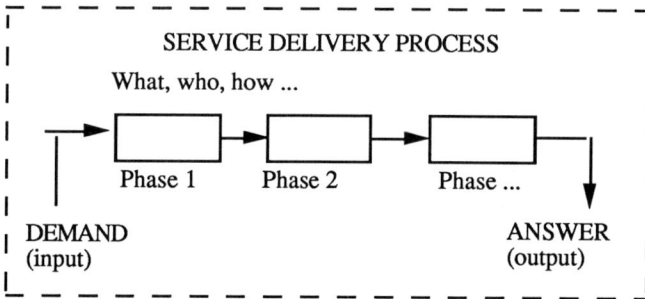

Figure 3 : Spider's web

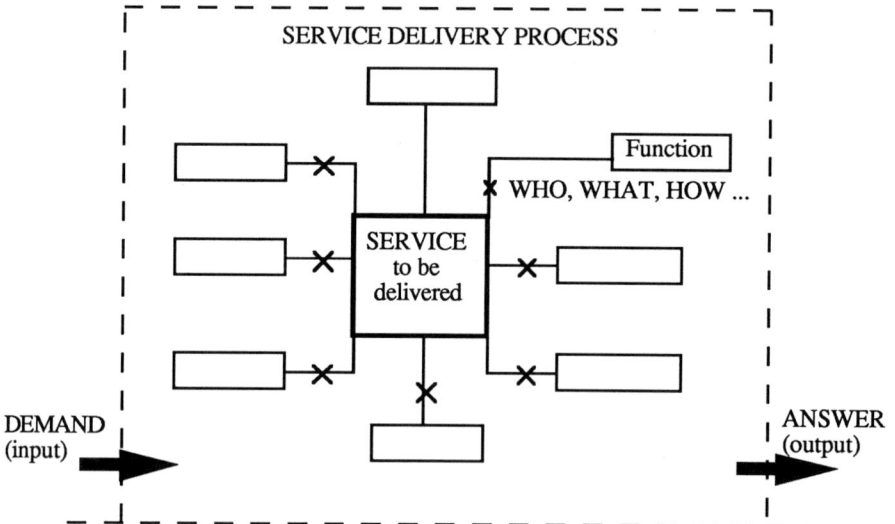

In the **cycle approach**, each phase of the cycle has to be described in terms of "documented procedures and instructions that define the execution and control of work". Feedback on the quality of the process comes from both supplier and customer by means of a questionnaire.

In the **spider's web** approach, each link between a function and the subject under study has to be described in terms of "documented procedures and instructions that define the execution and the control of work" as well.

Both approaches help to define the organization that brings a right answer to the "implied or stated needs". Again the feedback on the quality of the process comes from both supplier and customer by means of a questionnaire. In this logic it is assumed that the progress from demand to answer is carried out without any problems.

The support to service process logic : Many problems may arise within an organization. It is not that easy to progress from the Demand to the Answer without any non conformities. All the "documented procedures and instructions that define the execution and the control of work "that have been identified in the service process logic are not sufficient ; those to **"support the service process"** have to be created

For example, a **service process** will not work properly :
     - if the sub-contractors, if any, are not qualified,
     - if the non conformities cannot be handled,
     - if a traceability in the service process to initiate corrective actions cannot be provided,
     - etc.

Each element of the **support to service process** will be described in terms of "documented procedures and instructions" too.

The company organization logic :Most of the time a company organizational chart exists and authorities to be delegated to individuals to carry out their designated responsibilities are described. This information has to be cross-checked with the knowledge of the **service process** and **support to service process** that has been acquired in terms of "who does what and how" as seen in the two preceding logics. Decisions have to be taken when both sources of information do not fit well. **At that time it is possible to construct the DESIGN PROCESS phase with accuracy.**

The DESIGN PROCESS is the static description of the service to be delivered : supplier's and customer's assessments will help to correct it when necessary. Corrections apply both to the organization itself and to the customer needs appraisal which could have changed with time (the SERVICE NEEDS phase in the quality loop). ISO norm 9004-2 "guidelines for services" is of good help to explain the DESIGN PROCESS content in terms of service specifications, service delivery specifications and quality control specifications.

QUALITY ASSURANCE MANUAL

All the necessary information for the DESIGN PROCESS are known and the quality assurance manual can be constructed and all the "documented procedures and instructions" gathered in procedures manuals.

Figure 4 shows how the service process, support to service process, company organization approach must "feed" the different chapters of norms ISO on quality assurance to describe the DESIGN PROCESS phase.

Figure 4 : Quality assurance manual
(ISO 9001)

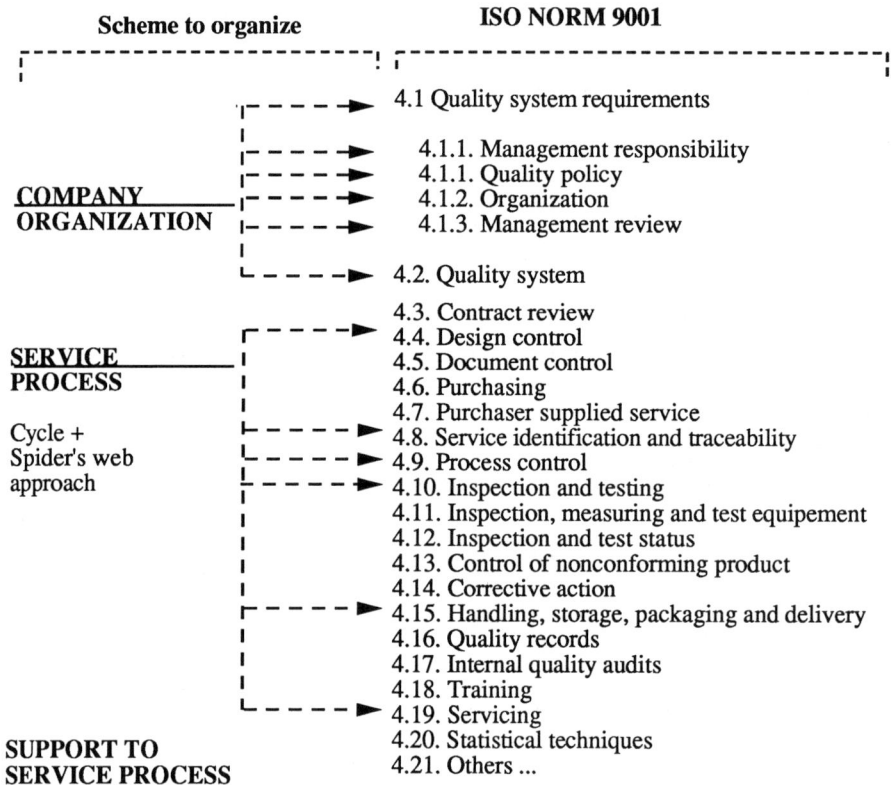

Scheme to organize   **ISO NORM 9001**

4.1 Quality system requirements

4.1.1. Management responsibility
4.1.1. Quality policy
COMPANY   4.1.2. Organization
ORGANIZATION   4.1.3. Management review

4.2. Quality system

4.3. Contract review
4.4. Design control
SERVICE   4.5. Document control
PROCESS   4.6. Purchasing
                                         4.7. Purchaser supplied service
Cycle +   4.8. Service identification and traceability
Spider's web   4.9. Process control
approach   4.10. Inspection and testing
                                         4.11. Inspection, measuring and test equipement
                                         4.12. Inspection and test status
                                         4.13. Control of nonconforming product
                                         4.14. Corrective action
                                         4.15. Handling, storage, packaging and delivery
                                         4.16. Quality records
                                         4.17. Internal quality audits
                                         4.18. Training
                                         4.19. Servicing
SUPPORT TO   4.20. Statistical techniques
SERVICE PROCESS   4.21. Others ...

Chapters :

4.3	4.12	4.17
4.5	4.13	4.18
4.6	4.14	4.20
4.7	4.16	4.21

are concerned

EXAMPLES

Ski Resort

A spider's web illustrates the tourist bureau's ability to answer any question and provide accurate service

Ski Resort (simplified)

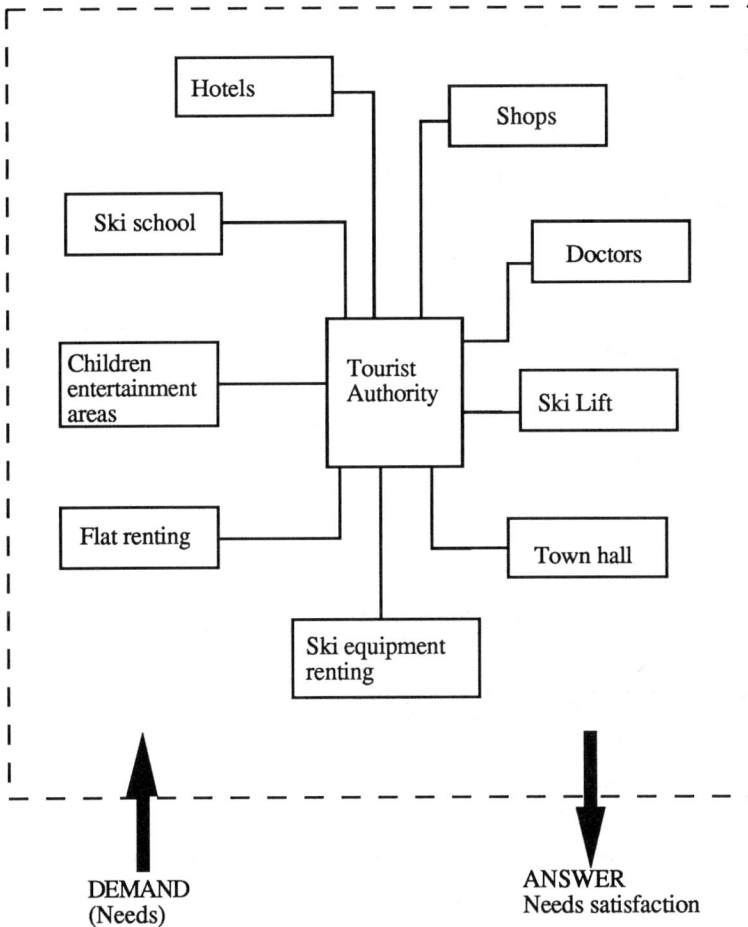

DEMAND
(Needs)

ANSWER
Needs satisfaction

Each link is described in terms of "documented procedures and instructions". The needs in the dynamic part have been identified as renting an appartement, hotel reservation, ski school, etc... The result of the study of the service delivery process shows the organizational requirements that the Tourist Authority office should meet to satisfy customer's needs. The **Design process** can then be constructed.

Insurance Company

Insurance Company (simplified)

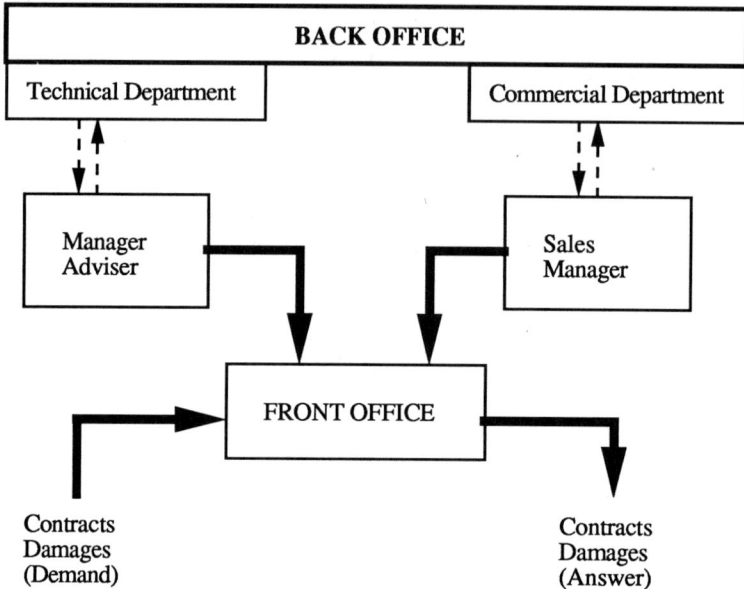

In this example, a cycle approach allowed to pinpoint part of the organization aimed at the customer's requirements in terms of contracts avaibility and damages declaration and follow up. A spider's web approach crosslinked with the cycle approach studied the organization aimed at the internal requirements that support the best service to the customer. Again, all the "documented procedures and instructions" have been gathered in a procedures manual.

Hotel Reception

This is a simplified example of a "documented procedure and instructions". A documented procedure tells exactly "who does what and how" as a rule. the procedure can include one or several check-lists, control sheets, which help apply the procedure correctly. In this case a check-list about the "Give customer details" will avoid mistakes.

Hotel Reception (simplified)

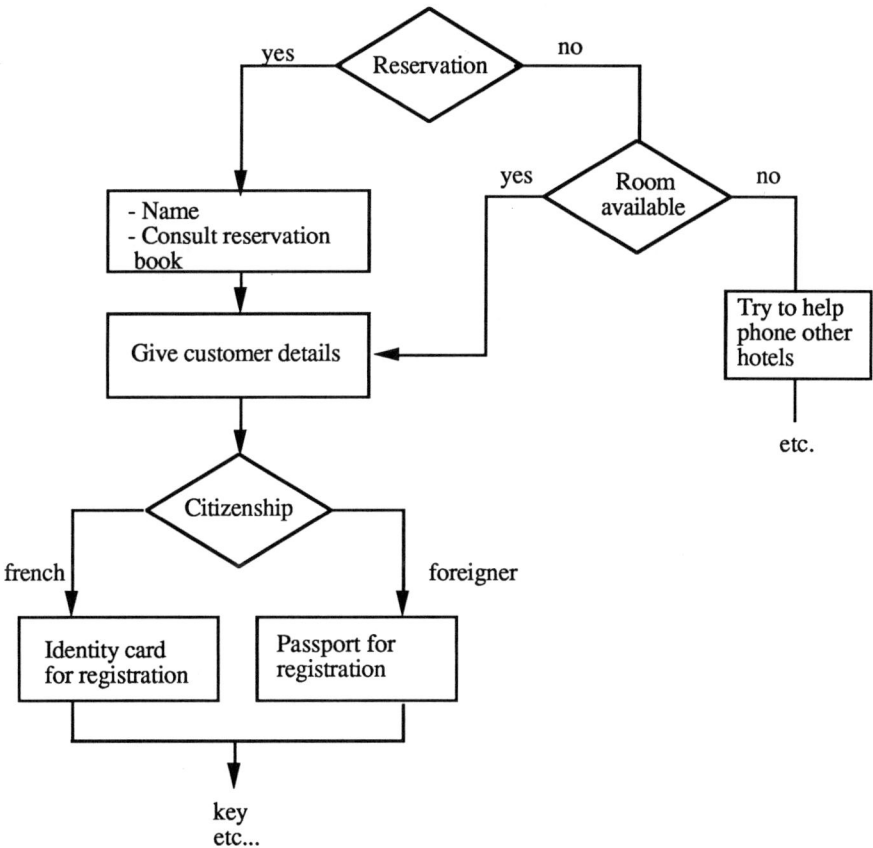

CONCLUSION

Quality assurance means transparency in an organization. The confidence that a company builds in its organization can be transferred to the customer. It is an obligation of means not a guarantee for result. One can only say that the guarantee of means leads to a high degree of confidence in the result.

So far, strong quality and productivity gains were mainly tied up to technology jumps and companies used to equaly compete on a higher level of technology. In the case of an organization based on the quality assurance methodology, productivity gains are based on people willingness to work properly according to the established rules.

Thanks to the ISO norms quality assurance is a worldwide language. Therefore the discrepancy in quality and productivity gains will be obvious from one organization to another according to people professionalism and motivation in the industrial field and even more in the service field.

BIOGRAPHICAL SKETCHES OF AUTHORS

Mr. C.P. LACAZE (49 years old) worked in the industry in the United States and in Europ. Since 1980, he has been senior consultant in project management and quality assurance in both industrial and service fields (public or private organization). He is associate professor at Aix-Marseille University-France.

Miss J.P. GAZERIAN (36 years old) (PhD in Organic Chemistry) is associate professor at Aix-Marseille University- France in Project Management and Industrial Engineering.

Mr. F.L. RIGAUD (55 years old) (PhD in Sciences) is associate professor at Aix-Marseille University- France in Project management and Industrial Engineering.

Mr. J.M. RUIZ (39 years old) (Doctorate in Organic Chemistry) is Professor at Aix-Marseille University- France in Project management and Industrial Engineering.

Productivity & Quality Management Frontiers-IV, edited by Sumanth, Edosomwan, Poupart, and Sink. ©1993
Institute of Industrial Engineers.

Investigating the Quality Message in Selected Advertisements

R.P. Kudar and R.R. Britney
University of Western Ontario
London, Ontario CANADA

ABSTRACT

This paper presents the results of two experiments
investigating the use of Garvin's Dimensions of Quality
Classification system on advertisements. The experiments were
conducted with three different groups of participants,
marketing managers, operations managers, and graduate business
students.

One experiment examined the use of the classification system on
video advertisements. The second experiment looked at the
application of the classification system on print
advertisements for automobiles.

In the video advertisements, the three different groups of
participants agreed on the least effective quality
advertisement. However, the different groups selected different
ads as the most effective quality advertisements. In addition,
the women managers in one group selected a different ad as
being the most effective than the male managers in the same
group.

In the print advertisements, the respondents indicated that
most of the advertisements appeared to present multiple quality
messages to the reader. However, the most important dimensions
of quality for automobiles, namely performance and reliability
were not the most frequently used dimensions in the
advertisements. Instead, features was found to be the most
common quality dimension used in the ads. Generally, each
advertisment appeared to present a dominant quality message on
one dimension.

Further work is needed to link the intended quality message in
the advertisements with the perceived quality message as
indicated by the respondents. As well, there is a need to
extend the analysis to identify the desired quality dimension
for various types of outputs in the advertisements.

KEY WORDS

advertising, quality dimensions, automobiles,

INTRODUCTION

It is an accepted tenet of business today that the customer defines quality for a good or service (1). The task of management is to discover what the customer means by quality, how much is needed, and to deliver that level of quality in a highly productive manner.

Unfortunately, all customers are not alike. Different segments of customers define quality for the same output in different ways. This presents problems for management. The result is that quality becomes a multi-dimensional concept for management. How does a firm deliver quality to the customer if there is no single definition of quality for the output? As well, how does a company communicate its quality message to the customer if quality is defined in the eye of the beholder?

One answer is to develop a classification system that can address the multi-dimensional aspect of quality. One such system has been developed by Garvin (2). The system defines quality in terms of eight dimensions. These are presented in Exhibit 1.

TABLE 1 DIMENSIONS OF QUALITY	
PERFORMANCE	The primary operating characteristic of the good or service
FEATURES	Those characteristics that supplement the basic functioning of the output
RELIABILITY	The probability of a malfunction within a specified time period
CONFORMANCE	The degree to which the output meets standards for its operating characteristics
DURABILITY	The extent of the life of the output
SERVICEABILITY	The speed, courtesy, ease, and competence of repairs for the output
AESTHETICS	How the output looks, sounds, tastes, smells
PERCEIVED QUALITY	Attributes that must be inferred because no direct information can be observed

Using this classification system as a framework, Garvin contends that management should compete offensively on the basis of quality. This means identifying which dimensions of quality are most relevant to the customer and ensuring that the customer knows that these dimensions are being achieved to their satisfaction. This is one of the primary roles of the marketing function of a firm. At the same time, he points out that the firm must avoid the introduction of quality dimensions that are not relevant to the customer's definition of quality for the output. While it is relatively easy to create a classification system, it is more difficult to determine if the classification system is useful to address management's problem.

PURPOSE OF EXPERIMENTS

The purpose of this study was to investigate the managerial usefulness of the Garvin classification system. Did the system allow the respondent to describe or identify a quality message? Did the classification system operate for several outputs or was it confined to one output? Two experiments are reported in this paper. Both focus on the use of advertising as a communication link between the firm and its customers regarding the quality of the firm's output. One experiment used video advertisements of several different outputs. The other experiment used print advertisements of one output, automobiles.

Three different groups of respondents were used in the experiments. All three groups were used for the video experiment. Only one group was used for the print experiment. The three groups of respondents consisted of practising managers in the field of marketing, production operations, and a group of full time graduate business students in the second year of a two year MBA program. The two practising managers' groups were attenders at residential executive management programs being held at the university. The managers were employed at several different firms across Canada. The full time graduate business students were enroled in an elective course on Quality and Productivity. These students entered the MBA program with an average of 43 months of full time work experience.

EXPERIMENTAL PROCEDURE

Video Experiment

The video experiment was undertaken as a regular class session within the program of the respondents. As a preliminary assignment for the class, the respondents were asked to read the Garvin article in the Harvard Business Review describing the classification system. In the classroom session, the instructor led a discussion of the article with the purpose of clarifying the meanings for all the dimensions in the classification system to ensure that all the participants had the same interpretation of the terms.

The video consisted of a set of five advertisements for a set of outputs. The different outputs were power lawn mowers, spark plugs, a hospital emergency room, automobiles, and tires. Each advertisement involved a well known firm. Each advertisement was of standard length for viewing on commercial television.

Prior to a viewing of each advertisement, the participants were told the generic output upon which the advertisement was based. The respondents were asked to identify the most important quality dimension for that output. The responses were given orally in class. After identification of the quality dimension, the respondents were shown the advertisement. After seeing the advertisement, the respondents were asked to identify the nature of the quality message. The responses were given orally. A discussion regarding the quality message in the advertisement was held for each video advertisement. This process was repeated for each advertisement and for each of the three different groups of respondents.

At the conclusion of viewing all five advertisements, the respondents were asked to identify the most effective and least effective quality message among the five advertisements. The responses were given through a showing of hands.

Print Experiment

A similar process was undertaken for the print experiment as for the video experiment. The experiment was conducted as part of a regular class session in the elective course on Quality and Productivity for the full time graduate business students. As an assignment for the class session, the respondents were asked to read the Garvin article. This article was then discussed in the class session, with an emphasis on understanding the terminology and classification system.

For the print experiment, a set of 14 advertisements on automobiles presented in a single issue of a magazine were selected. A booklet was prepared including a copy of each of the advertisements. These were presented in random order. Thus each participant received a slightly different order of the print advertisements. The advertisement was placed on the left hand page and the Garvin Classification system was placed on the right hand page.

The respondents were asked to indicate on the front page of the booklet the two most important dimensions of quality that they desired in an automobile, using the Garvin Classification system. They were then instructed to look at each advertisement in the booklet, and identify what the quality message was in the advertisement. They were to select one or more of the eight dimensions on the facing page for each advertisement. If they felt that there was no quality message in the advertisement, they were to indicate this on the page with the Garvin Classification for the advertisement.

When the participant had completed the booklet, the booklets were collected by the instructor and the results analyzed.

RESULTS

Video Experiment

There was no strong sense of consistency among any of the three groups of respondents regarding a single dominant quality dimension for each of the generic products presented in the advertisements. Despite efforts by the instructor to find consensus among each of the groups of respondents, the class discussion on the perceived dominant dimension of quality for each product resulted in the generation of a list of quality dimensions. Each of the groups tended to generate similar lists in terms of contents and magnitude for each of the outputs. Only the marketing managers had a tendency to include "meeting or exceeding customer expectations" as a quality dimension for the outputs.

The overall assessment of the video advertisements is presented in Exhibit 2. Once the video advertisement had been seen by the respondents, the subsequent discussion of the dominant dimension of quality present in the advertisement was much clearer. The dominant dimension for each advertisement is presented in Table 2. The majority of each of the groups of respondents identified this dimension in the advertisement. Other dimensions were also identified, but not by a majority of any group of respondents.

Each of the three groups of participants indicated that the spark plug advertisement was the least effective of the ads. Discussions in class indicated that the negative message of the advertisement emphasizing the large number of defective units did not engender a positive feeling of quality in the eyes of the respondents. With respect to effective advertisements, there were some differences. The marketing managers were divided on the basis of sex. The women indicated that the tire ad (Michelin) was the most effective while the men indicated that the automobile ad (BMW) was the most effective. In the case of the production-operations managers, there were no women present. These managers indicated that the gas lawn mower ad (Honda) was the most effective ad in terms of a quality message. The graduate students favoured the automobile advertisement.

Only the Hospital advertisement dealt with a service as opposed to a tangible product. As well, the advertisement's quality dimension was on the aesthetics of the emergency room as opposed to the more tangible dimensions associated with products. None of the groups selected this ad as being effective. In the class discussions, the quality message was not always clearly seen and articulated by the participants.

TABLE 2				
EFFECTIVE (+) OR NON-EFFECTIVE (X) ADS				
PRODUCT	MKTG	OPS	MBA	DIMENSION
Lawn mower		+		Performance
Sparkplugs	X	X	X	Conformance
Hospital				Aesthetics
Automobile	+(m)		+	Features
Tires	+(f)			Performance

Print Experiment

There were 23 graduate students who participated in the experiment. All were asked to complete the booklet. The participants were asked to identify the two most important dimensions of quality that they associated with automobiles. All respondents selected either performance (18) or reliability (18) as one of their most important dimensions. Over half of these respondents (13) selected both performance and reliability. Five participants who selected performance also selected features (1), durability (1), aesthetics (2), and perceived quality (1). Five participants who selected reliability also selected durability (2), serviceability (1), and aesthetics (2).

Each participant was asked to identify the dimensions of quality that were perceived in each of the print advertisements. Thus it was possible for each quality dimension to be cited 322 times. Table 3 identifies the frequency with which each of the dimensions of quality was cited by the respondents. The pattern for the citations of the dimensions was interesting. The two most frequently cited dimensions, features and performance were almost twice as frequent as the next set of dimensions, aesthetics and perceived quality. Similarly, these two dimensions were cited almost twice as frequently as the next three dimensions, durability, reliability, and serviceability. Conformance was cited less than half as often as the third group of dimensions.

This frequency likely results from the advertising approach of firms for print advertisements of automobiles. These results would suggest that from a marketing perspective, the dimension of features of the automobile appears to be an easier way to present an advertising quality message to the customer. It is interesting that this pattern is not consistent with the opinion of the respondents regarding the two most important dimensions of quality for this product.

<table>
<tr><td colspan="5" align="center">TABLE 3
FREQUENCY OF RESPONSE BY DIMENSION</td></tr>
<tr><td>DIMENSION</td><td>NUMBER OF
CITATIONS</td><td>NUMBER OF
ADVERTS</td><td>AV CITES
PER AD</td><td>RANGE
L - H</td></tr>
<tr><td>Features</td><td>139</td><td>11</td><td>12.6</td><td>3 - 20</td></tr>
<tr><td>Performance</td><td>123</td><td>12</td><td>10.3</td><td>3 - 18</td></tr>
<tr><td>Aesthetics</td><td>77</td><td>9</td><td>8.5</td><td>3 - 18</td></tr>
<tr><td>Perceived Quality</td><td>70</td><td>14</td><td>5.0</td><td>1 - 11</td></tr>
<tr><td>Durability</td><td>48</td><td>13</td><td>3.7</td><td>1 - 14</td></tr>
<tr><td>Reliability</td><td>47</td><td>13</td><td>3.6</td><td>1 - 9</td></tr>
<tr><td>Serviceability</td><td>42</td><td>8</td><td>5.3</td><td>1 - 15</td></tr>
<tr><td>Conformance</td><td>18</td><td>9</td><td>2.0</td><td>1 - 4</td></tr>
<tr><td>No Quality Message</td><td>17</td><td>6</td><td>2.8</td><td>2 - 4</td></tr>
</table>

A frequency count was made of the number of times that each dimension of quality was identified by a respondent for an individual advertisement. The intent was to determine if there was a dominant quality message in the advertisement. For each advertisement, we identified the most frequently cited dimension of quality. The results of the classification of the most dominant quality dimension in each advertisement is presented in Table 4.

ADVERTISEMENT	DIMENSION	FREQUENCY	PERCENTAGE
DOMESTIC CARS			
Buick *	Features	21	91.3
Chrysler	Features	20	90.9
Pontiac	Performance	18	78.2
Ford Truck *	Performance	18	78.2
Taurus *	Features	17	73.9
Saturn	Features	16	72.7
Oldsmobile	Serviceability	15	68.6
Ford	Aesthetics	10	43.4
FOREIGN CARS			
Mazda 929	Aesthetics	18	78.2
Isuzu	Features	18	78.2
Hyundai	Serviceability	15	68.6
Mazda MX-3	Aesthetics	12	52.1
Nissan	Perceived Quality	11	43.4
Volvo	Features	11	43.4

TABLE 4
DOMINANT QUALITY DIMENSION IN EACH AD

  * Also had a high response rate on a second quality dimension

As this table indicates, the dimension of features was
identified by the respondents as the most dominant quality
message in six specific advertisements for automobiles. It was
the second most frequently cited dimension for two other
advertisements. The results also suggest that the domestic
firms appear to be doing a better job of presenting a clear
quality message to the reader. Seven of the domestic automobile
ads were seen to have a clear quality message as perceived by a
majority of the respondents while only four of the foreign
automotive advertisements were perceived by the majority of the
respondents to have the same quality dimension in the
advertisement.

It would appear from these results that the classification
system is useful in identifying the quality message that is
present in communications between the firm and its customers.
There was a high degree of agreement between the respondents
regarding the quality message in some of the advertisements.

One of the expectations in the experiment was that the quality
dimension of the advertisements would be confined to a single
dimension. This was not the case. Each of the advertisements
were cited by the respondents as having multiple quality
dimensions. The results of the responses are presented in Table
5.

TABLE 5
MULTIPLE QUALITY MESSAGES

ADVERTISEMENT	FREQUENCY OF RESPONSES	PERCENTAGE OF RESPONSES	NUMBER OF DIMENSIONS
Hyundai	23	100	8
Taurus	20	86.9	8
Mazda 929	19	82.6	7
Buick	18	78.2	6
Pontiac	16	69.5	8
Mazda MX-3	16	69.5	7
Ford Trucks	13	56.5	4
Isuzu	11	47,8	7
Oldsmobile	11	47.8	6
Volvo	11	47.8	6
Nissan	11	47.8	5
Saturn	10	43.4	8
Ford	6	26.0	4
Chrysler	6	26.0	4

While all of the advertisements were perceived to have multiple
dimensions in the quality message, over half of the respondents
detected multiple messages in seven of the fourteen
advertisements. The Hyundai advertisement was identified by all
of the respondents as having multiple dimensions of quality. In
fact, all eight dimensions of quality were identified as being
associated with the advertisement. By contrast, only six

respondents identified multiple dimensions of quality in the message for the Chrysler advertisement. Only four dimensions of quality were identified in the Chrysler advertisement.

It is not clear from this experiment whether the identification of multiple dimensions in the advertisements results from the classification system being too specific in terms of the dimensions. or whether it is a deliberate strategy of the advertisement to have multiple dimensions of quality in order to convey a message to a wider group of customers.

CONCLUSIONS

Based on these results, it would appear that the classification system for the dimensions of quality developed by Garvin can be used to identify a quality message. This would suggest that firms interested in communicating their quality efforts to the customer can consider using this classification method as a framework for approaching the task. In the case of the video advertisements and the print advertisements, the respondents were able to achieve reasonable convergence regarding the dominant dimension of quality present.

It is also clear from the results, that certain dimensions of quality such as conformance are not regarded as important, from the customers' perspective as might previously have been thought. This concept of conformance is a production oriented perspective of quality that may be important in a business to business arrangement, but appears to have little weight in a consumer good business. In both experiments, we were hard pressed to find examples of conformance as a relevant dimension of quality.

In the area of determining specific dimensions of quality for an output, the classification system may be beneficial. While the discussions on the important dimensions of quality associated with the video advertisements did not result in overall consensus among the respondents, we found that in the print experiment, there was a strong sense of the important dimensions of quality for the automobile. It might be feasible for management to work with focus groups to identify relevant dimensions of quality for their outputs using the Garvin classification.

FUTURE WORK

There is a need to develop a stronger methodology to assess the suitability of the classification system for outputs and the impact on advertisement messages. It would be useful to identify the intent of the quality message in an advertisement from the creator and then test to determine if the respondent identifies the same quality message. A second interesting question would focus on the impact of using multiple or highly focused single quality messages in the advertisements.

If the Garvin classification system is to be relevant to management, it must be capable of helping management determine what quality message is needed by the customer, and what quality message is being received by the customer through the advertising channel. This knowledge should assist management in being able to better compete on the critical dimensions of quality that are most relevant to the customer.

REFERENCES

1.   Kudar R.P. and Britney R.R. "Total Quality Management and the Customer", Productivity and Quality Management Frontiers III, Sumanth et al (editors), Industrial Engineers and Management Press, Institute of Industrial Engineers (Norcross, Georgia), 1991, pp 377-382.

2.   Garvin J. "Competing on the Eight Dimensions of Quality", Harvard Business Review, November-December 1987, pp 101-109.

AUTHORS

Randy Kudar is an Associate Professor of Management Accounting. He has extensive experience in Management Development in Africa, South America, China, and Saudi Arabia. He has conducted seminars for firms in Canada, and has presented material on Quality and Productivity at National meetings in both Canada and the United States. He, together with Bob Britney have presented at the International Productivity Research Conference each time it has been held.

Bob Britney is a Professor of Operations Management. He is the recent editor of the OMA Review. He has extensive experience in management development with Operations managers. He has recently had a book published, Price and Discount Schedule Analysis with P.Kuzdrall.

Productivity & Quality Management Frontiers-IV, edited by Sumanth, Edosomwan, Poupart, and Sink. ©1993 Institute of Industrial Engineers.

The Application of TQM in the U.K. Service Sector

R. Maull	R. Cliffe	J. Marsh
University of Plymouth	Trustees Savings Bank	Avon TEC
Plymouth, England U.K.	Birmingham, England U.K.	Bristol, England U.K.

The 1980's saw Total Quality Management (TQM) being applied in a wide variety of manufacturing applications; chemicals, electronics, capital goods, light engineering etc, the 1990's is the decade when TQM is applied in the service sector. Deming has said that *"Improving our standard of living is highly dependant on better quality in the service sector"*.

Far too often service professionals and manufacturing consultants focus only on the similarities between services and manufacturing. It is essential that TQM is adapted to fit the organisation and not the other way around. The opposite approach has failed dismally when implementing Information systems so why should it work with TQM?

In this paper the authors will identify how TQM has been applied in a 2 major UK service organisations;

1   Training and Enterprise Council (TEC) a public funding body
2   Trustees Savings Bank, the UK's 6th largest bank

All the authors have had considerable experience with applying TQM methods in manufacturing prior to their experience in the service sector. As a result we will draw out similarities between manufacturing and service sectors and more importantly the key differences eg the differences in objectives, the difficulties in measuring service quality etc. We will also highlight how the Baldridge award has affected the development of strategies for quality and its assessment within these service organisations. We will conclude by highlighting our key learning experiences for those applying TQM in the service sector.

Productivity & Quality Management Frontiers-IV, edited by Sumanth, Edosomwan, Poupart, and Sink. ©1993
Institute of Industrial Engineers.

Productivity for Poland

I. Eriksson
Swedish Federation of Productivity Services (SRF)
Stockholm, SWEDEN

ABSTRACT

The Swedish Federation of Productivity Services, SRF, is working with training and consultancy in the field of total productivity e.g. labour productivity, capital productivity and quality both in Sweden and in other countries. It was with this background that SRF accepted an offer from its Polish sister organization to assist it in the transition of Polish industry into a market economy. A program containing both theoretical training and implementation assistance was established and financed by Polish and Swedish government bodies. Stage 1 of the program which was completed in April 92 involved two manufacturing companies and one hospital. The program has greatly increased the enterprizes ability to stay in business and also produced a staff of Polish consultants who can be responsible for a continuation of the program. This will be done in stage 2 and 3 of the program which is expected to start in the fall of 1992 and be finalized in June 1993.

Keywords: Profitability, Productivity, Transition of knowledge

Productivity & Quality Management Frontiers-IV, edited by Sumanth, Edosomwan, Poupart, and Sink. ©1993 Institute of Industrial Engineers.

National Strategies for Quality Improvement: The Case of Greece

N. Kastrinos
The University, PREST
Manchester, England UNITED KINGDOM

ABSTRACT

This paper stems from a study sponsored by the SPRINT programme of the Commission of the European Communities, investigating quality promotion measures and schemes in the 12 European Community countries. It analyzes the emergence of the quality issue in the agendas of the Greek government and industry. It draws on the way the quality issue has been dealt with in the international management literature and in the various Greek fora, and it presents and discusses the activities for quality improvement that were initiated by the Greek government and industry. These activities are analyzed and lessons are being drawn about the factors that bear on the promotion of quality improvement in a national environment.

KEY WORDS

Greece, quality, standardization, quality management, total quality management,

INTRODUCTION

This paper owes its existence to a project investigating measures and schemes for quality promotion in Europe, sponsored by the Commission of the European Communities. It analyzes the forces that led to the emergence of quality as an issue in Greece, in both the private and public sector, and presents and discusses the activities induced.

The first section of the paper discusses the rise of the quality issue as it has been presented in the international management literature. In this literature the challenge posed by Japanese competitive strategies is considered to be the stimulus for changes in firms' quality management practices and national policies. However, in Greece the issue of quality has emerged within a quite different framework, which is discussed in the second section of the paper. Greek production is virtually untouched by Japanese competition but is affected by the changes taking place at a European level. Thus, quality as an issue emerged with some delay in Greece compared with other European countries. The focal points of discussions comprise the changes in quality management practices at a European level that bear on the competitive performance of firms, and the establishment of a European standardization system.

The responses of the Greek public and private sectors to the emergence of the quality issue are discussed in the third and fourth section. The third section presents the discussions and developments related to the development of a Greek infrastructure that would be able to accommodate both the needs of Greek industry in its European environment, and the demands of this environment. The fourth section discusses the specific activities that are related to the promotion of product quality and quality management in Greek firms.

The fifth and concluding section discusses the Greek situation in the light of the activities presented. In particular it draws lessons about the factors that bear on the successful promotion of quality conscious competitive strategies in Greek firms.

THE EMERGENCE OF QUALITY AS AN ISSUE

Lascelles and Dale (1988) argue that recent years have seen a shift in the market paradigm that renders acceptable quality a minimum requirement for market entry. Following Friesecke (1983) they suggest that this shift was driven largely by Japanese competitive strategies which combined great efficiency in bringing innovations to the market with high quality products.

Quality improvement lies at the centre of Japanese competitive strategies. ISO 8402 defines quality as "the totality of features and characteristics of a product or a service that bear on its ability to satisfy stated or implied needs". Accordingly quality improvement can be defined as "the totality of possible improvements in product or service characteristics". Watanabe (1990) argues that Japanese management goes even further by including the improvements in production processes. In Japanese terms quality implies "anything that can be improved".

This explains why Japanese firms are known for their ability to introduce incremental innovations rather than new products (Wagasugi 1992). As Lundvall (1988) and Teubal et al (1991) argue, incremental innovations are the result of a communication process between producers and users through which user needs and product characteristics are articulated to ever greater degrees of specificity. Standards are an essential part of this process. A standard is a set of articulated user needs corresponding to a set of product characteristics. Once established, it can be diffused horizontally through the engineering communities, resulting in savings in the costs of communication between producers and users.

While the intermediation of standards between producers and users provides easy access to market entry requirements, it does not substitute for the communication processes that are essential for quality improvements. On the contrary, it involves the danger that firms can get trapped into a situation in which quality is interpreted as compliance with standards. In this case, the intermediation of standards reduces the flexibility of firms and their ability to respond in rapidly changing market conditions.

The extent to which this is the case relates to the way quality is managed by firms. Quality controls at the end of the production process can, by their nature, only deal with compliance to standards. In this case, incremental innovation requires a constant upgrading of the standards of quality control, which in turn requires very good interfaces between the quality control and the design departments within the firm, combined with close monitoring of markets and technologies.

In Japan statistical quality controls were introduced immediately after the Second World War. The practice was rapidly diffused throughout the industry via the Japanese Union of Scientists and Engineers (JUSE). In the late 1950's - early 1960's, JUSE played a major role in the diffusion of the Japanese version of Feigenbaum's concept of Total Quality Control, called Company Wide Quality Control (CWQC) or Total Quality Management (TQM). This quality management style is committed to the improvement, rather than the satisfactory execution of a given task (Watanabe 1990). This is achieved through the use of the concepts of the internal and external customer, and a transfer of the responsibility for quality control from the end of the production process to the quality circles which operate within the teams that deal with individual production stages. Essentially, quality circles are workshops on product and production improvements. The interfaces between the various departments and production stages are dealt with through frequent staff rotations (Aoki 1990, Watanabe 1990). Overall, while the firm's aim is to satisfy both sets of "customers", the employees (internal customers) become committed to the external customer with the intermediation of the firm.

The success of Japanese firms in rapidly managing change and gaining competitive advantages through innovation, brought about TQM as a new management paradigm. This is where the paradigm shift actually appeared, that

1247

is in management practices rather than in market processes. Quality standards are by nature "minimum requirements for market entry". Furthermore they have often been used by governments as a means of protecting their markets from foreign products. The only identifiable shift in the market paradigm relates to the ferocity of Japanese competition.

This competition brought European standardization systems face to face with ever shorter product life-cycles, that meant that standards had to be constantly devised and updated. Their response came with the establishment of quality management process standards in the form of BS 5750 in Britain and subsequently its international versions, the ISO 9000 and EN 29000 series. These standards certify quality assurance mechanisms in a firm rather than the quality of its product. In this they are similar to the practices of TQM. Their codification in standards means that they can be diffused via the engineering communities connected through the national standardization channels. Their imposition in markets, as in the case of British public procurement contracts, provides the inducement mechanism for the adoption by firms.

These standards represent commitment to quality assurance rather than quality improvement. However, their diffusion at a European level together with the harmonization of national standards are considered as a very important part of the idea of a Common Market consisting of internationally competitive firms. Both the public and the private sectors of the Member States are faced with the challenge of adapting to the needs of a European standardization system. At the same time they are increasingly faced with an environment in which markets are less stable and protected by technical regulations, and more open to competition from incremental innovations. This challenges them to promote a quality improvement generating production system.

THE EMERGENCE OF QUALITY AS AN ISSUE IN GREECE

The Greek economy is characterized by a predominance of the service sector. Its industry consists mainly of small firms in traditional industrial sectors. This has been increasingly the case since 1974, with industrial production showing a growing concentration in labour intensive activities. Virtually no part of the Greek production system has been faced with Japanese competition.

Perhaps as a reflection of this, only a very small number of firms in Greece perceive quality as a major issue in their competitive strategies. In particular, while in most firms some means are employed to guarantee an acceptable level of quality in the products that reach the customer, this is by no means systematic. Where they are in place, quality tends to be managed in a static sense (Mouzopoulos 1992). This is true for both large and small firms. A recent study addressed quality management practices in the 400 industrial, trading and service firms operating in Greece, which had the largest turn-over in 1989 (Vitantzakis et al 1992). Some 131 firms responded, 11 of which were subsidiaries of multinationals. The study found that while all the respondent firms consider the quality of their products and services essential for their performance, 65 % of them

1248

do not have a manager responsible for quality. A striking result was that only the 11 subsidiaries of multinationals had moved beyond statistical quality controls and were involved in TQM related programmes. This picture is supported by the fact that only 5 firms are certified to standards of the ISO 9000 series, 3 by the Greek Standards Organization (ELOT) and 2 by the Bureau Veritas Quality International (BVQI). Of these, 3 are subsidiaries and 2 are Greek transnational enterprises. Some 25 companies have applied to ELOT for certification.

Although ELOT was set up in 1976, it took quite some time until it found a role in Greek public policy-making, as standardization has not been a viable industrial policy option in Greece. As the Greek industry is not close to the leading edge of technological developments, the imposition of standards as barriers to entry in Greek markets would have selected out Greek firms. Thus, market protection relied entirely on tariff and non-tariff barriers to trade.

Standardization became an issue for Greece in the mid 1980's with the harmonization of the national standards, the mutual recognition of certification bodies and the consequent harmonization of national accreditation practices in the European Community. Within this framework, however, standardization acquires a new meaning, because the accredited bodies are called to certify compliance of national products to international standards and not *vice versa*. As a result, the national standardization systems are transformed from a means of protecting national markets to a means of accessing European and international markets. This issue is currently emerging in Greece and has induced a major discussion, mainly in the public sector, about setting up a "quality infrastructure" that will enable Greece to satisfy the demands of the emerging European standardization system.

THE QUALITY INFRASTRUCTURE

The quality infrastructure is emerging through creation of new institutions and the coordination of existing institutions. The latter have been created largely on an *ad hoc* basis, when the government has been faced with specific articulated sectoral demands. Today coherent structure is required that would be able to satisfy the needs of the European standardization system and, at the same time, articulate and respond to the needs of the Greek industry. In this framework, testing, certification and accreditation needs are considered to be three different but interdependent themes.

Testing is seen as a serious problem given that the bulk of Greek companies do not have the means to perform simple quality controls. This was regarded as a major deficiency of the Greek technological infrastructure, which was tackled in the National Technological Development Plan 1983-1987. A major reorganization of the scientific and technological system was initiated. This included programmes that would increase the cooperation between industry and scientific institutions including the setting up of applied research centres next to universities, and the creation of sectoral technology transfer companies as joint ventures of either the Ministry of Industry, Energy and Technology (MIET) or the Organization of Small and Medium-size Enterprises and Handicrafts (EOMMEX) [1] and firms in a number of sectors. A number of laboratories were thus set up which could be used by industry for quality testing. The technology transfer companies which were, by nature, closer to industry than any other research organization, were immediately faced with a very large demand for quality testing services (Kastrinos 1990).

In the mid 1980's, ELOT began to be perceived as an important actor in the National Technological Development Plan and set up four laboratories to perform its certification tests in the fields of low voltage electrical appliances and electronics, electric cable, toys, and plastic pipes. Facing increasing demand for certification tests in other areas, ELOT started using the services of two of the sectoral technology transfer companies in the fields of metallurgy, and ceramics and refractories, as well as those of the National Research Centre for Nuclear Research "Democritos", and the State Laboratory of Public Works (KEDE), the construction materials laboratory of the Ministry of Spatial Planning and Public Works.

A problem arose in relation to the authority of these four laboratories to certify compliance with standards, as ELOT is the only organization accredited by the Greek government. This raised the issue of accreditation which is being addressed at three levels. The first refers to the laboratories of the public sector which are capable of performing certification tests. Being under governmental control, these laboratories can be easily accredited. The second level refers to accreditation of laboratories of the private sector. This is a very debatable issue in Greece as it effectively involves the delegation of authority from the state to industry. Already one industrial association, the Greek Aluminium Association, is certifying its members in standards of international non-governmental organizations that are very well established in the international aluminium market. This brings about the third level of the accreditation issue which becomes important in view of the changing role of the national standardization systems in the European Community. A number of transnational organizations like the BVQI, being accredited by foreign National Accreditation Systems, operate in Greece and compete with ELOT without being accredited by the Greek government. While this issue can be resolved only at a European level, it creates additional pressures for the establishment of a National Accreditation System.

In 1989 an Accreditation Council was established comprising representatives from ELOT, MIET, The Federation of Greek Industries (SEB), the National Chemical Laboratory of the State, the Association of Greek Engineers, the National Technical University of Athens and one specialist appointed ad hoc from the Board of Directors of ELOT. ELOT holds the secretariat of the Council. While it is estimated that some 25 laboratories comply with the requirements of the standard series EN 45000 and thus are capable of certifying standards, still no accreditation has taken place. This is attributed to functional problems, such as the lack of staff and flexibility needed for the establishment of a suitable monitoring system as well as to the lack of a National Metrology System. This, together with the

---

[1] Acronyms are often derived from Greek initials

establishment of a number of testing laboratories, is being put forward to the European Community for funding under PRISMA, a programme aiming at assisting the industrial structures of the Member States in preparing for the Common Market.

QUALITY PROMOTION ACTIVITIES

In general quality promotion activities in Greece take place within the framework of the functions of institutions established under a variety of circumstances and with a variety of objectives. While the state plays a major role in quality promoting activities, there are neither any specific programmes in the area nor any organizations dealing specifically with quality promotion. However, quality promotion is *de facto* involved in the activities of a number of public sector organizations.

ELOT as part of its work in promoting the technological development of the Greek industry, has established an information directorate that diffuses information on technical standards and regulations and developments in the area at an international level. These are codified in data-bases that are accessible on line, and also printed in bulletins that are distributed in the industry. The scheme has been accompanied by minimal marketing effort and operates through subscriptions. Incentives were provided for firms to join in, as the charges for participation are minimal (in the range of ECU 50) and participating organizations can use the services of ELOT at greatly reduced prices. However, so far only 70 organizations from both the private and public sector have joined, and the scheme has not received the expected response. This is considered to be an indication of the low levels of awareness in Greek firms of the importance of quality and technical innovation for competitiveness.

This lack of awareness is recognized by a number of public sector organizations which provide technical, organizational and marketing support to businesses. However, there has not been a single awareness campaign by the Greek public sector. The only campaign was launched by the Federation of Greek Industries (SEB). It was called "1991-A Year of Quality for Greek Industry" and included a number of conferences in which specialists stressed the importance of Total Quality Management. The campaign also included the provision of awards to an academic and a journalist of the technical press for the best reports on TQM related subjects. A lot of discussion was stimulated and the campaign had a prominent representation in the technical and general press.

In the public sector, promotion of the importance of quality concepts for the competitiveness of firms is left to education and training schemes. During the eighties an increasing number of organizations which provide business support have been involved in providing professional training in the form of seminars to enterprises. Initially the Greek Productivity Centre (ELKEPA) provided training courses, which since the early 1980's include a course on quality management. More recently, other organizations such as EOMMEX, OPE (the Organization for the Promotion of Exports), OAED (the Organization for Employment) and EEDE (the Greek Management Association) have become involved. This increase in the number of organizations that offer training seminars on quality management is due to the fact that the European Community has began to subsidize professional training seminars via various mechanisms, particularly the Social Fund, while attaching increasing importance to the diffusion of TQM practices.

The most promising training programme is being implemented by EEDE. This consists of a series of workshops on quality management practices in which only high level managers participate. EEDE, which like SEB is a member of the European Foundation of Quality Management, has also organized a conference on TQM and intends to play a major role in the formulation of a quality management research community. For this it has planned to set up a Quality Association that will provide a focal point for Greek quality management research.

Research in quality management has been sporadic, usually taking place in *ad hoc* projects in university departments. Adhocracy has been supported by teaching practice. Engineering departments have quality control taught as part of courses on statistics course, while in management departments, if it exists at all, it is a low profile optional course. Breaching new ground in the area have been the DEREE College (a management school which does not have a university status in Greece, but is recognized by a number of universities in the UK and the US) and the University of Pereus, which have introduced strong quality management courses. Their efforts coincided with a growing interest on the subject stimulated by the launch of research projects sponsored by subsidiaries of multinational companies in support of their own TQM programmes.

FACTORS BEARING ON THE SUCCESS OF QUALITY PROMOTION MECHANISMS

The discussion of the quality issue in Greece has been essentially enclosed within two fora. In the first, discussions take place largely within the public sector and focus on the future of the Greek standardization system. While for the public sector this is inherently related to the future of Greek industry, as this system will address the needs of industry for certification and testing laboratories, there is surprisingly little participation of the private sector in this discussion. In the second forum, discussions focus on the need to promote TQM concepts and practices in Greek firms. While this discussion also addresses the future of Greek industry, it is enclosed within a relatively small community of quality management experts and large firms mainly subsidiaries of multinational companies.

The degree of closure demonstrated in these two fora can be explained with reference to the factors that prevent the formulation of a wide "quality community" in Greece. These can be traced to the ways in which the Greek economy and polity have been functioning in the past and to a certain extent today. The rise of standardization as a means of industrial policy and practice in the Western world has been supported by strong engineering communities which provided the nucleus for the diffusion of quality improvements. These communities have been organized in scientific organizations (e.g. The Association of German Engineers -

VDI) that interface with both industry and academia, and monitor and diffuse developments. The technological weakness of Greek industry and the subsequent implausibility of Greek standardization policies, combined with the absence of well organized scientific communities have resulted in a lack of a quality community that could play this role.

Furthermore, the subsequent absence of any standards from the Greek market (even in the cases of government procurement compliance with standards has hardly ever been mandatory), combined with a tradition of tariff and non-tariff barrier protection, created a market in which producers had little incentive to innovate and consumers were uneducated in demanding quality standards. It seems that these circumstances led industry to a passive attitude towards innovation and quality improvement which has very well grounded foundations. Characteristically in the two subsidiaries of multinational companies, which were suggested by people in the quality management community as the most dynamic in moving into TQM, the TQM projects were initiated after instruction from the parent company.

It is these well rooted attitudes that quality promotion measures and schemes come to fight against. In this framework, the "infrastructural" policies of the public sector, which builds organizations that wait for industry to go to them instead of going to industry themselves, seem to lack a necessary marketing strategy. At the other end of the spectrum, the discussions on TQM and the relevant awareness campaigns were targeted towards large and dynamic Greek firms which already attach a certain degree of priority to quality management. Thus, while some movement has been initiated it is confined to a small and dynamic population of firms.

A sign that developments are forthcoming lies in the quality management community which seems to be emerging around the TQM discussions. While still small, this community encompasses people from industry and universities and deals with a subject that appeals to a new generation of dynamic management executives. However, this can by no means substitute for a strong engineering quality community. While in Japan quality control circles, the heart of TQM, managed to cover up for a shortage of skilled engineers (Watanabe 1990), it is very unlikely that this would be the case in Greece. The attitudes of firms towards competition in the Japan of the late 1950's are very different to that of firms in present day Greece. While faced with increasing competition Greek firms will necessarily become more dynamic, what is needed is a widening of the quality management discussions to include the Greek engineering community and the creation of a wide quality community touching all firms and all industries.

BIBLIOGRAPHICAL REFERENCES

Aoki, M (1990) "Toward an Economic Model of the Japanese Firm", Journal of Economic Literature, vol XXVII, no 2, pp 1-27

Friesecke, R, F (1983) "The Quality Revolution: a challenge to management". Managerial Planning vol. 32, no 1, pp 7-9, p 26.

Kastrinos, N (1990) Research and Technology Policies in Greece and European Community Regional Development Assistance: an implementation study. MSc Thesis, University of Manchester.

Lascalles, D. M. and B. G. Dale (1988) "A Review of the issues involved in quality improvement" International Journal of Quality & Reliability Management, vol. 5 no. 5, pp 76-94

Lundvall, B. A. (1988)Innovation as an iterative process: from user-producer interaction to the national system of innovation, in G. Dosi et al / eds. Technical change and economic theory Pinter Publishers, London and New York.

Mouzopoulos, N (1992) "Quality award and Small-Medium Enterprises". Paper presented in the 3rd European Conference for Education, Training and Research, Rome, 9 & 10 April

Teubal, M et al (1991) "Networks and Market Creation", Research Policy, vol. 20, no. 5, pp 381-392

Vitantzakis, N et al (1992) Definition, measurement and improvement of quality in Greek enterprises. Technical College of Athens, Internal Paper

Wakasugi, R (1992) "Why are Japanese firms so innovative in engineering technology ?" Research Policy, vol 21, no 1, pp 1-12

Watanabe, S (1990) "Work organization, technical progress and culture with special reference to small group activities in Japanese industries". Paper presented in the Technology and Competitiveness Conference, organized by The French Ministry for Industry and Regional Planning, the French Ministry for Research and Technology and OECD, Paris 24-27 June.

BIOGRAPHICAL SKETCH OF AUTHOR

Nikolaos Kastrinos holds a BA in Political Science and an MSc in Technical Change and Industrial Strategy. He is currently a Research Associate with PREST, where he is also preparing a PhD Thesis on "Innovation and Diffusion through EC R&D programmes". He has performed work for the European Commission and the International Science Policy Foundation.

Productivity & Quality Management Frontiers-IV, edited by Sumanth, Edosomwan, Poupart, and Sink. ©1993 Institute of Industrial Engineers.

Stumble the Mumble: A Necessary Step before Walking the Talk of Quality Initiatives

S. Farrell

U.S. Army Construction Engineering Research Laboratories
Champaign, Illinois USA

ABSTRACT

Launching a Quality Initiative (QI) may seem overwhelming if viewed as a venture into uncharted territory. This paper illustrates the parallels between QI components and acknowledged family unit skills. Enlightened leaders, much like parents, will gently shepherd the organization through its growing pains while nurturing a vision of optimization. By reframing QI in terms of its familiarity, even those adult learners who find Statistical Process Control (SPC) tools daunting can approach QI with a new level of confidence--and a higher likelihood of success.

Productivity & Quality Management Frontiers-IV, edited by Sumanth, Edosomwan, Poupart, and Sink. ©1993 Institute of Industrial Engineers.

Management of Innovation Quality

H. Jaakkola and M. Lähdeniemi
Tampere University of Technology
Pori, FINLAND

Management of Innovation Quality

Quality system as a part of technological production is getting more importance. New technologies and innovation is necessary in the quality system itself because earlier applied methods are not any more useful or not enough qualified for communication surrounding. In the global market the key infrastructure aspects and best methods for technology transfer should be found to guarantee the tools for final product quality in limits of standards.

The paper includes analysis of the diffusion of quality methods. First principles of the diffusion of complicated technology, such as total quality management, are introduced. R&D activities, both in companies and in research organizations, are key factors in the process to develop methods for improved production processes and product proberties. Principles of the diffusion process are applied to manage the complicated process of technology transfer from research to the practice as a model of TQM adoption.

Productivity & Quality Management Frontiers-IV, edited by Sumanth, Edosomwan, Poupart, and Sink. ©1993 Institute of Industrial Engineers.

Creating and Sustaining a Local Quality Users' Network

R.P. Kudar, R.R. Britney, B. Portis, and J. Haywood-Farmer
University of Western Ontario
London, Ontario CANADA

ABSTRACT

In the past year, the Business School and several local businesses have combined to develop a Local Quality User's Network to share knowledge regarding ways to introduce quality improvement efforts within firms. The success of the network can be attributed to the low level of formal structure that has been used in the process.

We began the process with a day long workshop, attended by local business managers, and by a class of business students studying quality and productivity management. Part of the workshop was devoted to presentations by three firms on the efforts and results they had achieved in pursuing quality improvement in their organizations. A panel discussion highlighted different resources that were available to help the firms improve. The last part of the workshop involved an open discussion regarding the need and interest in developing a local network among the participants.

In the past year, the network has met every two months. The meetings are open to any firms that wish to attend. Various firms have volunteered to present their experience to the group. As well, the various firms within the community have offered their locations as meeting places for the network. The network has no membership fee, no officers, no fixed location or administration. It is simply an informal gathering of people who want to learn and are willing to share their findings with others. The major focus of the network has been on service businesses. This has proven to be most fascinating in terms of the lessons regarding suitable quality improvement techniques.

Over the year, the attendance at the meetings has increased as word of mouth regarding the group has spread. The only commitment asked is that the firm be willing to present their story and share their experience.

KEY WORDS

quality user network, service firms, informal, successful

Productivity & Quality Management Frontiers-IV, edited by Sumanth, Edosomwan, Poupart, and Sink. ©1993 Institute of Industrial Engineers.

Managing Sino-Western Joint Ventures: How to Implement Localization More Effectively

X. Jia, J. Bilderbeek, and E.J. de Bruijn
University of Twente
Enschede, THE NETHERLANDS

Abstract

With the development of China's economy in the 1980s, many Western firms aim to participate in such a world potential and risky market by creating a joint venture. Nowadays, increasing local content in a final product is a strategy usually pursued by many joint ventures. The central motives are to reduce the foreign exchange by replacing imported parts and to assimilate the Western Technology via this process, which is also called localization.

However, the evidence from many joint ventures in the automobile and electronics industries have revealed that the progress of localization frequently falls below the initial expectations. In general the underlying reasons are poor quality of locally made products, lack of motives from the Western partner, high cost of local production and poor industrial infrastructure. In addition, an optimistic progress is often planned by the joint ventures for the purpose of obtaining the approval from the Chinese government. Moreover, the Chinese partner usually ignores the difficulties in localization process and underestimates the poor local infrastructure.

It is important to note that the quality of the locally made product is a vital factor of the success of localization. The concept of quality is not as strong felt in China as is the Western world. As a consequence of that, not only the Western Technology should be transferred, but Western quality management also must be introduced to joint ventures.

The major objective of this paper is to present case studies to identify the main factors affecting the localization process. This study also provides a mode to manage the localization in an effective way.

Productivity & Quality Management Frontiers-IV, edited by Sumanth, Edosomwan, Poupart, and Sink. ©1993
Institute of Industrial Engineers.

Technology-Based Enterprise Incubator as an Instrument of Promotion for Regional Development: A Proposal for the Rio Grande do Norte State/Brazil

A.C.C.F. Campos, D.D.M.O. Souza, R.M.N. Bezerra, and R.C. da Costa
Universidade Federal do Rio Grande do Norte
Natal, RN BRAZIL

ABSTRACT

This work presents a proposal for setting up a technology-based incubator/innovation centre in the State of Rio Grande do Norte/Brazil, intended to stimulate and support the state development through the creation and development of enterprises. The importance of transfer of technologies originated from university research as well as an approach to the characteristics and peculiarities of the region are also discussed.

INTRODUCTION

One of the most remarkable changes in the world, brought about by the petrol world crisis, was in the field of regional development, which is now being oriented towards exploitation of the endogenous potential of underdeveloped regions or those in need of redevelopment. Within this scope, priority has been given to the creation of technology-based enterprises which in their majority are spin-off from universities. In fact, because of its primary and traditional functions comprising research, development and dissemination of knowledge, the university could be a key factor in this process. It could also assume new roles and for this purpose its potential is being surveyed. For some time now, all over the world and particularly in underdeveloped countries and/or economically depressed areas in developed countries, many universities are already contributing to the development of the region in which they are located, through technology transfer to enterprises.

At the same time, the productive sector is compelled to make a continuous and increasing effort in order to achieve a greater productivity, which will lead it to a greater competitiveness. In this context, the question of Quality is of vital importance, since the modern industrial society is becoming more demanding and selective. Also, promotion of Quality and Productivity depends on many factors, and the need for university-enterprise-government integration is of the utmost importance. Based on this, and considering the incipient stage of development of Rio Grande do Norte-(RN) (located in an economically depressed area in the Northeast of Brazil -

surface area=53.015 Km2 /inhabitants=2.200.000) and the
potential of the Federal University of Rio Grande do Norte
(UFRN), especially in terms of human resources, we believe
that the creation of a sector to support the establishment and
development of enterprises, which would provide goods and
services of a high - added - value, thus contributing to the
technological and socio-economic development of the RN State,
is of vital importance. Besides, it is necessary for the State
enterprises to attain higher levels of competitiveness, and
for this purpose they will need to incorporate the concepts of
TOTAL QUALITY and PRODUCTIVITY as central elements. In order
to support these changes, the following action lines should be
pursued :

- Support for creation of small enterprises. This would be
provided in the form of courses on "Business Projects",
comprising design, development and evaluation of projects;
market survey; selection of site; costs; revenue; economy
assessment, etc; Entrepreneurship; continuing education
courses and training courses. Establishment of Total Quality
Control programmes in the enterprises.

- Setting up an enterprise incubator to support the creation
of enterprises which otherwise would not be economically
viable, due to the lack of installation facilities, such as
suitable rooms, telephone, logistic support, technical
consultancy, etc. These facilities would be offered by the
incubator.

- Establishment of a databank to store and disseminate
information on Science and Technology, funding agencies,
patents, existing training courses and programmes in Quality
and Productivity in the country.

OBJECTIVES

a) The main objective of this Project is to offer the
potential entrepreneurs the opportunity to create, develop or
update their enterprise to help with the development of the RN
State. The credibility of the productive sector, either to the
external or to the internal buyer's market depends greatly on
its ability to offer durable goods, and services of good
quality and permanent character.

b) Transfer of technology arising from research work developed
by university academic staff, students or any other source
will be supported by the Enterprise Incubator and the
Technology Park. This support will be given to already
existing regional enterprises, as well as to the creation of
new ones.

c) The period of establishment of the Park will be divided
into stages. The Incubator will be set up at the initial stage

which is planned for a period of two years. Following this, the activities of the Park will be initiated.

d) The following services will be offered by the Incubator:

- Training courses, particularly in Quality and Productivity, besides technical courses in specific areas.
- Information on financing agencies, research and development;
- Technology transfer;
- Patenting;
- Information technology;
- Potential of the RN State;
- Survey of the priority sectors of the RN State economy for investment purposes, especially in the field of innovation.

The role of any Enterprise Incubator and/or Technology Park in promoting Quality and Productivity should be emphasized.

GENERAL PROFILE OF THE INCUBATOR

The main objective of the Incubator would be the rational use of a joint infrastructure which can provide basic support in planning, operating and developing new enterprises. This support would be in the form of:

- A well-known and respected address;
- Physical space (premises comprising modules and a common area including: reception, meeting room, auditorium, etc);
- Business advice (managerial and technical);
- Technical and marketing information;
- Technical and general services;
- Laboratories (or an agreement for using the UFRN laboratories or those located in any other institution involved in the programme);
- Logistic support offered by FUNPEC and the UFRN.

Another objective of the Incubator is to create opportunity for anyone who has developed a new technology or a new product to start his own enterprise.

In order to get a place at the Incubator the enterprises should go through a selection process (in the form of public tender) and should fall into one of the following categories:

- A STARTING UP ENTERPRISE STABLISHED BY AN INDIVIDUAL

It provides opportunity for a researcher who is developing a new technology, a good product, to start a technology-based enterprise.

- A NEW ENTERPRISE CREATED BY A LEGAL ENTITY

  A big enterprise or association which wants to start a technology-based enterprise.

- RELOCATED COMPANIES

  A regional technology-based enterprise or any enterprise from another region which needs suitable conditions to develop.

- R & D DEPARTMENT OF LARGE COMPANIES

  Big enterprises interested in establishing their division of product and process development.

  The incubating process should last approximately 2 to 3 years and should be divided into the following phases:

- IMPLANTATION

  Comprises the period of time (2 to 4 months) necessary for installation of the company, starting from the moment of assignment.

- DEVELOPMENT PHASE

  This phase comprises the period necessary for product improvement and marketing (1 to 2 years);

- CONSOLIDATION PHASE

  This phase concerns the time necessary for financial and administrative strengthening of the enterprises to the point of being mature enough to move to an independent address.

- LIQUIDATION PHASE

  At this stage the enterprise will start reverting the investment to the benefit of the Incubator (in case it does not move out of the Incubator).

INCUBATOR INFRASTRUCTURE

Structure

The incubator should dispose of an infrastructure to support its tenants to develop their products and to help them with the administrative and economic management of their business. For these purposes the Incubator will offer:

a) Purpose designed buildings for enterprise installation including common areas, such as meeting and training rooms, business services, warehouse, kitchen, administration room, xerox, fax, telephone, toilets, etc.;

b) Administrative support;

c) Technical support:

i) A technical team formed by academic staff from the Production Engineering, Economy, Management Science, Management Accounting and Social Science Courses of the Federal University of Rio Grande do Norte (UFRN);

ii) A team of consultants including the above mentioned academic staff and other researchers (accountants, jurists, bankers, bank managers, technitians, etc.);

iii) Community representatives;

iv) A databank to store information on these specialists and useful institutions.

Means

The Incubator policy for small and medium size enterprise creation is based on training and follow-up assistance.

FINANCING

Funds for the developmental phase of the Incubator will be granted by public and private institutions, such as:

- State Government;
- Local Government;
- Industry Federation;
- Superintendência de Desenvolvimento do Nordeste (SUDENE);
- Conselho Nacional de Desenvolvimento Científico e Tecnológico (CNPq);
- Private Companies;
- Others.

INCUBATOR MAIN FUCTIONS

The main functions of the Incubator are:

- To shelter potential entrepreneurs;
- To offer courses/training in the field of enterprise creation, Total Quality Control (TQC), etc.;
- To analyse enterprise creation projects;
- To provide consultancy on enterprise management;
- To provide continuous general upgrading programmes;

- To give consultancy on advanced management techniques;
- To carry out feasibility studies;
- To help with the working up of the project itself;
- To offer technical assistance within the scope of the project;
- To provide information on available resources;
- To survey potential areas for setting up enterprises;
- To give assistance to newly created enterprises;
- To encourage potential entrepreuners to start their business;
- To set up a programme intended to emphasize the importance of TQC for the productive sector;
- To provide training courses on TQC philosophy and techniques.

We believe that new entrepreuners can derive great benefit from a permanent and individualized assistance from the Incubator. For this purpose training courses on specific areas of interest will be offered on a regular basis. This procedure will help them to attain autonomy in their business.

As a whole, the public to be benefited from the Incubator will be the newly graduate students who want to develop the technology created in the University into business, thus using the Incubator as a starting point. In this process assistance from the academic staff will be available for them to continue the research activities previously initiated and/or to use technological innovation to enhance their chances of success.

Aiming at a policy at medium and long term the Incubator will also develop contracts on R&D with the help of the UFRN laboratories/research sectors.

Integration with other Institutions

By linking together the UFRN laboratories, research groups and other institutions such as Funding Banks, Government Bureau, RN Industry Federation, etc, the Incubator would be able to offer a variety of services, including:

- Management aid in elaborating surveys, budgets, market surveys;
- Assistance in obtaining funds from the State Government as well as from financing agencies;
- Availability of a "reception" structure to offer logistic services;
- Assistance to enterprise reorganization;
- Assistance to/and courses on Total Quality Control in the enterprises.

CONCLUSION

Taking into consideration the low degree of development of the Northeast Region of Brazil, its natural characteristics and potential, the innovative aspects of this project are basically identified as follows:

- The Technology Park/Enterprise Incubator will function as a tool to encourage and support technology-based enterprise creation, needed in developing regions.

- The technology Park/Enterprise Incubator will have a sector to promote actions intended to improve Quality and Productivity in the local enterprises. These actions would include motivation, awareness and training of the industrialists, and setting up a TQC programme in the local enterprises. Consequently, the Incubator will function as an instrument for promotion of Quality and Productivity in the local enterprises.

It is important to realize that in developed regions establishment of new enterprises are a natural process, while in underdeveloped regions, as in the case of Rio Grande do Norte State(RN), this is a slow process which needs encouragement and support from a sound and well structured institution. In this context the Incubator could function as a start up point to the establishment of technology-based enterprises due to the type of infrastructure it offers, including logistic and technical support, which are vital for new companies lacking funds for installation facilities. Therefore, it would contribute to the regional development through the services and products researched and developed by the tenant companies housed in its premises.

BIBLIOGRAPHY

1. Brescianini, E. A., Netto, E. J. **A incubadora tecnológica oportunizando o técnico empreendedor.** Tecnologia & Humanismo.

2. **CENTRE DE DESENVOLUPAMENT D'EMPRESES/INSTITUT DE TECNOLOGIA - BTC.** Parc tecnologic del Vallés. Barcelona, Espanha, Publicación interna.

3. **FUNDAÇÃO CENTRO REGIONAL DE TECNOLOGIA EM INFORMÁTICA DE SANTA CATARINA - CERTI.** (1991) Incubadora empresarial tecnológica. Santa Catarina, Brasil.

4. Medeiros, J. A. et al. (1991) **Perfil dos polos tecnológicos brasileiros.** Brasília, Brasil: IBICT, CNI/Dampi Sebrae.

Productivity & Quality Management Frontiers-IV, edited by Sumanth, Edosomwan, Poupart, and Sink. ©1993 Institute of Industrial Engineers.

Transfer of Technology: A Contribution for Improving Quality and Productivity in the Enterprises

D.D.M.O. Souza and A.C.C.F. Campos
Universidade Federal do Rio Grande do Norte
Natal, RN BRAZIL

The need to adopt efficient promotion instruments to be used as a tool to help in overcoming the obstacles to the creation and development of new enterprises in order to upgrade the Quality and Productivity, which will contribute to the regional development, has been considered.

It has been proved that in underdeveloped regions, lacking diversified promotion instruments, technology transfer from universities to enterprises has played an important part in improving Quality and Productivity for the developmental process of the region, since the results from academic researches are converted into marketable products with quality by the enterprises.

This work is focused on the potential university contribution to the economical development of a certain region, based on university/enterprise integration programmes aiming at Quality and Productivity.

Productivity & Quality Management Frontiers-IV, edited by Sumanth, Edosomwan, Poupart, and Sink. ©1993 Institute of Industrial Engineers.

The Impact of Brazil's Productivity & Quality Program on Business

E.I. Paulinyi
Strategic Affairs Office
Brasilia, DF BRAZIL

The Brazilian Productivity and Quality Program (PBQR) is different from other government programs, because it is an actual joint effort between government and business, whereby trade associations are the real 'distributors' of the Program, and because there are no funds in the Federal Budget allocated to the Program. Over 200 trade associations are actively engaged, supporting more than 200 industry-wide projects. Also 300 projects are active in all branches of the Federal government and 10 states have set up local productivity & quality programs of their own.

The Program is now going onto its third year. An assessment of the results achieved so far is based on a survey conducted in October 1992 among large and small businesses throughout the country, and among all trade associations. Over 100,000 questionnaires have been distributed.

Preliminary results show that today most large companies are engaged in efforts to improve productivity and quality and that these efforts are part of these companies business strategy. However, for half of these companies the organization chart does not yet confirm this fact. The vast majority of Brazilian companies does not know the Program. The diffusion of the quality movement in the economy though slow has doubled its pace in the last year. Management often blames the state of the domestic economy for in-house difficulties in implementing productivity and quality projects. A significant barrier to progress is labor's understanding and participation in each company's project and in the National Program.

In view of these results major changes are being introduced in the Program's strategy for 1993. Neighboring Latin American countries are studying the polices, management and accomplishments of the Brazilian Program.

Productivity & Quality Management Frontiers-IV, edited by Sumanth, Edosomwan, Poupart, and Sink. ©1993 Institute of Industrial Engineers.

How to Organize Quality Management in the Retail Enterprise

Z.Z. Chen
East China University of Chemical Technology
Shanghai, PEOPLE'S REPUBLIC OF CHINA

The role of the retail enterprise is to transfer the goods from producers to customers. For this purpose, the retail enterprise is mainly engaged in such business activities as procurement, selling, distribution and storing. Thus, while the quality management is considered focusing on the product quality in an industrial enterprise, it should be thought emphasizing the service quality in a retail enterprise. The service quality can be measured by the degree to which the customers' requirements are satisfied. For the retail enterprise to provide high quality of service, three aspects, i.e. goods inherent quality, business operation quality and business environmental quality should all be taken into account in organizing quality management. According to these three aspects, this paper is to identify the successes of quality management in Shanghai's largest retail enterprise -- Shanghai First Department Store (SFDS).

SFDS has the business area of 21,4000 square meters and over 3,000 employees. It deals with the selling of 54 major categories of goods, in which more than thirty thousand kinds of products are included. It has won the high reputation for its service quality and on the average, receives 250,000 customers every day. SFDS ranks first in terms of sales and profits in the retail area of China. The quality management in SFDS can be generalized into three main measures, i.e.

(1) implementing the standardization of quality management;
(2) intensifying the control of the operations on-the-spot; and
(3) improving the business environment.

From the theoretical study and the case study on SFDS, it has been concluded concerning the organizing of quality management in the retail enterprise that firstly, the principle of being systematic, preventative, effective and operational should be followed; secondly, out of the requirements set by National Organization for Standard and International Organization for Standard (ISO) 20 key elements, e.g. quality policy, market research, goods inspection and so on, are applicable and should be included; thirdly, the responsibility and tasks of quality management should be segmented and distributed to the different levels of the organization from top to bottom.

Part VI
FORMAL PRODUCTIVITY AND QUALITY EDUCATION

1. Formal Education Efforts in Universities, Colleges, and Schools

2. Formal Educational Efforts in Companies, Enterprises, and Productivity Centers

3. Integrative Productivity and Quality Management Education in Business and Engineering Schools

4. Reconfiguration of Industrial Engineering and Management Philosophies, Tools, and Techniques-Policy Debate Issues

Productivity & Quality Management Frontiers-IV, edited by Sumanth, Edosomwan, Poupart, and Sink. ©1993 Institute of Industrial Engineers.

A New Focus for Productivity and Quality Education

D.M. Rushforth
Educational Publications, Inc.
Fairfax, Virginia USA

ABSTRACT

The effort to improve the education of the nation's work force provides an opportunity to try new ideas with respect to productivity and quality in our school systems. The concepts of productivity and quality can and should be continuously taught, at an appropriate level, from Kindergarten through 12th grade and beyond.

This paper reviews the current National Education Goals, the AMERICA 2000 strategy to achieve the goals, and the U.S. Department of Labor Secretary's Commission On Achieving Necessary Skills (SCANS) model of competencies, skills and personal qualities that are needed for effective job performance. The author recommends courses of action, and demonstrates how the SCANS model can be used as a basis to introduce the concepts of productivity and quality; provide the requisite foundation of skills and personal qualities; and teach the needed competencies.

KEY WORDS

Competencies, competitiveness, education, effectiveness, foundation, productivity, quality, school, skill

INTRODUCTION

To improve American competitiveness in the world economy, a new focus on education for quality and productivity must begin in the elementary, middle and secondary schools. The AMERICA 2000 national education strategy provides an opportunity to achieve this objective. We cannot wait for the work force to come into industry to teach the foundations for productivity and quality in the work place. The future work force needs to learn the concepts and value of quality and productivity.

The first part of this paper is a review of the current National Education Goals, the AMERICA 2000 strategy to achieve the goals, and the U.S. Department of Labor Secretary's Commission On Achieving Necessary Skills (SCANS) model of competencies, skills and personal qualities that are needed for effective job performance. The second part is the author's recommended courses of action, consonant with the goals, for government, industry, schools, and families. Finally, a demonstration project is suggested which uses the SCANS model as a basis to introduce the concepts of productivity and quality, provide the requisite foundation of skills, personal qualities, and teach the needed competencies.

AMERICA 2000: EDUCATION GOALS

The National Education Goals set the target for an effort to produce a more educated work force. The goals are accompanied by a strategy and a model to improve the competencies of the work force. By the year 2000 it is anticipated that:[1]

1. All children in America will start school ready to learn.
2. The high school graduation rate will increase to at least 90 percent.
3. American students will leave grades four, eight, and twelve having demonstrated competency in challenging subject matter including English, mathematics, science, history and geography; and every school in America will ensure that all students learn to use their minds well, so they may be prepared for responsible citizenship, further learning, and productive employment in our modern economy.
4. U.S. students will be first in the world in science and mathematics achievement.
5. Every adult American will be literate and will possess the knowledge and skills necessary to compete in a global economy and exercise the rights and responsibilities of citizenship.
6. Every school in America will be free of drugs and violence and will offer a disciplined environment conducive to learning.

---

[1] U.S. Department of Education (1991) AMERICA 2000: An Education Strategy, Washington, D.C.

AMERICA 2000 EDUCATION STRATEGY

This consists of four concurrently-running parts:[2]

1. **For today's students,** we must radically improve today's schools by making all 110,000 of them better and more accountable for results.
2. **For tomorrow's students,** we must invent new schools to meet the demands of a new century with a New Generation of American Schools, bringing at least 535 of them into existence by 1996 and thousands by decade's end.
3. **For those of us already out of school and in the work force,** we must keep learning if we are to live and work successfully in today's world. A "Nation at Risk" must become a "Nation of Students."
4. **For schools to succeed,** we must look beyond our classrooms to our communities and families. Schools will never be much better than the commitment of their communities. Each of our communities must become a place where learning can happen.

The U.S. Department of Labor Secretary's Commission On Achieving Necessary Skills (SCANS) has completed an extensive study of <u>What Work Requires of Schools</u>. The commission proposed a model of five competencies and a three-part foundation of skills and personal qualities that are needed for "solid" job performance. While the SCANS model does an excellent job identifying the foundation and competencies that will help enhance productivity and quality, it does not directly address the basic concepts of productivity and quality. The skills are identified outside of the context in which they are to be used.

This provides an opportunity to introduce concepts of productivity and quality to the future work force. Given the framework of the goals and strategy, the new future for education with respect to productivity and quality requires the application of the SCANS model (in the proper context), by the employer, educator, student, and family.

The SCANS model appears in Figure 1.[3]

COURSES OF ACTION

There is a great opportunity to instill the concepts of productivity and quality in the current and future work force. The schools do not have the resources or expertise to introduce the concepts into the curriculum. A partnership is required of government, industry, schools, and families. Each partner must work as a member of a team to instill the concepts of productivity and quality at an appropriate level from Kindergarten through 12th grade.

---

[2]U.S. Department of Education (1992) <u>AMERICA 2000 Communities: Getting Started</u>, Washington, D.C.

[3]The Secretary's Commission on Achieving Necessary Skills (1991) <u>What Work Requires of Schools - A SCANS Report for AMERICA 2000</u>, Washington, D.C., U.S. Department of Labor

SCANS MODEL: THE FOUNDATION
Competence requires a three-part foundation of basic skills, thinking skills, and personal qualities:

1. Basic Skills - reading, writing, arithmetic and mathematics, speaking, and listening.
a. Reading - locates, understands, and interprets written information in prose and in documents such as manuals, graphs, and schedules.
b. Writing - communicates thoughts, ideas, information, and messages in writing; and creates documents such as letters, directions, manuals, reports, graphs and flow charts.
c. Arithmetic/Mathematics - performs basic computations and approaches practical problems by choosing appropriately from a variety of mathematical techniques.
d. Listening - receives, attends to, interprets, and responds to verbal messages and other cues.
e. Speaking - organizes ideas and communicates orally.

2. Thinking Skills - thinking creatively, making decisions, solving problems, seeing things in the mind's eye, knowing how to learn, and reasoning.
a. Creative Thinking - generates new ideas.
b. Decision Making - specifies goals and constraints, generates alternatives, considers risks, and evaluates and chooses best alternative.
c. Problem Solving - recognizes problems and devises and implements plan of action.
d. Seeing Things in the Mind's Eye - organizes, and processes symbols, pictures, graphs, objects and other information.
e. Knowing How to Learn - uses efficient learning techniques to acquire and apply new knowledge and skills.
f. Reasoning - discovers a rule or principle underlying the relationship between two or more objects and applies it to solving a problem.

3. Personal Qualities - individual responsibility, self-esteem, sociability, self-management, and integrity.
a. Responsibility - exerts a high level of effort and perseveres towards goal attainment.
b. Self-Esteem - believes in own self-worth and maintains a positive view of self.
c. Sociability - demonstrates understanding, friendliness, adaptability, empathy, and politeness in group settings.
d. Self-Management - assesses self accurately, sets personal goals, monitors progress, and exhibits self-control.
e. Integrity/Honesty - chooses ethical courses of action.

SCANS MODEL: THE COMPETENCIES
The five competencies require effective workers to productively use resources, interpersonal skills, information, systems, and technology:

1. Resources - allocating time, money, materials, space, and staff.
a. Time - Selects goal-relevant activities, ranks them, allocates time, and prepares and follows schedules.
b. Money - Uses or prepares budgets, makes forecasts, keeps records, and makes adjustments to meet objectives.
c. Material and Facilities - Acquires, stores, allocates, and uses materials or space efficiently.
d. Human Resources - Assesses skills and distributes work accordingly, evaluates performance and provides feedback.

2. Interpersonal Skills - working on teams, teaching others, serving customers, leading, negotiating, and working well with people from culturally diverse backgrounds.
a. Participates as Member of a Team - contributes to group effort.
b. Teaches Others New Skills
c. Serves Clients/Customers - works to satisfy customers' expectations.
d. Exercises Leadership - communicates ideas to justify position, persuades and convinces others, responsibly challenges existing procedures and policies.
e. Negotiates - works toward agreements involving exchange of resources, resolves divergent interests.
f. Works with Diversity - works well with men and women from diverse backgrounds.

3. Information - acquiring and evaluating data, organizing and maintaining files, interpreting and communicating, and using computers to process information.
a. Acquires and Evaluates Information
b. Organizes and Maintains Information
c. Interprets and Communicates Information
d. Uses Computers to Process Information

4. Systems - understanding social, organizational, and technological systems, monitoring and correcting performance, and designing or improving systems.
a. Understands Systems - knows how social, organizational, and technological systems work and operates effectively with them.
b. Monitors and Corrects Performance - distinguishes trends, predicts impacts on system operations, diagnoses deviations in systems' performance and corrects malfunctions.
c. Improves or Designs Systems - suggests modifications to existing systems and develops new or alternative systems to improve performance.

5. Technology - selecting equipment and tools, applying technology to specific tasks, and maintaining and troubleshooting technologies.
a. Selects Technology - Chooses procedures, tools or equipment including computers and related technologies.
b. Applies Technology to Task - Understands overall intent and proper procedures for setup and operation of equipment.
c. Maintains and Troubleshoots Equipment - Prevents, identifies, or solves problems with equipment, including computers and other technologies.

Figure 1. The SCANS Foundation and Competencies.

Government

The government must continue to communicate the vision to the people of the nation and provide resources. Informational materials must be developed and distributed to industry, schools, and families. The program has been announced, but the message has not been widely received. Many people (including teachers who are supposed to implement the program) do not know about any of the following: the National Education Goals; the AMERICA 2000 strategy to achieve the goals; the SCANS model to be used to improve the competencies of the work force. The Department of Education has a toll free number to call for information about AMERICA 2000: 1-800-872-5327.

The effort to improve the competency of the work force is not a free program. Schools are going to need more resources from the federal government than are currently being provided. A clearing house for information is a low cost way to help, similar to that of the drug demand reduction education program. Since all curricula are to be developed locally, it would be helpful to have access to successful materials that may have already been developed.

Telecommunications offers an efficient means of sharing information. The National Geographic Kids Network is a system that is funded by the National Science Foundation. Twenty-six percent of the nation's elementary schools and schools from ten nations are linked in the system. Educom, a nonprofit consortium of 600 universities and colleges, has a Kindergarten through 12th grade networking project. There are other projects being created for schools that may use telecommunications systems. Rather than having separate systems and dysfunctional efforts, the government should establish a national educational telecommunications system that would link all levels of education.

Industry

Industry resources are needed, but not necessarily in the form of a direct cash outlay. Expertise may be the most important contribution. The Industrial Engineer is a good candidate to be the corporate representative. The engineer can be a subject matter expert and advisor to the schools regarding the integration of concepts of productivity and quality into the curriculum. Supporting materials for the classroom can be developed by an industry-school partnership. Unless employers make a commitment to become actively involved in the education system, they are doomed to continue to receive the products of the system they have chosen to ignore.

Schools

The new approach to education is a top-down effort. Therefore, resistance can be expected from the staff and faculty. Also, teachers may not have the knowledge, skills, or time to develop curricula and supporting materials to make this new approach to education a reality. Schools will need to provide education, training and support for their teachers.

Families

Families must take a proactive approach to their children's education. The school cannot fulfill the parents' obligations to their children. Regardless of the parent's educational level, they can take an active role in improving the educational system by instilling values that support good citizenship, supporting budgets that provide needed resources, and working with Parent-Teacher-Student Associations.

Both parents and students must learn about the National Education Goals, the America 2000 strategy to achieve the goals, and the SCANS model foundation and competencies. Unless they know what is expected, their well-meaning efforts may be misdirected or even harmful.

The Partnership

Government, industry, schools and families need a framework to work together effectively. The SCANS model provides such a framework and is the basis for standards and evaluation. The application of the model requires thinking in a systems perspective and integrating the model across the Kindergarten through 12th grade. Applying the model only at an individual classroom level would be suboptimal.

A DEMONSTRATION PROJECT

A project as simple as a picnic can be used to demonstrate how the SCANS model can be used as a basis to introduce the concepts of productivity and quality, provide the foundation of skills and personal qualities, and teach the competencies in a Kindergarten through 12th grade system. Because of the scope of the project, only selected sections are presented in this paper.

The purpose is to identify a project that can be concurrently done by all grades in a school, within a school year or less. A picnic was chosen because it is something that children of all ages can understand. The project can be simple or detailed, according to the educational goals of the school. The most ambitious project would start in the fall and culminate just before the end of the school year. With International Summer Olympics as the theme, the project can include applications of English, foreign languages, history, mathematics, sciences, art, business, health, physical education, and many others.

While the materials presented are not developed for children in the early years of elementary school, they can be adapted for that age group. The objectives of the project are:

Main
1. To introduce the concepts of productivity and quality.
2. To demonstrate the relationship of the SCANS competencies to productivity and quality.

Ancillary
3. To relate the lessons learned in an academic environment to a potential "real world" application in terms of a project.
4. To encourage parents to become involved in their children's education, within their own ability.
5. To bring the faculty, parents and students together in a social environment.

A Model Instructor's Guide for teaching is presented. The guide facilitates academic freedom and creativity and keeps the instructor focused on the curriculum. Once developed, the guide provides the mechanism to continuously improve the quality of the curriculum and record the best practice to-date. It is always retained by the school so the teachers' experiences are not lost upon transfer or retirement. The Model Instructor's Guide is adapted from one developed by Dr. Marvin E. Mundel.[4] For purposes of this paper only part of the guide is presented. The guide has six major sections:

I. Introduction, which includes the purpose of the project or course; its description and outline.
II. List of classroom equipment
III. Instructor notes regarding equipment, materials, and homework.
IV. List of materials needed by each student
V. Summary course outline, by sessions
VI. Detailed daily teaching plans, including instructor notes

Also for purposes of this paper, the material has been condensed into two sessions, although these are too large for actual use.

PROJECT: PLANNING A PICNIC WITH THE INTERNATIONAL SUMMER
OLYMPICS AS A THEME

SESSION 1 INTRODUCTION TO PRODUCTIVITY
EQUIPMENT:
      1. Chalk board
      2. overhead projector
TOPICS:
      1. Introduce the picnic concept
      2. Describe the meaning of productivity
      3. Describe the importance of productivity
      4. The economics of productivity

1. INTRODUCE THE PICNIC CONCEPT

a. The theme is International Summer Olympics.
b. One country from each of the six most populated continents is selected to be represented at the International Summer Olympics Picnic.
c. The school must plan all aspects of the picnic to support the theme.

---

[4]Mundel, M.E. (1985) Instructor's Guide: Motion And Time Study, Sixth Edition, Englewood Cliffs, NJ, Prentice-Hall Inc.

2. DESCRIBE THE MEANING OF PRODUCTIVITY, EFFECTIVENESS, AND QUALITY

a. The educational materials and concepts presented must be at an appropriate age level. For older children, the concepts of productivity, effectiveness and quality can be more formally presented than with very young children.

b. Describe the three essential elements of productivity:
    (1) Productivity: Output divided by input, or goods and services produced divided by resources used to produce the output
    (2) Effectiveness: Do the goods and services help achieve the objective?
    (3) Quality: Degree or extent of fitness for use.

Describe the meaning of quality from two perspectives:
    (a) From the school's perspective, quality means the degree to which the SCANS foundation and competencies have been developed and applied to make the picnic project a success.
    (b) From an individual's perspective, quality means conformance to standards (specifications and procedures) that will produce a product or service that is acceptable to the customer.

c. Give examples of each:
    (1) Productivity: How many students does it take to prepare a hot dog sandwich?
    (2) Effectiveness: Does a given activity support the theme?
    (3) Quality:
        (a) Will the food appeal to the customers?
        (b) Is the food nutritious? (Relate to the food pyramid.)

3. DESCRIBE THE IMPORTANCE OF PRODUCTIVITY, EFFECTIVENESS, AND QUALITY

Relate the importance of productivity to the picnic project.
    (1) Productivity: A large project with limited resources and time
    (2) Effectiveness: All aspects of the picnic must support the theme
    (3) Quality:
        (a) Ask students to describe the importance of quality.
        (b) Describe examples found in the classroom (condition of equipment, books, etc.).
        (c) Ask students to describe the importance of quality as it relates to the picnic project. Food should appeal to the customers and games should not break.

4. THE ECONOMICS OF PRODUCTIVITY, EFFECTIVENESS, AND QUALITY

Describe the economics of productivity to the picnic project.
    (1) Productivity: Use example of 2b(1) and add costs.
    (2) Effectiveness: Time, effort, and the resulting cost that do not contribute to the objective (theme) are wasted.
    (3) Quality:
        (a) How is quality measured? The group should determine the criteria for the menu. This will establish the standards for production.

An example:

Criteria #	Too Broad	Better
1	Must be healthy.	Meet guideline of new food pyramid.

(b) What is the cost of poor quality? If the food does not appeal to the customers, there will be complaints and wasted food. They may not support a similar project in the future.

Food may spoil and have to be discarded. To determine the cost for food, a lesson can be developed with the following considerations:

a. Metric system and converting recipes.
b. Number of people to be served and total supplies needed.
c. Qualitative and quantitative considerations in food shopping.
d. Determining the best buy:
    (1) cost per unit of measure
    (2) coupons and net cost
    (3) quality/cost tradeoff

SESSION 2 PRODUCTIVITY, EFFECTIVENESS AND QUALITY IN PLANNING.
EQUIPMENT: 1. Chalk board
               2. Overhead projector
               3. Chart(s) of the SCANS model foundation and skills
TOPICS: 1. The concepts of productivity and quality
               2. The role of SCANS model foundation and skills

1. THE CONCEPTS OF PRODUCTIVITY, EFFECTIVENESS AND QUALITY

Review the concepts of productivity, effectiveness and quality.
See SESSION 1.

2. THE ROLE OF SCANS MODEL FOUNDATION AND COMPETENCIES

a. Review the SCANS model foundation and competencies, which are the basis of what the students need to know, what is expected of them, and how they will be evaluated.
(1) Discuss the three-part foundation and its importance in life and work: *basic skills, thinking skills, and personal qualities*.
(2) Discuss the five competencies required of workers to survive and be competitive in the work place: *resources, interpersonal skills, information, systems, and technology*.
(3) How does the foundation relate to the competencies?

b. Discuss the role of the SCANS foundation and competencies in the planning for productivity and quality. Use selected examples to illustrate.
(1) How does the foundation relate to planning for productivity?
Example: *Reading* - locates, understands, and interprets written information in prose and in documents such as manuals, graphs, and schedules.
(2) How does the foundation relate to planning for quality?

Examples: *Arithmetic/Mathematics* - performs basic computations and approaches practical problems by choosing appropriately from a variety of mathematical techniques.
Creative Thinking - generates new ideas.
(3) How do the competencies relate to planning for productivity?
Examples: *Time* - Selects goal-relevant activities, ranks them, allocates time, and prepares and follows schedules.
Participates as Member of a Team - contributes to group effort.
(4) How do the competencies relate to planning for quality?
Examples: *Monitors and Corrects Performance* - distinguishes trends, predicts impacts on system operations, diagnoses deviations in systems' performance and corrects malfunctions.
Improves or Designs Systems - suggests modifications to existing systems and develops new or alternative systems to improve performance.

CONCLUSION

The portions of the project just presented is a suggested application of an approach to teaching productivity and quality in a way that young students will be able to comprehend. Use the model as a shell to develop other approaches and applications. If you are able to try a demonstration project with a school, be sure to share both your successes and your failures. We should learn from each other and build upon a base of knowledge.

We cannot wait for the work force to come into industry before we teach the foundations for productivity and quality. Everyone must become part of the partnership to produce a quality work force. Use the SCANS model as a vehicle to instill the concepts of productivity and quality in the students.

REFERENCES

Juran, J.M. (1984) Upper Management and Quality, Fourth Edition, Fourth Printing, Wilton, CT, Juran Institute, Inc.

Mundel, M.E. (1985) Instructor's Guide: Motion and Time Study, Sixth Edition, Englewood Cliffs, NJ, Prentice-Hall Inc.

The Secretary's Commission on Achieving Necessary Skills (1991) What Work Requires of Schools - A SCANS Report for AMERICA 2000, Washington, D.C., U.S. Department of Labor

U.S. Department of Education (1992) AMERICA 2000 Communities: Getting Started, Washington, D.C.

BIOGRAPHICAL NOTE

Durward M. Rushforth is the Vice President of Educational Publications, Inc., and is responsible for government and military educational programs. He is the author of numerous articles, training guides, and informational publications. He has also worked with Dr. Mundel on a major white collar productivity measurement project.

Productivity & Quality Management Frontiers-IV, edited by Sumanth, Edosomwan, Poupart, and Sink. ©1993
Institute of Industrial Engineers.

An Examination of Course Content and Teaching Pedagogy of Quality Assurance Education in the Business School Curriculum

A.L. Guiffrida
Canisius College
Buffalo, New York USA

ABSTRACT

At a time when quality is emerging as the backbone of competitive business strategy, the academic literature and the practitioner community indicate that business school curricula are failing to provide their graduates with sufficient exposure to quality. This article reports the results of a study designed to audit industry's needs regarding the degree of training in quality assurance that is needed in business school graduates. We examine topical coverage and teaching pedagogy for a course in quality assurance for business students.

The results of the study indicate that practitioners feel that a quality assurance education gap exists between what is currently being taught in business school curricula and what is practiced in industry. Constructive ideas in the form of suggested course topics and teaching pedagogy are presented for improving the quality assurance education process in academia and closing the quality assurance education gap.

Key Words: Quality Assurance(QA) Education, QA Curriculum
           Design

INTRODUCTION

The successful implementation and administration of quality assurance programs in industry requires one basic raw material: a work force trained in the fundamentals of quality assurance. Leading authorities on quality such as Drs. W. Edwards Deming, Joseph M. Juran, and Kaoru Ishikawa all stress education as a key force in improving quality.

Business school curricula must keep pace with changes in industry's needs and provide entrants into the work force who are knowledgeable of quality assurance. However, most business students graduating from colleges and universities have had little, if any, exposure to quality assurance. Industry is the final market for business school graduates. Academia must communicate with the practitioner community and utilize the information it gains concerning industry's needs in quality education to provide curricula which responds to these needs.

This article reports the results of a study designed to i) gauge industry's needs regarding the degree of training in quality assurance that is needed in business school graduates, ii) examine topical coverage for a course in quality assurance for business students, and iii) reexamine traditional teaching pedagogy as it applies to quality assurance education.

LITERATURE REVIEW

Several studies have addressed the coverage of quality assurance and quality control topics in the business school curriculum. LaForge (1981) examined the coverage of quality control topics in 20 production and operations management textbooks. Each textbook was examined and an assessment was made as to the exposure in quality that the student would receive while completing the course. The study concluded that business students enrolled in courses using these textbooks would not know what workers in the quality control function actually do and would be unaware of how quality affects costs and contributes to the organizational goals of the firm.

Zimmerman (1984) investigated the coverage of quality and quality management topics in 42 textbooks which were considered appropriate for use in principles of management and business policy courses. This study concluded that the typical business student is unlikely to gain an appreciation of the importance of quality control. It further concluded that after completing courses in both principles of management and business policy, the student would most likely be unaware of how quality fits into the organization and fail to understand how it affects other functional areas in the firm.

Welki (1988) examined the extent to which quality control concepts are covered in 86 business and economic statistics textbooks that were published between 1945 and 1980. The study revealed that the coverage of quality control and its relationship to the production setting has been diluted in recent years by either excluding it altogether or incorporating it within other topical areas. Welki argues that de-emphasis of this material reduces the relative importance of quality in the minds of todays students.

Johnson and Winchell (1988) note that a large percentage of undergraduate and graduate students in business schools receive little or no exposure to quality concepts, and do not become knowledgeable of quality until they enter industry.

Doane (1992) analyzed the coverage of quality control topics in business statistics textbooks. Statistics on the number of pages devoted to quality control indicates that quality control topics are covered lightly in most business statistics textbooks. The study does identify that coverage of quality control topics in textbooks published since 1989 is on the rise.

Hart and Morrison (1992) address why quality principles are not taught with more emphasis in business schools. They note that business schools tend to be divided by function or discipline, while teaching quality management requires an interdisciplinary approach. Also, quality management is often perceived as a weak area for conducting academic research. Professors facing publish-or-perish tenure requirements tend not to engage in quality management as a field of specialization since its rewards in terms of scholarly publication are limited. This view is also shared by Salvia (1987).

The research findings discussed in the aforementioned studies suggests that most business schools are not providing students with an appropriate background in quality assurance. This educational gap is occurring at a time when quality is emerging as the backbone of competitive business strategy. The academic community must take the lead in developing and introducing quality assurance courses into business school curricula. However, the decision of what topics to teach should not be made in a vacuum. It is important that the instruction students receive addresses the skills that practitioners deem important. Thus, practitioners' input should be sought in the development of quality assurance curricula. The intent of the current study is to investigate the perceptions of quality assurance practitioners concerning curriculum development and teaching pedagogy for the quality assurance education process in business schools.

CURRENT STUDY

The study reported in this article consisted of two phases. Each phase of study utilized a mail questionnaire. In the first phase, a random sample of 250 quality assurance practitioners was selected from a sample frame of 7,500 members of the American Society for Quality Control(ASQC). The sample frame was composed of members who were listed under the job function of quality assurance for firms in the primary SIC Codes of 20-39, 45, 60, 63, 70, and 80. A total of 179 questionnaires were received for a 72% response rate.

A two page questionnaire was administered to gain practitioners' input concerning the need for, positioning of, and importance of a quality assurance course for business students. The respondents also ranked, in order of importance, 20 topics that might be covered in a quality assurance course. The list of topics was compiled from suggestions by practitioners in the pretest of the questionnaire and from the table of contents of the book Quality Planning and Analysis by J. M. Juran and F. M. Gryna. In the second phase of the study a sample of 150 practitioners was randomly selected from the 179 respondents who completed phase I of the study. A total of 75 completed questionnaires was received, representing a 50% response rate to the second phase of the study.

The second questionnaire investigated practitioner involvement in the quality assurance education process. An open-ended question also asked for input on how to bridge the perceived gap in quality assurance education which was identified in phase I.

The scope of this study was exploratory in nature. The effort was geared to obtain summary information for use by academicians in providing direction in curricula design and teaching pedagogy. The sample size used in both phases of the study was governed by the research budget available for the project.

RESULTS

Need And Positioning Of Course.

Table 1 summarizes practitioners' attitudes toward quality assurance education. Question one explores the issue of quality assurance education as a separate course of study. The responses suggest that the topic of quality assurance is important enough to be taught as a separate course with business school curricula.

Question two examines the issue of whether students studying quality assurance in an academic setting could be taught skills that are relevant in industry. The median response of 1 strongly suggests an agreement among practitioners that students can emerge with skills that are useful in industry.

Questions three and seven address the level of instruction (undergraduate versus graduate) for a quality assurance course. The frequency of responses for these questions indicates that quality assurance could be offered at both the graduate and undergraduate levels.

Business schools have been criticized for their performance in preparing students to meet the challenges and demands of a career in industry. The median response of 2 to question four suggests that practitioners agree that such a gap exists for the specific topic of quality assurance.

Questions five and eight examine the positioning of a quality assurance course in a business school curriculum. Medians of 1 and 2 for questions five and eight, respectively, indicate a positive response for requiring business students who major in production/operations management or general business to take a course in quality assurance. The results indicate a slightly stronger preference for requiring quality assurance for students who concentrate in production/operations management.

Question six examines the influence that a formal course in quality assurance would have on preparing a student for entry into the work force. The median response of 1 indicates that a student who has completed a course in quality assurance is better prepared to enter the work force than a student who has not.

Table 1
Practitioners' Attitudes Toward Quality Assurance Education

Note: All responses are based on a five-point scale
(1 strongly agree to 5 strongly disagree)

Question	Responses: Median	First Quartile	Third Quartile
1. The topic of quality assurance is important enough to warrant a separate course.	1	1	1
2. It is possible to teach industry relevant skills in an academic course.	1	1	2
3. Quality assurance should be taught only at the graduate level.	5	4	5
4. A gap exists between what is taught in academia and what is practiced in industry.	2	1	3
5. Course should be required of all business students majoring in production/operations management.	1	1	1
6. A student completing a course in quality assurance is better prepared to enter industry.	1	1	2
7. Quality assurance can be taught at the undergraduate level.	1	1	1
8. Course in quality assurance should be required for all business students.	2	1	3

Course Topics.
    Table 2 ranks topics according to their relative
importance for inclusion in a quality assurance course.
The total quality concept, quality planning, and Deming's 14
points for management are viewed as the most important topics.
Process capability analysis and statistical control charts are
the next most important. Coordination of the quality
function, quality cost categories, Pareto analysis, and the
product/service design process rank in the upper half of the
list.   Topics such as product liability, acceptance sampling,
and quality circles received low rankings. The topics of job
profiles in quality assurance, supplier certification, and
geometric dimensioning and tolerancing are viewed as least
important.

Table 2
Importance of Various Topics for a Quality Assurance Course

Topic	Ranking	Mean
Total quality control concept	1	2.79
Quality planning	2	5.13
Deming's 14 points	3	5.96
Process capability analysis	4	7.16
Statistical control charts	5	8.19
Coordination of quality function	6	8.27
Quality cost categories	7	8.92
Pareto analysis	8	9.62
Product/service design process	9	9.89
Quality information systems	10	10.00
Cause-and-effect diagrams	11	10.32
Quality audits	12	11.74
Reliability analysis	13	12.20
Taguchi Methods	14	12.26
Product liability	15	12.89
Acceptance sampling	16	13.44
Quality circles	17	14.38
Job profiles in quality assurance	18	15.29
Supplier certification	19	15.58
Geometric dim. and toleranceing	20	15.71

Practitioners' Involvement.
    Responses to twelve that examined the involvement of
practitioners in quality assurance education are summarized in
Table 3.

Question 1: Review and critique of topics. The positive
response to this question suggests that practitioners are
willing to assist the instructors of quality assurance courses
in the selection and organization of the topics to be included
in the course.

Questions 2 and 7: Participate on advisory board and in curriculum design. A high percentage of the respondents (82%) reported a willingness to serve on a quality assurance advisory board. A slightly lower percentage (78%) indicated that they would be willing to assist in the design of quality assurance curriculum. Time commitments and the lack of reimbursement for travel expenses by their employers were cited as the major reasons for not participating by those respondents answering no or undecided to either question.

Questions 3, 4, and 11: Internships for students and instructors. Slightly over 50% of the respondents stated that their firms would provide uncompensated internships to students. Respondents were less willing (28%) to offer students compensated internships. A high percentage of respondents (48%) reported that their firms would be willing to provide an internship for the instructor of the quality assurance course. Concerns about confidentiality, cost, and the lack of a formal internship program were cited as the major obstacles in offering internships to students and instructors of quality assurance courses.

Question 5: Development of case studies. The response to question five indicated that 68% of the respondents felt that their firms would be willing to assist instructors of quality assurance courses in the development of case studies. Concerns for confidentiality, time limitations, and lack of a company policy regarding case study development were identified as the major barriers to this form of participation.

Question 6: Serve as an outside reader for student projects. The majority of the practitioners surveyed (76%) expressed a willingness to serve as outside readers for a student quality assurance project. Time restrictions were cited as the major reason for not participating.

Question 8: Sponsor a student to a membership in ASQC. A high percentage of respondents (46%) indicated that their firms would be willing to sponsor the membership of one student in the quality assurance course in ASQC. Cost and the lack of a company policy were reported as the major reasons for not sponsoring a student. Several respondents indicated that they would personally be willing to sponsor the membership of one student in the event that their firms were unable to do so.

Questions 9 and 10: Provide guest lecturers and plant tours. The responses to questions 9 and 10 indicate that most firms would be willing to provide guest lecturers on quality assurance and allow students to tour their facilities and meet with members of the quality assurance staff. Major limitations to these actions included time considerations for guest lecturing, confidentiality concerns, and the lack of a company policy for student tours.

Question 12: Cooperate with quality assurance instructors on research projects. Response to this question suggests that most firms surveyed (56%) would be willing to participate in an academic research project with the instructor of a quality assurance course. Confidentiality and the content of the project were cited as the major concerns for not supporting this form of interaction.

Table 3
Practitioners' Involvement in Quality Assurance Education

Question	Responses	Yes	No	Undecided
1. Review and critique course outline of QA topics.	75	99%	1%	0%
2. Participate on a quality assurance advisory board.	75	82%	7%	11%
3. Provide uncompensated student internships/co-ops.	73	54%	8%	38%
4. Provide uncompensated faculty internships.	73	48%	10%	42%
5. Work with QA academicians to develop of QA case studies.	74	68%	12%	20%
6. Serve as an outside reader for QA student projects.	75	76%	12%	12%
7. Assist in curriculum design	75	78%	7%	15%
8. Sponsor student ASQC membership.	71	46%	27%	27%
9. Provide guest lecturers.	71	75%	4%	21%
10. Provide facility tours.	74	80%	8%	12%
11. Sponsor compensated student internships/co-ops.	72	28%	21%	51%
12. Cooperate with faculty on an academic research project.	73	56%	11%	33%

Bridging The Quality Assurance Education Gap.
    A total of 63 respondents in phase II of the study provided input on how to bridge the quality assurance education gap. Several of the respondents offered more than one idea. Three major themes emerged in the analysis of their responses. These themes address the content of the quality

assurance course, the teaching methodology used, and the interaction between the instructor of the course and industry.

Comments directed at the content of the quality assurance course were made 30 times. They identified the need for placing more emphasis on topics such as the total quality control concept, quality management, and the quality improvement process. Quality planning and the philosophies of Deming and Crosby were also stressed. Several of the respondents identified the need for a more applied and less theoretical coverage of statistics.

Suggestions concerning teaching methodologies were made 21 times. These suggestions called for the integration of case studies, plant tours, and guest lecturers from industry into the course. Internships and co-ops for students were also stressed. It was felt that these methodologies would be effective in introducing students to the "real-world" aspects of quality assurance.

The third theme identified the need for the instructor of the course to become more actively involved in industry. A total of 18 responses mentioned the need for the instructor to more actively communicate and interact with industry professionals. It was felt that these actions would give the instructor a better understanding of the educational needs of industry.

Five of the 63 respondents indicated that a quality assurance education gap between industry and academia should exist. This position was supported by two contentions. First, given the diversity of industry, it is impossible to design a quality assurance course which will meet the requirements of a specific industry. Second, within a specific industry the needs of individual firms are different. Academia can better serve industry by providing students with a well rounded background in quality. The emphasis of academia should be on theory which then can be brought to the organization and used to improve existing quality programs.

SUMMARY

It is clear, and as well as encouraging that the practitioner community is willing to get actively involved in the quality assurance education process. The practitioner community represents a valuable resource whom the academician should consult.

Based upon the information collected in this study, the following ideas may prove useful in the design and positioning of quality assurance courses in the business school. A major problem in teaching quality assurance is determining what topics to teach. Practitioners can assist academicians select topics for quality assurance courses. The list of topics identified in Table 2, and their relative rankings, will provide insights for academicians facing decisions regarding what topics to include in their courses.

Classroom lecture and discussion are the mainstay of practically all college courses. However, there are a variety of options that can be used to augment this form of instruction. This study has identified a willingness among practitioners' to work with faculty members in developing case studies, serving as guest lecturers, and providing plant tours. Additional practitioner interaction may come from internships with students and faculty, and service on quality assurance advisory boards. Each of these activities may further serve to help the instructor provide a learning and career-broadening experience for students.

The findings of this study are a starting point for bridging the quality assurance education gap. Success in bridging this gap will depend upon the implementation of ideas generated in this study, and other constructive ideas that may evolve based upon this initial study. By maintaining open lines of communication with industry, academicians involved in quality assurance education can provide their students with practical problems and issues. Students, faculty, and practitioners will all benefit.

BIBLIOGRAPHIC REFERENCES

Doane, D. P. (1992). "Quality Topics in the Business School Curriculum", ASQC Quality Congress Transactions-Nashville.

Hart, C. W. L. and Morrison, P. E. (1992). "Students Aren't Learning Quality Principles in Business Schools", Quality Progress, Vol. 25, No. 1, pp. 25-27.

Johnson, R. H. and Winchell, W. O. (1988). "Educating for Quality: A Different Approach", Quality Progress, Vol. 21, No. 10, pp. 48-50.

LaForge, R. L. (1981). "Production Textbooks: Are They Doing the Job for QC?", Quality Progress, Vol. 14, No. 6, pp. 12-15.

Salvia, A. A. (1987). "QC Education: Some Questions", Quality Progress, Vol. 20, No. 8, pp. 15-17.

Welki, A. M. (1988). "Quality Control and the College Business Statistics Course: Some Empirical Evidence", Journal of Education for Business, Vol. 63, No. 5, pp. 200-204.

Zimmerman, D. K. (1984). "Management Courses: Are They Overlooking Quality?", Quality Progress, Vol. 17, No. 5, pp. 26-28.

BIOGRAPHICAL SKETCH OF AUTHOR

Alfred L. Guiffrida is an assistant professor of management at Canisius College in Buffalo, NY. He holds a B.S.I.E from SUNY at Buffalo and an MBA from Virginia Tech.

Productivity & Quality Management Frontiers-IV, edited by Sumanth, Edosomwan, Poupart, and Sink. ©1993 Institute of Industrial Engineers.

Small Private College Surprises the Business Community with Academic Graduate Program in Total Quality Management

M.J. Byrd
Mobile College
Mobile, Alabama USA

Small Private College Surprises the Business Community
with Academic Graduate Program in Total Quality
Management

This paper is about the evolution and development of a Total Quality Management (TQM) track for graduate students within an existing Master of Business Administration (MBA) program. Members of the Mobile College faculty were constantly bombarded with requests for independent study courses in Quality Improvement or Management. Three MBA students from the field of hospital management were doing research and needed academic guidance for proposals in their field on the area of Quality Improvement. At this stage several area organizations were asking how to learn TQM.

With the leadership of the Academic Vice President, Mobile College began to participate in various ASQC seminars and the seed was planted! The MBA Director was compiling a library and clipping file on TQM. When students and other faculty members learned of this interest they in turn clipped and contributed. In the winter of 1991, several representatives of Mobile College, including the Academic Vice President, Chairman of the Business Administration/Computer Science Division (BA/CS), and the MBA Director met with a representative of the Mobile Area Chamber of Commerce who was very active in ASQC and the curriculum was born as a concentration for the MBA.

However, birthing of an idea does not create a program. The timing for adding this track to the MBA could not have been better. It was catalog revision time. As the idea began to take form the BA/CS faculty worked as a cohesive unit to help format and approve the program. All formalities were then easily achieved and the TQM track of the MBA was officially approved for implementation during the Fall of 1992.

INTRODUCTION

Mobile College offered its first ever course in Total Quality Management in the Spring Semester 1992. This was the result of a four month quest for a curriculum requested by several local organizations.

BACKGROUND

The summer of 1991 was a time in which several Master of Business Administration students asked the Master of Business Administration Director if she would make a course available to them in the area of Quality Assurance. These students represented a local state institution of mental health and were the hospital administrator and two key staff members. Shortly after this request a local chemical company inquired about a quality management course.

These two related incidents caused the Director to accumulate all information available in the area of Quality Improvement, Quality Assurance, and Total Quality Management. It was soon apparent that Total Quality was catching on like a "wild fire" in the Mobile Region.

In late September 1991, the Mobile Area Chamber of Commerce contacted the College administrators and requested that the school work in tandem with the Chamber in making seminars and courses in total quality available to area employers. Administration felt that the proper place to house the curriculum was within the Master of Business Administration program.

PROGRAM DEVELOPMENT

In researching for an existing program to use as a pattern, the Director soon learned the area was still too new to have been developed and added to business curriculums. Various colleges and universities conducted occasional seminars and a few even had specific courses in their catalogs.

Dr. James Pruett offered a specific course at Louisiana State University in Total Quality Management and very graciously shared information with Mobile College.

At this point Dr. Bryant Chow, who was with the Mobile Chamber o. Commerce at the time, was consulted and he helped brainstorm a Total Quality Management track for Mobile College's Master of Business

Administration program. Dr. Chow was an American Society Quality Control (ASQC) auditor and was hired by the Chamber to implement Total Quality Management in the Mobile area.

Current articles, buzz words, Louisiana State University course content, and student and industry inputs were assembled into a curriculum by November 1991. This program was approved and the "go-ahead" was given to implement the Total Quality Management Track of the Master of Business Administration.

PROGRAM CONTENT

The program includes three levels of courses. Level one: prerequisite courses, which must be completed before the student can move to levels two and three, include Principles of Accounting (six hours), Statistics (three hours), Computer Science Techniques and Applications (three hours), Macroeconomics (three hours), Microeconomics (three hours), and Principles of Management.

Level two: basic core courses include, Accounting for Managerial Decision Making (three hours), Managerial Economics (three hours), Financial Management (three hours), Organizational Communication (three hours), Organizational Behavior* (three hours), and Marketing Administration (three hours).

Level three: upper courses include, Total Quality Management* (three hours), Management Information Systems* (three hours), Production/Operations Management* (three hours), Total Quality Management electives* (six hours), Business Policy (three hours), a written comprehensive exam (one hour), and an oral comprehensive exam (one hour). Total Quality Management track courses are identified by "*"

Specific courses and their content are defined as follows:

Total Quality Management - The application of quality principles to all company endeavors, including satisfying internal "customers." The history, principles, and practices are also included in this course. Prerequisite for this course is Principles of Management. Credit: three hours.

Quantitative Methods - This course contains the statistical and mathematical methods necessary for the quality manager. (Pareto charts, PERT-CPM, regression analysis, etc.) Prerequisite is Total Quality Management, or documented work/experience. Credit: three hours.

Case Studies in Total Quality Management – This is a case analysis course for the quality manager. An actual business project is required for this course. Prerequisites for the course are Total Quality Management, Quantitative Methods, Managerial Finance, Accounting for Managerial Decision Making, Managerial Economics, Marketing Administration, Organizational Communication, Organizational Behavior, Production Operations Management, and Management Information Systems. Credit: three hours.

The courses are scheduled in sequence, and students are requested to take them "lock-step" in order to correlate the three levels of the program.

Graduation requirements include an application for a degree made in the Fall Semester prior to graduation. The application will be reviewed upon receipt of the application form, a recommendation from the MBA Director, recommendations from two MBA faculty members, satisfactory completion of the program requirements (a minimum of thirty-eight (38) semester hours), acceptable scores on the comprehensive examinations, and a minimum overall 3.0 (4.0) GPA on all work attempted. All requirements for a degree must be completed within six years from the time of initial enrollment.

ADMISSION REQUIREMENTS

Admission criteria are the same as for the existing Mobile College Master of Business Administration. A student seeking admission to the program should address all inquiries to the Office of Graduate Programs. The completed application and supporting documents should be received at least three weeks prior to the date on which the student wishes to enter. Applicants may be admitted in one of the following categories.

Unconditional admission requirements include: holding a Bachelor's degree in any discipline from an accredited institution of higher education; file the application for admission to the Graduate Programs and furnish the various materials listed in the instructions; pay a non-refundable application fee; furnish official transcript(s) from each institution attended, showing all credits previously earned; have an overall undergraduate GPA of 2.75 (4.0); submit an official report of test scores obtained on the Graduate Management Admissions Test (GMAT); acquiring at least a total of 1,000 on the formula (GMAT score and the GPA X 200), with the GMAT score being no lower than 400; and have successfully completed all prerequisites (level one), with no grade lower than "C".

Conditional admission may be granted to: an applicant with a GMAT no lower than 400; an applicant whose GPA is no lower than 2.50 (4.0); and an applicant who has a combined total of no less than 900 on the formula (GMAT score and GPA X 200). A student who is granted "Conditional Admission" is expected to maintain a "B" average at all times. A student who falls below this average may be subject to academic suspension. Appeals may be made to the Academic Vice-President, the area Graduate Director, and the area graduate faculty. The "Conditional" status may be changes upon the recommendation of the MBA advisor to "Unconditional Admission" for an individual who makes sufficient score on a retake of the GMAT, or makes a "B" or better grade on the first nine (9) hours of graduate courses in the program-provided at least six (6) hours are required graduate courses.

Clear-to-register admission is a temporary status and is granted for one semester and allows a student to enroll in classes prior to completing the admission process.

Mobile College also provides guidelines for special (non-degree) students and for transient admission.

A maximum of six semester hours of graduate credit earned from another institution accredited to offer graduate programs may be considered as part of the MBA degree. These credits will be evaluated by the Graduate Director, the Registrar, the Assistant to the Academic Vice-President and Dean. Additional hours may be accepted with the approval of the MBA Advisor and the Chair of the Business Administration/Computer Science Division. In truly exceptional cases, up to six (6) graduate hours may be satisfied by extensive documented, meaningful experience.

Graduate stu ents are allowed to repeat courses for graduate credit. All courses taken and all grades earned are permanently recorded on the student's permanent record. All grades earned on graduate level courses by an MBA student will be used in computing the grade point average.

MBA students are expected to make progress toward
the degree by making grades no lower than "A" or "B" on
graduate courses. Students may count only six (6)
graduate semester hours of work with grade "C" toward
the degree. When the six hour limit of grade "C" or
below is exceeded, the student will be automatically
dropped from the program. The student has the right to
appeal this decision with the Academic Vice-President
and Dean of the college. If the student is readmitted
to the program, he or she must repeat courses of grade
"C" in excess of the six hour limit and all courses on
which a grade of "F" was received.

Each student is assigned an academic faculty
advisor. The advisor will assist the student in program
planning by providing guidance in academic matters and
in approving course registration forms and degree plans.

A student who wishes to interrupt graduate study
for at least one semester should notify the Office of
Graduate Programs and the MBA director. He or she may
later return to the program with the same status held at
the time of the departure and under the same Bulletin.
This policy does not change the six year time limit
required for completion of the degree. A student
must apply for readmission if he or she has not
registered for three consecutive terms (whether summer
session or regular academic terms) before resuming
graduate work. A readmission application to graduate
study should be filed with the Office of Graduate
Programs at least three weeks before the opening session
in which the student wishes to continue in the
Graduate Program. Submitting a readmission request
does not automatically guarantee admission to the
Graduate Program.

IMPLEMENTATION

Total Quality Management was offered on Saturdays
from nine a.m. until twelve a.m. in the Spring
Semester of 1992. Thirteen students enrolled in this
course, which was taught by Myrlin Rohan.
Evaluations revealed comments which included: "Very
enjoyable class;" "would like to have a course involving
TQM and developing contracts;" "This has been a very
interesting class;" "I would like to take other classes
like this;" "easy understanding," "Excellent class;" "Of
all my graduate classes, I enjoyed this class the most."
Ninety-two percent responded "excellent" to the
instructor's knowledge of the field. The course was
labeled a success. Fall 1992 offers Quantitative

Methods, to be taught by Dr. Chow, and preregistration figures indicate adequate enrollment. Spring of 1993 will complete the cycle with Case Studies in Total Quality Management.

CONCLUSION

Response to Mobile College's Total Quality Management Track has been, and continues to be, quite positive, even utilizing a formerly unsuccessful time slot on Saturday mornings. Administration and staff cooperate fully and continue to work to maintain a learning track that is unique to the Gulf Coast area.

REFERENCES

Alexander, T. (1992). Product and Service Quality improves through Total Quality Management. Productivity Highlights, pp. 1-2.

Campbell, T. (1992, April). The pursuit of perfection. Business Tokyo, pp.14-19.

Chow, B. (personal communication, October 19, 1991).

Graduate Bulletin. (1992-1994 Bulletin). Graduate. Mobile College. pp. 76-85

Marchese, T. (1991, November). TQM reaches the academy. AAHE Bulletin. pp. 3-18.

Port, O. (1991, October). Questing for the best. Business Week. pp. 8-16.

Pruett, J. M. Correspondence (10-29-91). Course description of Total Quality Management to be offered by Louisiana State University, Spring 1992.

Woodruff, D. (1991, December). At Saturn, what workers want is...fewer defects. Business Week. pp.117-118.

AUTHOR

The author, M Jane Byrd, has a BS and MBA from the University of South Alabama, DBA from Nova University, and is MBA Director at Mobile College. She belongs to various organizations including American Society for Quality Control, Academy of Management and is included in Who's Who of American Women.

Productivity & Quality Management Frontiers-IV, edited by Sumanth, Edosomwan, Poupart, and Sink. ©1993 Institute of Industrial Engineers.

Latest Teaching Innovations

S. Martinez
Florida International University
Miami, Florida USA

Abstract

The "core" courses offered by different universities differ very little in content although titles may vary appreciably. It is for "non-core" courses that universities differ appreciably from each other; it is these courses that establish the "quality" of the specific program.

Recent new courses being taught will be analyzed. The study will include not only what material is actually covered but also why is such material included and how is industry benefitted. Comparison will be made between state and private universities; also between U.S. and foreign universities.

Topics to be discussed will include whether quality is required for productivity or viceversa. Also difference between "theoretical" approach based solely on educational procedures and "practical" approach where actual exposure to industry (or "real world") is a necessity.

Requirements of different industries as well as different countries will be discussed. Introduction of new topics such as JIT and TQC will be evaluated.

Productivity is usually associated with Automation and by reference with a decrease in work force. This would tend to indicate increased unemployment. It has been found that this is not the case. The cause will be discussed and evaluated.

Productivity & Quality Management Frontiers-IV, edited by Sumanth, Edosomwan, Poupart, and Sink. ©1993 Institute of Industrial Engineers.

In Search of Excellence in Engineering Education: Productivity Linked Bonus

Y.R. Babu
Gandhi Institute of Technology & Management
Visakhapatnam, INDIA

P.S. Rarmaiah
Andhra University
Visakhapatnam, Andhra Pradesh INDIA

ABSTRACT

The need of the hour for any Country is an army of engineers excelling in Quality to meet its needs. The present Technical Education System, especially in most of the asian countries, has a big stake in aiming at excellence in Engineering Education. To make this possible, our techniques for preparing engineers conversant with necessary theory and practice should change. This paper traces out the prevailing scenario of engineering education and suggests a module for the same giving all-out attention to search for excellence. The authors are interested in this context, to introduce a productivity Linked Bonus scheme for Engineering staff. This paper also deals with the selection of pararmeters which are functions of productivity in the Institutions. Once the parameters are decided, the relative weightages are decided and the Productivity Index in each year is determined. This index is then linked to the payment of annual bonus to the teaching staff. The basic objective of the scheme is to motivate the staff to perform better that in turn proves quality and productivity. The paper at this juncture, also highlights a future scenario with some inferences.

Key Words : Excellence, Module, Productivity Linked Bonus scheme, Parameters, Weightages, Productivity Index, Future Scenario, Inferences.

Productivity & Quality Management Frontiers-IV, edited by Sumanth, Edosomwan, Poupart, and Sink. ©1993
Institute of Industrial Engineers.

Productivity Measurement as a Tool of Management in all Organizational Levels in Finnish Forest Industry

H. Harjunkoski
Employers' Association of Finnish Forrest Industries
Helsinki, FINLAND

ABSTRACT

This paper tells experiences about the productivity measurement system adapted to the Finnish forest industry. The system has been in use over 10 years time. The measurement includes total and factor productivities. Almost all companies in paper industry in Finland are using the system nowadays. The aim and way, how they use the system, varies and so the experinces are also quite different. The main positive experiences are better consciousness of productivity and changes in attitudes. It is a pity that productivity operations are common during recessions but in booms top management seems to forget the importance of productivity.

Key words:
Total and factor productivities
Productivity measurement
Profitability
Attitudes
Computer systems for productivity measurement
Productivity comparisons

1. BACKGROUND

At the end of 1970's a new method to measure productivity was introduced in Finnish forest industry. The main principle was to calculate total productivity, which includes all factors as raw material, energy, labour capital etc. The former total productivity had excluded raw material and energy and normally productivity was understood only as labour productivity. The method was especially developed for the forest industry, which is the most important industry in Finland. The same calculating method was adapted on macro and micro level. On micro level it meant micro computer program to calculate the total and factor productivities from company's operational information systems. Companies have calculated productivity on machine, department and mill level. On macro level measurement has meant comparable productivity figures on both domestic and international forest industry level on the basis of general statistics.

It is not only a question of measurement principles and computer programs. Also other kind of material was made for teaching specialists and all other personnel to understand the importance of productivity.

2. THE ROLE OF PRODUCTIVITY AS A METHOD OF TOP LEVEL MANAGEMENT

The role of productivity and its' measurement is not clear on top level.
Most managers are more interested in economical measures. Instead of measurement most managers are eager to speak about bad productivity compared to others, especially in economic recession, but they do not define or have exact measures about productivity. If they have some measures, they have had measures only about labour procuctivity.

The new thinking of management, which seems to get air under the wings, is to have key measures on following main areas:

> profitability
> productivity
> guality
> personnel satisfaction

The connections between profitability and productivity must always be clear, because there are so many different ways to make analysis of changes. In Finnish productivity measurement system and its' relationship to profitability describes the following picture:

Figure 1

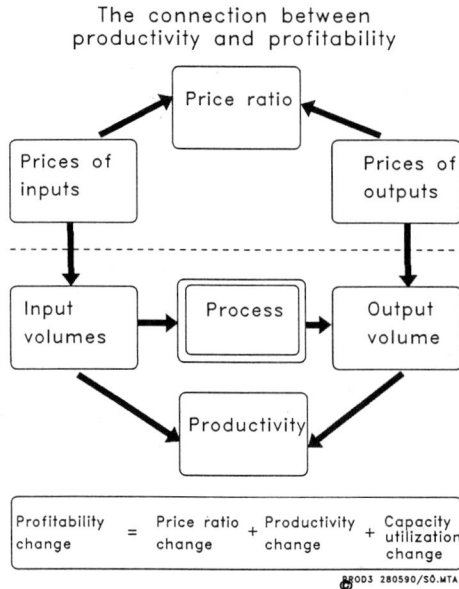

The connection between
productivity and profitability

Profitability = Price ratio + Productivity + Capacity
change   change   change   utilization
                                   change

PROD3 280590/SÖ.MTA

The measurement of factor and total productivities is based on values in
fixed prices. Many discussions have been concentrated on the relatiosship of the "old"
and the new productivity measures. Physical and factor productivities don't substitute but
complete each other. A common problem is that people don't understand this situation. It
can also mean that part of the personnel oppose factor productivities. Especially this
concerns the middle management with technical background.

The main use of productivity measurement at top level management is naturally to follow
the use of different inputs and analysis of profitability changes. Especially in forest
industry the changes of output and input prices are also important because of rapid
changes in outputprices. Also capacity utilization varies much during economic booms
and recessions and it has influence on both profitability and productivity. That is why the
Finnish productivity measurement system is an essential part of profitability analysis.

Productivity development in a company is not enough, if one cannot compare their own
figures to other companies. Companies use the same calculation principles in productivity
measurement and can make voluntarily comparisons. The differences in development of
factor productivities are big, although departments or machines have the same kind of
operational situation.

Productivity comparisons can also be made on international level to explain
competiveness of different countries. This information is necessary for instance in
domestic input-price negotiations and when making investment decisions.

3. THE USE OF PRODUCTIVITY MEASURES ON FLOOR LEVEL

On floor level productivity is usually seen very narrowly as speed of machines, quality, stoppages etc. Too seldom employees have information about use of energy, raw materials etc. Total and factor productivities cannot give any help to daily work. But new information can tell more largely about effectiveness, and the influence of input-/ outputmix on profitability.

The most important use of these new measures is on the area of attitudes. Quite often productivity information is easier to understand than profitability information, because the influence of price-development is such an essential part of profitability. After this kind of information employees are eager to develope productivity in their own working area. It is not easy to sell the idea "PRODUCTIVITY IS A STATE OF MIND" without good and comparable measures.

4. SOME EXPERIENCES DURING THE LAST 10 YEARS

The work has now lasted over 10 years and some main experiences can be noticed. As in Japan it takes years to change the attitudes for better productivity . When times are good even management almost forget the importance of productivity. But during recession productivity is very important and operations for better productivity are started eagerly. However, the results of these operations takes also months and so the real influence can't be seen until booms. Other personnel has often difficulties to understand these operations because of lack of continuity and fluctuations. So it is not very easy to get harmony in productivity operations during booms and recessions. The role of measurement is to inform about the development both during recessions and booms.

A new kind of thinking was easy to sell to the economists. The factor and total productivity measures are quite easy to get by computer programs. It is more difficult to analyse this information thoroughly and to start operations on mill level in order to get better productivity can be troublesome, if the attitudes are not ready for need of changes.

One positive result of the productivity campaign is a better knowledge of productivity. Nowadays productivity in forest industry is understood more largely and exactly. Figures are incorruptible. Companies know better now, how effectively they are using their inputs not only inside, but also compared to other companies in Finland and the main competitors outside Finland.

Management by objectives can be developed to MANAGEMENT BY PRODUCTIVITY OBJECTIVES. In forest industry the productivity differences can be big although the machines are the same. It is a question of attitudes among all personnel and positive attitudes are not selfevident. A typical situation is that technically the production is very good, but economically it can be disasterous because of too expensive machinery. The proportion between profitability and productivity is also better understood.

Although the productivity campaign has dured over ten years the acts have been concentrated to the recessions. Almost all paper companies use productivity measurement to some extent. There are differences, how largely and in which purpose companies are using this information. Productivity campaigns concerning the whole personnel are still quite uncommon. The unions in Finland are not against this. As in other countries they are more interested in wages and job security. Employees are otherwise quite interested to co-operate on mill level, if attitudes are positive and they are motivated by productivity training. This training includes both mill and floor level productivity measures. It must include organization for participation, operational technics for productivity development and involvement of management.

Productivity work takes years and trying to go too fast usually means failures. If attitudes in all levels are forgotten, the results are also poor.

The connection between productivity and profitability

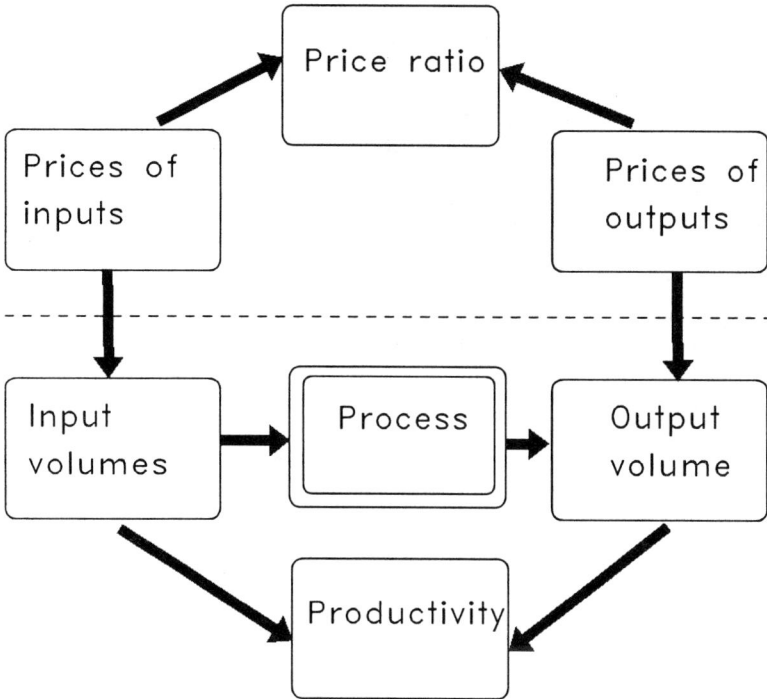

Price ratio

Prices of inputs

Prices of outputs

Input volumes

Process

Output volume

Productivity

| Profitability change | = | Price ratio change | + | Productivity change | + | Capacity utilization change |

Productivity & Quality Management Frontiers-IV, edited by Sumanth, Edosomwan, Poupart, and Sink. ©1993 Institute of Industrial Engineers.

Quality and Productivity: An Applied Research Intended for Teaching Activities

R.C. da Costa and A.C.C.F. Campos
Universidade Federal do Rio Grande do Norte
Natal, RN BRAZIL

The present paper describes the work carried out on civil engineering activities in the State of Rio Grande do Norte - RN (Brazil). The results were used on the structuring of a programme based on Quality and Productivity towards this sector (QCCRN - Qualidade e Produtividade na Construcao Civil do RN). They could also be used to update the Civil Engineering Course syllabus.

The main objective was to map out the difficulties confronted by the Engineers in carrying out their duties. The results show that these difficulties are mainly connected to the quality of their work and their productivity.

Productivity & Quality Management Frontiers-IV, edited by Sumanth, Edosomwan, Poupart, and Sink. ©1993 Institute of Industrial Engineers.

European Experiences of Productivity and Quality Teaching in Engineering Schools

C. Delvosalle and M. Vankerkem
Falculté Polytechnique de Mons
Mons, BELGIUM

J. Gazerian, F. Rigaud, and J.-M. Ruiz
Université de Droit
Marseille, FRANCE

ABSTRACT

This paper describes two European original experiences of Quality and Productivity teaching developed in close contact with industry and in the frame of the EEC internal market.
The engineer now actually appears at a key position in the industrial organisation: horizontally, he/she represents, from research to production, the link between customers' needs and customers' satisfaction; vertically, he/she plays a major role in the vertical communication of information. In this new general context, the need to fit *industrial needs* and *engineers' course* may be encountered by training in industrial engineering.
As a matter of fact, industrial engineering is a full discipline and must be taught as such.
Yet this approach is far from being common in Europe.
The *Faculté Polytechnique de Mons* in Belgium (F.P.Ms) and the *Ecole Nationale Supérieure de Synthèse, de Procédés et d'Ingéniérie Chimique d'Aix Marseille* in France (ENSSPICAM) developed very early original approaches to fulfil new industrial needs.
In both cases, programs were established with industrial participation and many professionals are involved in courses, seminars or thematic conferences.
Three different courses given by the Faculté Polytechnique de Mons directly concern Industrial Engineering. The *Engineering Degree in Information Systems and Management.* Created in 1969, this Degree acknowledges the importance of a managerial role within an engineering framework. The *Masters degree in Innovation Management.* Created in 1988, this Degree prepares engineers to stimulate creativity, stimulate the market and establish the profitability of innovative projects. The *Masters Degree in Total Quality Control.* Created in 1989, this Degree prepares engineers to implement and maintain the principles of Quality in their company.
L'Ecole Nationale Supérieure de Synthèse, de Procédés et d'Ingéniérie Chimique was the first in France, as soon as 1980, to propose an *one-year training in Project Management.* The course is opened to graduated engineers of various initial formations. Later, the ENSSPICAM opened an option in its traditional engineering curriculum specially oriented to industrial engineering (*"option ingéniérie"*) and, in 1985, a *Master* and a *Doctorate level* in *"Project Management Engineering"* was opened, promoting formation through research. Incidentally, the ENSSPICAM formalised its relationships with "the Project Management Master" of the University of Quebec.
These two experiences are encouraged by the Community namely through exchanges of students and professors in the frame of the European "ERASMUS" co-operation program between Universities.

INTRODUCTION

A fact: the *"technological phenomenon"*.

The *"technological phenomenon"* is probably one of the most noticeable characteristics of industrial context during the two last decades of the century. As a matter of fact, "Innovation", "Productivity" and "Quality" seem to be the only response against the world-wide competition challenge and constitute what can be called the *"technological phenomenon"*.

As explained by P. Desmarescaux (1992), R&D supervisor at Rhône-Poulenc : "the context is not simply competitive, it evolves more and more rapidly. Innovation is more than ever a strategic objective and time factor, an essential parameter".

The rapidly changing technological context leads to major evolution in the field of industrial management. After the age of *"technological production"* during the golden 1945-1975 years, appears the age of *"technology and innovation management"*. However, the technical evolution is surely not the only factor and the market internationalisation is also an accelerating factor. As noted by R.E. Miles (1989): " a piece of ice of hockey equipment designed in Scandinavia, engineered in the US to meet the requirements of the large US and Canadian market, manufactured in Korea and distributed through a multinational market network with initial distribution in Japan".

Productivity and quality: two major components of industrial engineering.

In the unceasing search for competitivity, production systems need to offer "even more": more productivity and more quality. This *search for excellence* requires the mobilisation of all the voluntary efforts and of all the skills and intelligence in the company. It implies a complete change in the management style through a post-Taylorian organisation (Enregle 1978). This represents, in our opinion, a major aspect in the mutation of industrial systems.

As a matter of fact, taking workers' individual needs and goals as well as cultural evolution into account will induce new organisational structures which fit better current companies' needs namely in the Total Quality Control field.

A second aspect related with productivity and quality is the generalisation of the *"supplier-customer"* relationship. This phenomenon concerns the external as well as the internal of a company.

The external customer's needs must be satisfied and therefore the product must fit its use. Moreover, the company must remain aware of the fact that the customer's needs are continually evolving. All these aspects of the "Quality spiral" are to be translated in technical activities by many tools such as market analysis, innovation management, value analysis, functional analysis, experimental design, statistical process control, sampling inspection, supplier partnership,... It also needs to be translated through Quality Assurance methods in the whole company and through its corollary the *"Quality System Certification"* which is, at the present time, a must for most European companies.

Inside the company, the introduction of the *"supplier-customer"* relationship formalises all the relations between departments and between people as well as it clearly defines authorities and responsibilities at any level.

The engineer : an evolving function.
Traditionally, the engineer was employed in functions in which his technical knowledge was enough; often, in fact, he was employed in one particular function such as research, production, construction, ... without any overall vision of his company and with no direct relationships with the market and the customers.
But now the engineer must be considered as the corner-stone of the technology and innovation management, on a technical level as well as on a management level. While remaining a skilled technician, his job is now to anticipate, analyse and manage, from a global point of view, all the customers' needs and all the developments required by the customers .

The engineer now actually appears at a key position in the industrial organisation: horizontally, he represents, from research to production, the link between customers' needs and customers' satisfaction; vertically, he works at the border between the shop floor and the top management. He therefore plays a major role in the vertical communication of information and in the horizontal co-ordination of efforts to reach all the designed goals.

This "new" engineer must not only be a technical expert but he must also be an expert in productivity and in quality management.
In a more and more complex technical context, the role of the engineer evolves. Some of his usual functions are rendered commonplace (C.A.D., simulation software, artificial intelligence, ...) and he must integrate these new tools but moreover he must redefine his own place in the company. Liberated from many technical aspects of his works, he shall assume his new vertical and horizontal roles in the company.

An adapted formation: considerations on industrial engineering.
In this new general industrial context, the need to fit *"industrial needs-engineers"* and *"engineers-engineers' training"* has to be analysed. Universities should take all the previously discussed changes into account in the field of industrial organisation and provide engineers with a new approach to their function in a company in order to enhance their competitonness.

DEVELOPMENT OF A DISCIPLINE : THE SITUATION IN EUROPE.

Characteristics
Industrial engineering must be considered a scientific subject for engineers and constitutes an horizontal science (integrating other fields).
Its "gravity centre" lies in technique and is based on the different engineering disciplines (chemical, civil electrical, mechanical, ... engineering) but it incorporates new tools (innovation management, quality control) and allied knowledge (marketing, finances, economics, ... and even psychology) which must be integrated in a common language.

Present development (Gousty (1981), Jacques (1988), Guvenen (1981))
While industrial engineering is well developed in US, Australia and Japan, it is not really the case in Europe (except northern Europe).

In France and in Belgium, industrial engineering was "discovered" only in the eighties and very few universities have incorporated it in their courses. Contrary to US and Canada, only classical fields such as chemistry, physics, mathematics or biology are recognised as initial formations at the BAC level (end of secondary school). Most educational efforts in industrial engineering are therefore only found at the master and the doctorate levels. In this frame, its is not surprising that most people performing research or providing courses in industrial engineering, like the authors of this paper, are officially Professors or Associate Professors in "classical" engineering.

TWO ORIGINAL EXPERIENCES IN BELGIUM AND IN FRANCE

Introduction

The most relevant features of industrial engineering probably concern production management and project management.

The *Faculté Polytechnique de Mons* in Belgium (F.P.Ms) and the *Ecole Nationale Supérieure de Synthèse, de Procédés et d'Ingéniérie Chimique d'Aix Marseille* in France (ENSSPICAM) developed very early original approaches to fulfil new industrial needs, namely for chemical process industries.

In both cases, programs were established with industrial participation and many professionals are involved in courses, seminars or thematic conferences. As most modern training (Smith (1991)), these teachings propose active learning integrating communication skills and group activities.

In the frame of the European Economic Community, these schools already exchanges students and professors (through ERAMUS program).

La Faculté Polytechnique de Mons (F.P.Ms)

Three different courses given by the Faculté Polytechnique de Mons directly concern Industrial Engineering:

- the Engineering Degree in Information Systems and Management
- the Masters degree in Innovation Management
- the Masters Degree in Total Quality Control

Moreover, courses on project and production management have been introduced in many classic engineering curriculum (namely chemical, electrical and mechanical engineering).

The Engineering Degree in Information Systems & Management at the F.P.Ms

In 1969, the F.P.Ms created a degree in Information Systems & Management. The profile of this "new" type of engineer seemed original at the time in that it acknowledged *the importance of a managerial role within an engineering framework.*

The professional objective of the Information Systems & Management engineer is twofold:
- to prepare in a scientific manner for decision-making in the context of a choice between economic alternatives.
- to study, be advisor, or act out the management role in the "integrated" management of firm's activities.

Note that such a specialisation corresponds to a *defined role*, whereas training in most other branches of engineering refers to a *specific area* of activity.

One must distinguish between the taking of a decision and the preparation leading up to it. Decision-making itself is the essence of the practice of power. Management, as such, cannot be scientifically based. What remains amenable to scientific approach, however, thanks to modern methods of operational research and economic calculation, and using the powerful techniques provided by information management systems, is the study of the alternatives and the analysis of their consequences.

The program of this engineering degree therefore includes, besides classic engineering sciences, lectures on economics, accounting, human resources management, operational research, applied mathematics and statistics, information management systems (computers, electronics and software). It also includes many personal or team works concerning project management.

The information Systems & Management engineer is often called upon to fulfil the global functions of manager and analyst. These tasks are bound to encounter twin concerns:

- to ensure an evolution as normal and as smooth as possible the total activity, with special attention to the avoidance of any bottlenecks (commercial, technical, financial or administrative).
- to establish, by means of profitability and partial productivity analysis, the corporate performance, and the openings which exist for its improvement.

This program is also open to graduated engineers who can obtain this diploma in eighteen months.

The Masters Degree in Innovation Management at the F.P.Ms

In 1988, the F.P.Ms created a Masters Degree in Innovation Management. This degree prepares the engineer for the three vital steps to successful innovation:

- *Stimulate creativity* (generate new ideas, encourage others to share these ideas, and win through);
- *Stimulate the market* (help customers through their evolution and invest the products with new commercial added value);
- *Establish the profitability of innovative projects* (define the relevant costs of the innovation and draw from this a clear vision of the profitability of the activities).

This Masters Degree is a post-university course. Since it is aimed at executives and managers, it is organised into evening and weekend classes. The course takes a minimum two years to complete.

From the very beginning the authorities of the Walloon Region in Belgium have given their support to this Masters Degree. Specifically, the Ministry of Research and New Technologies acted to subsidise the course. It therefore appears that this training is in fact perceived as a micro-economic way of solving a serious macro-economic problem: the relative paucity of innovation in Belgium, and in general in the countries of the EEC.

This lack of innovative spirit in Wallonia, compared, for example, to the Pacific Rim, is paradoxical in the light of increased tendency of executive and technical staff towards a scientific and technical background.

To liberate this potential, and run a project from the germ of an idea to its successful completion is a complex task which demands particular attention. It is precisely the mission of the Masters Degree in Innovation Management to develop the capacity for such innovation in public and private industry.

The pedagogic program includes those disciplines necessary to negotiate the three steps on the road to successful innovation. By comparison to the major components of traditional management training, "*stimulation of creativity*" falls into the domain of human resources management, "stimulation of the market" is an advanced development of marketing skills, whilst "*establishment of profitability*" is an extension of the financial management role within the company.

The final aim of the Masters Degree in Innovation Management is to have each participant carry out an innovative project within or exterior to his company.

The award of the diploma depends on the successful completion of a dissertation the subject of which must be an innovative project.

Around half of the teaching staff come from an industrial, economic or financial background. University professors and managers together give a complete inventory of the innovative approach. Experts, from varied industrial sectors, add to the training with their direct experience and specific case studies. The pedagogic technique is the opposite of the authoritative statement, and encourages participatory communication.

Since 1991, this Masters Degree, though essentially a post-university training, has also been recognised as a professional qualification by the Ministry of Employment. This particularity results from the fact that the training has a favourable impact on employment.

At the present time, more than one hundred students have followed this course.

The Masters Degree in Total Quality Control at the F.P.Ms

The concept of Quality has deeply changed in Europe during the last decade. As a matter of fact, the role of quality specialists and of the management as a whole is changing.

The role of the "new" quality specialists is to implement and maintain the principles of the TQM in their company. It namely means a new customer-oriented quality management process that everyone, in the company, understands, believes and is part of.

It also implies a clear and effective involvement of the managers of any departments in this challenge.

The new quality specialists and the whole management need to be specially educated and trained to succeed and overcome any form of "cultural or behavioural obstacles".

Consequently, *there is an obvious need of a university level education in TQM.*

In 1988, such a training was not available in Wallonia. Aware of these facts, the "Association Wallonne pour la Gestion de la Qualité" (AWQ), a non-profit-making association whose objective is to promote TQM in Wallonia, came into contact with the "Faculté Polytechnique de Mons" (a Walloon engineering university).
Following this initiative, a Masters degree in Total Quality Management was created in Wallonia at the end of 1989.

Using the very first principles of quality management, it appeared that the best way to fit the actual needs of our future "customers" was to involve them early in our research. This was a major point in our approach.
To achieve this goal, a working group of both university and industry specialists in TQM was formed. This group begun its work in April 1988.
More than twenty meetings took place between April 1988 and April 1989 until the objectives and the program of the course were completely achieved.
During the first meetings, the working group recognised that quality control has evolved over the years into a unique blend of disciplines including applied statistics, engineering sciences, management and human sciences.
Therefore, it became clear that we had to develop a course covering all the TQM disciplines and that this course should be embodied in an original and coherent education program.
The depth and extent of the required program correspond to a Masters Degree.

As the Walloon industry is lacking TQM specialists and management trained at the TQM concepts, the program must encounter that need as soon as possible. The course must therefore be primarily intended for working professionals who could rapidly put their knowledge into practice.
The courses, though of university level, should not be too theoretical but, conversely, must be based on case studies and personal works. Therefore, most of the professors were required to have an actual practical experience of TQM methods and were found outside of the University.

The basis of the training represents the basic knowledge needed by a quality professional, regardless of whether he/she is management or technically oriented. Each course contains a phase in which students are expected to perform a personal or a team work as a practical application of the information they have to learn. A large part of the training is devoted to a research project. The students may select a project chosen from a list proposed by the professors but they are strongly encouraged to propose themselves a topic based on their current professional activities.

The program of the masters degree is divided in four blocks and thirteen sub-blocks.
Each block corresponds to a semester while each sub-block corresponds to a main topic.

The first semester introduces students to the main Quality management concepts, history and philosophy. It also includes some basic courses on marketing and elementary statistics.
The second semester is concerned with the numerous quality tools which can be used through a product (or service) life, from the R&D to the sales and customers services.
The third semester covers the theory and practice of the implementation and management of a quality improvement program in a company as well as an introduction to human and communication sciences.
The last semester is devoted to the research project.

The total length of the course is about 450 hours for two years. Nearly 300 hours are devoted to tutorial classes, exercises and case studies and 150 hours to the research work.
As the master degree is mainly intended to working professionals, the courses take place on evenings and on Saturday mornings.
Students holding a university degree in engineering, sciences, mathematics, business or other fields with some years of work experience can apply for admission to the master degree program.

Students are evaluated during each phase of the formation mainly on the base of personal or team works.
The final grade is mainly based on the results of the research project which is publicly defended.
At the time, about seventy students have followed this training.

L'Ecole Nationale Supérieure de Synthèse, de Procédés et d'Ingéniérie Chimique
L'Ecole Nationale Supérieure de Synthèse, de Procédés et d'Ingéniérie Chimique was the first in France, as soon as 1980, to propose an one-year formation in Project Management. The course is opened to graduated engineers of various initial formations.
The courses were created for and with the industry, they are based on three main modules of tutorial classes:

* Basic formation
    -economics (national and international)
    - laws (national and international)
    - accountancy
    - human resources management
* Industrial organisation
    - project management
    - project economic evaluation
    - planning and cost control
    - quality assurance
    - data analysis

* Industrial engineering
    - economic feasibility of a project
    - contacts management
    - operational tolls
    - industrial management software

Other specific and thematic tutorial courses are also included in the training. Moreover students must perform an 11 week placement in industry and a large part of the training is devoted to the management of an actual project (often in direct connection with industry).

Later, the ENSSPICAM opened an option in its traditional engineering curriculum specially oriented to industrial engineering ("option ingéniérie") and therefore increased threefold its graduated engineers. Many of the courses given in the previously discussed graduation have been included in this specialisation.

In 1985, a Master and a Doctorate level in "Project Management Engineering" was opened, promoting formation through research. Incidentally, the ENSSPICAM formalised its relationships with "the Project Management Master" of the University of Quebec by establishing a possibility to be simultaneously graduated from both universities through exchanges of students and professors.

The central column of the course for students and graduated engineers is *Project Management* and is based on the study and realisation of industrial projects. In this frame, Productivity is naturally taken into account at each phases of the project development (feasibility, planning, control, ...). Total quality control is discussed in the training. From a rather theoretical point of view, the program describes the technical aspects (normalisation, applied statistics), the human aspects (team work, quality circles, participative management) and the information aspects (data collect and analysis, communication, ...). From a practical point of view, usual quality tools are used, such as pareto diagrams, Ishikawa diagrams, control charts, statistical inspection, ...
Moreover, as many engineering companies try to obtain a "Quality System Certification", a specific course on quality assurance for project management is also included in the program.

Over twelve years, eighty percent of these graduated engineers actually practice in the industrial engineering field for the majority of the French chemical companies.

CONCLUSIONS

The Industrial Engineering is *a full discipline and must be taught as such.*
It acknowledges the new roles of the engineer in industrial organisations and proposes an integrated image of companies. In the search for excellence which characterises all winning firms in a more and more competitive world, engineers should not only remain skilled technicians. They must pay a special attention to their new managerial roles which include the horizontal co-ordination of project development and production management as well as the vertical transmission of information "top-down" and "bottom-up".
Productivity and Quality are embodied in this vision and must be translated in practice through specific training.
Besides their technical formation, the "new" engineers must be trained for project and production management, in technical, economical and human areas.
Yet this approach remains far from being common in Europe, especially in a course dedicated for engineers.
Few schools in Belgium and in France promote Industrial Engineering and we believe that the two experiences described in this paper are largely original.
While the approach of the F.P.Ms and the ENSSPICAM are somewhat different, they are closely related in fundamentals. In both cases, these universities have detected new unsatisfied industrial needs and, in close connection with the industrial world, they developed new training corresponding to these needs.
The theme of these courses is Productivity in the broadest sense of the word, covering the interaction between technical production, industrial organisation and economy. At any level (graduated engineers or masters degrees), research is closely linked with teaching and any student has to perform a personal work in direct relation with industrial practice.

In the context of the coming EEC internal market, these approaches are encouraged by the Community namely through exchanges of students and professors in the frame of the European "ERASMUS" co-operation program between Universities.

REFERENCES

Desmarescaux P. (1992) "Evaluer la recherche et les chercheurs", Industries et Techniques, n°724, pp 16.

Enregle Y. and Thietart R.A. (1978) Précis de direction et de gestion, Paris, Les Editions de l'Organisation.

Gousty Y., Kieffer J.P. and Ronis M. (1981) "Le génie industriel", Actes du Colloque Franco-Québécois, Marseille.

Guvenen O., Labys W.C. and Lesourd J.B. (1981) International Market Models, Chapman and Hall.

Jacques J.K., Lesourd J.B. and Ruiz J.M. (1988) Modern Applied Energy Conservation: New Directions in Energy Conservation Management, Chichester, Ellis Horwood Pub.

Miles R.E. (1989) "Adapting to Technology and Competition: A New Industrial Relations System for 21st Century", California Management Review, vol. 31, n°2.

Smith R.A. (1991) Innovation and Teaching in Engineering, Chichester, Ellis Horwood Pub.

BIOGRAPHICAL SKETCHES OF AUTHORS

Christian Delvosalle is Chemical Engineer and holds a Ph.D. in Applied Sciences. He is Professor at the F.P.Ms and co-ordinator of the Masters in Total Quality Control organised by the F.P.Ms.

Michel Vankerkem is Electrical Engineer and holds a Ph.D. in Applied Economics. He is Professor at the F.P.Ms and co-ordinator of the Masters Degree in Innovation Management.

Joëlle Gazerian holds a Ph.D. in Sciences and is lecturer in Process Engineering at ENSS-PICAM.

François Rigaux holds a Ph.D. in Sciences and is lecturer in Process Engineering at ENSS-PICAM.

Jean-Michel Ruiz is "Docteur es Sciences" . He is Professor at ENSSPICAM and head of the industrial engineering project department of ENSSPICAM.

Productivity & Quality Management Frontiers-IV, edited by Sumanth, Edosomwan, Poupart, and Sink. ©1993 Institute of Industrial Engineers.

Feasibility Study on the Establishment of an Integration Programme between UFRN/Productive Sector of Rio Grande do Norte State (RN), Brazil

A.C.C.F. Campos and R.M.N. Bezerra
Universidade Federal do Rio Grande do Norte
Natal, RN BRAZIL

A feasibility study is being carried out aiming at the promotion and development of the productive sector of Rio Grande do Norte State (RN), Brazil. The focus of this study is the use of the state endogenous potential, including the UFRN (Federal University of RN) which acts as a key factor as a traditional instrument of development and knowledge.

This work presents a proposal for an integration programme between the university - state productive sector with emphasis on Quality & Productivity which are vital to achieve increasing levels of competitivity. Technological innovation has also been considered.
Through a survey on the potential areas to be acted upon and tools to be used by the university as a collaborator to the state development, the need for technological innovation and better quality of products and processes has become a link between the UFRN and the local enterprises. This approach has been used with the aim to minimize the existing problems related to the creation and survival of enterprises.

Based on the developed methodology, a preliminary analysis of the UFRN potential and a survey on data concerning some sectors of the local enterprises were carried out, as a first step to the establishment of an integration programme between UFRN and the RN Productive Sector.

Productivity & Quality Management Frontiers-IV, edited by Sumanth, Edosomwan, Poupart, and Sink. ©1993 Institute of Industrial Engineers.

Refining of Teaching Productivity and Quality Management in Alternative Business School

O. Borisov
Odessa Politechnic Institute
Odessa, UKRAINE

ABSTRACT

The paper deals with peculiarities of the alternative business school system in the ex-USSR. Submitted is a novel method for classifying the essence of business school activity. The problems of teaching Productivity and Quality Management in the alternative business schools are outlined. The scientific and educational training blocks are formulated. The reserves for improving PQM teaching are determined.

Business schools. Productivity and Quality Management. Improvement of training.

Within the states of the ex-USSR a formation of private and co-operative business schools (BSs) that present the alternative for the state education system is being completed.

The most complicated social and economic problem of the alternative education formation is that of objectively caused conflict between the most acute requirement of the society in diversified market economy specialists and the indifference in finding ways to solve the problem. Psychological alienation of a part of the society from market economy is one of the obstacles in the way of promoting alternative education (study of market economy).

The BSs have been established because of permanent lack of knowledge, abilities and skills across a wide spectrum of sciences dedicated to enterprising and private business.

Western countries conduct a number of programs in order to assist the countries of the ex-USSR in economic education. These programs that are completely or partially financed by government or non-state funds have no common concept. They must have clearly defined time-fixed aims and be customer-oriented. Means allocated by Western countries are spent to pay western lecturers, advisors and contractors. Unfortunately, these programs do not pay great attention to publishing literature on business in Russian, Ukrainian and other languages. Western countries have organized the assistance in the field of business education so that they are handsomely combined with assisting their own business schools.

The major part of this assistance is allocated to the capitals - Moscow and Kiev - and, as a rule, to elite schools that do not lack attention from the governments of Russia and the Ukraine. Western programs do not pay adequate attention to provincial business schools that are, frequently, treated as "province".

A novel method of study investigates the essence of the BSs activity. Four types have been classified. The first type of BSs (as a rule, in capitals) is that of specialized in overseas economic aspects. The second type of schools is specialized in managerial and economic training of accountants, commercial agents and brokers with the single basic subject. The third type of BSs is that of dealing with preparing specialists for the alternative sector of economy. These schools deal with teaching Productivity and Quality Management (PQM). The fourth type of BSs graduates comprise secretaries and assistant managers.

The business schools of the third type have developed in several stages. At the first stage the training programs have been formed, staff of lecturers selected and information block accumulated. At the second stage the school's own educational market sector is defined and the list of specialists that can be trained or have extension courses is determined. The third stage deals with training specialists to orders of co-operative and private enterprises, selection of trainees, determination of their individual ratings and lecturing following the programs approved by the customer enterprises. A basis of such training course is a study of Productivity and Quality Management. Training process is conducted individually. Aim, targets and contents of training are clearly defined. Great attention is attached to formation of a "portfolio" of methodical and reference literature and a package of application programs.

The main bulk of people who need PQM knowledge are the employees of small enterprises, their number in the Ukraine exceeds 40,000. The small enterprise is a structural and economical novelty that has been in use for several years.

The interest and requirement in knowledge and experience of the Western countries in the field of PQM is caused by the following factors:
    1. PQM has not been taught in the system of higher education of the ex-USSR.
    2. More than 80% of the managers of the alternative economics in the southern region of the Ukraine have higher technical education. In the higher technical institutions only from 4 to 6% of the curriculum had been allocated for managerial and economic subjects.

The level of teaching PQM in business schools has been studied. Generally, it can be characterized by the following grades:
    1. Teaching is effected by national specialists that had been trained (had mastered a short-term course, as a rule) abroad - in Germany, Italy, Finland, less often in USA.
    2. Teaching is effected by use of foreign books.
    3. Teaching is effected by western specialists. PQM takes in this case from 18 to 26 hrs.
    4. Teaching is effected by the scientists working in industry, mainly in scientific and production associations.
    5. Teaching is effected by the lecturers of higher institutions.

Within each of the presented grades of classification there are its own peculiarities and single and particular regularities.

A certain experience in PQM training indicates a requirement in conceptually new approach to a formation of economic culture raising the importance of general economic education. Paradoxical situation is due to the fact that "knowledge" of mar-

ket economy is based not upon the science and experience of
the developed countries but upon the emotional perception of
hard and complex economic realities.

In this respect we have suggested to the Association of "Production Management" of the Commonwealth of Independent States
to develop and prepare three scientific and educational blocks.

The first block includes information and education material
and literature on PQM intended for general education.

The second block comprises materials on PQM intended for specialists of various levels to be trained in the higher education system and in alternative business schools. PQM knowledge
block is included into an obligatory training.

The third block deals with PQM intended for professional fun-
ctionaries.

Proposals as to selecting PQM materials for teenagers to be
trained as future entrepreneures are formulated separately.

When analysing and synthesizing aspects and trends of development of entrepreneuring and establishing of small business,
determined on the basis of systematic and functional analysis
are the groups of reserves in teaching and implementation of
PQM achievements in entrepreneuring practice:
    1. Formulation of a concept for implementation and teach-
ing of PQM achievements on a national basis.
    2. Determination of forms, methods and trends of PQM im-
plementation from the viewpoint of system adaptation and
structural/logical completeness by the relevant stages.
    3. Determination of education market capacity in PQM
subject.
    4. Mass publication of foreign literature on PQM.
    5. Development of monitoring systems for selecting nati-
onal achievements in PQM.
    6. Integration of national research and practical achie-
vements in the world system of PQM.

Utilization of the best world experience in PQM when applied
to national peculiarities will facilitate integration of the
countries of the ex-USSR into the World economic system.

Dr.Oleg Gr.Borisov
Associate Professor, Department of Industrial Organization,
Odessa Polytechnical Institute, Head of Odessa Commercial
and Co-Operative Business School (Private)
Member of Prezidium and Leadership of Soviet Association of
Industrial Organization. Author of 85 research publications.

Productivity & Quality Management Frontiers-IV, edited by Sumanth, Edosomwan, Poupart, and Sink. ©1993 Institute of Industrial Engineers.

A Proposal for TQM Education within Higher Education Institutions

O. Usabiaga
Instituto Tecnologico de Estudios Superiores
Querétaro, Qro MEXICO

ABSTRACT:

What is happening to many organizations in this continuously evolving world where we live in? Many of them are losing their makets, or for the moment they still keep them at a very high cost staying in a very risky position, all of these conditions leading to the wear of the organization as a total entity.

We believe that any system of higher education is one of the most powerful competitive weapons that any country can have in order to struggle and seek for a leading position in this dynamic and integrated world. What do we (higher education institutions) do globaly in order to prepare our graduates to face this challenging world?   In particular, in engineering schools are we aware of the tremendous "human energy" that every organization needs in order to be competitive? What is this human energy and what is the best way to handle it leading the organization to a superior performance?. In this paper we propose an integrative model for TQM education in general and particulary addressed to engineering programs.

Productivity & Quality Management Frontiers-IV, edited by Sumanth, Edosomwan, Poupart, and Sink. ©1993 Institute of Industrial Engineers.

Integrative Education for Productivity and Quality Management: The Role of Business and Engineering Schools

S.B-S.K. Adjibolosoo
Trinity Western University
Langley, British Columbia CANADA

ABSTRACT

American productivity has been on a continuous decrease in the last few years. The rate of this decline is frightening. As globalization process continues, it is necessary for American businesses to reverse the trend of declining productivity and also deal with quality problems in order to compete effectively in the global marketplace. To achieve this goal, the role of integrative education is very essential. However, it is not just mere education that is required, but a relevant education for productivity and quality management. It is therefore necessary for American business and engineering schools to team up together in order to provide the necessary education for ensuring effective and efficient productivity and quality management. Since this issue is important for success in both domestic and global markets, it is crucial to identify and promote the role business and engineering schools must jointly play in the education process. In view of this, this paper presents a detailed analysis of how business and engineering schools must have to work hand-in-hand with business men and women to foster creatively integrated education required not only for productivity and quality management, but also essential for effective utilization of resources, global competitiveness, and customer satisfaction. A model for accomplishing productive integrated productivity and quality management education is developed and used to explain how American businesses can achieve and maintain global competitiveness through effective and efficient productivity and quality management.

1. INTRODUCTION

It has not only become quite evident that one major problem of the American economy is declining productivity and low quality of goods and services, but also that the Japanese have almost surpassed Americans in better management of productivity and quality. It is a widely held view in the United States that if this problem of declining productivity and quality issue is not properly dealt with immediately, American living standards may continue to plummet drastically. This decline would be accompanied with rising costs of living, worsening medicare programs, declining global competitiveness, etc. In a world which is reverting into a Global Village speedily, American businesses cannot continue to blame their lack of global competitiveness on government macroeconomic policies.

For example, Bond (1981), in a letter to the editor of the

Wall Street Journal wrote that "Productivity usually depends on relations between the producing technology and the people operating the system. Though complex, these relations are fairly well known. For instance, quality and quantity of production are influenced by the goals which people set for themselves. The information system which supervises the production must be perceived as fair and reliable; it must have "teeth", so that inadequate output can be tied to specific behaviors of specific people, and so that exceptional performance can be quickly recognized. Intragroup social relations can play a part. Some of the most productive work groups in the world are made up of people who have strong shared work values and commitments. Often, special techniques can be used: reinforcement schemes, job enrichment, and providing the challenge that comes from encouraging workers to develop a new method, product, or service."

In view of Bond's observation, the basic objective of this paper is to develop and present an integrated education model that has potentials for training and producing productivity and quality managers required by American businesses for successfully achieving productivity growth, quality improvement and improved global competitiveness. The remainder of the paper is presented in the following manner. While section 2 reviews briefly the manager's role in the business enterprise, section 3 discusses the attainment of management objectives. In section 4, a model of integrated education is developed, presented and utilized to explain how to produce effective and efficient productivity and quality managers for the United States. Section 5 contains summary and conclusions.

2. ROLE OF THE MANAGER IN THE BUSINESS ENTERPRISE

The regaining of American global competitiveness requires a special calibre of managers. They must be able to effectively and efficiently manage people and resources to enhance productivity and quality. They must be capable of successfully placing the organization on the pathway towards higher performance.

In the management literature, managers are usually classified into various categories, usually depicting what they do and at what level. Three basic categorizations include: (1). Line managers: these usually influence the actual production processes and act to achieve it. (2). Staff managers: they employ their expertise to assist line managers in the production process (i.e., personnel managers look for the best labour force). (3). Functional managers: among these are finance managers, accountants, marketing managers, production managers, personnel managers, sales managers, etc. Managers, in order to enhance productivity and quality, have to make sure that each employee is able to use available resources in the most efficient and effective manner.

Regarding what the roles of productivity and quality managers actually are, Schermerhorn et al (1988) suggested that "Managers are in a position to directly influence the productivity of individuals and groups under their supervison. They are also in a position to help to integrate these

1324

performance contributions to facilitate high productivity for the organization as a whole. A major part of every manager's job, therefore, is to establish and maintain the conditions for productivity. High productivity, in turn, requires more than appropriate technology and skilled workers. It requires their creative and successful combination into a well-functioning total performance system. High-performing individuals and groups are the foundations of organizational productivity. Facilitating individual and group performance, accordingly, is the ultimate test of managerial competence." The manager must therefore be interested in nurturing employees and fostering job satisfaction to reduce absenteeism and high job turnover.

3. PRODUCING EFFECTIVE PRODUCTIVITY AND QUALITY MANAGERS

In training American business managers for productivity and quality management, it is necessary to educate them to learn to effectively use and carefully control the management process (i.e., planning, organizing, leading and controlling resource use- the four major categories of management functions).

In the education process, emphasis must be placed on the acquisition of proper and productive skills. From management perspective, the required skills for effective management include (a) Technical Skills: ability to utilize expertise to effect goals, (b) Human Skills: ability to work in cooperation with others (i.e., human relations skills), and (c) Conceptual Skills: ability to identify problems and opportunities to be able to analytically solve these problems and/or take advantage of these opportunities.

In the case of technical skills, it is necessary that both business and engineering schools provide an integrated education necessary for equipping prospective productivity and quality managers. In a sense, a mutual relationship between both business and engineering institutions on one side and businesses on the other must be able to provide the required environment within which this new generation of managers would learn about the technical aspects of productivity and quality management. By so doing, the new breed of productivity and quality managers would learn to combine technical, engineering and managerial expertise to foster the company's global competitiveness. While in training, the emphasis must not only be placed on the acquisition of technical skills alone, but also on how to utilize these skills to achieve productivity and quality goals. For example, students must not only learn about marketing techniques, accounting processes, manufacturing procedures, designs, etc., but also be assisted in learning to apply the acquired managerial and technical expertise in a more productive way.

The Japanese have been very successful at this. Although they try to achieve this goal (i.e., the ability to apply technical skills) through business and engineering schools, they also provide appropriate job environments for their employees to enable them to acquire relevant skills by going through different functional areas of the business and spending part of their life-time working years in each of these functional areas. While doing this, employees are able to obtain first hand information and learn to apply it effectively. While engineering students must be provided with the opportunity to develop skills for managing, communicating, organizing, etc., business students must also learn to understand technical and/or engineering processes. An educational provision that facilitates the attainment of this goal will help develop productivity and quality managers for American businesses.

Similarly, it can hardly be denied that successful business activities and global competitiveness require managers with intense and effective conceptual skills. These skills can easily be provided through formally instituted integrated business and engineering education. In doing so, it is necessary for business and engineering schools to identify the manufacturing needs and the expectations of production managers. In trying to produce effective future productivity and quality managers, practical education cannot be neglected. Practical education here refers to the ability of these institutions to make it possible for their trainees to make frequent visits to production spots (i.e., the factories) and have first hand information and/or knowledge about what the needs and problems of businesses are. As they visit production sites, they must be made to know (or told) the existing current (practical?) problems being faced at the design and the manufacturing point. When this becomes a perpetual and integral part of the training process, prospective (future?) productivity and quality managers may gradually learn to develop the necessary conceptual skills required for effective productivity and quality management.

Although case studies may be helpful, they are not the best way for helping students to develop conceptual skills because in many cases, case studies deal with issues that have already been resolved. They are just studied posthumously! By telling students about how such problems were resolved does not necessarily assist them to develop the necessary conceptual skills required for effective and efficient productivity and quality management. Robinson (1985, p 116) noted that " many case studies dealing with the practical problems of specific organizations are available from a variety of sources, but the use of these does of course restrict trainees of studying situations which are not always easily related to their own problems and indeed may never be repeated elsewhere. There are therefore advantages in using case studies derived from the experiences of the group's own organization, where there is first-hand information about its successes and failures". Practical visits to the factory and learning about actual designing and manufacturing problems and thinking solutions to them would help America to develop effective productivity and quality managers. As times and business problems and needs change, it is necessary that America's traditional educational methods and/or procedures also change to effectively address new demands and needs of society.

One area where business and engineering schools are making meaningful progress is co-operative training education. This type of education probably has more power in accomplishing the practical education process for conceptual skill acquisition than the case study method of business training and/or education. Co-operative training education can be a strong link between classroom education and practical business. In a sense, it is capable of bringing business and engineering schools and businesses together. In both Canada and the United States, many businesses and engineering schools and corporations are engaging in this fruitful education-business co-operation.

Co-op education, as it is usually called, has the potential to aid business and engineering students to develop conceptual skills by providing them with the environment and/or opportunities through which they can obtain practical experience. In this way, co-op students can put theories learnt at school into practice. This is an integrated approach to both business and engineering education. One of the main problems of co-op education is that it does not provide all students with this meaningful experience. Co-op education is, in this sense, very selective. It goes after students who make good grades at school. Unfortunately, the program forgets that other students of average intelligence can also be assisted to develop their potentials for becoming excellent productivity and quality managers in the future. In view of this, it is necessary that co-op education programs be expanded and extended to all students in participating institutions regardless of their academic course grades. Let each student prove himself/herself. We would not be surprised when co-op programs that include all students turn out better productivity and quality managers than those which restrict their programs to "A" average students.

Not only must practical workshops be included in this type of training, but also global dimensions of business. Since we are educating America's future productivity and quality managers for a globally competitive marketplace, their education must also be global in vision. To accomplish this, American business and engineering schools, in addition to cultural, language and international studies, must also include international co-op internships. Such internships must be carefully designed to provide opportunities for each student to work abroad in order to develop global skills and/or experience required for successful management of global business ventures and competition. International co-op and/or practical workshops must form part of the core of business and engineering education in all American schools.

It is necessary for business and engineering schools to be in constant dialogues with men and women in the business environment. Professors of these institutions must be in constant touch with business and engineering firms. It is hoped that this would allow business and engineering professors to decipher what current business needs are. It would not be out of place for businesses to organize seminars in their workshops and/or at factory floors and convey to professors and students what their current industry problems and pressing needs are. Businesses need to communicate their needs to business and engineering schools. Programs can be designed to meet specific needs of both businesses and students. Business and engineering students must be permitted to design their own study programs. This would provide them with opportunities to decide on what they want to do.

Businesses must not only convey to business and engineering schools what their pressing needs and problems are, but also must contribute to the development of business and engineering curricula.

4.1. THE NEW MODEL FOR TRAINING EFFECTIVE MANAGERS

What follows is a proposed extensive educational paradigm which has the potential to turn America's productivity and quality problems around. Leboeuf (1982, p 26 and p 54) suggested that "good managers are made, not born. To increase long term productivity we must change the way we train, evaluate, and reward our managers. Management training needs to place less emphasis on cognitive techniques such as reading and implementing computerized mathematical decision models. A good manager has to be a creative visionary, a sound decision-maker, and - most important- a team-builder who knows how to motivate and lead individuals. These skills that can be taught and improved with practice. Evaluation must take a longer-range focus and managers will have to be rewarded on their contribution to both the long haul and the short run. Every organization needs outstanding leaders to bring out the best people...If there's one lesson we can learn from Japan, it's that productivity improvement begins with people improvement. Once you have a trained, organized, and committed workforce pulling together, productivity takes care of itself." This is the main basis for the integrated education required for productivity and quality management. This kind of integrative education must be purposive. At the onset, those who are involved with this education must have a vision of what graduates produced by the program must be capable of doing and the confidence with which they must do it. The education must equip them to deal effectively with problem issues.

In the integrated training education for effective and efficient productivity and quality management model presented in Figure 1, note the processes for preparing future productivity and quality managers. The actual preparation process goes through seven major levels of transition. As students transition through the first five levels, they are expected to be well-prepared and fully equipped for effective and efficient productivity and quality management. The model suggests that proper preparation must employ a mixture of co-op training education, conferences, workshops, seminars, internships, projects, case studies, incident processes, role playing, sensitivity training, simulation exercises, socratic method of questioning and answering, brainstorming, fieldtrips, etc. This education, training and socialization model is expected to use an effective combination (i.e., mix) of all transforming agents (at level 3). Due to the multifaceted nature of this educational program, this model of education is a problem-solving approach and appeals to all senses and stores of knowledge. By ingeneously balancing management training techniques, each student is expected to develop skills for logical analysis; ability to spot problems and deal with them effectively; developing insights into business, engineering and human relations problems; knowing how to look for

1328

FIGURE 1: INTEGRATIVE EDUCATION FOR EFFECTIVE AND EFFICIENT
PRODUCTIVITY AND QUALITY MANAGEMENT

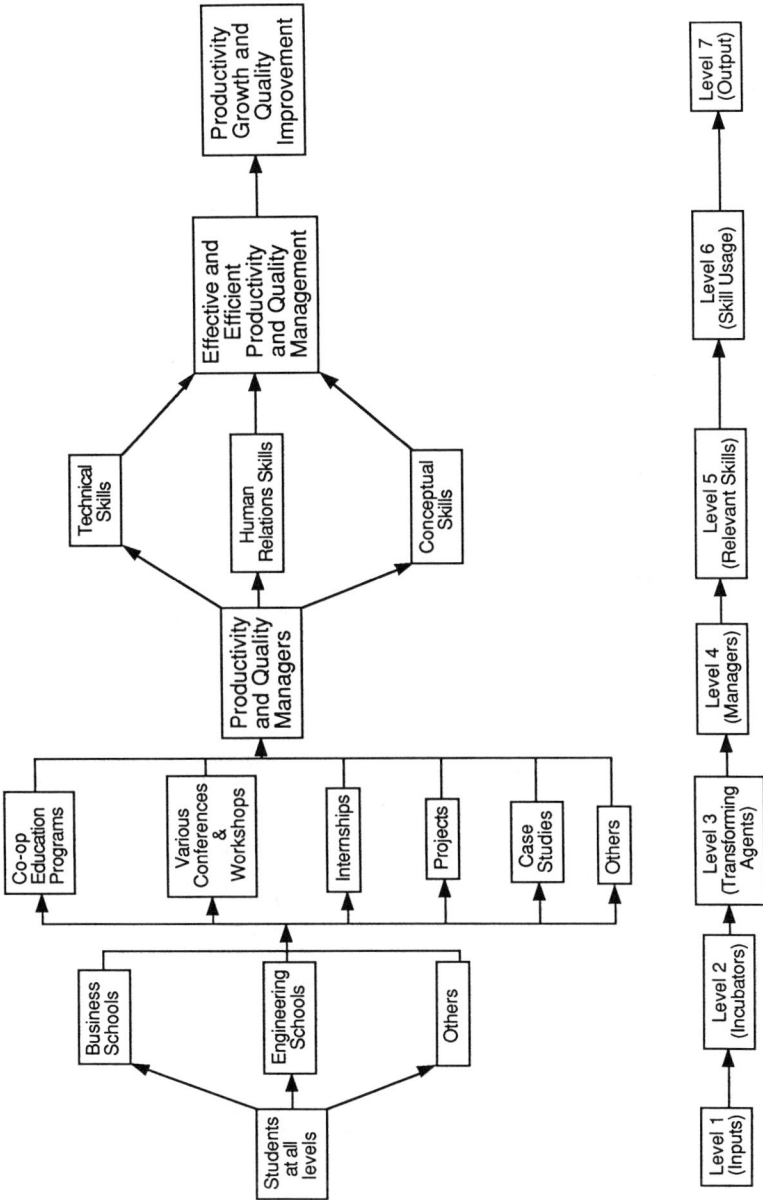

relevant information for problem-solving; develop skills for comprehending management perspectives in terms of the interdependency that exists in all functional areas of the business organization; understanding, communication and interpersonal skills. If students who graduate from the program are unable to draw information and/or knowledge from all subjects studied for solving real life business and engineering problems, then the educational process would have failed.

In both business and engineering schools, the teaching of rigorous quality control techniques in practical terms must always be emphasized. As technologies are contemplated and designed in these institutions, opportunities must be provided for engineering students to have these technologies and techniques tested. In every group setting, opportunities must be frequently provided for each student to learn to role-play in providing leadership to others. As they take turns to do this, each student will acquire leadership qualities required for managing productivity and quality.

By properly combining and effectively using these agents at level 3, major deficiencies would be spotted (and probably dealt with) before each trainee reaches crucial managerial positions. This model is not concerned with fault-finding. It is rather aimed at the discovery of managerial deficiencies in every student trainee. A successful application of the model would educate each trainee in all functional areas of the business organization. By the time each student successfully crosses over level 5, he/she must not only be ready for effective and efficient productivity and quality management, but also must understand the processes of productivity growth and quality improvement for world-class competitiveness.

Figure 2 presents a model for integrated result-inducing examination processes. As at now, traditional examination processes are mainly concerned with regurgitation of facts with very little applications and careful analysis. The model in Figure 2 suggests that in order to effectively educate and produce productivity and quality managers, it is necessary (as noted in Figure 1) to use educational, training and socialization examination techniques which have the capability for assisting students to review their value, belief and ideological systems; develop critical and analytic thinking; develop the ability to apply theories and principles learnt to solving practical problems; and to gain the ability to confidently confront practical business and engineering problems and risks. Examination processes that can help achieve these goals include thorough and intensive oral and written examinations, practical program designing, analytic, intuitive and applications examination questions, practical problem-solving on the factory floor, etc. (see Figure 2).

A successful implementation of these examination techniques has a great potential for producing business chief executive officers who can manage productivity growth, quality improvement, and global competitiveness.

In sum, Integrative education must, therefore, train and equip managers to be able to:

FIGURE 2: AN INTEGRATED RESULT-INDUCING EXAMINATION PROCESSES

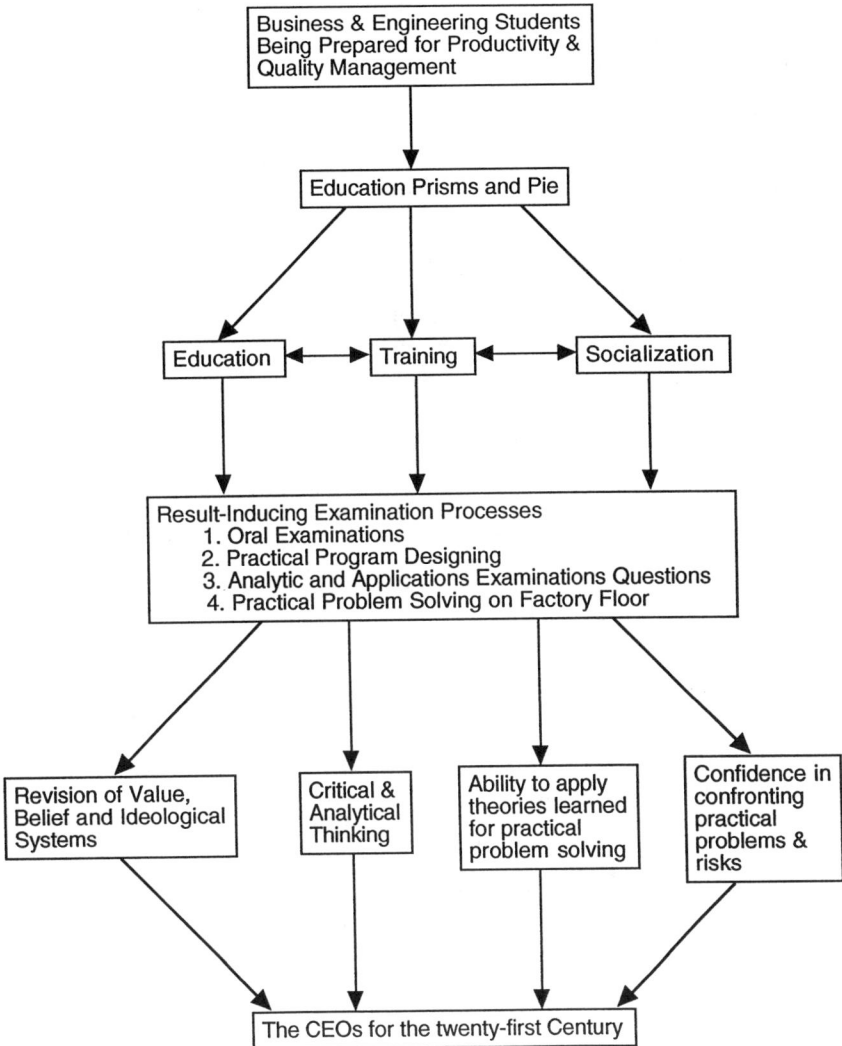

```
┌─────────────────────────────────┐
│ Business & Engineering Students  │
│ Being Prepared for Productivity &│
│ Quality Management               │
└─────────────────────────────────┘
              │
              ▼
      ┌───────────────────────┐
      │ Education Prisms and Pie│
      └───────────────────────┘
```

Business & Engineering Students Being Prepared for Productivity & Quality Management

Education Prisms and Pie

Education ←→ Training ←→ Socialization

Result-Inducing Examination Processes
   1. Oral Examinations
   2. Practical Program Designing
   3. Analytic and Applications Examinations Questions
   4. Practical Problem Solving on Factory Floor

Revision of Value, Belief and Ideological Systems

Critical & Analytical Thinking

Ability to apply theories learned for practical problem solving

Confidence in confronting practical problems & risks

The CEOs for the twenty-first Century

1331

a). analyze and understand existing organizational structure, its effectiveness and weaknesses,

b). to identify any existing problems that affect productivity and quality,

c). perceive existing employee morale, attitudes, feelings, expectations, values and norms, and

d) ingeneously carve out plans and/or suggestions for dealing with any productivity and quality problems in the organization. It is important for future managers of American business to be trained and well-equipped to spot and quickly deal with problematic issues (in their infancies) before they develop into crisis stage. By adopting this attitude of "prevention is better than cure", productivity and quality managers can be adequately prepared in advance in relation to when they may need to use acquired skills.

Although this involves a lot of work, the promises this evaluation model holds for America cannot be compared with the costs of extensive efforts and programs required for its implementation. Truly, from business and economic perspectives, **THERE IS NO SANTA CLAUS!** America must either go through the birthing pains now for future successes in the global marketplace or postpone this viable educational alternative to the traditional model to the detriment of her future productivity and quality management. It is our time and turn to change, **AMERICA!**

4.2. COMMITMENT FOR SUCCESS

The key to the accomplishment of these is commitment. When businesses, business and engineering schools give themselves to the educational approach put forward in this paper, productive and encouraging results will be attained. The role of integrative productivity and quality education in business and engineering schools is of a crucial importance in preparation for increased productivity and quality enhancement. When American managers are educated to learn to be passionately committed to goals, ideologies and values underlying effective management, the war against declining productivity and quality will be won because ideologies and values help managers to develop organized patterns of thought and analysis. Ideologies and values help prepapre managers for steadfastness, dedication and sacrifice in order to achieve productivity and quality enhancement goals. As noted by Rogow and Lasswell (1963) and reiterated by McFarland (1982), an ideology helps to solve problems by intellectually stimulating the individual in many different ways.

American businesses need people who have the qualities to lead the workforce into the productivity and quality revolution in the twenty-first century. Since values are not only useful, but also are developed over a long period of time, formal business and engineering education in American schools must be able to train and educate men and women properly for this job. If these issues are left to time and chance, we may be disappointed in the long run. It is an undeniable fact that managers who are committed to productivity and quality improvement must have to be men and women of character and commitment to company ideals and values.

We need to train and educate management personnel who are not only married to jobs and/or positions, but also be adaptable and committed to duty as is usually the case in Japan. These individuals must be nurtured to learn to offer total commitment to productivity and quality management in the company for effective results. Managers must be committed to character and personality development. It is necessary that business and engineering schools produce men and women who do not only have skills required by business, but must also have characteristics that are necessary for perpetual productivity growth and quality enhancement. Armed with such men and women at the forefront of American business, improvement in productivity and quality would be easily accomplished. The pressure to produce men and women of high calibre rests heavily on these institutions. American managers must be men and women who must be committed to strong moral and ethical value systems. These value systems must be demonstrated practically in their dealings with subordinates, superiors and customers. Managing for productivity and quality requires character and personality; ability to use knowledge and/or information; ambition and commitment, steadfastness and single-mindedness; dedication and sacrifice.

5. SUMMARY AND CONCLUSIONS

We, educators, need to realize that the world is changing moment by moment. The implication is that ideas, theories, principles, etc. that worked a few years ago may not necessarily be applicable to the present era. In view of this, it is necessary that the contents of American business and engineering schools curricula must change moment by moment to be relevant and also to enhance effectiveness in preparing people to adequately face the challenges of the current time period. If America fails to do so, she may produce educated elites who will be equipped to solve the problems of yesterday and yet, unfortunately, be incapable of dealing with those of the present and future times.

ACKNOWLEDGEMENT

I am thankful to Ms. Cynthia Macleans for her constructive suggestions for improvement after having read the first draft.

REFERENCES

Bond, N. A., Jr. (1981) "A Letter to the Editor." Wall Street Journal, March 10, 1981, p 23 (also quoted in Schermerhorn et al (1988, p 17).

LeBoeuf, M. (1982) The Productivity Challenge: How to Make it Work for America and You, New York, McGraw-Hill Book Company.

McFarland, D. E. (1982) Management and Society: An Institutional Framework, Englewood Cliffs, Prentice-Hall.

Robinson, R. K. (1985) A Handbook of Training Management, London, Kogan Page, pp 96-151.

Rogow, A. A. and Lasswell, H. D. (1963) Power, Corruption, and

Rectitude, Englewood Cliffs, Prentice-Hall.

Schermerhorn, J. R., Jr., Cattaneo, R. J. and Smith, R. E. (1988) Management for Productivity, Toronto, John Wiley & Sons, pp 5-30.

BIOGRAPHICAL SKETCH OF AUTHOR
Senyo Adjibolosoo is an associate professor of Business and Economics at Trinity Western University, where his research interests include Heteroskedasticity Pretest Estimation, Global Competitiveness, Pre-Classical Economic Analysis, Human Factor Engineering and Technology Transfer in Economic Development.

Productivity & Quality Management Frontiers-IV, edited by Sumanth, Edosomwan, Poupart, and Sink. ©1993 Institute of Industrial Engineers.

Developing the Joint MBA/MSE Program Capstone Course

R.M. Haynes, E.C. Keller, R. Pouraghabagher, and D. White
California Polytechnic State University
San Luis Obispo, California USA

ABSTRACT

This year, faculty from the Schools of Business and Engineering are completing work on the "learn-by-doing" component of the MBA/MS in Engineering program. This final segment will integrate academic concepts from business and engineering with real-world problems and opportunities. Teams of students will address specific industry problems based on projects identified during their prior summer internships.

The focus of these projects has been the consideration of productivity and quality issues within the context of sustainable competitive advantage in a global marketplace. The capstone course is the final, comprehensive exercise following 18 months of classroom instruction and a 3-month industry internship for each student enrolled in the Engineering Management Program (EMP).

An executive seminar format will be used with classes held on Thursday, Friday and Saturday for a total of 12 class/seminar sessions. Each three-day seminar will feature one of the four current themes selected. The presentation concept is to have academic perspectives from both business and engineering faculty followed by several "integration" sessions presented by industry executives. Each seminar day will end with either a workshop or panel discussion involving all presenters and attendees. The class has been designated as a Graduate School of Business (GSB) experimental course, GSB 559x. The title of the class will be "Sustaining Global Competitive Advantage" with each of the four seminar themes designed to be boundary-spanning in nature. The design is to focus the students on integration and macro-concepts rather than individual, limited subject areas.

The team-structured lectures will provide equal attention to both manufacturing and service components of the deliverable package. The student projects must cover all operational facets including the production and service necessary to bring a deliverable to market in an international business framework.

F4: Integrative productivity and quality management education in business and engineering schools.

INTRODUCTION

The establishment of a demand-driven MBA/MS in Engineering Program is a result of a grass-roots effort initiated by faculty from the Schools of Business and Engineering. The first ten graduates will complete requirements in August 1992. Several have already accepted positions and the others are actively considering offers. One of the metrics established for a successful program was the quantity and quality of job offers to graduates and at this writing, the Engineering Management Program (EMP) appears to be meeting the goals. Given the current state of the economy, placement of all graduates is considered an excellent indicator of the program's success.

While the culminating course is the primary focus of this paper, an understanding of the environmental setting is critical to seeing how the course integrates many of the facets of both the University and the Engineering Management Program.

Program History

The EMP accepted the first class in Fall 1990 after two years of planning and today has 25 students enrolled. The filter for incoming students has been to consider only engineering or other technical degrees, such as physics, as acceptable undergraduate credentials. As the program evolves, the plan is to place additional criteria on admittance including some years of work experience. Students who successfully complete the 24-month program earn both an MBA and MS Engineering degree with a specialization in Engineering Management. The program focus is strongly aligned with the University's "learn-by-doing" emphasis. And in addition to six quarters of coursework, EMP students take part in a structured Graduate Internship Program during their first summer quarter. Industry-driven projects are assigned for the second year on a team basis and finally, a capstone, culminating class is taken during the final summer quarter. Throughout the program, students have the opportunity to work in teams consisting of other students, faculty from both Schools and industry Partners. The integration of academic approaches from the Schools of Business and Engineering, exposure to other experienced students and direct involvement with industry participants gives the EMP a unique, integrative perspective.

The University

California Polytechnic State University is one of the 20 campuses of the California State University System (CSU). The CSU serves nearly 350,000 students and in the United States is second in size only to the State University of New York System which has 23 campuses. Today, the 3500 U.S. universities are the envy of the world and in the past year were flooded with more than 400,000 foreign students representing 193 countries (Elson 1992 and Smolowe 1992).

Cal Poly was established in 1901 and continues to offer a "polytechnic" approach to education. Seven schools have a student body of approximately 18,000 students. The Engineering School has gained worldwide attention for innovative research in man-powered helicopters, human-powered submarines, solar-powered cars and other areas including transportation management and fiber-optics research. The School of Business was formed in 1960 and offers concentrations in business administration, management, accounting and economics. All programs are accredited by the AACSB. Cal Poly graduates from both Business and Engineering are highly recruited and over the past five years, starting salaries have averaged nearly 20% more than the national averages as reported by the College Placement Council in their annual survey of 418 universities. In fact, Cal Poly has a long-time tradition of providing the industry customer a high-quality "product" and graduates are distinctive and highly valued in the corporate marketplace. However, the external environment continues to offer opportunities for creative programs in the pursuit of excellence in higher education (Smolowe 1992).

THE CHALLENGE FOR EDUCATION

Education in this decade is at a crossroads relative to direction. The U.S. media barrages the public with statistical data on how poorly K-12 students are performing. College graduates are finding the job market the worst in 30 years. Research universities such as Stanford and the University of California system are rocked with scandals on how funds had been mis-used, resignations and re-structuring are rampant. Virtually every American institution of higher learning is facing severe budget cuts, these are particularly ominous in state schools depending on legislative funding for survival. Quality in the educational process appears to be highly suspect (Elson 1992). Industry has continued to prod the higher education system and tell what is needed (Akers, et al 1991). Academics have responded with a list of reciprocal needs from industry (Hayes and Singhal 1992). Faculty are often blamed for the declining quality (Sykes 1990) but the nay-sayers offer little in the way of constructive suggestions. Meanwhile, some schools are pursuing quality oriented programs. Spanbauer (1992) documents the positive results of a total quality management (TQM) program undertaken at one community college. Seymour (1992) offers a recipe book for higher edcuation TQM programs. The quality issue in higher edcuation is receiving increased focus in the literature relative to assesment (Seymour and Collett 1991) and reports of success stories (Stratton 1991). In many instances this attention to quality practices is coincident with what is taking place in industry itself (Shepard 1991). The Baldrige Quality Award has made the public aware of quality management issues in business. At the very root of quality is the need to continuously focus on the customer. Many universities are taking this customer orientation seriously and offering new and exciting programs. The list grows each day but the general direction taken appears to be a realization that universities must consider both a student customer and industry customer perspective and involve both constituencies in the education process. Notable highlights include the Leaders for Manufacturing program at MIT, the MBA-quality concentration at The University of Chicago, the executive-MBA orientation at the University of Tennessee and the Engineering Management Program at Cal Poly in California. Most of these programs share common values in that industry partners have contributed to their development with both time and funding. The tendency is to share results of many of the innovative programs in conference presentations (Calista 1991 and Haynes 1991) and universities are increasingly paying attention to the quality steps that can be taken by all. Higher education in the United States is a $100 million business. No other nation matches the system that has 156 universities, 1953 four-year colleges and 1378 two-year colleges and technical schools (Elson 1992). Collectively they employ nearly 800,000 faculty and accomodate more than 14 million students. However, there is general concensus that the higher education must get better.

"By the Year 2000, American colleges and universities will be lean and mean, service oriented and science minded, multicultural and increasingly diverse--if they intend to survive their fiscal agony." Elson (1992).

The common method to accomplish this goal is to pay increased attention to quality issues and infuse total quality management (TQM) throughout the systems.

Considering that TQM requires continuous process improvement, the faculty involved with Cal Poly's EMP graduate courses decided to get industry partners and student customers committed to the design and development of the culminating class that would provide the springboard for students making the transition from graduate school to the real world.

THE CAPSTONE COURSE: GSB 559X

From the beginning the focus of the course was on integration from the perspective of prior courses taken in both business and engineering disciplines and consideration of the business environment that would be facing graduates. Course design began with student polls to identify what would be useful in terms of coverage. At the same time, Andersen Consulting became an unofficial part of the faculty task force and functioned as an consultant and event facilitator.

Evolution

Six companies were chosen from a list of about 100 corporations that regularly recruited at Cal Poly for both business and engineering graduates. These six companies were involved in several rounds of friendly focus sessions that were used to identify what the "industry customer" needed from the school. Based on these various inputs, the culminating course was designed over a six-month period. It should be noted that the friendly group included electronics, public utilities, computer manufacturing, software engineering, aerospace and government industries and many of the meetings were facilitated by a management consulting company.

One key factor was the early realization that a course taught by the equivalent of three full-time faculty to 10 students would not generate sufficient student-hours to fund the faculty time. Once again, we turned to the industry customers and devised a program wherein they could become funding "partners" in the EMP that would provide the resources to enable the faculty involvement in the program.

Structure

From the outset, the course was conceived as being not only an academic class but potentially offering industry an opportunity to present topics and participate in the panel discussions and workshops to be included. The only constraint was that the course must fit within an established summer quarter of 10 weeks. Initial plans for a series of nine short seminars was distilled over the planning cycle into a final product which will feature four, three-day seminars to be held every other week. After several iterations, the structure of the summer "seminar" course was developed and is presented in Figure 1.

Figure 1

SUMMER SEMINAR STRUCTURE

THURSDAY:	Keynote speaker(s) from industry	1:00-3:00 p.m.
	Panel discussion/workshop/social	3:00-6:00 p.m.
FRIDAY:	Business/Engineering/Industry presentations	a.m.
	Business/Engineering/Industry presentations	p.m.
	Panel/workshop	4:00-5:00 p.m.
SATURDAY:	Two Industry Application Success Stories	a.m.
	(One service and one manufacturing)	
	Panel/workshop	1:00-3:00 p.m.

The game plan is to offer presentations from an engineering perspective and a business perspective followed by an industry speaker that can provide an integration of the two academic viewpoints. Ideally, the industry speaker will show

1339

how elements from each area need to be coordinated into an actual implementation or application plan in the real world. Somewhat concurrently, the themes and topics of each seminar were also developed with the direct involvement of both students and industry partners. These have taken on a strategic focus with boundary spanning topics designed to incorporate the lastest in academic thought plus the reality of the environment in the global economy. The title of the summer seminar series is now "Sustaining Global Competitive Advantage" and features the four themes and 20 topic areas identified in Figure 2. Dates are shown to document how the course will actually take place during the summer of 1992.

Figure 2

SUSTAINING GLOBAL COMPETITIVE ADVANTAGE

July 9-11: TIME TO MARKET PROFITABILITY (Topics: concurrent engineering; criticality of time-to-market; cycle time management; fast response organization; quality function deployment)

July 23-25: CULTURAL TRANSFORMATIONS (Topics: breakthrough thinking; cultural diversity; empowerment; recognition & rewards; team-based organization)

August 6-8: MANAGING CRITICAL TECHNOLOGIES (Topics: benchmarking; competitive intelligence; high technology startups; market redefinitions; new technology strategy)

August 20-22: WORLD CLASS ORGANIZATIONS-YEAR 2000+ (Topics: business metrics; continuous improvement; customer driven; high performance teams; vision-proactive vs. reactive)

The concept of the jointly taught seminar segments is to provide both the industry and student customer insight into state-of-the- art topics from several perspectives. The design and development of the program and the culminating course has been considered a model for serving the university customer(s) in the future and as such is completely in line with what is being done throughout the higher education community (Elson 1992).

Status
     The GSB 559X course will be taught for the first time in the summer of 1992. The "x" designation stands for experimental and allows a new course to be introduced in somewhat of an exploratory mode with respect to content and structure. There are 10 EMP students registered for this course and several MBA and MS Engineering students have registered for independent study courses that will feature specific segments of GSB 559x as part of their lesson plan.
     There are currently ten EMP Industry Partners that have

helped to design the initial course offerings for Summer 1992. These include Andersen Consulting, Hewlett-Packard, Intel, Pacific Bell, Pacific Gas & Electric Company, Santa Barbara Research Center, Southern California Edison, Sun Microsystems, Tandem Computers and the U.S. Navy.

As is apparent, this group represents a broad base of manufacturing, service, and government industries generally focused in high technology systems. For instance, Pacific Gas & Electric is represented by the Nuclear Power Generation Group that operates the Diablo Canyon Reactor.

Each Partner has joined the program because of their desire to be involved in the education process and exposure to leading edge ideas from both academia and other Partners. They offer varying perspectives based on their own industry orientations that are useful in providing flexibility in the curriculum for the summer seminars and the ongoing evolution of the EMP classes.

CONCLUSION

This paper offers a limited perspective on a specialized graduate course that is part of a ongoing graduate studies program. The uniqueness of the summer course is based on the concept of team teaching using business and engineering faculty plus industry experts as the delivery mechanism. Additional differentiation is that the forum for delivery will be an executive seminar setting with both graduate students and industry attendees in the audience. However, from a conceptual point of view, this course embodies many of the principles that are becoming increasingly more associated with TQM in education, particularly the direct involvement of the customer in design and development of the "product" to be delivered. The goal is to deliver high quality, well-rounded graduates who are facilitators of change and integrators of engineering, business and people functional areas regardless of the industry they choose for a career.

BIBLIOGRAPHIC REFERENCES

Akers, J.F., Allaire, P.A., Artz, E.L., Galvin, R.W., Poling, H.A. and Robinson, J.D. III, (1991) "An open letter: TQM on campus", Harvard Business Review, November/December, pp. 94-95.

Calista, D.J. (Editor) (1991) "Total Quality Management Symposium-Special Section", Journal of Management Science & Policy Analysis, vol. 8, nos. 3&4, pp. 195-284.

Elson, J. (1992) "Campus of the future", Time, April 13, pp. 54-58.

Hayes, R. and Singhal, K. (1992) "An open response to `TQM on the campus': We need TQM...and more" Production and Operations Management, vol. 1, no. 1, pp. 124-125.

Haynes, R.M. (Editor) (1991) Management of Quality Conference, San Luis Obispo, California, Cal Poly School of Business Publication.

Seymour, D.T. (1992) On Q--Causing Quality in Higher Education, New York, MacMillan Publishing.

Seymour, D.T. and Collett, C. (1991) "Total quality management in higher education: A critical assessment", Goal/QPC, pp. 1-18.

Shepard, S.B. (1991) "Defining the Q-word", Business Week, October, pp. 4 [1991 Bonus Issue: The Quality Imperative].

Smolowe, J. (1992) "The pursuit of excellence", Time, April 13, pp. 59-60.

Spanbauer, S.J. (1992) A Quality System for Education, Milwaukee, ASQC Quality Press.

Stratton, B. (Editor) (1991) "Quality in education-Special Section", Quality Progress, October, pp. 34-74.

Sykes, C.J. (1990) Profscam: Professors and the Demise of Higher Education, New York, St. Martin's Press.

BIOGRAPHICAL SKETCHES OF AUTHORS

Ray Haynes is an Associate Professor of Management. He has 20 years industry experience and extensive consulting background in TQM and technology areas. He is currently Associate Director of the Cal Poly CIM Center.

Earl Keller is a Professor of Accounting. He has many years industry experience in telecommunications and accounting. He is currently Head of the Accounting Department and Director of Graduate Programs for the School of Business.

Reza Pouraghabagher is a Professor of Industrial Engineering. He has extensive consulting experience in the areas of JIT and continuous improvement. He is the Advisor for APICS at Cal Poly.

Don White is an Associate Professor of Industrial Engineering and has many years of industry experience in energy and tele-communications. He is the Coordinator for the Engineering Management Program for the School of Engineering.

This EMP Task Force has raised over $100,000 during 1991-92.

Productivity & Quality Management Frontiers-IV, edited by Sumanth, Edosomwan, Poupart, and Sink. ©1993 Institute of Industrial Engineers.

Public Policies and Schemes in Quality-Related Activities in France and the United Kingdom

B.G. Barker
PREST, The University
Manchester, England UNITED KINGDOM

J.-J. Chanaron
University of Grenoble, CNRS-IREP-D
Grenoble, FRANCE

ABSTRACT

This paper examines public policies and schemes introduced in France and the United Kingdom in order to improve quality. First we examine the relationship between quality and competitive performance and the reasons why governments become involved in quality promotion. Next we investigate the role played by private and public organisations in placing quality and, more recently, Total Quality Management (TQM) on the political agenda in both countries. We then examine the role played by these organisations in the definition and implementation of the various public sector schemes and initiatives dealing with quality promotion, consultancy, education and training, awareness etc. These schemes and initiatives are examined in terms of their objectives, activities and outcomes. Finally, likely future developments in the two countries are discussed. This paper is based on some of the results of a study to review in European Community member states national and regional schemes and measures in the field of quality. This study was supported by DG XIII of the Commission of the European Communities within its SPRINT (Strategic Programme for Innovation and Technology Transfer) initiative.

Key Words: Quality Management, Public Policy, Standards, France, UK.

INTRODUCTION

This paper examines public policies and schemes introduced in France and the United Kingdom in order to improve quality. First we examine the relationship between quality and competitive performance and the reasons why governments become involved in quality promotion. Next we investigate the role played by private and public organisations in placing quality and, more recently, Total Quality Management (TQM) on the political agenda in both countries. We then examine the role played by these organisations in the definition and implementation of the various public sector schemes and initiatives dealing with quality promotion, consultancy, education and training, awareness etc. These schemes and initiatives are examined in terms of their objectives, activities and outcomes. Finally, likely future developments in the two countries are discussed.

Quality and Competitive Performance

Ultimately, the performance of any economy depends on the success with which its individual firms produce products and services that are more competitive than those of their international competitors. High quality has long been recognised as an important element in achieving this competitive success. In an increasingly competitive world the existing quality management approach of many firms is no longer sufficient to guarantee quality that is superior to that of their competitors. To remain competitive these firms need to adopt a system of quality management that better ensures that the performance of their products or services satisfies and continues to satisfy customer requirements. These requirements do not remain static - as new products come onto the market and as fashions change, they develop over time. In order to survive and prosper, firms need to position their products or services so that they consistently fall within the boundaries of these developing requirements. Recognition that quality is not a static concept, but rather a dynamic one, involving a process of continuous improvement represents a paradigm shift - first understood by a number of Japanese companies and most clearly articulated in Total Quality Management (TQM). (Lascelles and Dale, 1988) Attempting to match the success of these companies an increasing number of organisations in the West have adopted approaches based on the TQM concept.

Government Promotion of Quality

Unassisted market forces cannot be relied upon to ensure that best practice quality-management will effectively diffuse throughout the economy. Government intervention may be justified in order to promote this diffusion. Such intervention may also occur in support of more strategic aims. (Stoneman and Vickers, 1988) Historically, European countries have shown significant national differences in their approach to quality policy formulation and implementation. To a large extent this reflects different national traditions in the relationship between government and industry. In some countries state involvement in industry is seen as a major part of a process of strategic planning. Essentially this characterises the situation in France. In other countries industrial policy is seen as part of a general economic policy, aiming to create a favourable climate for industrial development. Within Europe, the UK most clearly articulates this policy. Throughout the 1980s and thus far into the 1990s, UK public policy has been essentially hands-off in nature, being directed towards creating an environment conducive to industrial development. (Rothwell and Dodgson, 1991)

Governments typically promote quality through a range of schemes and initiatives. Quality promotion can be defined as the set of policies involving government intervention in the economy with the **intent** of improving the quality of firms' products and services. These range from the 'direct' promotion of quality, quality management guidelines (including standards) and training schemes to more general training, financial incentives and innovation promotion schemes that may include a significant quality element. Thus, many areas of government policy can have an influence on quality improvement. In general terms however, quality promotion activities can be characterised in terms of those which support research; those promoting awareness; those designed to increase the rate of adoption through the use of subsidies; those supporting education and training; and, those which attempt to improve quality through public procurement practices. (Stoneman and Vickers, 1988)

It should be noted that although the primary focus of the our survey has been the public sector we recognise the significant role played by private organisations (particularly large firms) in shaping the quality 'environment'. Furthermore, industrial and professional associations are actively involved in quality promotion schemes complementing public sector activities in both countries.

QUALITY PROMOTION IN FRANCE AND THE UK

In this section we look at the emergence of quality as an issue in France and the UK, how this has been reflected in the quality supporting infrastructure that has evolved in the two countries and how this has, in turn, shaped current quality promotion schemes and initiatives.

The United Kingdom
The UK Government has long been active in quality issues related to defence procurement, but only recently has its attention been drawn to the importance of quality in industry generally. In the late 1960s, the Government appointed two committees. One, under Colonel Raby, examined quality in the military domain, the other, under Sir Eric Mensforth, recommended measures for wider civilian applications. The Raby report of 1969, although unpublished, had a significant effect on the development of quality assurance in the public sector. In particular, the purchasing and quality systems in the Ministry of Defence (MOD) were reorganised as responsibility for quality was transferred from the MOD to its suppliers. The Mensforth report, published in 1970, expressed concern about national arrangements for the attainment of quality in the engineering industries, but had relatively little impact.

In the mid-1970s, the Government launched an Industrial Strategy with the aim of transforming the United Kingdom into a high output/high wage economy by improving the industrial performance and productive potential of manufacturing industry. In 1977, Sir Frederick Warner, under the aegis of the National Economic Development Organisation (NEDO), produced a paper 'The Role of Standards in the Industrial Strategy'. Warner argued that the development and use of standards was potentially a major contributory factor to the competitiveness of British products particularly in relation to their quality and reliability. He went on to argue for a widely accepted third party-certified standard for quality. The idea for a quality standard dated from the 1950s when procurement bodies devised standards of manufacture and products. During the 1960s, quality schemes evolved for particular sectors, operated by such organisations as the Central Electricity Generating Board, the National Coal Board and the Post Office. The emphasis, however, was still on inspection, and the direct cost of the schemes was borne by the purchaser. In the late 1970s, after studies of Japanese methods of quality control and following the success of retailers such as Marks and Spencers in requiring suppliers to introduce quality systems, the British Standards Institution (BSI) produced its standard for quality systems - BS 5750 (first published in 1979). In 1982, the Government published the White Paper, 'Standards, Quality and International Competitiveness'. The Paper promoted the concept that quality management systems should be installed to a recognised international standard and assessed by an impartial external body. A National Accreditation Council for Certification Bodies (NACCB) was subsequently established. The Paper also provided for a closer and more formal relationship between the government and the BSI - in particular, the Government agreed to make more reference to BSI standards, rather than drawing up its own. Finally, the Paper announced support for a National Quality Campaign.

The concept of such a campaign had originated in 1978 with a meeting of industrialists and government representatives organised by the Institute of Quality Assurance. Subsequently, a consultative document ('A National Strategy for Quality') was circulated by the then Department of Prices and Consumer Protection (1978). The report estimated that the cost to British industry of not adopting a quality approach, in terms of unnecessary extra work and replacement due to faults was some £10 billion, or 10 per cent of GDP. The report called for a national quality strategy having three priorities: the promotion of awareness of quality in meeting market needs; support for the implementation and assessment of modern quality management systems; and, support for national arrangements for the specification, testing and certification of goods to meet overseas market needs. This early initiative for a national quality strategy was lost with the change of government following the 1979 General Election.

In 1983, the then Department of Industry (DoI) announced the launch of its National Quality Campaign. The Campaign led to the creation of a wide variety of promotional literature and videos and the establishment of a National Quality Information Centre. Financial assistance was made available to firms. An essential part of the Campaign were efforts by the DoI to encourage the establishment of a structure to support quality achievement, and make companies better able to demonstrate this to their customers. Registers of quality assessed UK companies and of lead assessors were prepared and a Directory of Quality Assurance Education and Training was published. In addition, a British Quality Awards Scheme was created. In 1988, the National Quality Campaign was incorporated within the new Department of Trade and Industry's (DTI) 'Enterprise Initiative'.

The Enterprise Initiative is primarily concerned with spreading best practice management methods in small and medium sized enterprises (SMEs) in England and Wales (similar schemes have been introduced in Scotland and Northern Ireland). It has two main elements: awareness and consultancy help. The 'Managing into the 1990s' programme provides practical information and advice on the management of design, quality, purchasing and production. Having a budget of about £3 million per year, it offers a range of events backed up by written and audio/visual material. These include: a Strategy Roadshow - a free half day presentation which identifies factors including quality that will help improve companies' competitive performance; 'Inside UK Enterprise' - visits to companies employing best practice in a wide range of areas; workshops and seminars on TQM; and, a booklet 'Total Quality Management and Effective Leadership'.

The main focus of the Enterprise Initiative, however, is the provision of subsidized consultancy services. The aim of is to help companies identify and resolve barriers to their competitive performance. Consultancies cover the following topics: marketing; design; quality; advanced manufacturing; business planning; and management of financial and information systems. Under each initiative a maximum of 15 days of assisted consultancy is allowed for each assignment. A 50 per cent subsidy (rising to 66 per cent in regionally assisted areas) is provided toward the cost of the consultancy package. To date, the DTI has received about 100,000 applications for consultancy help. Total public expenditure is running at between £55-60 million per year. Of the six areas within the Initiative, most applications have been received for help with marketing (38%), and quality (21%). The Quality Consultancy offers expert advice on the introduction of better or more appropriate quality management systems and procedures. Since June 1989, the scheme has included support for the development of TQM, providing assistance with the introduction and implementation of a strategy for company-wide quality improvement. This can include an analysis of company culture and advice on motivational and management techniques designed to enable the company to effectively introduce TQM. Advice on TQM is not widely taken up, however. Certification to BS 5750 or equivalent standards is the primary purpose for consultancy in 85 per cent of cases; TQM is the primary purpose in only about 2 per cent. Most of the rest are requested by companies seeking to satisfy specific customer requirements. (Segal, Quince, Wickstead, 1989, 1991)

The Department of Employment through its Training Enterprise and Education Directorate (TEED), and the Training and Enterprise Councils (TECs) provide companies with help and advice on training. This includes information on courses and seminars (both full- and part-time) available locally and nationally on quality management. The Department of Employment Investors in People (IIP) initiative is designed to encourage firms to develop and train their employees to produce a highly skilled and motivated workforce. The initiative has been developed by the National Training Task Force working with local Training and Enterprise Councils (TECs), the Confederation of British Industry (CBI), and other business and training organisations. The focus of the initiative is the Investor in People Standard designed to assist companies achieve higher standards of quality and productivity.

A number of non-Government bodies play a significant role in quality promotion in the UK. Perhaps the most important is the Institute of Quality Assurance (IQA). The IQA played a leading role in the National Quality Campaign. The British Quality Awards scheme was launched in 1984 to give impetus to the government's initiatives arising from the 1982 White Paper. The intention was to create a national award which would encourage the adoption of TQM. Since its inception, 22 companies have won the award. In addition, the IQA runs an extensive training programme and prepares syllabuses for the institute's qualifying examinations. The Institute maintains a Directory of Quality Assurance Education and Training Facilities in the UK for the DTI. IQA recognised assessor training courses are run at Cranfield Institute, Sheffield and Portsmouth Polytechnics. Additional requirements have arisen from the application of quality management systems to the IT sector. Working with the British Computer Society and DTI, the institute has agreed plans to validate certification auditors in this sector.

The role of the universities and polytechnics in quality-related activities is widespread, but only a few institutions play any significant part. Most education and training takes place within HE/FE colleges and some in business schools and university departments of management education. Many of these courses are technician- rather than management-oriented. Most comprehensive educational work is done at postgraduate or post-experience level. At post graduate level two approaches are discernable. First, specialist technological universities, which teach quality management in the context of their expertise in particular sectors of industry. Second, business schools teach elements of quality management as a subset of general management programmes. In general, the business schools tend to stress the motivational and organisational aspects of the subject, whereas the technology-based schools tend to relate the subject more to manufacturing processes and systems and manufacturing management. (Rogerson, 1991)

France

From the beginning of the 1970s, the French government began to express concern about the key role of product quality in competitiveness and became aware of the necessity of public involvement in the definition of a national policy towards quality. In 1975 a Directorate for Quality of Industrial Products and Normalisation (SQUALPI - Sous-Direction de la Qualite pour L'Industrie et de la Normalisation) was set up within the Ministry of Industry (now the Ministry of Industry and International Trade - MICE). A report by the AFQ (Association Francaise des Qualiticiens) on "the cost of nonquality in industrial and commercial SMEs" was published in 1983 on behalf of the MICE. From a survey of 130 SMEs, it was estimated that the cost of product nonquality was FFRbn 150 in manufacturing and building and FFRbn 270 over the economy as a whole. This nonquality cost was 4.2 per cent of turnover and 9.7 per cent of total added value. In 1986, these estimates were revised to 5 to 15% of turnover or 15 to 40% of added value.

In 1983 the French national standards authority (AFNOR) published the French quality standards, NF 109-110-111-112. A National Committee for Maintenance was set up in 1986 and the MICE decided to support several bodies: National Laboratory for Tests (LNE); French Association for Quality Certification (Association Francaise pour l'Assurance Qualite - AFAQ); French Association for Value Analysis (Association Francaise pour l'Analyse de la Valeur - AFAV), French Quality Centre (Mouvement Francais pour la Qualite - MFQ).

In 1984, a report by G. Bapt surveyed the conditions for an improvement of quality in French industry. He found a high degree of consensus on the importance of quality amongst managers in SMEs, large corporations and public institutions. All agreed that there was a considerable amount of quality improvement to be achieved. Bapt concluded that quality had to be interpreted in a dynamic and global way dealing with technology, management methods, human attitudes and behaviours, relationships with suppliers and customers and organisation. In his report, Bapt made several recommendations to the French government in terms of public initiatives - national promotion campaigns, education and training, and fiscal and financial support.

SQUALPI's activities increased in scope and variety throughout the 1980s and is now the main body supporting French policy toward quality management and standards. The Directorate currently has several missions; promoting the concept of quality, structuring the institutional environment, funding and sustaining the implementation of quality management systems in SMEs. Under SQUALPI information has been disseminated through advertising and more particularly through the 1985 'Train for Quality'. Over the last few years France has adopted a global quality promotion strategy at the national level. Quality is defined in a comprehensive way ('Qualite Totale') and covers both the service and manufacturing sector. As in the UK, SMEs have been targeted in state and private initiatives for quality promotion.

Financial support for quality promotion has come from a variety of sources. In 1984, the FRAC (Fonds Regionaux d'Aide au Conseil) was set up. This provided regional funding for SMEs seeking consultancy (50% of the cost). In 1985, the "Tertiaire Industriel" (Industrial Services) was established in order to increase the skills of consulting companies in quality management. In 1986, a financial support scheme was set up to support the recruitment of skilled executives by SMEs. In 1988, "Partnership 92" (from 1992 renamed "Partners for Europe") was created to support collective projects. In 1989, the EDDF scheme, a Commitment to Develop Professional Training, was set up supporting 30 to 70 per cent of the training cost. From 1990, an R&D tax refund scheme has allowed companies to deduct

50 per cent of the increase in their standardisation expenditures from their operating income.

ANVAR, - the National Agency for Innovation and R&D, supports quality-related initiatives as far as new product or processes are concerned. Financial support can begin with market research and continue up to third party certification. Any company is eligible for this scheme providing a detailed and comprehensive project plan is presented. ANVAR is also using the National Fund for Modernisation and the so-called PPT initiative - Public Technological Venture Capital - to support projects improving process quality through investment in automation, training, and quality assurance.

In 1987, the Mission for the Teaching of Industrial Quality (MEQUI) (replacing a Club for Teaching and Quality [Enseignement et Qualite], and a working group on education and training of quality management systems) was set up under the auspices of the Ministry of Education. 65 of the 350 GRETA (GRoupements d'ETAblissements) under the Ministry of Education deal with adult training and education and quality training courses were first set up in 1985. In addition, the Ministry of Education also has responsibility for the CNED (Centre National pour l'Enseignement a Distance) providing distance training and education.

As in the UK, a number of non-government organisations promote quality and quality management in industry. They organise conferences, seminars and visits, publish books and reports, support databases and advertise quality through various media and grant awards. Some of the more important organisations are described below.

The Association Francaise pour L'Analyse de la Valeur (AFAV) was set up in 1978 to promote value analysis methods throughout French industry, disseminate relevant practical experiences (through the journal 'La Valeur', conferences and workshops), develop methods and standards definition. The Association Francaise pour L'Assurance Qualite (AFAQ) is an independent non-profit organisation set up in 1988 to have responsibility for quality certification to international quality standards (eg ISO 9001-9002-9003). AFAQ stresses its formal independence between suppliers and customers. Its boards consist of 50 members from 3 groups: suppliers (industry federations), buyers (major industrial groups) and quality bodies. AFAQ has 9 sectoral committees: chemicals; agro-food; transportation; civil engineering; electricity and electronics; engineering and consultancy; mechanicals; casting; building industry; and a pluri-sectoral committee - a joint-venture with AFNOR - for all other sectors. By May 1992, 500 firms had been certified by AFAQ (with a further 1,500 being considered for certification).

The Mouvement Francais pour la Qualite (MFQ), was set up in March 1991, through the merger of AFCIQ-AFQ (Association Francaise des Qualiticiens) and AFCERQ (Association Francaise pour les Cercles de Quality). It is a non-profit organisation dealing with promotion, training, communication, documentation, information and research on quality management systems through professional sections, working groups and two institutions (Institute for Safety Operating [Institut pour la Surete de Fonctionnement] and the Institute for Management through Quality [Institut pour le Management par la Qualite]. The MFQ has responsibility for several quality awards. The Institut de Recherche et de Developpement de la Qualite (IRDQ), was set up in 1986. It undertakes research on quality management systems, including practical in-company testing, documentation and training.

The ACFCI (National Association of Chambers of Trade and Industry) is involved in two national promotion schemes: the RNPQ (Reseau National de Promotion de la Qualite =

National Network for the Promotion of Quality) set up in 1984 by ACFCI, CNPF (national industry confederation) and CGPME (national SMEs confederation); and the "sur-contracting" initiative set-up in 1992 to promote quality within the relationship between manufacturers and suppliers: the objective is to help French SMEs to become suppliers of Japanese "transplants" in Europe in a first stage, and of Japanese manufacturers in Japan in a second stage. The target is to promote TQM culture and methods within 100 SMEs by 1993.

AFNOR is the main training body dealing with quality-related issues. It has 7 training centers in France, one in Paris and one in each of its regional delagation. In 1992, there were more than 300 training seminars in six major topics. MFQ is also strongly involved in quality management training. It provides its members with advice in training and is organising more than 50 national training courses in quality control and quality management. ACFCI, CRCI and CCI are involved in quality-related education through their 273 business schools and education centers. At university level, the most quality-dedicated centers are: IPIA (Auch), IFCC (Fougeres), CFSA (Bourges), Ecole de la Qualite (Charleville-Mezieres), EIA (Marseille), CERELOG (Metz), CHAMFOR (Reims), CEFOPE (Troyes) and UIEQT (Vichy).

THE DIFFUSION OF QUALITY

In this section we briefly examine evidence on the diffusion of new quality management approaches throughout France and the United Kingdom.

The United Kingdom
The major focus of the DTI campaign has been the promotion of BS 5750/ISO 9000 standards. The 1992 DTI QA Register lists around 13,500 companies in the UK and abroad whose quality systems have been assessed to BS 5750 or an equivalent standard (for instance, the NATO Defence AQAP series standards) by a UK Certification Body. There is some additional evidence on the diffusion of TQM techniques throughout UK industry. In 1991, 3000 companies were asked about their quality programmes, if any. 15 per cent responded, of whom nearly all had embarked, or were embarking, on TQM. After seven years or more, only 30 per cent had fully met their objectives in improving competitiveness: only half had improved suppliers' quality to the desired standards: there were also shortfalls in customer service and reducing the cost of failure. A 1991 study by Jay Communications found two-thirds of UK companies viewed quality as a strategic necessity, others responded to pressures from trade associations or purchasers, and a third category were driven by changed market conditions. Only 12 per cent had been spurred into action by export requirements. In the last 12 months there has been what is described as an 'explosion of interest' in quality in the service sector led by local government, health and other public authorities, and private consultancies.

France
Recently, two major surveys were carried out on behalf of the French Ministry of Industry and Trade. The first, "the cost of nonquality", assessed the diffusion of quality management systems throughout French industry. From the beginning of the 1980s, most French SMEs had paid great attention to the role of quality for their survival. However, only since the mid 1980s had they begun formally to implement structured quality management systems. A 1989 survey by ARACQ (Association Regionale pour l'Amelioration de la Competitive par la Qualite) pointed out that 45% of SMEs did not use any quality control systems and 71% did not have a quality improvement programme. Another survey, carried out in 1988 by the French Confederation of Industry (CNPF) pointed out that 41% of SMEs had set up a quality

improvement programme.

The second major survey, "Quality in SMEs", was published in October 1991. It found that the SMEs typically sought help from public bodies and quality institutions only after an increase in internal awareness of the importance of quality. In seeking help, the SMEs preferred to go to relevant technical centers and public administrations or associations they felt were independent. Amongst the 41 SMEs surveyed, quality improvement occurred for one of four reasons: management initiative; prompted by cooperation or partnership; compelled by customers; and a survival following bankruptcy! Implementation led both to an improvement in internal performance and to an increase in competitive advantage. The main obstacles to implementing improvements were employee inertia, organisational bottlenecks and insufficient training capabilities.

A 1992 document published by the SQUALPI estimates that 60 per cent of SMEs do not have any formal quality department or action. It is also pointed out that most SMEs are restricting quality management to two issues only: product control and human resources management.

SUMMARY AND FUTURE DEVELOPMENTS

A key aim of UK Government policy has been to support the development of a comprehensive quality supporting structure. This has meant closer involvement in standards-making, encouraging the adoption of quality management systems, and of assessment, certification and accreditation schemes. In general, however, recent government philosophy has been against direct intervention. Support for quality consultancy is justified in terms of market failure - ie. without this scheme smaller firms would find consultancy services to be costly, relevant consultants difficult to identify, and advice difficult to incorporate into their activities. The current DTI Enterprise Consultancy Initiative is due to end in March 1994. The original aim of encouraging a self-sustaining market amongst SMEs for consultants is felt to have been very successful. As yet there is little indication as to what, if anything, will follow it, although any follow-up scheme is likely to place more emphasis on TQM.

The activities on quality in France are diverse. In France, the quality community is characterised by a clear division of responsibility. Public bodies are only concerned with promotion of quality awareness at a 'global' level (and at a sectoral level where there is a specific government responsibility). Public associations are dealing with the 'hard core' of the implementation process of total quality management systems: standardisation, certification, accreditation, tests and control, training, consultancy and research. The private sector is strongly involved both in implementing TQM and in consultancy. This basic pattern of a strictly defined division of responsibility - with a decentralised structure - has been advocated since the 1970s and is likely to continue for the next few years.

Over the next five years, MICE's strategy is likely to remain unchanged. This will involve the promotion of a greater awareness of quality by all economic sectors, the fostering of an efficient technical and cultural institutional environment and support for firms in their efficient use of quality management systems. MICE will emphasize several priorities: The development of education and adult training, support for research in quality management concepts and methods, the creation of a national award for quality achievement, support for the MFQ, expansion of the operation "Partnership 92", and support for the AFAQ in increasing the number of certified firms.

Public policy promotion initiatives in both countries have emphasised the use of quality standards. While recognising that there is more to good quality management than simply achievement of certification, it is argued that the development and application of standards represents one of the most effective ways to approach the problem of improving quality across the economy as a whole. The coupling of national standards to international ones (ie. ISO 9000/EN 29000) has the further effect of reducing barriers to trade. With moves towards the European Single Market (and with it the harmonisation of European standards), it is likely that European bodies (including the European Commission) will come to play an increasingly important role in the promotion of quality throughout Europe.

BIBLIOGRAPHIC REFERENCES

AFNOR: (1991) Gerer et Assurer la Qualite, Recueil de Normes Francaises, Paris, AFNOR.
AFNOR: (1992) ISO 9000: Application Symposium, Paris, 26/27 March.
AFQ: (1983) Le Cout de la Non-Qualite dans les Petites et Moyennes Entreprises Industrielles et Commerciales, Paris, 31 March.
Bapt, G.: (1984) Les Conditions de l'Amelioration de la qualite dans l'Industrie Francaise, Paris, La Documentation Francaise.
Department of Prices and Consumer Protection: (1978) A National Strategy for Quality, London, HMSO.
Department of Industry: (1982) Standards, Quality and International Competitiveness, London, HMSO.
Doucet, C.: (1986) Rapport d'Etude Concernant la Certification des Systemes d'Assurance dela Qualite des Entreprises, Paris, MIPTT.
Jay Communications: (1991) Attitudes within British Business to Quality Management Systems, London.
Lascalles, D.M.; Dale, B.: (1988) "A Review of the Issues Involved in Quality Improvement", International Journal of Quality and Reliability Management, Vol. 15, No. 5, pp. 76-94.
Rogerson, J.H.: (November 14, 1991) The Times, London, p. 36.
Rothwell, R.; Dodgson, P: (1991) Industrial Innovation and Public Policy, Francis Pinter, London.
Segal, Quince and Wickstead: (1989) Evaluation of the Consultancy Initiatives, HMSO, London.
Segal, Quince and Wickstead: (1989) Evaluation of the Consultancy Initiatives - second stage, HMSO, London.
Stoneman, P.; Vickers, J.: (1988) "The Assessment: The Economics of Technology Policy", Oxford Review of Economic Policy, Vol. 4, No. 4, pp. i-xvi.
Warner, F.: (1977) Standards and Specifications in the Engineering Industries, NEDO.

BIOGRAPHICAL SKETCHES OF AUTHORS

Brendan Barker is a Research Fellow with the Programme for Policy Research in Engineering, Science and Technology (PREST), at the University of Manchester, UK. His research interests include government policy and business strategy in relation to new materials. He is coordinator of an EC project on Quality Promotion Initiatives in Europe.

Jean-Jacques Chanaron is a Senior Researcher with the National Centre for Scientific Research (CNRS-IREPD), at the University of Grenoble, France. His research interests include industrial organisation and technology management. He is a specialist on the automobile industry.

Part VII
AWARDS FOR PRODUCTIVITY AND/OR QUALITY EXCELLENCE

1. The Malcolm Baldrige Quality Award and its Impact on Enterprises in Productivity and Quality Improvement

2. State, Regional, and Local Awards, and their Impact on Awareness, Participation, and Performance

Productivity & Quality Management Frontiers-IV, edited by Sumanth, Edosomwan, Poupart, and Sink. ©1993 Institute of Industrial Engineers.

Applying Malcolm Baldrige Criteria at the Departmental Level

J.C. Parks

IBM Corporation

Poughkeepsie, New York USA

ABSTRACT

Baldrige criteria are not only useful at the corporate level, they provide a road map for improvement at the departmental level. At IBM East Fishkill, a competition for a departmental quality award judged individual departments using Baldrige criteria. The categories were fundamentally similar to those in the National Quality Award but were modified slightly to be more applicable at the departmental level. For example, the leadership category addressed the leadership qualities of the department manager and the supplier quality section addressed not only outside suppliers but also intra-company suppliers (ie. other departments). The assessment process was much the same as that for the National Quality Award. Applications were assessed by internally trained Baldrige assessors and the finalists were visited by a team of assessors. Finalists were classified as either bronze level (501-625), silver level (626-750), or gold level (751-1000). The departments were given a feedback range and a +/- assessment for each category. The assessment process highlighted the strengths and weaknesses that are inherent in every department. This information was used to affect change where it is most realizable, at the lowest level in the organization. This change from below can oftentimes be more valuable in today's empowered environment than a decree for change at the corporate level. The application process forced departments to map out their key business processes, which was important because business process mapping is not done on a widespread basis at the departmental level. Process mapping provided a thorough understanding of the fine points of each process and facilitated process improvements.

INTRODUCTION

Malcolm Baldrige criteria can be a useful tool for quality improvement when applied at the departmental level. Many quality programs are most effective when applied at the lowest level of an organization because they empower individuals to make decisions that improve quality in every process they control. Quality driven from the lower levels of an organization also generates enthusiasm for a quality program that would otherwise be viewed as rhetoric. Departmental level quality programs based on Baldrige criteria also reinforce a total quality management system and provide an incentive for widespread adoption of Baldrige principles throughout the organization. And a department program promotes better cooperation between internal suppliers and customers.

A departmental quality program is useful because it facilitates entry into the National Quality award competition. Each department maps out its key processes and key quality and service features, which helps because much of the process and results data can be summarized for inclusion in the National Award write-up.

IBM East Fishkill implemented a departmental level quality competition that used Baldrige criteria as a basis for judging the quality levels of a department. Each competing department submitted a 12 page write-up that was similar in content to those submitted by a corporation for the National Quality Award. The application write-ups were assessed by trained Baldrige examiners using an assessment process similar to that used by National Quality Award assessors.

IMPLEMENTATION

The IBM East Fishkill Departmental Baldrige Competition was first announced six months prior to the application write-up deadline. The competition guidelines and intent were posted on site bulletin boards and specific guidelines (including copies of the award application) were handed out to all site managers.

The specific guidelines had a cover letter written by the Site General Manager which reinforced his commitment to IBM's quality programs. The guidelines also outlined the intent of the award, which included:

- focus on quality
- think of each department as an individual business
- achieve a better understanding of requirements for total quality excellence
- improve the quality of materials and services received
- improve the quality of the department's output
- share information and techniques between departments

The guidelines listed the scoring process and maximum length for application write-ups.

The departmental award was based on 1991 National Baldrige application criteria. The items were greatly simplified and reduced in scope by combining all the areas to address from the National application into one smaller area to address per item. General keywords were modified for each category to suit the nature of the departmental level award. For instance, obvious changes such as the words "company" and "organization" to "department" were made.

General changes were made to some items before incorporation into the departmental application. Item 1.1, Senior Executive Leadership, was changed to address the department manager's leadership goals and attributes. Items 5.6 and 5.7, Business Process Support Service Quality and Supplier Quality, were changed to address the fact that most support services and suppliers of a department are internal to IBM. Similarly, item 6.3, Supplier Quality Results, was changed to reflect the fact that most departmental suppliers are internal IBM departments.

ASSESSMENT AND RECOGNITION

The scoring for the departmental applications was similar to that of the National Quality Award. As in the National Award, the departmental award maximum score was 1000 points and the scores for each category and item were the same as the category and item scores in the National Award. For the first level of competition, three internally trained assessors scored each application write-up independently. The assessors then met as a group and assigned a consensus score to each write-up. Write-ups that received a score of 500 or above advanced to the second level of competition.

At the second level of competition, three different assessors graded each write-up independently and met to assign a new team consensus score. The assessors also made a recommendation as to which department should be the final winner and which departments should receive a bronze, silver, or gold award.

In the third level of competition, members of the IBM East Fishkill Site Advisory Council (SAC) visited the top scoring departments and asked similar questions that National examiners ask when visiting top scoring companies. Top scoring departments also presented their write-ups to the Site Executive Committee (SEC). The final winner was selected from the results of the third phase of competition.

Each department whose write-up was assigned a bronze, silver, or gold award was selected for recognition at the site level. The Site General Manager and members of the SAC hosted an informal recognition event for each department where they awarded a departmental plaque and individual certificates commemorating the level achieved (ie. bronze, silver, or gold). A picture of each department and a short description of its quality philosophy were posted on site bulletin boards. Each member of the winning department also received a monetary award.

The examiners provided a +/- feedback report to all departments that submitted a write-up. The report highlighted strengths and weaknesses for each department the same way that feedback reports for the National Award write-ups highlight strengths and weaknesses for corporations. However, the +/- items were generally more specific due to the relatively small size of each area to address and its corresponding write-up.

RESULTS AND DISCUSSION

A departmental quality award program has both intrinsic and extrinsic value to any organization or company. Intrinsically, the award helps a department develop a specific quality agenda and provides the capability to assess the quality of its products and services. The Leadership category shows a department that the department's manager or supervisor plays a pivotal role in helping to set departmental goals. It also makes the department aware of its commitment to help others outside the business community.

The Information and Analysis category makes the fact apparent that a department must have a mature benchmarking process so it has realistic targets to shoot for based on the performance of other organizations or departments that provide similar products or services. The Strategic Planning category emphasizes the importance of having long and short range planning processes that constantly improve. The Human Resource category stresses the importance of a full educational plan for each department member. More importantly, it measures how well each employee participates in making everyday decisions that affect the quality of departmental products and services (empowerment).

The Quality Assurance category is by far the most important of the seven. It forces a department to map all processes, even though they may be taken for granted or deemed too simple for analysis. Process mapping is important because processes can only be improved if they are thoroughly understood. The Quality Assurance category also forces a department to identify all support services and suppliers and the degree of cooperation (interlock) between them.

The Quality Results category shows to what extent a department measures the quality of its products and services. Key quality measures for a department are dependent on current quality programs and could include statistical process control measurements, product cycle time measurements, design of experiment measurements, etc. The Quality Results category also forces a department to examine the quality of all supplier and support service products and services.

The Customer Satisfaction Results category shows a department that the way in which it deals with its customers on a daily basis affects the degree to which its customers are delighted. This need for customer satisfaction forces a department to survey customers and analyze trends in customer satisfaction and dissatisfaction.

The extrinsic value of a departmental level quality award is evident if a company (or organization within a company) that has such an award program applies for the National Quality Award or an intra-company Baldrige award (self-assessment). The departmental award helps in both horizontal and vertical quality deployment. Horizontal deployment is "the extent or spread of the quality effort across an organization" and vertical deployment is "the extent to which strategic, customer-oriented objectives have made their way from the CEO to lower levels of the organization." [1] Since both types of deployment are necessary for a successful quality program and, hence, the success of a Baldrige write-up, a departmental Baldrige competition shows the breadth and depth of an organization's quality program. A departmental quality award program also helps in Baldrige site visits because all departments will be integrated, or "speak the same (quality) language" [2] and be consistent when examiners are present.

A departmental award program aids in Baldrige competition because many medium size companies use "packaged programs or off the shelf solutions: employee suggestion programs, customer surveys, or statistical process control packages." [3] On the other hand, top scoring companies have high levels of integration and deployment, [4] both of which are enhanced by a departmental quality award program.

CONCLUSIONS

The IBM East Fishkill Departmental Award used modified Baldrige application criteria and a Baldrige-like winner selection method that helped individual departments assess the quality of their everyday processes and products. The application process also provided a barometer with which each department could measure quality trends and provided a road map to quality excellence that, if followed, could lead to tremendous improvements in product and service quality and customer-supplier relations.

The departmental quality award program enhanced the awareness of Baldrige criteria at the departmental level. This awareness will lead to

---

[1] Garvin (1991). [2] Ibid. [3] Ibid. [4] Ibid.

increased competitiveness in IBM self-assessment Baldrige competition and ultimately, it is hoped, to the increased competitiveness of IBM in the National Quality Award competition.

ACKNOWLEDGEMENT

The author would like to acknowledge Gil Currie of the IBM East Fishkill Site Advisory Council for his help in preparing this paper.

BIBLIOGRAPHY

Garvin, D. A. (1991) "How the Baldrige Award Really Works", Harvard Business Review, vol. 69, no. 6, pp. 80-93.

Parks, J. C. (1991) "Malcolm Baldrige Competition at the Departmental Level", Creativity!, vol. 10, no. 4, pp. C3-C4.

AUTHOR BIOGRAPHY

Jonathan Parks is a computer engineer in the Product Design Area at IBM East Fishkill. He received his B. S. degree in electrical engineering from Drexel University in 1989 and his M. S. degree in computer engineering from Syracuse University in 1991.

Productivity & Quality Management Frontiers-IV, edited by Sumanth, Edosomwan, Poupart, and Sink. ©1993 Institute of Industrial Engineers.

Quality and Innovation at 3M:
A Strategy for Customer Satisfaction

D.N. Anderson
3M Corporate Quality Services
St. Paul, Minnesota USA

ABSTRACT

For many years, 3M has regarded its total quality process as a positive business strategy for achieving competitive advantage, market share and financial goals in global markets.

Customer focus is fundamental to 3M's philosophy of quality as a business strategy. Customer focus means that customer expectations define quality, and customer focus provides a definition of the behaviors and improvement activities for exceeding customer expectations.

A second focus of our quality process has emerged in recent years: competition. With competitors rapidly deploying customer-focused strategies throughout global markets, our quality strategy must also include what competitors are doing to satisfy customer expectations.

The result is that innovation -- the ability to provide products and services differentiated from competition in ways that are valued by the customer -- is a critical component of the quality process. The challenge is to further accelerate innovation in order to perform better than competition and be the clear customer choice.

At 3M, we have learned that quality and innovation work synergistically to create a powerful competitive strategy. We manage the similar dynamics of quality and innovation as the means to providing greater customer value, and, through customer satisfaction, greater profitability.

With customer demands and competitive challenges escalating at a much greater pace than ever before, our response must be to manage within ever-shrinking time frames with no loss of quality or innovation.

INTRODUCING THE CHALLENGE

Quality and innovation are seldom considered as mutually supportive processes. Quality is seen as a product and service conformance issue, innovation as an R&D imperative. They proceed along separate paths. But do they really?

3M has learned that quality and innovation are partners, mutually supportive elements in the quest for customer satisfaction. A company that is good at either one and not the other is positioned for the short-term only. A company that is good at both, and knows how to manage the synergistic relationship between them, is positioned for long-term success.

This paper describes the partnership of quality and innovation at 3M, and the benefits of understanding and managing their relationship.

BEGINNING WITH SANDPAPER

3M began in 1902 as a manufacturer of a single product -- sandpaper. Today it is a worldwide company with $13 billion in annual revenues, 53 operating units, 58 international subsidiaries and 88,000 employees. Fifty percent of revenues come from outside the U.S.

We produce 60,000 different products based on 100-plus base technologies. Our first laboratory was established in 1916. Today we have labs in the U.S. and 21 other countries. We invest approximately 7 percent of sales revenues in R&D -- about twice the rate of the average U.S. company.

Our corporate theme is "Innovation Working for You." That theme reflects our view of ourselves as not a producer of products, but rather as a provider of customer satisfaction. Our fundamental objective is "uncompromising commitment to customer satisfaction." This requires both quality, which is a focus on the customer, and innovation, which is the ability to bring something new and useful to the customer.

DEVELOPING A CULTURE OF INNOVATION AND QUALITY

The McKnight Management Policy
In 1944, 3M CEO william McKnight, who is remembered as the founder of the modern 3M, wrote a management policy to formally establish the importance of innovation:

"As our business grows, it becomes increasingly necessary to delegate responsibility and to encourage men and women to exercise their initiative. This requires considerable tolerance. Those men and women to whom we delegate authority and responsibility, if they are good people, are going to want to do their jobs in their own way."

"Mistakes will be made. But if a person is essentially right, the mistakes he or she makes are not as serious as the mistakes management will make if it undertakes to tell those in authority exactly how they must do their jobs."

"Management that is destructively critical when mistakes are made kills initiative. And it's essential that we have people with initiative if we are to continue to grow."

McKnight's policy made innovation a formal part of 3M's culture.

The Impetus for Total Quality
Lew Lehr, 3M's CEO from 1979-1986, sought new ways to strengthen innovation and to position quality as a customer focus rather than an internally defined issue.

3M had grown by being consistently superior in quality and technological innovation. But by the late 1970s, more competitors emerged, and more began to catch up. Long-time 3M positions in several key technologies and product lines were being threatened. Though we had built our success on quality and innovation, we realized we needed to more fully understand the dynamics of both processes.

Lehr wanted improvement. He knew that unless we understood innovation and quality better and managed them more effectively, 3M's overall competitive position would be threatened.

3M renewed its emphasis on quality. At first, we tried to incorporate factory-driven quality control concepts into a total organizational approach. But we soon understood that control was antithetical to the new understanding of quality improvement. We needed a process that focused the entire organization on the customer, and then provided the system for defining customer expectations and delivering customer satisfaction.

From that understanding came the process of "managing total quality," a 3M discipline for meeting and exceeding customer expectations. We learned that total quality requires customer-driven values, behaviors and practices that are common throughout the organization. Managing total quality incorporates these into a systematic process for continuous improvement.

3M's Innovation Study
To better understand innovation, Lehr formed the Innovation Steering Committee in the early 1980s. The committee examined the climate for innovation at 3M, identified supports and barriers, and recommended ways to foster innovation and entrepreneurship.

The committee identified five fundamental supports for the innovation process.

Significantly, these five supports (listed in the next section of this paper) were the same organizational supports emerging as central to a total quality culture.

At that point, we realized that quality and innovation were paired in a way not previously recognized, thus giving tremendous implications for our long-range competitive strategy. Common roots and common elements mean common approaches to managing the two processes. Even more important, commonalities mean synergy, and this can be leveraged for tremendous advantage in providing the differentiation and customer value that drive price and profit levels.

Allen Jacobson, 3M CEO form 1986-1991, further reinforced the strategic relationship of quality and innovation when he said, "We have found that quality belongs at the center of our drive for innovation -- as a resource for our innovation."

SUPPORTING QUALITY AND INNOVATION

The five supports fundamental to both quality and innovation at 3M are:
- Values and goals
- Controls and approvals
- Boundary crossing
- Sponsorship
- Rewards and recognition

Values and goals
An organization's values and goals are critical to its ability to produce quality products and to innovate. The values and goals must directly support the processes that generate customer-focused quality improvement and innovation.

As mentioned earlier, CEO McKnight established a culture in which innovation was valued at the highest levels in the company. Through the years, his principles have become ingrained into 3M's culture.

Proof of the importance of innovation is our company-wide goal of achieving 25 percent of our sales from products introduced within the past five years. It is a goal we regularly achieve every year and have exceeded in the past three years. New product objectives are included in all executive plans.

Another very visible proof of management's belief in the importance of innovation is the 15 percent rule: 3M employees are encouraged to spend 15 percent of their work time on activities and projects beyond the boundaries of their defined responsibilities. There is a strong cultural belief that both quality and innovation are everybody's job.

Both quality and innovation are processes, and they prosper to the degree that the organization's values and goals support them.

Controls and approvals
Quality and innovation both thrive on empowerment. McKnight's advice from the '40s to give an employee the freedom to do a job his or her own way has never been more true than in an organization seeking total quality and innovation. Employees who are closest to the customer need the freedom to make improvements, prevent problems and enhance the product or service to meet rapidly changing customer expectations. Employees with innovative, customer-driven ideas need the freedom to develop those ideas.

We continuously examine the system of controls and approvals within which 3M employees work. We want to improve that system so that employees will have more freedom and encouragement to serve the customer.

Boundary crossing
A prime factor in both quality and innovation is the ability to bring together an organization's resources, both functionally and cross-functionally. But within an organization, there is a tendency to create barriers and create turf.

We have a continuous need to identify common objectives and benefits that transcend turf. Focusing on the customer does this. The common need to satisfy the customer necessitates cross-functional teams and teamwork, new initiatives, open communications and a strong emphasis on problem solving.

Real Progress in both quality and innovation requires cross-functional, cross-departmental and cross-divisional efforts.

Sponsorship
Few things have so powerful an impact on quality and innovation as sponsorship. Neither can prosper without the committed leadership and involvement of management -- especially top management.

Management involvement requires risk. A sponsor must be willing to support an employee in halting a manufacturing process because the process is out of control. A sponsor must be willing to support a new idea -- often solely on faith -- in order to give it the resources to progress.

Vigorous sponsorship of quality and innovation initiatives is pivotal to the success of both.

<u>Rewards and recognition</u>
Rewards and recognition reinforce and validate the importance quality and
innovation hold for the company.

The conventional approach of recognizing those who solve problems, while
valuable in itself, does not foster a high-quality, innovative organization. We must
reward and recognize behaviors that support quality and innovation.

By recognizing those who are customer focused, those who take intelligent risk to
better meet customer expectations, and those who venture outside the normal
organizational paths to achieve customer satisfaction, we create powerful role
models. Such recognition needs to be frequent and meaningful -- not just annual,
but day-to-day.

At 3M, quality achievers and innovators are rewarded through a variety of
recognition and career-growth avenues. For example, the annual 3M Quality
Achievement Awards recognize top achievements by individuals and teams in
improving quality and customer satisfaction. Division and department awards
support the annual recognition, and managers are given considerable freedom and
encouragement to recognize achievements on the spot.

Outstanding technical achievement is recognized with the Carlton Society Award.
3M Alpha and Genesis Awards fund new product and service development activities
by individual 3M employees.

ACCELERATING THE PROCESS

Customer demands and competitive responses are increasing exponentially. The
time taken to invent, develop, manufacture and market a product must be
compressed to points inconceivable even a year ago.

In the past we have relied on the premise that with a continuous supply of
successful "hits." Products like Post-it brand notes, masking tape and x-ray imaging
film are evidence of our past successes.

But today, producing the right product isn't enough. It must also be produced at the
right time -- when the market is ready and the competition is not. To this end, 3M
has instituted a number of time compression best practices.

In order to leverage resources, 3M identifies high priorities for resources needed to
get the product to market as quickly as possible.

Since the company's traditional culture found comfort in the breadth of diversity,
focusing the greater part of company resources on fewer efforts means greater

risk -- a sense of "putting all the eggs in one basket." We minimize the risks (and raise comfort levels) by developing a better understanding of customers and then leveraging the voice of the customer to make decisions.

Beginning with Europe, 3M has surveyed customers and potential customers in all major markets throughout the world to help in this heightened need for focusing resource deployment decisions on customer expectations.

The most essential tool in speeding the process of product introduction is communications. Customer surveys communicate market needs, and cross-functional teams communicate the requirements of every function that is or will be involved in the product. Working in parallel has speeded time dramatically while giving each function a better understanding of the other functions involved.

Being first to market has a great many benefits: the lion's share of the market, a longer presence in the market, better pricing control, and a reputation for innovation.

As mentioned earlier, 3M's corporate theme is "Innovation Working for You." To the customer, being first is perceived as being innovative. Innovation has been a part of 3M's 90-year history, and in order to keep that perception among customers, we must compress time in order to be first to market.

TAKING QUALITY AND INNOVATION INTO THE FUTURE

Customers and the global market continue to change. The world in the year 2000 will be significantly different from today. We cannot accurately predict what the competitive environment will be, nor the specific customer expectations we will need to meet and exceed. We do know that quality and innovation will be more important than they are today.

3M CEO L. D. DeSimone said about 3M's approach to the future: "Let's quit talking about surviving global competition, and talk instead about thriving and winning it. We must use quality and innovation as strategies for competitive advantage and growth rather than tools for survival."

In order to continue creating product and service differentiation and value, competitive advantage and profit, 3M has established a global management system, called "Q90s." It is designed to foster a nimble, highly responsive organization quick to anticipate and meet both changing customer expectations and evolving competition.

Through continuously improved performance in critical areas such as time to market new products, product and order cycle time, unit cost, and others, 3M will have the tools and capabilities to deliver value and customer satisfaction well into the future.

Fostering quality and innovation is at the core of 3M's global management system. As change accelerates, the need for quality and innovation will accelerate along with it -- as will the need to effectively manage these two synergistic forces.

CONCLUSION

When quality and innovation are seen as interrelated management processes, a company realizes significant performance benefits. When each is leveraged by customer focus and common cultural dynamics, the result is a powerful synergy.

The key to improving quality and innovation lies in understanding and fostering the key supports common to both. Supportive values and goals, controls and approvals, boundary crossing, sponsorship, and rewards and recognition are pivotal to quality and innovation.

Quality and innovation are partners in the quest for customer satisfaction. Building the synergy between them results in competitive strength and customer satisfaction.

REFERENCES

"Closing the Quality Gap"
by Alexander Hiam, The Conference Board
Pages 149 - 172

"Beyond Quality: How 50 Winning Companies Use Continuous Improvement"
Jerry Bowles and Joshua Hammond
Pages 157 - 194

"The Baldrige Quality System: The Do-It-Yourself Way to Transform Your Business"
Stephen George
Pages 135-151

Productivity & Quality Management Frontiers-IV, edited by Sumanth, Edosomwan, Poupart, and Sink. ©1993 Institute of Industrial Engineers.

Lockheed and the NASA Excellence Award Process: A Roadmap for Improvement

S.H. Prud'homme
Lockheed Engineering & Sciences Company
Houston, Texas USA

Abstract

Lockheed Engineering & Sciences Company (LESC) became the first services company to win a major national quality award in 1989 as the recipient of the NASA Excellence Award for Quality and Productivity. LESC provides high technology services to government and industry, and is headquartered in Houston, Texas.

LESC applied for the award twice before winning, and found the process of self-examination, application preparation, and validation by an outside party to be extremely beneficial. The self-examination of company activities against the award criteria revealed both strong and weak points. The assembly of quality and productivity data in a single application document allowed the company to assess activities in the context of overall organizational functioning. The validation by an outside panel of experts from within NASA and industry provided an illuminating perspective on both strengths and weaknesses. The award process activities served to strengthen and accelerate improvement activities.

The award process helped to coalesce a number of disparate improvement activities into a more purposeful, united entity. Linkages were developed between developmental training courses and the Total Quality Management Office, which provides a forum for people to take action on their ideas for improvement. In addition, the award requirements increased the awareness that a number of activities, such as peer review and technical forums, were actually "quality" activities but not labeled as such.

The net result of the award process has been an increased awareness and enthusiasm for continuous improvement. Voluntary participation in improvement activities has steadily increased from 25% in 1987 to 74% in 1991 in a workforce consisting mostly of engineers and scientists. Training for teams in the high technology services business has been refined and improved, and is frequently requested by NASA customers who wish to form improvement teams. A course for all employees has been developed, which provides the skills to make improvements and measurements for tasks in a research and engineering environment.

Productivity & Quality Management Frontiers-IV, edited by Sumanth, Edosomwan, Poupart, and Sink. ©1993 Institute of Industrial Engineers.

Virginia's Quality and Productivity Award Process

E.H. Ingold and C.S. Johnston
Virginia Polytechnic Institute & State University
Blacksburg, Virginia USA

ABSTRACT

In December 1982, the United States Senate passed Resolution 503, which established the United States Senate Productivity Award. This award was intended to foster awareness of the need for productivity improvement, and to recognize organizations, at the state level which demonstrated such improvement.

Although every state is eligible to have a Senate Productivity Award, very few have taken advantage of this opportunity. Virginia's is the longest continuously running award process, and throughout the years, this state has served as a model and a resource for other states establishing similar awards. More significant, however, is the impact Virginia's process has within its own borders.

Continuous improvement principles have been applied to the award process from its inception. The number of award categories increased from two in 1983 to four as of 1988. Any public or private sector organization practicing continuous improvement of quality and productivity within the Commonwealth of Virginia is eligible. Three years ago the Award for Continuing Excellence was established, which is Virginia's equivalent of the Malcolm Baldrige award. Any organization that is a previous recipient of the Senate Productivity Award is eligible to apply for this award.

Each year the number of applicants has increased. This year, 49 applications were submitted. On the basis of on a survey conducted by David Luther of Corning, this is the largest number of applications received for a state award. The Annual Awards Conference, held each April in Alexandria, Virginia, has also experienced consistent growth in attendance.

Virginia's Senate Productivity Award reaches beyond just the application for, and presentation of awards. Previous winners of the award are expected to speak across the state about their successful efforts. During National Quality Month the Senate Productivity Award Board is involved in a state-wide video-teleconference, featuring previous award recipients. Videotapes of the Conference are also available for educational purposes. Virginia organized the first State Quality Network meeting in 1991. The Governor's office recognizes the U.S. Senate Productivity Board for Virginia as Virginia's quality and productivity improvement council.

Virginia is a leader in the state award arena; many organizations have benefited from the award process, and the network of ideas generated about quality and productivity improvement. This paper addresses the infrastructure through which Virginia administers its process and the impact on awareness, participation and performance outlined above.

In December 1982, one year after the airing of the NBC White Paper, "If Japan Can, Why Can't We?" (1981) in which Dr. W. Edwards Deming and his ideas of continuous improvement were introduced formally to the United States, the United States Senate passed Resolution 503, which established the United States Senate Productivity Award (SPA). This award was intended to foster awareness of the need for productivity improvement, and to recognize organizations, at the state level which demonstrated such improvement.

GENERAL INFORMATION

Unlike the popular Malcolm Baldrige National Award for Quality, Virginia's SPA is open to any public or private sector organization practicing continuous improvement of quality and productivity, within the Commonwealth. There are no restrictions based on number of employees, revenue figures, or profit or not for profit status. Subsidiaries or divisions of organizations with headquarters outside the state are also eligible, as long as the improvement effort for which they want to be recognized is currently underway in Virginia. Organizations are not permitted to use information pertaining to activities outside the state.

Every state is eligible to have this award, however, few do. Established immediately following the Senate Resolution, Virginia's is the longest continuously running award process. Throughout the years, this state has served as a model and a resource for other states establishing similar awards. Both Alabama and Nevada used Virginia's process model extensively when initiating their award processes. Other states have consulted with Virginia, and Virginia has a reputation for willingness to share information and lessons learned from experience.

Administration of the award process varies considerably from state to state. In Virginia, the Virginia Productivity Center (VPC) at Virginia Tech assumes responsibility for the coordination and administration of the award. An 18-member Board of Directors reviews applications, makes site visits, and selects award recipients. The Program Manager and Information Coordinators for the process are provided by VPC. Additional support is provided by Board-member organizations and previous recipients of the award. In Virginia, the U.S. Senate Productivity Award is completely self-supporting and receives no federal or state financial support. This is not true for all participating states.

Although Senators John Warner and Paul Trible appointed the original Board, today the Board is self-perpetuating. New members are appointed for a term of three years and are often representatives of award winning organizations. However, the Board is very careful to ensure balanced representation from the public and private sector, small and large organizations, the major geographic regions of the state, and academia. There are three permanent Board seats, which are held by the Virginia Chamber of Commerce, the U.S. Small Business Administration and the Virginia Productivity Center.

When the award was established, there were only two award categories (i.e., manufacturing and non-manufacturing). As the award progressed, the Board recognized the need to expand these categories. In 1986, the categories of manufacturing and non-manufacturing were changed to manufacturing and service, for the private sector, and a third category, for state and federal agencies evolved. Interest from the public sector continued to such an extent that a fourth category, for local agencies, was created in 1988. See Figure 1 for award categories.

Another indication of the Board's efforts to keep pace with the advancements in continuous improvement is the U.S. Senate Productivity Award for Continuing Excellence. Created in 1989, this award recognizes previous recipients of the U.S. Senate Productivity Award for

Virginia. Three years from the date it was awarded the Senate Productivity Award, an organization may apply for the Award for Continuing Excellence (ACE). For this award, an organization competes only against itself and its previous application, to demonstrate a sustained, continuous improvement effort.

Any organization, regardless of size or profit status, practicing continuous improvement of quality and productivity in the Commonwealth of Virginia is eligible to apply for the U.S. Senate Productivity Award for Virginia.

- Private Sector Manufacturing

- Private Sector Service

- Public Sector State and Federal Agencies

- Public Sector Local Agencies

Three years from the date on which it received a previous Senate Productivity Award, an organization may reapply, and compete only against itself and its previous applicaton for the:

- Award for Continuing Excellence

Figure 1
U.S. Senate Productivity Award for Virginia
Award Categories

APPLICATION CRITERIA

Many applicants believe that the process of applying is as valuable and important as receiving the award. Several organizations have used this process as preparation for future application to the Malcolm Baldrige award. It is no coincidence that these opinions are connected to the rigor of this program.

The criteria for this award have changed substantially over the years, as the Board applies the concepts of continuous improvement to the award process. At first, productivity, and not quality, was stressed. Consequently, the criteria focused on productivity as the goal. As our understanding of the relationship between quality and productivity evolves, so do the criteria for this award. We now view increased productivity as an outcome of improved quality. All literature and materials for the award (U.S. Senate Productivity Award Application, 1992) clearly state the focus is quality and productivity. It would take an act of Congress, literally, to change the name of this award, but the emphasis has definitely changed.

To maintain the reputation of the program, the criteria are re-evaluated periodically to ensure applicants are being evaluated on the most important and relevant information, and to be sure they are not biased toward any of the four sectors. The criteria have been updated for the 1992 award year, and are presented in Figure 2. These criteria address the same areas of interest as the Baldrige award. (See Figure 3 for a comparison of the SPA criteria with Deming's Fourteen Points.)

Interest in this process started out strong in 1983 and has continued to be high. The profile of progress can be seen in Figure 4. This year, 49 applications were submitted. On the basis of on a survey conducted by David Luther of Corning (1992), this is the largest number of applications received for a state award. The number of repeat applicants, who have not yet received the medallion, is high; about 10% of the applicants during the past three years have reapplied. Applicants are made aware that it sometimes takes two or three years of applying before they receive the award.

PROGRAM PROCESS

The award cycle begins in August with the distribution of the new application. (See Figure 5 for calendar.) Completed applications are due, along with the application fee of $100 (used to offset administrative costs, such as printing), by November 30. Copies of the applications are distributed to Board members. Each Board member is on a team for one of the award categories.

Board members thoroughly review the applications in their category, and familiarize themselves with the Executive Summaries of the other applications. Board members review applications between mid-December and mid-January. In January, the Board meets to select those organizations deemed worthy of a site visit.

Site visits are conducted during January and February. Up to four organizations are visited, per category, for approximately 4-6 hours each. Site visits are designed to allow the Board to confirm information contained in the application, as well as to ask questions and gather data on issues not reflected in the written application. At site visits, Board members expect to have time to speak with anyone in the organization whom they encounter.

Following the conclusion of the site visits, the Board reconvenes to determine which organizations should be selected as finalists. Up to three organizations may be selected in each category. Those organizations selected as finalists are expected to make a presentation at the Awards Conference, which is held each April. At the time finalists are selected, the Board also decides which organization will receive the medallion in each category. It is important to note that there can be up to three finalists per category, and up to one medallion awarded per category. *Medallions are not automatically given in each of the four sectors.* Organizations must meet a certain level of requirements, as measured against the criteria and Board member assessment during the site visit. (See Figure 6 for Levels of Recognition.)

1. Maturity of Effort

When was the organization's improvement effort initiated? How was the effort conceived? Is the organization's approach original, or was an existing approach tailored to fit the organization's needs? How extensive is the effort within the company?

2. Top Management Commitment and Involvement (Leadership)

Describe resource commitments/allocation. How are the quality values of the organization epitomized by the leaders? What are specific examples of the level of commitment and involvement by top management?

3. Employee Involvement, Development and Management of Participation

How is employee involvement encouraged by top management? What types of quality and productivity training opportunities are provided to employees? How are teams used? To what degree are teams empowered? Are employee development plans derived from quality and company performance plans?

4. Recognition/Rewards Systems

How are contributors to and participants in the quality/productivity improvement effort recognized? Is there an established method for sharing gains? Who shares the gains of these efforts?

5. Plan for Continuous Improvement

How do the quality and productivity efforts integrate with the organization's vision, long range plans, business plans, and human resources programs? Are the individuals responsible for implementing these plans involved in developing them? Are targets, or long term goals established? Are self-evaluations made or conducted against other successful efforts? Does the process link plans to action? And how are they implemented?

6. Performance Measurement Process (Use of Information)

What types of measures are in place? How are they linked to the overall improvement effort? How are these measures communicated to the organization? What, specifically, is measured? How do you determine what to measure? What categories of information do you collect? Is the quality of the product or service measured at the customer's and supplier's location? Is quality measured internally from a customer perspective? Is there evidence of statistical thinking? Is competitive benchmarking evident?

7. Results Over Time

What are the specific results from the organization's quality and productivity improvement efforts? (NOTE: Please describe results from both quantitative and qualitative perspectives.)

8. Customer/Supplier Involvement

How do you assess supplier quality? How are customers and suppliers involved in your organization's ongoing efforts to improve quality and productivity? Are customers and suppliers recognized for their efforts? Is customer satisfaction measured? How? What use is made of this information?

Figure 2
U.S. Senate Productivity Award for Virginia
1992 Award Criteria

Deming's 14 Points \ SPA Criteria	Maturity of Effort	Top Mgmt. Commitment	Employee Involv., Dev., & Part.	Recognition/Rewards Systems	Plan for Cont. Improvement	Performance Meas. Process	Results Over Time	Customer/Supplier Involv.
Constancy of Purpose	•	•			•		•	
Adopt new philosophy	•	•	•					
Cease dependence on inspection					•	•		
End use of price tag alone		•						•
Improve constantly production & svc.			•		•			•
Institute Training and Retraining			•		•			
Institute Leadership	•	•	•					
Drive out fear	•	•			•		•	•
Break down barriers between staff areas	•	•	•		•	•		•
Eliminate slogans and exhortations	•	•						
Eliminate numerical quotas					•	•		
Remove barriers to pride of workmanship		•			•			
Institute prg. of educ. & training			•		•			
Take action to accomplish transform.	•				•		•	

Figure 3
U.S. Senate Productivity Award for Virginia Criteria
Compared to Deming's 14 Points

1375

	1983	1984	1985	1986	1987	1988	1989	1990	1991
Applicants	35	40	29	30	45	24	40	38	49
Attendance									
•Awards Ceremony	154	175	140	213	153	128	164	212	240
•Conference	n/a	n/a	64	85	79	94	86	149	164
•Workshop	n/a	n/a	n/a	53	50	59	53	63	62

Figure 4
U.S. Senate Productivity Award for Virginia
Profile of Progress

August	Applications available for distribution
November 30	Application deadline
January	Selection by Board of organizations to be site-visited
January/February	Site visits conducted
February	Selection of finalists and final evaluation
April (3rd week)	Awards Conference and Banquet
Spring	Planning meeting for next year and selection of new SPA Board members

Figure 5
U.S. Senate Productivity Award for Virginia
Application Process Calendar

There are three levels of recognition that may be awarded in each of the four categories:

•U.S. Senate Productivity Award Medallion   Awarded to the outstanding organization in each category. (It is not mandatory to have a medallion recipient in each category.)

•U.S. Senate Productivity Award Plaque   Awarded to up to three finalists in each category.

•U.S. Senate Productivity Award   The number awarded varies each
   Certificate of Merit   year.

U.S. Senate Productivity
Award for Continuing Excellence

There is no limit to the number awarded each year, as applicants only compete against themselves and their previous applications. However, to be eligible to apply, an organization must wait three years from the date they received their Senate Productivity Award Medallion.

Figure 6
U.S. Senate Productivity Award for Virginia
Levels of Recognition

When finalists have been notified of their selection, the program manager provides specifications for their Conference presentations and supporting materials. Organizations prepare for the Conference during March and April. The two-day Awards Conference and Banquet are held the third week of April, each year. Planning for the next year begins immediately following the conclusion of the Conference and Banquet.

AWARDS CONFERENCE AND CEREMONY

The Awards Conference and Banquet are an integral part of this process. On the first day of the two day conference, VPC conducts a workshop, the topic of which varies yearly. The workshop is an intensive session that allows participants to learn from the instructor, as well as each other, about different aspects of continuous improvement.

Educational opportunities continue on the second day of the conference with presentations from the finalists. Willingness to share information about their efforts is one of the requirements of finalists in this process. Each presentation is supplemented by printed materials. Following the presentations from a particular category, there is a question and answer session in which presenters address questions submitted by the audience. (The presentations have no bearing on the outcome of the award. As was mentioned earlier, the Board selects the medallion recipient, if there is to be one, well ahead of the conference.

However, the outcome remains confidential until the evening of the awards banquet.) The format of this conference allows the audience to hear from a significant number of outstanding organizations (usually 12-15) about their successes and failures. The benefits of such an opportunity are not only for the applicants of the process but for organizations at all stages of continuous improvement efforts. Videotapes of the Conference are made available. They are useful as educational tools as well as for assistance in preparing applications and presentations.

A banquet is held on the evening of the second day of the Conference, to recognize the finalists and medallion recipients. Each year the Senators are scheduled to make the presentations of the awards. Senators Warner and Robb are committed to visiting the medallion and ACE recipients during the months following the ceremony.

FEEDBACK

Each year they take part in this process, an organization learns more about what is still to be accomplished and gains knowledge on possible methods. This information is gained both from the Conference presentations and from feedback provided to the organizations by the Board members from their particular category.

Feedback is a critical part of the Senate Productivity Award process. At the conclusion of the application review process, those organizations not selected for site visits are notified of their status, and provided feedback on their application by the Board. Following the Awards ceremony, feedback is also provided to the finalists. In April 1992, an innovation was introduced to the award process, to help improve the timeliness of the feedback. The day following the award presentations, Feedback Sessions were held for each category and the Award for Continuing Excellence. All applicants were invited to participate and ask questions of the Board members who reviewed their application. This was a very popular activity with those who attended, and it will be improved and repeated in the future.

FOLLOW-UP

Virginia's Senate Productivity Award reaches beyond just the application for, and presentation of awards. Previous winners of the award are expected to speak across the state about their successful efforts. During National Quality Month the Senate Productivity Award Board is involved in a state-wide video-teleconference featuring previous award recipients. Both of these activities require organizations to update their progress. Speaking engagements include local chapters of professional organizations, business and civic clubs, National Quality Month activities, and any other appropriate opportunities.

The Award for Continuing Excellence, in addition to being a significant level of recognition, provides a structured process for following up with organizations on their continuous improvement efforts. The Board established a three-year waiting period from receipt of the SPA medallion (or previous ACE) prior to applying the ACE. Three years allows enough time for an organization to demonstrate sustained, continuous improvement. Evidence of this is obtained through a written application which is reviewed by a team of Board Members. If the organization does not merit a site visit, it is dropped from consideration.

The site visit for an ACE applicant is much more rigorous than that for an SPA applicant. ACE candidates are expected to have well developed systems and processes for monitoring and ensuring continuous improvement, and these should require little top management participation to run smoothly. To date there have been three recipients of the ACE - Norfolk

Naval Shipyard, ComSonics, Inc., and TRW Systems Division. It should be noted that since this award was initiated in 1989, there have been few eligible applicants due to the three-year waiting period.

Recipients of the SPA medallion and ACE are the "best of the best" in Virginia and are recognized as such. They are called upon to share their experiences and expertise with other organizations, and their communities.

CONCLUSION

Organizations that have benefited from the award process consider it an obligation to make others aware of their efforts to improve quality and productivity. Virginia is a leader in the area of state quality awards and considers it a responsibility to share information and lessons learned with other states. Virginia organized the first State Quality Network meeting in 1991. This group, comprised of about 15 states, has met three times and is an excellent source of information about awards processes at the state level.

Virginia's SPA Board works with the Governor's office to disseminate information and encourage economic development. The Governor's office recognizes the U.S. Senate Productivity Board for Virginia as Virginia's quality and productivity improvement council.

Quality and productivity improvement initiatives are more sophisticated and impressive every year. Virginia's Senate Productivity Award process will continue to recognize and publicize the efforts of outstanding organizations, in addition to continuing to improve its own award process and assist other states with their programs.

REFERENCES

Deming, W. Edwards, Ph.D. (1981) "If Japan Can, Why Can't We?", Films Incorporated, Wilmette, Illinois.

Luther, David, Survey conducted for state level quality awards, 1992, Corning, Inc., Corning, New York.

U.S. Senate Productivity Award Application, 1992.

BIOGRAPHICAL SKETCHES

Elizabeth Holmes Ingold is a Research Associate with VPC and has been Program Manager of the U.S. Senate Productivity Award for Virginia for four years.

Cynthia S. Johnston is a Research Associate with VPC and has been Information Director for the U.S. Senate Productivity Award for Virginia for three years.

Productivity & Quality Management Frontiers-IV, edited by Sumanth, Edosomwan, Poupart, and Sink. ©1993 Institute of Industrial Engineers.

State, Regional, and Local Awards in India and Their Impact on Improvement of Productivity in Industry

Y.S.M. Maheswar and M. Mallipeddi
J.N.T. University
Hyderabad, Andhra Pradesh INDIA

Awards as a means to motivate and ensure sustained performance is not something new. Their effectiveness in servicing the objective of optimal performance has been widely acknowledged. The Indian Industry is no exception and there are a host of awards instituted by both Government and Private organisations at State, Regional and Local levels. The increasing importance of awards as a means of promoting quality and productivity levels is evidenced by the fact that the number of awards has increased to over 30 at present from a meagre 10 five years ago at the national level covering varied categories of industries viz., Core Sector, Small Scale Sector, Food Processing Sector and Agricultural Sector. Similarly, there has been a significant increase in the number of awards for productivity instituted at regional and local levels too. Further confirming the crucial role of awards in achieving higher levels of productivity is the fact that the number of contenders entering the fray to earn the coveted awards has been increasing at an astounding rate, especially in the recent past.

The present paper is an attempt to evaluate the impact of various productivity awards at State, Regional and Local levels on awareness, participation and post award performance and various industries. While the necessary secondary data is collected from the awarding institutions such as National Productivity Council, Indian Chamber of Commerce etc., the primary data for evaluating the effectiveness of various awards is elicited through the administration of a questionnaire to a representative sample of awardee organisations. The paper based on the findings of the study attempts to putforth suggestions that may help improve the impact of the awards.

AUTHOR INDEX